## TAKING SIDES

Clashing Views in

# Race and Ethnicity

### SEVENTH EDITION

**Selected, Edited, and with Introductions by**

**Raymond D'Angelo**
*St. Joseph's College*

**Herbert Douglas**
*Rowan University*

**McGraw-Hill**
**Higher Education**

Boston   Burr Ridge, IL   Dubuque, IA   New York   San Francisco   St. Louis
Bangkok   Bogotá   Caracas   Kuala Lumpur   Lisbon   London   Madrid   Mexico City
Milan   Montreal   New Delhi   Santiago   Seoul   Singapore   Sydney   Taipei   Toronto

The McGraw-Hill Companies

# McGraw-Hill
# Higher Education

TAKING SIDES: CLASHING VIEWS IN RACE AND ETHNICITY, SEVENTH EDITION

Published by McGraw-Hill, a business unit of The McGraw-Hill Companies, Inc., 1221 Avenue
of the Americas, New York, NY 10020. Copyright © 2009 by The McGraw-Hill Companies, Inc.
All rights reserved. Previous edition(s) 1994–2008. No part of this publication may be reproduced
or distributed in any form or by any means, or stored in a database or retrieval system, without
the prior written consent of The McGraw-Hill Companies, Inc., including, but not limited to, in
any network or other electronic storage or transmission, or broadcast for distance learning.

Some ancillaries, including electronic and print components, may not be available to customers
outside the United States.

Taking Sides® is a registered trademark of the McGraw-Hill Companies, Inc.
Taking Sides is published by the **Contemporary Learning Series** group within the McGraw-Hill
Higher Education division.

1 2 3 4 5 6 7 8 9 0 DOC/DOC 0 9 8

MHID: 0-07-351537-X
ISBN: 978-0-07-351537-3
ISSN: 95-83858

Managing Editor: *Larry Loeppke*
Senior Managing Editor: *Faye Schilling*
Developmental Editor: *Jade Benedict*
Editorial Assistant: *Nancy Meissner*
Production Service Assistant: *Rita Hingtgen*
Permissions Coordinator: *Shirley Lanners*
Senior Marketing Manager: *Julie Keck*
Marketing Communications Specialist: *Mary Klein*
Marketing Coordinator: *Alice Link*
Project Manager: *Jane Mohr*
Design Specialist: *Tara McDermott*
Cover Graphics: *Kristine Jubeck*

Compositor: ICC Macmillan Inc.
Cover Image: © Marty Bahamonde/FEMA (left);
Library of Congress [LC-USZ62-12595] (top right);
© The McGraw-Hill Companies, Inc./John Flournoy, photographer (bottom right).

**Library of Congress Cataloging-in-Publication Data**

Main entry under title:
    Taking sides: clashing views in race and ethnicity/selected, edited, and with introductions
    by Raymond D'Angelo and Herbert Douglas.—7th ed.

    Includes bibliographical references.
    1. Race awareness, 2. Ethnicity. I. D'Angelo, Raymond, *comp*. II. Douglas, Herbert, *comp*.

                                                                                    305.8

www.mhhe.com

# TAKING SIDES

Clashing Views in

## Race and Ethnicity

SEVENTH EDITION

Clashing Views in
# Race and Ethnicity
### SEVENTH EDITION

**Raymond D'Angelo**
*St. Joseph's College*

**Herbert Douglas**
*Rowan University*

## Advisory Board

# Preface

This edition of *Taking Sides: Clashing Views in Race and Ethnicity* offers 20 selected issues and 40 readings dealing directly with race and ethnic relations in America. We have selected from historians, sociologists, political scientists, public intellectuals, and others to reflect a wide range of perspectives. The interdisciplinary nature of the selections provides students with much-needed different perspectives on issues. At the same time, the issues will be attractive to the different disciplines in colleges and universities that offer courses in race and ethnic relations. We anticipate that this edition may be used in history, sociology, political science, ethnic studies, and psychology courses. We have followed the standard *Taking Sides* format, which includes an issue introduction and postscript. The introduction to each issue prepares the student with a brief background and questions to be considered when reading the selections. The postscript summarizes the debate, and suggests additional sources for research on the topic.

This reader is intended to supplement other texts or case studies in college courses dealing with race and ethnicity. As such, it is designed to provide a range of readings within a framework.

Students are encouraged to develop and structure their own ideas about race and ethnicity. The introductions and postscripts of each issue intentionally do not contain definitive answers. Students should consider the selections along with our editorial comments, and then formulate responsible thinking and discussion.

**Changes to this Edition**   New to this edition of *Taking Sides: Clashing Views in Race and Ethnicity* are four issues that deal with the role of place for Native Americans, bilingual education in American schools, diversity, and the relationship between Latino immigration and African American labor opportunities. Reflecting a constantly changing culture, we tried to include the most central and historically relevant questions that affect race and ethnicity today. Indeed, there were choices to be made given the wide range of topics touched by race and ethnic matters. This edition has been expanded to 20 issues to accommodate the increasing and varied interest. We feel that the issues examined in this edition are of major significance and need to be studied carefully. These issues have been organized into five units. Unit 1 deals with race, ethnicity, and American identity. Unit 2 explores the extent to which race still matters and affects life chances in today's society. Unit 3 examines different cases involving the persistence of discrimination. Unit 4 looks at persistent challenges in a changing American culture. Unit 5 highlights important twenty-first-century policy issues.

**Supplements**   An *Instructor's Resource Guide with Test Questions* is available from the publisher for instructors who have adopted *Taking Sides: Clashing*

*Views in Race and Ethnicity* for their course. Also, a general guidebook offers information on methods and techniques for using the debate format in a classroom setting. Interested instructors should contact the publisher. There is an online version of *Using Taking Sides in the Classroom* along with a correspondence service for adopters at http://www.mhcls.com/usingts/.

*Taking Sides: Clashing Views in Race and Ethnicity* is only one title of many in the series. Any readers interested in viewing the table of contents for any other titles in the *Taking Sides* series should visit the Web site at http://www.mhcls.com/takingsides/.

**Acknowledgements** This book would not have been possible without many stimulating discussions about race and ethnicity that we have had with students, colleagues, and family members over the years. We wish to recognize the many students we have taught over the years at St. Joseph's College and Rowan University. It is their interest and curiosity that helped stimulate our research in this area.

Raymond D'Angelo recognizes former professors Eugene Schneider, Judith Porter, and Robert Washington of Bryn Mawr College, all of whom helped to provide the intellectual framework that has enabled me to teach and do research in the fields of race relations and ethnic studies. Thanks to historian and former St. Joseph's College colleague Jana Lipman for her critique and suggestions early on in the revision of this edition. Stephen Rockwell, political scientist and departmental colleague, was responsible for the initial research and selections on the topic of Native Americans. Additional departmental colleagues Kenneth Bauzon and Mirella Landriscina offered suggestions, support and critiques as well. Charles Gallagher of Georgia State University continues to provide insight and vigor to this field. Thanks to Stephen Steinberg of Queens College of the City University of New York, who recommended that this edition include the issue of Latino immigration and African American labor. Special appreciation goes to my wife, Susan, for her support and patience throughout this project. Also, my children, Adam and Olivia, deserve mention as they directly and indirectly offer their reactions to contemporary race and ethnic relations. Perhaps most importantly, deepest thanks go to my mother and late father, who in their own way have shed light and understanding for me on the many controversies stemming from race and ethnic differences within American society.

Herb Douglas acknowledges the support and encouragement over the years from his siblings, especially Ms. Doris Douglas and Dr. Sheila Douglas. Dr. Corann Okorodudu and the members of the Steering Committee of Africana Studies of Rowan University are recognized for their part to my development as a contributor to the discourse on race and ethnicity. Dr. Nadine Bitar, professor of sociology, University of Toledo, is recognized for the mentoring, guidance, and support he has provided for many years. Roy Silver, professor of sociology, Southeast Community and Technical College of the University of Kentucky, offered his comments and support. The late Ernest Anderson of the Vineland, New Jersey, NAACP is extended recognition for the significant role he played in the sharpening of my insight into race and ethnicity.

We both appreciate the assistance, diligence, and patience of Jade Benedict, Senior Developmental Editor, and Jane Mohr, Project Manager in the McGraw-Hill Contemporary Learning Series. We extend our thanks to them.

Together, Raymond D'Angelo and Herb Douglas wish to acknowledge the contribution our parents have made to any successes we have achieved in our academic lives and careers. Without the values that they instilled in us, including a commitment to life-long learning, this important project  would not have been possible for us to achieve.

**Raymond D'Angelo**
*St. Joseph's College*

**Herbert Douglas**
*Rowan University*

*For Our Parents*

# Contents In Brief

# Contents

Arthur Schlesinger, Jr., historian, asserts that America needs a common identity. In that context, he views multiculturalism as an attack on the basic values that have made America what it is today. For him, Western-rooted values, whether we like it or not, form the fabric of American society. The values of democracy, freedom, rule of law, human rights, and so forth are unfairly unchallenged under the guise of multiculturalism. He makes the argument for continuing the assimilation creed. Michael Walzer, professor at the Institute for Advanced Study, makes the pluralist argument that America cannot avoid its multicultural identity. He explores the ways in which citizenship and nationality are compatible with the preservation of one's ethnic identity, culture, and community.

Philippe Legrain is a journalist, economist, and author of *Immigrants: Your Country Needs Them* and *Open World: The Truth about Globalisation*. He makes the case that immigration contributes to a better America as well as a better world. His economic argument primarily emphasizes that the flow of immigrants within the global system brings both talent and labor to areas of need. Peter Brimelow, senior editor at *Forbes* and *National Review* magazines, argues that the United States is being overrun by a growing tide of aliens who are changing the character and composition of the nation in manners that are threatening and destructive to its well-being and prospects for future advancement.

Charles A. Gallagher, author and sociology professor at Georgia State University, argues that America is currently undergoing a "racial redistricting" in which the boundaries of whiteness are expanding to include lighter-skinned people of color (i.e., Asians and some Latinos). Ellis Cose, an African American journalist, argues that the traditional boundaries that determine race and skin color are not what they once were. Although he does not specifically cite ethnicity, Cose furthers the claim that American identity today is an expanding category. The boundaries of whiteness have expanded and are no longer hard and fast.

Carlos Fuentes, prominent Mexican writer and social commentator, argues that much of the current immigration debate is racist. For example, he criticizes Samuel Huntington's assessment that Mexican immigrants exploit the United States and represent an unjust burden to the nation. This "mask" of racism appears under the guise of a concern with American national unity. Samuel Huntington, political scientist, and Albert J. Weatherhead III, University Professor at Harvard University, expresses the concern that Mexican immigrants and, by implication, other Latinos, are creating significant problems for America, specifically with reference to assimilation, as their numbers continue to increase within the population. In general, he believes that Latino immigration is a threat to America's national unity.

# UNIT 2   RACE STILL MATTERS   83

Herbert Blumer, a sociologist, asserts that prejudice exists in a sense of group position rather than as an attitude based on individual feelings. The collective process by which a group comes to define other racial groups is the focus of Blumer's position. Gordon Allport, a psychologist, makes the case that prejudice is the result of a three-stage learning process.

Beverly Daniel Tatum, an African American clinical psychologist and president of Spelman College, examines identity development among adolescents, especially black youths, and the behavioral outcomes of this phenomenon. She argues that black adolescents' tendency to view themselves in racial terms is due to the totality of personal and environmental responses that they receive from the larger society. Peter Beinart, senior editor for *The New Republic*, examines the complexity of the issues of multiculturalism and diversity on the nation's campuses, and he asserts that one examine how a broad spectrum of groups responds to the challenges of identity and "fitting in" within increasingly multicultural and diverse communities.

Ward Connerly is a strong critic of all attempts at racial classification and believes that in order to achieve a racially egalitarian, unified American society, the government and private citizens must stop assigning people to categories delineated by race. To achieve this goal, Mr. Connerly is supporting the enactment of a "Racial Privacy Initiative." Eduardo Bonilla-Silva argues that "regardless of whites' sincere fictions, racial considerations shade almost everything in America" and, therefore, color-blind ideology is a cover for the racism and inequality that persist within contemporary American society.

Paul Kivel, a teacher, a writer, and an anti-violence/anti-racist activist, asserts that many benefits accrue to whites based solely on skin color. These benefits range from economic to political advantages and so often include better residential choice, police protection, and education opportunities. Tim Wise, an author of two books on race, argues that whites do not acknowledge privilege. Instead, whites are often convinced that the race card is "played" by blacks to gain their own privilege, something that whites cannot do. Hence, whites simply do not see discrimination and do not attach privilege to their skin color.

Derrick Bell, a prominent African American scholar and authority on civil rights and constitutional law, argues that the prospects for achieving racial equality in the United States are "illusory" for blacks. Dinesh D'Souza, John M. Ohlin Scholar at the American Enterprise Institute, believes that racial discrimination against blacks has substantially eroded within American society and that lagging progress among them is due to other factors, such as culture, rather than racism.

## Issue 10.   Is Racial Profiling Defensible Public Policy?   193

Scott Johnson, conservative journalist and an attorney and fellow at the Clermont Institute, argues in favor of racial profiling. He claims that racial profiling does not exist "on the nation's highways and streets." Johnson accuses David Harris of distorting the data on crimes committed and victimization according to race. For him, law enforcement needs to engage in profiling under certain circumstances in order to be effective. David A. Harris, law professor and leading authority on racial profiling, argues that racial profiling is ineffective and damaging to our diverse nation. He believes it hinders effective law enforcement.

## Issue 11.   Did Hurricane Katrina Expose Racism in America?   210

Adolph Reed, professor of political science at the University of Pennsylvania, and Stephen Steinberg, professor of sociology at Queens College in New York City, challenge the tendency of policy makers and other commentators to focus on blacks as the source of the problems faced by New Orleans in the wake of Hurricane Katrina and emphasize the need to address race and poverty concerns effectively. Shelby Steele, a research fellow at the Hoover Institution and political commentator, argues that blacks of New Orleans along with other blacks should focus on meaningful methods for overcoming their underdevelopment as revealed by Hurricane Katrina, rather than emphasizing the shame of white racism as the cause of their plight.

## Issue 12.   Is the Reservation the Only Source of Community for Native Americans?   224

Frank Pommersheim lived and worked on the Rosebud Sioux Reservation for 10 years and currently teaches at the University of South Dakota School of Law where he specializes in Indian law. Additionally, he is currently providing legal services within India. Emphasizing the critical role played by land in Indian culture, he develops the argument for the significance of "measured separatism." Susan Lobo, a cultural anthropologist and an expert on Native American studies, presents the case of Native Americans in the Bay Area in California. She demonstrates the richness of Indian community life that extends beyond the reservation.

# UNIT 4    PERSISTENT CHALLENGES IN A CHANGING AMERICA    245

Gary Orfield, professor of education and social policy at the Harvard Graduate School of Education, and Susan E. Eaton, author, demonstrate that America's public schools are resegregating. Their argument is based on a series of legal decisions beginning in the 1970s that have successfully reversed the historic *Brown* decision. Ingrid Gould Ellen, writer for *The Brookings Review*, argues that neighborhood racial integration is increasing. She thinks researchers must balance their pessimistic findings of resegregation with increased integration.

Kendra Hamilton, editor of *Black Issues in Higher Education*, argues that the studies available for assessing the quality of such programs are inconclusive. She makes the argument that the outcomes of bilingual education programs are often jeopardized by the quality of the instruction provided. Thus, the significant question of the quality of the programs is being ignored. Rosalie Pedalino Porter, author of *Forked Tongue: The Politics of Bilingual Education* and affiliate of The Institute for Research in English Acquisition and Development (READ), makes the case against bilingual education. She presents a negative view of the contributions of such programs to the academic achievement of non–English speaking students. Also, she is greatly concerned that such programs retard the integration of such students within the larger, English-speaking society.

Walter Benn Michaels, a literary theorist and English professor, is concerned that the emphasis on diversity and race obscures the scientific reality that there is only one race of which we all are members. As such, we tend to focus on racial identities instead of emphasizing that race does not or should not matter. Lastly, Michaels is concerned that the focus on diversity obscures the very real problems of class distinctions within American society.   Henry A. Giroux is an author on multiculturalism and related topics and current chair of Communication Studies at McMaster University, Ontario, Canada. He emphasizes the need to focus on the cultural categories (black vs. white) that are promoted within multiculturalism and diversity in order to understand power relations and other issues that are reflective of racialized identities in society. For Giroux, one significant way to get to the problem of inequality is through identity politics.

David A. Bell, journalist and historian, agrees that Asian Americans are a "model minority" and expresses a great appreciation for the progress and prominence they have achieved within the nation. Frank H. Wu, Howard University law professor, rejects the characterization of Asian Americans as a "model minority" based on the belief that this characterization tends to obscure problems facing Asians in America.

Douglas P. Woodward, director of the Division of Research and Professor of Economics, and Paulo Guimarães, a Clinical Research Professor of

Economics, both of the Moore School of Business at the University of South Carolina, in a strongly researched case study of the impact of Latino immigration on the workers of South Carolina, present significant statistical evidence that African American workers have lost both jobs and wages. David C. Ruffin, a writer and political analyst in Washington, D.C., interviews five black leaders who respond negatively to this question. It is their considered judgment that other factors including technological advancement and high rates of incarceration are major contributors to the lagging prospects of African American workers.

William G. Bowen, former president of Princeton University, and Neil L. Rudenstine, former president of Harvard University, make the case for race-sensitive admissions in higher education. With a focus on selective colleges, they cite empirical data that demonstrate the success of beneficiaries of race-sensitive admission policies. In their opinion, both public and private selective colleges should continue such policies. Roger Clegg, general counsel of the Center for Equal Opportunity in Sterling, Virginia, and contributor to *The Chronicle of Higher Education,* argues that universities should put racial groupings aside and give "individualized consideration" to all applicants. His center serves as a place where students can file complaints about illegal racially approved programs.

Robert Staples, an African American sociologist, views affirmative action as a positive policy designed to provide equal economic opportunities for women and other minorities. Roger Clegg, general counsel of the Center for Equal Opportunity in Sterling, Virginia and contributor to *The Chronicle of Higher Education,* argues against affirmative action, citing the 2003 Supreme Court decision. He makes the case for universities to hire the best-qualified faculty.

Robert L. Allen, professor and senior editor of *The Black Scholar,* argues that reparations for African Americans are necessary to achieve an economically just society within the United States. Staff writers from *The Economist* oppose reparations and question whether such a policy is appropriate in a nation where the victims of slavery are difficult to identify and the perpetrators of past racial oppressions are no longer among us.

# Correlation Guide

The *Taking Sides* series presents current issues in a debate-style format designed to stimulate student interest and develop critical thinking skills. Each issue is thoughtfully framed with an issue summary, an issue introduction, and a postscript. The pro and con essays—selected for their liveliness and substance—represent the arguments of leading scholars and commentators in their fields.

**Taking Sides: Clashing Views in Race and Ethnicity, 7/e** is an easy-to-use reader that presents issues on important topics such as *multiculturalism and democracy, immigration,* and *white privilege.* For more information on *Taking Sides* and other *McGraw-Hill Contemporary Learning Series* titles, visit www.mhcls.com.

This convenient guide matches the issues in **Taking Sides: Race and Ethnicity, 7/e** with the corresponding chapters in two of our best-selling McGraw-Hill Sociology textbooks by Aguirre/Turner and Kottak/Kozaitis.

| Taking Sides: Race and Ethnicity, 7/e | American Ethnicity: The Dynamics and Consequences of Discrimination, 6/e by Aguirre/Turner | On Being Different: Diversity and Multiculturalism in the North American Mainstream, 3/e by Kottak/Kozaitis |
|---|---|---|
| **Issue 1:** Do Americans Need a Common Identity? | **Chapter 2:** : Explaining Ethnic Relations | **Chapter 3:** Globalization and Identity |
| **Issue 2:** Does Immigration Contribute to a Better America? | **Chapter 10:** The Future of Ethnicity in America | **Chapter 4:** The Multicultural Society |
| **Issue 3:** Do Recent Immigration Trends Threaten Existing Ideas of America's White Identity? | **Chapter 10:** The Future of Ethnicity in America | **Chapter 4:** The Multicultural Society |
| **Issue 4:** : Is Today's Immigration Debate Racist? | **Chapter 1:** Ethnicity and Ethnic Relations | **Chapter 2:** Culture |
| **Issue 5:** : Is Race Prejudice a Product of Group Position? | **Chapter 1:** Ethnicity and Ethnic Relations | **Chapter 5:** Ethnicity |
| **Issue 6:** Do Minorities and Whites Engage in Self-segregation? | **Chapter 3:** The Anglo-Saxon Core and Ethnic Antagonism **Chapter 4:** White Ethnic Americans | **Chapter 4:** The Multicultural Society |
| **Issue 7:** Is the Emphasis on a Color-Blind Society an Answer to Racism? | **Chapter 1:** Ethnicity and Ethnic Relations | **Chapter 4:** The Multicultural Society |
| **Issue 8:** Is the Claim of White Skin Privilege a Myth? | **Chapter 2:** Explaining Ethnic Relations **Chapter 3:** The Anglo-Saxon Core and Ethnic Antagonism | **Chapter 7:** Race: Its Social Construction |
| **Issue 9:** Is Racism a Permanent Feature of American Society? | **Chapter 1:** Ethnicity and Ethnic Relations **Chapter 3:** The Anglo-Saxon Core and Ethnic Antagonism | **Chapter 7:** Race: Its Social Construction **Chapter 16:** Families |

| Taking Sides: Race and Ethnicity, 7/e | American Ethnicity: The Dynamics and Consequences of Discrimination, 6/e by Aguirre/Turner | On Being Different: Diversity and Multiculturalism in the North American Mainstream, 3/e by Kottak/Kozaitis |
| --- | --- | --- |
| **Issue 10:** Is Racial Profiling Defensible Public Policy? | | **Issue 7:** Race: Its Social Construction |
| **Issue 11:** Did Hurricane Katrina Expose Racism in New Orleans? | **Chapter 5:** African Americans | **Chapter 5:** Ethnicity **Issue 7:** Race: Its Social Construction |
| **Issue 12:** Is the Reservation the Only Source of Community for Native Americans? | **Chapter 6:** Native Americans | **Chapter 14:** Places and Spaces |
| **Issue 13:** Are America's Public Schools Resegregating? | **Chapter 5:** African Americans | **Chapter 13:** Class |
| **Issue 14:** Is There Room for Bilingual Education in American Schools? | **Chapter 7:** Latinos | **Chapter 15:** Linguistic Diversity |
| **Issue 15:** Is It Time to De-emphasize Diversity? | **Chapter 10:** The Future of Ethnicity in America | **Chapter 2:** Culture **Chapter 3:** Globalization and Identity |
| **Issue 16:** Are Asian Americans a Model Minority? | **Chapter 8:** Asian and Pacific Island Americans | **Chapter 4:** The Multicultural Society |
| **Issue 17:** Does Latino Immigration Threaten African American Workers? | **Chapter 7:** Latinos | **Chapter 5:** Ethnicity |
| **Issue 18:** Should Race Be Included Among the Many Factors Considered for Admission to Selective Colleges? | **Chapter 10:** The Future of Ethnicity in America | **Chapter 5:** Ethnicity |
| **Issue 19:** : Is Affirmative Action Necessary to Achieve Racial Equality in the United States Today? | **Chapter 10:** The Future of Ethnicity in America | **Chapter 7:** Race: Its Social Construction **Chapter 8:** Race: Its Biological Dimensions |
| **Issue 20:** Is Now the Time for Reparations for African Americans? | **Chapter 5:** African Americans | **Chapter 5:** Ethnicity |

# Introduction

Raymond D'Angelo and Herbert Douglas

"America is woven of many strands. Our fate is to become one, and yet many."

—Ralph Ellison (1952)

"Neither the life of an individual nor the history of a society can be understood without understanding both."

—C. Wright Mills

## History

### Immigration

From its inception, America emerged as a multi-ethnic nation. The Anglo-Saxons and other European ethnic groups who came to America during the Colonial Era were met by aboriginal people who had been residing on these lands for thousands of years prior to their arrival. As the colonies developed and their economies began to emerge, African slaves were imported to provide labor for the agrarian economy that would emerge. As the economy of the new nation evolved from agrarian pursuits to industrial capitalism, more and more ethnic groups were attracted to these shores to expand the ranks of labor and to pursue their American dream. Over time, the United States experienced multiple waves of immigration, from the old immigration of pre–Civil War times to the new immigrants of the post–Reconstruction Era, extending to include the most recent immigration of Asians and Hispanics that the nation experienced during the 1990s. So, America has developed as a nation of diverse ethnicities and races derived from virtually every corner of the known world. How does one accommodate the interests and the goals of these diverse ethnic and racial groups while maintaining a unified society? What is an American? How is one to define American identity? (See Issues 1 and 2.)

The United States gained its reputation in the world as a land of freedom and justice for all who arrived on its shores. This quality of the nation's experience has made America a magnet for peoples seeking liberty, justice, and opportunity for improving the quality of their lives.

In the shifting sands of vocabulary that describe the race and ethnic components of American culture, one contemplates "diversity" and "multi-culturalism." Public discourse on these matters takes us on a conceptual journey to explain who we are and who we are not. For all who are in America—the most recent arrivals together with descendants of the very first to arrive—the meaning of what is an American requires us to reflect upon and analyze the history of race and ethnicity.

Political authority and control of the means of economic production by a dominant Anglo group presented challenges to new immigrants, and later in the nineteenth century, former slaves along with other people of color, especially Native Americans. The popular notion of the American melting pot was problematic. The dominant group demonstrated a sense of superiority over subordinate groups. Ethnocentrism, xenophobia, and nativism were common in early American culture and soon resulted in policy efforts to restrict opportunities for those who did not look like white, Anglo-Saxon Protestants or practice their values. What price would a non-Anglo have to pay to "become" an American?

An early twentieth century effort to control American identity can be seen in the Immigration Act of 1924. The Act created immigration quotas based on the percentage of each ethnic group present in America at that time. This legislation had the effect of restricting the immigration of less-favored European ethnic groups such as the Italians and the Poles and created space for the great migration of African Americans from the South to the urban, industrial centers of the North.

We see the struggle for American identity encompassing European ethnics and American blacks as remarkably similar. Both groups were attracted to the northern industrial centers of the United States, seeking economic opportunity that was shrinking in their rural backgrounds. Both groups were deeply religious and anchored by the church in a new urban environment. At the same time, both were vulnerable to being exploited within the labor markets in which they were competing. The competition among racial and ethnic groups within prevailing labor markets is a significant feature of capitalist economies, and the United States was no exception.

## Race Segregation

Segregation emerged as the social and legal framework of race relations at the end of the nineteenth century. In the legal arena, the 1896 *Plessy v. Ferguson* became the law of the land and therefore public policy in race relations. The resulting race segregation that proliferated throughout American cities isolated blacks from European ethnic immigrants. It is in this context that an understanding of early twentieth century race and ethnic relations should be framed. Hence, the early notion of American identity for the most part excluded blacks. Consequently, the late nine-teenth to early twentieth century debate within the black community emerged between Booker T. Washington and W.E.B. DuBois. These leaders were concerned with issues of racial advancement, and they offered competing philosophies and strategies for African Americans to achieve these goals.

The intensity and divisiveness of the race issue in American life was manifested in thousands of lynchings of blacks, forced labor camps, and an ideology of white supremacy. This ideology extended to other peoples of color as seen when Japanese Americans were isolated in internment camps during World War II. Increasingly, blacks and other people of color resided in segregated barrios and ghettos within the core cities of the country. Douglas Massey and Nancy Denton, in *American Apartheid and the Urban Underclass*, refer to this housing segregation as American apartheid.

## The Civil Rights Movement and Desegregation

During the slave era, some questioned whether this peculiar institution was compatible with important American values such as those of the Christian religion and the nation's democratic ethos. The abolitionists were among the first to raise such questions, and their movement was a significant historical precursor to the civil rights movement of the post–World War II period. Indeed, the war itself contributed to changing race relations in the states. It was Executive Order 1199 issued by President Harry S. Truman that integrated the armed forces. This was significant in that it is an early example of the employment of an egalitarian principle to effect the racial reform of an American institution. Black soldiers receiving equal treatment while fighting the war would return home to face segregation.

During the 1940s, the NAACP's legal defense team under the leadership of Charles Hamilton Houston mapped out a strategy to dismantle Jim Crow. Public education became the battleground to overturn the "separate but equal" law of the land. Eventually, in 1954 the Supreme Court overturned *Plessy* in the *Brown v. Board of Education* decision. This decision was a watershed of progress in American race relations. Soon, the civil rights movement would address many issues including public accommodations and perhaps, most importantly, voting rights among others.

Gunnar Myrdal's *An American Dilemma* (1944), a landmark critique of American race relations, contributed significantly to the depth and breadth of knowledge on race in that it argued that America lacked the will to change and enforce its creed of equality and justice within the common life of society, C. Vann Woodward's *The Strange Career of Jim Crow* (1955) became a classic study of segregation.

In the 1960s and beyond, the civil rights movement forced America to recognize and confront the phenomenon of institutional racism. There was more to the problem of racial injustice than just individual attitude and behavior. The Civil Rights Act of 1964, along with the Voting Rights Act of 1965 and the Fair Housing Act of 1968, were key legislative initiatives advanced to address racial inequality.

## Multiculturalism

With new immigrants of color arriving in significant numbers in the 1990s—coming together with existing minorities within desegregated America—an emphasis on multiculturalism and diversity emerged. So, for example, the 2000 U.S. Census shows a population breakdown of 12% Hispanic, 12% African American, 3% Asian American, and 70% white. This contrasts with the demographic profile of the mid-twentieth century in which the minority population consisted primarily of 12% black.

Today, we see a country with an increasing Latino population. In this context, multicultural and diversity concerns are affecting a broad spectrum of American institutions extending from the private corporate sector to public education. Further, this calls into question traditional definitions of race and ethnicity. American demographers predict that increasing diversification of the population of the United States will continue unabated for the foreseeable future. Thus, the challenges to the institutional leaders of America to manage diversity properly will be a major challenge of the twenty-first century. The large numbers of recent Latino immigrants have rekindled the debate over national identity. It has exposed fault lines within the Congress, leading to divisions within each political party; it has forced the corporate elite into a defensive position over hiring practices; it has provoked a mass reaction as reflected in the Minutemen, a volunteer group that has assumed a role of southern border security; and it has become a major arena of media presentation.

## Trends in the Study of Race and Ethnicity

Race and ethnicity were not focal concerns of American scholarship prior to the dawn of the twentieth century; thus, there was a dearth of course offerings on this subject matter within American colleges and universities. The Chicago School of Sociology is credited with introducing the formal study of race relations in American colleges and universities in the 1920s. Beginning with Robert Park, a journalist turned sociologist, along with Ernest Burgess and their colleagues, the study of race and ethnic groups emerged as a primary area in the twentieth century history and sociology due to their introduction of such courses at the University of Chicago. Park's race relations cycle and the idea of assimilation served the country well in terms of policy, as immigrants believed they, and especially their children, would eventually be accepted in their new culture.

Much later in the twentieth century, a pluralist perspective emerged that offered a challenge to the notion of assimilation. Cultural pluralism, a concept noted by Milton Gordon in 1964, refers to the many different cultural systems within the framework of the larger society. When contrasted to assimilation theory, pluralism offers an explanation for the lack of mixing and merging of cultural groups.

It should be noted that Ulrich B. Phillip's *American Negro Slavery* and William Dunning's (*Reconstruction, Political and Economic: 1865–1877*) work on Reconstruction were the primary influences of research and teaching on race prior to the 1950s. The revisionist/reformist scholars who followed them consider both as apologists for slavery and racism. African American intellectuals whose scholarship challenged the perspectives on race presented by Phillips and Dunning found it very difficult to secure publication of their own works. Despite these challenges, black scholars such as Rayford Logan (*The Betrayal of the Negro: From Rutherford B. Hayes to Woodrow*

*Wilson*) and E. Franklin Frazier (*The Negro Family in the United States*) were able to publish works that challenged the traditional notions of race promoted by white scholars of the earlier period.

Some of the most significant challenges to the scholarship and teaching of race that prevailed during the Segregation Era came from white scholars of a leftist orientation. Two prime examples of this scholarly tradition are the multiple-volume work, *A Documentary History of the Negro People in the United States* by the Marxist historian Herbert Aptheker, and Philip Foner's *Mrs. Lincoln and Mrs. Keckly: The Remarkable Story of the Friendship between a First Lady and a Former Slave.* In contrast to traditional history books, Howard Zinn, in *A People's History of the United States: 1492– Present,* highlights the contributions of people of color, women, and immigrants to American culture.

Increasingly, the scholarly literature places immigration in the larger context of globalization. For some, immigration has been promoted directly and indirectly by the idea that global trade is the key to economic prosperity. This is seen as the case for rich as well as poor nations and has stimulated the movement of people from sex slaves to field hands. Thus, there is concern with the economic impact of immigration on the existing workforce (Issues 2, 4, and 17). The impact of a revitalized conservatism in politics, government, and society has been attended by challenges to diversity and multiculturalism and a reemphasis on an "American" identity and its concomitant impact on immigration and immigrants (Issues 1, 3, and 15).

Immigrants who came to the United States often received an "industrial welcome." This positive participation in certain labor markets was facilitated by existing shortages of labor within certain sectors of the economy dominated by menial jobs of law status and offering minimal remuneration. A good example of this orientation toward low-wage workers can be seen in the situation faced by immigrant labor from Latin America in agriculture. Workers from the existing American labor markets tend to find farm labor as undesirable and thus they are quite willing for Mexicans and other Latinos to do this "dirty work" of society. However, when immigrants begin to compete with native-born workers for higher status jobs in pursuit of upward mobility, the result is social conflict between and among such groups.

Social conflict theories offer us important insights into significant areas of race and ethnic relations. Theories of economic competition and cultural conflict are important theoretical perspectives for examining such intergroup relations. Also, Herbert Blumer's theory of group position became another important analytical construct that can be profitably employed to examine competition and conflict within race and ethnic relations (Issue 5).

The inevitable conflicts between and among immigrant groups and racial minorities living in a new country were examined by the emerging social sciences. Within these disciplines, Theodore Adorno, Gordon Allport, Robert Merton, and others applied social scientific thought to prejudice, discrimination, and racism. Some of these problems and issues are explored in this edition (see Issue 5).

In the wake of the landmark decision of the United States Supreme Court of 1954 and the Civil Rights Movement, new opportunities for advancing the study of race and ethnicity emerged. In the wake of this opening, other scholars including Eric Foner, John Hope Franklin, Thomas Pettigrew, Thomas F. Gossett, and Cornel West and many others proliferated within the academic community to advance this interdisciplinary area of scholarly concern. Emerging in academia now were new programs and college majors whose primary focus is on the unique history and experiences of racial and ethnic groups.

Renewed interest in immigration has emerged in response to the changing American demographics. Consider that recent immigration trends show significant growth of the Asian, and especially the Latino components, of the American population (Issues 4 and 16). The increasing racial and ethnic diversity of America today is not without its controversy. What is the role of race in an increasingly multicultural society? How does the shift in dominant-subordinate relations affect members of the dominant group? These questions are reviewed in the book under the following issues: resegregation (Issue 13), who gets into college? (Issues 18 and 19), and is multiculturalism compatible with a democratic ethos (Issue 13)?

More recent developments in the study of race and ethnicity include the increasing research and publication on white skin privilege (Issue 8), racial profiling (Issue 10), and reparations for African Americans (Issue 20). The emerging scholarship from underrepresented minority scholars of Asian, Latino, and Native American backgrounds suggest an expanding group of thinkers bringing new perspectives and adding to the scholarship of race and ethnic studies. At the same time, we see the proliferation of influential conservative think tanks and media-based talk shows. Thus, current scholarship reflects some of these divisions regarding immigration, national identity, race, and ethnicity in the popular culture.

## To the Student

Emphasis on diversity and multiculturalism may reflect a fundamental shift in American culture in terms of the language and vocabulary of American identity. At the same time, healing racial and ethnic issues takes more than changing labels. It requires attitude changes, which are not easy, and institutional changes, which develop slowly in conjunction with public and private policy change. Clearly, disparities in education and economic opportunity persist. Let us begin a reasonable, respectful discussion about important issues, their causes, and possible ways to move forward.

Does "American" constitute multicultural and multiethnic ancestry? Or does it constitute one dominant racial and ethnic group together with many (growing) subordinate groups? We would like to move beyond the blame the individual versus blame society dichotomy and engage in a discourse that includes the past, along with the present, along with the demographic reality of the future.

It is our hope that, in the end, students will gain a greater understanding of the diversity that is the American experience. Further, we hope that students will develop the skills to elevate the discourse of race and ethnic issues through reading, respectful discussion, and critical analysis. These issues need sociological scrutiny because without critical thinking, they are so often determined by popular culture and media-influenced ideas. At the same time the student is assessing American culture, he or she can then grasp the individual issue of identity. Without theory and historical perspective, one essentially has no context for ideas that otherwise may reflect a narrow, incomplete picture of the culture.

Some limitations in this didactic approach of study, which positions one selection against another for the purpose of "debate," must be recognized. At times, one side of the issue is clearly and articulately stated, while the opposite position lacks these qualities. We have tried to find scholarly representations of different points of view. In the process, however, we have found this to be easier said than done. Also, we are aware that the issues may have greater complexity than the two positions offered. Clearly, we run the risk of creating a false dichotomy. It is our expectation that the positions included in the reader will generate interest and insight for the student. Indeed, issues should be explored more comprehensively.

Some of the analytical questions may strike the reader as simplistic or even trivial. For example, how can scholars evaluate the condition of Asians in America with the question, Are Asian Americans a model minority? Clearly, a definitive yes or no answer ignores a growing body of scholarship concerning this and related issues. Further it ignores the extensive and significant ethnic differences among Asians in America, along with the social class composition of these communities. Further, it ignores the extensive diversity of the Asian community. Thus, we seek further understanding by placing the issue in a format that enables the student to organize and express his or her ideas while, at the same time, addressing the given points of view.

Despite the potential limitations, the *Taking Sides* format serves as an introduction to the student as he or she tries to structure thoughts and ideas in these controversial areas. We consider America as a society whose unifying identity is rooted in ethnic and racial diversity. How the diversity plays out—that is, the structures and the forms it takes—is of sociological interest to us. In sum, we want students to explore critically the historical and contemporary experiences of racial and ethnic groups in America.

## Issues in This New Edition

This edition builds on our previous two editions (fifth and sixth) in consideration of the most recent American trends in the field of race and ethnicity. Our search to locate and balance two sides of a topic covers a wide variety of sources and, at times, we are limited in the selection process due to considerations of space, permissions, and availability of college-level articles. We seek to elevate the treatment of issues on race and ethnicity to a level of responsible scholarship. From time to time, polar opposite positions on a given issue may lead to a more vituperative debate. At other times, after careful study and discussion, different positions may not be viewed as opposite, but closer to a middle range. Nevertheless, the different positions reflect the development of American culture and deserve to be debated. The net result, we hope, is a deeper and greater understanding of race and ethnicity.

The student or professor familiar with the previous two editions will note that our focus continues to be in American race and ethnic issues. Clearly, in the larger picture, the study of race and ethnicity benefits from a cross-national approach. While we do not ignore global trends, especially in consideration of immigration, we can only do justice to American race and ethnicity in one volume. We have suggested to our senior editor that global issues of race and ethnicity be considered for a separate publication. Our decision to focus on American issues is based on the judgment that race, ethnicity, and immigration are fundamental to understanding the American experience and that unresolved issues on these fronts continue to challenge society in the twenty-first century. We have made a concerted effort to move beyond the black–white dichotomy in clear recognition that issues of race and ethnicity are more complex and extensive.

This edition is organized around five concepts: (1) race, ethnicity, and American identity, (2) race still matters, (3) the persistence of discrimination, (4) persistent challenges in a changing America, and (5) policy issues for the twenty-first century.

Unit 1, "Race, Ethnicity, and American Identity," introduces the student to the classic question of American identity. What is an American? Specifically, students will contemplate, in the context of race, ethnicity, and American identity, "Who am I?" or "Who are we?" From the early years of the new nation, immigration and slavery confronted both newcomers and those who preceded them. Thus, how to understand the making of an American identity includes consideration of both. Each of the issues in this unit of the book deals with immigration, while three issues incorporate race in the dilemma of American identity. Students should develop a broad historical perspective of these issues, which are still with us today.

Unit 2, "Race Still Matters," deals with the impact of prejudice and the lingering effect of race on minority groups as well as on the larger society. Why does self-segregation occur, not only among minorities but also within the white majority? What exactly is white skin privilege? Why is there a recent emphasis on a color-blind society? Is this emphasis a new form of racism? Or is it an effort to transcend race differences politically as well as sociologically? Students should examine these issues both conceptually and empirically.

Unit 3, "The Persistence of Discrimination," critically asks and applies examples of institutional discrimination to contemporary problems. Each issue raises the question of discrimination. The question about the permanence of racism may at first seem audacious, but its examination will benefit student understanding. A consideration of Hurricane Katrina, the natural disaster of 2005 that beset New Orleans and the Gulf coast, gives us the opportunity to assess race prejudice and discrimination in a unique context. The inclusion of the important issue of place for Native Americans forces the reader to examine the early years of the American attitude and policy dealing with non-whites. Further, it encourages the student to include an often-neglected group in the study of race and ethnicity.

Unit 4, "Persistent Challenges in a Changing America," raises relevant questions about fairness, equity, and opportunity as American society changes demographically, politically, and culturally. Insurgent multiculturalism and diversity are essential concepts to explore as we move to resolve the challenges of equity and opportunity. The resegregation of public schools and the issue of bilingualism confront public education in many American communities. Indeed, segregated neighborhoods make for segregated public schools. Is resegregation taking place? Should bilingualism continue? How are these challenges being met? The inclusion of the issue of Asians in America allows students to examine critically race and ethnic concepts such as stereotypes beyond the black–white paradigm.

Unit 5, "Policy Issues for the Twenty-First Century," focuses on what we think are significant controversial issues bearing on public policy for the twenty-first century. What policies should be developed concerning Latino immigration, race and selective college admissions, affirmative action, and reparations for African Americans? Two of the issues deal directly with education. They reflect changes in racial and ethnic diversity leading to the recognition of multiculturalism in contemporary American society. Thus, the policy of affirmative action is evaluated along with the related issue of race (and other factors) and its role in selective college admissions. The final issue of reparations for African Americans may not be resolved until far into this century. Students should see the persistent role of race and ethnicity in American society throughout this part of the book and its likely impact on public policy.

## Editors' Note

We have been engaged in a fascinating and endless four-decade dialogue about race and ethnicity in American society. Putting together this reader has given us the opportunity to examine and frame some of the critical problems and issues in the field. We welcome feedback from our readers. Email responses to rdangelo@sjcny.edu.

# Internet References . . .

## United States Census Bureau

The U.S. Census Bureau Web site presents useful demographic information on ancestry, citizenship, and foreign-born citizens. The links to Hispanic and Asian minority data are extensive. This site is a very good starting point for the serious student to gain background information on race and ethnicity.

**www.uscensus.gov**

## American Ethnic Studies: Yale Library Research Guide

At Yale University, this site provides sources for researching ethnic identity including research guides in African American, Latino, Native American, Asian American, and American studies. It is a valuable site for students to begin research in race and ethnic relations, offering multiple links to college libraries and scholarly journals. Includes links to guides, encyclopedias, and dictionaries, along with connections to museums, centers, institutes, and databases.

**www.library.yale.edu/rsc/ethnic/internet.html**

## United States Citizenship and Immigration Services

This is the home page of the United States Citizenship and Immigration Services (USCIS). It offers up-to-date information on U.S. immigration law and policy.

**http://uscis. gov/graphics/index.htm**

## Ellis Island Foundation

The Web site of the Ellis Island Foundation enables almost everyone a chance to research his or her family history. It contains an American family immigration history center.

**http://www.ellisisland.org/**

## Immigration History Research Center: University of Minnesota

The University of Minnesota Immigration Research Center, with a focus on research sources for European immigrants, seeks to promote the history of the American immigrant experience. It offers an extensive bibliography of manuscripts and monographs on European immigrant groups.

**http://www.ihrc.umn.edu/**

## Guide to Sociological Resources

SocioWeb is an excellent starting place for information and research opportunities in the field of sociology including race relations, demography, and population, all of which relate directly to clashing views on race and ethnicity.

**http://www.socioweb.com**

# Race, Ethnicity, and American Identity

*T* *here are a number of concerns that have challenged the American nation throughout its history. Given the fact that immigration has been a significant factor in shaping the nation, significant concerns with immigration and immigration policies have confronted the American body politic over time. Immigration has challenged the traditional notion of American identity and raises serious issues concerning the maintenance of an American unum. The diversity of the American population to which immigration has been a major contributor has brought substantial issues of race relations to the fore. Most recently, Latino immigration has emerged as a major domestic issue presenting new challenges to American identity and culture. Racial minorities have challenged the nation to live up to the true meaning of its creed where issues of equity and social justice are concerned and these issues and concerns have been illuminated within the experiences of African Americans and those of the peoples of color that have swelled the ranks of America's immigrant populations. The efforts of immigrants to advance within the institutional domains of the American society have been ongoing challenges to our national experience. Prejudice and discrimination still remain as obstacles for new immigrants and existing minorities to overcome in pursuit of the American dream.*

- Do Americans Need a Common Identity?

- Does Immigration Contribute to a Better America?

- Do Recent Immigration Trends Threaten Existing Ideas of America's White Identity?

- Is Today's Immigration Debate Racist?

1

# ISSUE 1

# Do Americans Need
# a Common Identity?

**YES: Arthur M. Schlesinger, Jr.,** from *The Disuniting of America: Reflections on a Multicultural Society* (W.W. Norton Co., 1992)

**NO: Michael Walzer,** from "What Does It Mean to Be an 'American'?" *Social Research* (Fall 1990)

### ISSUE SUMMARY

**YES:** Arthur Schlesinger, Jr., historian, asserts that America needs a common identity. In that context, he views multiculturalism as an attack on the basic values that have made America what it is today. For him, Western-rooted values, whether we like it or not, form the fabric of American society. The values of democracy, freedom, rule of law, human rights and so forth are unfairly challenged under the guise of multiculturalism. He makes the argument for continuing the assimilation creed.

**NO:** Michael Walzer, professor at the Institute for Advanced Study, makes the pluralist argument that America cannot avoid its multicultural identity. He explores the ways in which citizenship and nationality are compatible with the preservation of one's ethnic identity, culture, and community.

**G**iven the varied background differences of the many groups of people who have become Americans, the question of a common identity is inevitable. What is an American? When does an immigrant become an "American"? This edition of *Taking Sides, Race and Ethnicity* begins with the complex issue of American identity. Indeed, the parallel issues of race and ethnicity are at the heart of the American experience. Hence, to understand American identity is to consider the uniqueness of American culture along with what holds it together. A common American identity began as a European immigrant culture that dealt with racial differences through the institution of slavery and isolating Native Americans on reserve land. Throughout American history, the idea of a common American culture has constantly changed. Central to the changes is, on one hand, the firm notion that there must be a common American identity, while on the other is the recognition of several different, sometimes competing, cultural groups who are part of the same culture. This dilemma has emerged conceptually in the form of the assimilation versus pluralism debate.

Arthur Schlesinger, Jr., is concerned about what he sees as an attack on the common American identity, which was initially launched by European immigrants of non-British origin, and continued by later immigrants of non-European origin. For Schlesinger, a common American identity is based on values that originated in Europe and developed fully in America. Values such as individual freedom, tolerance, liberty, equality, and human rights are part of Western culture. They have become the core of a common American identity.

How are racial and ethnic differences included in American culture? The dominant culture is rooted in Anglo-Saxon foundations. Nevertheless, the different immigrant groups ("a nation of immigrants") reflect many different cultures. Culturally, what does an immigrant experience to become an American? How much assimilation is possible? And, what are the perceived costs and rewards of assimilation?

In the same context that Schlesinger critiques the interest in multiculturalism, he cites the democratic principle of tolerance. He assumes that all races are included in the common American identity.

Michael Walzer argues that America has no singular national identity. Further, he writes, that to be an American is "to know that and to be more or less content with it." Using the ideas of Horace Kallen, Walzer furthers the argument that the United States is less a union of states than a union of ethnic, racial, and religious groups.

Walzer maintains that these "unrelated natives" constitute a permanent "manyness." A dissimilation or unique cultural consciousness does not threaten American culture. Given the tremendous diversity of American people, the common culture of the nation is seen through its citizenship. Hence, the need for a common American identity is limited.

As you read this issue, keep in mind that each new wave of immigrants raises the question of American identity. Again and again, the culture and contributions of new immigrants pushes America to ask, should we stress our similarities or encourage diversity? Should we insist on a common American identity or celebrate our differences? Consider Schlesinger's critique of multiculturalism and contrast it with Walzer's ideas of pluralism. Is Schlesinger trying to protect and preserve a dominant group culture? Or is he intolerant of cultural differences? Does Walzer truly favor pluralism? Or does he think a common American identity is impossible?

# YES                 Arthur M. Schlesinger, Jr.

# E Pluribus Unum?

The attack on the common American identity is the culmination of the cult of ethnicity. That attack was mounted in the first instance by European Americans of non-British origin ("unmeltable ethnics") against the British foundations of American culture; then, latterly and massively, by Americans of non-European origin against the European foundations of that culture. As Theodore Roosevelt's foreboding suggests, the European immigration itself palpitated with internal hostilities, everyone at everybody else's throats—hardly the "monocultural" crowd portrayed by ethnocentric separatists. After all, the two great "world" wars of the twentieth century began as fights among European states. Making a single society out of this diversity of antagonistic European peoples is a hard enough job. The new salience of non-European, nonwhite stocks compounds the challenge. And the non-Europeans, or at least their self-appointed spokesmen, bring with them a resentment, in some cases a hatred, of Europe and the West provoked by generations of Western colonialism, racism, condescension, contempt, and cruel exploitation.

&bull;&#10086;&bull;

Will not this rising flow of non-European immigrants create a "minority majority" that will make Eurocentrism obsolete by the twenty-first century? This is the fear of some white Americans and the hope (and sometimes the threat) of some nonwhites.

Immigrants were responsible for a third of population growth during the 1980s. More arrived than in any decade since the second of the century. And the composition of the newcomers changed dramatically. In 1910 nearly 90 percent of immigrants came from Europe. In the 1980s more than 80 percent came from Asia and Latin America.

Still, foreign-born residents constitute only about 7 percent of the population today as against nearly 15 percent when the first Roosevelt and Wilson were worrying about hyphenated Americans, Stephan Thernstrom doubts that the minority majority will ever arrive. The black share in the population has grown rather slowly—9.9 percent in 1920, 10 percent in

1950, 11.1 percent in 1970, and 12.1 percent in 1990. Neither Asian-Americans nor Hispanic-Americans go in for especially large families; and family size in any case tends to decline as income and intermarriage increase. "If today's immigrants assimilate to American ways as readily as their predecessors at the turn of the century—as seems to be happening," Thernstrom concludes, "there won't be a minority majority issue anyway."

America has so long seen itself as the asylum for the oppressed and persecuted—and has done itself and the world so much good thereby—that any curtailment of immigration offends something in the American soul. No one wants to be a Know-Nothing. Yet uncontrolled immigration is an impossibility; so the criteria of control are questions the American democracy must confront. We have shifted the basis of admission three times this century—from national origins in 1924 to family reunification in 1965 to needed skills in 1990. The future of immigration policy depends on the capacity of the assimilation process to continue to do what it has done so well in the past: to lead newcomers to an acceptance of the language, the institutions, and the political ideals that hold the nation together.

·✦·

Is Europe really the root of all evil? The crimes of Europe against lesser breeds without the law (not to mention even worse crimes—Hitlerism and Stalinism—against other Europeans) are famous. But these crimes do not alter other facts of history: that Europe was the birthplace of the United States of America, that European ideas and culture formed the republic, that the United States is an extension of European civilization, and that nearly 80 percent of Americans are of European descent.

When Irving Howe, hardly a notorious conservative, dared write, "The Bible, Homer, Plato, Sophocles, Shakespeare are central to our culture," an outraged reader ("having graduated this past year from Amherst") wrote, "Where on Howe's list is the *Quran*, the *Gita*, Confucius, and other central cultural artifacts of the peoples of our nation?" No one can doubt the importance of these works nor the influence they have had on other societies. But on American society? It may be too bad that dead white European males have played so large a role in shaping our culture. But that's the way it is. One cannot erase history.

These humdrum historical facts, and not some dastardly imperialist conspiracy, explain the Eurocentric slant in American schools. Would anyone seriously argue that teachers should conceal the European origins of American civilization? Or that schools should cater to the 20 percent and ignore the 80 percent? Of course the 20 percent and their contributions should be integrated into the curriculum too, which is the point of cultural pluralism.

But self-styled "multiculturalists" are very often ethnocentric separatists who see little in the Western heritage beyond Western crimes. The Western tradition, in this view, is inherently racist, sexist, "classist," hegemonic; irredeemably repressive, irredeemably oppressive. The spread of Western culture is due not to any innate quality but simply to the spread of Western power. Thus the popularity of European classical music around the world—and, one supposes, of American jazz and rock too—is evidence not of wide appeal but of "the pattern of imperialism, in which the conquered culture adopts that of the conqueror."

Such animus toward Europe lay behind the well-known crusade against the Western-civilization course at Stanford ("Hey-hey, ho-ho, Western culture's got to go!"). According to the National Endowment for the Humanities, students can graduate from 78 percent of American colleges and universities without taking a course in the history of Western civilization. A number of institutions—among them Dartmouth, Wisconsin, Mt. Holyoke—require courses in third-world or ethnic studies but not in Western civilization. The mood is one of divesting Americans of the sinful European inheritance and seeking redemptive infusions from non-Western cultures.

❧

One of the oddities of the situation is that the assault on the Western tradition is conducted very largely with analytical weapons forged in the West. What are the names invoked by the coalition of latter-day Marxists, deconstructionists, poststructuralists, radical feminists, Afrocentrists? Marx, Nietzsche, Gramsci, Derrida, Foucault, Lacan, Sartre, de Beauvoir, Habermas, the Frankfurt "critical theory" school—Europeans all. The "unmasking," "demythologizing," "decanonizing," "dehegemonizing" blitz against Western culture depends on methods of critical analysis unique to the West—which surely testifies to the internally redemptive potentialities of the Western tradition.

Even Afrocentrists seem to accept subliminally the very Eurocentric standards they think they are rejecting. "Black intellectuals condemn Western civilization," Professor Pearce Williams says, "yet ardently wish to prove it was founded by their ancestors." And, like Frantz Fanon and Léopold Senghor, whose books figure prominently on their reading lists, Afrocentric ideologues are intellectual children of the West they repudiate. Fanon, the eloquent spokesman of the African wretched of the earth, had French as his native tongue and based his analyses on Freud, Marx, and Sartre. Senghor, the prophet of Negritude, wrote in French, established the Senegalese educational system on the French model and, when he left the presidency of Senegal, retired to France.

Western hegemony, it would seem, can be the source of protest as well as of power. Indeed, the invasion of American schools by the Afrocentric curriculum, not to mention the conquest of university departments of English and comparative literature by deconstructionists, poststructuralists, etc., are developments that by themselves refute the extreme theory of "cultural hegemony." Of course, Gramsci had a point. Ruling values do dominate and permeate any society; but they do not have the rigid and monolithic grip on American democracy that academic leftists claim.

Radical academics denounce the "canon" as an instrument of European oppression enforcing the hegemony of the white race, the male sex, and the capitalist class, designed, in the words of one professor, "to rewrite the past and construct the present from the perspective of the privileged and the powerful." Or in the elegant words of another—and a professor of theological ethics at that: "The canon of great literature was created by high Anglican assholes to underwrite their social class."

The poor old canon is seen not only as conspiratorial but as static. Yet nothing changes more regularly and reliably than the canon: compare, for example, the canon in American poetry as defined by Edmund Clarence Stedman in his *Poets of America* (1885) with the canon of 1935 or of 1985 (whatever happened to Longfellow and Whittier?); or recall the changes that have overtaken the canonical literature of American history in the last half-century (who reads Beard and Parrington now?). And the critics clearly have no principled objection to the idea of the canon. They simply wish to replace an old gang by a new gang. After all, a canon means only that because you can't read everything, you give some books priority over others.

Oddly enough, serious Marxists—Marx and Engels, Lukacs, Trotsky, Gramsci—had the greatest respect for what Lukacs called "the classical heritage of mankind." Well they should have, for most great literature and much good history are deeply subversive in their impact on orthodoxies. Consider the present-day American literary canon: Emerson, Jefferson, Melville, Whitman, Hawthorne, Thoreau, Lincoln, Twain, Dickinson, William and Henry James, Henry Adams, Holmes, Dreiser, Faulkner, O'Neill. Lackeys of the ruling class? Apologists for the privileged and the powerful? Agents of American imperialism? Come on!

It is time to adjourn the chat about hegemony. If hegemony were as real as the cultural radicals pretend, Afrocentrism would never have got anywhere, and the heirs of William Lyon Phelps would still be running the Modern Language Association.

⋅⟨⊙⟩⋅

Is the Western tradition a bar to progress and a curse on humanity? Would it really do America and the world good to get rid of the European legacy?

No doubt Europe has done terrible things, not least to itself. But what culture has not? History, said Edward Gibbon, is little more than the register of the crimes, follies, and misfortunes of mankind. The sins of the West are no worse than the sins of Asia or of the Middle East or of Africa.

There remains, however, a crucial difference between the Western tradition and the others. The crimes of the West have produced their own antidotes. They have provoked great movements to end slavery, to raise the status of women, to abolish torture, to combat racism, to defend freedom of inquiry and expression, to advance personal liberty and human rights.

Whatever the particular crimes of Europe, that continent is also the source—the *unique* source—of those liberating ideas of individual liberty, political democracy, the rule of law, human rights, and cultural freedom that constitute our most precious legacy and to which most of the world today aspires. These are *European* ideas, not Asian, nor African, nor Middle Eastern ideas, except by adoption.

The freedoms of inquiry and of artistic creation, for example, are Western values. Consider the differing reactions to the case of Salman Rushdie: what the West saw as an intolerable attack on individual freedom the Middle East saw as a proper punishment for an evildoer who had violated the mores of his group. Individualism itself is looked on with abhorrence and dread by collectivist cultures in which loyalty to the group overrides personal goals—cultures that, social scientists say, comprise about 70 percent of the world's population.

There is surely no reason for Western civilization to have guilt trips laid on it by champions of cultures based on despotism, superstition, tribalism, and fanaticism. In this regard the Afrocentrists are especially absurd. The West needs no lectures on the superior virtue of those "sun people" who sustained slavery until Western imperialism abolished it (and, it is reported, sustain it to this day in Mauritania and the Sudan), who still keep women in subjection and cut off their clitorises, who carry out racial persecutions not only against Indians and other Asians but against fellow Africans from the wrong tribes, who show themselves either incapable of operating a democracy or ideologically hostile to the democratic idea, and who in their tyrannies and massacres, their Idi Amins and Boukassas, have stamped with utmost brutality on human rights.

Certainly the European overlords did little enough to prepare Africa for self-government. But democracy would find it hard in any case to put down roots in a tribalist and patrimonial culture that, long before the West invaded Africa, had sacralized the personal authority of chieftains and ordained the submission of the rest. What the West would call corruption is regarded through much of Africa as no more than the prerogative of power. Competitive political parties, an independent judiciary, a free press, the rule of law are alien to African traditions.

It was the French, not the Algerians, who freed Algerian women from the veil (much to the irritation of Frantz Fanon, who regarded deveiling as symbolic rape); as in India it was the British, not the Indians, who ended (or did their best to end) the horrible custom of *suttee*—widows burning themselves alive on their husbands' funeral pyres. And it was the West, not the non-Western cultures, that launched the crusade to abolish slavery— and in doing so encountered mighty resistance, especially in the Islamic world (where Moslems, with fine impartiality, enslaved whites as well as blacks). Those many brave and humane Africans who are struggling these days for decent societies are animated by Western, not by African, ideals. White guilt can be pushed too far.

The Western commitment to human rights has unquestionably been intermittent and imperfect. Yet the ideal remains—and movement toward it has been real, if sporadic. Today it is the *Western* democratic tradition that attracts and empowers people of all continents, creeds, and colors. When the Chinese students cried and died for democracy in Tiananmen Square, they brought with them not representations of Confucius or Buddha but a model of the Statue of Liberty.

⋅⟨◉⟩⋅

The great American asylum, as Crèvecoeur called it, open, as Washington said, to the oppressed and persecuted of all nations, has been from the start of an experiment in a multiethnic society. This is a bolder experiment than we sometimes remember. History is littered with the wreck of states that tried to combine diverse ethnic or linguistic or religious groups within a single sovereignty. Today's headlines tell of imminent crisis or impending dissolution in one or another multiethnic polity—the Soviet Union, India, Yugoslavia, Czechoslovakia, Ireland, Belgium, Canada, Lebanon, Cyprus, Israel, Ceylon, Spain, Nigeria, Kenya, Angola, Trinidad, Guyana. . . . The list is almost endless. The luck so far of the American experiment has been due in large part to the vision of the melting pot. "No other nation," Margaret Thatcher has said, "has so successfully combined people of different races and nations within a single culture."

But even in the United States, ethnic ideologues have not been without effect. They have set themselves against the old American ideal of assimilation. They call on the republic to think in terms not of individual but of group identity and to move the polity from individual rights to group rights. They have made a certain progress in transforming the United States into a more segregated society. They have done their best to turn a college generation against Europe and the Western tradition. They have imposed ethnocentric, Afrocentric, and bilingual curricula on public schools, well designed to hold minority children out of American society. They have told young people from minority groups that the Western democratic tradition is not for them. They have encouraged minorities to see themselves as victims and to live by alibis rather than to claim the opportunities opened for them by the potent combination of black protest and white guilt. They have filled the air with recrimination and rancor and have remarkably advanced the fragmentation of American life.

Yet I believe the campaign against the idea of common ideals and a single society will fail. Gunnar Myrdal was surely right: for all the damage it has done, the upsurge of ethnicity is a superficial enthusiasm stirred by romantic ideologues and unscrupulous hucksters whose claim to speak for their minorities is thoughtlessly accepted by the media. I doubt that the ethnic vogue expresses a reversal of direction from assimilation to apartheid among the minorities themselves. Indeed, the more the ideologues press the case for ethnic separatism, the less they appeal to the mass of their own groups. They have thus far done better in intimidating the white majority than in converting their own constituencies.

"No nation in history," writes Lawrence Fuchs, the political scientist and immigration expert in his fine book *The American Kaleidoscope*, "had proved as successful as the United States in managing ethnic diversity. No nation before had ever made diversity itself a source of national identity and unity." The second sentence explains the success described in the first, and the mechanism for translating diversity into unity has been the American Creed, the civic culture—the very assimilating, unifying culture that is today challenged, and not seldom rejected, by the ideologues of ethnicity.

A historian's guess is that the resources of the Creed have not been exhausted. Americanization has not lost its charms. Many sons and daughters of ethnic neighborhoods still want to shed their ethnicity and move to the suburbs as fast as they can—where they will be received with far more tolerance than they would have been 70 years ago. The desire for achievement and success in American society remains a potent force for assimilation. Ethnic subcultures, Stephen Steinberg, author of *The Ethnic Myth,* points out, fade away "because circumstances forced them to make choices that undermined the basis for cultural survival."

Others may enjoy their ethnic neighborhoods but see no conflict between foreign descent and American loyalty. Unlike the multiculturalists, they celebrate not only what is distinctive in their own backgrounds but what they hold in common with the rest of the population.

The ethnic identification often tends toward superficiality. The sociologist Richard Alba's study of children and grandchildren of immigrants in the Albany, New York, area shows the most popular "ethnic experience" to be sampling the ancestral cuisine. Still, less than half the respondents picked that, and only one percent ate ethnic food every day. Only one-fifth acknowledged a sense of special relationship to people of their own ethnic background; less than one-sixth taught their children about their ethnic origins; almost none was fluent in the language of the old country. "It is hard to avoid the conclusion," Alba writes, "that ethnic experience is shallow for the great majority of whites."

If ethnic experience is a good deal less shallow for blacks, it is because of their bitter experience in America, not because of their memories of Africa. Nonetheless most blacks prefer "black" to "African-Americans," fight bravely and patriotically for their country, and would move to the suburbs too if income and racism would permit.

As for Hispanic-Americans, first-generation Hispanics born in the United States speak English fluently, according to a Rand Corporation study; more than half of second-generation Hispanics give up Spanish altogether. When *Vista,* an English-language monthly for Hispanics, asked its readers what historical figures they most admired, Washington, Lincoln, and Theodore Roosevelt led the list, with Benito Juárez trailing behind as fourth, and Eleanor Roosevelt and Martin Luther King Jr. tied for fifth. So much for ethnic role models.

Nor, despite the effort of ethnic ideologues, are minority groups all that hermetically sealed off from each other, except in special situations, like colleges, where ideologues are authority figures. The wedding notices in any newspaper testify to the increased equanimity with which people these days marry across ethnic lines, across religious lines, even, though to a smaller degree, across racial lines. Around half of Asian-American marriages are with non-Orientals, and the Census Bureau estimates one million interracial—mostly black-white—marriages in 1990 as against 310,000 in 1970.

♦

The ethnic revolt against the melting pot has reached the point, in rhetoric at least, though not I think in reality, of a denial of the idea of a common culture and a single society. If a large number of people really accept this, the republic would be in serious trouble. The question poses itself: how to restore the balance between *unum* and *pluribus?*

The old American homogeneity disappeared well over a century ago, never to return. Ever since, we have been preoccupied in one way or another with the problem, as Herbert Croly phrased in 80 years back in *The Promise of American Life,* "of preventing such divisions from dissolving the society into which they enter—of keeping such a highly differentiated society fundamentally sound and whole." This required, Croly believed, an "ultimate bond of union." There was only one way by which solidarity could be restored, "and that is by means of a democratic social ideal. . . . "

The genius of America lies in its capacity to forge a single nation from peoples of remarkably diverse racial, religious, and ethnic origins. It has done so because democratic principles provide both the philosophical bond of union and practical experience in civic participation. The American Creed envisages a nation composed of individuals making their own choices and accountable to themselves, not a nation based on inviolable ethnic communities. The Constitution turns on individual rights, not on group rights. Law, in order to rectify past wrongs, has from time to time (and in my view often properly so) acknowledged the claims of groups; but this is the exception, not the rule.

Our democratic principles contemplate an open society founded on tolerance of differences and on mutual respect. In practice, America has been more open to some than to others. But it is more open to all today than it was yesterday and is likely to be even more open tomorrow than today. The steady movement of American life has been from exclusion to inclusion.

Historically and culturally this republic has an Anglo-Saxon base; but from the start the base has been modified, enriched, and reconstituted by transfusions from other continents and civilizations. The movement from exclusion to inclusion causes a constant revision in the texture of our culture. The ethnic transfusions affect all aspects of American life—our politics, our literature, our music, our painting, our movies, our cuisine, our customs, our dreams.

Black Americans in particular have influenced the ever-changing national culture in many ways. They have lived here for centuries, and, unless one believes in racist mysticism, they belong far more to American culture than to the culture of Africa. Their history is part of the Western democratic tradition, not an alternative to it. Henry Louis Gates Jr. reminds us of James Baldwin's remark about coming to Europe to find out that he was "as American as any Texas G.I." No one does black Americans more disservice than those Afrocentric ideologues who would define them out of the West.

The interplay of diverse traditions produces the America we know. "Paradoxical though it may seem," Diane Ravitch has well said, "the United States has a common culture that is multicultural." That is why unifying political ideals coexist so easily and cheerfully with diversity in social and cultural values. Within the overarching political commitment, people are free to live as they choose, ethnically and otherwise. Differences will remain; some are reinvented; some are used to drive us apart. But as we renew our allegiance to the unifying ideals, we provide the solvent that will prevent differences from escalating into antagonism and hatred.

One powerful reason for the movement from exclusion to inclusion is that the American Creed facilitates the appeal from the actual to the ideal. When we talk of the American democratic faith, we must understand it in its true dimensions. It is not an impervious, final, and complacent orthodoxy, intolerant of deviation and dissent, fulfilled in flag salutes, oaths of allegiance, and hands over the heart. It is an ever-evolving philosophy, fulfilling its ideals through debate, self-criticism, protest, disrespect, and irreverence; a tradition in which all have rights of heterodoxy and opportunities for self-assertion. The Creed has been the means by which Americans have haltingly but persistently narrowed the gap between performance and principle. It is what all Americans should learn, because it is what binds all Americans together.

Let us by all means in this increasingly mixed-up world learn about those other continents and civilizations. But let us master our own history first. Lamentable as some may think it, we inherit an American experience, as America inherits a European experience. To deny the essentially European origins of American culture is to falsify history.

Americans of whatever origin should take pride in the distinctive inheritance to which they have all contributed, as other nations take pride in their distinctive inheritances. Belief in one's own culture does not require disdain for other cultures. But one step at a time: no culture can hope to ingest other cultures all at once, certainly not before it ingests its own. As we begin to master our own culture, then we can explore the world.

Our schools and colleges have a responsibility to teach history for its own sake—as part of the intellectual equipment of civilized persons—and not to degrade history by allowing its contents to be dictated by pressure groups, whether political, economic, religious, or ethnic. The past may sometimes give offense to one or another minority; that is no reason for rewriting history. Giving pressure groups vetoes over textbooks and courses betrays both history and education. Properly taught, history will convey a sense of the variety, continuity, and adaptability of cultures, of the need for understanding other cultures, of the ability of individuals and peoples to overcome obstacles, of the importance of critical analysis and dispassionate judgment in every area of life.

Above all, history can give a sense of national identity. We don't have to believe that our values are absolutely better than the next fellow's or the next country's, but we have no doubt that they are better *for us,* reared as we are—and are worth living by and worth dying for. For our values are not matters of whim and happenstance. History has given them to us. They are anchored in our national experience, in our great national documents, in our national heroes, in our folkways, traditions, and standards. People with a different history will have differing values. But we believe that our own are better for us. They work for us; and, for that reason, we live and die by them.

It has taken time to make the values real for all our citizens, and we still have a good distance to go, but we have made progress. If we now repudiate the quite marvelous inheritance that history bestows on us, we invite the fragmentation of the national community into a quarrelsome spatter of enclaves, ghettos, tribes. The bonds of cohesion in our society are sufficiently fragile, or so it seems to me, that it makes no sense to strain them by encouraging and exalting cultural and linguistic apartheid.

The American identity will never be fixed and final; it will always be in the making. Changes in the population have always brought changes in the national ethos and will continue to do so; but not, one must hope, at the expense of national integration. The question America confronts as a pluralistic society is how to vindicate cherished cultures and traditions without breaking the bonds of cohesion—common ideals, common political institutions, common language, common culture, common fate—that hold the republic together.

Our task is to combine due appreciation of the splendid diversity of the nation with due emphasis on the great unifying Western ideas of individual freedom, political democracy, and human rights. These are the ideas that define the American nationality—and that today empower people of all continents, races, and creeds.

"What then is the American, this new man? . . . Here individuals of all nations are melted into a new race of men." Still a good answer—still the best hope.

Michael Walzer

# What Does It Mean to Be an "American"?

There is no country called America. We live in the United States *of America,* and we have appropriated the adjective "American" even though we can claim no exclusive title to it. Canadians and Mexicans are also Americans, but they have adjectives more obviously their own, and we have none. Words like "unitarian" and "unionist" won't do; our sense of ourselves is not captured by the mere fact of our union, however important that is. Nor will "statist," even "united statist," serve our purposes; a good many of the citizens of the United States are antistatist. Other countries, wrote the "American" political theorist Horace Kallen, get their names from the people, or from one of the peoples, who inhabit them. "The United States, on the other hand, has a peculiar anonymity."[1] It is a name that doesn't even pretend to tell us who lives here. Anybody can live here, and just about everybody does—men and women from all the world's peoples. (The *Harvard Encyclopedia of American Ethnic Groups* begins with Acadians and Afghans and ends with Zoroastrians.[2]) It is peculiarly easy to become an American. The adjective provides no reliable information about the origins, histories, connections, or cultures of those whom it designates. What does it say, then, about their political allegiance?

## Patriotism and Pluralism

American politicians engage periodically in a fierce competition to demonstrate their patriotism. This is an odd competition, surely, for in most countries the patriotism of politicians is not an issue. There are other issues, and this question of political identification and commitment rarely comes up; loyalty to the *patrie,* the fatherland (or motherland), is simply assumed. Perhaps it isn't assumed here because the United States isn't a *patrie.* Americans have never spoken of their country as a fatherland (or a motherland). The kind of natural or organic loyalty that we (rightly or wrongly) recognize in families doesn't seem to be a feature of our politics. When American politicians invoke the metaphor of family they are usually making an argument about our mutual responsibilities and welfarist

From *Social Research,* vol. 57, no. 3, Fall 1990, pp. 591–614. Copyright © 1990 by New School for Social Research. Reprinted by permission.

obligations, and among Americans, that is a controversial argument.[3] One can be an American patriot without believing in the mutual responsibilities of American citizens—indeed, for some Americans disbelief is a measure of one's patriotism.

Similarly, the United States isn't a "homeland" (where a national family might dwell), not, at least, as other countries are, in casual conversation and unreflective feeling. It is a country of immigrants who, however grateful they are for this new place, still remember the old places. And their children know, if only intermittently, that they have roots elsewhere. They, no doubt, are native grown, but some awkward sense of newness here, or of distant oldness, keeps the tongue from calling this land "home." The older political uses of the word "home," common in Great Britain, have never taken root here: home counties, home station, Home Office, home rule. To be "at home" in America is a personal matter: Americans have homesteads and homefolks and hometowns, and each of these is an endlessly interesting topic of conversation. But they don't have much to say about a common or communal home.

Nor is there a common *patrie,* but rather many different ones—a multitude of fatherlands (and motherlands). For the children, even the grandchildren, of the immigrant generation, one's *patrie,* the "native land of one's ancestors," is somewhere else. The term "Native Americans" designates the very first immigrants, who got here centuries before any of the others. At what point do the rest of us, native grown, become natives? The question has not been decided; for the moment, however, the language of nativism is mostly missing (it has never been dominant in American public life), even when the political reality is plain to see. Alternatively, nativist language can be used against the politics of nativism, as in these lines of Horace Kallen, the theorist of an anonymous America:

> Behind [the individual] in time and tremendously in him in quality are his ancestors; around him in space are his relatives and kin, carrying in common with him the inherited organic set from a remoter common ancestry. In all these he lives and moves and has his being. They constitute his, literally, *natio,* the inwardness of his nativity.[4]

But since there are so many "organic sets" (language is deceptive here: Kallen's antinativist nativism is cultural, not biological), none of them can rightly be called "American." Americans have no inwardness of their own; they look inward only by looking backward.

According to Kallen, the United States is less importantly a union of states than it is a union of ethnic, racial, and religious groups—a union of otherwise unrelated "natives." What is the nature of this union? The Great Seal of the United States carries the motto *E pluribus unum,* "From many, one," which seems to suggest that manyness must be left behind for the sake of oneness. Once there were many, now the many have merged or, in Israel Zangwell's classic image, been melted down into one. But the Great Seal presents a different image: the "American" eagle holds a sheaf of arrows. Here there is no merger or fusion but only a fastening, a putting together: many-in-one. Perhaps the adjective "American" describes this kind of oneness. We might say, tentatively, that it points to the citizenship, not the nativity or nationality, of the men and women it designates. It is a political adjective, and its politics is liberal in the strict sense: generous, tolerant, ample, accommodating—it allows for the survival, even the enhancement and flourishing, of manyness.

On this view, appropriately called "pluralist," the word "from" on the Great Seal is a false preposition. There is no movement from many to one, but rather a simultaneity, a coexistence—once again, many-in-one. But I don't mean to suggest a mystery here, as in the Christian conception of a God who is three-in-one. The language of pluralism is sometimes a bit mysterious—thus Kallen's description of America as a "nation of nationalities" or John Rawls's account of the liberal state as a "social union of social unions"—but it lends itself to a rational unpacking.[5] A sheaf of arrows is not, after all, a mysterious entity. We can find analogues in the earliest forms of social organization: tribes composed of many clans, clans composed of many families. The conflicts of loyalty and obligation, inevitable products of pluralism, must arise in these cases too. And yet, they are not exact analogues of the American case, for tribes and clans lack Kallen's "anonymity." American pluralism is, as we shall see, a peculiarly modern phenomenon—not mysterious but highly complex.

In fact, the United States is not a "nation of nationalities" or a "social union of social unions." At least, the singular nation or union is not constituted by, it is not a combination or fastening together of, the plural nationalities or unions. In some sense, it includes them; it provides a framework for their coexistence; but they are not its parts. Nor are the individual states, in any significant sense, the parts that make up the United States. The parts are individual men and women. The United States is an association of citizens. Its "anonymity" consists in the fact that these citizens don't transfer their collective name to the association. It never happened that a group of people called Americans came together to form a political society called America. The people are Americans only by virtue of having come together. And whatever identity they had before becoming Americans, they retain (or, better, they are free to retain) afterward. There is, to be sure, another view of Americanization, which holds that the process requires for its success the mental erasure of all previous identities—forgetfulness or even, as one enthusiast wrote in 1918, "absolute forgetfulness."[6] But on the pluralist view, Americans are allowed to remember who they were and to insist, also, on *what else they are.*

They are not, however, bound to the remembrance or to the insistence. Just as their ancestors escaped the old country, so they can if they choose escape their old identities, the "inwardness" of their nativity. Kallen writes of the individual that "whatever else he changes, he cannot change his grandfather."[7] Perhaps not; but he can call his grandfather a "greenhorn," reject his customs and convictions, give up the family name, move to a new neighborhood, adopt a new "life-style."

He doesn't become a better American by doing these things (though that is sometimes his purpose), but he may become an American simply, an American and nothing else, freeing himself from the hyphenation that pluralists regard as universal on this side, though not on the other side, of the Atlantic Ocean. But, free from hyphenation, he seems also free from ethnicity: "American" is not one of the ethnic groups recognized in the United States census. Someone who is only an American is, so far as our bureaucrats are concerned, ethnically anonymous. He has a right, however, to his anonymity; that is part of what it means to be an American.

For a long time, British-Americans thought of themselves as Americans simply—and not anonymously: they constituted, so they would have said, a new ethnicity and a new nationality, into which all later immigrants would slowly assimilate. "Americanization" was a political program designed to make sure that assimilation would not be too slow a process, at a time, indeed, when it seemed not to be a recognizable *process* at all. But though there were individuals who did their best to assimilate, that is, to adopt, at least outwardly, the mores of British-Americans, that soon ceased to be a plausible path to an "American" future. The sheer number of non-British immigrants was too great. If there was to be a new nationality, it would have to come out of the melting pot, where the heat was applied equally to all groups, the earlier immigrants as well as the most recent ones. The anonymous American was, at the turn of the century, say, a placeholder for some unknown future person who would give cultural content to the name. Meanwhile, most Americans were hyphenated Americans, more or less friendly to their grandfathers, more or less committed to their manyness. And pluralism was an alternative political program designed to legitimate this manyness and to make it permanent—which would leave those individuals who were Americans and nothing else permanently anonymous, assimilated to a cultural nonidentity.

## Citizens

But though these anonymous Americans were not better Americans for being or for having become anonymous, it is conceivable that they were, and are, better American *citizens*. If the manyness of America is cultural, its oneness is political, and it may be the case that men and women who are free from non-American cultures will commit themselves more fully to the American political system. Maybe cultural anonymity is the best possible grounding for American politics. From the beginning, of course, it has been the standard claim of British-Americans that their own culture is the best grounding. And there is obviously much to be said for that view. Despite the efforts of hyphenated Americans to describe liberal and democratic politics as a kind of United Way to which they have all made contributions, the genealogy of the American political system bears a close resemblance to the genealogy of the Sons and Daughters of the American Revolution—ethnic organizations if there ever were any![8] But this genealogy must also account for the flight across the Atlantic and the Revolutionary War. The parliamentary oligarchy of eighteenth-century Great Britain wasn't, after all, all that useful a model for America. When the ancestors of the Sons and Daughters described their political achievement as a "new order for the ages," they were celebrating a break with their own ethnic past almost as profound as that which later Americans were called upon to make. British-Americans who refused the break called themselves "Loyalists," but they were called disloyal by their opponents and treated even more harshly than hyphenated Americans from Germany, Russia, and Japan in later episodes of war and revolution.

Citizenship in the "new order" was not universally available, since blacks and women and Indians (Native Americans) were excluded, but it was never linked to a single nationality. "To be or to become an American," writes Philip Gleason, "a person did not have to be of any particular national, linguistic, religious, or ethnic background. All he had to do was to commit himself to the political ideology centered on the abstract ideals of liberty, equality, and republicanism."[9] These abstract ideals made for a politics separated not only from religion but from culture itself or, better, from all the particular forms in which religious and national culture was, and is, expressed—hence a politics "anonymous" in Kallen's sense. Anonymity suggests autonomy too, though I don't want to claim that American politics was not qualified in important ways by British Protestantism, later by Irish Catholicism, later still by German, Italian, Polish, Jewish, African, and Hispanic religious commitments and political experience. But these qualifications never took what might be called a strong adjectival form, never became permanent or exclusive qualities of America's abstract politics and citizenship. The adjective "American" named, and still names, a politics that is relatively unqualified by religion or nationality or, alternatively, that is qualified by so many religions and nationalities as to be free from any one of them.

It is this freedom that makes it possible for America's oneness to encompass and protect its manyness. Nevertheless, the conflict between the one and the many is a pervasive feature of American life. Those Americans who attach great value to the oneness of citizenship and the centrality of political allegiance must seek to constrain the influence of cultural manyness; those who value the many must disparage the one. The conflict is evident from the earliest days of the republic, but I will begin my own account of it with the campaign to restrict immigration and naturalization in the 1850s. Commonly called "nativist" by historians, the campaign was probably closer in its politics to a Rousseauian republicanism.[10] Anti-Irish and anti-Catholic bigotry played a large part in mobilizing support for the American (or American Republican) party, popularly called the Know-Nothings; and the political style of the party, like that of contemporary abolitionists and free-soilers, displayed many of the characteristics of Protestant moralism. But in its self-presentation, it was above all republican, more concerned about the civic virtue of the new immigrants than about their ethnic lineages, its religious critique focused on the ostensible connection between Catholicism and tyranny. The legislative program of the Know-Nothings had to do largely with questions of citizenship at the national level and of public education at the local level. In Congress, where the party had 75 representatives (and perhaps another 45 sympathizers, out of a total of 234) at the peak of its strength in 1855, it seemed more committed to restricting the suffrage than to cutting off immigration. Some of its members would have barred "paupers" from entering the United States, and others would have required an oath of allegiance from all immigrants immediately upon landing. But their energy was directed mostly toward revising the naturalization laws.[11] It was not the elimination of manyness but its disenfranchisement that the Know-Nothings championed.

Something like this was probably the position of most American "nativists" until the last years of the nineteenth century. In 1845, when immigration rates were still fairly low, a group of "native Americans" meeting in Philadelphia declared that they would "kindly receive [all] persons who came to America, and give them every privilege except office and suffrage."[12] I would guess that the nativist view of American blacks was roughly similar. Most of the northern Know-Nothings (the party's greatest strength was in New England) were strongly opposed to slavery, but it did not follow from that opposition that they were prepared to welcome former slaves as fellow citizens. The logic of events led to citizenship, after a bloody war, and the Know-Nothings, by then loyal Republicans, presumably supported that outcome. But the logic of republican principle, as they understood it, would have suggested some delay. Thus a resolution of the Massachusetts legislature in 1856 argued that "republican institutions were especially adapted to an educated and intelligent people, capable of *and accustomed to* self-government. Free institutions could be confined safely only to free men. . . . "[13] The legislators went on to urge a twenty-one-year residence requirement for naturalization. Since it was intended that disenfranchised residents should nonetheless be full members of civil society, another piece of Know-Nothing legislation would have provided that any alien free white person (this came from a Mississippi senator) should be entitled after twelve months residence "to all the protection of the government, and [should] be allowed to inherit, and hold, and transmit real estate . . . the same manner as though he were a citizen."[14]

Civil society, then, would include a great variety of ethnic and religious and perhaps even racial groups, but the members of these groups would acquire the "inestimable" good of citizenship only after a long period of practical education (but does one learn just by watching?) in democratic virtue. Meanwhile, their children would get a formal education. Despite their name, the Know-Nothings thought that citizenship was a subject about which a great deal had to be known. Some of them wanted to make attendance in public schools compulsory, but, faced with constitutional objections, they insisted only that no public funding should go to the support of parochial schools. It is worth emphasizing that the crucial principle here was not the separation of church and state. The Know-Nothing party did not oppose sabbatarian laws.[15] Its members believed that tax money should not be used to underwrite social manyness—not in the case of religion, obviously, but also not in the case of language and culture. Political identity, singular in form, would be publicly inculcated and defended; the plurality of social identities would have to be sustained in private.

I don't doubt that most nativists hoped that plurality would not, in fact, be sustained. They had ideas, if not sociological theories, about the connection of politics and culture—specifically, as I have said, republican politics and British Protestant culture. I don't mean to underestimate the centrality of these ideas: this was presumably the knowledge that the Know-Nothings were concealing when they claimed to know nothing. Nonetheless, the logic of their position, as of any "American" republican position, pressed toward the creation of a politics independent of all the ethnicities and religions of civil society. Otherwise too many people would be excluded; the political world would look too much like Old England and not at all like the "new order of the ages," not at all like "America." Nor could American nativists challenge ethnic and religious pluralism directly, for both were protected (as the parochial schools were protected) by the constitution to which they claimed a passionate attachment. They could only insist that passionate attachment should be the mark of all citizens—and set forth the usual arguments against the seriousness of love at first sight and in favor of long engagements. They wanted what Rousseau wanted: that citizens should find the greater share of their happiness in public (political) rather than in private (social) activities.[16] And they were prepared to deny citizenship to men and women who seemed to them especially unlikely to do that.

No doubt, again, public happiness came easily to the nativists because they felt so entirely at home in American public life. But we should not be too quick to attribute this feeling to the carry-over of ethnic consciousness into the political sphere. For American politics in the 1850s was already so open, egalitarian, and democratic (relative to European politics) that almost anyone could feel at home in it. Precisely because the United States was no one's *national* home, its politics was universally accessible. All that was necessary in principle was ideological commitment, in practice, a good line of talk. The Irish did very well and demonstrated as conclusively as one could wish that "British" and "Protestant" were not necessary adjectives for American politics. They attached to the many, not to the one.

For this reason, the symbols and ceremonies of American citizenship could not be drawn from the political culture or history of British-Americans. Our Congress is not a Commons; Guy Fawkes Day is not an American holiday; the Magna Carta has never been one of our sacred texts. American symbols and ceremonies are culturally anonymous, invented rather than inherited, voluntaristic in style, narrowly political in content: the flag, the Pledge, the Fourth, the Constitution. It is entirely appropriate that the Know-Nothing party had its origin in the Secret Society of the Star-Spangled Banner. And it is entirely understandable that the flag and the Pledge continue, even today, to figure largely in political debate. With what reverence should the flag be treated? On what occasions must it be saluted? Should we require school children to recite the Pledge, teachers to lead the recitation? Questions like these are the tests of a political commitment that can't be assumed, because it isn't undergirded by the cultural and religious commonalities that make for mutual trust. The flag and the Pledge are, as it were, all we have. One could suggest, of course, alternative and more practical tests of loyalty—responsible participation in political life, for example. But the real historical alternative is the test proposed by the cultural pluralists: one proves one's Americanism, in their view, by living in peace with all the other "Americans," that is, by agreeing to respect social manyness rather than by pledging allegiance to the "one and indivisible" republic. And pluralists are led on by the logic of this argument to suggest that citizenship is something less than an "inestimable" good.

## Hyphenated Americans

Good it certainly was to be an American citizen. Horace Kallen was prepared to call citizenship a "great vocation," but he clearly did not believe (in the 1910s and '20s, when he wrote his classic essays on cultural pluralism) that one could make a life there. Politics was a necessary, but not a spiritually sustaining activity. It was best understood in instrumental terms; it had to do with the arrangements that made it possible for groups of citizens to "realize and protect" their diverse cultures and "attain the excellence appropriate to their kind."[17] These arrangements, Kallen thought, had to be democratic, and democracy required citizens of a certain sort—autonomous, self-disciplined, capable of cooperation and compromise. "Americanization" was entirely legitimate insofar as it aimed to develop these qualities; they made up Kallen's version of civic virtue, and he was willing to say that they should be common to all Americans. But, curiously perhaps, they did not touch the deeper self. "The common city-life, which depends upon like-mindedness, is not inward, corporate, and inevitable, but external, inarticulate, and incidental . . . not the expression of a homogeneity of heritage, mentality, and interest."[18]

Hence Kallen's program: assimilation "in matters economic and political," dissimilation "in cultural consciousness."[19] The hyphen joined these two processes in one person, so that a Jewish-American (like Kallen) was similar to other Americans in his economic and political activity, but similar only to other Jews at the deeper level of culture.[20] It is clear that Kallen's "hyphenates," whose spiritual life is located so emphatically to the left of the hyphen, cannot derive the greater part of their happiness from their citizenship. Nor, in a sense, should they, since culture, for the cultural pluralists, is far more important than politics and promises a more complete satisfaction. Pluralists, it seems, do not make good republicans—for the same reason that republicans, Rousseau the classic example, do not make good pluralists. The two attend to different sorts of goods.

Kallen's hyphenated Americans can be attentive and conscientious citizens, but on a liberal, not a republican, model. This means two things. First, the various ethnic and religious groups can intervene in political life only in order to defend themselves and advance their common interests—as in the case of the NAACP or the Anti-Defamation League—but not in order to impose their culture or their values. They have to recognize that the state is anonymous (or, in the language of contemporary political theorists, neutral) at least in this sense: that it can't take on the character or the name of any of the groups that it includes. It isn't a nation-state of a particular kind and it isn't a Christian republic. Second, the primary political commitment of individual citizens is to protect their protection, to uphold the democratic framework within which they pursue their more substantive activities. This commitment is consistent with feelings of gratitude, loyalty, even patriotism of a certain sort, but it doesn't make for fellowship. There is indeed *union* in politics (and economics) but union of a sort that precludes intimacy. "The political and economic life of the commonwealth," writes Kallen, "is a single unit and serves as the foundation and background for the realization of the distinctive individuality of each *natio*."[21] Here pluralism is straightforwardly opposed to republicanism: politics offers neither self-realization nor communion. All intensity lies, or should lie, elsewhere.

Kallen believes, of course, that this "elsewhere" actually exists; his is not a utopian vision; it's not a case of "elsewhere, perhaps." The "organic groups" that make up Kallen's America appear in public life as interest groups only, organized for the pursuit of material and social goods that are universally desired but sometimes in short supply and often unfairly distributed. That is the only appearance countenanced by a liberal and democratic political system. But behind it, concealed from public view, lies the true significance of ethnicity or religion: "It is the center at which [the individual] stands, the point of his most intimate social relations, therefore of his intensest emotional life."[22] I am inclined to say that this is too radical a view of ethnic and religious identification, since it seems to rule out moral conflicts in which the individual's emotions are enlisted, as it were, on both sides. But Kallen's more important point is simply that there is space and opportunity *elsewhere* for the emotional satisfactions that politics can't (or shouldn't) provide. And because individuals really do find this satisfaction, the groups within which it is found are permanently sustainable: they won't melt down, not, at least, in any ordinary (non-coercive) social process. Perhaps they can be repressed, if the repression is sufficiently savage; even then, they will win out in the end.

Kallen wasn't entirely unaware of the powerful forces making for cultural meltdown, even without repression. He has some strong lines on the effectiveness of the mass media—though he knew these only in their infancy and at a time when newspapers were still a highly localized medium and the foreign-language press flourished. In his analysis and critique of the pressure to conform, he anticipated what became by the 1950s a distinctively American genre of social criticism. It isn't always clear whether he sees pluralism as a safeguard against or an antidote for the conformity of ethnic-Americans to that spiritless "Americanism" he so much disliked, a dull protective coloring that destroys all inner brightness. In any case, he is sure that inner brightness will survive, "for Nature is naturally pluralistic; her unities are eventual, not primary. . . . "[23] Eventually, he means, the American union will prove to be a matter of "mutual accommodation," leaving intact the primacy of ethnic and religious identity. In the years since Kallen wrote, this view has gathered a great deal of ideological, but much less of empirical, support. "Pluralist principles . . . have been on the ascendancy," writes a contemporary critic of pluralism, "precisely at a time when ethnic differences have been on the wane."[24] What if the "excellence" appropriate to our "kind" is, simply, an American excellence? Not necessarily civic virtue of the sort favored by nativists, republicans, and contemporary communitarians, but nonetheless some local color, a brightness of our own?

## Peripheral Distance

This local color is most visible, I suppose, in popular culture—which is entirely appropriate in the case of the world's first mass democracy. Consider, for example, the movie *American in Paris,* where the hero is an American simply and not at all an Irish- or German- or Jewish-American. Do we drop our hyphens when we travel abroad? But what are we, then, without them? We carry with us cultural artifacts of a quite specific sort: *"une danse americaine,"* Gene Kelly tells the French children as he begins to tap dance. What else could he call it, this melted-down combination of Northern English clog dancing, the Irish jig and reel, and African rhythmic foot stamping, to which had been added, by Kelly's time, the influence of the French and Russian ballet? Creativity of this sort is both explained and celebrated by those writers and thinkers, heroes of the higher culture, that we are likely to recognize as distinctively American: thus Emerson's defense of the experimental life (I am not sure, though, that he would have admired tap dancing), or Whitman's democratic inclusiveness, or the pragmatism of Peirce and James.

"An American nationality," writes Gleason, "does in fact exist."[25] Not just a political status, backed up by a set of political symbols and ceremonies, but a full-blooded nationality, reflecting a history and a culture—exactly like all the other nationalities from which Americans have been, and continue to be, recruited. The ongoing immigration makes it difficult to see the real success of Americanization in creating distinctive types, characters, styles, artifacts of all sorts which, were Gene Kelly to display them to his Parisian neighbors, they would rightly recognize as "American." More important, Americans recognize one another, take pride in the things that fellow Americans have made and done, identify with the national community. So, while there no doubt are people plausibly called Italian-Americans or Swedish-Americans, spiritual (as well as political) life—this is Gleason's view—is lived largely to the right of the hyphen: contrasted with real Italians and real Swedes, these are real Americans.

This view seems to me both right and wrong. It is right in its denial of Kallen's account of America as an anonymous nation of named nationalities. It is wrong in its insistence that America is a nation like all the others.

But the truth does not lie, where we might naturally be led to look for it, somewhere between this rightness and this wrongness—as if we could locate America at some precise point along the continuum that stretches from the many to the one. I want to take the advice of that American song, another product of the popular culture, which tells us: "Don't mess with mister in-between."[26] If there are cultural artifacts, songs and dances, styles of life and even philosophies, that are distinctively American, there is also an idea of America that is itself distinct, incorporating oneness and manyness in a "new order" that may or may not be "for the ages" but that is certainly for us, here and now.

The cultural pluralists come closer to getting the new order right than do the nativists and the nationalists and the American communitarians. Nonetheless, there is a nation and a national community and, by now, a very large number of native Americans. Even first- and second-generation Americans, as Gleason points out, have graves to visit and homes and neighborhoods to remember *in this country,* on this side of whatever waters their ancestors crossed to get here.[27] What is distinctive about the nationality of these Americans is not its insubstantial character—substance is quickly acquired—but its nonexclusive character. Remembering the God of the Hebrew Bible, I want to argue that America is not a jealous nation. In this sense, at least, it is different from most of the others.

Consider, for example, a classic moment in the ethnic history of France: the debate over the emancipation of the Jews in 1790 and '91. It is not, by any means, a critical moment; there were fewer than 35,000 Jews in revolutionary France, only 500 in Paris. The Jews were not economically powerful or politically significant or even intellectually engaged in French life (all that could come only after emancipation). But the debate nonetheless was long and serious, for it dealt with the meaning of citizenship and nationality. When the Constituent Assembly voted for full emancipation in September 1791, its position was summed up by Clermont-Tonnerre, a deputy of the Center, in a famous sentence: "One must refuse everything to the Jews as a nation, and give everything to the Jews as individuals. . . . It would be repugnant to have . . . a nation within a nation."[28] The Assembly's vote led to the disestablishment of Jewish corporate existence in France, which had been sanctioned and protected by the monarchy. "Refusing everything to the Jews as a nation" meant withdrawing the sanction, denying the protection. Henceforth Jewish communities would be voluntary associations, and individual Jews would have rights against the community as well as against the state: Clermont-Tonnerre was a good liberal.

But the Assembly debate also suggests that most of the deputies favoring emancipation would not have looked with favor even on the voluntary associations of the Jews, insofar as these reflected national sensibility or cultural difference. The future Girondin leader Brissot, defending emancipation, predicted that Jews who became French citizens would "lose their particular characteristics." I suspect that he could hardly imagine a greater triumph of French *civisme* than this—as if the secular Second Coming, like the religious version, awaited only the conversion of the Jews. Brissot thought the day was near: "Their eligibility [for citizenship] will regenerate them."[29] Jews could be good citizens only insofar as they were regenerated, which meant, in effect, that they could be good citizens only insofar as they became French. (They must, after all, have some "particular characteristics," and if not their own, then whose?) Their emancipators had, no doubt, a generous view of their capacity to do that but would not have been generous in the face of resistance (from the Jews or from any other of the corporate groups of the old regime). The price of emancipation was assimilation.

This has been the French view of citizenship ever since. Though they have often been generous in granting the exalted status of citizen to foreigners, the successive republics have been suspicious of any form of ethnic pluralism. Each republic really has been "one and indivisible," and it has been established, as Rousseau thought it should be, on a strong national oneness. Oneness all the way down is, on this view, the only guarantee that the general will and the common good will triumph in French politics.

America is very different, and not only because of the eclipse of republicanism in the early nineteenth century. Indeed, republicanism has had a kind of afterlife as one of the legitimating ideologies of American politics. The Minute Man is a republican image of embodied citizenship. Reverence for the flag is a form of republican piety. The Pledge of Allegiance is a republican oath. But emphasis on this sort of thing reflects social disunity rather than unity; it is a straining after oneness where oneness doesn't exist. In fact, America has been, with severe but episodic exceptions, remarkably tolerant of ethnic pluralism (far less so of racial pluralism).[30] I don't want to underestimate the human difficulties of adapting even to a hyphenated Americanism, nor to deny the bigotry and discrimination that particular groups have encountered. But tolerance has been the cultural norm.

Perhaps an immigrant society has no choice; tolerance is a way of muddling through when any alternative policy would be violent and dangerous. But I would argue that we have, mostly, made the best of this necessity, so that the virtues of toleration, in principle though by no means always in practice, have supplanted the singlemindedness of republican citizenship. We have made our peace with the "particular characteristics" of all the immigrant groups (though not, again, of all the racial groups) and have come to regard American nationality as an addition to rather than a replacement for ethnic consciousness. The hyphen works, when it is working, more like a plus sign. "American," then, is a name indeed, but unlike "French" or "German" or "Italian" or "Korean" or "Japanese" or "Cambodian," it can serve as a second name. And as in those modern marriages where two patronymics are joined, neither the first nor the second name is dominant: here the hyphen works more like a sign of equality.

We might go farther than this: in the case of hyphenated Americans, it doesn't matter whether the first or the second name is dominant. We insist, most of the time, that the "particular characteristics" associated with the first name be sustained, as the Know-Nothings urged, without state help—and perhaps they will prove unsustainable on those terms. Still, an ethnic American is someone who can, in principle, live his spiritual life as he chooses, *on either side of the hyphen*. In this sense, American citizenship is indeed anonymous, for it doesn't require a full commitment to American (or to any other) nationality. The distinctive national culture that Americans have created doesn't underpin, it exists alongside of, American politics. It follows, then, that the people I earlier called Americans simply, Americans and nothing else, have in fact a more complicated existence than those terms suggest. They are American-Americans, one more group of hyphenates (not quite the same as all the others), and one can imagine them attending to the cultural aspects of their Americanism and refusing the political commitment that republican ideology demands. They might still be good or bad citizens. And similarly, Orthodox Jews as well as secular (regenerate) Jews, Protestant fundamentalists as well as liberal Protestants, Irish republicans as well as Irish Democrats, black nationalists as well as black integrationists—all these can be good or bad citizens, given the American (liberal rather than republican) understanding of citizenship.

One step more is required before we have fully understood this strange America: it is not the case that Irish-Americans, say, are culturally Irish and politically American, as the pluralists claim (and as I have been assuming thus far for the sake of the argument). Rather, they are culturally Irish-American and politically Irish-American. Their culture has been significantly influenced by American culture; their politics is still, both in style and substance, significantly ethnic. With them, and with every ethnic and religious group except the American-Americans, hyphenation is doubled. It remains true, however, that what all the groups have in common is most importantly their citizenship and what most differentiates them, insofar as they are still differentiated, is their culture. Hence the alternation in American life of patriotic fevers and ethnic revivals, the first expressing a desire to heighten the commonality, the second a desire to reaffirm the difference.

At both ends of this peculiarly American alternation, the good that is defended is also exaggerated and distorted, so that pluralism itself is threatened by the sentiments it generates. The patriotic fevers are the symptoms of a republican pathology. At issue here is the all-important ideological commitment that, as Gleason says, is the sole prerequisite of American citizenship. Since citizenship isn't guaranteed by oneness all the way down, patriots or superpatriots seek to guarantee it by loyalty oaths and campaigns against "un-American" activities. The Know-Nothing party having failed to restrict naturalization, they resort instead to political purges and deportations. Ethnic revivals are less militant and less cruel, though not without their own pathology. What is at issue here is communal pride and power—a demand for political recognition without assimilation, an assertion of interest-group politics against republican ideology, an effort to distinguish this group (one's own) from all the others. American patriotism is always strained and nervous because hyphenation makes indeed for dual loyalty but seems, at the same time, entirely American. Ethnic revivalism is also strained and nervous, because the hyphenates are already Americans, on both sides of the hyphen.

In these circumstances, republicanism is a mirage, and American nationalism or communitarianism is not a plausible option; it doesn't reach to our complexity. A certain sort of communitarianism is available to each of the hyphenate groups—except, it would seem, the American-Americans, whose community, if it existed, would deny the Americanism of all the others. So Horace Kallen is best described as a Jewish (-American) communitarian and a (Jewish-) American liberal, and this kind of co-existence, more widely realized, would constitute the pattern he called cultural pluralism. But the different ethnic and religious communities are all of them far more precarious than he thought, for they have, in a liberal political system, no corporate form or legal structure or coercive power. And, without these supports, the "inherited organic set" seems to dissipate—the population lacks cohesion, cultural life lacks coher-ence. The resulting "groups" are best conceived, John Higham suggests, as a core of activists and believers and an expanding periphery of passive members or followers, lost, as it were, in a wider America.[31] At the core, the left side of the (double) hyphen is stronger; along the periphery, the right side is stronger, though never fully dominant. Americans choose, as it were, their own location; and it appears that a growing number of them are choosing to fade into the peripheral distances. They become Ameri-can-Americans, though without much passion invested in the becoming. But if the core doesn't hold, it also doesn't disappear; it is still capable of periodic revival.

At the same time, continued large-scale immigration reproduces a Kallenesque pluralism, creating new groups of hyphenate Americans and encouraging revivalism among activists and believers in the old groups. America is still a radically unfinished society, and for now, at least, it makes sense to say that this unfinishedness is one of its distinctive features. The country has a political center, but it remains in every other sense decen-tered. More than this, the political center, despite occasional patriotic fevers, doesn't work against decentering elsewhere. It neither requires nor demands the kind of commitment that would put the legitimacy of ethnic or religious identification in doubt. It doesn't aim at a finished or fully co-herent Americanism. Indeed, American politics, itself pluralist in character, *needs* a certain sort of incoherence. A radical program of Americanization would *really* be un-American. It isn't inconceivable that America will one day become an American nation-state, the many giving way to the one, but that is not what it is now; nor is that its destiny. America has no singu-lar national destiny—and to be an "American" is, finally, to know that and to be more or less content with it.

# Notes

1. Horace M. Kallen, *Culture and Democracy in the United States* (New York: Boni & Liveright, 1924), p. 51.

2. *Harvard Encyclopedia of American Ethnic Groups,* ed. Stephan Thernstrom (Cambridge, Mass.: Harvard University Press, 1980).

3. Mario Cuomo's speech at the 1984 Democratic party convention provides a nice example of this sort of argument.

4. Kallen, *Culture and Democracy,* p. 94.

5. *Ibid.,* p. 122 (cf. 116); John Rawls. *A Theory of Justice* (Cambridge, Mass.: Harvard University Press, 1971), p. 527.

6. Quoted in Kallen, *Culture and Democracy,* p. 138; the writer was superintendent of New York's public schools.

7. Kallen, *Culture and Democracy,* p. 94.

8. See Kallen's account of how British-Americans were forced into ethnicity: *Culture and Democracy,* pp. 99f.

9. Philip Gleason. "American Identity and Americanization," in *Harvard Encyclopedia,* p. 32.

10. On the complexities of "nativism," see John Higham, *Send These to Me: Jews and Other Immigrants in Urban America* (New York: Atheneum, 1975). pp. 102–115. For an account of the Know-Nothings different from mine, to which I am nonetheless indebted, S.M. Lipset and Earl Raab, *The Politics of Unreason: Right-wing Extremism in America, 1790–1970* (New York: Harper & Row, 1970), ch. 2.

11. Frank George Franklin, *The Legislative History of Naturalization in the United States* (New York: Arno Press, 1969), chs. 11–14.

12. *Ibid.,* p. 247.

13. *Ibid.,* p. 293.

14. Ibid.

15. Lipset and Raab, *Politics of Unreason,* p. 46.

16. Jean-Jacques Rousseau, *The Social Contract,* trans. G. D. H. Cole (New York: E. P. Dutton, 1950), bk. III, ch. 15, p. 93.

17. Kallen, *Culture and Democracy,* p. 61.

18. *Ibid.,* p. 78.

19. *Ibid.,* pp. 114–115.

20. It is interesting that both nativists and pluralists wanted to keep the market free of ethnic and religious considerations. The Know-Nothings, since they thought that democratic politics was best served by British ethnicity and Protestant religion, set the market firmly within civil society, allowing full market rights even to new and Catholic immigrants. Kallen, by contrast, since he understands civil society as a world of ethnic and religious groups, assimilates the market to the universality of the political sphere, the "common city-life."

21. Kallen, *Culture and Democracy,* p. 124.

22. *Ibid.,* p. 200.

23. *Ibid.,* p. 179.

24. Stephen Steinberg, *The Ethnic Myth: Race, Ethnicity, and Class in America* (Boston: Beacon Press, 1981), p. 254.

25. Gleason, "American Identity," p. 56.

26. The song is "Accentuate the Positive," which is probably what I am doing here.

27. Gleason, "American Identity," p. 56.

28. Quoted in Gary Kates, "Jews into Frenchmen: Nationality and Representation in Revolutionary France," *Social Research* 56 (Spring 1989): 229. See also the discussion in Arthur Hertzberg, *The French Enlightenment and the Jews: The Origins of Modern Anti-Semitism* (New York: Schocken, 1970), pp. 360–362.

29. Kates, "Jews into Frenchmen," p. 229.

30. The current demand of (some) black Americans that they be called African-Americans represents an attempt to adapt themselves to the ethnic paradigm—imitating, perhaps, the relative success of various Asian-American groups in a similar adaptation. But names are no guarantees; nor does antinativist pluralism provide sufficient protection against what is all too often an *ethnic*-American racism. It has been argued that this racism is the necessary precondition of hyphenated ethnicity: the inclusion of successive waves of ethnic immigrants is possible only because of the permanent exclusion of black Americans. But I don't know what evidence would demonstrate *necessity* here. I am inclined to reject the metaphysical belief that all inclusion entails exclusion. A historical and empirical account of the place of blacks in the "system" of American pluralism would require another paper.

31. Higham, *Send These to Me,* p. 242.

# POSTSCRIPT

## Do Americans Need
## a Common Identity?

The classic issue of American identity—assimilation versus pluralism—is alive and well today with the issue of multiculturalism. Today's emphasis on diversity is the latest manifestation of the issue.

Who is eligible to become an American? Until the Civil War, only European American males who owned property could exercise full citizenship. People of color living in the United States were isolated. Africans were isolated as slaves on southern plantations while Native Americans were confined to areas of land reserves. The abolishment of slavery led to an immediate—and temporary—citizenship inclusion for former slaves, but the brief historical period known as the Reconstruction Era soon gave way to a century of Jim Crow culture. Native Americans continued to be sequestered on reservations. Clearly, racial minority groups were separated from whites. So an honest treatment of African Americans escaped us until the 1950s. To what extent did a common American identity ever exist? Does Schlesinger confuse the dominant Anglo-Saxon culture of the past with a common American identity?

Neither Walzer nor Schlesinger address the question of a common American identity in terms of race and racism. Walzer refers to the difficulties of racial minorities in becoming part of the *unum*. But both positions are challenged when we consider the legacy of slavery and the long Jim Crow period of American history. The complexity of an American identity is illuminated when we recognize the divergence of the immigrant experience with that of African Americans.

Arthur Schlesinger, Jr., laments the development of race-conscious politics and public policies due to their impact of promoting divisions within society. These concerns are buttressed by the assumption that significant unity of blacks and whites had been achieved prior to the development and implementation of affirmative action programs. This proposition is not supported by evidence. In contrast, Walzer's approach views race and ethnic-conscious politics as an inevitable and important part of American identity.

It is interesting to observe ethnic holiday celebrations in America. It would appear that the concern with core values and identity emerges substantially in response to African American gains. Do celebrations such as St. Patrick's Day and Columbus Day threaten a common American identity? In the same context, what can we say about the celebration of Martin Luther King Day or Black History Month? How much of this celebration of ethnicity is "symbolic," as the sociologist Herbert Gans writes, or do these ethnic celebrations threaten American identity?

Both Walzer and Schlesinger employ the Great Seal of the United States along with the motto *E pluribus unum* to illustrate different positions on a common American identity. The title of Schlesinger's selection, "E Pluribus Unum?" suggests that the concern of minority group racial and ethnic issues is at the expense of unity. For Walzer, the motto is questioned differently. His emphasis is on the question mark. In contrast, "from many, one" suggests "that manyness must be left behind for the sake of oneness." Are differences melted down into one? Here, Walzer offers another look. The American eagle holds a sheaf of arrows—many in one. "On the pluralist view, Americans are allowed to remember who they were and to insist, also, on *what else they are.*"

Oscar Handlin's classic study, *The Uprooted* (1951), is a good place to begin further reading on this issue. He explains how a new American culture replaced immigrant values. *The Ordeal of Assimilation,* edited by Stanley Feldstein and Lawrence Costello (Anchor Books, 1974), presents more on the rise of ethnic consciousness. A pictorial history of immigration can be found in Bernard Weisberger's *The American People* (American Heritage, 1971). More scholarly information appears in *International Migration Review, The Population Bulletin,* and *Migration Today.*

For further classic reading on Schlesinger's perspective, one can explore Milton Gordon's *Assimilation in American Life* (Oxford University Press, 1964) and Robert Park's noted essay "On Assimilation" in *Race and Culture: Essays on the Sociology of Contemporary Man* (Free Press, 1950). Gordon's *Human Nature, Class, and Ethnicity* (Oxford U. Press, 1978) looks at conflict and cooperation found in all human societies. It is relevant to the question of an American identity in that the reader is exposed to more general issues of racial and ethnic group conflict. *Beyond the Melting Pot* by Nathan Glazer and Daniel Patrick Moynihan (MIT Press, 1970) became a classic when it was first written. It represents a close look at race and ethnic issues in New York City. A useful discussion of the current tension of ethnic identity and a common American identity can be found in Mary Waters' *Ethnic Options: Choosing Identities in America* (University of California Press, 1990).

Michael Novak's *The Rise of the Unmeltable Ethnics: Politics and Culture in the Seventies* (Collier, 1973) is an assessment of the American identity issue. He notes the rise of "ethnic consciousness" in America. Stephen Steinberg's *The Ethnic Myth* offers a labor analysis of immigration and American identity using both assimilation and pluralism. Michael Parenti's essay, "Assimilation and Counter-Assimilation" in Philip Green and Stanford Levison's collection, *Power and Community: Dissenting Essays in Political Science* (Vintage Books, 1970) is an interesting assessment of the assimilation dilemma.

Immigration continues to influence American cultural reality. The newest immigrants who contribute to the "browning" of our society (see Issue 4) present new challenges to American identity.

# ISSUE 2

## Does Immigration Contribute to a Better America?

**YES: Philippe Legrain**, from "The Case for Immigration: The Secret to Economic Vibrancy," *The International Economy* (vol. 21, issue 3, Summer 2007)

**NO: Peter Brimelow**, from *Alien Nation: Common Sense About America's Immigration Disaster* (Random House, 1995)

### ISSUE SUMMARY

**YES:** Philippe Legrain is a journalist, economist, and author of *Immigrants: Your Country Needs Them* and *Open World: The Truth about Globalisation*. He makes the case that immigration contributes to a better America as well as a better world. His economic argument primarily emphasizes that the flow of immigrants within the global system brings both talent and labor to areas of need.

**NO:** Peter Brimelow, senior editor at *Forbes* and *National Review* magazines, argues that the United States is being overrun by a growing tide of aliens who are changing the character and composition of the nation in manners that are threatening and destructive to its well-being and prospects for future advancement.

**D**espite the fact that virtually all members of the current population of the United States are either immigrants or their descendants, concerns with immigrants and immigration policies have confronted the nation throughout history. One reason for this reality is the fact that the United States has promoted the imagery within the world that the nation is a welcoming bastion of *freedom* and *democracy* and a land of virtually unlimited economic opportunities. Not surprisingly, this nation has served as a magnet for peoples seeking freedom from tyranny and oppression and opportunities to improve the material circumstances of their lives. Thus, the United States has experienced continuing waves of immigration throughout its history, and these influxes of new peoples have raised concerns within segments of the public and political leadership over the potential for deleterious impacts of these foreigners upon American culture and society.

The current immigration debate has revealed a broad spectrum of opinion regarding this issue. Immigration hawks—people hostile to the new immigrants—pressure elected officials to tighten restrictions, making illegal immigration a felony offense, and to protect the border with fencing. Some hawks would like to see illegal immigrants returned to their country of origin. Interestingly, President Bush, a conservative, takes a middle-ground position on the issue. He proposes a guest worker program and opportunities for resident illegal immigrants to gain citizenship.

On the other side, "immigration doves" are favorable to new immigrants. These doves oppose "criminalizing" illegal immigrants and propose an amnesty program for undocumented aliens. The supporters of new immigrants oppose the tendency to blame some of America's economic problems on the new arrivals. Immigrant supporters claim that immigrants make America a better place through cultural enrichment, economic advancement through both labor and entrepreneurial initiatives, and enhancement of the political culture.

Philippe Legrain argues that immigrant labor is essential to the maintenance of economic vitality and the continuing prosperity of societies. He claims that nations gain economically from accepting both low- and high-skilled immigrant labor. In support of his argument, Legrain cites evidence that immigrants do not harm American workers. He views immigrant labor as beneficial to both rich and poor countries. The rich nations acquire needed labor and an enriched talent pool. The poor nations receive remittances that lift some of their people from abject poverty and provide a boost for the local economy.

In contrast, Peter Brimelow is disturbed by the current immigration policies of the U.S. government and, according to his view, the self-inflicted problems they present to the nation. Among his concerns are the increasing numbers of predominately Hispanics and Asians, who are exerting a negative impact upon the demographic composition and character of the American society and its culture. Brimelow also expresses more traditional concerns that tend to link immigrant populations to crime and expanding prison populations, and to the rising costs of the health care, education, and other human services that these newcomers require.

Peter Brimelow views the nation's current immigration policies as out of control and permitting millions of foreign-born persons, both legal and illegal, to arrive on America's shores. He views immigrants as persons who are distorting the demographic composition of society and requiring increasing levels of financial expenditures to support human services and other social support systems while contributing little or nothing economically beneficial or required to the nation. Thus, Brimelow advocates substantial reform of current immigration policy with an emphasis on restricting newcomers from the global South.

In evaluating this issue, readers are urged to balance the country's historical immigrant past with contemporary patterns of immigration. At the same time, readers should note that there has always been a native reaction to immigration, whether it was nineteenth century nativism or twenty-first century new nativism. Why do some support immigration? Why do others oppose it? What is it that really makes for a better America? To what extent does immigration factor into the equation?

# YES

Philippe Legrain

# The Case for Immigration: The Secret to Economic Vibrancy

There is a contradiction at the heart of our globalizing world: while goods, services, and capital move across borders ever more freely, most people cannot. No government except perhaps North Korea's would dream of banning crossborder trade in goods and services, yet it is seen as perfectly normal and reasonable for governments to outlaw the movement across borders of most people who produce goods and services. No wonder illegal immigration is on the rise: most would-be migrants have no other option.

This is perverse. Immigrants are not an invading army; they are mostly people seeking a better life. Many are drawn to rich countries such as the United States by the huge demand for workers to fill the low-end jobs that their increasingly well-educated and comfortable citizens do not want. And just as it is beneficial for people to move from Alabama to California in response to market signals, so too from Mexico to the United States.

Where governments permit it, a global labor market is emerging: international financiers cluster in New York and London, information technology specialists in Silicon Valley, and actors in Hollywood, while multinational companies scatter skilled professionals around the world. Yet rich-country governments endeavor to keep out Mexican construction workers, Filipino care workers, and Congolese cooks, even though they are simply service providers who ply their trade abroad, just as American investment bankers do. And just as it is often cheaper and mutually beneficial to import information technology services from Asia and insurance from Europeans, it often makes sense to import menial services that have to be delivered on the spot, such as cleaning. Policymakers who want products and providers of high-skilled services to move freely but people who provide less-skilled services to stay put are not just hypocrites, they are economically illiterate.

From a global perspective, the potential gains from freer migration are huge. When workers from poor countries move to rich ones, they too can make use of advanced economies' superior capital and technologies, making them much more productive. This makes them—and the world—much better off. Starting from that simple insight, economists calculate that removing immigration controls could more than double the size of the world economy. Even a small relaxation of immigration controls would yield disproportionately big gains.

Yet many people believe that while the world would gain, workers in rich countries would lose out. They fear that foreigners harm the job prospects of local workers, taking their jobs or depressing their wages. Others fret that immigrants will be a burden on the welfare state. Some seem to believe that immigrants somehow simultaneously "steal" jobs and live off welfare.

Governments increasingly accept the case for allowing in highly skilled immigrants. The immigration bill before the Senate would tilt U.S. policy in that direction, establishing a points system that gives preference to university graduates. Such skills-focused points systems are in vogue: Canada and Australia employ one; Britain is introducing one; and other European countries are considering them.

For sure, as the number of university graduates in China, India, and other emerging markets soars in coming decades, it will be increasingly important for the United States to be able to draw on the widest possible pool of talent—not just for foreigners' individual skills and drive, but for their collective diversity.

It is astonishing how often the exceptional individuals who come up with brilliant new ideas happen to be immigrants. Twenty-one of Britain's Nobel Prize winners arrived in the country as refugees. Perhaps this is because immigrants tend to see things differently rather than following the conventional wisdom, perhaps because as outsiders they are more determined to succeed.

Yet most innovation nowadays comes not from individuals, but from groups of talented people sparking off each other—and foreigners with different ideas, perspectives, and experiences add something extra to the mix. If there are ten people sitting around a table trying to come up with a solution to a problem and they all think alike, then they are no better than one. But if they all think differently, then by bouncing ideas off each other they can solve problems better and faster. Research shows that a diverse group of talented individuals can perform better than a likeminded group of geniuses.

Just look at Silicon Valley: Intel, Yahoo!, Google, and eBay were all co-founded by immigrants, many of whom arrived as children. In fact, nearly half of America's venture capital-backed start-ups have immigrant founders. An ever-increasing share of our prosperity comes from companies that solve problems, be they developing new drugs, video games, or pollution-reducing technologies, or providing management advice. That's why, as China catches up, America and Europe need to open up further to foreigners in order to stay ahead.

Diversity also acts as a magnet for talent. Look at London: it is now a global city, with three in ten Londoners born abroad, from all over the world. People are drawn there because it is an exciting, cosmopolitan place. It's not just the huge range of ethnic restaurants and cultural experiences on offer, it's the opportunity to lead a richer life by meeting people from different backgrounds: friends, colleagues, and even a life partner.

Yet it is incorrect to believe that rich countries only need highly skilled immigrants, still less that bureaucrats can second-guess through a points system precisely which people the vast number of businesses in the economy need. America and Europe may increasingly be knowledge-based economies, but they still rely on low-skilled workers too. Every hotel requires not just managers and marketing people, but also receptionists, chambermaids, and waiters. Every hospital requires not just doctors and nurses, but also many more cleaners, cooks, laundry workers, and security staff. Everyone relies on road-sweepers, cabdrivers, and sewage workers.

Many low-skilled jobs cannot readily be mechanized or imported: old people cannot be cared for by a robot or from abroad. And as people get richer, they increasingly pay others to do arduous tasks, such as home improvements, that they once did themselves, freeing up time for more productive work or more enjoyable leisure. As advanced economies create high-skilled jobs, they inevitably create low-skilled ones too.

Critics argue that low-skilled immigration is harmful because the newcomers are poorer and less-educated than Americans. But that is precisely why they are willing to do low-paid, low-skilled jobs that Americans shun. In 1960, over half of American workers older than 25 were high school dropouts; now, only one in ten are. Understandably, high-school graduates aspire to better things, while even those with no qualifications don't want to do certain dirty, difficult, and dangerous jobs. The only way to reconcile aspirations to opportunity for all with the reality of drudgery for some is through immigration.

Fears that immigrants threaten American workers are based on two fallacies: that there is a fixed number of jobs to go around, and that foreign workers are direct substitutes for American ones. Just as women did not deprive men of jobs when they entered the labor force too, foreigners don't cost Americans their jobs—they don't just take jobs; they create them too. When they spend their wages, they boost demand for people who produce the goods and services that they consume; and as they work, they stimulate demand for Americans in complementary lines of work. An influx of Mexican construction workers, for instance, creates new jobs for people selling building materials, as well as for interior designers. Thus, while the number of immigrants has risen sharply over the past twenty years, America's unemployment rate has fallen.

But do some American workers lose out? Hardly any; most actually gain. Why? Because, as critics of immigration are the first to admit, immigrants are different to Americans, so that they rarely compete directly with them in the labor market; often, they complement their efforts—a foreign child-minder may enable an American nurse to go back to work, where her productivity may be enhanced by hard-working foreign doctors and cleaners—while also stimulating extra capital investment.

Study after study fails to find evidence that immigrants harm American workers. Harvard's George Borjas claims otherwise, but his partial approach is flawed because it neglects the broader complementarities between immigrant labor, native labor, and capital. A recent National Bureau of Economic Research study by Gianmarco Ottaviano and Giovanni Peri finds that the influx of foreign workers between 1990 and 2004 raised the average wage of U.S.-born workers by 2 percent. Nine in ten American workers gained; only one in ten, highschool dropouts, lost slightly, by 1 percent.

Part of the opposition to immigration stems from the belief that it is an inexorable, once-and-for-all movement of permanent settlement. But now that travel is ever cheaper and economic opportunities do not stop at national borders, migration is increasingly temporary when people are allowed to move freely. That is true for globe-trotting businessmen and it is increasingly so for poorer migrants too: Filipino nurses as well as Polish plumbers.

Britain's experience since it opened its borders to the eight much poorer central and eastern European countries which joined the European Union in 2004 is instructive. All 75 million people there could conceivably have moved, but in fact only a small fraction have, and most of those have already left again. Many are, in effect, international commuters, splitting their time between Britain and Poland. Of course, some will end up settling, but most won't. Most migrants do not want to leave home forever: they want to go work abroad for a while to earn enough to buy a house or set up a business back home.

Studies show that most Mexican migrants have similar aspirations. If they could come and go freely, most would move only temporarily. But perversely, U.S. border controls end up making many stay for good, because crossing the border is so risky and costly that once you have got across you tend to stay.

Governments ought to be encouraging such international mobility. It would benefit poor countries as well as rich ones. Already, migrants from poor countries working in rich ones send home much more—$200 billion a year officially, perhaps twice that informally (according to the Global Commission on International Migration)—than the miserly $100 billion that Western governments give in aid. These remittances are not wasted on weapons or siphoned off into Swiss bank accounts; they go straight into the pockets of local people. They pay for food, clean water, and medicines. They enable children to stay in school, fund small businesses, and benefit the local economy more broadly. What's more, when migrants return home, they bring new skills, new ideas, and capital to start new businesses. Africa's first internet cafes were started by migrants returning from Europe.

The World Bank calculates that in countries where remittances account for a large share of the economy (11 percent of GDP on average), they slash the poverty rate by a third. Even in countries which receive relatively little (2.2 percent of GDP on average), remittances can cut the poverty rate by nearly a fifth. Since the true level of remittances is much higher than official figures, their impact on poverty is likely to be even greater.

Remittances can also bring broader economic benefits. When countries are hit by a hurricane or earthquake, remittances tend to soar. During the Asian financial crisis a decade ago, Filipino migrants cushioned the blow on the Philippines' economy by sending home extra cash-and their dollar remittances were worth more in devalued Filipino pesos. Developing country governments can even borrow using their country's expected future remittances as collateral. Even the poorest countries, which receive $45 billion in remittances a year, could eventually tap this relatively cheap form of finance, giving them the opportunity of faster growth.

By keeping kids in school, paying for them to see a doctor, and funding new businesses, remittances can boost growth. A study by Paola Guiliano of Harvard and Marta Ruiz-Arranz of the International Monetary Fund finds that in countries with rudimentary financial systems, remittances allow people to invest more and better, and thus raise growth. When remittances increase by one percentage point of GDP, growth rises by 0.2 percentage points.

John Kenneth Galbraith said, "Migration is the oldest action against poverty. It selects those who most want help. It is good for the country to which they go; it helps break the equilibrium of poverty in the country from which they come. What is the perversity in the human soul that causes people to resist so obvious a good?"

Part of the answer is that people tend to focus their fears about economic change on foreigners. Other fears are cultural; more recently, these have got mixed up with worries about terrorism. Mostly, this is illogical: Christian Latinos are scarcely likely to be a fifth column of al Qaeda operatives, as Pat Buchanan has suggested. But logic scarcely comes into it. Psychological studies confirm that opposition to immigration tends to stem from an emotional dislike of foreigners. Intelligent critics then construct an elaborate set of seemingly rational arguments to justify their prejudice.

In *Who Are We: The Challenges to America's National Identity*, Harvard academic Samuel Huntington warns that Latino immigrants are generally poor and therefore a drain on American society, except in Miami, where they are rich and successful, at Americans' expense. Ironically, when he shot to fame by warning about a global "clash of civilizations," he lumped Mexicans and Americans together in a single civilization; now he claims that Latinos in the United States threaten a domestic clash of civilizations. He frets that Latinos have until recently clustered in certain cities and states, and then that they are starting to spread out. Immigrants can't win: they're damned if they do and damned if they don't.

Rich-country governments should not let such nonsense define their policies. Opening up our borders would spread freedom, widen opportunity and enrich the economy, society, and culture. That may seem unrealistic, but so too, once, did abolishing slavery or giving women the right to vote.

Peter Brimelow

# Immigration: Dissolving the People

There is a sense in which current immigration policy is Adolf Hitler's posthumous revenge on America. The U.S. political elite emerged from the war passionately concerned to cleanse itself from all taints of racism or xenophobia. Eventually, it enacted the epochal Immigration Act (technically, the Immigration and Nationality Act Amendments) of 1965.

And this, quite accidentally, triggered a renewed mass immigration, so huge and so systematically different from anything that had gone before as to transform—and ultimately, perhaps, even to destroy—the one unquestioned victor of World War II: the American nation, as it had evolved by the middle of the 20th century.

Today, U.S. government policy is literally dissolving the people and electing a new one. You can be for this or you can be against it. But the fact is undeniable.

"Still," *Time* magazine wrote in its fall 1993 "Special Issue on Multiculturalism," "for the first time in its history, the U.S. has an immigration policy that, for better or worse, is truly democratic."

As an immigrant, albeit one who came here rather earlier than yesterday and is now an American citizen, I find myself asking with fascination: What can this possibly mean? American immigration policy has always been democratic, of course, in the sense that it has been made through democratic procedures. Right now, as a matter of fact, it's unusually undemocratic, in the sense that Americans have told pollsters long and loudly that they don't want any more immigration; but the politicians ignore them.

The mass immigration so thoughtlessly triggered in 1965 risks making America an alien nation—not merely in the sense that the numbers of aliens in the nation are rising to levels last seen in the 19th century; not merely in the sense that America will become a freak among the world's nations because of the unprecedented demographic mutation it is inflicting on itself; not merely in the sense that Americans themselves will become alien to each other, requiring an increasingly strained government to arbitrate between them; but, ultimately, in the sense that Americans

From *Alien Nation: Common Sense About America's Immigration Disaster* by Peter Brimelow (Random House, 1995). Copyright © 1995 by Peter Brimelow. Reprinted by permission of Wylie Agency.

will no longer share in common what Abraham Lincoln called in his first inaugural address "the mystic chords of memory, stretching from every battlefield and patriotic grave, to every living heart and hearth stone, all over this broad land."

Alexander James Frank Brimelow is an American, although I was still a British subject and his mother a Canadian when he shot into the New York delivery room, yelling indignantly, one summer dawn in 1991. This is because of the 14th Amendment to the U.S. Constitution. It states in part:

"All persons born or naturalized in the United States, and subject to the jurisdiction thereof, are citizens of the United States and of the State wherein they reside."

The 14th Amendment was passed after the Civil War in an attempt to stop Southern states denying their newly freed slaves the full rights of citizens. But the wording is general. So it has been interpreted to mean that any child born in the United States is automatically a citizen. Even if its mother is a foreigner. Even if she's just passing through.

I am delighted that Alexander is an American. However, I do feel slightly, well, guilty that his fellow Americans had so little choice in the matter.

But at least Maggy and I had applied for and been granted legal permission to live in the United States. There are currently an estimated 3.5 million to 4 million foreigners who have just arrived and settled here in defiance of American law. When these illegal immigrants have children in the United States, why those children are automatically American citizens too.

And right now, two-thirds of births in Los Angeles County hospitals are to illegal-immigrant mothers.

All of which is just another example of one of my central themes:

The United States has lost control of its borders—in every sense. A series of institutional accidents, of which birthright citizenship is just one, has essentially robbed Americans of the power to determine who, and how many, can enter their national family, make claims on it—and exert power over it.

In 1991, the year of Alexander's birth, the Immigration and Naturalization Service reported a total of over 1.8 million legal immigrants. That was easily a record. It exceeded by almost a third the previous peak of almost 1.3 million, reached 84 years earlier at the height of the first great wave of immigration, which peaked just after the turn of the century.

The United States has been engulfed by what seems likely to be the greatest wave of immigration it has ever faced. The INS [Immigration and Naturalization Service] estimates that 12 million to 13 million legal and illegal immigrants will enter the United States during the 1990s. The Washington, D.C.-based Federation for American Immigration Reform (FAIR), among the most prominent of the groups critical of immigration policy, thinks the total will range between 10 million and 15 million.

It's not just illegal immigration that is out of control. So is legal immigration. U.S. law in effect treats immigration as a sort of imitation civil right, extended to an indefinite group of foreigners who have been selected arbitrarily and with no regard to American interests.

The American immigration debate has been a one-way street. Criticism of immigration, and news that might support it, just tends not to get through.

For example, the United States is in the midst of a serious crime epidemic. Yet almost no Americans are aware that aliens make up one-quarter of the prisoners in federal penitentiaries—almost three times their proportion in the population at large.

Indeed, many problems that currently preoccupy Americans have an unspoken immigration dimension.

Two further instances:

- The health care crisis. Americans have been told repeatedly that some 30 million to 40 million people in the country have no health insurance at any one point in time. Typically, nobody seems to know how many are immigrants. But immigrants certainly make up a disproportionate share—particularly of the real problem: the much smaller hard core, perhaps 6 million, that remains uninsured after two years.
- The education crisis. Americans are used to hearing that their schools don't seem to be providing the quality of education that foreigners get. Fewer of them know that the U.S. education system is also very expensive by international standards. Virtually none of them know anything about the impact of immigration on that education system.

Yet the impact of immigration is clearly serious. For example, in 1990 almost one child in every 20 enrolled in American public schools either could not speak English or spoke it so poorly as to need language-assistance programs. This number is increasing with striking speed: Only six years earlier, it had been one child in 31.

Current law is generally interpreted as requiring schools to educate such children in their native language. To do so, according to one California estimate, requires spending some 65 percent more per child than on an English-speaking child. And not merely money but, more importantly, teacher time and energy are inevitably being diverted from America's children.

My thesis is that the immigration resulting from current public policy:

- Is dramatically larger, less skilled and more divergent from the American majority than anything that was anticipated or desired.
- Is probably not beneficial economically—and is certainly not necessary.
- Is attended by a wide and increasing range of negative consequences, from the physical environment to the political.
- Is bringing about an ethnic and racial transformation in America without precedent in the history of the world—an astonishing social experiment launched with no particular reason to expect success.

Some of my American readers will be stirring uneasily at this point. They have been trained to recoil from any explicit discussion of race.

Because the term "racist" is now so debased, I usually shrug off such smears by pointing to its new definition: anyone who is winning an argument with a liberal. Or, too often, a libertarian. And, on the immigration issue, even some confused conservatives.

This may sound facetious. But the double standards are irritating. Anyone who has got into an immigration debate with, for example, Hispanic activists must be instantly aware that some of them really are consumed by the most intense racial animosity—directed against whites. How come what's sauce for the goose is not sauce for the gander?

I have indeed duly examined my own motives. And I am happy to report that they are pure. I sincerely believe I am not prejudiced—in the sense of committing and stubbornly persisting in error about people, regardless of evidence—which appears to be the only rational definition of "racism." I am also, however, not blind.

Race and ethnicity are destiny in American politics. And, because of the rise of affirmative action quotas, for American individuals too.

My son, Alexander, is a white male with blue eyes and blond hair. He has never discriminated against anyone in his little life (except possibly young women visitors whom he suspects of being baby-sitters). The sheer size of the so-called "protected classes" that are now politically favored, such as Hispanics, will be a matter of vital importance as long as he lives. And their size is basically determined by immigration.

For Americans even to think about their immigration policy, given the political climate that has prevailed since the 1960s, involves a sort of psychological liberation movement. In Eugene McCarthy's terms, America would have to stop being a colony of the world. The implications are shocking, even frightening: that Americans, without feeling guilty, can and should seize control of their country's destiny.

If they did, what would a decolonized American immigration policy look like? The first step is absolutely clear:

The 1965 Immigration Act, and its amplifications in 1986 and 1990, have been a disaster and must be repealed.

It may be time for the United States to consider moving to a conception of itself more like that of Switzerland: tolerating a fairly large foreign presence that comes and goes, but rarely, if ever, naturalizes. It may be time to consider reviving a version of the bracero program, the agricultural guest-worker program that operated from the 1940s to the 1960s, allowing foreign workers to move in and out of the country in a controlled way, without permanently altering its demography and politics.

This new conception may be a shock to American sensibilities. Many Americans, like my students at the University of Cincinnati Law School, are under the charming impression that foreigners don't really exist. But they also tend to think that, if foreigners really do exist, they ought to become Americans as quickly as possible.

However, the fact is that we—foreigners—are, in some sense, all Americans now, just as Jefferson said everyone had two countries, his own and France, in the 18th century. That is why we are here, just as the entire world flocked to Imperial Rome. The trick the Americans face now is to be an empire in fact, while remaining a democratic republic in spirit. Avoiding the Romans' mistake of diluting their citizenship into insignificance may be the key.

# POSTSCRIPT

## Does Immigration Contribute to a Better America?

**A** common reference concerning the nature of American society is to characterize it as a nation of immigrants. Virtually all of the people of the United States are either immigrants or their descendants. So, immigration is a significant theme of the American experience. These newcomers have made innumerable contributions to the creation and development of the American nation. The earliest European immigrant populations converted the lands that they colonized into viable Western-style political and economic entities, which were transformed by the American Revolution into an independent republic, the United States of America. Foreign-born peoples explored the West, broke the sod of the prairie lands by the sweat of their brows, and contributed to those developments that resulted in the establishment of agriculture as a vital component of economic progress while expanding the frontiers/boundaries of this emergent and dynamic nation.

As capitalist industrial and commercial developments emerged to dominate the U.S. economy, immigrants and their children provided the requisite labor to extract the resources necessary to operate the factories producing the goods and services of this emergent economy. Ultimately, "Americanized" children of immigrants made significant contributions to the building of modern American institutions while exerting leadership to move this nation forward to achieve a preeminent position in the world.

The anti-immigration position taken by descendants of immigrants is revealing of the American experience. At what point does an immigrant, or his descendants, identify more with the dominant culture than with his immigrant culture? Perhaps an answer to this question will aid in understanding the immigration issue. Are those who are already here fearful of losing jobs? Is there a perceived cultural threat in terms of language, customs, and values? We need to address these questions in order to understand people, like Peter Brimelow, who oppose immigration.

Brimelow is concerned that America is becoming an "alien nation." He believes that mass immigration is out of control and inflicting harm on the nation. In this context, Brimelow raises concern for American social problems that are heavily affected by immigrants, such as crime, health care, and education. For him, the benefits of immigration do not outweigh the social costs.

Legrain, in contrast to Brimlow, places great emphasis upon the economic contributions of new immigrants to American life. His argument directly challenges Brimlow's in that the benefits of immigration clearly outweigh the social costs.

This is an important issue in that immigration has re-emerged as a major policy concern of American government. The public debate has entertained topics such as border patrol, quotas, English-only demands, labor competition, amnesty, national security, and cost-benefit analysis. These issues have been the source of controversy throughout history and are likely to continue.

Oscar Handlin's *The Uprooted: The Epic Story of the Great Migrations That Made the American People* (Grossett and Dunlap, 1951) is a good starting point for further research on immigration to America. A general understanding can be found in *A History of Immigration and Ethnicity in American Life* (Harper Perrennial, 1990) by Roger Daniel. A recent issue of *CQ Journal* was devoted to contemporary immigration. It presents a factual comparison of immigration in the 1990s to immigration of the 1890s. *The Emigration Dialectic* (1980) by J. Maldonado Denis provides an interesting examination of the dynamic of Puerto Rican immigration to the mainland United States.

A comprehensive reference book on immigrants and ethnic groups is the *Harvard Encyclopedia of American Ethnic Groups* (Harvard University Press, 1980) by Stephan Thernstrom. *We Are the People: An Atlas of America's Ethnic Diversity* (Macmillan, 1988) by James Paul Allen and Eugene James Turner shows the settlement patterns of immigrants with over 100 maps. A useful pamphlet, *Ethnicity and Immigration* (American Historical Association 1997), by James P. Shenton and Kevin Kenny, provides an overview and an extensive bibliography. An article that deals with Asians, immigration, and assimilation can be found in *Commentary* (July–August 2000), "In Asian America" by Tamar Jacoby.

The most recent immigration debate is argued in "Where Are My Juice and Crackers," by Glynn Custard in *The American Spectator* (July/August 2005). Custard describes the neighborhood watch scene along the southwestern border and the role of a small group of civilian volunteers, the Minutemen. Mark Krikorian discusses the problems with immigration and amnesty in "Amnesty Again" in *National Review* (January 26, 2004). Also in *National Review* (September 12, 2005), John O'Sullivan discusses immigration and American politics in "The GOP's Immigration Problem." The NAACP publication, *The Crisis* (July/August 2006) devotes its feature article to "Immigration: Should African Americans Be Worried?" In this article, five African American leaders engage the topic with a sympathetic view toward the new immigration. Also in *National Review* (May 23, 2005), Mark Krikorian offers a conservative 10-point plan on immigration in "Re: Immigration." In "Border War," John B. Judis, argues the liberal perspective on immigration and national identity in *The New Republic* (January 16, 2006). For an overview of global migration, students will find a recent volume of *Population Bulletin* (March 2008) dedicated to an assessment of the international implications of migration and immigration. "Managing Migration: The Global Challenge," by Philip Martin and Gottfried Zurcher, focuses on the consequences of population movement in different areas of the world, including the United States. Using the most recently available data from the United Nations and related sources, the researchers discuss international migration, which peaked in 2005.

# ISSUE 3

## Do Recent Immigration Trends Threaten Existing Ideas of America's White Identity?

**YES: Charles A. Gallagher,** from "Racial Redistricting: Expanding the Boundaries of Whiteness," in Heather M. Dalmage, ed., *The Politics of Multiracialism: Challenging Racial Thinking* (State University of New York Press, 2004)

**NO: Ellis Cose,** from "What's White, Anyway?" *Newsweek* (September 18, 2000)

### ISSUE SUMMARY

**YES:** Charles A. Gallagher, author and sociology professor at Georgia State University, argues that America is currently undergoing a "racial redistricting" in which the boundaries of whiteness are expanding to include lighter-skinned people of color (i.e., Asians and some Latinos).

**NO:** Ellis Cose, an African American journalist, argues that the traditional boundaries that determine race and skin color are not what they once were. Although he does not specifically cite ethnicity, Cose furthers the claim that American identity today is an expanding category. The boundaries of whiteness have expanded and are no longer hard and fast.

$C$urrently a debate is raging in the United States regarding 12 million alleged illegal immigrants. A recent issue of the *Population Bulletin* devoted to immigration cites recent U.S. Census data that over 1 million immigrants came to the United States in 2001. Over half of these immigrants came from Latin America, while 30% came from Asia. Thus, 81% of recent immigrants are classified as non-white. What are the implications of this trend? Along with the social and demographic issues is the question of race and American identity. Americans have always been concerned with strangers and new immigrants. In one sense, the current concern about white identity and American culture repeats history.

Clearly, one of the consequences of recent immigration patterns is a renewal of the question of race and American identity. Issue 1 in this book deals with the historic question of the need for a common American identity. This issue involves the contemporary tensions of how to incorporate non-European immigrants within an American identity. How do recent immigration trends challenge existing ideas of white identity? The argument made by Gallagher suggests that dominant whites in America view Asians as "driven to assimilate and move up the socioeconomic ladder." Along with some Latinos, Asians are viewed as having values similar to those of the dominant American culture, including hard work, family values, and willingness to assimilate. Gallagher's interpretation of this leads to his notion of racial redistricting. By this, he means expanding the boundaries of whiteness to include these groups.

The late twentieth and early twenty-first centuries' reaction to the preponderance of non-European immigrants to America has been seen by many as a threat to majority status. Race, however the concept is defined today, is assumed to be included in an American identity. Specifically, whites tend to take for granted that the majority status of whiteness is synonymous with American identity. Demographically, that has always been easy to ascertain. For example, as recently as the 1950s, blacks were 12% of the population, while Hispanics were 3%, and Asians were less than 1%. America was, statistically speaking, nearly 85% white. In contrast, today whites constitute approximately 70% of the population with blacks and Hispanics both at approximately 13% and Asians approaching 5%.

Charles Gallagher views the unintended consequence of recent immigration trends as the creation of a new racial landscape that is characterized in a nonblack–black dichotomy in place of the older white–black dichotomy. Racial redistricting means expanding those who are accepted as white. This development will benefit some new immigrants and leave others behind because of skin color.

Beginning with his citation of the McCarran-Walter Act of 1952, Ellis Cose argues that non-white immigrants no longer have to "paint themselves white in order to become Americans." His position is that American identity increasingly is no longer defined by whiteness. Rather, American identity is slowly changing as the definition of what is white expands its boundaries. In contrast, Gallagher argues that American identity continues to be defined by whiteness. Despite his agreement with Cose that the boundaries of what is considered white are expanding, Gallagher strongly disagrees with his view that whiteness is increasingly irrelevant.

The reader should first try to connect Issue 1 with the contemporary ideas of Gallagher and Cose. Does Gallagher further the assimilation argument, or does he challenge it? How accurate is Cose in his position that for recent immigrants, race means less than in the past? Does he make the case for a modern pluralist argument? Is he correct in his assumption that whiteness is fading into irrelevance?

# YES

**Charles A. Gallagher**

# Racial Redistricting: Expanding the Boundaries of Whiteness

My family would object to a biracial relationship if the person I was seeing were African American. I'm dating someone from El Salvador now
and they are okay with the relationship.

> —nineteen-year-old white female college student

My dad would be more upset if the guy was black than if he was Asian.
I think this is because of the slavery situation in America, the hatred
towards black and vice versa.

> —eighteen-year-old white female college student

We are most likely to see something more complicated: a white-Asian-
Hispanic melting pot—a hard to differentiate group of beige Americans—
offset by a minority consisting of blacks who have been left out of the
melting pot once again.

> —Political Analyst Michael Lind on the future of interracial relationships

The multiracial movement has raised public awareness that millions of individuals with mixed-race backgrounds do not fit into the racial categories
established by the government. What this movement has ignored however, are the ways in which existing racial categories expand to incorporate
groups once considered outside of a particular racial category. The social
and physical markers that define whiteness are constantly in a state of flux,
shifting in response to sociohistoric conditions. Groups once on the margins of whiteness, such as Italians and the Irish, are now part of the dominant group. National survey data and my interviews with whites suggest a
process similar to the incorporation of Southern and Eastern Europeans into
the "white" race is taking place among certain parts of the Asian and Latino
populations in the United States. I argue that the racial category "white" is
expanding to include those ethnic and racial groups who are recognized as
being socially, culturally, and physically similar to the dominant group.

How borders of whiteness have evolved over time provides theoretical insight into how racial categories are redefined and how this process

From *The Politics of Multiracialism: Challenging Racial Thinking* by Heather M. Dalmage, ed.,
(SUNY Press, 2004), pp. 59–76. Copyright © 2004 by State University of New York Press. All
rights reserved. Reprinted by permission.

affects the relative mobility of racial and ethnic groups.[1] Not long ago Italian and Irish immigrants and their children had a racial status that placed them outside the bounds of whiteness.[2] Both of these groups now fit unambiguously under the umbrella of whiteness. Like the process of racialization[3] that transformed Italians and Irish into whites, some light-skinned, middle-class Latinos and multiracial Asians are being incorporated into the dominant group as they define themselves, their interests, and are viewed by others as being like whites. As white respondents in my study made clear, Asians, and to a lesser extent Latinos, were viewed as having the cultural characteristics (a strong work ethic, commitment to family, focus on schooling) that whites believe (or imagine) themselves as possessing. In what was an extension of the model minority myth, many whites in this study saw Asians as potential partners in the demonization of African Americans, further legitimating the existing racial hierarchy.

I argue that we are currently experiencing a "racial redistricting" where the borders of whiteness are expanding to include those groups who until quite recently would have been outside the boundaries of the dominant group. Within the context of contemporary race relations those groups who do not "conform" to cultural and physical expectations of white middle-class norms, namely blacks and dark-skinned Latinos who are poor, will be stigmatized and cut off from the resources whites have been able to monopolize; good public schools, social networks, safe neighborhoods and access to primary sector jobs. These expanding borders serve to maintain white or nonblack privilege by casting blacks in negative, stereotypical terms. As whites and other nonblack groups inhabit a common racial ground the stigma once associated with interracial relationships between these groups is diminishing. These trends in racial attitudes and how these perceptions may influence mate selection have important implications for multiracial individuals and how racial categories will be defined in the near future.

The initial focus of the twenty individual interviews and eight focus groups (a total of seventy-five randomly picked white college students at a large northeastern urban university) was to examine the political and cultural meaning they attached to being white. What emerged in the interviews was a narrative about their whiteness that was intricately tied to how similar or dissimilar respondents saw other racial groups, why discussions of race relations tended to focus only on blacks and whites, and why Asians, and not blacks, could be absorbed or folded into the dominant group. These interviews revealed that many whites saw Asians and blacks in starkly different terms. At another large urban university in the southeast I administered an open-ended survey to a large undergraduate sociology class asking white respondents if they or any family members would have any reservations about them dating or marrying across the color line. The questionnaire was designed to examine to what extent, if any, white respondents' views about interracial relationships varied by race of the potential partner. Fifty-nine white students of traditional college age participated in the open-ended survey. The trends in these two samples point to how racial attitudes, social distance, and the perception of assimilation may shape dating preferences and how the cultural and phenotypical expectations that define racial categories change.

## Multi or Mono Racial: National Trends

Over the next twenty years we are likely to witness the children of Asian/white and Latino/white unions identifying themselves as many of their parents have already; as whites with multiple heritages where expressions of ancestry are "options" that do not limit or circumscribe life chances. According to the 1990 census, native-born Asian wives were almost equally likely (45 percent) to have a white *or* Asian husband. Almost one third (31.4 percent) of native-born Latinas had white husbands while 54 percent of married American Indian women had white husbands. Only 2.2 percent of black wives had white husbands. The percentage of husbands who had white wives was also quite high; 36 percent of native born Asian, 32 percent of Latino, and 53 percent of American Indian men married white women. Only 5.6 percent of black husbands, however, had white wives.[4]

Self-identifying as white rather than a combination of races is the choice made by a sizable number of multiracial offspring. In fact, a 2000 study by the National Health Interview Surveys allowed respondents to select more than one race but were then asked in a follow-up interview to choose their "main race." More than 46 percent of those who marked white and Asian as their racial identity chose white as their "main race," 81 percent of those who marked white and American Indian marked white as their "main race," whereas only 25 percent of those who marked black and white marked chose white as their "main race."[5] In the 2000 census almost half (48 percent) of the nation's Latino population defined themselves as white.[6]

What is perhaps more important for understanding how the contours of racial categories expand and contract is an examination of the racial definition parents in interracial marriages give to their children. A significant proportion of interracial couples where one partner is white and the other is Asian or Latino choose to define their offspring as white.[7] In families where the father was white and the mother was Asian Indian, 93 percent defined their children as white. Where the father was white, 51 percent of Native American, 67 percent of Japanese and 61 percent of Chinese mixed-race families defined their children as white. Only 22 percent white father and black mother unions defined their children as white. Among white mothers who married nonwhite husbands Waters found "50 percent of the offspring of white mothers and Native American fathers are reported to be white, 43 percent of Japanese/white children are reported as white, 35 percent of Chinese/white children are reported as white, and 58 percent of Korean/white children are reported *by* their parents to be white" while only 22 percent of black/white children were defined as white.[8] Given these trends, it is possible that the progeny of some of these relationships will have the option to self-identify as white and live their lives in white social networks, occupy white neighborhoods, and marry white partners. It is possible then that the white race can "grow" without an influx of "white" immigrants.

## Asian Assimilation Versus Black Separatism

One theme that emerged in my interviews was that whites viewed Asians as model minorities driven to assimilate and move up the socioeconomic ladder while blacks were viewed as refusing to adopt the styles, mannerisms, and habits that would aid in their upward mobility. The sense that Asians were working to be part of system while blacks were not was evident in the following focus group discussion:

*Interviewer:*   Why is our conversation mostly about blacks.

*Theresa:*   Because [Asians] are so quiet.

*Martha:*   That's exactly what I was going to say. They don't make a big deal like the blacks do. They don't jump up and down and scream and yell. They just do their thing.

*Theresa:*   [Asians] don't want to be bothered. They want to get through so that they can have a chance to get into the system, figure it out, work up to what they want and they don't need anyone to bother them. They'll be fine. They can depend on themselves. They know that. I think they figure that if they try and depend on other people or try to make a voice about it they'll just get pushed down.

*Interviewer:*   So why don't they make demands on the system?

*Kathleen:*   I don't think they particularly lose out like the blacks did. And now the American Indians are starting to get more vocal because they've just been pushed down so much. I don't know that [Asians] ever have. I know that during World War II when they were put in the camps and stuff, whatever, but I don't see discrimination against them.

Theresa's comments point to the stages of assimilation some whites believe groups need or should pass through in order to gain upward mobility. The expectation is that groups will learn to work within the ethnic and racial hierarchy, not challenge it. The reference that blacks "jump up and down and scream and yell" suggests that organized resistance and opposition by African Americans to racial inequality is not a legitimate way to bring about social change or create economic opportunity for blacks. If Asians are no longer discriminated against, as Kathleen argues, the reason must be that they have properly integrated themselves in a dominant group. What was implied in many of these exchanges was that whites perceived blacks as not trying hard enough to mirror the beliefs and behaviors of the dominant group while Asians did. Culturally, then, whites view Asians (and Latinos) as fellow immigrants who also worked their way up the racial and ethnic hierarchy; these groups are, as implied by my respondents, kindred spirits.

In sharp contrast to the idea that Asians have been accepted because of individual self-reliance, blacks' wearing clothing that expressed black unity, black nationalism, or critiques of institutional racism (e.g., wearing

Malcolm X shirts or caps) was perceived as intimidating to whites and the antithesis of the assimilation narrative whites see blacks rejecting. The view that Asians wished to be mainstream culturally where blacks did not was evident in this exchange:

*Mitch:*   They just go about and do what they have to do and blend in with the background. They're not so much asserting themselves. They kind of work around you to get done what they have to get done, more than trying to break through a whole blockade of stuff.

*Interviewer [addressing Frances]:*   Were you going to say something about intimidation?

*Frances:*   I mean, [Asians] don't intimidate us. They don't walk around with Oriental hats or clothes. They don't make a big issue of it. They keep their culture to themselves. If you want to join their culture they don't have a problem with that. If you want to marry an Oriental, granted, that can be a problem. A lot of times that can really be a problem. But, the only problem we would run into would be the parents of the kids our age, because most of them have come from their country but the second generation, *they're American and they know American ways*. There's no pressure.

*Mitch:*   I think there's a lot in the press about discrimination and its time is coming. I mean it's true, though. But, I mean, it's all over the place, stuff about discrimination. It's just becoming like really, really popular for black students to be black and proud and racist. But with Asians it's not that way. I mean there is a magazine *Ebony* for strictly black people—I've never really read it. I mean there is no magazine for just Asian people. There's nothing saying, like, Asian power. But it's [a black focus] all over the place.

That which makes race a salient form of social identity, such as wearing a Malcolm X cap or "black theme" shirts that call for pan-African unity, was viewed by some whites as a form of racial intimidation. The perception that blacks self-segregate and promote separatism by reading a black magazine such as *Ebony* while Asians do not, reflects the belief that Asians and whites have rejected race politics and share a common vision of what it means to being an American. It is important to note that dozens of magazines exist that are directed primarily at Asian and Asian Americans on a wide range of social, cultural, and business topics.

Having a strong work ethic, taking responsibility for your own mobility and embracing assimilation was a point Sharie made to contrast why she believes Koreans have been more successful than blacks:

*Interviewer:*   Why do you think the Koreans have succeeded where the blacks haven't?

*Sharie:*   Because they don't blame anybody. They try. They work, work, work and they succeed. And if they don't succeed they take it and they accept it and they don't blame anybody for it. They just take it and they don't cause any problems. And we don't blame them for anything. They don't do anything to us wrong. They're nice to us. You know what I mean? There shouldn't be a struggle. The black people have every opportunity. We try to give them every opportunity. Look at the schools—if you are a black person you can practically go to school free here, practically. And, uh, and I'm glad to see that there's so many black people going to college and that they're all trying to succeed but they can't blame us all the time.

*Interviewer:*   Whom do they blame?

*Sharie:*   The white society, that we're not giving them enough opportunity. I don't know. I think that's why the Koreans . . .

*Interviewer:*   What do you think that does, the blaming, in terms of what whites think about blacks?

*Sharie:*   That they're losers. That they're putting the blame on somebody who's not—it's an excuse for them—it's your fault; it's the white society's fault. I think it just makes them think less of them. It makes them think that they don't have a work ethic. I mean when we came to this country no one had anything—I mean, they had less than the blacks when they came over to this country, way less. And look at where this country has come. They can work just as hard and succeed way above their expectations if they just stopped and looked at themselves.

This depiction of Asians collectively starting out with "way less" than African Americans yet achieving the American Dream because they are the model minority serves a number of functions; it minimizes social distance between whites and Asians while crafting a narrative where each group can point to the other's immigration experiences and shared upward mobility. What is also shared however, as evidenced in surveys of perceived social distance racial attitudes, is the tendency for both whites and Asians to stereotype blacks.[9]

## Asian Passivity, Black Intimidation: Reflections of Social Distance

The theme of black racial intimidation and Asian passivity emerged in this focus group exchange:

*James:*   It's because—I think they're quiet and they're smaller in stature than black people and they seem less threatening. I mean, that's not all of them. You know, I have a couple Asian friends, and they can be loud sometimes, but, I think, as a group they're all right.

*Rita:*   They don't walk around with Mao Tse-tung hats on or shirts that say Asian Power. They're not being threatening. They're acting, they're making themselves useful, not making themselves useful, that's really awful to say, but they're working within the framework that they're given and they're making the best of their opportunities.

*James:*   Maybe it's because of their culture.

*Interviewer:*   So does that mean that since they're not asking for anything so they're not a threat? Is that what goes on?

*Jeff:*   They're not demanding anything—a lot of the time in dealing with the black cause it won't work—please, "can we have equal rights," demanding . . .

*Interviewer:*   So, why is that so different?

*Jeff:*   Because demanding takes on an aggressive stature whereas asking doesn't.

And if I personally see someone being aggressive to me my first impulse is to be aggressive back and, again, that's another vicious circle.

As Rita sees it, Asians work "within the framework" where blacks presumably do not, and unlike blacks, Asians do not use past racial injustices to explain current racial inequities. Rita's reference that Asians do not use racial identity politics (no Mao Tse-tung hats) to advance group interests taps a strong sentiment among whites that the assertion of group rights (demanding "equal rights") to ameliorate racial inequality is a rejection of the ideals that made America great: rugged individualism, embracing an achievement ideology, and believing the socioeconomic playing field is level for all. In the last exchange Jeff explains that race relations between black and whites are tense because blacks are "aggressive" where Asians are not.

The amount of perceived social distance between whites, blacks, and Asians was evident in this exchange concerning which groups whites view as a threat:

*Mike:*   Asians are different about being Asians and blacks are different about being black.

*Joshua:*   You don't usually see Asian Power T-shirts.

*Mike:*   And they're just not militant—that's not the word I'm looking for but it seems like the Asians are like, scholars.

*Christel:*   They seem more complacent.

*Lori:*   Yeah. They laugh at us. You know, they can say, make fun of me now, but . . .

*Mike:*   They're so academic. I don't really think they're worried about finding a place and getting up in the university.

*Lori:*   They're not as concerned with social issues. It doesn't seem like it, anyway.

*Interviewer:*   Are they less threatening as a group?

*Mike:*   They're not threatening, I don't think, to anybody.

Rejecting identity politics, blending in, not being threatening or militant; all these characteristics serve to make blacks cultural outsiders and by contrast, make Asians insiders. In addition to James's earlier comment about Asians being less threatening because they are smaller in stature, a few other respondents identified appearance as central to race relations.

One of the few nontraditional-aged students in the interviews, Pauline, a thirty-eight-year-old student, links color and culture in her explanation of group dynamics.

*Interviewer:*   And why don't we talk about white and Asian?

*Pauline:*   Like I said, I think it's because they're a little more accepted than the blacks.

*Interviewer:*   Why are they more accepted?

*Pauline:*   I think because their skin color is not as dark.

*Interviewer:*   Do you think it's just that, just the skin color?

*Pauline:*   Uh, maybe their culture is more accepted.

*Interviewer:*   In what way?

*Pauline:*   Well, you hear about how, like the Asians, a lot of them have families that believe in respect, respect for the family, so maybe their ideas in those ways are more accepted than the ways that blacks have lived.

Rob uses what he perceives as the physical similarities between whites and Asians also as the reason there seems to be less hostility between whites and Asians than whites and blacks.

*Interviewer:*   It seems that I don't really hear students, that is, white students talk about Asian students that much. They don't seem to be an issue about anything. What's your take on that? I mean, why do you think that is?

*Rob:*   I don't know. That is an interesting perspective. I don't know. I don't know. Maybe it gets down to something as simple as, you know, the contrast of skin color. Maybe it's just that blunt. I don't know.

*Interviewer:*   What do you mean by that, though?

*Rob:*   I mean that if you had a mass of people, just a crowd of people standing right there you could obviously pick out black Americans much easier than you might an Asian. You know what I mean? Because there is an obvious difference. Maybe it's something like that. I don't know. I really don't know.

These exchanges suggest that whites view Asians as having made every effort to assimilate by embracing a work ethnic, striving for the American Dream, and doing so in a color-blind fashion.

Many whites in this study saw Asians as possessing similar attitudes, beliefs, ambitions and even viewed Asians as being physically similar to whites, while blacks were seen as aggressive, threatening, and demanding. Herbert Blumer succinctly described how racial identities are constructed and understood by observing: "To characterize another racial group is, by opposition, to define one's own group."[10] However, groups are not only defined through an oppositional relationship; solidarity between groups can emerge when social distance between two groups is less than the social distance of a different, and often more stigmatized group. My respondents' comments suggest that a racial repositioning is taking place where whites imagine Asians as occupying a place within the existing racial hierarchy that minimizes the social distance between whites and Asians, while blacks are placed farther on the social margins.[11]

## Shades of Romance: Color, Preference, and Stigma

The focus group interviews above suggest that many whites view Asians as being culturally more similar to them than blacks, a finding that mirrored my survey on interracial relationships. My open-ended questionnaire asked respondents if any family members would "object to you bringing home a romantic partner that was from a different race." An overwhelming majority (86 percent) of the fifty-nine white respondents in my survey said that at least one family member would object to dating outside the white race but most wrote that being involved with Asians and Latinos would be viewed as less of a problem for family members. This finding is consistent with national survey data on intermarriage rates. A Knight Ridder poll in 1997 found that although whites were generally accepting of interracial marriage, 30 percent of respondents opposed black and white unions but were less critical of interracial marriages involving Latinos and Asians.[12] Mary Waters reports that "one in five whites still believes interracial marriage should be outlawed, and a majority of whites, 66 percent, said they would oppose a close relative marrying a black."[13] In their analysis of 1990 General Social Survey data, Herring and Missah found that whites, Jews, Asians, and Hispanics had the greatest opposition to one of their own marrying someone who was black.[14] While there was variation in the levels of opposition to interracial marriages for all groups, marrying someone who was white generated the least amount of disapproval. Using data from a 1992 study of Los Angeles County, Bobo and Smith found an "unambiguously greater average level of hostility to contact with blacks among nonblacks than occurs in reference to any other group."[15] Their survey found that whites, Asians, and Hispanics were more likely to oppose residential integration and interracial marriage with blacks and viewed blacks as being more dependent on welfare, harder to get along with, and less intelligent than other racial and ethnic groups. These attitudes serve as an important backdrop in understanding which racial groups whites might consider as romantic partners and how the resulting multiracial families would be positioned in the U.S. racial hierarchy.

## My Father Would Disown Me, . . .

The responses below typify the anger that crossing the color line was imagined to trigger with family members, especially when it was a white female being involved with a black male:

> If I were to bring home a black man or a man of any other racial group home with me, my father would disown me! My father would kick me out of the house and would financially disown me, and never talk to me again. He was raised in a very old fashioned traditional blacks are slaves, lower on the social scale and not anywhere close to being on the same level as the rest of the world. I have never been involved with a black man, but I did go to my senior prom with a black friend. It started a big fight between everyone in my family. (eighteen-year-old white female)
>
> If I were to bring someone home from a different racial background as my boyfriend, my family would be very confused. The person that would be most upset would be my dad. He would completely object to me having a black male date his daughter. My dad grew up in Atlanta, and now works in Atlanta. He is surrounded by the black race all day. He has set in his mind there are blacks and there are niggers. He says the black men and women that speak where people can understand them, and that have respect for people and their things are respectable black people. He will then explain that the niggers in the world that are lazy, disrespectful, stealing, cheating, Ebonics speaking blacks who will never earn respect by him. Don't get me wrong. My dad has black friends too. (nineteen-year-old white female)
>
> My father would object, my mom and dad will both be upset. They said that it looks bad when a white girl is dating a black guy because it looks like she cannot do any better than a black guy. (eighteen-year-old white female)
>
> We moved, as part of the white flight, to a whiter area. A part of why we moved was so that I would date a white girl, in my opinion. (nineteen-year-old white male)

What stands out in these survey responses was that blacks, but not Asian, American Indian, or Latino were the reference group these white respondents used to explain how family members might react to an interracial relationship. Perhaps that as the quintessential racial "other" in the United States "black" was automatically inserted as what was understood as a worst-case scenario for their families. Only a minority of white respondents (14 percent) wrote that their family would be indifferent or supportive of an interracial relationship, a finding that calls into question recent national surveys that suggest America has come to accept interracial relationships.

# Asian or Latino—But No Blacks

A number of respondents made it clear that crossing the color line would *only* be a problem if their partner were black.

> My dad and brother. I think men are intimidated by other men that are different from them. I do think that there is a big difference from Asian or Latin to black. My dad would be more upset if the guy was black than if he was Asian. I think this is because of the slavery situation in America, the hatred towards black and vice versa. (eighteen-year-old white female)
>
> My ultra-liberal parents wouldn't care. I assume the only race that would shock them (assuming I was still living in the south) is black. Considering the drastic habitual differences and tastes on a general level they would question our compatibility. As for Asians, Latino, Middle Eastern, etc., I've had a diverse group of friends so neither of us would feel awkward. My family would object to a biracial relationship if the person I was seeing was African American. I'm dating someone from El Salvador now and they are okay with the relationship. (nineteen-year-old white female)
>
> Most of my family is pretty open-minded. To be honest, my step-father wouldn't care unless my partner were African American (black). (twenty-year-old white male)
>
> My dad would object to the relationship the most. He is very traditional. Especially towards a relationship between myself and a guy of African American decent. I have had a relationship with a Filipino-American and he addressed little objection however it was clear that he wasn't thrilled about it. (nineteen-year-old white female)

These last open-ended survey responses and the responses in the epigraph underscore trends in the national survey data discussed at the beginning of this chapter; whites are more willing to cross the color line when their potential mate is not black.

# Growing the White Race: Theoretical Predictions

The Multiracial Movement seeks to highlight how the existing racial categories used by government and state agencies deny multiracial people the right to self-definition. Moreover rejecting the monoracial categories imposed on multiracial people is taken as an act of revolution and ultimately such insurgency can bring about positive social change by acknowledging how the idea of race as a socially constructed category reflects power, politics, and the maintenance of white privilege.[16] In a society fixated on creating an infinite amount of consumer choices and willing to impose free market principles on almost every social interaction, the beliefs that undergird the Multiracial Movement would appear to fit easily into post–civil rights race politics. This however, has not happened as evidenced by the relatively small number of multiracial people who could have defined themselves as multiracial in the 2000 census but did not. What appears to be taking place is a reconfiguring of existing racial categories. Richard Alba advises that "rather than speak of the decreasing White population," our collective notion of majority group might undergo a profound redefinition as "some Asians and Hispanics join what has been viewed as 'White' European population."[17] Herbert Gans makes a similar yet more problematic prediction about the future of racial categories:

> [T]oday's multiracial hierarchy could be replaced by what I think of as a dual or bimodal one consisting of "nonblack" and "black" population categories, with a third "residual," category for the groups that do not, or do not yet, fit into the basic dualism. More important, this hierarchy may be based not just on color or other visible bodily features, but also on the distinction between undeserving and deserving, or stigmatized and respectable, races. The hierarchy is new only insofar as the old white-nonwhite dichotomy may be replaced by a nonblack one, but it is hardly new for blacks, who are likely to remain at the bottom once again.[18]

Gans's collapsing of our current racial hierarchy into a dichotomous one where a sizable part of the population is placed in an intergenerational racial holding pattern is consistent with cultural critic Michael Lind's comment in the epigraph which suggests that racial borders may be fluid but the end result will be a further cementing of blacks to the bottom of the racial and economic hierarchy.

Sociologist Mary Waters writes that "[i]n general in the United States, those who are nonwhite racially have not been granted this opportunity by society but have been identified racially *by* others even if they wanted to disregard their racial or ethnic identity" (emphasis hers).[19] What is of particular importance in Waters's analysis is that the inability to select from the full range of the racial or ethnic options is imposed by "others," a point that underscores the racism on which the one-drop rule was founded. But just as the dominant group can impose measures that exclude individuals from their ranks so too can it create discourse, privilege traits, and stereotypes that assume group behavior. It is not that nonblacks aspire to be white but "in the racial context of the United States, in which Blacks are the defining other, the space exists for significant segments of groups today defined as non-White to become White."[20] What is suggested here is that educated, assimilated Asians and Latinos will be accepted into the dominant group. Those Asians and light-skinned Latinos who are well educated, economically secure, and/or with a white partner, may be able to take advantage of and exploit the perks, privileges, and prerogatives of being a member of the dominant group.

Access to amenities such as suburban housing and good schools are linked to race. Reynolds Farley notes that when Asians and Latinos move to metropolitan areas "they find themselves less residentially segregated than blacks."[21] More than one-half of all Asians (50.6 percent) in 1998 lived in suburban areas. Douglas Massey found that "the largest and most segregated Asian communities in the United States are much less isolated than the most integrated Black communities." In addition, he found that class did not lessen the extent to which black communities were racially segregated. "The most affluent blacks," Massey explains, "appear to be more segregated than the poorest Hispanics and Asians; and in contrast to the case of Blacks, Hispanic and Asian segregation levels fall steadily as income rises, reaching low or moderate levels of $50,000 or more."[22] Adelman and associates found that "even when group differences in socio-demographic are controlled, blacks were located in neighborhoods with higher levels of poverty and female headship and fewer college-educated residents than were their non-Hispanic white counterparts."[23] It is likely Asian/white and Latino/white families are part of these suburbanization trends.

But these assertions concerning residential segregation, social isolation, and which racial minorities are denied access to the resource rich middle-class white suburbs also miss what is slowly taking place: white suburbs are absorbing, even welcoming certain multiracial families because they are viewed as being culturally similar to the dominant group. Sociologist Orlando Patterson chides African Americans for not creating the rich and dense web of social networks that result from interethnic and interracial marriages. He argues that "[a]ll other American ethnic groups, including the more recently arrived Asians are intermarrying at record rates. . . . [W]hen one marries into another ethnic group one greatly expands one's social networks."[24] He advises, "[A]fter four centuries of imposed social—although not sexual reproductive—endogamy, Afro-Americans could do with a good deal of exogamy."[25] But Patterson's inability to understand why interracial marriage rates look as they do is analogous to the Multiracial Movement's blind spot on how a sizable part of the multiracial population define themselves or go on to define their children as white rather than multiracial. Patterson suggests that each racial group has a cultural dowry they bring to their marriages. The problem is that in a society structured around white racial dominance Asians and Latinos are defined as having those traits while blacks do not. We are now (or perhaps again) at a unique juncture in the history of racial and ethnic identity construction where racial categories may be mutating. Expanding the boundaries of whiteness to include those groups who subscribe to the existing racial status quo is one way racial dominance is "reorganized." White privilege is not being challenged by the incorporation of new groups into the category "white." It is revitalized as potential challengers to the existing hierarchy are co-opted and rewarded with the perks of membership in the dominant group. What is typically required, however, is that the racist beliefs and practices of the dominant group are internalized by those who join the ranks of the dominant group. In the end the Multiracial Movement may not be able to count on assimilated, economically successful light-skinned Latinos or Asians or their even lighter-skinned multiracial children, because like the Italians and Irish before them, racial redistricting will have allowed them to glide easily into the category "white."

# Notes

Michael Lind, "The Beige and the Black," New York Times Magazine, September 6, 1998, 39.

1. See Roediger and Ignatiev. See also Ruth Frankenberg, *White Women, Race Matters: The Social Construction of Whiteness* (Minneapolis: University of Minnesota Press, 1993); Birgit Brander, ed., *The Making and Unmaking of Whiteness* (Durham: Duke University Press, 2001); Ashley W. Doane Jr., "Dominant Group Identity in the United States: The Role of "Hidden" Ethnicity in Intergroup Relations," *The Sociological Quarterly,* 38, no. 3; Charles A. Gallagher, "White Reconstruction in the University," *Socialist Review* 24 (1995); Amanda Lewis, "Whiteness Studies: Past Research and Future," *African American Research Perspectives,* 8, no. 1 (2002).

2. See David Roediger; *Towards an Abolition of Whiteness: Essays on Race, Politics, and the Working Class* (New York: Verso, 1994); David Roediger, *The Wages of Whiteness: Race and the Making of the American Working Class* (New York: Verso, 1991); Noel Ignatiev, *How the Irish Became White* (New York: Routledge, 1995); Karen Brodkin Sacks, "How Did Jews Become White Folks?" in *Race,* ed. Steven Gregory and Roger Sanjek (New Brunswick: Rutgers University Press, 1994); Charles A. Gallagher, "White Racial Formation: Into the Twenty-First Century," in *Critical White Studies: Looking Behind the Mirror,* ed. Richard Delgado and Jean Stefancic (Philadelphia: Temple University Press, 1997).

3. Omi and Winant define this process as a "socio-historical process by which racial categories are created, inhabited, transformed and destroyed." Michael Omi and Howard Winant, *Racial Formation in the United States: From the 1960s to the 1990s* (New York: Routledge, 1994), 55.

4. Reynolds Farley, "Racial Issues: Recent Trends in Residential Patterns and Intermarriage," in *Diversity and Its Discontents: Cultural Conflict and Common Ground in Contemporary American Society,* ed. Neil Smelser and Jeffrey Alexander (Princeton: Princeton University Press, 1999), 114–15.

5. Annie E. Casey Foundation, "Using New Racial Categories in the 2000 Census. . . .

6. U.S. Census.

7. Mary Waters, "Multiple Ethnic Identity Choices," in *Beyond Pluralism: The Conception of Groups and Group Identities in America,* ed. Wendy F. Katlin, Ned Landsman, and Andrea Tyree (Chicago: University of Chicago Press, 1998).

8. Waters, 41.

9. Cedric Herring and Charles Amissah, "Advance and Retreat: Racially Based Attitudes and Public Policy," in *Racial Attitudes in the 1990s: Continuity and Change,* ed. Steven A. Tuch and Jack Martin (Westport: Praeger, 1997), 139.

10. Herbert Blumer, "Race Prejudice as a Sense of Group Position," in *Rethinking the Color Line: Readings in Race and Ethnicity,* ed. Charles A. Gallagher (Mountain View, CA: Mayfield Press, 1999).

11. Michael Omi argues that we should not think about increased rates of intermarriage between white men and Asian women as an "indicator of assimilation" because such a description negates "differences in group power." It may be, as Omi suggests, that the assimilation framework masks patriarchy, sexist stereotypes of Asian women, and group-based

inequalities in the name of minimizing social distance but it does not alter the fact that these marriages and the children of these unions challenge and blur existing racial categories. The ability to have both racial and ethnic options in how these individuals construct their identity suggests that under certain conditions the one-drop rule will cease to accurately describe the experiences of certain mixed race individuals. See Michael Omi, "The Changing Meaning of Race," in *America Becoming: Racial Trends and Their Consequences,* ed. Neil Smelser, William J. Wilson, and Faith Mitchell (Washington, DC: National Academy Press, 2001), 258.

12. Anne-Marie Connor, "Interracial Unions Have a Ripple Effect on Families, Society," *Los Angeles Times.* . . .

13. Waters, 43.

14. Cedric Herring and Charles Amissah, "Advance and Retreat: Racially Based Attitudes and Public Policy," in *Racial Attitudes in the 1990s: Continuity and Change,* ed. Steven A. Tuch and Jack Martin (Westport: Praeger, 1997), 139.

15. Lawrence Bobo and Ryan Smith, "From Jim Crow Racism to Laissez-Faire Racism: The Transformation of Racial Attitudes," in *Beyond Pluralism: The Conception of Groups and Group Identities in America,* ed. Wendy Katlin, Ned Landsman, and Andrea Tyree (Chicago: University of Illinois Press), 202.

16. Root, 7.

17. Omi, 258.

18. Herbert Gans, "The Possibility of a New Racial Hierarchy in the Twenty-First Century United States," in *The Cultural Territories of Race,* ed. Michele Lamont (Chicago: University of Chicago Press, 1999), 371.

19. Waters, 29.

20. Jonathan W. Warren and France Winddance Twine, "White Americans, the New Minority?: Non-Blacks and the Ever-Expanding Boundaries of Whiteness," *Journal of Black Studies,* 28, no. 2 (Nov. 1997).

21. Farley, 102.

22. Douglas Massey, "Residential Segregation and Neighborhood Conditions," in *America Becoming: Racial Trends and Their Consequences,* ed. Neil Smelser, William J. Wilson, and Faith Mitchell (Washington, DC: National Academy Press, 2001), 411.

23. Robert Adelman, Hui-shien Tsao, Stewart Tolnay, and Kyle Crowder, "Neighborhood Disadvantage Among Racial and Ethnic Groups: Residential Location in 1970 and 1980," *The Sociological Quarterly,* 42, no. 4.

24. Orlando Patterson, *The Ordeal of Integration: Progress and Resentments in America's Racial Crisis* (Washington, DC: Civitas, 1997), 195.

25. Patterson, 197.

**Ellis Cose**

# What's White, Anyway?

**I**n Argentina, where he was born, my acquaintance had always been on solid taxonomic ground. His race was no more a mystery than the color of the clouds. It was a fact, presumably rooted in biology, that he was as white as a man could be. But his move to the United States had left him confused. So he turned to me and sheepishly asked in Spanish, "Am I white or am I Latino?"

Given his fair complexion and overall appearance, most Americans would deem him white, I replied—that is, until he opened his mouth, at which point his inability to converse in English would become his most salient feature. He would still be considered white, I explained, but his primary identity would be as a Latino. For his U.S.-raised children, the relevant order will likely be reversed: in most circles they will simply be white Americans, albeit of Argentine ancestry, unless they decide to be Latino. At any rate, I pointed out, the categories are not exclusive—although in the United States we often act as if they are.

He said he understood, though something in his manner told me he was more confused than ever. Playing the game of racial classification has a way of doing that to you. For though the question—*who is white?*—is as old as America itself, the answer has often changed. And it is shifting yet again, even as the advantages of whiteness have become murkier than ever.

In the beginning, the benefits were obvious. American identity itself was inextricably wrapped up in the mythology of race. The nation's first naturalization act (passed during the second session of the first Congress in March 1790) reserved the privilege of naturalization for "aliens being free white persons." Only after the Civil War were blacks allowed to present themselves for citizenship, and even then other suspect racial groups were not so favored. Thus, well into the 20th century persons of various ethnicities and hues sued for the purpose of proving themselves white.

In 1922 the case of a Japanese national who had lived in America for two decades made its way to the Supreme Court. Takao Ozawa argued that the United States, in annexing Hawaii, had embraced people even darker than the Japanese—implicitly recognizing them as white. He also made the rather novel, if bizarre, claim that the dominant strain of Japanese were "white persons" of Caucasian root stock who spoke an "Aryan tongue."

The high court disagreed. Nonetheless, the following year a high-caste Hindu, Bhagat Singh Thind, asked the same court to accept him as a white Aryan. In rejecting his claim Justice George Sutherland, writing for the court, declared: "It may be true that the blond Scandinavian and the brown Hindu have a common ancestor in the dim reaches of antiquity, but the average man knows perfectly well that there are unmistakable and profound differences between them today." While the children of Europeans quickly became indistinguishable from other Americans, "it cannot be doubted that the children born in this country of Hindu parents would retain indefinitely the clear evidence of their ancestry," concluded Sutherland.

The McCarran-Walter Act, passed in 1952, finally eliminated racial restrictions on citizenship. No longer were East Indians, Arabs and assorted other non-Europeans forced, in a figurative sense, to paint themselves white in order to become Americans.

Today such an exercise seems weird beyond words. But it's worth recalling that even Europeans were not exempt from establishing their racial bona fides. The great immigration debates of the first part of the 20th century were driven in large measure by panic at the prospect of American's gene pool becoming hopelessly polluted with the blood of inferior European tribes. Many of the leading scientists and politicians of the day worried that immigrants from Eastern and Southern Europe—people considered intellectually, morally and physically inferior—would debase America's exalted Anglo-Saxon-Germanic stock. Such thinking was influenced, among other things, by the rise of eugenics. "The Races of Europe," a book published in 1899 by sociologist William Z. Ripley, was a typical text. Ripley classified Europeans into three distinct races: blond, blue-eyed Teutonics (who were at the highest stage of development); stocky, chestnut-haired Alpines, and dark, slender Mediterraneans. No less a personage than Stanford University president David Starr Jordan bought into the scheme, along with some of the leading lights of Congress. And though "undesirable" European races were never flatly prohibited from eligibility for citizenship, American immigration laws were crafted to favor those presumed to be of finer racial stock. While all whites might be deemed superior to those who were black, yellow or brown, all white "races" were not considered equal to each other.

Gradually America learned to set aside many of its racial preconceptions. Indeed, much of American history has been a process of embracing previously reviled or excluded groups. At one time or another, various clans of Europeans—Poles, Italians, Jews, Romanians—were deemed genetically suspect; but they were subsequently welcomed. They were all, in essence, made white. The question today is whether that process will extend to those whose ancestors, for the most part, were not European.

To some extent it certainly will. That reality struck me some years ago when, in a moment of unguarded conversation, a radio host observed that "white Asians" were in demand for certain jobs. Initially I had no idea what the man was talking about, but as he rattled on I realized he was saying that he considered some Asian-Americans (those with a lighter complexion) to be, for all intents and purposes, as white as himself. In his mind at least, the definition of whiteness has expanded well beyond its old parameters. And I suspect he is far from alone. This is not to say that Takao Ozawa would be better able today than in 1922 to convince a court that he is Aryan; but he almost certainly could persuade most Americans to treat him like a white person, which essentially amounts to the same thing. America's cult of whiteness, after all, was never just about skin color, hair texture and other physical traits. It was about where the line was drawn between those who could be admitted into the mainstream and those who could not.

Those boundaries clearly are no longer where they once were. And even as the boundaries of whiteness have expanded, the specialness of whiteness has eroded. Being white, in other words, is no longer quite what it used to be. So if Ozawa and his progeny have not exactly become white, they are no longer mired in America's racial wasteland. Indeed, even many Americans with the option of being white—those with, say, one Mexican parent or a Cherokee grandfather—are more than ever inclined to think of themselves as something else. And those for whom whiteness will likely never be an option (most blacks and many darker Hispanics, for instance) are freer to enjoy being whatever they are.

Society, in short, has progressed much since the days when Eastern Europeans felt it necessary to Anglicize their names, when Arabs and East Indians went to court to declare themselves white and when the leading scientists of the day had nothing better to do than to link morality and intelligence to preconceived notions of race. But having finally thrust aside 19th-century racial pseudo-science, we have not yet fully digested the science of the 21st, which has come to understand what enlightened souls sensed all along: that the differences that divided one race from another add up to a drop in the genetic ocean.

Recognizing the truth of that insight is only part of society's challenge. The largest part is figuring out what to do with it, figuring out how, having so long given racial categories an importance they never merited, we reduce them to the irrelevance they deserve—figuring out how, in short, to make real the abstraction called equality we profess to have believed in all along.

# POSTSCRIPT

## Do Recent Immigration Trends Threaten Existing Ideas of America's White Identity?

The racial and ethnic diversity of the United States in 2006 is obvious to anyone. Large metropolitan areas such as Los Angeles and New York, along with hundreds of other cities and suburbs, are becoming increasingly diverse. The diversity is marked by demographic changes in both race and ethnic groups. The most recent wave of immigrants from Latin America and Asia have added to the multicultural character of American identity. What has it added? How will the new groups reflect on their racial identity? How will these additions change our notion of minority groups?

Controversy is not new to immigration history. Nineteenth century reactions to "new" immigrants gave rise to nativism that opposed Roman Catholic and Chinese immigrants. The sentiment eventually produced a social and political reaction that led to the National Origins System, a highly restrictionist immigration policy directed at the growing immigration from southern Europe. The dominance of a white, Anglo-Saxon, Protestant culture asserted itself. Other European groups would be accommodated but in limited numbers so as to protect the majority culture rooted in Northern and Western European background.

Similarly today, Asian and Latin American immigration raises the question of American identity. With this contemporary immigration pattern, does race emerge as a major factor? Should the paradigm for looking at race relations extend beyond the black-white and include ethnicity? With all the issues surrounding nineteenth and early twentieth century immigration and its impact on a common American identity, race had much less significance than it has today. European immigrants and their descendants assimilated to the dominant group, and in the process, distanced themselves from the non-whites such as the Native Americans and African-Americans.

Just as certain segments of the population reacted to "new" immigrants in the two centuries past, today the reaction continues. Whiteness enables them to assimilate. The question of white identity (as American identity) is reflected in the shifting percentages of majority-minority groups. Once again the phrase, "They are not like us," manifests itself to distinguish resident groups from new immigrants.

A history of non-Anglo groups in the United States is found in *A Different Mirror: A History of Multicultural America* by Ronald Takaki (Little, Brown & Co., 1993).

An interesting and provocative chapter in Lillian Rubin's *Families on the Fault Line* (Harper Perennial, 1995) is "Is This a White Country, or What?" She contrasts current immigrants who are mostly nonwhite with nineteenth-century European immigrants, almost all of whom were considered white. *Are Italians White?* (Routledge, 2003), edited by Jennifer Guglielmo and Salvatore Salerno, offers a collection of readings dealing with Italian immigrants and the color line. This is a good reference to document the historical problems of assimilation that are relevant today with new immigrant groups. The natavist challenge to new immigrants is explored in *Immigrants Out! The New Nativism and the Anti-Immigrant Impulse in the United States* (New York Press, 1997), edited by Juan F. Perea. Particularly relevant to this issue is Mary Waters' "Multiple Ethnic Identity Choices," in *Beyond Pluralism: The Conception of Groups and Group Identities in America* (University of Chicago Press, 1998), edited by Wendy F. Katlin, Ned Landsman, and Andrea Tyree.

# ISSUE 4

## Is Today's Immigration Debate Racist?

**YES: Carlos Fuentes,** from "Huntington and the Mask of Racism," trans. Thomas D. Morin, *New Perspectives Quarterly* (Spring 2004)

**NO: Samuel P. Huntington,** from *The Clash of Civilizations and the Remaking of World Order* (Simon & Schuster, 1996)

### ISSUE SUMMARY

**YES:** Carlos Fuentes, prominent Mexican writer and social commentator, argues that much of the current immigration debate is racist. For example, he criticizes Samuel Huntington's assessment that Mexican immigrants exploit the United States and represent an unjust burden to the nation. This "mask" of racism appears under the guise of a concern with American national unity.

**NO:** Samuel Huntington, political scientist and Albert J. Weatherhead III, University Professor at Harvard University, expresses the concern that Mexican immigrants and, by implication, other Latinos, are creating significant problems for America, specifically with reference to assimilation, as their numbers continue to increase within the population. In general, he believes that Latino immigration is a threat to America's national unity.

$I$t is an undeniable historical fact that the vast majority of the 300 million people comprising the population of the United States migrated to this country or are descendants of migrants from a foreign land. Most came voluntarily, impelled by the promise of a better life, while others arrived in the chains of bondage of American slavery. However, despite the fact that the United States is a nation whose people are mostly descendants of migrants, immigrants and the policies that define and regulate their status within society are a continuing source of controversy.

Those who favor immigrants offer many arguments in support of the thesis that these newcomers are good for the nation. Immigrants are viewed by supporters as sources of cultural enrichment and renewal. Immigrants are also viewed as cheap labor that can contribute to continuing economic vitality, especially within societies with aging populations. In today's urban America, immigrants are given credit for the revitalization of neglected and deteriorating neighborhoods. Opponents of immigration base their negative assessments on claims including alleged contribution to crime, welfare dependency, taking jobs from America's poor and minorities, among other concerns.

The often-unstated claim is that Mexican immigrants threaten Anglo-Saxon heritage. For example, a reaction to Mexican and other Latino immigrants has resulted in the creation of an English-only movement. There is considerable criticism of bilingualism today (see Issue 14). In many states, local initiatives aim to reduce or eliminate signs and forms in Spanish.

Huntington notes that immigrants arriving in the United States are increasingly from non-Western societies with cultures that are distant from America's dominant culture. This cultural distance that he observes is viewed as a major barrier to assimilation and the unity of the nation.

The current controversy over immigration is intertwined with issues of homeland security, especially border security. Despite the fact that the northern border—Canada—is much longer, the focus on the United States' southern border—Mexico—has become the major domestic political issue regarding immigration policy. Would Swedes concentrated on our borders constitute the same reactions as Latinos? Why is there less concern with security on the Canadian border?

Swirling about this issue are concerns with low wages, crime, a permanent underclass, linguistic ethnocentrism, and the issue of race. Hence, the current controversy is a continuation of restrictive immigration policy aimed primarily at people of color. In this regard, one should note the passage of the Chinese Exclusion Act of 1882 and the anti-Japanese Gentleman's Agreement of 1907. Both were directed at potential immigrants of color.

Fuentes defends current immigration trends and attacks Huntington for developing a mask of racism. He accuses Huntington of promoting an image of Mexican immigrants as "the brown menace"—a major threat to American society. In contrast to Huntington and other critics of Latino immigrants including Mexicans, Fuentes stresses economic and cultural benefits of Mexican and other Latino immigrants.

In April 2006, there were major demonstrations throughout the country in support of immigrants' rights. Since Latinos tend to be concentrated within the southwestern states of Texas, New Mexico, Arizona, and California, along with Florida, then these states are the major focus for this issue. At the same time the Latino population is spreading throughout the country.

We recommend that this issue be studied in both a social and an economic context. For example, contemporary political solutions dealing with the current illegal immigration debate includes additional issues such as amnesty for illegal immigrants, guest worker programs, border security, and concern with the extensive use of the Spanish language in the United States.

Students should consider Issues 1 and 2 as background to a fuller comprehension of this issue. Additionally, students should consider the following questions that arise from this issue: Do immigrants take jobs? Do immigrants contribute to economic expansion? Do immigrants serve as a reserve "army" of the unemployed and thus drag down wages? Do immigrants create opportunity? How much of a factor do you think race contributes to the current public reaction to immigration—both legal and illegal?

# YES

**Carlos Fuentes**

# Huntington and the Mask of Racism

"The best Indian is a dead Indian." "The best nigger is a nigger slave." "The yellow threat." "The red threat." The Puritanism one finds at the base of WASP culture (White, Anglo Saxon, and Protestant) in the United States of America expresses itself, from time to time, with shocking color. Now, another of these forceful and freely expressed simplistic ideas can be added to the colorful expressions already mentioned: "The Brown Menace."

The proponent of this idea is Professor Samuel P. Huntington, the tireless voice of alarm with respect to the menace that the idea of the "other" represents for the foundational soul of white, protestant, Anglo-Saxon United States of America. That there existed (and, still, exists) an indigenous-"America" (Huntington uses the United States as a name for the entire continent) prior to the European colonization is of no concern to him. That besides Anglo-America, there existed a prior French-"America" (Louisiana) and, even, a Russian-America (Alaska) is of no inter-est to Huntington. What worries him is Hispanic-America, the America of Ruben Dario, the America that speaks Spanish and believes in God. For Huntington, this brown danger is an indispensable danger for a nation that requires, in order to exist, an identifiable external menace. Moby Dick, the white whale, is a symbol of this attitude which, fortunately, not all North Americans share, including John Quincy Adams, the sixth president of the North American nation, who warned his countrymen: "Let us not go out into the world in search of monsters to destroy."

Huntington, in his *Clash of Civilizations,* discovers his necessary external monster (once the USSR and "the red danger" disappeared) in an Islam poised to assault the borders of Western Civilization, in an attempt to outdo the feats of Saladino, the Sultan, who captured Jerusalem in 1187. As a result, Huntington outdoes the Christian Crusade of Richard the Lion Hearted in the Holy Land. Huntington the Lion Hearted's anti-Islamic Crusade expresses the profound racism in his heart and, in similar manner, his profound ignorance of the true *kulturkampf* evident in the Islamic world. Islam is not poised to invade the West. Islam is living, from Algeria to Iran, its own cultural and political battle between conservatives and Islamic liberals. It is a vertical battle, deep within, not a horizontal one of expansion.

From *New Perspectives Quarterly,* Spring 2004, pp. 77–81. Copyright © 2004 by NPQ. Reprinted by permission.

# The Mexican as Exploiter

Huntington's new crusade is directed against Mexico and the Mexicans that live, work, and enrich life in the northern nation. As far as Huntington is concerned, Mexicans do not live—they invade; they do not work—they exploit; and, they do not enrich—they impoverish, since poverty is part a Mexican's natural condition. All of this, when taking into account the number of Mexicans and Latin Americans in the United States, constitutes a cultural threat for that which Huntington dares to mention: the Anglo-American, Protestant, and Anglo speaking white race.

Are Mexicans invading the US? No, they are simply obeying the laws of the job market. There are job offers for Mexicans because there is a North American labor need. If some day, there were to exist full employment in Mexico, the US would have to find cheap labor from another country for the jobs whites, Saxons, and Protestants—naming them as does Huntington—do not want to fill, since they have either surpassed these levels of employment, or because they have grown old, due to the fact that the economy of the US has passed from the industrial period, to the post-industrial, technological, information age.

Do Mexicans exploit the US? According to Huntington, Mexicans constitute an unjust burden for the US economy: they receive more than they give back.

All of this is false. California earmarks a billion dollars a year to educate the children of immigrants. But if it were to do otherwise—listen up, Schwarzenegger—the state would lose $16 billion a year in federal aid to education. Similarly, Mexican migrant workers pay $29 billion a year more in taxes than the services they receive.

The Mexican immigrant, far from being an impoverishing burden, as assumed by Huntington, creates wealth for all economic levels. At the most humble worker level, the expulsion of Mexican immigrants would be ruinous for the US. John Kenneth Galbraith (the kind of North American that Huntington cannot be) writes the following: "If all the undocumented people in the US were to be expelled, the effect on the North American economy . . . would be nothing less than disastrous . . . Fruit and vegetables in Florida, Texas and California would not be harvested. The price of food products would rise to incredible levels. The Mexican people that want to come to the US are necessary, and clearly add to everyone's well-being." (The Nature of Mass Poverty)

On another level, the Hispanic migrant, as Gregory Rodriguez from Pepperdine University tells us, has the highest number of salaried individuals per family than any other ethnic group. So, too, is his level of family cohesiveness. The result is that, while the father of the family may have arrived barefoot and soaking wet, the descendents of migrants have attained income levels comparable to those of Asian and Caucasian laborers. By the second and third generation, 55 percent of Hispanic households are owners of their own homes, compared to 71 percent of white households and 44 percent of black households.

I would like to add to the figures given by Professor Rodriguez the fact that in Los Angeles County alone, the number of businesses created by Hispanic migrants rose from 57,000 in 1987 to 210,000 last year. Since 1990, the purchasing power of Hispanics has risen 65 percent. Furthermore, the Hispanic American economy in the US generates almost $400 billion a year—more than the Gross National Product of Mexico.

Do we Hispanics exploit or contribute, Mr. Huntington?

# Mexican Balkanization

According to Huntington, the sheer numbers and customs of Mexican migrants will end up Balkanizing the US. North American unity has absorbed the European immigrant (including Jews and Arabs, who are not specifically mentioned by Huntington) because the immigrant of old, such as Chaplin in the movie of the same name, came from Europe, crossed the ocean and being white and Christian assimilated quickly into Anglo-Saxon culture and forgot his language and native customs, something which might surprise the Italians in *The Godfather* and the Central Europeans in *The Deer Hunter*.

No. Only the Mexicans and the Hispanics, in general, are separatists. These people have conspired to create a separate Hispanic American nation, the soldiers of a re-conquest of the territories lost in the Mexican-American War of 1848.

If we were to turn the page over, we would find English to be the most spoken Western language. Does Huntington ever think that this fact reveals to all a silent North American invasion of the entire world? Would we Mexicans, Chileans, French, Egyptians, Japanese and Hindi be justified in prohibiting English to be spoken in our respective countries? To stigmatize the Spanish language as a divisive, practically subversive, factor demonstrates the racist, divisive and provocative spirit of Professor Huntington.

To speak a second (or a third or fourth language) is a sign of culture throughout the world excepting, it would seem, in the Monolingual Eden invented by Huntington. To establish the requirement of a second language in the US (as occurs in Mexico and in France) would eliminate the Satanic effects that Huntington attributes to the language of Cervantes. Hispanic speakers in the US do not form impenetrable nor aggressive groups. They adapt themselves rapidly to English and, at times, conserve the use of Spanish, thus, enriching the accepted multiethnic and multicultural character of the US.

All in all, mono-lingualism is a curable disease. Many of us Latin Americans speak English without fear of being contaminated. Huntington presents us with an image of the US as a fearful trembling giant attacked by Spanish speakers. His tactic is fear of the "other," so favored by fascist mentalities.

No: The Mexican and the Hispanic, in general, contribute to the wealth of the US. They give more than they receive. They wish to integrate themselves in the North American nation. They attenuate the cultural isolationism that has led the governments in Washington to so many disastrous international situations. They advocate a political diversification that has been brought about by Afro-Americans, Native Americans, the Irish, Poles, Russians and Italians, Swedes and Germans, Arabs and Jews.

## The Mexican Menace

Huntington brings to the fore a musty anti-Mexican racism that I knew, all to well, as a child studying in the North American capital. *The Volume Library*, a one volume encyclopedia published in 1928 in New York, said the following: "One reason for Mexican poverty is the predominance of its racial inferiority." "No dogs nor Mexicans allowed," read the signs written on numerous restaurant facades in Texas during the Thirties. Today, the Latino electorate is seduced with mixed phrases in Spanish by many candidates, among them Gore and Bush during the last electoral process. It is an electoral campaign tactic (similar to Bush's recent migration proposal).

But for us, Mexicans, Spaniards and Hispanic Americans, what is certain is that language is a factor of pride and unity. Five hundred million men and women speak Spanish around the world. But, it is not a fear factor, nor a menace. If Huntington fears the Hispanic Balkanization of the US and wishes to blame Latin American for its incapacity to establish democratic governments and economic development, we, at least, have lived without nationalistic separatisms since the dawn of Independence.

Perhaps what unites us is what Huntington believes disunites: the multicultural nature of the Spanish language. As Hispanic Americans and Spanish speakers, we are, also, Indo-European and Afro-American. We are the descendants of one nation, Spain, which cannot be understood without its racial multiplicity and Celt-Iberian, Greek, Phoenician, Roman, Arabic, Judaic, Gothic linguistic system. We speak a language with Celt-Iberian followed by Latin roots, enriched by a good portion of Arabic words and set in place by the Jews of the 13th century in the court of Alphonse the Wise.

With all we have mentioned, we are winners, not losers. The loser is Huntington, isolated in his imaginary land of Anglo speaking, white and Protestant racial purity. Even, if, in a curiously benevolent way, he offers his space to "Christianism." Most assuredly, Israel and Islam are menaces to be equally condemned as are Mexico and Hispanic America, and, by extension today's Spain, for their undesirable incursions into the old territories of Huntington's Kingdom.

An idle question: Who will become the next Moby Dick of Captain Ahab Huntington?

Samuel P. Huntington  **NO**

# The Clash of Civilizations and the Remaking of World Order

## Immigration

If demography is destiny, population movements are the motor of history. In centuries past, differential growth rates, economic conditions, and governmental policies have produced massive migrations by Greeks, Jews, Germanic tribes, Norse, Turks, Russians, Chinese, and others. In some instances these movements were relatively peaceful, in others quite violent. Nineteenth-century Europeans were, however, the master race at demographic invasion. Between 1821 and 1924, approximately 55 million Europeans migrated overseas, 34 million of them to the United States. Westerners conquered and at times obliterated other peoples, explored and settled less densely populated lands. The export of people was perhaps the single most important dimension of the rise of the West between the sixteenth and twentieth centuries.

The late twentieth century has seen a different and even larger surge in migration. In 1990 legal international migrants numbered about 100 million, refugees about 19 million, and illegal migrants probably at least 10 million more. This new wave of migration was in part the product of decolonization, the establishment of new states, and state policies that encouraged or forced people to move. It was also, however, the result of modernization and technological development. Transportation improvements made migration easier, quicker, and cheaper; communications improvements enhanced the incentives to pursue economic opportunities and promoted relations between migrants and their home country families. In addition, as the economic growth of the West stimulated emigration in the nineteenth century, economic development by non-Western societies has stimulated emigration in the twentieth century. Migration becomes a self-reinforcing process. "If there is a single 'law' in migration," Myron Weiner argues, "it is that a migration flow, once begun, induces its own flow. Migrants enable their friends and relatives back home to migrate by providing them with information about how to migrate, resources to facilitate movement, and assistance in finding jobs and housing." The result is, in his phrase, a "global migration crisis." . . .

In the United States immigrants constituted 8.7 percent of the population in 1994, twice that of 1970, and made up 25 percent of the people in California and 16 percent of those in New York. About 8.3 million people entered the United States in the 1980s and 4.5 million in the first four years of the 1990s. . . .

Public opposition to immigration and hostility toward immigrants manifested itself at the extreme in acts of violence against immigrant communities and individuals, which particularly became an issue in Germany in the early 1990s. More significant were increases in the votes for right-wing, nationalist, anti-immigration parties. . . .

The immigration issue came to the fore somewhat later in the United States than it did in Europe and did not generate quite the same emotional intensity. The United States has always been a country of immigrants, has so conceived itself, and historically has developed highly successful processes for assimilating newcomers. In addition, in the 1980s and 1990s unemployment was considerably lower in the United States than in Europe, and fear of losing jobs was not a decisive factor shaping attitudes toward immigration. The sources of American immigration were also more varied than in Europe, and thus the fear of being swamped by a single foreign group was less nationally, although real in particular localities. The cultural distance of the two largest migrant groups from the host culture was also less than in Europe: Mexicans are Catholic and Spanish-speaking; Filipinos, Catholic and English-speaking.

Despite these factors, in the quarter century after passage of the 1965 act that permitted greatly increased Asian and Latin American immigration, American public opinion shifted decisively. In 1965 only 33 percent of the public wanted less immigration. In 1977, 42 percent did; in 1986, 49 percent did; and in 1990 and 1993, 61 percent did. Polls in the 1990s consistently show 60 percent or more of the public favoring reduced immigration. While economic concerns and economic conditions affect attitudes toward immigration, the steadily rising opposition in good times and bad suggests that culture, crime, and way of life were more important in this change of opinion. "Many, perhaps most, Americans," one observer commented in 1994, "still see their nation as a European settled country, whose laws are an inheritance from England, whose language is (and should remain) English, whose institutions and public buildings find inspiration in Western classical norms, whose religion has Judeo-Christian roots, and whose greatness initially arose from the Protestant work ethic." Reflecting these concerns, 55 percent of a sample of the public said they thought immigration was a threat to American culture. While Europeans see the immigration threat as Muslim or Arab, Americans see it as both Latin American and Asian but primarily as Mexican. When asked in 1990 from which countries the United States was admitting too many immigrants, a sample of Americans identified Mexico twice as often as any other, followed in order by Cuba, the Orient (nonspecific), South America and Latin America (nonspecific), Japan, Vietnam, China, and Korea.

Growing public opposition to immigration in the early 1990s prompted a political reaction comparable to that which occurred in Europe.

Given the nature of the American political system, rightist and anti-immigration parties did not gain votes, but anti-immigration publicists and interest groups became more numerous, more active, and more vocal. Much of the resentment focused on the 3.5 million to 4 million illegal immigrants, and politicians responded. As in Europe, the strongest reaction was at the state and local levels, which bear most of the costs of the immigrants. As a result in 1994, Florida, subsequently joined by six other states, sued the federal government for $884 million a year to cover the education, welfare, law enforcement, and other costs produced by illegal immigrants. In California, the state with the largest number of immigrants absolutely and proportionately, Governor Pete Wilson won public support by urging the denial of public education to children of illegal immigrants, refusing citizenship to U.S.-born children of illegal immigrants, and ending state payments for emergency medical care for illegal immigrants. In November 1994 Californians overwhelmingly approved Proposition 187, denying health, education, and welfare benefits to illegal aliens and their children.

Also in 1994 the Clinton administration, reversing its earlier stance, moved to toughen immigration controls, tighten rules governing political asylum, expand the Immigration and Naturalization Service, strengthen the Border Patrol, and construct physical barriers along the Mexican boundary. In 1995 the Commission on Immigration Reform, authorized by Congress in 1990, recommended reducing yearly legal immigration from over 800,000 to 550,000, giving preference to young children and spouses but not other relatives of current citizens and residents, a provision that "inflamed Asian-American and Hispanic families." Legislation embodying many of the commission's recommendations and other measures restricting immigration was on its way through Congress in 1995–96. By the mid-1990s immigration had thus become a major political issue in the United States, and in 1996 Patrick Buchanan made opposition to immigration a central plank in his presidential campaign. The United States is following Europe in moving to cut back substantially the entry of non-Westerners into its society. . . .

Can either Europe or the United States stem the migrant tide? France has experienced a significant strand of demographic pessimism, stretching from the searing novel of Jean Raspail in the 1970s to the scholarly analysis of Jean-Claude Chesnais in the 1990s and summed up in the 1991 comments of Pierre Lellouche: "History, proximity and poverty insure that France and Europe are destined to be overwhelmed by people from the failed societies of the south. Europe's past was white and Judeo-Christian. The future is not."*

---

*Raspail's *Le Camp des Saints* was first published in 1973 (Paris. Editions Robert Laffront) and was issued in a new edition in 1985 as concern over immigration intensified in France. The novel was dramatically called to the attention of Americans as concern intensified in the United States in 1994 by Matthew Connelly and Paul Kennedy, "Must It Be the Rest Against the West?" *Atlantic Monthty,* v. 274 (Dec. 1994). pp. 61ff., and Raspail's preface to the 1985 French edition was published in English in *The Social Contract,* v. 4 (Winter 1993–94). pp. 115–117.

*Table 1*

## U.S. Population by Race and Ethnicity (in percentages)

|  | 1995 | 2020 Est. | 2050 Est. |
|---|---|---|---|
| Non-Hispanic White | 74% | 64% | 53% |
| Hispanic | 10 | 16 | 25 |
| Black | 12 | 13 | 14 |
| Asian & Pacific Islander | 3 | 6 | 8 |
| American Indian & Alaskan Native | <1 | <1 | 1 |
| Total (Millions) | 263 | 323 | 394 |

Source: U.S. Bureau of the Census. *Population Projections of the United States by Age, Sex, Race, and Hispanic Origin: 1995 to 2050* (Washington: U.S. Government Printing Office, 1996), pp. 12–13.

The future, however, is not irrevocably determined; nor is any one future permanent. The issue is not whether Europe will be Islamicized or the United States Hispanicized. It is whether Europe and America will become cleft societies encompassing two distinct and largely separate communities from two different civilizations, which in turn depends on the numbers of immigrants and the extent to which they are assimilated into the Western cultures prevailing in Europe and America.

While Muslims pose the immediate problem to Europe, Mexicans pose the problem for the United States. Assuming continuation of current trends and policies, the American population will, as the figures in Table 1 show, change dramatically in the first half of the twenty-first century, becoming almost 50 percent white and 25 percent Hispanic. As in Europe, changes in immigration policy and effective enforcement of anti-immigration measures could change these projections. Even so, the central issue will remain the degree to which Hispanics are assimilated into American society as previous immigrant groups have been. Second and third generation Hispanics face a wide array of incentives and pressures to do so. Mexican immigration, on the other hand, differs in potentially important ways from other immigrations. First, immigrants from Europe or Asia cross oceans; Mexicans walk across a border or wade across a river. This plus the increasing ease of transportation and communication enables them to maintain close contact and identity with their home communities. Second, Mexican immigrants are concentrated in the southwestern United States and form part of a continuous Mexican society stretching from Yucatan to Colorado. Third, some evidence suggests that resistance to assimilation is stronger among Mexican migrants than it was with other immigrant groups and that Mexicans tend to retain their Mexican identity, as was evident in the struggle over Proposition 187 in California in 1994. Fourth, the area settled by Mexican migrants was annexed by the United States after it defeated Mexico in the mid-nineteenth century. Mexican economic development will almost certainly generate Mexican revanchist sentiments. In due course, the results of American military expansion in the nineteenth century could be threatened and possibly reversed by Mexican demographic expansion in the twenty-first century.

The changing balance of power among civilizations makes it more and more difficult for the West to achieve its goals with respect to weapons proliferation, human rights, immigration, and other issues. To minimize its losses in this situation requires the West to wield skillfully its economic resources as carrots and sticks in dealing with other societies, to bolster its unity and coordinate its policies so as to make it more difficult for other societies to play one Western country off against another, and to promote and exploit differences among non-Western nations. The West's ability to pursue these strategies will be shaped by the the nature and intensity of its conflicts with the challenger civilizations, on the one hand, and the extent to which it can identify and develop common interests with the swing civilizations, on the other.

# POSTSCRIPT

## Is Today's Immigration Debate Racist?

The current immigration debate is focused on the approximately 12 million illegal immigrants living in the United States today. Despite the fact that the discussion of this issue so often occurs within the juxtaposition of legal versus illegal immigration, the social concerns generated by these new immigrants are not limited to the dichotomy indicated. Students should note that the 12 million illegal immigrants are disproportionately Latinos as distinct from the European immigrants that preceded them. Clearly, these newcomers are changing the demographic character; that is, the color composition of American society and their impact upon social structure, culture, economy, and politics is transparent and can only increase in the future. Some American citizens view these newcomers and the impact they are having upon society as uplifting. Others view the new immigrants as potential threats to order and progress.

In 1959, when Oscar Handlin, foremost scholar on American immigrants, wrote *The Newcomers: Negroes and Puerto Ricans in a Changing Metropolis*, he described the prejudice and discrimination working against both groups. Further, Handlin pointed out how the new arrivals to New York City "assumed the role formerly played by European immigrants." Almost fifty years later, we see the issue of prejudice and racism repeated with the arrival of Latinos.

For further reading consider "The Immigration Equation," by Roger Lowenstein in *The New York Times Magazine* (July 9, 2006). An interesting work on immigration and race is David R. Roediger's *Working Toward Whiteness: How America's Immigrants Became White* (Basic Books, 2005). Also, in *The New Republic* (January 16, 2006) John B. Judis, in "Border War," argues the liberal perspective on immigration and national identity. An article on the subject of black-Latino relations is "Strength in Numbers," by Lori Robinson, Paul Cuadros, and Alysia Tate (*The Crisis*, January/February 2004).

# Internet References . . .

## Southern Poverty Law Center

This is the Web site for the Southern Poverty Law Center (SPLC), which was founded by Morris Dees and Joe Levin. Located in Alabama, the Center is internationally known for many tolerance programs including education programs, tracking of hate groups, and its legal victories against white supremacists. It offers educational and community programs for those interested in dismantling bigotry.

**http://www.splcenter. org**

## NAACP

This Web site offers information, news, and trends dealing with African Americans. The 50th year commemoration of the 1954 decision, *Brown v. Board of Education,* is explored in detail on the site. The official NAACP publication, *The Crisis,* is available, as are past issues through the site's archives section. Additional information revolving around race relations is presented daily, including a Congressional Report.

**www.naacp.org**

## Museum of Racist Memorabilia

This is the Web site for the Jim Crow Museum of Racist Memorabilia located in Michigan. It contains information and illustrations on popular cultural racist memorabilia. The site promotes the scholarly examination of historical and contemporary expressions of racism. The virtual tour reveals several caricatures and an informative essay on racist images.

**http://www.ferris.edu/news/jimcrow/menu.html**

## Black Agenda Report

*The Journal of African American Thought and Action* is published every Wednesday on this Web site. It promotes a critically progressive agenda and offers links to approximately 75 progressive Web sites. Twenty-first century policy issues including labor, immigration, and reparations for African Americans are discussed. Glen Ford is the executive editor.

**http://www.blackagendareport.com**

# Race Still Matters

*A*t a time when an African American candidate has a realistic prospect of being elected the president of the United States, one may find it difficult to accept that race still matters in this country. However, as is routinely the case, this candidate may give a speech in the future, citing significant racial progress in America, but also acknowledging, "that we still have a long way to go." What aspects of social reality might elicit such a response? Issues of race have challenged the nation from the Colonial era to the present. Traditionally, race developed as a biological concept. The criteria that were established to place human beings within distinct racial categories were biological in nature and included such features as skin color, prognathism, and cranial config- uration, among others. As a result of research and scientific discovery, including the human genome project that is currently underway, the biological basis of racial categories has been destroyed. Yet race has been retained as a social construction that provides a basis for distin- guishing and treating human groups other than one's own. So, race still matters. How does it matter? Race affects where one lives, goes to school, and worships. Race is a factor in the distribution of income and wealth. Race is a factor in terms of crime and punishment. Race influences one's life chances.

- Is Race Prejudice a Product of Group Position?

- Do Minorities Engage in Self-Segregation?

- Is the Emphasis on a Color-Blind Society an Answer to Racism?

- Is the Claim of White Skin Privilege a Myth?

# ISSUE 5

## Is Race Prejudice a Product of Group Position?

**YES: Herbert Blumer,** from "Race Prejudice as a Sense of Group Position," *The Pacific Sociological Review* (Spring 1958)

**NO: Gordon W. Allport,** from *The Nature of Prejudice* (Perseus Books, 1979)

### ISSUE SUMMARY

**YES:** Herbert Blumer, a sociologist, asserts that prejudice exists in a sense of group position rather than as an attitude based on individual feelings. The collective process by which a group comes to define other racial groups is the focus of Blumer's position.

**NO:** Gordon Allport, a psychologist, makes the case that prejudice is the result of a three-stage learning process.

**W**here does prejudice come from? When do we learn it? What are its characteristics? Is prejudice an individual personality trait or, is it a product of structural factors such as group position or economic factors? Ill feelings and overt hostility can reflect prejudice, but so can quiet benign beliefs. The many theories that explain prejudice can be categorized into those that attribute prejudice to individual personality, and those theories that see prejudice resulting from larger structural factors.

Blumer begins his group position argument in the context of dominant-subordinate group analysis. Members of the dominant group will, in addition to feelings of superiority, "feel a proprietary claim to certain areas of privilege and advantage." Suspicions of subordinate group members exist because of a fear that the minority group "harbors designs on the prerogatives of the dominant race." Although Blumer uses psychological concepts such as feelings, superiority, and distinctiveness, his focus is not on the individual. Rather it rests on the process of image formation. Image formation takes place in the public domain including newspapers, film, and other media. "Careless ignorance of the facts" is often part of the image formation. Surely Blumer believes that prejudice is learned. Nevertheless, his analysis transcends mere "learning."

The analysis of the collective process through which one group defines another involves a historical process. Group position is formed in a process defined by the dominant group and redefines subordinate groups. Hence, attitudes are formed from the dominant group perspective.

When the position of the dominant group is challenged, race prejudice emerges. According to Blumer this may occur in different ways. For example, it may be an affront to feelings or an attempt to transgress racial boundaries. Reaction to interracial marriage or the racial integration of a neighborhood may provoke a "defensive reaction" on the part of the dominant group. Generalizations of the minority group that often lead to fear emerge. Disturbed feelings are marked by hostility. Thus, Blumer suggests that race prejudice becomes a protective device. Prejudice is associated with the belief that gains for other (racial and ethnic) groups will result in losses for one's own—a zero sum game.

Examining how prejudice is learned, Gordon Allport stresses the first six years of a child's life, especially the role of the parents in transferring ideas as creating an atmosphere in which the child "develops prejudice as his style of life." The psychological factors exhibited during child rearing, including how the child is disciplined, loved, and threatened, translate into fear or hatred that may ultimately be directed at minorities. A rigid home environment in which parents exercise strict control is more likely to lead to prejudice among the children than a less rigid upbringing. Tolerance results from a less strict child-rearing style.

Allport explains that there are three stages of learning prejudice. In the first stage, the pre-generalized learning period, the child learns linguistic categories before he is ready to apply them. For example, ethnic and racial slurs are not yet applied to specific groups. Nevertheless, the categories are learned. The second stage in learning prejudice, the period of total rejection, occurs when children connect the labels of groups to be rejected with the individuals in minority groups. For example, Allport argues, by the fifth grade, children tend to choose their own racial group. However, as children grow older and mature, they lose the tendency to overgeneralize minorities. The third stage, differentiation, sets in often during the latter years of high school. By then, the "escape clauses" or exceptions to stereotypes are incorporated into the individual's attitude. So, the limited early learning experiences are replaced by the wider experiences that come with adolescence.

This selection from Allport is part of his more comprehensive social psychological account of how prejudice is learned. The emphasis on personality traits formed during early childhood contrasts with Blumer's group position thesis. We recommend that the student consider both positions to complete a study of prejudice. In this issue we urge students to search for similarities, along with the differences, between Allport and Blumer. Does Blumer reject the notion that prejudice is learned? Does Allport ignore the collective process? If your answer is "no" to these two questions, then how can you build a theory of prejudice?

# YES

Herbert Blumer

# Race Prejudice as a Sense of Group Position

In this paper I am proposing an approach to the study of race prejudice different from that which dominates contemporary scholarly thought on this topic. My thesis is that race prejudice exists basically in a sense of group position rather than in a set of feelings which members of one racial group have toward the members of another racial group. This different way of viewing race prejudice shifts study and analysis from a preoccupation with feelings as lodged in individuals to a concern with the relationship of racial groups. It also shifts scholarly treatment away from individual lines of experience and focuses interest on the collective process by which a racial group comes to define and redefine another racial group. Such shift, I believe, will yield a more realistic and penetrating understanding of race prejudice.

There can be little question that the rather vast literature on race prejudice is dominated by the idea that such prejudice exists fundamentally as a feeling or set of feelings lodged in the individual. It is usually depicted as consisting of feelings such as antipathy, hostility, hatred, intolerance, and aggressiveness. Accordingly, the task of scientific inquiry becomes two-fold. On one hand, there is a need to identify the feelings which make up race prejudice—to see how they fit together and how they are supported by other psychological elements, such as mythical beliefs. On the other hand, there is need of showing how the feeling complex has come into being. Thus, some scholars trace the complex feelings back chiefly to innate dispositions; some trace it to personality composition, such as authoritarian personality; and others regard the feelings of prejudice as being formed through social experience. However different may be the contentions regarding the make-up of racial prejudice and the way in which it may come into existence, these contentions are alike in locating prejudice in the realm of individual feeling. This is clearly true of the work of psychologists, psychiatrists, and social psychologists, and tends to be predominantly the case in the work of sociologists.

Unfortunately, this customary way of viewing race prejudice overlooks and obscures the fact that race prejudice is fundamentally a matter of relationship between racial groups. A little reflective thought should make

From *The Pacific Sociological Review,* Spring 1958. Copyright © 1958 by NPQ. Reprinted by permission.

86

this very clear. Race prejudice presupposes, necessarily, that racially prejudiced individuals think of themselves as belonging to a given racial group. It means, also, that they assign to other racial groups those against whom they are prejudiced. Thus, logically and actually, a scheme of racial identification is necessary as a framework for racial prejudice. Moreover, such identification involves the formation of an image or a conception of one's own racial group and of another racial group, inevitably in terms of the relationship of such groups. To fail to see that racial prejudice is a matter (a) of the racial identification made of oneself and of others, and (b) of the way in which the identified groups are conceived in relation to each other, is to miss what is logically and actually basic. One should keep clearly in mind that people necessarily come to identify themselves as belonging to a racial group; such identification is not spontaneous or inevitable but a result of experience. Further, one must realize that the kind of picture which a racial group forms of itself and the kind of picture which it may form of others are similarly products of experience. Hence, such pictures are variable, just as the lines of experience which produce them are variable.

The body of feelings which scholars, today, are so inclined to regard as constituting the substance of race prejudice is actually a resultant of the way in which given racial groups conceive of themselves and of others. A basic understanding of race prejudice must be sought in the process by which racial groups form images of themselves and of others. This process, as I hope to show, is fundamentally *a collective process*. It operates chiefly through the public media in which individuals who are accepted as the spokesmen of a racial group characterize publicly another racial group. To characterize another racial group is, by opposition, to define one's own group. This is equivalent to placing the two groups in relation to each other, or defining their positions *vis-à-vis* each other. It is the *sense of social position* emerging from this collective process of characterization which provides the basis of race prejudice. The following discussion will consider important facets of this matter.

I would like to begin by discussing several of the important feelings that enter into race prejudice. This discussion will reveal how fundamentally racial feelings point to and depend on a positional arrangement of the racial groups. In this discussion I will confine myself to such feelings in the case of a dominant racial group.

There are four basic types of feelings that seem to be always present in race prejudice in the dominant group. They are (1) a feeling of superiority, (2) a feeling that the subordinate race is intrinsically different and alien, (3) a feeling of proprietary claim to certain areas of privilege and advantage, and (4) a fear and suspicion that the subordinate race harbors designs on the prerogatives of the dominant race. A few words about each of these four feelings will suffice.

In race prejudice there is a self-assured feeling on the part of the dominant racial group of being naturally superior or better. This is commonly shown in a disparagement of the qualities of the subordinate racial group. Condemnatory or debasing traits, such as laziness, dishonesty, greediness, unreliability, stupidity, deceit and immorality, are usually imputed to it. The second feeling, that the subordinate race is an alien and fundamentally different stock, is likewise always present. "They are not of our kind" is a common way in which this is likely to be expressed. It is this feeling that reflects, justifies, and promotes the social exclusion of the subordinate racial group. The combination of these two feelings of superiority and of distinctiveness can easily give rise to feelings of aversion and even antipathy. But in themselves they do not form prejudice. We have to introduce the third and fourth types of feeling.

The third feeling, the sense of proprietary claim, is of crucial importance. It is the feeling on the part of the dominant group of being entitled to either exclusive or prior rights in many iolmmportant areas of life. The range of such exclusive or prior claims may be wide, covering the ownership of property such as choice lands and sites; the right to certain jobs, occupations or professions; the claim to certain kinds of industry or lines of business; the claim to certain positions of control and decision-making as in government and law; the right to exclusive membership in given institutions such as schools, churches and recreational institutions; the claim to certain positions of social prestige and to the display of the symbols and accoutrements of these positions; and the claim to certain areas of intimacy and privacy. The feeling of such proprietary claims is exceedingly strong in race prejudice. Again, however, this feeling even in combination with the feeling of superiority and the feeling of distinctiveness does not explain race prejudice. These three feelings are present frequently in societies showing no prejudice, as in certain forms of feudalism, in caste relations, in societies of chiefs and commoners, and under many settled relations of conquerors and conquered. Where claims are solidified into a structure which is accepted or respected by all, there seems to be no group prejudice.

The remaining feeling essential to race prejudice is a fear or apprehension that the subordinate racial group is threatening, or will threaten, the position of the dominant group. Thus, acts or suspected acts that are interpreted as an attack on the natural superiority of the dominant group, or an intrusion into their sphere of group exclusiveness, or an encroachment on their area of proprietary claim are crucial in arousing and fashioning race prejudice. These acts mean "getting out of place."

It should be clear that these four basic feelings of race prejudice definitely refer to a positional arrangement of the racial groups. The feeling of superiority places the subordinate people *below;* the feeling of alienation places them *beyond;* the feeling of proprietary claim excludes them from the prerogatives of position; and the fear of encroachment is an emotional recoil from the endangering of group position. As these features suggest, the positional relation of the two racial groups is crucial in race prejudice. The dominant group is not concerned with the subordinate group as such but it is deeply concerned with its position *vis-à-vis* the subordinate group. This is epitomized in the key and universal expression that a given race is all right in "its place." The sense of group position is the very heart of the relation of the dominant to the subordinate group. It supplies the dominant group with its framework of perception, its standard of judgment, its patterns of sensitivity, and its emotional proclivities.

It is important to recognize that this sense of group position transcends the feelings of the individual members of the dominant group, giving such members a common orientation that is not otherwise to be found in separate feelings and views. There is likely to be considerable difference between the ways in which the individual members of the dominant group think and feel about the subordinate group. Some may feel bitter and hostile, with strong antipathies, with an exalted sense of superiority and with a lot of spite; others may have charitable and protective feelings, marked by a sense of piety and tinctured by benevolence; others may be condescending and reflect mild contempt; and others may be disposed to politeness and considerateness with no feelings of truculence. These are only a few of many different patterns of feeling to be found among members of the dominant racial group. What gives a common dimension to them is a sense of the social position of their group. Whether the members be humane or callous, cultured or unlettered, liberal or reactionary, powerful or impotent, arrogant or humble, rich or poor, honorable or dishonorable—all are led, by virtue of sharing the sense of group position, to similar individual positions.

The sense of group position is a general kind of orientation. It is a general feeling without being reducible to specific feelings like hatred, hostility or antipathy. It is also a general understanding without being composed of any set of specific beliefs. On the social psychological side it cannot be equated to a sense of social status as ordinarily conceived, for it refers not merely to vertical positioning but to many other lines of position independent of the vertical dimension. Sociologically it is not a mere reflection of the objective relations between racial groups. Rather, it stands for "what ought to be" rather than for "what is." It is a sense of where the two racial groups *belong*.

In its own way, the sense of group position is a norm and imperative—indeed a very powerful one. It guides, incites, cows, and coerces. It should be borne in mind that this sense of group position stands for and involves a fundamental kind of group affiliation for the members of the dominant racial group. To the extent they recognize or feel themselves as belonging to that group they will automatically come under the influence of the sense of position held by that group. Thus, even though given individual members may have personal views and feelings different from the sense of group position, they will have to conjure with the sense of group position held by their racial group. If the sense of position is strong, to act contrary to it is to risk a feeling of self-alienation and to face the possibility of ostracism. I am trying to suggest, accordingly, that the locus of race prejudice is not in the area of individual feeling but in the definition of the respective positions of the racial groups.

The source of race prejudice lies in a felt challenge to this sense of group position. The challenge, one must recognize, may come in many different ways. It may be in the form of an affront to feelings of group superiority; it may be in the form of attempts at familiarity or transgressing the boundary line of group exclusiveness; it may be in the form of encroachment at countless points of proprietary claim; it may be a challenge to power and privilege; it may take the form of economic competition. Race prejudice is a defensive reaction to such challenging of the sense of group position. It consists of the disturbed feelings, usually of marked hostility, that are thereby aroused. As such, race prejudice is a protective device. It functions, however shortsightedly, to preserve the integrity and the position of the dominant group.

It is crucially important to recognize that the sense of group position is not a mere summation of the feelings of position such as might be developed independently by separate individuals as they come to compare themselves with given individuals of the subordinate race. The sense of group position refers to the position of group to group, not to that of individual to individual. Thus, *vis-à-vis* the subordinate racial group the unlettered individual with low status in the dominant racial group has a sense of group position common to that of the elite of his group. By virtue of sharing this sense of position such an individual, despite his low status, feels that members of the subordinate group, however distinguished and accomplished, are somehow inferior, alien, and properly restricted in the area of claims. He forms his conception as a representative of the dominant group; he treats individual members of the subordinate group as representative of that group.

An analysis of how the sense of group position is formed should start with a clear recognition that it is an historical product. It is set originally by conditions of initial contact. Prestige, power, possession of skill, numbers, original self-conceptions, aims, designs and opportunities are a few of the factors that may fashion the original sense of group position. Subsequent experience in the relation of the two racial groups, especially in the area of claims, opportunities and advantages, may mould the sense of group position in many diverse ways. Further, the sense of group position may be intensified or weakened, brought to sharp focus or dulled. It may be deeply entrenched and tenaciously resist change for long periods of time. Or it may never take root. It may undergo quick growth and vigorous expansion or it may dwindle away through slow-moving erosion. It may be firm or soft, acute or dull, continuous or intermittent. In short, viewed comparatively, the sense of group position is very variable.

However variable its particular career, the sense of group position is clearly formed by a running process in which the dominant racial group is led to define and redefine the subordinate racial group and the relations between them. There are two important aspects of this process of definition that I wish to single out for consideration.

First, the process of definition occurs obviously through complex interaction and communication between the members of the dominant group. Leaders, prestige bearers, official, group agents, dominant individuals and ordinary laymen present to one another characterizations of the subordinate group and express their feelings and ideas on the relations. Through talk, tales, stories, gossip, anecdotes, messages, pronouncements, news accounts, orations, sermons, preachments and the like definitions are presented and feelings are expressed. In this usually vast and complex interaction separate views run against one another, influence one another, modify each other, incite one another and fuse together in new forms. Correspondingly, feelings which are expressed meet, stimulate each other, feed on each other, intensify each other and emerge in new patterns. Currents of view and currents of feeling come into being; sweeping along to positions of dominance and serving as polar points for the organization of thought and sentiment. If the interaction becomes increasingly circular and reinforcing, devoid of serious inner opposition, such currents grow, fuse and become strengthened. It is through such a process that a collective image of the subordinate group is formed and a sense of group position is set. The evidence of such a process is glaring when one reviews the history of any racial arrangement marked by prejudice.

Such a complex process of mutual interaction with its different lines and degrees of formation gives the lie to the many schemes which would lodge the cause of race prejudice in the make-up of the individual—whether in the form of innate disposition, constitutional make-up, personality structure, or direct personal experience with members of the other race. The collective image and feelings in race prejudice are forged out of a complicated social process in which the individual is himself shaped and organized. The scheme, so popular today, which would trace race prejudice to a so-called authoritarian personality shows a grievous misunderstanding of the simple essentials of the collective process that leads to a sense of group position.

The second important aspect of the process of group definition is that it is necessarily concerned with *an abstract image* of the subordinate racial group. The subordinate racial group is defined as if it were an entity or whole. This entity or whole—like the Negro race, or the Japanese, or the Jews—is necessarily an abstraction, never coming within the perception of any of the senses. While actual encounters are with individuals, the picture formed of the racial group is necessarily of a vast entity which spreads out far beyond such individuals and transcends experience with such individuals. The implications of the fact that the collective image is of an abstract group are of crucial significance. I would like to note four of these implications.

First, the building of the image of the abstract group takes place in the area of the remote and not of the near. It is not the experience with concrete individuals in daily association that gives rise to the definitions of the extended, abstract group. Such immediate experience is usually regulated and orderly. Even where such immediate experience is disrupted the new definitions which are formed are limited to the individuals involved. The collective image of the abstract group grows up not by generalizing from experiences gained in close, first-hand contacts but through the transcending characterizations that are made of the group as an entity. Thus, one must seek the central stream of definition in those areas where the dominant group as such is characterizing the subordinate group as such. This occurs in the "public arena" wherein the spokesmen appear as representatives and agents of the dominant group. The extended public arena is constituted by such things as legislative assemblies, public meetings, conventions, the press, and the printed word. What goes on in this public arena attracts the attention of large numbers of the dominant group and is felt as the voice and action of the group as such.

Second, the definitions that are forged in the public arena center, obviously, about matters that are felt to be of major importance. Thus, we are led to recognize the crucial role of the "big event" in developing a conception of the subordinate racial group. The happening that seems momentous, that touches deep sentiments, that seems to raise fundamental questions about relations, and that awakens strong feelings of identification with one's racial group is the kind of event that is central in the formation of the racial image. Here, again, we note the relative unimportance of the huge bulk of experiences coming from daily contact with individuals of the subordinate group. It is the events seemingly loaded with great collective significance that are the focal points of the public discussion. The definition of these events is chiefly responsible for the development of a racial image and of the sense of group position. When this public discussion takes the form of a denunciation of the subordinate racial group, signifying that it is unfit and a threat, the discussion becomes particularly potent in shaping the sense of social position.

Third, the major influence in public discussion is exercised by individuals and groups who have the public ear and who are felt to have standing, prestige, authority and power. Intellectual and social elites, public figures of prominence, and leaders of powerful organizations are likely to be the key figures in the formation of the sense of group position and in the characterization of the subordinate group. It is well to note this in view of the not infrequent tendency of students to regard race prejudice as growing out of the multiplicity of experiences and attitudes of the bulk of the people.

Fourth, we also need to perceive the appreciable opportunity that is given to strong interest groups in directing the lines of discussion and setting the interpretations that arise in such discussion. Their self-interests may dictate the kind of position they wish the dominant racial group to enjoy. It may be a position which enables them to retain certain advantages, or even more to gain still greater advantages. Hence, they may be vigorous in seeking to manufacture events to attract public attention and to set lines of issue in such a way as to predetermine interpretations favorable to their interests. The role of strongly organized groups seeking to further special interest is usually central in the formation of collective images of abstract groups. Historical records of major instances of race relations, as in our South, or in South Africa, or in Europe in the case of the Jew, or on the West Coast in the case of the Japanese show the formidable part played by interest groups in defining the subordinate racial group.

I conclude this highly condensed paper with two further observations that may throw additional light on the relation of the sense of group position to race prejudice. Race prejudice becomes entrenched and tenacious to the extent the prevailing social order is rooted in the sense of social position. This has been true of the historic South in our country. In such a social order race prejudice tends to become chronic and impermeable to change. In other places the social order may be affected only to a limited extent by the sense of group position held by the dominant racial group. This I think has been true usually in the case of anti-Semitism in Europe and this country. Under these conditions the sense of group position tends to be weaker and more vulnerable. In turn, race prejudice has a much more variable and intermittent career, usually becoming pronounced only as a consequence of grave disorganizing events that allow for the formation of a scapegoat.

This leads me to my final observation which in a measure is an indirect summary. The sense of group position dissolves and race prejudice declines when the process of running definition does not keep abreast of major shifts in the social order. When events touching on relations are not treated as "big events" and hence do not set crucial issues in the arena of public discussion; or when the elite leaders or spokesmen do not define such big events vehemently or adversely; or where they define them in the direction of racial harmony; or when there is a paucity of strong interest groups seeking to build up a strong adverse image for special advantage—under such conditions the sense of group position recedes and race prejudice declines.

The clear implication of my discussion is that the proper and the fruitful area in which race prejudice should be studied is the collective process through which a sense of group position is formed. To seek, instead, to understand it or to handle it in the arena of individual feeling and of individual experience seems to me to be clearly misdirected.

# The Young Child

**H**ow is prejudice learned? We have opened our discussion of this pivotal problem by pointing out that the home influence has priority, and that the child has excellent reasons for adopting his ethnic attitudes ready-made from his parents. We likewise called attention to the central role of identification in the course of early learning. In the present chapter we shall consider additional factors operating in preschool years. The first six years of life are important for the development of all social attitudes, though it is a mistake to regard early childhood as alone responsible for them. A bigoted personality may be well under way by the age of six, but by no means fully fashioned.

Our analysis will be clearer if at the outset we make a distinction between *adopting* prejudice and *developing* prejudice. A child who adopts prejudice is taking over attitudes and stereotypes from his family or cultural environment. Most of the cases cited in the previous chapter are instances in point. Parental words and gestures, along with their concomitant beliefs and antagonisms, are transferred to the child. He adopts his parents' views. Some of the principles of learning discussed in this and the following chapter will help explain further how this transfer comes about.

But there is also a type of training that does not transfer ideas and attitudes directly to the child, but rather creates an atmosphere in which he *develops* prejudice as his style of life. In this case the parents may or may not express their own prejudices (usually they do). What is crucial, however, is that their mode of handling the child (disciplining, loving, threatening) is such that the child cannot help acquire suspicions, fears, hatreds that sooner or later may fix on minority groups.

In reality, of course, these forms of learning are not distinct. Parents who *teach* the child specific prejudices are also likely to *train* the child to develop a prejudiced nature. Still it is well to keep the distinction in mind, for the psychology of learning is so intricate a subject that it requires analytical aids of this type.

## Child Training

We consider now the style of child training that is known to be conducive to the *development* of prejudice. (We shall disregard for the time being the learning of specific attitudes toward specific groups.)

---

One line of proof that a child's prejudice is related to the manner of his upbringing comes from a study of Harris, Gough, and Martin.[1] These investigators first determined the extent to which 240 fourth, fifth, and sixth grade children expressed prejudiced attitudes toward minority groups. They then sent questionnaires to the mothers of these children, asking their views on certain practices in child training. Most of these were returned with the mothers' replies. The results are highly instructive. Mothers of prejudiced children, *far more often* than the mothers of unprejudiced children, held that

> Obedience is the most important thing a child can learn.
>
> A child should never be permitted to set his will against that of his parents.
>
> A child should never keep a secret from his parents.
>
> "I prefer a quiet child to one who is noisy."
>
> (In the case of temper tantrums) "Teach the child that two can play that game, by getting angry yourself."

In the case of sex-play (masturbation) the mother of the prejudiced child is much more likely to believe she should punish the child; the mother of the unprejudiced child is much more likely to ignore the practice.

All in all, the results indicate that pervasive family atmospheres do definitely slant the child. Specifically, a home that is suppressive, harsh, or critical—where the parents' word is law—is more likely to prepare the groundwork for group prejudice.

It seems a safe assumption that the mothers who expressed their philosophies of child training in this questionnaire actually carried out their ideas in practice. If so, then we have strong evidence that children are more likely to be prejudiced if they have been brought up by mothers who insist on obedience, who are suppressive of the child's impulses, and who are sharp disciplinarians.

What does such a style of child training do to a child? For one thing it puts him on guard. He has to watch his impulses carefully. Not only is he punished for them when they counter the parents' convenience and rules, as they frequently do, but he feels at such times that love is withdrawn from him. When love is withdrawn he is alone, exposed, desolate. Thus he comes to watch alertly for signs of parental approval or disapproval. It is they who have power, and they who give or withhold their conditional love. Their power and their will are the decisive agents in the child's life.

What is the result? First of all, the child learns that power and authority dominate human relationships—not trust and tolerance. The stage is thus set for a hierarchical view of society. Equality does not really prevail. The effect goes even deeper. The child mistrusts his impulses: he must not have temper tantrums, he must not disobey, he must not play with his sex organs. He must fight such evil in himself. Through a simple act of projection . . . the child comes to fear evil impulses in others. They have dark designs; their impulses threaten the child; they are not to be trusted.

If this style of training prepares the ground for prejudice, the opposite style seems to predispose toward tolerance. The child who feels secure and loved whatever he does, and who is treated not with a display of parental power (being punished usually through shaming rather than spanking), develops basic ideas of equality and trust. Not required to repress his own impulses, he is less likely to project them upon others, and less likely to develop suspicion, fear, and a hierarchical view of human relationships.[2]

While no child is always treated according to one and only one pattern of discipline or affection, we might venture to classify prevailing home atmospheres according to the following scheme:

Permissive treatment by parents

Rejective treatment

    suppressive and cruel (harsh, fear-inspiring)

    domineering and critical (overambitious parents nagging and dissatisfied with the child as he is)

Neglectful

Overindulgent

Inconsistent (sometimes permissive, sometimes rejective, some-times overindulgent)

Although we cannot yet be dogmatic about the matter, it seems very likely that rejective, neglectful, and inconsistent styles of training tend to lead to the development of prejudice.[3] Investigators have reported how impressed they are by the frequency with which quarrelsome or broken homes have occurred in the childhood of prejudiced people.

> Ackerman and Jahoda made a study of anti-Semitic patients who were undergoing psychoanalysis. Most of them had had an unhealthy homelife as children, marked by quarreling, violence, or divorce. There was little or no affection or sympathy between the parents. The rejection of the child by one or both parents was the rule rather than the exception.[4]

These investigators could not find that specific parental indoctrination in anti-Semitic attitudes was a necessary element. It is true that the parents, like the children, were anti-Semitic, but the authors explain the connection as follows:

> In those cases where parents and children are anti-Semitic, it is more reasonable to assume that the emotional predispositions of the parents created a psychological atmosphere conducive to the development of similar emotional dispositions in the child, than to maintain the simple imitation hypothesis.[5]

In other words, prejudice was not *taught* by the parent but was *caught* by the child from an infected atmosphere.

Another investigator became interested in paranoia. Among a group of 125 hospital patients suffering from fixed delusional ideas, he found that the majority had a predominantly suppressive and cruel upbringing. Nearly three-quarters of the patients had parents who were either suppressive and cruel or else domineering and overcritical. Only seven percent came from homes that could be called permissive.[6] Thus many paranoia in adult years be traceable to a bad start in life. We cannot, of course, equate paranoia and prejudice. Yet the rigid categorizing indulged in by the prejudiced person, his hostility, and his inaccessibility to reason are often much like the disorder of a paranoiac.

Without stretching the evidence too far, we may at least make a guess: children who are too harshly treated, severely punished, or continually criticized are more likely to develop personalities wherein group prejudice plays a prominent part. Conversely, children from more relaxed and secure homes, treated permissively and with affection, are more likely to develop tolerance.

## Fear of the Strange

Let us return again to the question whether there is an inborn source of prejudice. . . . [We] reported that as soon as infants are able (perhaps at six months of age) to distinguish between familiar and unfamiliar persons, they sometimes show anxiety when strangers approach. They do so especially, if the stranger moves abruptly or makes a "grab" for the child. They may show special fear if the stranger wears eyeglasses, or has skin of an unfamiliar color, or even if his expressive movements are different from what the child is accustomed to. This timidity usually continues through the preschool period— often beyond. Every visitor who has entered a home where there is a young child knows that it takes several minutes, perhaps several hours, for the child to "warm up" to him. But usually the initial fear gradually disappears.

We reported also an experiment where infants were placed alone in a strange room with toys. All of the children were at first alarmed and cried in distress. After a few repetitions they became entirely habituated to the room and played as if at home. But the biological utility of the initial fear reaction is obvious. Whatever is strange is a potential danger, and must be guarded against until one's experience assures one that no harm is lurking.

The almost universal anxiety of a child in the presence of strangers is no more striking than his rapid adaptability to their presence.

> In a certain household a Negro maid came to work. The young children in the family, aged three and five, showed fear and for a few days were reluctant to accept her. The maid stayed with the family for five or six years and came to be loved by all. Several years later, when the children were young adults, the family was discussing the happy period of Anna's services in the household. She had not been seen for the past ten years, but her memory was affectionately held. In the course of the conversation it came out that she was colored. The children were utterly astonished. They insisted that they had never known this fact, or had completely forgotten it if they ever knew it.

Situations of this type are not uncommon. Their occurrence makes us doubt that instinctive fear of the strange has any necessary bearing upon the organization of permanent attitudes.

## Dawn of Racial Awareness

The theory of "home atmosphere" is certainly more convincing than the theory of "instinctive roots." But neither theory tells us just when and how the child's ethnic ideas begin to crystallize. Granted that the child possesses relevant emotional equipment, and that the family supplies a constant undertone of acceptance or rejection, anxiety or security, we still need studies that will show how the child's earliest sense of group differences develops. An excellent setting for such a study is a biracial nursery school.

In investigations conducted in this setting, it appears that the earliest age at which children take any note of race is two and a half.

> One white child of this age, sitting for the first time beside a Negro child, said, "Dirty face." It was an unemotional remark, prompted only by his observing a wholly dark-skinned visage—for the first time in his life.

The purely sensory observation that some skins are white, some colored, seems in many cases to be the first trace of racial awareness. Unless there is the quiver of fear of the strange along with this observation, we may say that race difference at first arouses a sense of curiosity and interest—nothing more. The child's world is full of fascinating distinctions. Facial color is simply one of them. Yet we note that even this first perception of racial difference may arouse associations with "clean" and "dirty."

The situation is more insistent by the age of three and a half or four. The sense of dirt still haunts the children. They have been thoroughly scrubbed at home to eradicate dirt. Why then does it exist so darkly on other children? One colored boy, confused concerning his membership, said to his mother, "Wash my face clean; some of the children don't wash well, especially colored children."

> A first grade teacher reports that about one white child in ten refuses to hold hands during games with the solitary Negro child in the classroom. The reason apparently is not "prejudice" in any deep-seated sense. The rejective white children merely complain that Tom has dirty hands and face.

Dr. Goodman's nursery school study shows one particularly revealing result. Negro children are, by and large, "racially aware" earlier than are white children.[7] They tend to be confused, disturbed, and sometimes excited by the problem. Few of them seem to know that they are Negroes. (Even at the age of seven one little Negro girl said to a white playmate, "I'd hate to be colored, wouldn't you?")

The interest and disturbance take many forms. Negro children ask more questions about racial differences; they may fondle the blond hair of a white child; they are often rejective toward Negro dolls. When given a white and Negro doll to play with, they almost uniformly prefer the white doll; many slap the Negro doll and call it dirty or ugly. As a rule, they are more rejective of Negro dolls than are white children. They tend to behave self-consciously when tested for racial awareness. One Negro boy, being shown two baby dolls alike save for color, is asked, "Which one is most like you when you were a baby?"

> Bobby's eyes move from brown to white; he hesitates, squirms, glances at us sidewise—and points to the white doll. Bobby's perceptions relevant to race, feeble and sporadic though they are, have some personal meaning— some ego-reference.

Especially interesting is Dr. Goodman's observation that Negro children tend to be fully as active as white children at the nursery school age. They are on the whole more sociable—particularly those who are rated as high on "racial awareness." A larger proportion of the Negro children are rated as "leaders" in the group. Although we cannot be certain of the meaning of this finding, it may well come from the fact that Negro children are more highly stimulated by the dawning awareness of race. They may be excited by a challenge they do not fully understand, and may seek reassurance through activity and social contacts for the vague threat that hangs over them. The threat comes not from nursery school, where they are secure enough, but from their first contacts with the world outside and from discussions at home, where their Negro parents cannot fail to talk about the matter.

What is so interesting about this full-scale activity at the nursery school age is its contrast to the adult demeanor of many Negroes who are noted for their poise, passivity, apathy, laziness—or whatever the withdrawing reaction may be called. . . . [We] noted that the Negro's conflicts sometimes engender a quietism, a passivity. Many people hold that this "laziness" is a biological trait of Negroes—but in the nursery school we find flatly contradictory evidence. Passivity, when it exists as a Negro attribute, is apparently a learned mode of adjustment. The assertive reaching out of the four-year-old for security and acceptance is ordinarily doomed to failure. After a period of struggle and suffering the passive mode of adjustment may set in.

Why is there, even in the dawning race-awareness of four-year-olds, a nebulous sense of inferiority associated with dark skin? A significant part of the answer lies in the similarity between dark pigmentation and dirt. A third of Dr. Goodman's children (both Negro and white) spoke of this matter. Many others no doubt had it in their minds, but did not happen to mention it to the investigators. An additional part of the answer may lie in those subtle forms of learning—not yet fully understood—whereby value-judgments are conveyed to the child. Some parents of white children may, by word or act, have conveyed to their children a vague sense of their rejection of Negroes. If so, the rejection is still only nascent in the four-year-old, for in virtually no case could the investigators find anything they were willing to label "prejudice" at this age level. Some of the Negro parents, too, may have conveyed to their children a sense of the handicaps of people with black skin, even before the children themselves knew their own skin was black.

The initial damage of associated ideas seems inescapable in our culture. Dark skin suggests dirt—even to a four-year-old. To some it may suggest feces. Brown is not the aesthetic norm in our culture (in spite of the popularity of chocolate). But this initial disadvantage is by no means insuperable. Discriminations in the realm of color are not hard to learn: a scarlet rose is not rejected because it is the color of blood, nor a yellow tulip because it is the color of urine.

To sum up: four-year-olds are normally interested, curious, and appreciative of differences in racial groups. A slight sense of white superiority seems to be growing, largely because of the association of white with cleanness—cleanliness being a value learned very early in life. But contrary associations can be, and sometimes are, easily built up.

> One four-year-old boy was taken by train from Boston to San Francisco. He was enchanted by the friendly Negro porter. For fully two years thereafter he fantasied that he was a porter, and complained bitterly that he was not colored so that he could qualify for the position.

## Linguistic Tags: Symbols of Power and Rejection

Earlier we discussed the immensely important role of language in building fences for our mental categories and our emotional responses. This factor is so crucial that we return to it again—as it bears on childhood learning.

In Goodman's study it turned out that fully half the nursery school children knew the word "nigger." Few of them understood what the epithet culturally implies. But they knew that the word was potent. It was forbidden, taboo, and always fetched some type of strong response from the teachers. It was therefore a "power word." Not infrequently in a temper tantrum a child would call his teacher (whether white or colored) a "nigger" or a "dirty nigger." The term expressed an emotion—nothing more. Nor did it always express anger—sometimes merely excitement. Children wildly racing around, shrieking at play might, in order to enhance their orgies, yell "nigger, nigger, nigger." As a strong word it seemed fit to vocalize the violent expenditure of energy under way.

One observer gives an interesting example of aggressive verbalization during wartime play:

> Recently, in a waiting room, I watched three youngsters who sat at a table looking at magazines. Suddenly the smaller boy said: "Here's a soldier and an airplane. He's a Jap." The girl said: "No, he's an American." The little fellow said: "Get him, soldier. Get the Jap." The older boy added, "And Hitler too." "And Mussolini," said the girl. "And the

Jews," said the big boy. Then the little fellow started a chant, the others joining in: "The Japs, Hitler, Mussolini, and the Jews! The Japs, Hitler, Mussolini, and the Jews!"[8] It is certain that these children had very little understanding of their bellicose chant. The names of their enemies had an expressive but not a denotative significance.

One little boy was agreeing with his mother, who was warning him never to play with niggers. He said, "No, Mother, I never play with niggers. I only play with white and black children." This child was developing aversion to the term "nigger," without having the slightest idea what the term meant. In other words, the aversion is being set up prior to acquiring a referent.

Other examples could be given of instances where words appear strong and emotionally laden to the child (goy, kike, dago). Only later does he attach the word to a group of people upon whom he can visit the emotions suggested by the word.

We call this process "linguistic precedence in learning." The emotional word has an effect prior to the learning of the referent. Later, the emotional effect becomes attached to the referent.

Before a firm sense of the referent is acquired, the child may go through stages of puzzlement and confusion. This is particularly true because emotional epithets are most likely to be learned when some exciting or traumatic experience is under way. Lasker gives the following example:

> Walking across the playground, a settlement worker found a little Italian boy crying bitterly. She asked him what was the matter. "Hit by Polish boy," the little man repeated several times. Inquiry among the bystanders showed that the offender was not Polish at all. Turning again to her little friend, she said, "You mean, hit by a big naughty boy." But he would not have it thus and went on repeating that he had been hit by a Polish boy. This struck the worker as so curious that she made inquiries of the little fellow's family. She learned that it lived in the same house with a Polish family and that the Italian mother, by constantly quarreling with her Polish neighbor, had put into the heads of her children the notion that "Polish" and "bad" were synonymous terms.[9]

When this lad finally learns who Poles are, he already will have a strong prejudice against them. Here is a clear case of linguistic precedence in learning.

Children sometimes confess their perplexity concerning emotional tags. They seem to be groping for proper referents. Trager and Radke, from their work with kindergarten, first and second grade children, give several examples:[10]

**Anna**   When I was coming out of the dressing room, Peter called me a dirty Jew.

**Teacher**   Why did you say that, Peter?

**Peter (earnestly)**   I didn't say it for spite. I was only playing.

*Johnny (helping Louis pull off his leggings)*   A man called my father a goy.

*Louis*   What's a goy?

*Johnny*   I think everybody around here is a goy. But not me. I'm Jewish.

> On being called a "white cracker" by a Negro boy in the class, the teacher said to her class, "I am puzzled by the meaning of two words. Do you know what 'white cracker' means?"
>
> A number of vague answers were received from the children, one being "You're supposed to say it when you're mad."

Even while the child is having difficulty with words, they have a great power over him. To him they are often a type of magic, of verbal realism. . . .

> A little boy in the South was playing with the child of the washer-woman. Everything was going smoothly until a neighbor white child called over the fence, "Look out, you'll catch it."
>
> "Catch what?" asked the first white child.
>
> "Catch the black. You'll get colored too."
>
> Just this assertion (reminding the child, no doubt, of expressions such as "catch the measles") frightened him. He deserted his colored companion then and there, and never played with him again.

Children often cry if they are called names. Their self-esteem is wounded by any epithet: naughty, dirty, harum-scarum, nigger, dago, Jap, or what not. To escape this verbal realism of early childhood, they often reassure themselves, when they are a little older, with the self-restorative jingle: Sticks and stones may break my bones, but names can never hurt me. But it takes a few years for them to learn that a name is not a thing-in-itself. As we saw earlier verbal realism may never be fully shaken off. The rigidity of linguistic categories may continue in adult thinking. To some adults "communist" or "Jew" is a dirty word—and a dirty thing—an indis-soluble unity, as it may be to a child.

## The First Stage in Learning Prejudice

Janet, six years of age, was trying hard to integrate her obedience to her mother with her daily social contacts. One day she came running home and asked, "Mother, what is the name of the children I am supposed to hate?"

Janet's wistful question leads us into a theoretical summary of the present chapter.

Janet is stumbling at the threshold of some abstraction. She wishes to form the right category. She intends to oblige her mother by hating the right people when she can find out who they are.

In this situation we suspect the preceding stages in Janet's develop-mental history:

1. She identifies with the mother, or at least she strongly craves the mother's affection and approval. We may imagine that the home is not "permissive" in atmosphere, but somewhat stern and critical. Janet may have found that she must be on her toes to please her parent. Otherwise she will suffer rejection or punishment. In any event, she has developed a habit of obedience.

2. While she has apparently no strong fear of strangers at the present time, she has learned to be circumspect. Experiences of insecurity with people outside the family circle may be a factor in her present effort to define her circle of loyalties.

3. She undoubtedly has gone through the initial period of curiosity and interest in racial and ethnic differences. She knows now that human beings are clustered into groups—that there are important distinctions if only she can identify them. In the case of Negro and white the visibility factor has helped her. But then she discovered that subtler differences were also important; Jews somehow differed from gentiles; wops from Americans; doctors from salesmen. She is now aware of group differences, though not yet clear concerning all the relevant cues.

4. She has encountered the stage of linguistic precedence in learning. In fact, she is now in this stage. She knows that group X (she knows neither its name nor its identity) is somehow hate-worthy. She already has the emotional meaning but lacks the referential meaning. She seeks now to integrate the proper content with the emotion. She wishes to define her category so as to make her future behavior conform to her mother's desires. As soon as she has the linguistic tag at her command, she will be like the little Italian boy for whom "Polish" and "bad" were synonymous terms.

Up to the present, Janet's development marks what we might call the first stage of ethnocentric learning. Let us christen it the period of *pregeneralized* learning. This label is not altogether satisfactory, but none better describes the potpourri of factors listed above. The term draws attention primarily to the fact that the child has not yet generalized after the fashion of adults. He does not quite understand what a Jew is, what a Negro is, or what his own attitude toward them should be. He does not know even what *he* is—in any consistent sense. He may think he is an American only when he is playing with his toy soldiers (this type of categorizing was not uncommon in wartime). It is not only in ethnic matters that thoughts are prelogical from an adult point of view. A little girl may not think that her mother is her mother when the latter is working at the office; and may not regard her mother as an officeworker when she is at home tending the family.[11]

The child seems to live his mental life in specific contexts. What exists here and now makes up the only reality. The strange-man-who-knocks-at-the-door is something to be feared. It does not matter if he is a delivery man. The Negro boy at school is dirty. He is not a member of a race.

Such independent experiences in concrete procession seem to furnish the child's mind. His pregeneralized thinking (from the adult's point of view) has sometimes been labeled "global," or "syncretistic," or "prelogical."[12]

Now the place of linguistic tags in the course of mental development is crucial. They stand for adult abstractions, for logical generalizations of the sort that mature adults accept. The child learns the tags before he is fully ready to apply them to the adult categories. They prepare him for prejudice. But the process takes time. Only after much fumbling—in the manner of Janet and other children described in this chapter—will the proper categorizing take place.

## The Second Stage in Learning Prejudice

As soon as Janet's mother gives a clear answer to Janet, she will in all probability enter a second period of prejudice—one that we may call the period of *total rejection*. Suppose the mother answers, "I told you not to play with Negro children. They are dirty; they have diseases; and they will hurt you. Now don't let me catch you at it." If Janet by now has learned to distinguish Negroes from other groups, even from the dark-skinned Mexican children, or Italians—in other words, if she now has the adult category in mind—she will undoubtedly reject all Negroes, in all circumstances, and with considerable feeling.

The research of Blake and Dennis well illustrates the point.[13] It will be recalled that these investigators studied Southern white children in the fourth and fifth grades (ten- and eleven-year-olds). They asked such questions as, "Which are more musical—Negroes or white people?" "Which are more clean?"—and many questions of a similar type. These children had, by the age of ten, learned to reject the Negro category *totally*. No favorable quality was ascribed to Negroes more often than to whites. In effect, whites had all the virtues; Negroes, none.

While this totalized rejection certainly starts earlier (in many children it will be found by the age of seven or eight), it seems to reach its ethnocentric peak in early puberty. First- and second-grade children often elect to play with, or sit beside, a child of different race or ethnic membership. This friendliness usually disappears in the fifth grade. At that time children choose their own group almost exclusively. Negroes select Negroes, Italians select Italians, and so on.[14]

As children grow older, they normally lose this tendency to total rejection and overgeneralization. Blake and Dennis found that in the 12th grade the white youth ascribed several favorable stereo-types to Negroes. They considered them more musical, more easygoing, better dancers.

## The Third Stage

Thus, after a period of *total rejection*, a stage of *differentiation* sets in. The prejudices grow less totalized. Escape clauses are written into the attitude in order to make it more rational and more acceptable to the individual.

One says, "Some of my best friends are Jews." Or, "I am not prejudiced against Negroes—I always loved my black Mammy." The child who is first learning adult categories of rejection is not able to make such gracious exceptions. It takes him the first six to eight years of his life to learn total rejection, and another six years or so to modify it. The actual adult creed in his culture is complex indeed. It allows for (and in many ways encourages) ethnocentrism. At the same time, one must give lip service to democracy and equality, or at least ascribe some good qualities to the minority group and some-how plausibly justify the remaining disapproval that one expresses. It takes the child well into adolescence to learn the peculiar double-talk appropriate to prejudice in a democracy.

Around the age of eight, children often *talk* in a highly prejudiced manner. They have learned their categories and their totalized rejection. But the rejection is chiefly verbal. While they may damn the Jews, the wops, the Catholics, they may still *behave* in a relatively democratic manner. They may play with them even while they talk against them. The "total rejection" is chiefly a verbal matter.

Now when the teaching of the school takes effect, the child learns a new verbal norm: he must talk democratically. He must profess to regard all races and creeds as equal. Hence, by the age of 12, we may find *verbal* acceptance, but *behavioral* rejection. By this age the prejudices have finally affected conduct, even while the verbal, democratic norms are beginning to take effect.

The paradox, then, is that younger children may talk undemocratically, but behave democratically, whereas children in puberty may talk (at least in school) democratically but behave with true prejudice. By the age of 15, considerable skill is shown in imitating the adult pattern. Prejudiced talk and democratic talk are reserved for appropriate occasions, and rationalizations are ready for whatever occasions require them. Even conduct is varied according to circumstances. One may be friendly with a Negro in the kitchen, but hostile to a Negro who comes to the front door. Double-dealing, like double-talk, is hard to learn. It takes the entire period of childhood and much of adolescence to master the art of ethnocentrism.

## Notes and References

1. D. B. Harris, H. G. Gough, W. E. Martin. Children's ethnic attitudes: II, Relationship to parental beliefs concerning child training. *Child Development,* 1950, 21, 169–181.

2. These two contrasting styles of child training are described more fully by D. P. Ausubel in *Ego Development and the Personality Disorders.* New York: Grune & Stratton, 1952.

3. The most extensive evidence is contained in researches conducted at the University of California. See: T. W. Adorno, Else Frenkel-Brunswik, D. J. Levinson, R. N. Sanford, *The Authoritarian Personality,* New York: Harper, 1950; also, Else Frenkel-Brunswik, Patterns of social and cognitive outlook in children and parents, *American Journal of Orthopsychiatry,* 1951, 21, 543–558.

4. N. W. Ackerman and Marie Jahoda. *Anti-Semitism and Emotional Disorder.* New York: Harper, 1950, 45.

5. *Ibid.,* 85.

6. H. Bonner. Sociological aspects of paranoia. *American Journal of Sociology,* 1950, 56, 255–262.

7. Mary E. Goodman. *Race Awareness in Young Children.* Cambridge: Addison-Wesley, 1952. Other studies have confirmed the fact that Negro children are race-aware before white children: e.g., Ruth Horowitz, Racial aspects of self-identification in nursery school children, *Journal of Psychology,* 1939, 7, 91–99.

8. Mildred M. Eakin. *Getting Acquainted with Jewish Neighbors.* New York: Macmillan, 1944.

9. B. Lasker. *Race Attitudes in Children.* New York: Henry Holt, 1929, 98.

10. Helen G. Trager and Marian Radke. Early childhood airs its views. *Educational Leadership,* 1947, 5, 16–23.

11. E. L. Hartley, M. Rosenbaum, and S. Schwartz. (Children's perceptions of ethnic group membership. *Journal of Psychology,* 1948, 26, 387–398.

12. *Cf.* H. Werner. *Comparative Psychology of Mental Development.* Chicago: Follett, 1948. J. Piaget. *The Child's Conception of the World.* New York: Harcourt, Brace, 1929, 236. G. Murphy. Personality. New York: Harper, 1947, 336.

13. R. Blake and W. Dennis. The development of stereotypes concerning the Negro. *Journal of Abnormal and Social Psychology,* 1943, 38, 525–531.

14. J. H. Criswell. A sociometric study of race cleavage in the classroom. *Archives of Psychology,* 1939, No. 235.

# POSTSCRIPT

## Is Race Prejudice a Product of Group Position?

Clearly, there is no one theory that offers a complete explanation of prejudice. However, when we consider theories together or debate differing positions advanced in this issue, we gain insight and understanding. The basic dilemma is whether or not prejudice results from personality traits best revealed through psychological theories, or whether prejudice is more social and cultural, reflecting Blumer's idea of group position. Utilizing both approaches will help us see how social learning takes place. At this point we can ask another question concerning the relationship between attitudes and behavior.

To study race prejudice is to consider the role of attitudes and individual feelings in one's life. Still unclear to us is the relationship of attitudes to behavior. Does race prejudice lead to discriminatory practice? Does the prejudiced person behave differently from the non-prejudiced person? Sociologist Robert Merton suggests that prejudice and discrimination are linked in ways that are determined by different social environments. He developed categories to demonstrate that one can be prejudice and not discriminate, or one is not prejudice but nevertheless discriminates.

Blumer's position shifts the investigation of prejudice away from the psychological to something more sociological, which looks at the relationship of racial groups to each other. His theory is illustrated in the educational videos *Ethnic Notions* and *Color Adjustment* by Marlon Riggs (California Newsreel). They show how racial images of blacks after the Civil War were formed in the white community. In the late nineteenth century the media, largely newspapers and silent movies, depicted blacks as savages or brutes for which freedom from slavery was not a good thing. The movie, *The Birth of a Nation*, directed by D. W. Griffith, presented to the country's dominant white population an image of free-from-slavery blacks with exaggerated physical features associated with negative behavior patterns. The stereotyped images of black men included an alleged desire for white women, and they were to be feared. In the Jim Crow America that evolved after Reconstruction, many whites formed such images of blacks derived from available popular cultural images.

Both Blumer and Allport associate prejudice with attitudes of individuals, whether the cause is personality or social. Beyond individual prejudice is institutional prejudice, which along with institutional discrimination, cannot be ignored in the study of prejudice. For example, institutional racism was the law of the land before the 1954 *Brown* decision.

The "separate but equal" doctrine stemming from the landmark *Plessy* case enabled institutions such as schools to discriminate. Institutional prejudice was a "normal" part of American culture and reflected the negative stereotyping of blacks. One of the consequences of institutional prejudice led to self-segregation. Although the country has moved away from legal segregation, the latent effect of institutional prejudice today leads to self-segregation. Students will find Issue 6 ("Do Minorities and Whites Engage in Self-Segregation?") closely related to this discussion of prejudice.

For a historical account of the psychological understanding of prejudice, see "Psychology and Prejudice: A Historical Analysis and Integrative Framework," by John Duckett in *American Psychologist* (October 1992). Readers are encouraged to consult the entire classic, *The Nature of Prejudice* (Perseus, 1979), by Gordon Allport. It is a comprehensive and detailed account of prejudice. Another detailed account of the prejudiced personality appears in *The Authoritarian Personality* (Harper & Row, 1950) by Theodor Adorno. Also recommended is "Prejudice" by Thomas Pettigrew in *Harvard Encyclopedia of Ethnic Groups* (Harvard University Press, 1980) edited by Stephen Thornstrom.

Several important videos to further one's understanding of prejudice are available to the student. *The Color of Fear* (Stir-Fry Productions, 1994) by L. M. Wah shows an intense dialogue about race, prejudice, and racism. Jane Elliot's *Blue-Eyed* (California Newsreel) depicts the learning and unlearning process of prejudice for a class of elementary school children. Marlon Riggs' two videos, *Ethnic Notions* and *Color Adjustment* (California Newsreel, 1986), trace the stereotyping of blacks over the nineteenth and twentieth centuries.

To build upon the study of prejudice and look at theories of racism, Christopher Bates Doob's book, *Racism: An American Cauldron* (HarperCollins, 1996) offers a cross-cultural comparison of race relations. Students interested in the politics of race prejudice may find *The Racial Attitudes of American Presidents: From Abraham Lincoln to Theodore Roosevelt* (Anchor, 1972) by George Sinkler informative. He analyzes the role of the presidency in relation to racial problems. *The First R: How Children Learn Race and Racism* by Debra Van Ausdale and Joe Feagin argues that children learn racial attitudes at a very young age. *Race Manners: Navigating the Minefield Between Black and White Americans* (Arcade, 1999) by Bruce A. Jacobs provides a contemporary look at prejudice, racism, and discrimination. A lively feminist perspective is offered by Patricia Williams' *The Rooster's Egg: On the Persistence of Prejudice* (Harvard University Press, 1995).

# ISSUE 6

## Do Minorities and Whites Engage in Self-Segregation?

**YES: Beverly Daniel Tatum,** from *Why Are All the Black Kids Sitting Together in the Cafeteria?* (Basic Books, 1977)

**NO: Peter Beinart,** from "Degree of Separation at Yale," *The New Republic* (November 3, 1997)

### ISSUE SUMMARY

**YES:** Beverly Daniel Tatum, an African American clinical psychologist and president of Spelman College examines identity development among adolescents, especially black youths, and the behavioral outcomes of this phenomenon. She argues that black adolescents' tendency to view themselves in racial terms is due to the totality of personal and environmental responses that they receive from the larger society.

**NO:** Peter Beinart, senior editor for *The New Republic,* examines the complexity of the issues of multiculturalism and diversity on the nation's campuses, and he asserts that one examine how a broad spectrum of groups responds to the challenges of identity and "fitting in" within increasingly multicultural and diverse communities.

The continuing legacy of racial segregation and the Jim Crow lifestyles mandated within this system of intergroup relations poses significant challenges to the development of contemporary race relations within the United States. In the wake of the civil rights movement, out of which came a vision of a desegregated and equalitarian nation, many Americans are perplexed by the persistence of racial and ethnic separation.

American colleges and universities are major institutional domains in which the isolation of African American students and other ethnic groups is a reality that has generated interest, concern, and controversy. African American students tend to be the primary focus of such concerns on our campuses, though they are not the only group involved in what many Americans, both scholars and others, characterize as "self-segregation." The clustering and grouping together of whites can also be seen as self-segregation. The focal concern of this social issue is often stated within the question: "Why are all the black kids sitting together in the cafeteria?" However, the larger and perhaps more relevant question is why do all racial groups tend to congregate together.

Beverly Daniel Tatum notes that the quest for personal identity is a fundamental aspect of human experience. As black youth proceed in their development from childhood through adolescence, the question of identity evolves and grows, according to Tatum and other psychologists.

This identity development of black youth is influenced by an evolving racial consciousness within their perceptions of self. According to Tatum, these racially focused self-perceptions and identities that black youth develop in response to their experiences within an environment intensify due to messages and treatments they receive in interacting with white America. The challenges facing black youth in their attempts to engage this dominant white world range from having to confront and effectively deal with prejudice and discrimination to resisting stereotypes and affirming other more positive definitions of themselves. In response to these challenges, Tatum examines significant coping strategies that are developed by these youth including self-segregation.

Tatum maintains that black youth develop strategies to affirm and protect themselves from the deleterious effects of their involvement within a society with embedded stereotypes concerning blacks. So, Tatum answers the question, "Why all the black kids are sitting together in the cafeteria?" She does so by exploring the responses of black youth to the stresses of race in our society, and their need to seek meaning, sensitivity, understanding, and support from their black peers.

Peter Beinart examines the concerns with multiculturalism, diversity, and self-segregation on the campuses of colleges and universities. Beinart asserts that African American students are not the only ones to engage in overt and voluntary disassociation from whites and other ethnic groups in various social settings within these institutions. In addition to African-American and Latino students who seek separate dorms and cultural centers to foster their group identities, there are other groups who desire to be accorded similar sensitivity and accommodation of their needs and desires for separation from others within residential or other social settings. Beinart is critical of America's political/social conservatives who decry separatism among secular black or Latino students, while supporting such tendencies among Orthodox Jewish students and other religious conservatives. To Beinart, this is a clear example of the selectivity, hypocrisy, and significant contradictions within the thinking and policies advocated by America's conservatives with regard to this issue.

Although Beinart recognizes that many groups seek accommodation on campus in support of the maintenance of their identities and cultures, he views such separatist arrangements as undermining society's quest to build a nation of common core values, principles, and goals that identify and unify us as citizens with an American identity.

Both Beinart and Tatum offer the reader insight into the complex problem of race and American identity. Is self-segregation truly voluntary? To what extent is self-segregation on campuses a threat to a common America? Do the social psychological factors cited by Tatum outweigh Beinart's concern with self-segregation? Are the views of these two writers mutually exclusive? Why does Beinart fail to ask this question of whites?

# YES

**Beverly Daniel Tatum**

# Identity Development in Adolescence

**W**alk into any racially mixed high school cafeteria at lunch time and you will instantly notice that in the sea of adolescent faces, there is an identifiable group of Black students sitting together. Conversely, it could be pointed out that there are many groups of White students sitting together as well, though people rarely comment about that. The question on the tip of everyone's tongue is "Why are the Black kids sitting together?" Principals want to know, teachers want to know, White students want to know, the Black students who aren't sitting at the table want to know.

How does it happen that so many Black teenagers end up at the same cafeteria table? They don't start out there. If you walk into racially mixed elementary schools, you will often see young children of diverse racial backgrounds playing with one another, sitting at the snack table together, crossing racial boundaries with an ease uncommon in adolescence. Moving from elementary school to middle school (often at sixth or seventh grade) means interacting with new children from different neighborhoods than before, and a certain degree of clustering by race might therefore be expected, presuming that children who are familiar with one another would form groups. But even in schools where the same children stay together from kindergarten through eighth grade, racial grouping begins by the sixth or seventh grade. What happens?

One thing that happens is puberty. As children enter adolescence, they begin to explore the question of identity, asking "Who am I? Who can I be?" in ways they have not done before. For Black youth, asking "Who am I?" includes thinking about "Who am I ethnically and/or racially? What does it mean to be Black?"

As I write this, I can hear the voice of a White woman who asked me, "Well, all adolescents struggle with questions of identity. They all become more self-conscious about their appearance and more concerned about what their peers think. So what is so different for Black kids?" Of course, she is right that all adolescents look at themselves in new ways, but not all adolescents think about themselves in racial terms.

The search for personal identity that intensifies in adolescence can involve several dimensions of an adolescent's life: vocational plans, religious beliefs, values and preferences, political affiliations and beliefs, gender roles, and ethnic identities. The process of exploration may vary across these identity domains. James Marcia described four identity "statuses" to characterize the variation in the identity search process: (1) *diffuse,* a state in which there has been little exploration or active consideration of a particular domain, and no psychological commitment; (2) *foreclosed,* a state in which a commitment has been made to particular roles or belief systems, often those selected by parents, without actively considering alternatives; (3) *moratorium,* a state of active exploration of roles and beliefs in which no commitment has yet been made; and (4) *achieved,* a state of strong personal commitment to a particular dimension of identity following a period of high exploration.

An individual is not likely to explore all identity domains at once, therefore it is not unusual for an adolescent to be actively exploring one dimension while another remains relatively unexamined. Given the impact of dominant and subordinate status, it is not surprising that researchers have found that adolescents of color are more likely to be actively engaged in an exploration of their racial or ethnic identity that are White adolescents.

Why do Black youths, in particular, think about themselves in terms of race? Because that is how the rest of the world thinks of them. Our self-perceptions are shaped by the messages that we receive from those around us, and when young Black men and women enter adolescence, the racial content of those messages intensifies. A case in point: If you were to ask my ten-year-old son, David, to describe himself, he would tell you many things: that he is smart, that he likes to play computer games, that he has an older brother. Near the top of his list, he would likely mention that he is tall for his age. He would probably not mention that he is Black, though he certainly knows that he is. Why would he mention his height and not his racial group membership? When David meets new adults, one of the first questions they ask is "How old are you?" When David states his age, the inevitable reply is "Gee, you're tall for your age!" It happens so frequently that I once overheard David say to someone, "Don't say it, I know. I'm tall for my age." Height is salient for David because it is salient for others.

When David meets new adults, they don't say, "Gee, you're Black for your age!" If you are saying to yourself, of course they don't, think again. Imagine David at fifteen, six-foot-two, wearing the adolescent attire of the day, passing adults he doesn't know on the sidewalk. Do the women hold their purses a little tighter, maybe even cross the street to avoid him? Does he hear the sound of the automatic door locks on cars as he passes by? Is he being followed around by the security guards at the local mall? As he stops in town with his new bicycle, does a police officer hassle him, asking where he got it, implying that it might be stolen? Do strangers assume he plays basketball? Each of these experiences conveys a racial message. At ten, race is not yet salient for David, because it is not yet salient for society. But it will be.

# Understanding Racial Identity Development

Psychologist William Cross, author of *Shades of Black: Diversity in African American Identity,* has offered a theory of racial identity development that I have found to be a very useful framework for understanding what is happening not only with David, but with those Black students in the cafeteria. According to Cross's model, referred to as the psychology of nigrescence, or the psychology of becoming Black, the five stages of racial identity development are *pre-encounter, encounter, immersion/emersion, internalization,* and *internalization-commitment.* For the moment, we will consider the first two stages as those are the most relevant for adolescents.

In the first stage, the Black child absorbs many of the beliefs and values of the dominant White culture, including the idea that it is better to be White. The stereotypes, omissions, and distortions that reinforce notions of White superiority are breathed in by Black children as well as White. Simply as a function of being socialized in a Eurocentric culture, some Black children may begin to value the role models, lifestyles, and images of beauty represented by the dominant group more highly than those of their own cultural group. On the other hand, if Black parents are what I call race-conscious—that is, actively seeking to encourage positive racial identity by providing their children with positive cultural images and messages about what it means to be Black—the impact of the dominant society's messages are reduced. In either case, in the pre-encounter stage, the personal and social significance of one's racial group membership has not yet been realized, and racial identity is not yet under examination. At age ten, David and other children like him would seem to be in the pre-encounter stage. When the environmental cues change and the world begins to reflect his Blackness back to him more clearly, he will probably enter the encounter stage.

Transition to the encounter stage is typically precipitated by an event or series of events that force the young person to acknowledge the personal impact of racism. As the result of a new and heightened awareness of the significance of race, the individual begins to grapple with what it means to be a member of a group targeted by racism. Though Cross describes this process as one that unfolds in late adolescence and early adulthood, research suggests that an examination of one's racial or ethnic identity may begin as early as junior high school.

In a study of Black and White eighth graders from an integrated urban junior high school, Jean Phinney and Steve Tarver found clear evidence for the beginning of the search process in this dimension of identity. Among the forty-eight participants, more than a third had thought about the effects of ethnicity on their future, had discussed the issues with family and friends, and were attempting to learn more about their group. While White students in this integrated school were also beginning to think about ethnic identity, there was evidence to suggest a more active search among Black students, especially Black females. Phinney and Tarver's research is consistent with my own study of Black youth in predominantly White communities, where the environmental cues that trigger an examination of racial identity often become evident in middle school or junior high school.

Some of the environmental cues are institutionalized. Though many elementary schools have self-contained classrooms where children of varying performance levels learn together, many middle and secondary schools use "ability grouping," or tracking. Though school administrators often defend their tracking practices as fair and objective, there usually is a recognizable racial pattern to how children are assigned, which often represents the system of advantage operating in the schools. In racially mixed schools, Black children are much more likely to be in the lower track than in the honors track. Such apparent sorting along racial lines sends a message about what it means to be Black. One young honors student I interviewed described the irony of this resegregation in what was an otherwise integrated environment, and hinted at the identity issues it raised for him.

> It was really a very paradoxical existence, here I am in a school that's 35 percent Black, you know, and I'm the only Black in my classes. . . . That always struck me as odd. I guess I felt that I was different from the other Blacks because of that.

In addition to the changes taking place within school, there are changes in the social dynamics outside school. For many parents, puberty raises anxiety about interracial dating. In racially mixed communities, you begin to see what I call the birthday party effect. Young children's birthday parties in multiracial communities are often a reflection of the community's diversity. The parties of elementary school children may be segregated by gender but not by race. At puberty, when the parties become sleepovers or boy-girl events, they become less and less racially diverse.

Black girls, especially in predominantly White communities, may gradually become aware that something has changed. When their White friends start to date, they do not. The issues of emerging sexuality and the societal messages about who is sexually desirable leave young Black women in a very devalued position. One young woman from a Philadelphia suburb described herself as "pursuing White guys throughout high school" to no avail. Since there were no Black boys in her class, she had little choice. She would feel "really pissed off" that those same White boys would date her White friends. For her, "that prom thing was like out of the question."

Though Black girls living in the context of a larger Black community may have more social choices, they too have to contend with devaluing messages about who they are and who they will become, especially if they are poor or working-class. As social scientists Bonnie Ross Leadbeater and Niobe Way point out,

> The school drop-out, the teenage welfare mother, the drug addict, and the victim of domestic violence or of AIDS are among the most prevalent public images of poor and working-class urban adolescent girls. . . .

Yet, despite the risks inherent in economic disadvantage, the majority of poor urban adolescent girls do not fit the stereotypes that are made about them.

Resisting the stereotypes and affirming other definitions of themselves is part of the task facing young Black women in both White and Black communities.

As was illustrated in the example of David, Black boys also face a devalued status in the wider world. The all too familiar media image of a young Black man with his hands cuffed behind his back, arrested for a violent crime, has primed many to view young Black men with suspicion and fear. In the context of predominantly White schools, however, Black boys may enjoy a degree of social success, particularly if they are athletically talented. The culture has embraced the Black athlete, and the young man who can fulfill that role is often pursued by Black girls and White girls alike. But even these young men will encounter experiences that may trigger an examination of their racial identity.

Sometimes the experience is quite dramatic. *The Autobiography of Malcolm X* is a classic tale of racial identity development, and I assign it to my psychology of racism students for just that reason. As a junior high school student, Malcolm was a star. Despite the fact that he was separated from his family and living in a foster home, he was an A student and was elected president of his class. One day he had a conversation with his English teacher, whom he liked and respected, about his future career goals. Malcolm said he wanted to be a lawyer. His teacher responded, "That's no realistic goal for a nigger," and advised him to consider carpentry instead. The message was clear: You are a Black male, your racial group membership matters, plan accordingly. Malcolm's emotional response was typical—anger, confusion, and alienation. He withdrew from his White classmates, stopped participating in class, and eventually left his predominately white Michigan home to live with his sister in Roxbury, a Black community in Boston.

No teacher would say such a thing now, you may be thinking, but don't be so sure. It is certainly less likely that a teacher would use the word *nigger,* but consider these contemporary examples shared by high school students. A young ninth-grade student was sitting in his homeroom. A substitute teacher was in charge of the class. Because the majority of students from this school go on to college, she used the free time to ask the students about their college plans. As a substitute she had very limited information about their academic performance, but she offered some suggestions. When she turned to this young man, one of few Black males in the class, she suggested that he consider a community college. She had recommended four-year colleges to the other students. Like Malcolm, this student got the message.

In another example, a young Black woman attending a desegregated school to which she was bussed was encouraged by a teacher to attend the upcoming school dance. Most of the Black students did not live in the neighborhood and seldom attended the extracurricular activities. The young woman indicated that she wasn't planning to come. The well-intentioned teacher was persistent. Finally the teacher said, "Oh come on, I know you people love to dance." This young woman got the message, too.

## Coping with Encounters: Developing an Oppositional Identity

What do these encounters have to do with the cafeteria? Do experiences with racism inevitably result in so-called self-segregation? While certainly a desire to protect oneself from further offense is understandable, it is not the only factor at work. Imagine the young eighth-grade girl who experienced the teacher's use of "you people" and the dancing stereotype as a racial affront. Upset and struggling with adolescent embarrassment, she bumps into a White friend who can see that something is wrong. She explains. Her White friend responds, in an effort to make her feel better perhaps, and says, "Oh, Mr. Smith is such a nice guy, I'm sure he didn't mean it like that. Don't be so sensitive." Perhaps the White friend is right, and Mr. Smith didn't mean it, but imagine your own response when you are upset, perhaps with a spouse or partner. He or she asks what's wrong and you explain why you are offended. Your partner brushes off your complaint, attributing it to your being oversensitive. What happens to your emotional thermostat? It escalates. When feelings, rational or irrational, are invalidated, most people disengage. They not only choose to discontinue the conversation but are more likely to turn to someone who will understand their perspective.

In much the same way, the eighth-grade girl's White friend doesn't get it. She doesn't see the significance of this racial message, but the girls at the "Black table" do. When she tells her story there, one of them is likely to say, "You know what, Mr. Smith said the same thing to me yesterday!" Not only are Black adolescents encountering racism and reflecting on their identity, but their White peers, even when they are not the perpetrators (and sometimes they are), are unprepared to respond in supportive ways. The Black students turn to each other for the much needed support they are not likely to find anywhere else.

In adolescence, as race becomes personally salient for Black youth, finding the answer to questions such as, "What does it mean to be a young Black person? How should I act? What should I do?" is particularly important. And although Black fathers, mothers, aunts, and uncles may hold the answers by offering themselves as role models, they hold little appeal for most adolescents. The last thing many fourteen-year-olds want to do is to grow up to be like their parents. It is the peer group, the kids in the cafeteria, who hold the answers to these questions. They know how to be Black. They have absorbed the stereotypical images of Black youth in the popular culture and are reflecting those images in their self-presentation.

Based on their fieldwork in U.S. high schools, Signithia Fordham and John Ogbu identified a common psychological pattern found among

African American high school students are this stage of identity development. They observed that the anger and resentment that adolescents feel
in response to their growing awareness of the systematic exclusion of Black
people from full participation in U.S. society leads to the development
of an oppositional social identity. This oppositional stance both protects
one's identity from the psychological assault of racism and keeps the dominant group at a distance. Fordham and Ogbu write:

> Subordinate minorities regard certain forms of behavior and certain
> activities or events, symbols, and meanings as *not appropriate* for them
> because those behaviors, events, symbols, and meanings are character-
> istic of white Americans. At the same time they emphasize other forms
> of behavior as more appropriate for them because these are *not* a part
> of white Americans' way of life. To behave in the manner defined as
> falling within a white cultural frame of reference is to "act white" and
> is negatively sanctioned.

Certain styles of speech, dress, and music, for example, may be embraced as "authentically Black" and become highly valued, while attitudes
and behaviors associated with Whites are viewed with disdain. The peer
groups's evaluation of what is Black and what is not can have a powerful
impact on adolescent behavior.

Reflecting on her high school years, one Black woman from a White
neighborhood described both the pain of being rejected by her Black classmates and her attempts to conform to her peer's definition of Blackness:

> "Oh you sound White, you think you're White," they said. And the
> idea of sounding White was just so absurd to me. . . . So ninth grade
> was sort of traumatic in that I started listening to rap music, which I
> really just don't like. [I said] I'm gonna be Black, and it was just that
> stupid. But it's more than just how one acts, you know. [The other
> Black women there] were not into me for the longest time. My first year
> there was hell.

Sometimes the emergence of an oppositional identity can be quite
dramatic, as the young person tries on a new persona almost overnight. At
the end of one school year, race may not have appeared to be significant,
but often some encounter takes place over the summer and the young person returns to school much more aware of his or her Blackness and ready
to make sure that the rest of the world is aware of it, too. There is a certain "in your face" quality that these adolescents can take on, which their
teachers often experience as threatening. When a group of Black teens are
sitting together in the cafeteria, collectively embodying an oppositional
stance, school administrators want to know not only why they are sitting
together, but what can be done to prevent it.

We need to understand that in racially mixed settings, racial grouping
is a developmental process in response to an environmental stressor, racism.
Joining with one's peers for support in the face of stress is a positive coping

strategy. What is problematic is that the young people are operating with a very limited definition of what it means to be Black, based largely on cultural stereotypes.

## Oppositional Identity Development and Academic Achievement

Unfortunately for Black teenagers, those cultural stereotypes do not usually include academic achievement. Academic success is more often associated with being White. During the encounter phase of racial identity development, when the search for identity leads toward cultural stereotypes and away from anything that might be associated with Whiteness, academic performance often declines. Doing well in school becomes identified as trying to be White. Being smart becomes the opposite of being cool.

While this frame of reference is not universally found among adolescents of African descent, it is commonly observed in Black peer groups. Among the Black college students I have interviewed, many described some conflict or alienation from other African American teens because of their academic success in high school. For example, a twenty-year-old female from a Washington, D.C., suburb explained:

> It was weird, even in high school a lot of the Black students were, like, "Well, you're not really Black." Whether it was because I became president of the sixth-grade class or whatever it was, it started pretty much back then. Junior high, it got worse. I was then labeled certain things, whether it was "the oreo" or I wasn't really Black.

Others described avoiding situations that would set them apart from their Black peers. For example, one young woman declined to participate in a gifted program in her school because she knew it would separate her from the other Black students in the school.

In a study of thirty-three eleventh-graders in a Washington, D.C., school, Fordham and Ogbu found that although some of the students had once been academically successful, few of them remained so. These students also knew that to be identified as a "brainiac" would result in peer rejection. The few students who had maintained strong academic records found ways to play down their academic success enough to maintain some level of acceptance among their Black peers.

Academically successful Black students also need a strategy to find acceptance among their White classmates. Fordham describes one such strategy as *racelessness,* wherein individuals assimilate into the dominant group by de-emphasizing characteristics that might identify them as members of the subordinate group. Jon, a young man I interviewed, offered a classic example of this strategy as he described his approach to dealing with his discomfort at being the only Black person in his advanced classes. He said, "At no point did I ever think I was White or did I ever want to be White. . . . I guess it was one of those things where I tried to de-emphasize the fact that I was Black." This strategy led him to avoid activities that were associated with Blackness. He recalled, "I didn't want to do anything that was traditionally Black, like I never played basketball. I ran cross-country. . . . I went for distance running instead of sprints." He felt he had to show his White classmates that there were "exceptions to all these stereotypes." However, this strategy was of limited usefulness. When he traveled outside his home community with his White teammates, he sometimes encountered overt racism. "I quickly realized that I'm Black, and that's the thing that they're going to see first, no matter how much I try to de-emphasize my Blackness."

A Black student can play down Black identity in order to succeed in school and mainstream institutions without rejecting his Black identity and culture. Instead of becoming raceless, an achieving Black student can become an *emissary,* someone who sees his or her own achievements as advancing the cause of the racial group. For example, social scientists Richard Zweigenhaft and G. William Domhoff describe how a successful Black student, in response to the accusation of acting White, connected his achievement to that of other Black men by saying, "Martin Luther King must not have been Black, then, since he had a doctoral degree, and Malcolm X must not have been Black since he educated himself while in prison." In addition, he demonstrated his loyalty to the Black community by taking an openly political stance against the racial discrimination he observed in his school.

It is clear that an oppositional identity can interfere with academic achievement, and it may be tempting for educators to blame the adolescents themselves for their academic decline. However, the questions that educators and other concerned adults must ask are, How did academic achievement become defined as exclusively White behavior? What is it about the curriculum and the wider culture that reinforces the notion that academic excellence is an exclusively White domain? What curricular interventions might we use to encourage the development of an empowered emissary identity?

An oppositional identity that disdains academic achievement has not always been a characteristic of Black adolescent peer groups. It seems to be a post-desegregation phenomenon. Historically, the oppositional identity found among African Americans in the segregated South included a positive attitude toward education. While Black people may have publicly deferred to Whites, they actively encouraged their children to pursue education as a ticket to greater freedom. While Black parents still see education as the key to upward mobility, in today's desegregated schools the models of success—the teachers, administrators, and curricular heroes—are almost always White.

Black Southern schools, though stigmatized by legally sanctioned segregation, were often staffed by African American educators, themselves visible models of academic achievement. These Black educators may have presented a curriculum that included references to the intellectual legacy of other African Americans. As well, in the context of a segregated school, it was a given that the high achieving students would all be Black. Academic achievement did not have to mean separation from one's Black peers.

## The Search for Alternative Images

This historical example reminds us that an oppositional identity discouraging academic achievement is not inevitable even in a racist society. If young people are exposed to images of African American academic achievement in their early years, they won't have to define school achievement as something for Whites only. They will know that there is a long history of Black intellectual achievement.

This point was made quite eloquently by Jon, the young man I quoted earlier. Though he made the choice to excel in school, he labored under the false assumption that he was "inventing the wheel." It wasn't until he reached college and had the opportunity to take African American studies courses that he learned about other African Americans besides Martin Luther King, Malcolm X, and Frederick Douglass—the same three men he had heard about year after year, from kindergarten to high school graduation. As he reflected on his identity struggle in high school, he said:

> It's like I went through three phases. . . . My first phase was being cool, doing whatever was particularly cool for Black people at the time, and that was like in junior high. Then in high school, you know, I thought being Black was basically all stereotypes, so I tried to avoid all of those things. Now in college, you know, I realize that being Black means a variety of things.

Learning his history in college was of great psychological importance to Jon, providing him with role models he had been missing in high school. He was particularly inspired by learning of the intellectual legacy of Black men at his own college:

> When you look at those guys who were here in the Twenties, they couldn't live on campus. They couldn't eat on campus. They couldn't get their hair cut in town. And yet they were all Phi Beta Kappa. . . . That's what being Black really is, you know, knowing who you are, your history, your accomplishments. . . . When I was in junior high, I had White role models. And then when I got into high school, you know, I wasn't sure but I just didn't think having White role models was a good thing. So I got rid of those. And I basically just, you know, only had my parents for role models. I kind of grew up thinking that we were on the cutting edge. We were doing something radically different than everybody else. And not realizing that there are all kinds of Black people doing the very things that I thought we were the only ones doing. . . . You've got to do the very best you can so that you can continue the great traditions that have already been established.

This young man was not alone in his frustration over having learned little about his own cultural history in grade school. Time and again in the research interviews I conducted, Black students lamented the absence of courses in African American history or literature at the high school level and indicated how significant this new learning was to them in college, how excited and affirmed they felt by this newfound knowledge. Sadly, many Black students never get to college, alienated from the process of education long before high school graduation. They may never get access to the information that might have helped them expand their definition of what it means to be Black and, in the process, might have helped them stay in school. Young people are developmentally ready for this information in adolescence. We ought to provide it.

## Not at the Table

As we have seen, Jon felt he had to distance himself from his Black peers in order to be successful in high school. He was one of the kids *not* sitting at the Black table. Continued encounters with racism and access to new culturally relevant information empowered him to give up his racelessness and become an emissary. In college, not only did he sit at the Black table, but he emerged as a campus leader, confident in the support of his Black peers. His example illustrates that one's presence at the Black table is often an expression of one's identity development, which evolves over time.

Some Black students may not be developmentally ready for the Black table in junior or senior high school. They may not yet have had their own encounters with racism, and race may not be very salient for them. Just as we don't all reach puberty and begin developing sexual interest at the same time, racial identity development unfolds in idiosyncratic ways. Though my research suggests that adolescence is a common time, one's own life experiences are also important determinants of the timing. The young person whose racial identity development is out of synch with his or her peers often feels in an awkward position. Adolescents are notoriously egocentric and assume that their experience is the same as everyone else's. Just as girls who have become interested in boys become disdainful of their friends still interested in dolls, the Black teens who are at the table can be quite judgmental toward those who are not. "If I think it is a sign of authentic Blackness to sit at this table, then you should too."

The young Black men and women who still hang around with the White classmates they may have known since early childhood will often be snubbed by their Black peers. This dynamic is particularly apparent in regional schools where children from a variety of neighborhoods are brought together. When Black children from predominantly White neighborhoods go to school with Black children from predominantly Black neighborhoods, the former group is often viewed as trying to be White by the latter group. We all speak the language of the streets we live on. Black children living in White neighborhoods often sound White to their Black peers from across town, and may be teased because of it. This can be a very painful experience, particularly when the young person is not fully accepted as part of the White peer group either.

One young Black woman from a predominantly White community described exactly this situation in an interview. In a school with a lot of racial tension, Terri felt that "the worst thing that happened" was the rejection she experienced from the other Black children who were being bussed to her school. Though she wanted to be friends with them, they teased her, calling her an "oreo cookie" and sometimes beating her up. The only close Black friend Terri had was a biracial girl from her neighborhood.

Racial tensions also affected her relationships with White students. One White friend's parents commented, "I can't believe you're Black. You don't seem like all the Black children. You're nice." Though other parents made similar comments, Terri reported that her White friends didn't start making them until junior high school, when Terri's Blackness became something to be explained. One friend introduced Terri to another White girl by saying, "She's not really Black, she just went to Florida and got a really dark tan." A White sixth-grade "boyfriend" became embarrassed when his friends discovered he had a crush on a Black girl. He stopped telling Terri how pretty she was, and instead called her "nigger" and said, "Your lips are too big. I don't want to see you. I won't be your friend anymore."

Despite supportive parents who expressed concern about her situation, Terri said she was a "very depressed child." Her father would have conversations with her "about being Black and beautiful" and about "the union of people of color that had always existed that I needed to find. And the pride." However, her parents did not have a network of Black friends to help support her.

It was the intervention of a Black junior high school teacher that Terri feels helped her the most. Mrs. Campbell "really exposed me to the good Black community because I was so down on it" by getting Terri involved in singing gospel music and introducing her to other Black students who would accept her. "That's when I started having other Black friends. And I thank her a lot for that."

The significant role that Mrs. Campbell played in helping Terri open up illustrates the constructive potential that informed adults can have in the identity development process. She recognized Terri's need for a same-race peer group and helped her find one. Talking to groups of Black students about the variety of living situations Black people come from, and the unique situation facing Black adolescents in White communities, helps to expand the definition of what it means to be Black and increases intragroup acceptance at a time when that is quite important.

For children in Terri's situation, it is also helpful for Black parents to provide ongoing opportunities for their children to connect with other Black peers even if that means traveling outside the community they live in. Race-conscious parents often do this by attending a Black church or maintaining ties to Black social organizations such as Jack and Jill. Parents who make this effort often find that their children become bicultural, able to move comfortably between Black and White communities, and able to sit at the Black table when they are ready.

Implied in this discussion is the assumption that connecting with one's Black peers in the process of identity development is important and should be encouraged. For young Black people living in predominantly Black communities, such connections occur spontaneously with neighbors and classmates and usually do not require special encouragement. However, for young people in predominantly White communities they may only occur with active parental intervention. One might wonder if this social connection is really necessary. If a young person has found a niche among a circle of White friends, is it really necessary to establish a Black peer group as a reference point? Eventually it is.

As one's awareness of the daily challenges of living in a racist society increase, it is immensely helpful to be able to share one's experiences with others who have lived it. Even when White friends are willing and able to listen and bear witness to one's struggles, they cannot really share the experience. One young woman came to this realization in her senior year of high school:

> [The isolation] never really bothered me until about senior year when I was the only one in the class. . . . That little burden, that constant burden of you always having to strive to do your best and show that you can do just as much as everybody else. Your White friends can't understand that, and it's really hard to communicate to them. Only someone else of the same racial, same ethnic background would understand something like that.

When one is faced with what Chester Pierce calls the "mundane extreme environmental stress" of racism, in adolescence or in adulthood, the ability to see oneself as part of a larger group from which one can draw support is an important coping strategy. Individuals who do not have such a strategy available to them because they do not experience a shared identity with at least some subset of their racial group are at risk for considerable social isolation.

Of course, who we perceive as sharing our identity may be influenced by other dimensions of identity such as gender, social class, geographical location, skin color, or ethnicity. For example, research indicates that first-generation Black immigrants from the Caribbean tend to emphasize their national origins and ethnic identities, distancing themselves from U.S. Blacks, due in part to their belief that West Indians are viewed more positively by Whites than those American Blacks whose family roots include the experience of U.S. slavery. To relinquish one's ethnic identity as West Indian and take on an African American identity may be understood as downward social mobility. However, second-generation. West Indians without an identifiable accent may lose the relative ethnic privilege their parents experienced and seek racial solidarity with Black American peers in the face of encounters with racism. Whether it is the experience of being followed in stores because they are suspected of shoplifting, seeing people respond to them with fear on the street, or feeling overlooked in school, Black youth can benefit from seeking support from those who have had similar experiences.

# An Alternative to the Cafeteria Table

The developmental need to explore the meaning of one's identity with others who are engaged in a similar process manifests itself informally in school corridors and cafeterias across the country. Some educational institutions have sought to meet this need programmatically. Several colleagues and I recently evaluated one such effort, initiated at a Massachusetts middle school participating in a voluntary desegregation program known as the Metropolitan Council for Educational Opportunity (METCO) program. Historically, the small number of African American students who are bussed from Boston to this suburban school have achieved disappointing levels of academic success. In an effort to improve academic achievement, the school introduced a program, known as Student Efficacy Training (SET) that allowed Boston students to meet each day as a group with two staff members. Instead of being in physical education or home economics or study hall, they were meeting, talking about homework difficulties, social issues, and encounters with racism. The meeting was mandatory and at first the students were resentful of missing some of their classes. But the impact was dramatic. Said one young woman,

> In the beginning of the year, I didn't want to do SET at all. It took away my study and it was only METCO students doing it. In the beginning all we did was argue over certain problems or it was more like a rap session and I didn't think it was helping anyone. But then when we looked at records. . . . I know that last year out of all the students, sixth through eighth grade, there was, like, six who were actually good students. Everyone else, it was just pathetic, I mean, like, they were getting like Ds and Fs. . . . The eighth grade is doing much better this year. I mean, they went from Ds and Fs to Bs and Cs and occasional As. . . . And those seventh-graders are doing really good, they have a lot of honor roll students in seventh grade, both guys and girls. Yeah, it's been good. It's really good.

Her report is borne out by an examination of school records. The opportunity to come together in the company of supportive adults allowed these young Black students to talk about the issues that hindered their performance—racial encounters, feelings of isolation, test anxiety, homework dilemmas—in the psychological safety of their own group. In the process, the peer culture changed to one that supported academic performance rather than undermined it, as revealed in these two students' comments:

> Well, a lot of the Boston students, the boys and the girls, used to fight all the time. And now, they stopped yelling at each other so much and calling each other stupid.

> It's like we've all become like one big family, we share things more with each other. We tease each other like brother and sister. We look out for each other with homework and stuff. We always stay on top of each other 'cause we know it's hard with African American students to go to a predominantly White school and try to succeed with everybody else.

The faculty, too, were very enthusiastic about the outcomes of the intervention, as seen in the comments of these two classroom teachers:

> This program has probably produced the most dramatic result of any single change that I've seen at this school. It has produced immediate results that affected behavior and academics and participation in school life.

> My students are more engaged. They aren't battling out a lot of the issues of their anger about being in a White community, coming in from Boston, where do I fit, I don't belong here. I feel that those issues that often came out in class aren't coming out in class anymore. I think they are being discussed in the SET room, the kids feel more confidence. The kids' grades are higher, the homework response is greater, they're not afraid to participate in class, and I don't see them isolating themselves within class. They are willing to sit with other students happily. . . . I think it's made a very positive impact on their place in the school and on their individual self-esteem. I see them enjoying themselves and able to enjoy all of us as individuals. I can't say enough, it's been the best thing that's happened to the METCO program as far as I'm concerned.

Although this intervention is not a miracle cure for every school, it does highlight what can happen when we think about the developmental needs of Black adolescents coming to terms with their own sense of identity. It might seem counterintuitive that a school involved in a voluntary desegregation program could improve both academic performance and social relationships among students by *separating* the Black students for one period every day. But if we understand the unique challenges facing adolescents of color and the legitimate need they have to feel supported in their identity development, it makes perfect sense.

Though they may not use the language of racial identity development theory to describe it, most Black parents want their children to achieve an internalized sense of personal security, to be able to acknowledge the reality of racism and to respond effectively to it. Our educational institutions should do what they can to encourage this development rather than impede it. When I talk to educators about the need to provide adolescents with identity-affirming experiences and information about their own cultural groups, they sometimes flounder because this information has not been part of their own education. Their understanding of adolescent development has been limited to the White middle-class norms included in most textbooks, their knowledge of Black history limited to Martin Luther King, Jr., and Rosa Parks. They sometimes say with frustration that parents should provide this kind of education for their children. Unfortunately Black parents often attended the same schools the teachers did and have the same informational gaps. We need to acknowledge that an important part of interrupting the cycle of oppression is constant re-education, and sharing what we learn with the next generation.

Peter Beinart  **NO**

# Degree of Separation at Yale

**F**or decades at Cornell University, minority students have opted out of regular dorms and into ethnic theme houses. Last year, Cornell's president proposed changing that slightly: students should wait to enter the Ujamaa house or the Latino Living Center until after their freshman year. The response? Fifteen undergrads went on a hunger strike, hundreds laid down in the street, and Reverend Al Sharpton dropped in to accuse the administration of trying to make black and Latino students "merge in with everyone else so we don't know they're here."

This is the kind of thing that gives conservative critics of political correctness a reason to get up in the morning. And it occasioned the usual shoutfest about diversity, forced integration, and self-segregation—followed by a weak-kneed administration compromise.

So far, so predictable. But right-wing outrage separatism at Cornell raises an interesting question: Why on Earth are conservatives supporting the five Orthodox Jewish students who won't live in the regular dormitories at Yale? The answer is one of the ironies of the culture war: when it comes to religion, the real multiculturalists are all on the Right.

The Yale case and the Cornell case are essentially the same. It's true that the Yalies are asking to move off campus, but that's only because Yale doesn't have specialty houses. If it had a single sex dorm, or a "no-premarital sex" dorm, the Orthodox five would live there. And it's true that the Cornell radicals say they're fleeing racism while the Yale faithful say they're fleeing condoms. But it amounts to the same thing. Yale freshman Elisha Dov Hack's older brother told him that dorm life has made previous Orthodox students less observant. Hunger-striking black senior Dana Miller told *The New York Times* last year that Cornell's proposed change was "an attempt to socialize students into a homogeneous group." Hack and Miller are both really fleeing assimilation.

That's why it's so remarkable that champions of the melting pot like Charles Krauthammer, William Buckley, Kate O'Beirne, and the editors of *The Weekly Standard* have risen to the Yale Five's defense. This, after all, is the same Charles Krauthammer who recently decried "the tragic turn towards black separatism," and the same *Standard* which in September coined the phrase, "diversity gulag."

From *The New Republic*, November 3, 1997, pp. 314–316. Copyright © 1997 by The New Republic, LLC. Reprinted by permission of The New Republic.

Conservative views about separatism, it turns out, depend on who's doing the separating. Consider these words, written in September by frequent *National Review* contributor Jacob Neusner: "cripples have their ramps, homosexuals their K-Y dispensers and double beds, blacks their ghettos, Hispanics their barrios, voyeurs their unisex toilets, all courtesy of university housing directors. But rather than extend the same 'sensitivity' to scarcely a minyan—a quorum—of Orthodox Jews, Yale would rather humiliate itself." This tasteful nugget gets to the heart of the issue. All this time everyone thought conservatives opposed "ghettos" and "barrios" on principle. But now it turns out they're just mad that P.C. radicals get them and prudish believers do not.

A good example of this multicultural me-tooism is the Right's support for charter schools. On August 16, 1996, *The Washington Times* called the accreditation of charter schools in the District of Columbia a "ray of hope." Three and a half months later, the principal of the Afrocentric Marcus Garvey Public Charter School assaulted a *Washington Times* reporter. A *Times* commentator, Ernest Lefever, called the attack "the latest in a long string of outrages committed in the name of multiculturalism."

He's right, but the *Times* was asking for it. Multiculturalism isn't just the ideology of the Marcus Garvey charter school, it's the ideology of charter schools, period. Charter schools are based on the idea that communities should be able to fashion their own institutions with minimal interference from outsiders. They represent a rejection of the principle that public schools educate all students in a common curriculum or a common culture. That is why Michael Kelly wrote in this space last December that charter schools "take from the pluribus to destroy the unum." In their mania for local autonomy, conservative educational reformers have recreated the publicly funded black nationalist schools that arose in late 1960s New York under radical chic Mayor John Lindsey—most notoriously in Ocean Hill-Brownsville, Brooklyn.

Their motivation, of course, is different. For liberals, multiculturalism offered emancipation from racial oppression; for conservatives, it's about religion. Charter schools, combined with vouchers for private and parochial schools, and subsidies for home schooling, constitute the multiculturalist Right's assault on a common school system. Many Christian conservatives believe that regular public schools promote an immoral, godless ideology. Like the Orthodox Jews at Yale, they want to separate—and take their money with them. And just as liberals are instinctively (sometimes mindlessly) sympathetic to demands made in the name of anti-racism, secular conservatives jump to defend the beleaguered faithful. In so doing, they end up supporting a multiculturalism of their own. Once upon a time, liberals and conservatives believed in Norman Podhoretz's "brutal bargain." Assimilation was hard and even demeaning, but it bought you entrance into a common American culture. That didn't mean the culture was static; over time it might absorb a bit of your particular ethos. But you pushed from the inside, conscious that you could not both reject assimilation and expect its fruits.

In the 1960s, the Left decided this model wouldn't work for blacks. It believed, naively, that African Americans could remain separate from whites while making ever greater moral claims on them. The result, of course, was a tremendous backlash, as working-class whites learned how to stake the claims of identity themselves.

As conservatives line up behind their own brand of separatism, they should take care not to be similarly naive. The options are these: you either commit to common institutions, and accept the old, painful disjuncture between home and school, or you accept marginality. It is a far different thing to call for prayer in public schools than it is to demand that the citizenry fund religious schools. And it is a far different thing to participate fully in a university while maintaining your identity than it is to expect a university to accept you fully while refusing to give yourself fully to it. If conservatives really cared about the Yale Five, they would tell them what they told the hunger-strikers at Cornell: assimilation is the American way.

# POSTSCRIPT

## Do Minorities and Whites
## Engage in Self-Segregation?

The separation of blacks from whites within American society is the prevailing context within which race relations develop throughout history. There is a long-standing tradition of segregated schools, neighborhoods, and even churches in the United States. Segregation and racial stereotyping are parts of the American experience, and African-Americans and other minorities have had to resist racist stereotypes throughout history.

The issue of self-segregation is linked to Issue 1, "Do We Need a Common American Identity?", in that it extends the assimilation-pluralism debate. The debate here is compounded by voluntary segregation in contrast to exclusion. Given the goal of equality, what are the functions of self-segregation? On one hand, as Tatum points out, it offers a means to cope with rejection. However, as Beinart points out, it can undermine the goal of assimilation. Beinart's argument against self-segregation raises further questions about multiculturalism. Does self-segregation contribute to a common American identity, or does it lead to disunity?

The United States has a legacy of conflict-ridden race and ethnic relations rooted in such institutions as slavery, segregation, and related policies and practices of discrimination. Despite this legacy, the idea of assimilation is very strong in America. To Beinart, assimilation is beneficial to a common culture. His concern with self-segregation is that it threatens the *unum*. Beinart's argument is based on social categories such as American cultural identity, viable institutions, and social cohesion. Despite his concerns, Beinart does not recognize and therefore does not criticize the white tendency to congregate together. In contrast, Tatum addresses the issue from a social psychological perspective.

Many of the nation's campuses have not achieved multicultural sensitivity. We still have hate crimes and other manifestations of race and ethnic conflict. Confederate flags and other incendiary symbols of American racist tradition are still able to penetrate communities of higher learning. Given such realities, the black "table in the cafeteria" is expected to persist within the educational institutions of the United States. Essentially, Tatum describes black students congregating around these tables as engaging in positive identity formation. Their peers provide them with the reaffirmation and support that they need to affirm that their blackness is a positive quality. The immersion of these youth within the circle of their peers around the black table can facilitate their development of positive senses of self-esteem and self-worth to serve as effective antidotes to the negativity that they often encounter in dealing with the dominant society. Thus Tatum argues that self-segregation is a social adaptation by blacks and other youth in order to function effectively on campus.

Issues 1 ("Do We Need a Common American Identity?") and 3 ("Do Recent Immigration Trends Challenge Existing Ideas of America's White Identity?") share an important theme with this issue of self-segregation. In each case, one side challenged the other of threatening American unity, the *unum*, with some form of multiculturalism. So, whether it's a hyphenated identity, or immigrants of color, or the lunch table, the concern remains.

Readers will find a discussion regarding the self-segregation issue in *The Rage of a Privileged Class* (HarperCollins, 1993) by Ellis Cose. Deidre A. Royster, in *Race and the Invisible Hand: How White Networks Exclude Black Men from Blue Collar Jobs* (University of California, 2003), illustrates how blacks are excluded from many blue-collar trades because of segregation. From another perspective, what Royster describes can be viewed as white self-segregation that results from discrimination against black workers. William Julius Wilson's acclaimed study, *The Declining Significance of Race* (University of Chicago, 1980), offers the view that race is becoming less and less important in the economic lives of blacks.

# ISSUE 7

## Is the Emphasis on a Color-Blind Society an Answer to Racism?

**YES: Ward Connerly,** from "Don't Box Me In," *National Review* (April 16, 2001)

**NO: Eduardo Bonilla-Silva,** from *Racism Without Racists: Color-Blind Racism and the Persistence of Racial Inequality in the United States* (Rowman & Littlefield, 2003)

### ISSUE SUMMARY

**YES:** Ward Connerly is a strong critic of all attempts at racial classification and believes that in order to achieve a racially egalitarian, unified American society, the government and private citizens must stop assigning people to categories delineated by race. To achieve this goal, Mr. Connerly is supporting the enactment of a "Racial Privacy Initiative."

**NO:** Eduardo Bonilla-Silva argues that "regardless of whites' sincere fictions, racial considerations shade almost everything in America" and, therefore, color-blind ideology is a cover for the racism and inequality that persists within contemporary American society.

S kin color has played a pivotal role in determining the legal and social status of individuals and groups throughout American history. Slavery within the United States developed as a racial institution in which blackness defined one's status as a bonded person and the distinction between black and white facilitated the establishment of the social controls necessary to maintain the effectiveness of this mode of economic production. The miscegenation among blacks and whites during the Slave Era resulted in the production of persons of biracial identities, octoroons and quadroons, and these interracial groups were components of a racial hierarchy based upon skin color. The status of the free African Americans of this period was above that of the slaves but below the biracial groups, thus reflecting the color-based status differentiations that informed the social structure of antebellum American society.

In the wake of the Civil War and Reconstruction, racial segregation emerged as the defining mode of race relations within the United States. The Segregation Era was defined by a color-caste system of race relations that was designed to promote the overt exclusion of blacks from meaningful institutional participation and power within society in order to maintain white dominance within society. Signs that read "whites only" and "colored" were quite common throughout this period and defined employment opportunities available to members of the two races and the access of blacks to housing, schools, and other public accommodations that were available within the society.

The *de jure* segregation of American society persisted until it was overtaken by the civil rights movement of the 1960s, but *de facto* segregation remains a prominent feature of the social order of the United States despite the reforms of the last half-century. Baby boomers within today's African American population bear memories of being socialized and conditioned by the restraining values of this color-caste system of race relations.

Ward Connerly strongly argues in favor of the promise of a color-blind society. For him, America is becoming increasingly homogeneous where race is concerned and color categories are seen as irrelevant today.

In contrast, Eduardo Bonilla-Silva views color-blind ideology as a fiction and a new manifestation of racism. For him, the question remains, how do whites explain the contradiction between the notion of a color-blind society and the color-coded inequality that persists in America? For Bonilla-Silva, it is color-blind racism, the new racial ideology.

**Ward Connerly**

# Don't Box Me In

**A** few weeks ago, I was having dinner with a group of supporters following a lecture. One of those in attendance was a delightful woman who applauded my efforts to achieve a colorblind government. She strongly urged me to stay the course, promised financial support for my organization—the American Civil Rights Institute—and proclaimed that what we are doing is best for the nation.

Then, an odd moment occurred, when she said, "What you're doing is also best for your people." I flinched, took a couple of bites of my salad, and gathered my thoughts. I thought: *"My people"? Anyone who knows me knows that I abhor this mindset. But this dear lady doesn't know all my views or the nuances of race. She has innocently wandered into a racial thicket and doesn't have a clue that she has just tapped a raw nerve. Do I risk offending her by opening this issue for discussion? Do I risk losing her financial support by evidencing my distaste for what she has said? Perhaps it would be best to ignore the moment and let my staff follow up in pursuit of her support.*

I concluded that the situation demanded more of me than to believe that she was incapable of understanding what troubled me about her comment. So, I did what comes naturally in such situations—I politely confronted her. "What did you mean when you referred to 'my people' a moment ago?" I asked. "The black race," she responded. "What is your 'race'?" I asked. She said, "I'm Irish and German." I plowed ahead. "Would it affect your concept of my 'race' if I told you that one of my grandparents was Irish and American Indian, another French Canadian, another of African descent, and the other Irish? Aren't they all 'my people'? What about my children? They consist of my ingredients as well as those of their mother, who is Irish. What about my grandchildren, two of whom have a mother who is half Vietnamese?" The lady was initially awestruck. But that exchange produced one of the richest conversations about race I have ever had.

This discussion is one that an increasing number of Americans are having across our nation. It is one that many more would *like* to have. Thanks to the race questions placed in the 2000 Census, a great number of people are beginning to wonder about this business of their "race."

From its inception, America has promised equal justice before the law. The Declaration of Independence and the Constitution stand as monuments to the Founders' belief that we can fashion a government of colorblind laws, a unified nation without divisible parts. Unfortunately, they had to compromise on that vision from the beginning. To create a government, they had to protect the international slave trade until 1808. After that time, with the slave trade forever banned, they hoped and believed the slave system would wither away.

In a second concession of their principles to material interests, the Founders also agreed to count slaves as only three-fifths of a person. This compromise stemmed not from a belief that slaves were less than human; rather, slaveowning states wanted to count slaves as whole persons in deciding how large their population was, but not count them at all in deciding how much the states would pay in taxes. The infamous three-fifths compromise was the unfortunate concession.

To distinguish slaves from non-slaves, governments established various race classifications. Unfortunately, these classifications continued long after the Civil War amendments formally repudiated them. After all, once everyone was free to enjoy all the privileges and immunities of American citizenship, there was no longer a need to classify people by race. In hindsight, we recognize that, after nearly a century of race classifications imposed by the state, these classifications had become part of the way average Americans saw themselves, as well as others. Over the next half-century, scientists began to recognize that these race classifications don't exist in nature. We had created them, to justify an inhuman system.

Even as science reached these conclusions, however, these classifications played ever more important roles in American life. Poll taxes and literacy tests; separate bathroom facilities, transportation, water fountains, neighborhoods—the entire Jim Crow system relied on these state-imposed race classifications. And with science unable to distinguish a black person from a non-black person, the government relied on the infamous "one-drop rule": If you have just one drop of "black blood," you're black.

Although the Supreme Court struck down the "separate but equal" legal structure, the Court failed to eliminate the race classifications that sustained all the forms of segregation and discrimination the Court was trying to eliminate. We have seen the actual expansion of the groups being classified. On some level, though, I'm sure we really do want to become "one nation . . . indivisible." Witness the tenfold increase in "multiracial" families since 1967. In its decision that year—aptly named *Loving v. Virginia*—the Supreme Court ruled that anti-miscegenation laws (those forbidding people of different races to marry) were unconstitutional. While it took some time for us to shed the taboos against interracial dating and marriage, today there are more "multiracial" children born in California than there are "black" children. When Benjamin Bratt and Julia Roberts began dating, no one cared that they were an interracial couple. So too with Maury Povich and Connie Chung. Love has become colorblind.

The time has come for America to fulfill the promise of equal justice before the law and for the nation to renounce race classifications. To that end, I am preparing to place the Racial Privacy Initiative (RPI) before

California voters on the March 2002 ballot. This initiative would prohibit governments in California from classifying individuals by race, color, ethnicity, or national origin. Much to my surprise, just submitting RPI to the state in preparation for gathering signatures has generated controversy. The American Civil Liberties Union has called it a "racist" initiative, and various proponents of race preferences have said it will "turn back the clock on civil rights."

In drafting RPI, we have exempted medical research and have proposed nothing that would prevent law-enforcement officers from identifying particular individuals, so long as those methods are already lawful. To guarantee that laws against discrimination are enforced, we have exempted the Department of Fair Employment and Housing from the provisions of RPI for ten years.

Getting the government out of the business of classifying its citizens and asking them to check these silly little race boxes represents the next step in our nation's long journey toward becoming one nation. Getting rid of these boxes will strike a blow against the overbearing race industry that has grown like Topsy in America. It will help free us from the costly and poisonous identity politics and the racial spoils system that define our political process. It will clip the wings of a government that has become so intrusive that it classifies its citizens on the basis of race, even when citizens "decline to state." Enacting the Racial Privacy Initiative is the most significant step we can take to bring Americans together.

I ask all Americans who share the goal of a united America to join in this endeavor to fulfill our Founders' promise of colorblind justice before the law. For my part, I just don't want to be boxed in.

**Eduardo Bonilla-Silva**

 **NO**

# Racism without Racists: Color-Blind Racism and the Persistence of Racial Inequality in the United States

## The Strange Enigma of Race in Contemporary America

> There is a strange kind of enigma associated with the problem of racism. No one, or almost no one, wishes to see themselves as racist; still, racism persists, real and tenacious.
>
> —Albert Memmi, *Racism*

## Racism without "Racists"

Nowadays, except for members of white supremacist organizations, few whites in the United States claim to be "racist." Most whites assert they "don't see any color, just people"; that although the ugly face of discrimination is still with us, it is no longer the central factor determining minorities' life chances; and, finally, that like Dr. Martin Luther King Jr., they aspire to live in a society where "people are judged by the content of their character, not by the color of their skin." More poignantly, most whites insist that minorities (especially blacks) are the ones responsible for whatever "race problem" we have in this country. They publicly denounce blacks for "playing the race card," for demanding the maintenance of unnecessary and divisive race-based programs, such as affirmative action, and for crying "racism" whenever they are criticized by whites. Most whites believe that if blacks and other minorities would just stop thinking about the past, work hard, and complain less (particularly about racial discrimination), then Americans of all hues could "all get along."

But regardless of whites' "sincere fictions," racial considerations shade almost everything in America. Blacks and dark-skinned racial minorities lag well behind whites in virtually every area of social life; they are about three times more likely to be poor than whites, earn about 40 percent less than whites, and have about a tenth of the net worth that whites have. They also receive an inferior education compared to whites, even when they attend integrated institutions. In terms of housing, black-owned units comparable to white-owned ones are valued at 35 percent less. Blacks and Latinos also have less access to the entire housing market because whites, through a variety of exclusionary practices by white realtors and homeowners, have been successful in effectively limiting their entrance into many neighborhoods. Blacks receive impolite treatment in stores, in restaurants, and in a host of other commercial transactions. Researchers have also documented that blacks pay more for goods such as cars and houses than do whites. Finally, blacks and dark-skinned Latinos are the targets of racial profiling by the police that, combined with the highly racialized criminal court system, guarantees their overrepresentation among those arrested, prosecuted, incarcerated, and if charged for a capital crime, executed. Racial profiling in the highways has become such a prevalent phenomenon that a term has emerged to describe it: driving while black. In short, blacks and most minorities are, "at the bottom of the well."

How is it possible to have this tremendous degree of racial inequality in a country where most whites claim that race is no longer relevant? More important, how do whites explain the apparent contradiction between their professed color blindness and the United States' color-coded inequality? I contend that whites have developed powerful explanations—which have ultimately become justifications—for contemporary racial inequality that exculpate them from any responsibility for the status of people of color. These explanations emanate from a new racial ideology that I label *color-blind racism*. This ideology, which acquired cohesiveness and dominance in the late 1960s, explains contemporary racial inequality as the outcome of nonracial dynamics. Whereas Jim Crow racism explained blacks' social standing as the result of their biological and moral inferiority, color-blind racism avoids such facile arguments. Instead, whites rationalize minorities' contemporary status as the product of market dynamics, naturally occurring phenomena, and blacks' imputed cultural limitations. For instance, whites can attribute Latinos' high poverty rate to a relaxed work ethic ("the Hispanics are mañana, mañana, mañana—tomorrow, tomorrow, tomorrow") or residential segregation as the result of natural tendencies among groups ("Does a cat and a dog mix? I can't see it. You can't drink milk and scotch. Certain mixes don't mix.").

Color-blind racism became the dominant racial ideology as the mechanisms and practices for keeping blacks and other racial minorities "at the bottom of the well" changed. I have argued elsewhere that contemporary racial inequality is reproduced through "new racism" practices that are subtle, institutional, and apparently nonracial. In contrast to the Jim Crow era, where racial inequality was enforced through overt means (e.g., signs saying "No Niggers Welcomed Here" or shotgun diplomacy at the voting booth), today racial practices operate in "now you see it, now you don't" fashion. For example, residential segregation, which is almost as high today as it was in the past, is no longer accomplished through overtly discriminatory practices. Instead, covert behaviors such as not showing all the available units, steering minorities and whites into certain neighborhoods, quoting higher rents or prices to minority applicants, or not advertising units at all are the weapons of choice to maintain separate communities. In the economic field, "smiling face" discrimination ("We don't have jobs now, but please check later"), advertising job openings in mostly white networks and ethnic newspapers, and steering highly educated people of color into poorly remunerated jobs or jobs with limited opportunities for mobility are the new ways of keeping minorities in a secondary position. Politically, although the Civil Rights struggles have helped remove many of the obstacles for the electoral participation of people of color, "racial gerrymandering, multimember legislative districts, election runoffs, annexation of predominantly white areas, at-large district elections, and anti–single-shot devices (disallowing concentrating votes in one or two candidates in cities using at-large elections) have become standard practices to disenfranchise" people of color. Whether in banks, restaurants, school admissions, or housing transactions, the maintenance of white privilege is done in a way that defies facile racial readings. Hence, the contours of color-blind racism fit America's "new racism" quite well.

Compared to Jim Crow racism, the ideology of color blindness seems like "racism lite." Instead of relying on name calling (niggers, Spics, Chinks), color-blind racism otherizes softly ("these people are human, too"); instead of proclaiming God placed minorities in the world in a servile position, it suggests they are behind because they do not work hard enough; instead of viewing interracial marriage as wrong on a straight racial basis, it regards it as "problematic" because of concerns over the children, location, or the extra burden it places on couples. Yet this new ideology has become a formidable political tool for the maintenance of the racial order. Much as Jim Crow racism served as the glue for defending a brutal and overt system of racial oppression in the pre–Civil Rights era, color-blind racism serves today as the ideological armor for a covert and institutionalized system in the post–Civil Rights era. And the beauty of this new ideology is that it aids in the maintenance of white privilege without fanfare, without naming those who it subjects and those who it rewards. It allows a President to state things such as, "I strongly support diversity of all kinds, including racial diversity in higher education," yet, at the same time, to characterize the University of Michigan's affirmation action program as "flawed" and "discriminatory" against whites. Thus whites enunciate positions that safeguard their racial interests without sounding "racist." Shielded by color blindness, whites can express resentment toward minorities; criticize their morality, values, and work ethic; and even claim to be the victims of "reverse racism." This is the thesis I will defend to explain the curious enigma of "racism without racists."

## Whites' Racial Attitudes in the Post–Civil Rights Era

Since the late 1950s surveys on racial attitudes have consistently found that fewer whites subscribe to the views associated with Jim Crow. For example, whereas the majority of whites supported segregated neighborhoods, schools, transportation, jobs, and public accommodations in the 1940s, less than a quarter indicated they did in the 1970s. Similarly, fewer whites than ever now seem to subscribe to stereotypical views of blacks. Although the number is still high (ranging from 20 percent to 50 percent, depending on the stereotype), the proportion of whites who state in surveys that blacks are lazy, stupid, irresponsible, and violent has declined since the 1940s.

These changes in whites' racial attitudes have been explained by the survey community and commentators in four ways. First, are the *racial optimists*. This group of analysts agrees with whites' common sense on racial matters and believes the changes symbolize a profound transition in the United States. Early representatives of this view were Herbert Hyman and Paul B. Sheatsley, who wrote widely influential articles on the subject in *Scientific American*. In a reprint of their earlier work in the influential collection edited by Talcott Parsons and Kenneth Clark, *The Negro American*, Sheatsely rated the changes in white attitudes as "revolutionary" and concluded,

> The mass of white Americans have shown in many ways that they will not follow a racist government and that they will not follow racist leaders. Rather, they are engaged in the painful task of adjusting to an integrated society. It will not be easy for most, but one cannot at this late date doubt the basic commitment. In their hearts they know that the American Negro is right.

In recent times, Glenn Firebaugh and Kenneth Davis, Seymour Lipset, and Paul Sniderman and his coauthors, in particular, have carried the torch for racial optimists. Firebaugh and Davis, for example, based on their analysis of survey results from 1972 to 1984, concluded that the trend toward less anti-black prejudice was across the board. Sniderman and his coauthors, as well as Lipset, go a step further than Firebaugh and Davis because they have openly advocated color-blind politics *as the* way to settle the United States' racial dilemmas. For instance, Sniderman and Edward Carmines made this explicit appeal in their recent book, *Reaching Beyond Race*,

> To say that a commitment to a color-blind politics is worth undertaking is to call for a politics centered on the needs of those most in need. It is not to argue for a politics in which race is irrelevant, but in favor of one in which race is relevant so far as it is a gauge of need. Above all, it is a call for a politics which, because it is organized around moral principles that apply regardless of race, can be brought to bear with special force on the issue of race.

The problems with this optimistic interpretation are twofold. First, as I have argued elsewhere, relying on questions that were framed in the Jim Crow era to assess whites' racial views today produces an artificial image of progress. Since the central racial debates and the language used to debate those matters have changed, our analytical focus ought to be dedicated to the analysis of the new racial issues. Insisting on the need to rely on old questions to keep longitudinal (trend) data as the basis for analysis will, by default, produce a rosy picture of race relations that misses what is going on on the ground. Second, and more important, because of the change in the normative climate in the post–Civil Rights era, analysts must exert extreme caution when interpreting attitudinal data, particularly when it comes from single-method research designs. The research strategy that seems more appropriate for our times is mixed research designs (surveys used in combination with interviews, ethnosurveys, etc.), because it allows researchers to cross-examine their results.

A second, more numerous group of analysts exhibit what I have labeled elsewhere as the *racial pesoptimist* position. Racial pesoptimists attempt to strike a "balanced" view and suggest that whites' racial attitudes reflect progress and resistance. The classical example of this stance is Howard Schuman. Schuman has argued for more than thirty years that whites' racial attitudes involve a mixture of tolerance and intolerance, of acceptance of the principles of racial liberalism (equal opportunity for all, end of segregation, etc.) and a rejection of the policies that would make those principles a reality (from affirmative action to busing).

Despite the obvious appeal of this view in the research community (the appearance of neutrality, the pondering of "two sides," and this view's "balanced" component), racial pesoptimists are just closet optimists. Schuman, for example, has pointed out that, although "White responses to questions of principle are . . . more complex than is often portrayed . . . they nevertheless do show in almost every instance a positive movement over time." Furthermore, it is his belief that the normative change in the United States is real and that the issue is that whites are having a hard time translating those norms into personal preferences.

A third group of analysts argues that the changes in whites' attitudes represent the emergence of a *symbolic racism*. This tradition is associated with the work of David Sears and his associate, Donald Kinder. They have defined symbolic racism as "a blend of anti-black affect and the kind of traditional American moral values embodied in the Protestant Ethic." According to these authors, symbolic racism has replaced biological racism as the primary way whites express their racial resentment toward minorities. In Kinder and Sanders's words:

> A new form of prejudice has come to prominence, one that is preoccupied with matters of moral character, informed by the virtues associated with the traditions of individualism. At its center are the contentions that blacks do not try hard enough to overcome the difficulties they face and that they take what they have not earned. Today, we say, prejudice is expressed in the language of American individualism.

Authors in this tradition have been criticized for the slipperiness of the concept "symbolic racism," for claiming that the blend of antiblack affect and individualism is new, and for not explaining why symbolic racism came about. The first critique, developed by Howard Schuman, is that the concept has been "defined and operationalized in complex and varying ways." Despite this conceptual slipperiness, indexes of symbolic racism have been found to be in fact different from those of old-fashioned racism and to be strong predictors of whites' opposition to affirmative action. The two other critiques, made forcefully by Lawrence Bobo, have been partially addressed by Kinder and Sanders in their recent book, *Divided by Color*. First, Kinder and Sanders, as well as Sears, have made clear that their contention is not that this is the first time in history that antiblack affect and elements of the American Creed have combined. Instead, their claim is that this combination has become *central* to the new face of racism. Regarding the third critique, Kinder and Sanders go at length to explain the transition from old-fashioned to symbolic racism. Nevertheless, their explanation hinges on arguing that changes in blacks' tactics (from civil disobedience to urban violence) led to an onslaught of a new form of racial resentment that later found more fuel in controversies over welfare, crime, drugs, family, and affirmative action. What is missing in this explanation is a materially based explanation for why these changes occurred. Instead, their theory of prejudice is rooted in the "process of socialization and the operation of routine cognitive and emotional psychological processes."

Yet, despite its limitations, the symbolic racism tradition has brought attention to key elements of how whites explain racial inequality today. Whether this is "symbolic" of antiblack affect or not is beside the point and hard to assess, since as a former student of mine queried, "How does one test for the unconscious?"

The fourth explanation of whites' contemporary racial attitudes is associated with those who claim that whites' racial views represent a *sense of group position*. This position, forcefully advocated by Lawrence Bobo and James Kluegel, is similar to Jim Sidanius's "social dominance" and Mary Jackman's "group interests" arguments. In essence, the claim of all these authors is that white prejudice is an ideology to defend white privilege. Bobo and his associates have specifically suggested that because of socioeconomic changes that transpired in the 1950s and 1960s, *a laissez-faire racism* emerged that was fitting of the United States' "modern, nationwide, postindustrial free labor economy and polity." Laissez-faire racism "encompasses an ideology that blames blacks themselves for their poorer relative economic standing, seeing it as the function of perceived cultural inferiority."

Some of the basic arguments of authors in the symbolic and modern racism traditions and, particularly, of the laissez-faire racism view are fully compatible with my color-blind racism interpretation. As these authors, I argue that color-blind racism has rearticulated elements of traditional liberalism (work ethic, rewards by merit, equal opportunity, individualism, etc.) for racially illiberal goals. I also argue like them that whites today rely more on cultural rather than biological tropes to explain blacks' position in this country. Finally, I concur with most analysts of post–Civil Rights' matters in arguing that whites do not perceive discrimination to be a central factor shaping blacks' life chances.

Although most of my differences with authors in the symbolic racism and laissez-faire traditions are methodological, I have one central theoretical disagreement with them. Theoretically, most of these authors are still snarled in the prejudice problematic and thus interpret actors' racial views as *individual psychological* dispositions. Although Bobo and his associates have a conceptualization that is closer to mine, they still retain the notion of prejudice and its psychological baggage rooted in interracial hostility. In contrast, my model is not anchored in actors' affective dispositions (although affective dispositions may be manifest or latent in the way many express their racial views). Instead, it is based on a materialist interpretation of racial matters and thus sees the views of actors as corresponding to their systemic location. Those at the bottom of the racial barrel tend to hold oppositional views and those who receive the manifold wages of whiteness tend to hold views in support of the racial status quo. Whether actors express "resentment" or "hostility" toward minorities is largely irrelevant for the maintenance of white privilege. As David Wellman points out in his *Portraits of White Racism*, "[p]rejudiced people are not the only racists in America."

## Key Terms: Race, Racial Structure, and Racial Ideology

One reason why, in general terms, whites and people of color cannot agree on racial matters is because they conceive terms such as "racism" very differently. Whereas for most whites racism is prejudice, for most people of color racism is systemic or institutionalized. Although this is not a theory book, my examination of color-blind racism has etched in it the indelible ink of a "regime of truth" about how the world is organized. Thus, rather than hiding my theoretical assumptions, I state them openly for the benefit of readers and potential critics.

The first key term is the notion of *race*. There is very little formal disagreement among social scientists in accepting the idea that race is a socially constructed category. This means that notions of racial difference are human creations rather than eternal, essential categories. As such, racial categories have a history and are subject to change. And here ends the agreement among social scientists on this matter. There are at least three distinct variations on how social scientists approach this constructionist perspective on race. The first approach, which is gaining popularity among white social scientists, is the idea that because race is socially constructed, it is not a fundamental category of analysis and praxis. Some analysts go as far as to suggest that because race is a constructed category, then it is not real and social scientists who use the category are the ones who make it real.

The second approach, typical of most sociological writing on race, gives lip service to the social constructionist view—usually a line in the beginning of the article or book. Writers in this group then proceed to discuss "racial" differences in academic achievement, crime, and SAT scores as if they were truly racial. This is the central way in which contemporary scholars contribute to the propagation of racist interpretations of racial inequality. By failing to highlight the social dynamics that produce these racial differences, these scholars help reinforce the racial order.

The third approach, and the one I use in this book, acknowledges that race, as other social categories such as class and gender, is constructed but insists that it has a *social* reality. This means that after race—or class or gender—is created, it produces real effects on the actors racialized as "black" or "white." Although race, as other social constructions, is unstable, it has a "changing same" quality at its core.

In order to explain how a socially constructed category produces real race effects, I need to introduce a second key term, the notion of *racial structure*. When race emerged in human history, it formed a social structure (a racialized social system) that awarded systemic privileges to Europeans (the peoples who became "white") over non-Europeans (the peoples who became "nonwhite"). Racialized social systems, or white supremacy for short, became global and affected all societies where Europeans extended their reach. I therefore conceive a society's racial structure as *the totality of the social relations and practices that reinforce white privilege.* Accordingly, the task of analysts interested in studying racial structures is to uncover the particular social, economic, political, social control, and ideological mechanisms responsible for the reproduction of racial privilege in a society.

But why are racial structures reproduced in the first place? Would not humans, after discovering the folly of racial thinking, work to abolish race as a category as well as a practice? Racial structures remain in place for the same reasons that other structures do. Since actors racialized as "white"—or as members of the dominant race—receive material benefits from the racial order, they struggle (or passively receive the manifold wages of whiteness) to maintain their privileges. In contrast, those defined as belonging to the subordinate race or races struggle to change the status quo (or become resigned to their position). Therein lies the secret of racial structures and racial inequality the world over. They exist because they benefit members of the dominant race.

If the ultimate goal of the dominant race is to defend its collective interests (i.e., the perpetuation of systemic white privilege), it should surprise no one that this group develops rationalizations to account for the status of the various races. And here I introduce my third key term, the notion of *racial ideology.* By this I mean *the racially based frameworks used by actors to explain and justify* (dominant race) or *challenge* (subordinate race or races) *the racial status quo.* Although all the races in a racialized social system have the *capacity* of developing these frameworks, the frameworks of the dominant race tend to become the master frameworks upon which *all* racial actors ground (for or against) their ideological positions. Why? Because as Marx pointed out in *The German Ideology,* "the ruling *material* force of society, is at the same time its ruling *intellectual* force." This does not mean that ideology is almighty. In fact, ideological rule is always partial. Even in periods of hegemonic rule, such as the current one, subordinate racial groups develop oppositional views. However, it would be foolish to believe that those who rule a society do not have the power to at least color (pun intended) the views of the ruled.

Racial ideology can be conceived for analytical purposes as comprising the following elements: common frames, style, and racial stories. The frames that bond together a particular racial ideology are rooted in the group-based conditions and experiences of the races and are, at the symbolic level, the representations developed by these groups to explain how the world is or ought to be. And because the group life of the various racially defined groups is based on hierarchy and domination, the ruling ideology expresses as "common sense" the interests of the dominant race, while oppositional ideologies attempt to challenge that common sense by providing alternative frames, ideas, and stories based on the experiences of subordinated races.

Individual actors employ these elements as "building blocks . . . for manufacturing versions on actions, self, and social structures" in communicative situations. The looseness of the elements allows users to maneuver within various contexts (e.g., responding to a race-related survey, discussing racial issues with family, or arguing about affirmative action in a college classroom) and produce various accounts and presentations of self (e.g., appearing ambivalent, tolerant, or strong minded). This loose character enhances the legitimating role of racial ideology because it allows for accommodation of contradictions, exceptions, and new information. As Jackman points out about ideology in general: "Indeed, the strength of an ideology lies in its loose-jointed, flexible application. *An ideology is a political instrument, not an exercise in personal logic:* consistency is rigidity, the only pragmatic effect of which is to box oneself in."

Before I can proceed, two important caveats should be offered. First, although whites, because of their privileged position in the racial order, form a social group (the dominant race), they are fractured along class, gender, sexual orientation, and other forms of "social cleavage." Hence, they have multiple and often contradictory interests that are not easy to disentangle and that predict *a priori* their mobilizing capacity (Do white workers have more in common with white capitalists than with black workers?). However, because all actors awarded the dominant racial position, regardless of their multiple structural locations (men or women, gay or straight, working class or bourgeois) benefit from what Mills calls the "racial contract," *most* have historically endorsed the ideas that justify the racial status quo.

Second, although not every single member of the dominant race defends the racial status quo or spouts color-blind racism, *most* do. To explain this point by analogy, although not every capitalist defends capitalism (e.g., Frederick Engels, the coauthor of *The Communist Manifesto,* was a capitalist) and not every man defends patriarchy (e.g., *Achilles Heel* is an English magazine published by feminist men), *most* do in some fashion. In the same vein, although some whites fight white supremacy and do not endorse white common sense, *most* subscribe to substantial portions of it in a casual, uncritical fashion that helps sustain the prevailing racial order. . . .

If instead one regards racial ideology as in fact changing, the reliance on questions developed to tackle issues from the Jim Crow era will produce an artificial image of progress and miss most of whites' contemporary racial nightmares.

Despite my conceptual and methodological concerns with survey research, I believe well-designed surveys are still useful instruments to glance at America's racial reality. Therefore, I report survey results from my own research projects as well as from research conducted by other scholars whenever appropriate. My point, then, is not to deny attitudinal change or to condemn to oblivion survey research on racial attitudes, but to understand whites' new racial beliefs and their implications as well as possible. . . .

## One Important Caveat

The purpose of this book is not to demonize whites or label them "racist." Hunting for "racists" is the sport of choice of those who practice the "clinical approach" to race relations—the careful separation of good and bad, tolerant and intolerant Americans. Because this book is anchored in a structural understanding of race relations, my goal is to uncover the collective practices (in this book, the ideological ones) that help reinforce the contemporary racial order. Historically, many good people supported slavery and Jim Crow. Similarly, most color-blind whites who oppose (or have serious reservations about) affirmative action, believe that blacks' problems are mostly their own doing, and do not see anything wrong with their own white lifestyle are good people, too. The analytical issue, then, is examining how many whites subscribe to an ideology that ultimately helps preserve racial inequality rather than assessing how many hate or love blacks and other minorities.

. . . Since color-blind racism is the dominant racial ideology, its tentacles have touched us all and thus most readers will subscribe to some—if not most—of its tenets, use its style, and believe many of its racial stories. Unfortunately, there is little I can do to ease the pain of these readers, since when one writes and exposes an ideology that is at play, its supporters "get burned," so to speak. For readers in this situation (good people who may subscribe to many of the frames of color blindness), I urge a personal and political movement away from claiming to be "nonracist" to becoming "antiracist." Being an antiracist begins with understanding the institutional nature of racial matters and accepting that all actors in a racialized society are affected *materially* (receive benefits or disadvantages) and *ideologically* by the racial structure. This stand implies taking responsibility for your unwilling participation in these practices and beginning a new life committed to the goal of achieving real racial equality. The ride will be rough, but after your eyes have been opened, there is no point in standing still.

# POSTSCRIPT

## Is the Emphasis on a Color-Blind Society an Answer to Racism?

One of the highlights of the civil rights movement was the speech delivered by Dr. Martin Luther King, Jr. during the March on Washington of August 1963. Exhibiting the soaring oratory to which the nation and world had become accustomed, this drum major of civil rights advocacy espoused a profound vision of an American future in which people are not judged by the color of their skins, but, rather, by the content of their character as they seek civil rights, equity, and respect for their humanity and human dignity within society. King's words have been used and misused by both sides of the color-blind issue. Connerly would argue that if King were alive today, he would support the color-blind thesis. Bonilla-Silva, on the other hand, would argue that King would never recognize the current color-blind ideology as a basis for racial progress because of persistent race prejudice and discrimination within society.

Despite the efforts of Dr. King and other supporters of civil rights and social justice for African Americans and others of color, the United States is still a nation within which color-consciousness and color-coded decision making is broadly prevalent. The American language and culture are laden with color-coded references such as whites/people of color, black neighborhood/white neighborhood, chocolate cities/vanilla suburbs, and many others. As the Latino population grows and receives more public attention, white Latino references are increasingly found within linguistic expression. It is common to observe the white Latino versus the black Latino and increasingly Latinos collectively are assigned the identity of "brown." Note Issue 4 and Samuel Huntington's critique of Mexican immigration.

In June 1994, the publishers of *Time* magazine were so confident that the American public responds to color-coded communications that it darkened the image of OJ Simpson appearing on one of its covers. This dramatized the image of the sinister black male stereotype and crime. While part of the culture ramps up the idea of color-blindness, here we see mainstream publications use color to distinguish and define racial differences. This interesting paradox has the guise of appearing to be race-neutral. Also, some like Bonilla-Silva argue that it is a new form of racism—that is, on the one hand, a denial of race differences, but on the other, a perpetuation of racial stereotypes.

Students should be aware that the promotion of a color-blind ideology as social reform raises significant questions. Given the reality of a color-conscious American culture that has lasted for nearly four centuries,

146

how plausible is the achievement of this goal? Is the color-blind thesis as benign as it appears? What is the potential impact of color-blind ideology on black identity? Red? Yellow? Brown? Does color-blind ideology serve as a mask for white privilege? Does the promotion of color-blind ideology undermine civil rights and social justice organization and advocacy? These are among the salient questions that confront this issue.

There is also a plethora of research and published scholarship in a number of disciplines that is focused on the effects of skin color within society. For example, there are works being published in criminology and criminal justice to examine the effects of color-coded decision making— *The Color of Justice* by Walker, Spohn, and DeLeon; *The Color of Crime* by Katherine K. Russell; and *Images of Color, Images of Crime* by Mann, Zatz, and Rodriguez.

Additionally, students should be cognizant of the proliferation of literature within this new field, white studies involved in critical examinations of the meaning of whiteness, white identity, white privilege, the dynamic boundaries of whiteness, among other pertinent issues. For further reading David R. Roediger, in *Colored White: Transcending the Racial Past,* argues that racism is a creation of culture and politics. He shows the need for political activism that would transform both the social and political meaning of race. *Whiteness: Feminist Philosophical Reflections,* edited by Chris J. Cuomo and Kim Q. Hall, presents essays on whiteness and feminism. In *Who Is White?: Latinos, Asians, and the Black/Nonblack Divide,* George Yancey explores the shifting boundaries of whiteness in this significant work on white identity.

For a critical examination of white supremacist organizations, see *White Power, White Pride!: The White Separatist Movement in the United States* (Twayne Publishers, 1997) by Betty A. Dobratz and Stephanie L. Shanks-Meile. Robert Lovato's "A New Vision of Immigration" (*The Nation,* March 6, 2006) is a progressive examination of immigration policy concerns within a global context. Also interesting in this area are Cuomo and Hall's *Whiteness: Feminist Philosophical Reflections* (Rowman & Littlefield Publishers, 1999) and David Roediger's *Colored White: Transcending the Racial Past* (University of California Press, 2002). Lawrence Wright, in "One Drop of Blood" (*The New Yorker,* July 12, 1993), discusses multiracial groups who, in the 1990s, did not fit into the government's traditional categories of race and ethnicity and began to challenge them as too narrow and inaccurate.

To gain a context for the place of color-blind ideology in modern American history, students are urged to read Martin Luther King's *Stride Toward Freedom* (Harper Collins, 1987), *Why We Can't Wait* (Harper Collins, 1964), and *Where Do We Go from Here: Chaos or Community?* (Harper & Row, 1967). King notes that since color-conscious practices are the source of black disadvantage, policies that address these problems should be color-conscious. In *Black, White, and Southern: Race relations and Southern Culture 1940 to the Present* (Louisiana State University Press, 1990), D. R. Goldfield examines the development of race relations since World War II.

# ISSUE 8

## Is the Claim of White Skin Privilege a Myth?

**YES: Paul Kivel,** from *Uprooting Racism: How White People Can Work for Racial Justice* (New Society, 1996)

**NO: Tim Wise,** from "The Absurdity (and Consistency) of White Denial: What Kind of Card Is Race?" http://www.counterpunch.org/wise04242006.html (April 24, 2006)

### ISSUE SUMMARY

**YES:** Paul Kivel, a teacher, writer, and anti-violence/anti-racist activist, asserts that many benefits accrue to whites based solely on skin color. These benefits range from economic to political advantages and so often include better residential choice, police protection, and education opportunities.

**NO:** Tim Wise, an author of two books on race, argues that whites do not acknowledge privilege. Instead, whites are often convinced that the race card is "played" by blacks to gain their own privilege, something that whites cannot do. Hence, whites simply do not see discrimination and do not attach privilege to their skin color.

**W**.E.B. DuBois has reminded us of the centrality of skin color when he noted that issues of color would dominate human relations of the twentieth century. In the United States, African American children tend to develop a keen understanding of the impact of color in social/race relations when they sang from blues singer Big Bill Broonzy's 1951 composition "Black, Brown and White":

> If you're white, you're alright!
> If you're brown, stick around!
> And, if you're black, get back!

These lines were uttered routinely by black children during their developmental years within the United States. It reminds us of the salience of skin color for racial identity.

There is a consensus view among scholars that racial distinctions were not a primary factor influencing human relations in the premodern world. The more substantial influence of race within society tends to be a more recent phenomenon influencing modern cultures and civilizations, especially institutional arrangements such as slavery and segregation. So, the issue of white skin privilege falls in the larger context of race identity in American history.

Clearly, the formation of racial consciousness and its impact upon society is a vital area of scholarly investigation in a world characterized by nations of increasing racial/ethnic diversity. Naomi Zack, in *Thinking About Race*, explains the rise of whiteness studies in perspective. Most recent immigration and demographic trends have led to what has been called "the browning of America." A significant increase in Latino and Asian immigration, along with white-nonwhite intermarriage, symbolizes the decrease in the number of whites as a majority. Many scholars see this browning as having the effect of stimulating an increase of white self-awareness.

Minority groups are seen in terms of small numbers compared to the majority white population. More important, sociologically, is the dominant-subordinate relationship. Throughout the world, although whites do not constitute a majority, they represent a dominant group (people who have the most wealth, power, and possessions). The reality of privilege is so embedded within dominant group status that to recognize and admit its reality is alien to most whites.

Whites are often asked to think about race from a minority point of view. Throughout one's years of formal education, there is an emphasis upon tolerance and understanding, which enable dominant group whites to appreciate minority group experiences. Despite the built-in limitations of viewing things from the point of view of another race, color shifting can enable one to view one's own race differently. Paul Kivel sees race privilege as white, middle-class privilege. It is not something to be earned; it is viewed as a birthright. It comes with economic, social, and political benefits. Wise, in contrast, argues that whites are oblivious to the notion of skin privilege. Further, he uses the white allegation of "playing the race card," which is directed at blacks, to demonstrate that whites do not think skin privilege exists.

Many Americans believe that white skin privilege is a myth. It is common for such persons to assert that if such a privilege did exist in the past, it has been overtaken by the reforms of the civil rights era and the color-blind, race-neutral (deracialized) atmosphere that has resulted from these developments. Such observers of current social trends tend to cite the significant expansion of the African American middle class, the more visible presence of blacks and other people of color within American institutions most especially, within the professions, and the increasing profile of black/minority athletes in support of their claim.

Such assertions do not answer the question posed for this selection adequately. There is copious empirical evidence that significant inequity in such vital areas as wealth, income, education, employment, etc. exist between whites and people of color, especially blacks and Latinos. Both groups are disproportionately represented within the lower strata of the class structure. How can this persistent advantage of whites over others be explained? Is it due to white intellectual superiority? Can it be explained by the assertion that whites are more industrious and motivated? Or, is white privilege part of it?

# YES

**Paul Kivel**

# Uprooting Racism: How White People Can Work for Racial Justice

## White Benefits, Middle Class Privilege

It is not necessarily a privilege to be white*, but it certainly has its benefits. That's why so many of us gave up our unique histories, primary languages, accents, distinctive dress, family names and cultural expressions. It seemed like a small price to pay for acceptance in the circle of whiteness. Even with these sacrifices it wasn't easy to pass as white if we were Italian, Greek, Irish, Jewish, Spanish, Hungarian, or Polish. Sometimes it took generations before our families were fully accepted, and then usually because white society had an even greater fear of darker skinned people.

Privileges are the economic "extras" that those of us who are middle class and wealthy gain at the expense of poor and working class people of all races. Benefits, on the other hand, are the advantages that all white people gain at the expense of people of color regardless of economic position. Talk about racial benefits can ring false to many of us who don't have the economic privileges that we see many in this society enjoying. But just because we don't have the economic privileges of those with more money doesn't mean we haven't enjoyed some of the benefits of being white.

We can generally count on police protection rather than harassment. Depending on our financial situation, we can choose where we want to live and choose neighborhoods that are safe and have decent schools. We are given more attention, respect and status in conversations than people of color. We see people who look like us in the media, history books, news and music in a positive light. (This is more true for men than for women, more true for the rich than the poor.) We have more recourse to, and credibility within, the legal system (again taking into account class and gender). Nothing that we do is qualified, limited, discredited or acclaimed simply because of our racial background. We don't have to represent our race, and nothing we do is judged as a credit to our race, or as confirmation of its

---

*I draw on important work on privilege done by Peggy McIntosh, "White Privilege and Male Privilege: A Personal Account of Coming to See Correspondences Through Work in Women's Studies," Center for Research on Women, Wellesley College, MA 02181 (1988), as well as material from *Helping Teens Stop Violence*, Allan Creighton with Paul Kivel, Hunter House, Alameda CA (1992).

shortcomings or inferiority. There are always mitigating factors, and some of us have these benefits more than others. All else being equal, it pays to be white. We will be accepted, acknowledged and given the benefit of the doubt. Since all else is not equal we each receive different benefits or different levels of the same benefits from being white.

These benefits start early. Most of them apply less to white girls than white boys, but they are still substantial. Others will have higher expectations for us as children, both at home and at school. We will have more money spent on our education, we will be called on more in school, we will be given more opportunity and resources to learn. We will see people like us in the textbooks, and if we get into trouble adults will expect us to be able to change and improve, and therefore will discipline or penalize us less or differently than children of color.

These benefits continue today and work to the direct economic advantage of every white person in the United States. First of all, we will earn more in our lifetime than a person of color of similar qualifications. We will be paid $1.00 for every $.60 that a person of color makes. We will advance faster and more reliably as well.

There are historically derived economic benefits too. All the land in this country was taken from Native Americans. Much of the infrastructure of this country was built by slave labor, incredibly low-paid labor, or by prison labor performed by men and women of color. Much of the housecleaning, childcare, cooking and maintenance of our society has been done by low wage earning women of color. Further property and material goods were appropriated by whites through the colonization of the West and Southwest throughout the 19th century, through the internment of Japanese Americans during World War II, through racial riots against people of color in the 18th, 19th and 20th centuries, and through an ongoing legacy of legal manipulation and exploitation. Today men and women and children of color still do the hardest, lowest paid, most dangerous work throughout the country. And we white people, again depending on our relative economic circumstances, enjoy plentiful and inexpensive food, clothing and consumer goods because of that exploitation.

We have been taught history through a white-tinted lens which has minimized our exploitation of people of color and extolled the hardworking, courageous qualities of white people. For example, many of our foreparents gained a foothold in this country by finding work in such trades as railroads, streetcars, construction, shipbuilding, Wagon and coach driving, house painting, tailoring, longshore work, brick laying, table waiting, working in the mills, furriering or dressmaking. These were all occupations that Blacks, who had begun entering many such skilled and unskilled jobs, were either excluded from or pushed out of in the nineteenth century. Exclusion and discrimination, coupled with immigrant mob violence against Blacks in many northern cities (such as the anti-black draft riots of 1863), meant that recent immigrants had economic opportunities that Blacks did not. These gains were consolidated by explicitly racist trade union practices and policies which kept Blacks in the most unskilled labor and lowest paid work.

It is not that white Americans have not worked hard and built much. We have. But we did not start out from scratch. We went to segregated schools and universities built with public money. We received school loans, V.A. loans, housing and auto loans when people of color were excluded or heavily discriminated against. We received federal jobs, military jobs and contracts when only whites were allowed. We were accepted into apprenticeships, training programs and unions when access for people of color was restricted or nonexistent.

Much of the rhetoric against more active policies for racial justice stem from the misconception that we are all given equal opportunities and start from a level playing field. We often don't even see the benefits we have received from racism. We claim that they are not there.

Think about your grandparents and parents and where they grew up and lived as adults. What work did they do? What are some of the benefits that have accrued to your family because they were white?

Look at the following benefits checklist. Put a check beside any benefit that you enjoy that a person of color of your age, gender and class probably does not. Think about what effect not having that benefit would have had on your life. (If you don't know the answer to any of these questions, research. Ask family members. Do what you can to discover the answers.)

## White Benefits Checklist

- My ancestors were legal immigrants to this country during a period when immigrants from Asia, South and Central America or Africa were restricted.
- My ancestors came to this country of their own free will and have never had to relocate unwillingly once here.
- I live on land that formerly belonged to Native Americans.
- My family received homesteading or landstaking claims from the federal government.
- I or my family or relatives receive or received federal farm subsidies, farm price supports, agricultural extension assistance or other federal benefits.
- I lived or live in a neighborhood that people of color were discriminated from living in.
- I lived or live in a city where red-lining discriminates against people of color getting housing or other loans.
- I or my parents went to racially segregated schools.
- I live in a school district or metropolitan area where more money is spent on the schools that white children go to than on those that children of color attend.
- I live in or went to a school district where children of color are more likely to be disciplined than white children, or more likely to be tracked into nonacademic programs.
- I live in or went to a school district where the textbooks and other classroom materials reflected my race as normal, heroes and builders of the United States, and there was little mention of the contributions of people of color to our society.

- I was encouraged to go on to college by teachers, parents or other advisors.
- I attended a publicly funded university, or a heavily endowed private university or college, and/or received student loans.
- I served in the military when it was still racially segregated, or achieved a rank where there were few people of color, or served in a combat situation where there were large numbers of people of color in dangerous combat positions.
- My ancestors were immigrants who took jobs in railroads, street-cars, construction, shipbuilding, wagon and coach driving, house painting, tailoring, longshore work, brick laying, table waiting, working in the mills, furriering, dressmaking or any other trade or occupation where people of color were driven out or excluded.
- I received job training in a program where there were few or no people of color
- I have received a job, job interview, job training or internship through personal connections of family or friends.
- I worked or work in a job where people of color made less for doing comparable work or did more menial jobs.
- I have worked in a job where people of color were hired last, or fired first.
- I work in a job, career or profession, or in an agency or organization in which there are few people of color.
- I received small business loans or credits, government contracts or government assistance in my business.
- My parents were able to vote in any election they wanted without worrying about poll taxes, literacy requirements or other forms of discrimination.
- I can always vote for candidates who reflect my race.
- I live in a neighborhood that has better police protection, municipal services and is safer than that where people of color live.
- The hospital and medical services close to me or which I use are better than that of most people of color in the region in which I live.
- I have never had to worry that clearly labeled public facilities, such as swimming pools, restrooms, restaurants and nightspots were in fact not open to me because of my skin color.
- I see white people in a wide variety of roles on television and in movies.
- My race needn't be a factor in where I choose to live.
- My race needn't be a factor in where I send my children to school.
- I don't need to think about race and racism everyday. I can choose when and where I want to respond to racism.

What feelings come up for you when you think about the benefits that white people gain from racism? Do you feel angry or resentful? Guilty or uncomfortable? Do you want to say "Yes, but . . . "?

Again, the purpose of this checklist is not to discount what we, our families and foreparents, have achieved. But we do need to question any assumptions we retain that everyone started out with equal opportunity.

You may be thinking at this point, "If I'm doing so well how come I'm barely making it?" Some of the benefits listed previously are money in the bank for each and every one of us. Some of us have bigger bank accounts—much bigger. According to 1989 figures, 1 percent of the population controls about 40 percent of the wealth of this country (*New York Times*, April 17, 1995 "Gap in Wealth in United States called Widest in West"). In 1992, women generally made about 66 cents for every dollar that men made (Women's Action Coalition p. 59).

Benefits from racism are amplified or diminished by our relative privilege. People with disabilities, people with less formal education, and people who are lesbian, gay or bi-sexual are generally discriminated against in major ways. All of us benefit in some ways from whiteness, but some of us have cornered the market on significant benefits from being white to the exclusion of the rest of us.

The opposite of a benefit is a disadvantage. People of color face distinct disadvantages many of which have to do with discrimination and violence. If we were to talk about running a race for achievement and success in this country, and white people and people of color lined up side by side as a group, then every white benefit would be steps ahead of the starting line and every disadvantage would be steps backwards from the starting line before the race even began.

The disadvantages of being a person of color in the United States today include personal insults, harassment, discrimination, economic and cultural exploitation, stereotypes and invisibility, as well as threats, intimidation and violence. Not every person of color has experienced all the disadvantages described below, but they each have experienced some of them, and they each experience the vulnerability to violence that being a person of color in this country entails.

Institutional racism is discussed in detail in parts four, five, and six. But the personal acts of harassment and discrimination experienced directly from individual white people can also take a devastating toll. People of color never know when they will be called names, ridiculed or have comments made to them or about them by white people they don't know. They don't know when they might hear that they should leave the country, go home or go back to where they came from. Often these comments are made in situations where it isn't safe to confront the person who made the remark.

People of color also have to be ready to respond to teachers, employers or supervisors who have stereotypes, prejudices or lowered expectations about them. Many have been discouraged or prevented from pursuing academic or work goals or have been placed in lower vocational levels because of their racial identity. They have to be prepared for receiving less respect, attention or response from a doctor, police officer, court official, city official or other professional. They are not unlikely to be mistrusted or accused of stealing, cheating or lying, or to be stopped by the police because of their racial identity. They may also experience employment or housing discrimination or know someone who has.

There are cultural costs as well. People of color see themselves portrayed in degrading, stereotypical and fear-inducing ways on television and in the movies. They may have important religious or cultural holidays which are not recognized where they work or go to school. They have seen their religious practices, music, art, mannerisms, dress and other customs distorted, "borrowed," ridiculed, exploited or otherwise degraded by white people.

If they protest they may be verbally attacked by whites for being too sensitive, too emotional or too angry. Or they may be told they are different from other people of their racial group. Much of what people of color do, or say, or how they act in racially mixed company is judged as representative of their race.

On top of all this they have to live with the threat of physical violence. Some are the survivors of racial violence or have had close friends or family who are. People of color experience the daily toll of having to plan out how they are going to respond to racist comments and racial discrimination whenever it might occur.

In the foot race referred to above for jobs, educational opportunities or housing, each of these disadvantages would represent a step backward from the starting line *before the race even started.*

Although all people of color have experienced some of the disadvantages mentioned above, other factors make a difference in how vulnerable a person of color is to the effects of racism. Economic resources help buffer some of the more egregious effects of racism. Depending upon where one lives, women and men from different racial identities are treated differently. Discrimination varies in form and ranges from mild to severe depending on one's skin color, ethnicity, level of education, location, gender, sexual orientation, physical ability, age and how these are responded to by white people and white-run institutions.

Is it hard for you to accept that this kind of pervasive discrimination still occurs in this country? Which of the above statements is particularly hard to accept?

There is ample documentation for each of the effects of racism on people of color listed above. In many workshops we do a stand up exercise using a list of disadvantages for people of color to respond to. Those of us who are white are often surprised and disturbed about how many people of color stand when asked if they have experienced these things.

Most of us would like to think that today we have turned the tide and people of color have caught up with white people. We would like to believe (and are often told by other white people) that they enjoy the same opportunities as the rest of us. If we honestly add up the benefits of whiteness and the disadvantages of being a person of color, we can see that existing affirmative action programs don't go very far toward leveling the playing field.

The benefits of being white should be enjoyed by every person in this country. No one should have to endure the disadvantages that people of color experience. In leveling the playing field we don't want to hold anyone back. We want to push everyone forward so that we all share the benefits.

When we talk about the unequal distribution of benefits and disadvantages, we may feel uncomfortable about being white. We did not choose our skin color. Nor are we guilty for the fact that racism exists and that we have benefitted from it. We are responsible for acknowledging the reality of racist and for the daily choices we make about how to live in a racist society. We are only responsible for our own part, and we each have a part.

Sometimes, to avoid accepting our part, we want to shoot the bearer of bad news. Whether the bearer is white or a person of color, we become angry at whoever points out a comment or action that is hurtful, ignorant or abusive. We may accuse the person of being racist. This evasive reaction creates a debate about who is racist, or correct, or good, or well-intentioned, not about what to do about racism. It is probably inevitable that, when faced with the reality of the benefits and the harm of racism, we will feel defensive, guilty, ashamed, angry, powerless, frustrated or sad. These feelings are healthy and need to be acknowledged. Because they are uncomfortable we are liable to become angry at whoever brought up the subject.

Acknowledge your feelings and any resistance you have to the information presented above. Keep reading through this book and doing the exercises. Yes, it is hard and sometimes discouraging. For too long we have ignored or denied the realities of racism. In order to make any changes, we have to start by facing where we are and making a commitment to persevere and overcome the injustices we face.

We can support each other through the feelings. We need a safe place to talk about how it feels to be white and know about racism. It is important that we turn to other white people for this support. Who are white people you can talk with about racism?

When people say, "We all have it hard," or "Everyone has an equal opportunity," or "People of color just want special privileges," how can you use the information in this book to respond? What might be difficult about doing so? What additional information or resources will you need to be able to do this with confidence? How might you find those resources?

**Tim Wise**

# The Absurdity (and Consistency) of White Denial: What Kind of Card Is Race?

**R**ecently, I was asked by someone in the audience of one of my speeches, whether or not I believed that racism—though certainly a problem—might also be something conjured up by people of color in situations where the charge was inappropriate. In other words, did I believe that occasionally folks play the so-called race card, as a ploy to gain sympathy or detract from their own shortcomings? In the process of his query, the questioner made his own opinion all too clear (an unambiguous yes), and in that, he was not alone, as indicated by the reaction of others in the crowd, as well as survey data confirming that the belief in black malingering about racism is nothing if not ubiquitous.

It's a question I'm asked often, especially when there are several high-profile news events transpiring, in which race informs part of the narrative. Now is one of those times, as a few recent incidents demonstrate: Is racism, for example, implicated in the alleged rape of a young black woman by white members of the Duke University lacrosse team? Was racism implicated in Congresswoman Cynthia McKinney's recent confrontation with a member of the Capitol police? Or is racism involved in the ongoing investigation into whether or not Barry Bonds—as he is poised to eclipse white slugger Babe Ruth on the all-time home run list—might have used steroids to enhance his performance?*

Although the matter is open to debate in any or all of these cases, white folks have been quick to accuse blacks who answer in the affirmative of playing the race card, as if their conclusions have been reached not because of careful consideration of the facts as they see them, but rather, because of some irrational (even borderline paranoid) tendency to see racism everywhere. So too, discussions over immigration, "terrorist" profiling, and Katrina and its aftermath often turn on issues of race, and so give rise to the charge that as regards these subjects, people of color are "overreacting" when they allege racism in one or another circumstance.

Asked about the tendency for people of color to play the "race card," I responded as I always do: First, by noting that the regularity with which whites respond to charges of racism by calling said charges a ploy, suggests that the race card is, at best, equivalent to the two of diamonds. In other words, it's not much of a card to play, calling into question why anyone would play it (as if it were really going to get them somewhere). Secondly, I pointed out that white reluctance to acknowledge racism isn't new, and it isn't something that manifests only in situations where the racial aspect of an incident is arguable. Fact is, whites have always doubted claims of racism at the time they were being made, no matter how strong the evidence, as will be seen below. Finally, I concluded by suggesting that whatever "card" claims of racism may prove to be for the black and brown, the denial card is far and away the trump, and whites play it regularly: a subject to which we will return.

## Turning Injustice into a Game of Chance: The Origins of Race as "Card"

First, let us consider the history of this notion: namely, that the "race card" is something people of color play so as to distract the rest of us, or to gain sympathy. For most Americans, the phrase "playing the race card" entered the national lexicon during the O.J. Simpson trial. Robert Shapiro, one of Simpson's attorneys famously claimed, in the aftermath of his client's acquittal, that co-counsel Johnnie Cochran had "played the race card, and dealt it from the bottom of the deck." The allegation referred to Cochran's bringing up officer Mark Fuhrman's regular use of the 'n-word' as potentially indicative of his propensity to frame Simpson. To Shapiro, whose own views of his client's innocence apparently shifted over time, the issue of race had no place in the trial, and even if Fuhrman was a racist, this fact had no bearing on whether or not O.J. had killed his ex-wife and Ron Goldman. In other words, the idea that O.J. had been framed because of racism made no sense and to bring it up was to interject race into an arena where it was, or should have been, irrelevant.

That a white man like Shapiro could make such an argument, however, speaks to the widely divergent way in which whites and blacks view our respective worlds. For people of color—especially African Americans—the idea that racist cops might frame members of their community is no abstract notion, let alone an exercise in irrational conspiracy theorizing. Rather, it speaks to a social reality about which blacks are acutely aware. Indeed, there has been a history of such misconduct on the part of law enforcement, and for black folks to think those bad old days have ended is, for many, to let down their guard to the possibility of real and persistent injury.[1]

So if a racist cop is the lead detective in a case, and the one who discovers blood evidence implicating a black man accused of killing two white people, there is a logical alarm bell that goes off in the head of most any black person, but which would remain every bit as silent in the mind of someone who was white. And this too is understandable: for most whites, police are the helpful folks who get your cat out of the tree, or take you around in their patrol car for fun. For us, the idea of brutality or misconduct on the part of such persons seems remote, to the point of being fanciful. It seems the stuff of bad TV dramas, or at the very least, the past—that always remote place to which we can consign our national sins and predations, content all the while that whatever demons may have lurked in those earlier times have long since been vanquished.

To whites, blacks who alleged racism in the O.J. case were being absurd, or worse, seeking any excuse to let a black killer off the hook—ignoring that blacks on juries vote to convict black people of crimes every day in this country. And while allegations of black "racial bonding" with the defendant were made regularly after the acquittal in Simpson's criminal trial, no such bonding, this time with the victims, was alleged when a mostly white jury found O.J. civilly liable a few years later. Only blacks can play the race card, apparently; only they think in racial terms, at least to hear white America tell it.

## Anything But Racism: White Reluctance to Accept the Evidence

Since the O.J. trial, it seems as though almost any allegation of racism has been met with the same dismissive reply from the bulk of whites in the U.S. According to national surveys, more than three out of four whites refuse to believe that discrimination is any real problem in America.[2] That most whites remain unconvinced of racism's salience—with as few as six percent believing it to be a "very serious problem," according to one poll in the mid 90s[3]— suggests that racism-as-card makes up an awfully weak hand. While folks of color consistently articulate their belief that racism is a real and persistent presence in their own lives, these claims have had very little effect on white attitudes. As such, how could anyone believe that people of color would somehow pull the claim out of their hat, as if it were guaranteed to make white America sit up and take notice? If anything, it is likely to be ignored, or even attacked, and in a particularly vicious manner.

That bringing up racism (even with copious documentation) is far from an effective "card" to play in order to garner sympathy, is evidenced by the way in which few people even become aware of the studies confirming its existence. How many Americans do you figure have even heard, for example, that black youth arrested for drug possession for the first time are incarcerated at a rate that is forty-eight times greater than the rate for white youth, even when all other factors surrounding the crime are identical?[4]

How many have heard that persons with "white sounding names," according to a massive national study, are fifty percent more likely to be called back for a job interview than those with "black sounding" names, even when all other credentials are the same?[5]

How many know that white men with a criminal record are slightly more likely to be called back for a job interview than black men without one, even when the men are equally qualified, and present themselves to potential employers in an identical fashion?[6]

How many have heard that according to the Justice Department, Black and Latino males are three times more likely than white males to have their vehicles stopped and searched by police, even though white males are over four times more likely to have illegal contraband in our cars on the occasions when we are searched?[7]

How many are aware that black and Latino students are about half as likely as whites to be placed in advanced or honors classes in school, and twice as likely to be placed in remedial classes? Or that even when test scores and prior performance would justify higher placement, students of color are far less likely to be placed in honors classes?[8] Or that students of color are 2–3 times more likely than whites to be suspended or expelled from school, even though rates of serious school rule infractions do not differ to any significant degree between racial groups?[9]

Fact is, few folks have heard any of these things before, suggesting how little impact scholarly research on the subject of racism has had on the general public, and how difficult it is to make whites, in particular, give the subject a second thought.

Perhaps this is why, contrary to popular belief, research indicates that people of color are actually reluctant to allege racism, be it on the job, or in schools, or anywhere else. Far from "playing the race card" at the drop of a hat, it is actually the case (again, according to scholarly investigation, as opposed to the conventional wisdom of the white public), that black and brown folks typically "stuff" their experiences with discrimination and racism, only making an allegation of such treatment after many, many incidents have transpired, about which they said nothing for fear of being ignored or attacked.[10] Precisely because white denial has long trumped claims of racism, people of color tend to underreport their experiences with racial bias, rather than exaggerate them. Again, when it comes to playing a race card, it is more accurate to say that whites are the dealers with the loaded decks, shooting down any evidence of racism as little more than the fantasies of unhinged blacks, unwilling to take personal responsibility for their own problems in life.

# Blaming the Victims for White Indifference

Occasionally, white denial gets creative, and this it does by pretending to come wrapped in sympathy for those who allege racism in the modern era. In other words, while steadfastly rejecting what people of color say they experience—in effect suggesting that they lack the intelligence and/or sanity to accurately interpret their own lives—such commentators seek to assure others that whites really do care about racism, but simply refuse to pin the label on incidents where it doesn't apply. In fact, they'll argue, one of the reasons that whites have developed compassion fatigue on this issue is precisely because of the overuse of the concept, combined with what we view as unfair reactions to racism (such as affirmative action efforts which have, ostensibly, turned us into the victims of racial bias). If blacks would just stop playing the card where it doesn't belong, and stop pushing for so-called preferential treatment, whites would revert back to our prior commitment to equal opportunity, and our heartfelt concern about the issue of racism.

Don't laugh. This is actually the position put forward recently by James Taranto of the Wall Street Journal, who in January suggested that white reluctance to embrace black claims of racism was really the fault of blacks themselves, and the larger civil rights establishment.[11] As Taranto put it: "Why do blacks and whites have such divergent views on racial matters? We would argue that it is because of the course that racial policies have taken over the past forty years." He then argues that by trying to bring about racial equality—but failing to do so because of "aggregate differences in motivation, inclination and aptitude" between different racial groups—policies like affirmative action have bred "frustration and resentment" among blacks, and "indifference" among whites, who decide not to think about race at all, rather than engage an issue that seems so toxic to them. In other words, whites think blacks use racism as a crutch for their own inadequacies, and then demand programs and policies that fail to make things much better, all the while discriminating against them as whites. In such an atmosphere, is it any wonder that the two groups view the subject matter differently?

But the fundamental flaw in Taranto's argument is its suggestion—implicit though it may be—that prior to the creation of affirmative action, white folks were mostly on board the racial justice and equal opportunity train, and were open to hearing about claims of racism from persons of color. Yet nothing could be further from the truth. White denial is not a form of backlash to the past forty years of civil rights legislation, and white indifference to claims of racism did not only recently emerge, as if from a previous place where whites and blacks had once seen the world similarly. Simply put: whites in every generation have thought there was no real problem with racism, irrespective of the evidence, and in every generation we have been wrong.

# Denial as an Intergenerational Phenomenon

So, for example, what does it say about white rationality and white collective sanity, that in 1963—at a time when in retrospect all would agree racism was rampant in the United States, and before the passage of modern civil rights legislation—nearly two-thirds of whites, when polled, said they believed blacks were treated the same as whites in their communities—almost the same number as say this now, some forty-plus years later? What does it suggest about the extent of white folks' disconnection from the real world, that in 1962, eighty-five percent of whites said black children had just as good a chance as white children to get a good education in their communities?[12] Or that in May, 1968, seventy percent of whites said that blacks were treated the same as whites in their communities, while only seventeen percent said blacks were treated "not very well" and only 3.5 percent said blacks were treated badly?[13]

What does it say about white folks' historic commitment to equal opportunity—and which Taranto would have us believe has only been rendered inoperative because of affirmative action—that in 1963, three-fourths of white Americans told Newsweek, "The Negro is moving too fast" in his demands for equality?[14] Or that in October 1964, nearly two-thirds of whites said that the Civil Rights Act should be enforced gradually, with an emphasis on persuading employers not to discriminate, as opposed to forcing compliance with equal opportunity requirements?[15]

What does it say about whites' tenuous grip on mental health that in mid-August 1969, forty-four percent of whites told a Newsweek/Gallup National Opinion Survey that blacks had a better chance than they did to get a good paying job—two times as many as said they would have a worse chance? Or that forty-two percent said blacks had a better chance for a good education than whites, while only seventeen percent said they would have a worse opportunity for a good education, and eighty percent saying blacks would have an equal or better chance? In that same survey, seventy percent said blacks could have improved conditions in the "slums" if they had wanted to, and were more than twice as likely to blame blacks themselves, as opposed to discrimination, for high unemployment in the black community.[16]

In other words, even when racism was, by virtually all accounts (looking backward in time), institutionalized, white folks were convinced there was no real problem. Indeed, even forty years ago, whites were more likely to think that blacks had better opportunities, than to believe the opposite (and obviously accurate) thing: namely, that whites were advantaged in every realm of American life.

Truthfully, this tendency for whites to deny the extent of racism and racial injustice likely extends back far before the 1960s. Although public opinion polls in previous decades rarely if ever asked questions about the extent of racial bias or discrimination, anecdotal surveys of white opinion suggest that at no time have whites in the U.S. ever thought blacks or other people of color were getting a bad shake. White Southerners were all but convinced that their black slaves, for example, had it good, and had no reason to complain about their living conditions or lack of freedoms. After emancipation, but during the introduction of Jim Crow laws and strict Black Codes that limited where African Americans could live and work, white newspapers would regularly editorialize about the "warm relations" between whites and blacks, even as thousands of blacks were being lynched by their white compatriots.

# From Drapetomania to Victim Syndrome— Viewing Resistance as Mental Illness

Indeed, what better evidence of white denial (even dementia) could one need than that provided by "Doctor" Samuel Cartwright, a well-respected physician of the 19th century, who was so convinced of slavery's benign nature, that he concocted and named a disease to explain the tendency for many slaves to run away from their loving masters. Drapetomania, he called it: a malady that could be cured by keeping the slave in a "child-like state," and taking care not to treat them as equals, while yet striving not to be too cruel. Mild whipping was, to Cartwright, the best cure of all. So there you have it: not only is racial oppression not a problem; even worse, those blacks who resist it, or refuse to bend to it, or complain about it in any fashion, are to be viewed not only as exaggerating their condition, but indeed, as mentally ill.[17]

And lest one believe that the tendency for whites to psychologically pathologize blacks who complain of racism is only a relic of ancient history, consider a much more recent example, which demonstrates the continuity of this tendency among members of the dominant racial group in America.

A few years ago, I served as an expert witness and consultant in a discrimination lawsuit against a school district in Washington State. Therein, numerous examples of individual and institutional racism abounded: from death threats made against black students to which the school district's response was pitifully inadequate, to racially disparate "ability tracking" and disciplinary action. In preparation for trial (which ultimately never took place as the district finally agreed to settle the case for several million dollars and a commitment to policy change), the school system's "psychological experts" evaluated dozens of the plaintiffs (mostly students as well as some of their parents) so as to determine the extent of damage done to them as a result of the racist mistreatment. As one of the plaintiff's experts, I reviewed the reports of said psychologists, and while I was not surprised to see them downplay the damage done to the black folks in this case, I was somewhat startled by how quickly they went beyond the call of duty to actually suggest that several of the plaintiffs exhibited "paranoid" tendencies and symptoms of borderline personality disorder. That having one's life threatened might make one a bit paranoid apparently never entered the minds of the white doctors. That facing racism on a regular basis might lead one to act out, in a way these "experts" would then see as a personality disorder, also seems to have escaped them. In this way, whites have continued to see mental illness behind black claims of victimization, even when that victimization is blatant.

In fact, we've even created a name for it: "victimization syndrome." Although not yet part of the DSM-IV (the diagnostic manual used by the American Psychiatric Association so as to evaluate patients), it is nonetheless a malady from which blacks suffer, to hear a lot of whites tell it. Whenever racism is brought up, such whites insist that blacks are being encouraged (usually by the civil rights establishment) to adopt a victim mentality, and to view themselves as perpetual targets of oppression. By couching their rejection of the claims of racism in these terms, conservatives are able to parade as friends to black folks, only concerned about them and hoping to free them from the debilitating mindset of victimization that liberals wish to see them adopt.

Aside from the inherently paternalistic nature of this position, notice too how concern over adopting a victim mentality is very selectively trotted out by the right. So, for example, when crime victims band together—and even form what they call victim's rights groups—no one on the right tells them to get over it, or suggests that by continuing to incessantly bleat about their kidnapped child or murdered loved one, such folks are falling prey to a victim mentality that should be resisted. No indeed: crime victims are venerated, considered experts on proper crime policy (as evidenced by how often their opinions are sought out on the matter by the national press and politicians), and given nothing but sympathy.

Likewise, when American Jews raise a cry over perceived anti-Jewish bigotry, or merely teach their children (as I was taught) about the European Holocaust, replete with a slogan of "Never again!" none of the folks who lament black "victimology" suggests that we too are wallowing in a victimization mentality, or somehow at risk for a syndrome of the same name.

In other words, it is blacks and blacks alone (with the occasional American Indian or Latino thrown in for good measure when and if they get too uppity) that get branded with the victim mentality label. Not quite drapetomania, but also not far enough from the kind of thinking that gave rise to it: in both cases, rooted in the desire of white America to reject what all logic and evidence suggests is true. Further, the selective branding of blacks as perpetual victims, absent the application of the pejorative to Jews or crime victims (or the families of 9/11 victims or other acts of terrorism), suggests that at some level white folks simply don't believe black suffering matters. We refuse to view blacks as fully human and deserving of compassion as we do these other groups, for whom victimization has been a reality as well. It is not that whites care about blacks and simply wish them not to adopt a self-imposed mental straightjacket; rather, it is that at some level we either don't care, or at least don't equate the pain of racism even with the pain caused by being mugged, or having your art collection confiscated by the Nazis, let alone with the truly extreme versions of crime and anti-Semitic wrongdoing.

## See No Evil, Hear No Evil, Wrong as Always

White denial has become such a widespread phenomenon nowadays, that most whites are unwilling to entertain even the mildest of suggestions that racism and racial inequity might still be issues. To wit, a recent survey from the University of Chicago, in which whites and blacks were asked two questions about Hurricane Katrina and the governmental response to the tragedy. First, respondents were asked whether they believed the government response would have been speedier had the victims been white. Not surprisingly, only twenty percent of whites answered in the affirmative. But while that question is at least conceivably arguable, the next question seems so weakly worded that virtually anyone could have answered yes without committing too much in the way of recognition that racism was a problem. Yet the answers given reveal the depths of white intransigence to consider the problem a problem at all.

So when asked if we believed the Katrina tragedy showed that there was a lesson to be learned about racial inequality in America—any lesson at all—while ninety percent of blacks said yes, only thirty-eight percent of whites agreed.[18] To us, Katrina said nothing about race whatsoever, even as blacks were disproportionately affected; even as there was a clear racial difference in terms of who was stuck in New Orleans and who was able to escape; even as the media focused incessantly on reports of black violence in the Superdome and Convention Center that proved later to be false; even as blacks have been having a much harder time moving back to New Orleans, thanks to local and federal foot-dragging and the plans of economic elites in the city to destroy homes in the most damaged (black) neighborhoods and convert them to non-residential (or higher rent) uses.

Nothing, absolutely nothing, has to do with race nowadays, in the eyes of white America writ large. But the obvious question is this: if we have never seen racism as a real problem, contemporary to the time in which the charges are being made, and if in all generations past we were obviously wrong to the point of mass delusion in thinking this way, what should lead us to conclude that now, at long last, we've become any more astute at discerning social reality than we were before? Why should we trust our own perceptions or instincts on the matter, when we have run up such an amazingly bad track record as observers of the world in which we live? In every era, black folks said they were the victims of racism and they were right. In every era, whites have said the problem was exaggerated, and we have been wrong.

Unless we wish to conclude that black insight on the matter—which has never to this point failed them—has suddenly converted to irrationality, and that white irrationality has become insight (and are prepared to prove this transformation by way of some analytical framework to explain the process), then the best advice seems to be that which could have been offered in past decades and centuries: namely, if you want to know about whether or not racism is a problem, it would probably do you best to ask the folks who are its targets. They, after all, are the ones who must, as a matter of survival, learn what it is, and how and when it's operating. We whites on the other hand, are the persons who have never had to know a thing about it, and who—for reasons psychological, philosophical and material—have always had a keen interest in covering it up.

In short, and let us be clear on it: race is not a card. It determines whom the dealer is, and who gets dealt.

# Notes

*Personally, I have no idea whether or not Barry Bonds has used anabolic steroids during the course of his career, nor do I think the evidence marshaled thus far on the matter is conclusive, either way. But I do find it interesting that many are calling for the placement of an asterisk next to Bonds' name in the record books, especially should he eclipse Ruth, or later, Hank Aaron, in terms of career home runs. The asterisk, we are told, would differentiate Bonds from other athletes, the latter of which, presumably accomplished their feats without performance enhancers. Yet, while it is certainly true that Aaron's 755 home runs came without any form of performance enhancement (indeed, he, like other black ball-players had to face overt hostility in the early years of their careers, and even as he approached Ruth's record of 714, he was receiving death threats), for Ruth, such a claim would be laughable. Ruth, as with any white baseball player from the early 1890s to 1947, benefited from the "performance enhancement" of not having to compete against black athletes, whose abilities often far surpassed their own. Ruth didn't have to face black pitchers, nor vie for batting titles against black home run sluggers. Until white fans demand an asterisk next to the names of every one of their white baseball heroes—Ruth, Cobb, DiMaggio, and Williams, for starters—who played under apartheid rules, the demand for such a blemish next to the name of Bonds can only be seen as highly selective, hypocritical, and ultimately racist. White privilege and protection from black competition certainly did more for those men's game than creotine or other substances could ever do for the likes of Barry Bonds.

1. There is plenty of information about police racism, misconduct and brutality, both in historical and contemporary terms, available from any number of sources. Among them, see Kristian Williams, *Our Enemies in Blue*. Soft Skull Press, 2004. . . .

2. *Washington Post*. October 9, 1995: A22.

3. Ibid.

4. "Young White Offenders get Lighter Treatment," 2000. *The Tennessean*. April 26: 8A.

5. Bertrand, Marianne and Sendhil Mullainathan, 2004. "Are Emily and Greg More Employable Than Lakisha and Jamal? A Field Experiment in Labor Market Discrimination." June 20.

6. Pager, Devah. 2003. "The Mark of a Criminal Record." *American Journal of Sociology*. Volume 108: 5, March: 937–75.

7. Matthew R. Durose, Erica L. Schmitt and Patrick A. Langan, *Contacts Between Police and the Public: Findings from the 2002 National Survey*. U.S. Department of Justice, (Bureau of Justice Statistics), April 2005.

8. Gordon, Rebecca. 1998. *Education and Race*. Oakland: Applied Research Center: 48–49; Fischer, Claude S. et al., 1996. *Inequality by Design: Cracking the Bell Curve Myth*. Princeton, NJ: Princeton University Press: 163; Steinhorn, Leonard and Barabara Diggs-Brown, 1999. *By the Color of Our Skin: The Illusion of Integration and the Reality of Race*. NY: Dutton: 95–96.

9. Skiba, Russell J. et al., *The Color of Discipline: Sources of Racial and Gender Disproportionality in School Punishment*. Indiana Education Policy Center, Policy Research Report SRS1, June 2000; U.S. Centers for Disease Control and Prevention, *Youth Risk Behavior Surveillance System: Youth 2003*, Online Comprehensive Results, 2004.

10. Terrell, Francis and Sandra L. Terrell, 1999. "Cultural Identification and Cultural Mistrust: Some Findings and Implications," in *Advances in African*

*American Psychology*, Reginald Jones, ed., Hampton VA: Cobb & Henry; Fuegen, Kathleen, 2000. "Defining Discrimination in the Personal/Group Discrimination Discrepancy," *Sex Roles: A Journal of Research*. September; Miller, Carol T. 2001. "A Theoretical Perspective on Coping With Stigma," *Journal of Social Issues*. Spring; Feagin, Joe, Hernan Vera and Nikitah Imani, 1996. *The Agony of Education: Black Students in White Colleges and Universities*. NY: Routledge.

11. Taranto, James. 2006. "The Truth About Race in America—IV," Online Journal (*Wall Street Journal*), January 6.

12. The Gallup Organization, *Gallup Poll Social Audit, 2001. Black-White Relations in the United States, 2001 Update*, July 10: 7–9.

13. The Gallup Organization, *Gallup Poll*, #761, May, 1968.

14. "How Whites Feel About Negroes: A Painful American Dilemma," *Newsweek*, October 21, 1963: 56.

15. The Gallup Organization, *Gallup Poll* #699, October, 1964.

16. Newsweek/Gallup Organization, *National Opinion Survey*, August 19, 1969.

17. Cartwright, Samuel. 1851. "Diseases and Peculiarities of the Negro Race," *DeBow's Review*. (Southern and Western States: New Orleans), Volume XI.

18. Ford, Glen and Peter Campbell, 2006. "Katrina: A Study-Black Consensus, White Dispute," *The Black Commentator*, Issue 165, January 5.

# POSTSCRIPT

## Is the Claim of White Skin Privilege a Myth?

**W**ise cites several surveys to indicate white reluctance to acknowledge racism. Essentially, he argues that blacks and whites see the world differently. The white assertion that blacks play the race card is noted in many examples including the relationship between the police and both the black and white communities. Distrust of the police among blacks (see Issue 10) is more than conventional wisdom; it is a reflection of real-life experiences. At the same time, whites' view of the police reflects a different real-life experience, which Wise sees as white privilege. However, many do not recognize this as privilege. Thus, the idea of white privilege is difficult, if not impossible, for most whites to recognize because for centuries the culture has associated race with minority blacks in the United States. White privilege is taken for granted to the extent that one's life experiences are seen as universally normal.

The emerging body of literature in whiteness studies now raises questions of privilege in the context of being white. Wise links this with white denial of racism and a "blaming the victim" attitude of blacks. He writes that blacks use racism as a crutch for their own inadequacies.

In contrast, Kivel's straightforward presentation lists how whites benefit directly from color. He does not consider denial of racism and neither does he view playing the race card as a factor in white privilege.

This issue will challenge students in several ways. First, the notion of white privilege should expand the boundaries of discussion about race relations. Second, unlike most issues in this edition, the positions elicited are not strongly opposite each other. By using Kivel and Wise, the student will need to deconstruct the concepts and challenge both pieces. Kivel and Wise both write about white privilege and their ideas overlap. At the same time, Wise interprets the attitude held by whites that there is no such thing as white skin privilege.

Historically, since race in the United States has been divided into black or white—one had to be either—a black person was someone defined as someone having black ancestors. The increasing diversity of the American population has rendered traditional race and ethnic categories, regardless of how familiar they are, inadequate. Expanded populations of Asians, Hispanics, and Middle Easterners, for example, challenge the traditional black–white dichotomy. The historical mixing of the races that occurred in the United States resulted in the rule of hypo-descent, or "the one drop rule" and rigidly enforced the black–white dichotomy.

Why, in the American experience, did mixed-race people become categorized as black? How would you define whiteness? Why do blacks and whites have such divergent views on racial matters? Is the emphasis on examining white privilege another way to argue for minorities and against the majority group? Is white skin privilege a functional form of discrimination?

The rapid growth of studies in whiteness and white privilege offers the student a wide range of additional sources for reference. George Lipsitz, in *The Possessive Investment in Whiteness: How White People Profit From Identity Politics* (Temple University Press), explores several areas of white studies including white privilege, "color-blind" racism, and how color works into American culture. Linda Faye Williams's *The Constraint of Race: Legacies of White Skin Privilege in America* (The Pennsylvania State University Press, 2003), argues that there is "no race problem" per se; instead, "race problem" is a euphemism for "white skin privilege."

As early as 1970 Peter Binzen wrote *Whitetown, USA: A Firsthand Study of How the "Silent Majority" Lives, Learns, Works and Thinks* (Vintage). Anthropologist Brewton Berry's study, *Almost White* (Collier Books), demonstrated the preference for being classified as white because it was associated with privilege and advantage. For an extended discussion of white privilege and color-blind racism, see Eduardo Bonilla-Silva's *White Supremacy and Racism in the Post-Civil Rights Era* (Lynn Rienner Publishers). In the context of white privilege, he asks why blacks and other racial minorities lag behind whites in terms of income, wealth, educational attainment, and other social indicators. *Off White: Readings on Power, Privilege, and Resistance* (Routledge) edited by Fine, Weis, Pruitt, and Burns contains several selections on whiteness and multicultural issues. Winthrop Jordan, in *White Over Black*, develops a theme of white color preference over nonwhites, especially blacks, by examining how perceptions of blackness developed within white consciousness.

*White Like Me: Reflections on Race from a Privileged Son* (Soft Skull Press, 2005) by Tim Wise examines how whites benefit from "racial preferences." It is a critical assessment of race privilege. Stanley Crouch's *The Artificial White Man: Essays on Authenticity* (Basic Books, 2004) explores the problem of authenticity in the America. For Crouch, there is difficulty in distinguishing the real from the counterfeit in the lives of whites in the United States. In *Everyday Racism* (Sourcebooks, Inc., 2000), Annie S. Barnes tells the story of 150 middle-class black college students and their frequent encounters with racism. An interesting work on immigration and race is David R. Roediger's *Working Toward Whiteness: How America's Immigrants Became White* (Basic Books, 2005). Frantz Fanon's *Black Skin, White Masks* is about social, economic, and racial privilege.

# Internet References . . .

## The Civil Rights Project: Harvard University

The Civil Rights Project helps to renew the civil rights movement by "bridging the worlds of ideas and action, and by becoming a preeminent source of intellectual capital and a forum for building consensus within that movement." It is an excellent source of information and research findings in the field of race relations.

**http://www.civilrightsproject.harvard.edu/**

## Social Science Data Analysis Network (SSDAN)

The Social Science Data Analysis Network (SSDAN) runs this site to research segregation in local communities across the country. It offers students a chance to do original quantitative research on segregation by selecting neighborhoods in cities and then analyzing the data on race. This site is recommended for a wide range of research possibilities.

**http://www.censusscope.org/segregation.html**

## American Studies: Georgetown University

This site contains the largest bibliography of Web-based resources in the field of American Studies. The "Race, Ethnicity and Identity" section offers reference and research opportunity for students.

**http://cfdev.georgetown.edu/endls/asw/**

## Library of Congress (LOC)

This Web site offers an extensive online collection including areas of interest to students of race and ethnicity. The section titled "American Memory: U.S. History and Culture" presents a good deal of information to the student including an online exhibit of African American history. The LOC also offers an extensive collection in its Hispanic division.

**http://memory.loc.gov/ammem/aaohtml/exhibit/aointro.html**

## American Civil Liberties Union

This site covers current information on immigrants' rights and issues of civil rights, including voting rights. It reviews Supreme Court decisions and other legislative action. The archives section offers a wealth of information on race and ethnic legal cases throughout American history. There is an interesting section on racial profiling.

**http://www.aclu.org**

# The Persistence of Discrimination

*F*rom its inception, the American nation has struggled to achieve the goals of an egalitarian vision of society that has been enunciated by leaders from the Colonial era to the present. Economically, there is a significant racial gap in critical areas such as poverty, employment, median family income, and median family assets among other areas of consideration. Similar inequities attend the lives of Latinos and Native Americans. In fact, the conditions of lives of America's Indians are much worse than those of most other minorities. In the medical health care field and related areas of human welfare, there are significant inequities experienced by African Americans, Latinos, and Native Americans. The average life expectancy of each of these groups is significantly lower than that of their white counterparts. Despite many efforts to end both individual and institutional discrimination some issues persist. In the context of persistent institutional discrimination the permanence of racism, racial profiling, racism and government rescue efforts following Hurricane Katrina, and the unique role of place for Native Americans are considered. Why does discrimination persist?

- Is Racism a Permanent Feature of American Society?

- Is Racial Profiling a Defensible Public Policy?

- Did Hurricane Katrina Expose Racism in America?

- Is the Reservation the Only Source of Community for Native Americans?

# ISSUE 9

# Is Racism a Permanent Feature of American Society?

**YES: Derrick Bell,** from *Faces at the Bottom of the Well: The Permanence of Racism* (Basic Books, 1992)

**NO: Dinesh D'Souza,** from *The End of Racism: Principles for a Multiracial Society* (Free Press, 1995)

## ISSUE SUMMARY

**YES:** Derrick Bell, a prominent African-American scholar and authority on civil rights and constitutional law, argues that the prospects for achieving racial equality in the United States are "illusory" for blacks.

**NO:** Dinesh D'Souza, John M. Ohlin scholar at the American Enterprise Institute, believes that racial discrimination against blacks has substantially eroded within American society and that lagging progress among them is due to other factors, such as culture, rather than racism.

**R**acist ideology has been employed throughout the nation's history in attempts to justify institutional policies and practices such as slavery and segregation. Despite the substantial efforts of supporters of a racially egalitarian society, the reification of racism is a continuing reality of this nation.

The persistence of ideological and institutional racism within the United States has given rise to a debate over the prospects for ridding our society of this glaring contradiction. On one side of this debate are those who believe that a proper examination of the American experience and the treatment of African Americans and other peoples of color throughout history leads to the conclusion that racism is unlikely to be eroded in this country and will continue to challenge the American creed. The other side is comprised of those who advance the more optimistic view concerning race relations within the United States. Members of this camp claim that the destructive impact of racism is declining in this country, and that any lagging progress of African Americans is due to factors other than racial discrimination.

Derrick Bell is a proponent of the thesis that racism is a permanent feature of American society. His now classic thesis is supported by an analysis of some of the most important aspects of African Americans' historical development. Bell reminds us that despite the fact of significant progress for some blacks of the United States, the legacy of slavery has left a significant portion of the race "with life-long poverty and soul-devastating despair. . . ."

Bell believes that race consciousness is so imbedded in whites that it is virtually impossible to rise above it. He argues that "few whites are able to identify with blacks as a group" and tend to view them through "comforting racial stereotypes." Bell cites a number of examples of the destructive impact of racial bonding among whites upon blacks' efforts to progress within society. He points out that even poor whites have tended to support institutions such as slavery and segregation rather than coalescing with blacks to fight against common social disadvantages such as unemployment and poverty. Given this record of race relations, it is impossible for Bell to accept the claim that racism has been largely overcome in these United States. To the contrary, he feels strongly that a critical and proper examination of the history of black-white relations supports the conclusion that racism is a permanent feature of American society.

Dinesh D'Souza does not agree with Bell that racism is a permanent strain fabric of American society. D'Souza distinguishes between racial discrimination that is "irrational, motivated by bigotry" and that which is "rational from the point of view of the discriminator." While admitting that such discrimination may be harmful to individual blacks, D'Souza rejects any causal linkage between the lagging indicators of blacks' overall progress with racial discrimination. Since he believes that racism is a diminishing force within American life, D'Souza argues that factors other than racial discrimination are the sources of lagging progress toward the American dream. He is strongly supportive of the view that cultural factors contribute to social pathology, including crime, unwed motherhood, and others, and are the primary causes of the prevailing and persistent gap in socioeconomic achievement between blacks and whites.

D'Souza argues that the failure of blacks to observe and embrace certain cultural norms of the dominant American society is a major reason why the race is not achieving more in America. He argues that those blacks who are successful exhibit cultural values that promote success. Those who are not achieving are immersed in a defective culture that is antithetical to success. Thus, D'Souza would argue that blacks need to place a much greater emphasis on overcoming cultural barriers rather than continuing to assert that the race is being held back by a persistent racism that afflicts America.

The reader would benefit from expanding his or her perspective to include ideas and concepts dealing with social and cultural values. This is a debate in itself. That is, do structural conditions such as racism, discrimination, and lack of opportunity lead to inequality and poverty? Or, is poverty attributed to individual factors including socialization and value formation? Bell makes the structural argument while D'Souza offers a culture of poverty thesis.

# YES

Derrick Bell

# Faces at the Bottom of the Well: The Permanence of Racism

## Divining Our Racial Themes

> *In these bloody days and frightful nights when an urban warrior can find no face more despicable than his own, no ammunition more deadly than self-hate and no target more deserving of his true aim than his brother, we must wonder how we came so late and lonely to this place.*

—Maya Angelou

When I was growing up in the years before the Second World War, our slave heritage was more a symbol of shame than a source of pride. It burdened black people with an indelible mark of difference as we struggled to be like whites. In those far-off days, survival and progress seemed to require moving beyond, even rejecting slavery. Childhood friends in a West Indian family who lived a few doors away often boasted—erroneously as I later learned—that their people had never been slaves. My own more accurate—but hardly more praiseworthy—response was that my forebears included many free Negroes, some of whom had Choctaw and Blackfoot Indian blood.

In those days, self-delusion was both easy and comforting. Slavery was barely mentioned in the schools and seldom discussed by the descendants of its survivors, particularly those who had somehow moved themselves to the North. Emigration, whether from the Caribbean islands or from the Deep South states, provided a geographical distance that encouraged and enhanced individual denial of our collective, slave past. We sang spirituals but detached the songs from their slave origins. As I look back, I see this reaction as no less sad, for being very understandable. We were a subordinate and mostly shunned portion of a society that managed to lay the onus of slavery neatly on those who were slaves while simultaneously exonerating those who were slaveholders. All things considered, it seemed a history best left alone.

Then, after the Second World War and particularly in the 1960s, slavery became—for a few academics and some militant Negroes—a subject of fascination and a sure means of evoking racial rage as a prelude to righteously repeated demands for "Freedom Now!" In response to a resurrection

From *Faces At the Bottom of the Well: The Permanence of Racism,* (Basic Books, 1993), pp. 2–13. Copyright © 1993 by Derrick Bell. Reprinted by permission of Basic Books, a member of Perseus Books Group, L. L. C.

of interest in our past, new books on slavery were written, long out-of-print volumes republished. The new awareness reached its highest point in 1977 with the television version of Alex Haley's biographical novel, *Roots*. The highly successful miniseries informed millions of Americans—black as well as white—that slavery in fact existed and that it was awful. Not, of course, as awful as it would have been save for the good white folks the television writers had created to ease the slaves' anguish, and the evil ones on whose shoulders they placed all the guilt. Through the magic of literary license, white viewers could feel revulsion for slavery without necessarily recognizing American slavery as a burden on the nation's history, certainly not a burden requiring reparations in the present.

Even so, under pressure of civil rights protests, many white Americans were ready to accede to, if not applaud, Supreme Court rulings that the Constitution should no longer recognize and validate laws that kept in place the odious badges of slavery.

As a result, two centuries after the Constitution's adoption, we did live in a far more enlightened world. Slavery was no more. Judicial precedent and a plethora of civil rights statutes formally prohibited racial discrimination. Compliance was far from perfect, but the slavery provisions in the Constitution[1] did seem lamentable artifacts of a less enlightened era.

But the fact of slavery refuses to fade, along with the deeply embedded personal attitudes and public policy assumptions that supported it for so long. Indeed, the racism that made slavery feasible is far from dead in the last decade of twentieth-century America; and the civil rights gains, so hard won, are being steadily eroded. Despite undeniable progress for many, no African Americans are insulated from incidents of racial discrimination. Our careers, even our lives, are threatened because of our color. Even the most successful of us are haunted by the plight of our less fortunate brethren who struggle for existence in what some social scientists call the "underclass." Burdened with life-long poverty and soul-devastating despair, they live beyond the pale of the American Dream. What we designate as "racial progress" is not a solution to that problem. It is a regeneration of the problem in a particularly perverse form.

According to data compiled in 1990 for basic measures of poverty, unemployment, and income, the slow advances African Americans made during the 1960s and 1970s have definitely been reversed. The unemployment rate for blacks is 2.5 times the rate for whites. Black per-capita income is not even two thirds of the income for whites; and blacks, most of whom own little wealth or business property, are three times more likely to have income below the poverty level than whites. If trends of the last two decades are allowed to continue, readers can safely—and sadly—assume that the current figures are worse than those cited here.[2]

Statistics cannot, however, begin to express the havoc caused by joblessness and poverty: broken homes, anarchy in communities, futility in the public schools. All are the bitter harvest of race-determined unemployment in a society where work provides sustenance, status, and the all-important sense of self-worth. What we now call the "inner city" is, in fact, the American equivalent of the South African homelands. Poverty is less the source than the status of men and women who, despised because of their race, seek refuge in self-rejection. Drug-related crime, teenaged parenthood, and disrupted and disrupting family life all are manifestations of a despair that feeds on self. That despair is bred anew each day by the images on ever-playing television sets, images confirming that theirs is the disgraceful form of living, not the only way people live.

Few whites are able to identify with blacks as a group—the essential prerequisite for feeling empathy with, rather than aversion from, blacks' self-inflicted suffering, as expressed by the poet Maya Angelou in this introduction's epigraph. Unable or unwilling to perceive that "there but for the grace of God, go I," few whites are ready to actively promote civil rights for blacks. Because of an irrational but easily roused fear that any social reform will unjustly benefit blacks, whites fail to support the programs this country desperately needs to address the ever-widening gap between the rich and the poor, both black and white.

Lulled by comforting racial stereotypes, fearful that blacks will unfairly get ahead of them, all too many whites respond to even the most dire reports of race-based disadvantage with either a sympathetic headshake or victim-blaming rationalizations. Both responses lead easily to the conclusion that contemporary complaints of racial discrimination are simply excuses put forward by people who are unable or unwilling to compete on an equal basis in a competitive society.

For white people who both deny racism and see a heavy dose of the Horatio Alger myth as the answer to blacks' problems, how sweet it must be when a black person stands in a public place and condemns as slothful and unambitious those blacks who are not making it. Whites eagerly embrace black conservatives' homilies to self-help, however grossly unrealistic such messages are in an economy where millions, white as well as black, are unemployed and, more important, in one where racial discrimination in the workplace is as vicious (if less obvious) than it was when employers posted signs "no negras need apply."

Whatever the relief from responsibility such thinking provides those who embrace it, more than a decade of civil rights setbacks in the White House, in the courts, and in the critical realm of media-nurtured public opinion has forced retrenchment in the tattered civil rights ranks. We must reassess our cause and our approach to it, but repetition of time-worn slogans simply will not do. As a popular colloquialism puts it, it is time to "get real" about race and the persistence of racism in America.

To make such an assessment—to plan for the future by reviewing the experiences of the past—we must ask whether the formidable hurdles we now face in the elusive quest for racial equality are simply a challenge to our commitment, whether they are the latest variation of the old hymn "One More River to Cross." Or, as we once again gear up to meet the challenges posed by these unexpected new setbacks, are we ignoring a current message with implications for the future which history has already taught us about the past?

Such assessment is hard to make. On the one hand, contemporary color barriers are certainly less visible as a result of our successful effort to strip the law's endorsement from the hated Jim Crow signs. Today one can travel for thousands of miles across this country and never see a public facility designated as "Colored" or "White." Indeed, the very absence of visible signs of discrimination creates an atmosphere of racial neutrality and encourages whites to believe that racism is a thing of the past. On the other hand, the general use of so-called neutral standards to continue exclusionary practices reduces the effectiveness of traditional civil rights laws, while rendering discriminatory actions more oppressive than ever. Racial bias in the pre-*Brown* era was stark, open, unalloyed with hypocrisy and blank-faced lies. We blacks, when rejected, knew who our enemies were. They were not us! Today, because bias is masked in unofficial practices and "neutral" standards, we must wrestle with the question whether race or some individual failing has cost us the job, denied us the promotion, or prompted our being rejected as tenants for an apartment. Either conclusion breeds frustration and alienation—and a rage we dare not show to others or admit to ourselves.

Modern discrimination is, moreover, not practiced indiscriminately. Whites, ready and willing to applaud, even idolize black athletes and entertainers, refuse to hire, or balk at, working with blacks. Whites who number individual blacks among their closest friends approve, or do not oppose, practices that bar selling or renting homes or apartments in their neighborhoods to blacks they don't know. Employers, not wanting "too many of them," are willing to hire one or two black people, but will reject those who apply later. Most hotels and restaurants who offer black patrons courteous—even deferential—treatment, uniformly reject black job applicants, except perhaps for the most menial jobs. When did you last see a black waiter in a really good restaurant?

Racial schizophrenia is not limited to hotels and restaurants. As a result, neither professional status nor relatively high income protects even accomplished blacks from capricious acts of discrimination that may reflect either individual "preference" or an institution's bias. The motivations for bias vary; the disadvantage to black victims is the same.

Careful examination reveals a pattern to these seemingly arbitrary racial actions. When whites perceive that it will be profitable or at least cost-free to serve, hire, admit, or otherwise deal with blacks on a nondiscriminatory basis, they do so. When they fear—accurately or not—that there may be a loss, inconvenience, or upset to themselves or other whites, discriminatory conduct usually follows. Selections and rejections reflect preference as much as prejudice. A preference for whites makes it harder to prove the discrimination outlawed by civil rights laws. This difficulty, when combined with lackluster enforcement, explains why discrimination in employment and in the housing market continues to prevail more than two decades after enactment of the Equal Employment Opportunity Act of 1965 and the Fair Housing Act of 1968.

Racial policy is the culmination of thousands of these individual practices. Black people, then, are caught in a double bind. We are, as I have said, disadvantaged unless whites perceive that nondiscriminatory treatment for us will be a benefit for them. In addition, even when nonracist practices might bring a benefit, whites may rely on discrimination against blacks as a unifying factor and a safety valve for frustrations during economic hard times.

Almost always, the injustices that dramatically diminish the rights of blacks are linked to the serious economic disadvantage suffered by many whites who lack money and power. Whites, rather than acknowledge the similarity of their disadvantage, particularly when compared with that of better-off whites, are easily detoured into protecting their sense of entitlement vis-à-vis blacks for all things of value. Evidently, this racial preference expectation is hypnotic. It is this compulsive fascination that seems to prevent most whites from even seeing—much less resenting—the far more sizable gap between their status and those who occupy the lofty levels at the top of our society.

Race consciousness of this character, as Professor Kimberlè Crenshaw suggested in 1988 in a pathbreaking *Harvard Law Review* article, makes it difficult for whites "to imagine the world differently. It also creates the desire for identification with privileged elites. By focusing on a distinct, subordinate 'other,' whites include themselves in the dominant circle—an arena in which most hold no real power, but only their privileged racial identity."

The critically important stabilizing role that blacks play in this society constitutes a major barrier in the way of achieving racial equality. Throughout history, politicians have used blacks as scapegoats for failed economic or political policies. Before the Civil War, rich slave owners persuaded the white working class to stand with them against the danger of slave revolts—even though the existence of slavery condemned white workers to a life of economic privation. After the Civil War, poor whites fought social reforms and settled for segregation rather than see formerly enslaved blacks get ahead. Most labor unions preferred to allow plant owners to break strikes with black scab labor than allow blacks to join their ranks. The "them against us" racial ploy—always a potent force in economic bad times—is working again: today whites, as disadvantaged by high-status entrance requirements as blacks, fight to end affirmative action policies that, by eliminating class-based entrance requirements and requiring widespread advertising of jobs, have likely helped far more whites than blacks. And in the 1990s, as through much of the 1980s, millions of Americans—white as well as black—face steadily worsening conditions: unemployment, inaccessible health care, inadequate housing, mediocre education, and pollution of the environment. The gap in national incomes is approaching a crisis as those in the top fifth now earn more than their counterparts in the bottom four fifths combined. The conservative guru Kevin Phillips used a different but no less disturbing comparison: the top two million income earners in this country earn more than the next one hundred million.

Shocking. And yet conservative white politicians are able to gain and hold even the highest office despite their failure to address seriously any of these issues. They rely instead on the time-tested formula of getting needy whites to identify on the basis of their shared skin color, and suggest with little or no subtlety that white people must stand together against the Willie

Hortons, or against racial quotas, or against affirmative action. The code words differ. The message is the same. Whites are rallied on the basis of racial pride and patriotism to accept their often lowly lot in life, and encouraged to vent their frustration by opposing any serious advancement by blacks. Crucial to this situation is the unstated understanding by the mass of whites that they will accept large disparities in economic opportunity in respect to other whites as long as they have a priority over blacks and other people of color for access to the few opportunities available.

This "racial bonding" by whites means that black rights and interests are always vulnerable to diminishment if not to outright destruction. The willingness of whites over time to respond to this racial rallying cry explains—far more than does the failure of liberal democratic practices (re black rights) to coincide with liberal democratic theory—blacks' continuing subordinate status. This is, of course, contrary to the philosophy of Gunnar Myrdal's massive midcentury study *The American Dilemma*. Myrdal and two generations of civil rights advocates accepted the idea of racism as merely an odious holdover from slavery, "a terrible and inexplicable anomaly stuck in the middle of our liberal democratic ethos." No one doubted that the standard American policy making was adequate to the task of abolishing racism. White America, it was assumed, *wanted* to abolish racism.[3]

Forty years later, in *The New American Dilemma*, Professor Jennifer Hochschild examined what she called Myrdal's "anomaly thesis," and concluded that it simply cannot explain the persistence of racial discrimination. Rather, the continued viability of racism demonstrates "that racism is not simply an excrescence on a fundamentally healthy liberal democratic body, but is part of what shapes and energizes the body." Under this view, "liberal democracy and racism in the United States are historically, even inherently, reinforcing; American society as we know it exists only because of its foundation in racially based slavery, and it thrives only because racial discrimination continues. The apparent anomaly is an actual symbiosis."

The permanence of this "symbiosis" ensures that civil rights gains will be temporary and setbacks inevitable. Consider: In this last decade of the twentieth century, color determines the social and economic status of all African Americans, both those who have been highly successful and their poverty-bound brethren whose lives are grounded in misery and despair. We rise and fall less as a result of our efforts than in response to the needs of a white society that condemns all blacks to quasi citizenship as surely as it segregated our parents and enslaved their forebears. The fact is that, despite what we designate as progress wrought through struggle over many generations, we remain what we were in the beginning: a dark and foreign presence, always the designated "other." Tolerated in good times, despised when things go wrong, as a people we are scapegoated and sacrificed as distraction or catalyst for compromise to facilitate resolution of political differences or relieve economic adversity.

We are now, as were our forebears when they were brought to the New World, objects of barter for those who, while profiting from our existence, deny our humanity. It is in the light of this fact that we must consider the haunting questions about slavery and exploitation contained in Professor Linda Myers's *Understanding an Afrocentric World View: Introduction to an Optimal Psychology*, questions that serve as their own answers.

We simply cannot prepare realistically for our future without assessing honestly our past. It seems cold, accusatory, but we must try to fathom with her "the mentality of a people that could continue for over 300 years to kidnap an estimated 50 million youth and young adults from Africa, transport them across the Atlantic with about half dying unable to withstand the inhumanity of the passage, and enslave them as animals."

As Professor Myers reminds us, blacks were not the only, and certainly not America's most, persecuted people. Appropriately, she asks about the mindset of European Americans to native Americans. After all, those in possession of the land were basically friendly to the newcomers. And yet the European Americans proceeded to annihilate almost the entire race, ultimately forcing the survivors onto reservations after stealing their land. Far from acknowledging and atoning for these atrocities, American history portrays whites as the heroes, the Indian victims as savage villains. "What," she wonders, "can be understood about the world view of a people who claim to be building a democracy with freedom and justice for all, and at the same time own slaves and deny others basic human rights?"

Of course, Americans did not invent slavery. The practice has existed throughout recorded history, and Professor Orlando Patterson, a respected scholar, argues impressively that American slavery was no worse than that practiced in other parts of the world.[4] But it is not comparative slavery policies that concern me. Slavery is, as an example of what white America has done, a constant reminder of what white America might do.

We must see this country's history of slavery, not as an insuperable racial barrier to blacks, but as a legacy of enlightenment from our enslaved forebears reminding us that if they survived the ultimate form of racism, we and those whites who stand with us can at least view racial oppression in its many contemporary forms without underestimating its critical importance and likely permanent status in this country.

To initiate the reconsideration, I want to set forth this proposition, which will be easier to reject than refute: *Black people will never gain full equality in this country. Even those herculean efforts we hail as successful will produce no more than temporary "peaks of progress," short-lived victories that slide into irrelevance as racial patterns adapt in ways that maintain white dominance. This is a hard-to-accept fact that all history verifies. We must acknowledge it, not as a sign of submission, but as an act of ultimate defiance.*

We identify with and hail as hero the man or woman willing to face even death without flinching. Why? Because, while no one escapes death, those who conquer their dread of it are freed to live more fully. In similar fashion, African Americans must confront and conquer the otherwise deadening reality of our permanent subordinate status. Only in this way can we prevent ourselves from being dragged down by society's racial hostility. Beyond survival lies the potential to perceive more clearly both a reason and the means for further struggle.

In this book, Geneva Crenshaw, the civil rights lawyer—protagonist of my earlier *And We Are Not Saved: The Elusive Quest for Racial Justice,* returns in a series of stories that offer an allegorical perspective on old dreams, long-held fears, and current conditions. The provocative format of story, a product of experience and imagination, allows me to take a new look at what, for want of a better phrase, I will call "racial themes." Easier to recognize than describe, they are essentials in the baggage of people subordinated by color in a land that boasts of individual freedom and equality. Some of these themes—reliance on law, involvement in protests, belief in freedom symbols—are familiar and generally known. Others—the yearning for a true homeland, the rejection of racial testimony, the temptation to violent retaliation—are real but seldom revealed. Revelation does not much alter the mystique of interracial romance or lessen its feared consequences. Nor does the search ever end for a full understanding of why blacks are and remain this country's designated scapegoats. . . .

The goal of racial equality is, while comforting to many whites, more illusory than real for blacks. For too long, we have worked for substantive reform, then settled for weakly worded and poorly enforced legislation, indeterminate judicial decisions, token government positions, even holidays. I repeat. If we are to seek new goals for our struggles, we must first reassess the worth of the racial assumptions on which, without careful thought, we have presumed too much and relied on too long.

Let's begin.

## Notes

1. According to William Wiecek, ten provisions in the Constitution directly or indirectly provided for slavery and protected slave owners.

2. Not all the data are bleak. While the median family income for black families declined in the 1970s and 1980s, the proportion of African-American families with incomes of $35,000 to $50,000 increased from 23.3 to 27.5 percent. The proportion with incomes above $50,000 increased by 38 percent, from 10.0 to 13.8 percent. The overall median income for blacks declined though: while the top quarter made progress, the bottom half was sliding backward, and the proportion of blacks receiving very low income (less than $5,000) actually increased.

3. According to Myrdal, the "Negro problem in America represents a moral lag in the development of the nation and a study of it must record nearly everything which is bad and wrong in America. . . . However, . . . not since Reconstruction has there been more reason to anticipate fundamental changes in American race relations, changes which will involve a development toward the American ideals."

4. He suggests: "The dishonor of slavery . . . came in the primal act of submission. It was the most immediate human expression of the inability to defend oneself or to secure one's livelihood. . . . The dishonor the slave was compelled to experience sprang instead from that raw, human sense of debasement inherent in having no being except as an expression of another's being."

# The End of Racism

**R**acism undoubtedly exists, but it no longer has the power to thwart blacks or any other group in achieving their economic, political, and social aspirations. It cannot be denied that African Americans suffer slights in terms of taxidrivers who pass them by, pedestrians who treat them as a security risk, banks that are reluctant to invest in black neighborhoods, and other forms of continued discrimination. Some of this discrimination is irrational, motivated by bigotry or faulty generalization. Much of it, as we have seen, is behavior that is rational from the point of view of the discriminator and at the same time harmful for black individuals who do not conform to the behavioral pattern of their peers. Such incidents undoubtedly cause pain, and invite legitimate public sympathy and concern. But they do not explain why blacks as a group do worse than other groups in getting into selective colleges, performing well on tests, gaining access to rewarding jobs and professions, starting and successfully operating independent businesses, and maintaining productive and cohesive communities.

Racism cannot explain most of the contemporary hardships faced by African Americans, even if some of them had their historical roots in oppression. Activists like Derrick Bell may deny it, but America today is not the same place that it was a generation ago. African Americans now live in a country where a black man, Colin Powell, who three decades ago could not be served a hamburger in many Southern restaurants, became chairman of the Joint Chiefs of Staff; where an African American, Douglas Wilder, was elected governor of Virginia, the heart of the Confederacy; where a former Dixiecrat like Senator Strom Thurmond supported the nomination of Clarence Thomas, a black man married to a white woman, for the Supreme Court; and where an interracial jury convicted Byron De La Beckwith for killing civil rights activist Medgar Evers a generation after two all-white juries acquitted him.

Many scholars and civil rights activists continue to blame racism for African American problems; yet if white racism controls the destiny of blacks today, how has one segment of the black community prospered so much over the past generation, while the condition of the black underclass has deteriorated? Since black women and black men are equally exposed to white bigotry, why are black women competitive with white women in the workplace, while black men lag behind all other groups? In major cities in which blacks dominate the institutions of government, is it realistic to assume that white racism is the main cause of crime, delinquency, and dilapidation? It also is not at all clear how racism could prevent the children of middle-class blacks from performing as well as whites and Asians on tests of mathematical and logical reasoning. Black pathologies such as illegitimacy, dependency, and crime are far more serious today than in the past, when racism was indisputably more potent and pervasive. "No one who supports the contemporary racism thesis," William Julius Wilson acknowledges, "has provided adequate or convincing answers to these questions."[1]

Even if racism were to disappear overnight, the worst problems facing black America would persist. Single parenthood and welfare dependency among the black underclass would not cease. Crack and AIDS would continue to ravage black communities. The black crime rate, with its disproportionate impact on African American communities, would still extract a terrible toll.[2] Indeed drugs and black-on-black crime kill more blacks in a year than all the lynchings in U.S. history. Racism is hardly the most serious problem facing African Americans in the United States today. Their main challenge is a civilizational breakdown that stretches across class lines but is especially concentrated in the black underclass. At every socioeconomic level, blacks are uncompetitive on those measures of achievement that are essential to modern industrial society. Many middle-class African Americans are, by their own account, distorted in their social relations by the consuming passion of black rage. And nothing strengthens racism in this country more than the behavior of the African American underclass, which flagrantly violates and scandalizes basic codes of responsibility, decency, and civility. As far as many blacks are concerned, as E. Franklin Frazier once wrote, "The travail of civilization is not yet ended."[3]

Racism began in the West as a biological explanation for a large gap of civilizational development separating blacks from whites. Today racism is reinforced and made plausible by the reemergence of that gap within the United States. For many whites the criminal and irresponsible black underclass represents a revival of barbarism in the midst of Western civilization. If this is true, the best way to eradicate beliefs in black inferiority is to remove their empirical basis. As African American scholars Jeff Howard and Ray Hammond argue, if blacks as a group can show that they are capable of performing competitively in schools and the work force, and exercising both the rights and the responsibilities of American citizenship, then racism will be deprived of its foundation in experience.[4] If blacks can close the civilization gap, the race problem in this country is likely to become insignificant. African Americans in particular and society in general have the daunting mission to address the serious internal problems within black culture. That is the best antiracism now.

In private, some activists like Jesse Jackson will tentatively acknowledge black pathologies. Yet it is difficult for liberal whites and mainstream black leaders to confront these problems publicly because of the deep-rooted ideology of cultural relativism. If all cultures are equal, on what grounds can the standards of mainstream society be applied to evaluate the performance and conduct of African Americans? If such standards are entirely relative and culture-bound, on what basis can blacks who are productive and law-abiding establish valid norms for blacks who are not? As Elijah Anderson argues, the inner city is characterized by two rival cultures: a hegemonic culture of pathology and a besieged culture of decency. By refusing to acknowledge that one culture is better than another—by erasing the distinction between barbarism and civilization—cultural relativism cruelly inhibits the nation from identifying and working to ameliorate pathologies that are destroying the life chances of millions of African Americans. Thus we arrive at a singular irony: cultural relativism, once the instrument of racial emancipation for blacks, has now become an obstacle to confronting real problems that cannot be avoided. One may say that today the most formidable ideological barrier facing blacks is not racism but antiracism.

## Rethinking Relativism

As we have seen, liberals in the twentieth century embraced relativism because it offered a basis for affirming and working to secure racial equality. Undoubtedly the relativist proclamation of the equality of all cultures provided liberals with a powerful rationale to reject the classic racist assertion of white civilizational superiority. But as often happens, the solution to an old problem becomes the source of a new one. Relativism has now imprisoned liberals in an iron cage that prevents them from acknowledging black pathology, makes it impossible for them to support policies that uphold any standard of responsibility, and compels them to blame every problem faced by blacks on white racism or its institutional legacy. This explains the interminable liberal rhetoric about the "root causes" of poverty, the "bitter hoax" of the American dream, the mysterious disappearance of "meaningful" jobs, the prospect of a "resurgence" of "hate," the danger of "imposing one's morality," the need to avoid "code words," and how we should all "understand the rage." Pondering what he concedes are the shocking behavior patterns of the black underclass, columnist Michael Massing can only ask, "what has driven these people to engage in such excesses?"[5] By denying that blacks can fail on their own, cultural relativism denies them the possibility of achieving success. Seeking to cover up black failure, relativism suppresses cultural autonomy, refusing to grant blacks control over their destiny.

Modern liberals are well aware of the differences in academic achievement, economic performance, family structure, and crime rates between blacks and other groups. Given that these differences persist at all socioeconomic levels, there are three possible explanations: genes, culture, and racial discrimination (or some combination of these factors). Since many liberals are committed to the precept that all cultures are or should be equal, it follows that observable group differences are the product of either discrimination or genes. If discrimination cannot fully explain why blacks do not perform as well as whites on various measures of performance, then the conclusion cannot be escaped: according to the liberal paradigm, blacks must be genetically inferior. Arthur Jensen and Charles Murray wait in the wings.

Since relativism makes it impossible for liberals to confront the issue of black cultural pathology—to do so is seen as "blaming the victim"—the desire to avoid a genetic explanation forces liberals to blame group differences on racism. At first glance it seems difficult, if not impossible, to argue that African Americans as a group perform substantially worse in intellectual and economic ventures than whites and Asians of similar background because they are passed up by racist cabdrivers or because shopkeepers follow them around in stores. Yet despite their absurdity, such suggestions are required by a liberal ideology that requires white racism to explain black failure. If racism cannot be located in individuals, it must be diagnosed in institutional structures. The charge of racism becomes a kind of incantation intended to ward off the demons of black inferiority. It offers a bewitched understanding that makes nonsense of everyday perception and empirical reality by alleging the subtle workings of unfriendly ghosts. In this Ptolemaic universe, the idea of racism serves the function of corrective epicycles that need to be invoked constantly to preserve the liberal edifice of cultural relativism and liberal confidence in black capacity. Raising the question of "why so many young men are engaging in what amounts to self-inflicted genocide," Andrew Hacker provides the prescribed answer. "It is white America that has made being black so disconsolate an estate."[6]

Thus begins the liberal project to offer an elaborate and shifting rationale for black incapacity. If African Americans do not do well on tests, that is because the tests are biased, and because white society has deprived them of the necessary skills. If they drop out of school, they have been driven out by racism which injures black self-esteem. If they have illegitimate children, this is because society refuses to provide black males with steady jobs. If they are convicted of a disproportionate number of violent crimes, this is because the police, judges, and juries are racist. Those who have committed crimes have been pressured to do so by undeserved economic hardship. Riots are automatically attributed to legitimate outbursts of black rage. In short, the liberal position on black failure can be reduced to a single implausible slogan: Just say racism. Yet liberals recognize that old forms of segregation and overt discrimination have greatly eroded, so where is this racism that is supposedly holding African Americans back at every juncture? Bull Connor does not serve in the Princeton admissions office, where he keeps blacks out with hoses and dogs; Bull Connor is dead. The main obstacle to more blacks getting into Princeton is the university's selective admissions standards. Consequently many liberals find that they must now treat merit itself as a mere cover for racism. In case after case, liberals are destroying legitimate institutions and practices in order to conceal the embarrassing reality of black failure.

In the view of its founders, such as Locke, liberalism is a philosophy that seeks to establish fair rules so that people with different interests have the freedom to pursue their goals within a framework of state neutrality. In modern liberal society, democratic elections, free markets, and civil liberties are all instruments that aim at maximizing freedom without dictating results. Liberalism does not tell you who to vote for, what to buy, or how to exercise your freedom of religion and speech. Liberal procedures such as the jury system and the presumption of innocence are intended to secure basic rights. Yet in order to compel the relativist outcome of substantive racial equality, liberals are forced to subvert these very principles. The easiest way to ensure that more blacks enter selective colleges and receive well-paying jobs is to lower admissions and hiring standards. If companies prove recalcitrant, the civil rights laws invert the premise of Western justice and treat defendants who fail to hire a proportional number of blacks as "guilty until proven innocent." In order to ensure that blacks are elected to represent blacks, voting districts are drawn in such a way as to virtually foreordain the result. In some cases, free speech is subordinated to the goals of sensitivity and diversity, as in so-called hate speech and hate crimes laws. At every stage, fundamental liberal principles are being sacrificed at the altar of cultural relativism. In its fanatical commitment to the relativist ideology of group equality, liberalism is inexorably destroying itself.

In the 1960s, many liberals supported civil rights because of a deep confidence in color-blind rules that would give blacks a fair chance to compete on their merits. The results of the last few decades have eroded this faith, so that now many of these same white liberals mainly produce alibis for black failure. These apologies take on a ritualistic and sometimes comic aspect, and there is some question about whether they are even believed by their advocates. Shelby Steele points out that many of the same activists who offer extensive arguments for why grades and standardized aptitude and achievement tests are meaningless nevertheless demonstrate intense private concern about how their own sons and daughters do on such measures of performance. If this double standard exists, it shows that many activists don't want to get rid of standards altogether, they want to get rid of standards *for blacks*. Eventually such self-deception becomes corrosive; many liberals may cease to believe in their own ingenious excuses and become like lawyers who suspect, finally, that their client may be guilty. Indeed before the moral tribunal of liberalism, blacks seem to stand publicly exculpated but privately convicted. White liberals do not want blacks to fail but many seem to behave as though, in every competition that is not rigged, they expect them to do so. Moreover, the routine abridgment of standards for blacks makes it more likely that blacks will fail at tasks for which they are inadequately prepared. Liberalism, which began as an ideology of equal rights, has degenerated into the paternalism of rigged results.

While contemporary liberalism destroys its principles, it clears the pathway for various species of illiberalism. Ironically liberalism which has for much of this century been the ideology of antiracism is now establishing the foundation for a new racism, black and white. Today's invocations of white power are based upon an appeal to cultural integrity and racial pride; on what grounds can liberal relativists criticize groups like

Jared Taylor's "American Renaissance" which assert the right to defend their own cultural norms? Similarly white liberals find it difficult to condemn Afrocentric extremism and black racism because those ideologies are also constructed on the foundation of Boasian relativism. Instead, all the threats and actions of black racists must be blamed on societal racism or on liberalism itself: "Look what we made them do."[7] Not only does liberal relativism legitimate white and black racism, but it also concedes the high ground to the forces of bigotry: white racists become the unchallenged custodians of Western civilization, and black racists become the most clear-eyed diagnosticians of our social problems. . . .

## Rethinking Racism

So what about racism? . . . [Racism] is not reducible to ignorance or fear. Not only is the liberal remedy for racism incorrect; the basic diagnosis of the malady is wrong. Racism is what it always was: an opinion that recognizes real civilizational differences and attributes them to biology. Liberal relativism has been based on the denial of the differences. Liberals should henceforth admit the differences but deny their biological foundation. Thus liberals can continue to reject racism by preserving the Boasian distinction between race and culture. This is not a denial of the fact that individuals do differ or even the possibility that there are some natural differences between groups. Yet liberals can convincingly argue that whatever these may be, they are not significant enough to warrant differential treatment by law or policy. In other words, intrinsic differences are irrelevant when it comes to the ability of citizens to exercise their rights and responsibilities. Liberals can explain group differences in academic and economic performance by pointing to cultural differences, and acknowledging that some cultures are functionally superior to others. The racist fallacy, as Anthony Appiah contends, is the act of "biologizing what is culture."[8]

Yet this new liberal understanding should not make the present mistake—duplicated in thousands of sensitivity classes—of treating racism the way a Baptist preacher considers sin. Rather, it should recognize racism as an opinion, which may be right or wrong, but which in any case is a point of view that should be argued with and not suppressed. Antiracist education is largely a waste of time because it typically results in intellectual and moral coercion. Heavy-handed bullying may produce public acquiescence but it cannot compel private assent. Increasingly it appears that it is liberal antiracism that is based on ignorance and fear: ignorance of the true nature of racism, and fear that the racist point of view better explains the world than its liberal counterpart.

For a generation, liberals have treated racism as a form of psychological dementia in need of increasingly coercive forms of enlightenment. But liberal societies should not seek to regulate people's inner thoughts, nor should they outlaw ideas however reprehensible we find them. Hate speech and hate crime laws that impose punishment or enhanced penalties for proscribed motives and viewpoints are inherently illiberal and destructive of intellectual independence and conscience. Americans should recognize that racism is not what it used to be; it does exist, but we can live with it. This is not to say that racism does not do damage, only that the sorts of measures that would be needed to eradicate all vestiges of racist thought can only be totalitarian. Efforts to root out residual racism often create more injustice than they eliminate.

The crucial policy issue is what to do about discrimination. Irrational discrimination of the sort that inspired the civil rights laws of the 1960s is now, as we have seen, a relatively infrequent occurrence. Although such discrimination continues to cause harm, it is irrelevant to the prospects of blacks as a group because it is selective rather than comprehensive in scope. For a minority like African Americans, discrimination is only catastrophic when virtually everyone colludes to enforce it. Consider what would happen if every baseball team in America refused to hire blacks. Blacks would suffer most, because they would be denied the opportunity to play professional baseball. And fans would suffer, because the quality of games would be diminished. But what if only a few teams—say the New York Yankees and the Los Angeles Dodgers—refused to hire blacks? African Americans as a group would suffer hardly at all, because the best black players would offer their services to other teams. The Yankees and the Dodgers would suffer a great deal, because they would be deprived of the chance to hire talented black players. Eventually competitive pressure would force the Yankees and Dodgers either to hire blacks, or to suffer losses in games and revenue.[9] As Gary Becker has pointed out, in a free market, selective discrimination imposes the heaviest cost on the discriminator, which is where it should be. Some people will undoubtedly continue to eschew blacks because of their "taste for discrimination," but most will continue to deal with them because of their taste for profit.[10] Rational discrimination, on the other hand, is likely to persist even in a fully competitive market. . . .

What we need is a long-term strategy that holds the government to a rigorous standard of race neutrality, while allowing private actors to be free to discriminate as they wish. In practice, this means uncompromising color blindness in government hiring and promotion, criminal justice, and the drawing of voting districts. Yet individuals and companies would be allowed to discriminate in private transactions such as renting an apartment or hiring for a job. Am I calling for a repeal of the Civil Rights Act of 1964? Actually, yes. The law should be changed so that its nondiscrimination provisions apply only to the government.

## The End of Racism

Once we have set aside the false remedies premised on relativism—proportional representation and multiculturalism—it is possible to directly address America's real problem, which is partly a race problem and partly a black problem. The solution to the race problem is a public policy that is strictly indifferent to race. The black problem can be solved only through a program of cultural reconstruction in which society plays a supporting role but which is carried out primarily by African Americans themselves. Both projects need to be pursued simultaneously; neither can work by itself. If society is race neutral but blacks remain uncompetitive, then equality of rights for individuals will lead to dramatic inequality of result for groups, liberal embarrassment will set in, and we are back on the path to racial preferences. On the other hand, if blacks are going to reform their community, they have a right to expect that they will be treated equally under the law. Although America has a long way to go, many mistakes have been made, and current antagonisms are high, still there are hopeful signs that the nation can move toward a society in which race ceases to matter, a destination that we can term "the end of racism."

# Notes

1. William Julius Wilson, *The Truly Disadvantaged: The Inner City, the Underclass, and Public Policy,* University of Chicago, Chicago, 1987, p. 11.

2. "If all racial discrimination were abolished today, the life prospects facing many poor blacks would still constitute major challenges for public policy." Gerald David Jaynes and Robin M. Williams, *A Common Destiny: Blacks and American Society,* National Academy Press, Washington, DC, 1989, p. 4.

3. E. Franklin Frazier, *The Negro Family in the United States,* University of Chicago Press, Chicago, 1939, p. 487.

4. "When we react to the rumor of inferiority by avoiding intellectual engagement, and when we allow our children to do so, black people forfeit the opportunity for intellectual development which could extinguish the debate about our capacities, and set the stage for group progress." Jeff Howard and Ray Hammond, "Rumors of Inferiority," *The New Republic,* September 9, 1985.

5. Michael Massing, "Ghetto Blasting," *New Yorker,* January 16, 1995, p. 36.

6. Andrew Hacker, *Two Nations: Black and White, Separate, Hostile, Unequal,* Ballantine Books, New York, 1992, p. 218.

7. An example of this rhetoric is Joe Feagin and Hernan Vera's assertion that despite her incendiary rhetoric, "Sister Souljah is not the problem—she is only a messenger with bad news about the state of white racism." Joe Feagin and Hernan Vera, *White Racism: The Basics,* Routledge, New York, 1995, p. 131.

8. Anthony Appiah, *In My Father's House: Africa in the Philosophy of Culture,* Oxford University Press, New York, 1992, p. 45.

9. Jencks, *Rethinking Social Policy,* p. 41.

10. Gary S. Becker, *The Economics of Discrimination,* University of Chicago Press, Chicago, 1971.

# POSTSCRIPT

## Is Racism a Permanent Feature of American Society?

**R**acism has played a major role in the formation and ongoing development of the American society. Given this existential reality, it is not difficult to understand that some observers and analysts of American race relations, when confronted with the inequality that persists between blacks and whites in society would blame this phenomenon on racial discrimination. Those who support this argument view racism as a continuing and permanent reality of American society.

Derrick Bell is a proponent of this view. In the selection, Bell argues that "Black people will never gain full equality in this country." For him the legacy of institutional discrimination that was reflected in slavery continues through the exclusionary policies of racial segregation that has left blacks "at the bottom of the well." Additionally, Bell views certain roles that blacks play in the society, such as the scapegoat, as contributing to the permanence of racism. Who will play these roles? He also views the color-coded perceptions and behaviors that dominate social interaction between the "races" as so culturally imbedded as to be virtually impossible to overcome.

It is interesting to note that in the America of today there is substantial support, especially within the white population, for the goal of achieving a color-blind society (see Issue 7) as the proper response to the deleterious influences of an endemic and pervasive racism on the people and institutions of the nation. Such a policy recommendation is based on a clear recognition that white racism within the nation and throughout the world is reflective of a profound and entrenched color consciousness that has manifested itself in long-standing practices and policies of discrimination and exclusion, a sorting-out process that is primarily based on the color of one's skin. However, the debate over such a policy goal within society serves to illuminate the salience of "race" and the establishment of distinct color-coded racial categories in influencing the development of social relations within modern societies such as the United States and South Africa.

D'Souza, in contrast, argues that blacks who do not conform to the destructive behavior of their peers are making significant progress in the United States. So, he firmly believes that the blacks who are lagging in their pursuit of the American dream are afflicted by destructive impacts of black culture (i.e., the wrong values). The culture he refers to is that of the black underclass. D'Souza believes that the social pathology that it produces within African-American life is the primary source of the lagging progress of the race.

The 2007 racial controversy started by white radio talk show host Don Imus' on air comments about the predominantly black Rutgers University women's basketball team is instructive. The host referred to the team as "nappy-headed hoes" and "jiggaboos." Is this an example of media-perpetuated racism? Does it contribute to the continuity and perhaps permanence of racism in American culture? Moreover, increasingly, popular talk radio, which at times can promote public hatred of minority groups, is at the center of the controversy. Students may want to use talk radio examples in their discussion of the permanence of racism and the persistence of discrimination.

Overwhelmingly, white sports fans indicate that they are color-blind when it comes to teams and athletes, where winning and overall performance matter most. The attitude, as argued by *New York Times* columnist William C. Rhoden, "is that racism is something for the archives, especially in professional sports, in which so many black and brown athletes are richly compensated." (*NY Times*, May 25, 2008). Clearly, Rhoden's position gives support to Derrick Bell's argument for the permanence of racism. D'Souza would most likely challenge Rhoden's position.

To illustrate Bell's notion of the permanence of racism, students interested in race and sport will find a five-part series in the popular magazine *Sports Illustrated* entitled "The Black Athlete—A Shameful Story," (Volume 29, No. 1–5, July 1968) illuminating in documenting racism in professional and collegiate sports during the 1950s and 1960s. Also, the recently published *Forty Million Dollar Slaves: The Rise, Fall, and Redemption of the Black Athlete* (Crown Publishers 2006) written by *New York Times* sports columnist William C. Rhoden, offers an insightful analysis of both the excellence and exploitation of comtemporary black athletes.

A comprehensive reader entitled *Racism* (Oxford, 1999), edited by Martin Bulmer and John Solomos, offers students both classical and contemporary selections on racism. Gunnar Myrdal's *An American Dilemma* (Harper, 1944) is a classic that deconstructs post–World War II race relations. In agreement with Bell is Eduardo Bonilla-Silva's *Racism Without Racists: Color-Blind Racism and the Persistence of Racial Inequality in the United States* (Rowman & Littlefield, 2003). He argues that the emphasis on "color-blindness" is a new form of racism. Also, for an extended argument, see Bonilla-Silva's *White Supremacy and Racism in the Post Civil Rights Era* (Rienner, 2001). William Julius Wilson's *The Declining Significance of Race: Blacks and Changing American Institutions* (University of Chicago Press, 1978) emphasizes issues of class although it does not deny the existence of racism. Tomas Almaguer, in *Racial Fault Lines: The Historical Origins of White Supremacy in California* (University of California Press, 1994), develops a comparative, historical study of the racialization of Mexican Americans, Native Americans, Asian Americans, and others, which resulted in a society structured as a racial hierarchy influenced by white supremacy philosophy. This was the foundation of the state of California and the southwest overall. *Slavery by Another Name: The Re-Enslavement of Black Americans from the Civil War to World War II,* by Douglas A. Blackmon (Doubleday, 2008), is a groundbreaking account of how thousands of free black men labored without compensation for white southerners in a form of "neoslavery."

For literature dealing with cultural values and poverty, see *La Vida: A Puerto Rican Family in the Culture of Poverty, San Juan and New York* (Random House, 1966) by Oscar Lewis. Edward Banfield, in *The Unheavenly City* (Little, Brown, 1970) argues that cultural values are the major cause of urban poverty. Lawrence E. Harrison promotes the culture of poverty thesis in *Who Prospers? How Cultural Values Shape Economic and Political Success* (Basic Books, 1992). A critique of the culture of poverty perspective can be found in *Yo' Mama's Disfunktional: Fighting the Culture Wars in Urban America* (Beacon, 1997) by Robin Kelly. A structural explanation of poverty can be found in *The Truly Disadvantaged* (University of Chicago Press, 1990), written by William Julius Wilson, the leading authority on the black underclass.

Among the recent publications contributing to the issue of racism in America is James W. Loewen's *Sundown Towns: A Hidden Dimension of American Racism* (Touchstone 2006). It is a comprehensive history of all-white towns established in American between 1890 and 1968. *Medical Apartheid: The Dark History of Medical Experimentation on Black Americans from Colonial Times to the Present* (Doubleday 2007) by Harriet A. Washington is a groundbreaking study that documents the infamous Tuskegee experiments and New York State Psychiatric Institute and Columbia University drug experiments on African-American and black Dominican boys to determine a genetic predisposition for "disruptive behavior." In July 2008, Washington wrote an essay for the *New York Times* entitled "Apology Shines Light on Racial Schism in Medicine." The essay summarized the racism in medicine documented by the American Medical Association's exclusion of blacks. On July 10, 2008, the AMA made a public apology for "past wrongs." *Driven Out: The Forgotten War against Chinese Americans* (Random House, 2007) by Jean Pfaelzer describes the purging of thousands of Chinese immigrants in the Pacific Northwest and Rocky Mountain region between 1850 and 1906. *Buried in the Bitter Waters: The Hidden History of Racial Cleansing in America* (Basic Books, 2007) by Elliot Jaspin reveals a systematic racial cleansing that took place in the United States from the Civil War to the 1920s. These recently published sources make significant contributions to the literature on racism in America.

# ISSUE 10

# Is Racial Profiling Defensible Public Policy?

**YES: Scott Johnson,** from "Better Unsafe than (Occasionally) Sorry?" *The American Enterprise* (January/February 2003)

**NO: David A. Harris,** from *Profiles in Injustice: Why Police Profiling Cannot Work* (The New Press, 2002)

## ISSUE SUMMARY

**YES:** Scott Johnson, conservative journalist and an attorney and fellow at the Clermont Institute, argues in favor of racial profiling. He claims that racial profiling does not exist "on the nation's highways and streets." Johnson accuses David Harris of distorting the data on crimes committed and victimization according to race. For him, law enforcement needs to engage in profiling under certain circumstances in order to be effective.

**NO:** David A. Harris, law professor and leading authority on racial profiling, argues that racial profiling is ineffective and damaging to our diverse nation. He believes it hinders effective law enforcement.

$T$he issue of racial profiling has raised many questions concerning the society's commitment to the rule of law and the protection of individual rights as provided within the Constitution of the United States. This issue has gained greater salience in America in the wake of the events of September 11, 2001 that gave impetus to an overwhelming focus on national security both within and outside of government.

Scott Johnson suggests that racial profiling is a reasonable and appropriate response to the challenges that confront the nation in its attempts to prevent crime and to maintain social order effectively. In developing his argument in favor of profiling, Scott Johnson contends that the data available on crime rates and arrests by race does not support the claim of racially biased policing as claimed by David Harris and others. Johnson views the opponents of racial profiling as undermining the effectiveness of law enforcement by denying them such a tool. He claims that the restrictions upon profiling will impact disproportionately upon the security of minority victims of crime. Thus, Johnson believes that the profiling of members of certain groups as potential perpetrators of crime is reasonable and effective. From his perspective, "better safe than sorry."

In addition to viewing racial profiling as morally wrong, David Harris argues that there are other salient reasons for opposing this practice. Thus, he is concerned that the police are targeting persons with dark skins without proper reference to probable cause, an important principle of American law. To Harris, treating an entire group as potential criminals based on the wrong-doing of a small cohort of its members violates the equal protection principle of the XIV Amendment of the Constitution of the United States, a significant value of the nation's political culture.

Harris is also convinced that racial profiling is an ineffective practice of law enforcement, and he presents an empirical argument to support his claim. Additionally, David Harris is concerned that racial profiling is having a corrosive impact on the relationship between the police and the African American, Latino, and other minority communities they are responsible to protect and to serve. He believes that such treatment of minority groups can only result in a diminution of respect for law enforcement and a polarization between the police and members of these communities, thus making effective law enforcement more difficult to achieve.

To place this issue in perspective, readers must confront the topics of race, crime, national security, and criminal justice. How does our concern with effective law enforcement contribute to racial profiling? Does the culture of police contribute to racial profiling? Is racial profiling unequal treatment? Are minority police officers a response to this problem? On the other hand, is there an anti-police culture within the African-American community? The actions of the Oklahoma City bomber, Timothy McVeigh, a white American, did not result in racial profiling. What does that suggest about racial profiling? Are members of anti-government militias who congregate in remote areas and sharpen their military skills with live arms being targeted in accordance with a "white" profile? How can America balance its egalitarian commitment with the profiling of Arabs/Muslims?

# YES

Scott Johnson

# Better Unsafe than (Occasionally) Sorry?

**D**avid Harris is the University of Toledo law professor who provided much of the intellectual heft behind the war on racial profiling. His 1999 report for the American Civil Liberties Union, which has filed most of the anti-profiling law suits, was entitled "Driving While Black: Racial Profiling on the Nation's Highways." In 2002 he expanded his argument into a book.

The national ruckus Harris helped stir up has, among other results, made it hard for security personnel to use intelligent profiles to uncover potential terrorists in airports, at our national borders, and at visa offices abroad. That is a mistake that has already come to haunt the U.S. horribly (see sidebar). And so long as anti-profiling crusaders prevent law enforcement officials from carefully applying profiling tools, Americans will continue to be needlessly exposed to potential re-runs of September 11.

Harris and his compatriots are clever enough to present themselves as friends of law enforcement, who are just trying to help the police do a better job. Harris himself purports to object to racial profiling mostly because it's "ineffective." But the reality is that he has launched a broad and misguided attack on America's law enforcement and criminal justice systems. Like most of the activists who have turned the campaign against racial profiling into a crusade, Harris practices a shoddy form of racial politics with which we have become all too familiar.

The thesis at the heart of the anti-profiling complaint—that racial disparities in crime rates and arrests reflect racially biased policing—is torn to shreds by basic criminological data. David Harris argues that crime rates are equal among racial groups, and arrests, convictions, and incarcerations are unequal simply because police, prosecutors, and courts systematically pick on minorities because of the color of their skin. The logic of his argument ends in a demand for justice by racial quota.

The contention that crime is committed at equal rates by members of various ethnic groups is the central premise of the ACLU's anti-profiling argument. If that premise is false, their argument fails. And the stakes are high. The issue of alleged ethnic discrimination by police has taken on a heightened importance amidst the war on terrorism. Many of the profiling issues that began as farce over traffic enforcement stops are now replaying themselves in the war on terror as potential tragedies.

From *American Enterprise*, vol. 14, issue 1, January/February 2003, pp. 28–30. Copyright © 2006 by American Enterprise Institute. Reprinted by permission.

Contrary to the view of the world propounded by David Harris and the ACLU, racial disparities in law enforcement generally reflect racial disparities in crime rates. It is true that racial disparities exist at many stages of our criminal justice system. Blacks have been arrested, convicted, and incarcerated at rates far exceeding those of whites for as long as official data on the subject have been compiled. Middle Eastern Arabs have been disproportionately associated with air terrorism for more than a generation.

These disparities have been studied for evidence of systematic discrimination, and it is now widely accepted among serious scholars, such as Professor Michael Tonry of the University of Minnesota Law School, that higher levels of arrests and incarceration in the U.S. by ethnicity result substantially from higher levels of crime, not racial bias. Sometimes the magnitude of the racial disparities in crime rates is huge. The black murder rate is seven to ten times the white murder rate.

Harris claims that disparities in arrest and incarceration rates are a function of systemic law enforcement bias. Finding that the best national data do not agree, he arbitrarily declares the data wrong: Citing statistics from the National Crime Victimization Survey, he correctly states that more than 50 percent of violent crimes are unreported. Harris then absurdly implies that it is among these unreported crimes that the otherwise undetected white criminals are hiding.

Harris's argument on this basic point does not reflect well on his methods. He makes such claims not only against cops, but against all parts of our justice system. According to him, "Just as with arrest statistics, incarceration rates measure not crime but the activity of people and institutions responsible for determining criminal sentences." In other words: Judges are racists too, just trust me.

Harris implies that if law enforcers just weren't so darn fixated on Arabs, blacks, and other minority groups, officials would discover that comparable levels of crime and terrorism are committed by whites, and just left unpunished. But we have statistics on the race of perpetrators as identified by the victims of unreported crimes. And guess what? They closely track the racial identity of perpetrators in reported crimes. Harris omits this inconvenient fact brought to light by the National Crime Victimization Survey, even though he relies on that same survey to build other parts of his argument.

The anti-profilers' campaign against law enforcement is particularly bizarre and perverse given that minorities are vastly more likely to be victims of crimes. What kind of "civil rights campaign" prevents the police from incapacitating criminals who prey on minority groups? If police flinch from law enforcement for fear of generating bad arrest data that will label them racist, the great harm that follows will fall disproportionately on law-abiding residents of lower-income neighborhoods.

The controversy over "racial profiling" originated in data regarding traffic stops and airport searches that disproportionately affect blacks and ethnic minorities. In his book, Harris traces profiling back to Operation Pipeline, the 1986 Drug Enforcement Administration effort to enlist highway police in interdicting illegal drugs as they are transported by distributors on the nation's highways. Harris's argument that Operation Pipeline resulted in unfair racial profiling by highway patrollers in New Jersey, Maryland, and elsewhere is predicated on studies that falsely assume there are no ethnic differences in driving behavior, and that all ethnicities violate traffic laws at the same high rate. It is also based on the assertion that drug violations are roughly equal across groups.

But a definitive study commissioned by the New Jersey attorney general and designed by the Public Service Research Institute of Maryland found that on the New Jersey Turnpike blacks speed twice as much as white drivers-and are actually stopped less than their speeding behavior would predict. (The study was released after Harris's book had been published.) Elsewhere, Harris conflates statistics on drug use among racial groups (roughly equal) with statistics on drug distribution (as far as we can tell, not close to equal). It is drug distributors that highway patrol officers are seeking out, not drug users.

Several of the studies used by profiling opponents to indict police show nearly equal "hit" rates between whites and blacks despite the fact that blacks were searched at higher rates. (Hit rates are the rates at which searches result in the discovery of contraband.) In Maryland, "73 percent of those stopped and searched on a section of Interstate 95 were black, yet state police reported that equal percentages of the whites and blacks who were searched had drugs or other contraband," groused the New York Times. "Studies have shown that being black substantially raises the odds of a person being stopped and searched by the police-even though blacks who are stopped are no more likely than whites to be carrying drugs," complained the New Republic last year. What these statistically misleading statements overlook is that if the hit rates are about equal, there is no discrimination. It appears the police are focusing on legitimately suspicious behavior, and not simply picking on people by ethnicity.

The war on racial profiling has obscured two important facts: Racial profiling does not exist where the ACLU has persuaded everyone it does, such as on the nation's highways and streets. And it does not exist where it should, in the nation's airports and airlines.

Unfortunately, the facts have yet to catch up with the myths promoted by opponents of criminal profiling. Many Americans—including many of our leaders in politics and law enforcement—continue to treat profiling as illegitimate, as if it were disproved and discredited. That is the product of a political campaign, not of scholarly research. And it is a policy which leaves innocent Americans far more exposed to danger than they ought to be.

 **NO**

# Profiles in Injustice: American Life under the Regime of Racial Profiling

## Sergeant Rossano Gerald

Sergeant First Class Rossano Gerald, a black man, had made the United States Army his life. He served in Operation Desert Storm in Iraq, winning the Bronze Star, and in Operation United Shield in Somalia. His nineteen-year military career has included postings both in the United States and overseas. Military service runs deep in Sergeant Gerald's family; he describes himself as an "army brat" who grew up on military bases.

One blazing hot August day in 1998, Sergeant Gerald and his twelve-year-old son, Gregory, were on their way to a big family reunion in Oklahoma. Almost as soon as they crossed into Oklahoma from Arkansas, an Oklahoma Highway Patrol officer stopped their car. He questioned them, warning Sergeant Gerald not to follow cars in front of him too closely, then allowed him to leave. (Gerald denies following any other cars too closely; because he had noticed several highway patrol cars as he entered the state, he had been driving with extra caution.) But less than half an hour farther into Oklahoma, another highway patrol officer stopped Sergeant Gerald again, this time accusing him of changing lanes without signaling. Sergeant Gerald denied this, and he told the officer that another officer had just stopped him.

Despite Sergeant Gerald's having produced a valid driver's license, proof of insurance, and army identification, the troopers—several squad cars had arrived by now—asked to search his car. Sergeant Gerald politely refused; after answering numerous questions, Sergeant Gerald asked many times that the officer in charge call his commanding officer at his base. The highway patrol officers refused each request. Instead, the police put Sergeant Gerald and Gregory into a squad car, turned off the air conditioning, and turned on the car's fan, which blew suffocatingly hot air into the vehicle; they warned Sergeant Gerald and Gregory that the police dogs present would attack them if they tried to escape.

When Sergeant Gerald still refused to allow them to search his car, the troopers told him that Oklahoma statutes allowed them to search (a blatant misstatement of the law), and they had a drug-sniffing dog search the vehicle. Sergeant Gerald knew something about these animals; as part of his army duties, he'd worked with military police officers using drug-detection dogs. The dog never gave any signal that it smelled drugs, but the troopers told Sergeant Gerald that the dog had "alerted" to the presence of narcotics and that they were going to search his car.

For what seemed like hours in the oppressive heat, Sergeant Gerald—now in handcuffs in the backseat of a patrol car—watched as officers used a variety of tools to take apart door panels, consoles, even the inside of the car's roof; at one point they announced that they had found a "secret compartment" in the car's floor. (It was actually a factory-installed footrest.) The troopers attempted to block his view of the search by raising the hoods on their vehicles, and one of them deactivated a patrol car video-evidence camera. They went through every item in the luggage, questioning Sergeant Gerald about Gregory's plane tickets home, which they found in one of the suitcases. (Gregory lived with his mother in northern Indiana, and Sergeant Gerald planned to put him on a plane home after the reunion.) Meanwhile, Gregory was moved to another police car against his father's express wishes; he was made to sit in the front while a dog barked and growled at him from the backseat and a police officer asked him about his father's "involvement" in drug trafficking.

After two and a half hours—and no recovery of any drugs—the police released Sergeant Gerald with a warning ticket. When he asked them what they planned to do about the mess they had made of his car and his personal belongings, they gave him a screwdriver. Their parting words to him: "We ain't good at repacking." Damage to the car amounted to more than a thousand dollars.

Sergeant Gerald filed a lawsuit to contest his mistreatment. Although he has little taste or desire for litigation, he felt he owed it to his son, Gregory, to show that people who have power cannot abuse others with impunity. "I'm an authority figure myself," Sergeant Gerald says. "I don't want my son thinking for one minute that this kind of behavior by anyone in uniform is acceptable." The lawsuit ended with a settlement of seventy-five thousand dollars paid to Sergeant Gerald and Gregory, even as state officials still denied any wrongdoing. "I think I serve my country well," Sergeant Gerald said. "I never want my son to see racism like this happen." Gregory, he said, remains "scarred" by the experience.

## Judge Filemon Vela

In 1980, President Carter appointed Filemon Vela United States District Judge for the Southern District of Texas. Vela had been an elected state judge for six years before that, following a career in private practice. Judge Vela's chambers are in Brownsville, Texas, just across the Rio Grande from Matamoros, Mexico. Brownsville has a long history of connection with Mexico; many of its 130,000 citizens are of Mexican descent. Judge Vela's own great-grandfather came to Texas from Mexico in the 1860s. People know Judge Vela not only for what he does in his courtroom, but also for his activities in the community. His bedrock beliefs in education and straight talk led him to help organize and direct a program in which young male and female convicts serving drug sentences come to local high schools to tell the students how involvement with drugs and violence stole their futures. Judge Vela plays the Ted Koppel role in these sessions, asking the inmates about everything from their fear of prison rape to their shame at having embarrassed their families. Judge Vela's wife, Blanca Vela, is the mayor of Brownsville; between their friends, families, and their many personal and professional acquaintances, they know almost everyone in the city who is involved in politics and civic life.

In 1997, the area around Brownsville became the focus of intense immigration enforcement. "Operation Rio Grande" increased the number of agents in the area from seven hundred to twelve hundred by the end of 1999 and poured sophisticated equipment and resources into the effort. The stepped-up activity paralleled similar operations in California, West Texas, and other illegal immigration hot spots. The result was a strong, proactive Border Patrol presence, enough to affect almost everyone of Mexican descent.

During the summer of 1999, Judge Vela and three members of his staff drove to Laredo, one of the cities in south Texas where Judge Vela holds court on a regular basis. The four rode in a Ford Explorer. A Border Patrol agent, who'd been sitting in a vehicle parked next to the side of the road, pulled them over. The agent asked Judge Vela and the others in the car about their citizenship. After they had answered, Judge Vela asked the agent why he had stopped the car. "He said he stopped us because there were too many people in the vehicle," Vela says, though the Explorer could certainly have held more passengers. Only then did Judge Vela tell the agent who he was; he also said that he felt that the agent did not have legal grounds to stop them. Though the agent quickly ended the encounter, telling Judge Vela and his staff they could go, Vela made a complaint to the officer's superiors—not so much about the conduct of the particular officer involved but rather about the practices and policies that led him to make an unjustified stop. As a judge, he was keenly aware that for any search that uncovers contraband to "stand up in court," the stop of the car that led to the search had to be legal. If the stop was illegal, a judge would have to throw out the evidence—and a criminal would go free. It's not at all surprising that Judge Vela's complaint was taken seriously by the Border Patrol; he received assurances that Border Patrol agents would get more training and education to teach them to stop motorists only with a legal basis.

Almost exactly a year after his first encounter with the Border Patrol, Judge Vela was again on his way to Laredo to preside in court, driving on the same road, this time as the passenger of an assistant U.S. attorney. His staff was riding in another vehicle, traveling along with them. Again, a

Border Patrol agent pulled the car over; again, Judge Vela—an American citizen, an attorney, and a federal judge—had to answer questions about his citizenship. Once again, Judge Vela asked why the agent stopped them. The answer this time: the car had tinted windows. Judge Vela filed another complaint, but he was not surprised that a second incident had occurred.

Judge Vela talks about these experiences with candor and a touch of humor. He feels that although it is important to speak out, he cannot allow himself to be defined or embittered by what has happened. "If I ever catch myself being affected by these kinds of things, I should not allow myself to sit [as a judge]," he says. Yet it is clear that these experiences have confirmed for him that everyone in the Hispanic community is a target of immigration enforcement, regardless of whether they are citizens, or of their status or station in life. "If they stop us . . . we who are attorneys, we who study law . . . then my goodness, what will they do to persons who do not have our place?" he wonders. "If they can do it to you and me," he says, referring to himself, his staff, and the assistant U.S. attorney who were with him, "who won't they do it to?" Vela has taught American law and constitutionalism on behalf of the Unites States government to attorneys, judges, and other officials all over the world, particularly in Latin America, and he believes with all his heart that the United States and its Constitution are something special, something unique—something worth preserving. "But if you let these things happen, it will deteriorate." He worries that something is badly out of balance. Another Hispanic judge in Brownsville, who has also experienced the Border Patrol's tactics firsthand, puts it this way: "It feels like occupied territory. It does not feel like we're in the United States of America."

## Minhtran Tran and Quyen Pham

With school out for the year, Minhtran Tran and Quyen Pham went shopping one morning at a strip of stores in Garden Grove, a city of approximately 150,000 in Orange County, California. Neither girl, both fifteen-year-old honor students, had a police record or had had any contact at all with law enforcement. When they decided to leave and went to a pay phone outside the stores, police from Garden Grove's gang suppression unit drove up, got out of their cars, and confronted them and a third young Asian girl. The police accused them of making trouble and asked them whether they belonged to a gang, allegedly because they were wearing gang clothing. Officers then put the three girls up against a wall and took photographs of them with a Polaroid camera. None of the girls consented; in fact, the police never asked for their permission, let alone the permission of their parents. The "gang attire" they were alleged to have been wearing could have described the clothing of a million other teenagers that day: form-fitting shirts and oversized baggy pants. The police also took down information from the girls, including height, weight, age, hair and eye color, their home addresses, and the names of the schools they attended.

Minhtran Tran and Quyen Pham may have felt disturbed by their treatment that day, but they received a worse shock later. Other kids they knew who went to the Garden Grove Police Station later that day told the girls that they saw the Polaroid pictures the police had taken of them pinned up on a prominent bulletin board. The girls found this hard to understand; police had not charged or cited them, and they hadn't done anything. They felt that the police had labeled them criminals and treated them as gang members because they were Asians dressed in a certain way. Eventually, along with other young Asian Americans, the two girls became the plaintiffs in a lawsuit against the Garden Grove Police Department.

The photographing of the high school honor students by police did not happen by accident. Rather, it came about as part of a set of practices put in place as a deliberate effort to fight gangs in California. With an influx of Asian immigrants to the West Coast over the last twenty-five years, including refugees from Southeast Asia, the region's Asian population has surged. The growth of any immigrant population typically contributes to the problems one customarily finds in any city or suburban area, including crime and gangs. The Asian population is no different, despite the model minority stereotype, and in the early 1990s southern California communities began to make a concerted effort to combat what they saw as a rising menace.

One of the first examples of the effort came in a thirty-page report, entitled "Asian Gangs in Little Saigon: Identification and Methods of Operation." The document, written by Detective Mark Nye of the Westminster Police Department, explored many aspects of Orange County's Asian youth gangs, from what they did to how they dressed to which cars they drove. The report discussed many different demographic groups, including female gang members. Nye warned that "female gang members in some cases dress very similar to male gang members. They will wear baggy, loose fitting clothing, baggy pants, oversized shirts, usually untucked, and in some cases baseball caps." (Parents will recognize this description of clothing as the nearly ubiquitous uniform of the American teenager—Asian, African American, Hispanic, or white.) Female members of Asian gangs, Nye said, looked enough like their male counterparts that they "can be mistakenly identified as males." And in a catch-22 that makes it difficult to see how any young Asian woman could avoid being labeled as a gang member, Nye said that Asian girls who did not dress in typical gang attire were really just in "disguise."

## Robert Wilkins

In the early morning hours of a Monday in May 1992, Robert Wilkins and three members of his extended family were driving to Washington, D.C. from Chicago. The four, all African Americans, had traveled together to Chicago a few days before for the funeral of Wilkins's grandfather, the family patriarch. As they drove along an interstate highway outside of Cumberland, Maryland, a Maryland State Police car pulled them over. Wilkins's cousin had been at the wheel when Wilkins noticed that the stop had lasted some time and that the trooper had brought his cousin to the rear of their rental car, where he could not be seen. Wilkins and his uncle got out to see what was happening.

Wilkins's decision to get out of the car and investigate made perfect sense. He had exactly the right training to deal with a situation like this. A graduate of Harvard Law School, Wilkins was himself a criminal defense lawyer. He practiced with Washington, D.C.'s Public Defender Service, one of the most highly regarded public defender offices in the nation. Wilkins had considerable seasoning not only in the ins and outs of criminal and constitutional law, but also in the nuances of police tactics and street stops. He was a skilled trial lawyer, accustomed to speaking his mind in court crisply, authoritatively, and carefully, even though he was a soft-spoken person. He also had considerable experience dealing with police officers.

Wilkins's cousin, who had been driving, told him that the trooper wanted consent to search the car. It was true; the trooper showed Wilkins a consent-to-search form—a piece of paper that, if signed, would indicate that the trooper had obtained voluntary consent to a search of the car. "I explained to him who I was and that I was a public defender in Washington, D.C.," Wilkins said, "and I understood clearly what our rights were and what his rights were, and that we didn't want to have the car searched." The trooper's reply, though perhaps showing a lack of understanding of the law, was just as clear as Wilkins's statement had been. "He looked at me," Wilkins said, "and he said, 'Well, if you don't have anything to hide, then what's the problem?'"

Undoubtedly, most ordinary people would have given in to the officer's demand at this point, but Wilkins was not so easily intimidated. "I thought to myself that this is the exact, most inappropriate response that the law enforcement officer can give," he said. Just asserting your rights "shouldn't make you suspicious." Wilkins held firm; he told the officer that he and his family wanted to be left alone.

The trooper seemed genuinely puzzled and surprised. Giving the trooper credit for frankness, Wilkins remembers his explanation. "He said, 'Well, this is routine, no one ever objects.' I said I don't know what other people do and that may be the case that nobody else does, but we object." The trooper, perhaps sensing that he was not going to get to search the car the easy way, began to play hardball. He told Wilkins that he and his family would have to wait for a drug-sniffing dog. Wilkins continued to stand his ground, calmly but firmly. He told the trooper that *United States v. Sharpe,* a U.S. Supreme Court decision, said that he could not detain Wilkins and his family without some fact-based suspicion, and he asserted that there was nothing even remotely suspicious about the family. Though Wilkins clearly had the law on his side, the trooper didn't care to debate the issue. He told Wilkins that these searches were "just routine procedure" because the police had been having "problems with rental cars and drugs." (Wilkins and his family were driving a Virginia-registered rental car; the license plate, with its first letter *R,* showed this.) "He wasn't rude, he was firm," Wilkins recalls. "He just made clear, 'Look, you know, this is procedure. . . . You're gonna have to wait here for this dog.'" Even offering to show the trooper the program from his grandfather's funeral did not change anything. By this time, other troopers had arrived. Though they saw Wilkins begin to write down names and badge numbers on a pad, the troopers were undeterred; in fact, Wilkins remembers that at least one seemed quite amused by his insistence on his rights.

And the way the trooper wanted it was, in the end, the way it went. The family was held until the dog arrived. Despite their strenuous objections, all of them were forced to get out of the car and stand in the dark and the rain by the side of the road as the dog—so reminiscent to Wilkins and his family of the dogs turned loose on blacks in the South by police in civil rights confrontations—sniffed every inch of the exterior of the car. And only after this careful search turned up nothing were they allowed to leave—with a $105 ticket, though the trooper had originally told them they would receive only a warning. It was only later that Wilkins learned he'd been stopped because of a written profile (prepared by the Maryland State Police) that described him perfectly—a black male in a rental car.

༺◈༻

All four of these stories may sound like egregious examples of police run amok, the work of rogue officers. But the truth is that these situations were the result of a well-known, well-used law enforcement technique that has spread all over the country. It has become known as "racial profiling"—and it describes life for millions of Americans who happen to be black, brown, or Asian. What happened to Sergeant Gerald, Judge Vela, Minhtran Tran and Quyen Pham, and Robert Wilkins is not uncommon at all among people like them. They have lived with these practices for many years—even if the rest of the nation has become aware of racial profiling only recently.

*Racial* profiling grew out of a law enforcement tactic called *criminal* profiling. *Criminal* profiling has come into increasing use over the last twenty years, not just as a way to solve particular crimes police know about but also as a way to predict who may be involved in as-yet-undiscovered crimes, especially drug offenses. *Criminal* profiling is designed to help police spot criminals by developing sets of personal and behavioral characteristics associated with particular offenses. By comparing individuals they observe with profiles, officers should have a better basis for deciding which people to treat as suspects. Officers may see no direct evidence of crime, but they can rely on noncriminal but observable characteristics associated with crime to decide whether someone seems suspicious and therefore deserving of greater police scrutiny.

When these characteristics include race or ethnicity as a factor in predicting crimes, *criminal* profiling can become *racial* profiling. Racial profiling is a crime-fighting strategy—a government policy that treats African Americans, Latinos, and members of other minority groups as criminal suspects on the assumption that doing so will increase the odds of catching criminals. Many in law enforcement argue that it makes sense to use race or ethnicity in criminal profiles because there is a strong statistical association between membership in minority groups and involvement in crime. Having black or brown skin elevates the chances that any given person may be engaged in crime, especially drug crime, the thinking of police and many members of the public goes. The disproportionately large number of minorities reflected in arrest and incarceration statistics is further proof, the argument continues, that skin color is a valid indicator of a greater propensity to commit crime. Supporters of racial profiling arrive, therefore, at the conclusion that focusing police suspicion on blacks, Latinos, Asians, and other minorities makes perfect sense. Racial profiling is nothing more than rational law enforcement.

If racial profiling is what directs police suspicion at minorities, it is high-discretion police tactics that put these suspicions into action, turning profiles into police investigations. These high-discretion methods allow police to detain, question, and search people who have exhibited no concrete evidence of wrongdoing—something the law would almost never otherwise allow. But thanks to the U.S. Supreme Court, which has widened the permissible scope of police discretion and vastly increased law enforcement power at the same time that profiling has come into wide use, these tactics are all perfectly legal. For example, police officers can use traffic enforcement as a legal excuse to "fish" for evidence, even though officers have observed no criminal conduct. Officers can also ask for "voluntary" consent to search, without even a whisper of a reason to think the citizen asked has done anything wrong. And officers can also "stop and frisk" pedestrians without the probable cause they need in other circumstances.

Taken at face value, we could say that racial profiling is morally and ethically wrong. It is clearly unconscionable to treat an individual as a criminal suspect simply because a small number of individuals from the same racial or ethnic group are criminals. But in a society dedicated to equal justice under law, such a practice also undermines our commitment to individual civil rights. Enforcing the law on the basis of racial and ethnic calculations therefore also offends the Constitution. All Americans are guaranteed "the equal protection of the law"; there are few values closer to the core of our political culture. Enforcing the law in a racially or ethnically biased way violates this central principle.

Racial profiling also damages the relationship between police departments and the communities they serve. Almost all police departments today describe themselves as service oriented; community policing, a philosophy of law enforcement that features partnerships between police and the citizens they serve, has become the accepted and applauded orthodoxy everywhere. Yet profiling, which treats all citizens of particular racial and ethnic groups as potential criminals, can do nothing but alienate these same citizens from their police. It breaks down the trust that must be at the heart of any true partnership, and it threatens to defeat community policing's best efforts to fight crime and disorder. Racial profiling reinforces the preexisting fissures of race in our society. By putting citizens in categories by race and ethnicity to determine which ones should be regarded as suspicious and therefore worthy of greater police scrutiny, we divide ourselves into "the good" and "the bad," the citizen and the criminal.

. . . Apart from the moral, ethical, and constitutional arguments against racial profiling, which have increasingly been embraced by Americans of all colors in recent years, new data now offer an irrefutable statistical argument against the practice. Despite the widespread belief that racial profiling, reprehensible though it may be, is an effective and efficient way of catching criminals—a "rational" approach to law enforcement—newly collected information about "hit rates" gives the lie to this assumption: the numbers just don't add up. Data emerging from studies done over the last few years demonstrate conclusively that hit rates—the rates at which police actually find contraband on people they stop—run contrary to long-held "commonsense" beliefs about the effectiveness of racial profiling. The rate at which officers uncover contraband in stops and searches is *not* higher for blacks than for whites, as most people believe. Contrary to what the "rational" law enforcement justification for racial profiling would predict, *the hit rate for drugs and weapons in police searches of African Americans is the same as or lower than the rate for whites.* Comparing Latinos and whites yields even more surprising results. Police catch criminals among Latinos at *far lower rates* than among whites. These results hold true in studies done in New York, Maryland, New Jersey, and other places. We see the same results in data collected by the U.S. Customs Service, concerning the searches it does of people entering the country at airports: the hit rate is lower for blacks than it is for whites, and the hit rate for Latinos is lower still.

Other data also yield startling surprises. For example, while it is true that automobile stops sometimes result in large seizures of drugs, this rarely happens. In fact, police usually find nothing at all; when they do find drugs, it is almost always very small amounts. The quantities discovered seldom exceed enough for personal use and often amount to even less—so-called trace amounts that can be detected but not used. Of course, what we see on the evening news are the big seizures; we seldom hear about the small ones and never about the far more numerous times that officers come up empty-handed. We come away with the mistaken impression that these tactics are not only rational and fair but successful—when nothing could be further from the truth. All of this exposes the rational law enforcement argument as, at best, the product of a set of mistaken assumptions. If blacks and Latinos who are stopped as a result of racial profiling are no more likely or are even less likely to be in possession of drugs or other contraband than whites, it simply doesn't make sense to enforce the law in this way. And if the net results are not a constant parade of big-time seizures of contraband but mostly "dry holes" and tiny amounts, there's no real payoff. If "rational" law enforcement seems to make sense, that is only because we are selective in our interpretations of facts and limited in our vision of what police do and in the effects these actions have.

Even if we were to overlook racial profiling's moral, legal, and social flaws, it simply does not work as a law enforcement tactic. And it is a way of enforcing the law that we almost surely would not accept in other circumstances. Suppose, for example, that profiles focused not on race and ethnicity but on poverty. We can imagine appearance characteristics for poverty that would prove almost as easy to observe as skin color: clothing and personal appearance, the physical condition and age of vehicles, and the neighborhood in which a person lives. Yet we would almost certainly object if police consistently stopped, questioned, and searched almost everyone who looked poor. The assumption that police should treat *all* poor people as criminal suspects because *some* poor people commit crimes would—and should—outrage us. Yet this is precisely what is happening when we police with racial profiles—except, of course, that the burden is likely to be distributed not by poverty, but by race and ethnicity.

It would be easy to assume that racial profiling has its roots only in the racism of individual racist police officers—that the officers who engage in this practice are bigots whom we should simply root out of the police force. Surely there are bigots among police officers, but there are also bigots in every other profession. The great majority of police officers are good people who make use of racial profiling unintentionally. They do so not because they are bigoted or bad, but because they think it is the right way to catch criminals. Racial profiling is an institutional practice—a tactic accepted and encouraged by police agencies as a legitimate, effective crime-fighting tool. It is a method full of assumptions that have, for too long, gone untested, unexamined, and unchallenged. And when we do challenge it—push hard on its underlying premises and look at real data—policing with racial profiles cannot be said to be a rational response to crime. It is instead a misdirected attack on a difficult set of problems that causes its own damage to innocent individuals, to policing, to society, and to the law itself. Racial profiling is based not on real evidence but on distorted ideas about crime and an overly narrow view of how to attack it. We can do better; in fact, we must do better. The task of this book is to get us beyond the inaccurate, incorrect, and misleading ways in which we think about crime and how to fight it.

# POSTSCRIPT

## Is Racial Profiling Defensible Public Policy?

The debate over racial profiling serves to illuminate a major division in American politics between the advocates of human rights and individual liberties and others who are willing to relinquish the protection of certain rights in the interests of law and order and national security. Racial minorities tend to view such policies as unwarranted assaults on their human dignity, and counterproductive to achieving the goals of the wars on drugs, crime, and terrorism. Others are concerned that instead of promoting national security, this policy has alienated minorities and immigrant groups and has raised serious concerns around the world. There is a growing perception within the international community that racial profiling is compromising the U.S. government's commitments to the rule of law and to equal rights and social justice.

The current controversy over racial profiling entered the public consciousness when the issue emerged in New Jersey and other states that were forced to respond to mounting criticisms of law enforcement practices and policies. Due to the vigorous campaign that was launched against this policy by the Black Ministerial Conference of New Jersey, the ACLU, and other black and Latino leaders and organizations, racial profiling appeared to lose some support. However, due to the events of September 11, 2001, and the ensuing declaration of a war on terrorism, public attitudes on this issue seem to have shifted, and many Americans now view it as necessary to secure the nation against a growing threat to national security.

In response to the September 11 terrorist attacks, there has been a perceptible shift in the focus of racial profiling from the war on drugs to a war on terrorism that tends to target Arabs and Muslims, both citizens and immigrants, as suspects. The treatment that members of these groups have received from police, the Immigration and Naturalization Service, and other agents of national security has caused many of their members to reconsider their status and identity within the American society. So, racial profiling is having disconcerting effects on Arabs and Muslims of the United States and is producing negative perceptions of this country within their extended communities throughout the world.

Consider the following example. During a recent congressional primary race in Georgia (August 2006), a challenger to Representative Cynthia McKinney referred to an "abundant number of contributors to Ms. McKinney's campaign have Palestinian and Arab surnames. Now I could accuse her of being under the control of terrorists." Is this an ethnic slur that is the product of stereotyping and profiling? Does the use of Arab-baiting score political points? Why?

Significant evidence is available to demonstrate the ineffectiveness of racial profiling. Yet, people are standing in the netting of racial profiling based on suspicions derived from racial stereotyping, thus exposing the contradictory nature of this practice.

It is important to note that there was a significant increase in the Latino and Asian populations of the United States during the 1990s. As a result of this increase in immigration, the minority population of the nation has continued to grow and now approaches one hundred million. These demographic changes in the United States' population make it clear that managing diversity is one of the most significant challenges facing current and future leadership of the nation. Hence, the issue of racial profiling will become relevant in the future.

More reading critiquing racial profiling can be found in David Harris' *Profiles in Injustice: Why Racial Profiling Cannot Work* (The New Press, 2002). Journalist Kenneth Meek discusses racial profiling and incidents on the New Jersey Turnpike in *Driving While Black: What to Do if You Are a Victim of Racial Profiling* (Broadway Books, 2000). *Race, Crime and the Law* (Vintage, 1998) by Randall Kennedy suggests that liberals and conservatives have more in common than expected when it comes to crime. He argues that blacks do not receive adequate police protection. David Cole explains how law enforcement is a two-tiered system in America in *No Equal Justice: Race and Class in the American Criminal Justice System* (New Press, 2000). In contrast to Cole, Andrew McCarthy argues that policing without profiling does not make sense in "Unreasonable Searches," in *National Review* (August 29, 2005). For a complete and unbiased treatise on racial profiling, see Brian L. Withrow's *Racial Profiling: From Rhetoric to Reason* (Pearson Education, Inc. 2006). He traces the issue from its current rhetoric of exaggerated and unsupported conclusion into a reasoned and scientific inquiry.

A comprehensive and balanced examination of race, crime, and the criminal justice system is in *The Color of Justice: Race, Ethnicity, and Crime in America* (Wadsworth, 1999) by Samuel Walker, Merian Delone, and Cassia C. Spohn. Images of color and images of crime are addressed in *Race, Crime and Criminal Justice* (Roxbury Publishing Co., 2002) edited by Coramae Richey Mamr and Marjorie Sue Zatz. The March 2004 issue of *American Behavorial Scientist* (Sage Publications) is entitled "Critical Racial and Ethnic Studies: Profiling and Reparations." Six articles deal with examples of racial profiling.

Katheryn K. Rusell discusses crime hoaxes of both blacks and whites in *The Color of Crime: Racial Hoaxes, White Fear, Black Protectionism, Police Harassment, and Other Macroaggressions (Critical America Series)* (New York University Press, 1999). Heather MacDonald justifies police crime-control tactics and methods in *Are Cops Racist?* (Ivan R. Dee, Inc., 2003). Students are encouraged to research the growing literature in the area of race, crime, and criminology.

# ISSUE 11

# Did Hurricane Katrina Expose Racism in America?

**YES: Adolph Reed and Stephen Steinberg,** from "Liberal Bad Faith in the Wake of Hurricane Katrina," *The Black Commentator* (May 4, 2006)

**NO: Shelby Steele,** from "Witness: Blacks, Whites, and the Politics of Shame in America," *The Wall Street Journal* (October 26, 2005)

## ISSUE SUMMARY

**YES:** Adolph Reed, professor of political science at the University of Pennsylvania, and Stephen Steinberg, professor of sociology at Queens College in New York City, challenge the tendency of policy makers and other commentators to focus on blacks as the source of the problems faced by New Orleans in the wake of Hurricane Katrina and emphasize the need to address race and poverty concerns effectively.

**NO:** Shelby Steele, a research fellow at the Hoover Institution and political commentator, argues that blacks of New Orleans, along with other blacks, should focus on meaningful methods for overcoming their underdevelopment as revealed by Hurricane Katrina rather than emphasizing the shame of white racism as the cause of their plight.

**D**uring much of the nation's history, the status of the lives of African Americans as perceived within the majority white population of the United States was informed by imagery that extended from that of the impoverished field hands of both the Slave Era and Segregation Era of the agrarian South to the wretched conditions of life experienced by the ghetto underclass within urban America. The disparities of black life are inconsistent with the promise of the American dream, and the overcoming of these social contradictions has been a major focus of progressive reform of race relations within the nation. Poor whites too have had problems but did not have to deal with the additional obstacle of racism.

The lives of African Americans and their prospects for advancement within the society have been altered since the 1960s. Prior stark images of black life that dominated the public consciousness began to change, especially since the period of social reform of the post–World War II era, and were replaced by images of racial progress. Due to the impact and social impetus of the Civil Rights Movement, a substantial portion of the dominant-group population began to embrace images that reflected significant progress in reducing the inequities of life that attend the color line in America. Increasingly, some Americans tend to believe that racism and its overt manifestations of color prejudice and racial discrimination are phenomena of the past and that America is essentially being transformed into a truly egalitarian society. Others question this view.

Status and color have always been linked in New Orleans, which was a center of the American slave trade and a prominent component of the slavocracy. In the wake of emancipation, the city emerged as a bastion of racial segregation. The later conflict over school integration during the 1950s and 1960s punctuates the history of race and New Orleans. For example, in the fall of 1960, 6 years after the *Brown* decision, the New Orleans school system was still segregated. When four black girls began to integrate the public schools, there was a citywide riot. White flight soon followed and contributed to increased residential isolation of blacks and whites within the city. Hence, the racial distribution of New Orleans, as manifested by the concentrated population of poor and working class blacks within the Ninth Ward, clearly demonstrated that racial segregation is alive and well within that city.

In their article, Reed and Steinberg emphasize the tendency on the part of political leaders and other commentators, including certain academicians who utilized this natural disaster to focus on the shortcomings of the poor, black population of New Orleans as a basis for policy recommendations. They are very critical of those who would present the black poor of New Orleans as a major source of the city's problems and who propose that the best method for overcoming these problems is to "resettle" the black population in a manner that does not permit "the concentration of poverty" in the future. Steinberg and Reed present a contrarian analysis suggesting that poverty and proper policies for overcoming this phenomenon are the keys to overcoming the racial contradictions that Hurricane Katrina exposed within New Orleans.

In contrast, Shelby Steele rejects the notion that a focus on white racism is a proper response to the conditions of black life in New Orleans that were exposed by Katrina. Steele strongly believes that instead of playing "the shame of white racism" card, African Americans would be well advised to recognize that the hurricane exposed a condition of underdevelopment and inequality within black America for which the race must take major responsibility and find the proper policies to advance within society. Steele's argument is another manifestation of a classic social issue, which contrasts personal responsibility with social structural factors. Some would accuse Steele of "blaming the victim." Others would say that he illuminates the conservative argument of individual responsibility.

This century-old debate (personal responsibility versus government responsibility) now emerges in the discussion of race and Katrina.

# YES

Adolph Reed and
Stephen Steinberg

# Liberal Bad Faith in the Wake of Hurricane Katrina

So, Barbara Bush was right after all when she said, "So many of the people in the arena here, you know, were underprivileged anyway, so this, this is working very well for them." And Rep. Richard Baker, a 10-term Republican from Baton Rouge, was right when he was overheard telling lobbyists: "We finally cleaned up public housing in New Orleans. We couldn't do it, but God did." The publication of both statements elicited public condemnation and was followed by a flurry of hairsplitting denials. But it is now clear that their only transgression was to say in unvarnished language what many pundits, politicians, and policy wonks were thinking. Since then, there has been a stream of proposals in more circumspect language, first by conservatives and then by a liberal policy circle at Harvard, that also envision the resettlement of New Orleans' poverty population far from the Vieux Carré, Garden District and other coveted neighborhoods of the "new" New Orleans.

David Brooks weighed in first, in a September 8, 2005 column in the *New York Times* under the title, "Katrina's Silver Lining." How can such a colossal natural disaster that devastated an entire city and displaced most of its population have "a silver lining"? Because, according to Brooks, it provided an opportunity to "break up zones of concentrated poverty," and thus "to break the cycle of poverty." The key, though, is to relocate the poor elsewhere, and to replace them with middle class families who will rebuild the city. "If we just put up new buildings and allow the same people to move back into their old neighborhoods," Brooks warned, "then urban New Orleans will become just as rundown and dysfunctional as before."

OK, this is what we expect from the neocons. Enter William Julius Wilson, whose message in *The Declining Significance of Race* catapulted him to national prominence. In an appearance on *The News Hour*, Wilson began by diplomatically complimenting Bush for acknowledging the problems of racial inequality and persistent poverty, and then made a pitch for funneling both private and public sector jobs to low-income people. So far so good. But then Wilson shifted to some ominous language:

> "Another thing, it would have been good if he had talked about the need to ensure that the placement of families in New Orleans does not

reproduce the levels of concentrated poverty that existed before. So I would just like to underline what Bruce Katz was saying and that is that we do have evidence that moving families to lower poverty neighborhoods and school districts can have significant positive effects."

Wilson was referring to his fellow panelist on *The News Hour,* Bruce Katz, who was chief of staff for the Department of Housing and Urban Development in the Clinton administration. According to Katz, to build "a competitive healthy and viable city," we need "to break up the concentrations of poverty, to break up those federal enclaves of poverty which existed in the city and to really give these low income residents more choice and opportunity." Finally, it becomes clear what Katz is driving at:

> "*I think the city will be smaller and I'm not sure if that's the worst thing in the world.* I think we have an opportunity here to have a win-win. I think we have an opportunity to build a very different kind of city, a city with a much greater mix of incomes. And, at the same time, we have the opportunity, if we have the right principles and we have the right tools to give many of those low income families the ability to live in neighborhoods, *whether in the city, whether in the suburbs, whether in other parts of the state or in other parts of the country,* live in neighborhoods where they have access to good schools, safe streets and quality jobs." (Italics ours.)

Stripped of its varnish, what Wilson and Katz are proposing is a resettlement program that will result in a "smaller" New Orleans that is depleted of its poverty population.

This is not all. Together with Xavier Briggs, a sociologist and urban planner at MIT, Wilson posted a petition on the listserve of the Urban Sociology Section of the American Sociological Association, under the title "Moving to Opportunity in the Wake of Hurricane Katrina." After some hand wringing about the terrible impact of Katrina, we're presented with the silver lining: ". . . our goal for these low-income displaced persons, most of whom are racial minorities, should be to create a 'move to opportunity.'" Of course, this is followed by the necessary caveat: "we do not seek to depopulate the city of its historically black communities," et cetera, et cetera. But the main thrust of the petition touts "a growing body of research" that demonstrates the "significant positive effects" of "mobility programs" that break up "concentrated poverty." By happy coincidence, Briggs has just published an edited volume, *The Geography of Opportunity,* with a foreword by William Julius Wilson, which promotes such mobility programs.

The dangerous, reactionary implications of a government-sponsored resettlement program were apparently not evident to the 200-plus signatories, which include some of the most prominent names in American social science: First on the list was William Julius Wilson, followed by Christopher Jencks, Lawrence Katz, David Ellwood, Herbert Gans, Todd Gitlin, Alejandro Portes, Katherine Newman, Jennifer Hochschild, Sheldon Danziger, Mary Jo Bane, to mention some of the names on just the first of ten pages of signatories. With these luminaries at the head of the petition, given their unimpeachable liberal credentials, scores of urban specialists flocked to add their names. But how is the position laid out in the measured language of the petition different from the one expressed by Barbara Bush, Rep. Richard Baker, and David Brooks? This is a relocation scheme, pure and simple. Of course, the petition was careful to stipulate that this was a voluntary program, leaving people with a "choice" to return to New Orleans or to relocate elsewhere. However, as these anointed policy experts surely know, the ultimate outcome hinges on what policies are enacted. If public housing and affordable housing in New Orleans are not rebuilt, if rent subsidies are withheld, then what "choice" do people have but to relocate elsewhere? The certain result will be "a smaller and stronger New Orleans," depleted of its poverty population.

Already public officials are crowing about the "new" New Orleans. According to a recent article in the *New York Times,* "the bullets and drugs and the fear are gone now, swept away by Hurricane Katrina, along with the dealers and gangs and most of the people." Step forward another credentialed expert, Peter Scharf, executive director of the Center for Society, Law and Justice at the University of New Orleans. Hurricane Katrina, Scharf exults, "was one of the greatest crime-control tools ever deployed against a high-crime city," sweeping away, by his estimate, as many as 20,000 participants in the drug culture before the storm.

Here we see the first problem of the "moving to opportunity" discourse. It is a throwback to the crude environmental determinism of the Jacob Riis era, which equated urban pathology with the urban environment, and assumed that a more salubrious environment—more commodious housing, playgrounds, and clean streets—would provide a panacea for the "ills of the city." One Progressive Era book began with the instructive story about a lamppost that had been the site of a rash of suicides. Alas, the authorities removed the lamppost, and poof, the suicides ceased! Does anyone doubt that New Orleans' drug trade will not reestablish itself elsewhere?

On closer examination, the campaign against "concentrated poverty" is a scheme for making poverty invisible. The policy is based on an anti-urban bias that is as frivolous as it is deep-seated, as though the romanticized small towns across the nation are not plagued with the litany of "urban" problems. Wherever there is chronic joblessness and poverty, and no matter its color, there are high rates of crime, alcoholism, drugs, school dropouts, domestic violence, and mental health issues, especially among the poor youth who pass up the option to rescue themselves by joining the army and fighting America's imperial wars. To echo C. Wright Mills, when poverty is spread thin, then these behaviors can be dismissed as individual aberrations stemming from moral blemishes, rather than a problem of society demanding political action.

Besides, what kind of policy simply moves the poor into somebody else's back yard, without addressing the root causes of poverty itself, and in the process disrupts the personal networks and community bonds of these indigent people? Contrary to the claim of the petition, the "careful studies" that have evaluated the "moving to opportunity" programs report very mixed results, and why should one think otherwise? Unless the uprooted families are provided with jobs and opportunities that are the sine qua non of stable families and communities, "move to opportunity" is only a spurious theory and an empty slogan.

This brings attention to two other fatal flaws in the logic of "moving to opportunity" policy. It is based on a demonized image of the reprobate poor, who make trouble for themselves and others. Yes, the drug dealers are swept out of the 9th ward, but so are countless others, often single mothers with children, with an extended kin network of siblings, aunts, uncles, cousins, and that heroic grandmother, who indeed have deep roots in the communities from which they are being evicted. How is it that this Gang of 200, from their ivory towers and gilded offices, presume to speak for the poor? Tossing in a caveat to the effect that "we do not seek to depopulate the city or its historically black communities" must be read literally. They want only to depopulate the city of concentrated poverty, and they will leave intact middle-class black communities that will insulate them from charges of racism.

The great fallacy of the "moving to opportunity" programs is that, by definition, they reach only a small percentage of the poverty population (and typically those who are both motivated and qualified to participate in the program). Left behind are masses to fend for themselves, particularly since the "moving to opportunity" programs are themselves used as an excuse to disinvest in these poor black communities that are written off as beyond redemption. Moving to opportunity becomes a perverse euphemism for policy abdication of the poor people left behind who are in desperate need of programs, services, and jobs.

Here, finally, is what is most sinister and myopic about the "moving to opportunity" concept. It is not part of a comprehensive policy to attack poverty and racism: to rid the United States of impoverished ghettos that pockmark the national landscape. Rather the policy is enacted in places where poor blacks occupy valuable real estate, as was the case for Cabrini Green in Chicago. After Cabrini Green was imploded, and its displaced residents sent off with Section 8s, median sales prices of single-unit homes in the vicinity soared from $138,000 to $700,000 during the 1980s, and the area lost 7,000 African Americans and gained 4,000 whites. It is only a matter of time before we read upbeat news accounts about the gentrifying neighborhoods surrounding the Vieux Carré.

What is perhaps saddest and most reprehensible about the petition of the Gang of 200 is the solipsistic arrogance on which it rests. This initiative comes at a time when ACORN and other advocacy groups and grassroots activists in New Orleans have championed "the right of return" for even its poorest citizens displaced by Katrina. According to the National Low Income Housing Coalition, over 140,000 units of housing were destroyed, the majority of them affordable for low-income families. But the Housing Authority of New Orleans has shut down its public-housing operations, and informed landlords of people assisted by federal rent vouchers that government rent subsidies for impacted units have been suspended indefinitely. According to

Mike Howells, an organizer with a local human rights group, "sensing an opportunity to enhance the fortunes of real estate interests and to dump a form of public assistance that mainly benefits poor working class locals, Washington and local authorities are using Hurricane Katrina as a pretext for effectively gutting government subsidized housing in New Orleans."

Sure enough, the key player on Mayor Nagin's "Bring New Orleans Back Commission" is Joe Canizaro, a billionaire local developer and one of President Bush's "pioneers," i.e., individuals who raised at least $100,000 for the Bush presidential campaign. The commission initially retained the Urban Land Institute—a real estate development industry organization on whose board Canizaro sits—to propose a framework for pursuing reconstruction. Unsurprisingly, that proposal called for a form of market-based triage. It recommended that reconstruction efforts should be focused in proportion to areas' market value and further suggested that rebuilding of New Orleans East and the Lower Ninth Ward be deferred indefinitely. What else could we have expected? Asking such an outfit how to rebuild a devastated city is like asking a fox how to organize a chicken coop.

As we write, the fate of displaced poor New Orleanians is more precarious than ever. FEMA has terminated rent payments for thousands. Only 20 of the 117 public schools that existed before the hurricane are operating, and 17 of those 20 have opened as charter schools. The school board laid off all the teachers and staff months ago—so much for concerns about poverty. Most of the city remains empty, eerily quiet and covered with a gray, filmy residue that shows how high floodwaters were in each neighborhood. And the eerie quiet underscores the colossal failure of government at all levels to propose a plan for the hundreds of thousands of people who have been dislocated for six months and counting.

Tellingly, the outrage that Canizaro and the Urban Land Institute's proposal sparked among working-class homeowners only reinforced poor people's marginalization. The relevant unit of protest against the ULI plan, its moral center, became homeownership. But what of the tens of thousands who weren't homeowners before Katrina? Who is factoring their interests into the equation? Did Barbara Bush speak for history, ratified by the policy circle at Harvard, when she said, "So many of the people in the arena here, you know, were underprivileged anyway, so this, this is working very well for them."

The Gang of 200's petition reproduces and reinforces this disregard for the idea that poor people may have, or deserve to have, emotional attachments to a place they consider home. This is one way in which the stereotype of the "urban underclass"—which Wilson in particular has done so much to legitimize—is insidious: it defines poor people's lives as only objects for "our" administration (and just who makes up the circle of "we" anyway?). It effectively divests the poor of civic voice, thus reprising 19th century republican treatment of those without property as ineligible for full citizenship.

We are braced for the counterattack from the Gang of 200. First, they will howl about the obvious differences between Indian removal and the Negro removal that they advocate. We are more struck by the similarities.

Naiveté and hubris can go hand-in-hand. Wilson et al. rushed to tout their silly pet idea without a whit's thought of the social, political, and economic dynamics and tensions that might be at play in the debate over how to reconstruct New Orleans. Their sole proviso is the lame reassurance that the city's distinctive diversity should be preserved. They gave no thought that Republicans might link the city's repopulation to their desire to gut Democratic power in New Orleans and move Louisiana into the column of reliably Republican states. They apparently also failed to consider the potential that their idée fixe would play into the hands of real estate development interests and others who relish any opportunity to dissipate New Orleans's black electoral majority. Such talk began well before the floodwaters began to recede.

Recently, a politically-connected white lawyer in the city remarked that Katrina provided an opportunity to rebuild a smaller, quainter New Orleans, more like Charleston. (Charleston, of course, has an ample poor black servant class for its tourist economy, but a white electoral majority.) And speaking of Charleston, a low-income housing project near downtown was condemned and razed after Hurricane Hugo in 1989 because the flood and storm surge supposedly had rendered the land on which it stood too toxic to afford human habitation. The site subsequently became home to the aquarium, a key node in the Charleston's tourist redevelopment. Rumors abound that luxury condos may also now be in the works for the site.

Next, the Gang of 200 will accuse us of defending segregated housing and opposing their proposal to integrate blacks into mixed income and mixed race neighborhoods. This does not withstand even a moment's scrutiny. Without doubt, many poor black people aspire to move to a "better neighborhood," and they should have the option to do so. If the Gang of 200 were serious about helping them, first on their policy agenda would be a proposal for massive enforcement of existing laws against housing discrimination, in order to drive a wedge through the wall of white segregation. The problem here is that relocation is being enacted through a state-sponsored resettlement policy, and notwithstanding promises for "traditional support services," these poor families (and not all of them are poor!), will be relocated in poor, segregated neighborhoods. The only certain outcome is that New Orleans will be depleted of its poor black population in neighborhoods that are ripe for development.

It is astounding that the Gang of 200 do not see the expropriation of poor neighborhoods and the violation of human rights. And they remain strangely oblivious of their potential for playing into the hands of the retrograde political forces that would use their call to justify displacement. Well-intentioned, respectable scholars as they are, they live no less than anyone else within a political culture shaped largely by class experience and perception. And the poverty research industry, of which Wilson is an avatar and leading light, has been predicated for decades on the premise that poor people are defective, incapable of knowing their own best interests, that they are solely objects of social policy, never its subjects. Worst of all, they provide liberal cover for those who have already put a resettlement policy into motion that is reactionary and racist at its core.

Shelby Steele  **NO**

# Witness: Blacks, Whites, and the Politics of Shame in America

**P**robably the single greatest problem between blacks and whites in America is that we are forever witness to each other's great shames. This occurred to me in the immediate aftermath of Katrina, when so many black people were plunged into misery that it seemed the hurricane itself had held a racial animus. I felt a consuming empathy but also another, more atavistic impulse. I did not like my people being seen this way. Beyond the human mess one expects to see after a storm like this, another kind of human wretchedness was on display. In the people traversing waist-deep water and languishing on rooftops were the markers of a deep and static poverty. The despair over the storm that was so evident in people's faces seemed to come out of an older despair, one that had always been there. Here—40 years after the great civil rights victories and 50 years after Rosa Parks's great refusal—was a poverty that oppression could no longer entirely explain. Here was poverty with an element of surrender in it that seemed to confirm the worst charges against blacks: that we are inferior, that nothing really helps us, that the modern world is beyond our reach.

Of course, shame is made worse, even unbearable, when there is a witness, the eye of an "other" who is only too happy to use our shame against us. Whites and blacks often play the "other" for each other in this way, each race seeking a bit of redemption and power in the other's shame. And both races live with the permanent anxiety of being held to account for their shames by the other race. So, there is a reflex in both races that reaches for narratives to explain shame away and, thus, disarm the "other."

Therefore, it was only a matter of time before the images of deep black poverty that emerged in Katrina's aftermath were covered over in a narrative of racism: If Katrina's victims had not been black, the response to their suffering would have been faster. It did not matter that a general lack of preparedness, combined with a stunning level of governmental incompetence and confusion, made for an unforgivably slow response to Katrina's victims. What mattered was the invocation of the great white shame. And here, in white racism, was a shame of truly epic proportions—the shame of white supremacy that for centuries so squeezed the world with violence and oppression that white privilege was made a natural law.

Once white racism—long witnessed by blacks and acknowledged since the '60s by whites—was in play, the subject was changed from black weakness to white evil. Now accountability for the poverty that shamed blacks could be once again assigned to whites. If this was tiresome for many whites, it was a restoration of dignity for many blacks.

In the '60s—the first instance of open mutual witness between blacks and whites in American history—a balance of power was struck between the races. The broad white acknowledgment of racism meant that whites would be responsible both for overcoming their racism and for ending black poverty because, after all, their racism had so obviously caused that poverty. For whites to suggest that blacks might be in some way responsible for their own poverty would be to relinquish this responsibility and, thus, to return to racism. So, from its start in the '60s, this balance of power (offering redemption to whites and justice to blacks) involved a skewed distribution of responsibility: Whites, and not blacks, would be responsible for achieving racial equality in America, for overcoming the shames of both races—black inferiority and white racism. And the very idea of black responsibility would be stigmatized as racism in whites and Uncle Tomism in blacks.

President Johnson's famous Howard University speech, which launched the Great Society in 1965, outlined this balance of power by explicitly spelling out white responsibility without a single reference to black responsibility. In the 40 years since that speech no American president has dared correct this oversight.

The problem here is obvious: The black shame of inferiority (the result of oppression, not genetics) cannot be overcome with anything less than a heroic assumption of responsibility on the part of black Americans. In fact, true equality—an actual parity of wealth and ability between the races—is now largely a black responsibility. This may not be fair, but historical fairness—of the sort that resolves history's injustices—is an idealism that now plagues black America by making black responsibility seem an injustice.

And yet, despite the fact that greater responsibility is the only transforming power that can take blacks to true equality, this is an idea that deeply threatens the 40-year balance of power between the races. Bill Cosby's recent demand that poor blacks hold up "their end of the bargain" and do a better job of raising their children was explosive because it threatened this balance. Mr. Cosby not only implied that black responsibility was the great transforming power; he also implied that there was a limit to what white responsibility could do. He said, in effect, that white responsibility cannot overcome black inferiority. This is a truth so obvious as to be mundane. Yet whites won't say it in the interest of their redemption and blacks won't say it in the interest of historical justice. It is left to hurricanes to make such statements.

And black responsibility undermines another purpose of this balance of power, which is to keep the shames of both races covered. It was always the grandiosity of white promises (President Johnson's promise to "end poverty in our time," today's promises of "diversity" and "inclusion") that enabled whites and American institutions to distance themselves from the shame of white racism. But if black responsibility is the great transformative power, whites are no more than humble partners in racial reform, partners upon whom little depends. In this position they cannot make grandiose claims for what white responsibility can do. And without a language of grandiose promises, the shame of white racism is harder to dispel.

But it is the shame of blacks that becomes most transparent when black responsibility is given its rightful ascendancy. When this happens blacks themselves cannot look at New Orleans without acknowledging what Bill Cosby acknowledged in a different context, that poor blacks have not held up their end of the bargain. Responsibility always comes with the risk of great shame, the shame of failing to meet the responsibility one has assumed. A great problem in black American life is that we have too often avoided responsibility in order to avoid shame. This is understandable given the unforgiving pas de deux of mutual witness between blacks and whites in which each race prepares a face for the other and seizes on the other's weaknesses with ravenous delight. And four centuries of persecution have indeed left us with weaknesses, and even a degree of human brokenness, that is shaming. Nevertheless, it is only an illusion to think that we can mute the sting of shame by charging whites with responsibility for us. This is a formula for running into the shame you run from.

❧

Today it has to be conceded that whites have made more progress against their shame of racism than we blacks have made against our shame of inferiority. It took nothing less than four centuries, but in the '60s whites finally took open responsibility for their racism despite the shame this exposed them to. And they knew that ever-present black witness would impose on them an exacting accountability (Bill Bennett, Vicente Fox, Trent Lott) for diffusing this evil. But, in fact, racism has receded in American life because whites, at long last, took greater responsibility for making it recede despite the shame they endured. And wasn't it the certainty of shame, as much as anything else, that had kept them rationalizing their racism for so long, looking to the supposed inferiority of blacks to justify an evil?

No doubt it is easier to overcome racism than an inferiority of development grounded in centuries of racial persecution. Nevertheless, if New Orleans is a wake-up call to government, it is also a wake-up call to black America. If we want to finally erase the inferiority that oppression left us with, we have to first of all acknowledge it to ourselves, as whites did with their racism. Our scrupulous witness of whites helped them become more and more responsible for resisting the shame of racism.

And our open acknowledgment of our underdevelopment will clearly give whites a power of witness over us. It will mean that whites can hold us accountable for overcoming inferiority as we hold them accountable for overcoming racism. They will be able to openly shame us when we are not fully at war with our underdevelopment, just as Bill Bennett was shamed for no more than giving a false impression of racism. If this prospect feels terrifying to many blacks, we have to remember that whites witness and judge us anyway, just as we have witnessed and judged their shame for so long. Mutual witness will go on no matter what balances of power we strike. It is best to be open, and allow the "other's" witness to inspire rather than shame.

# POSTSCRIPT

## Did Hurricane Katrina Expose Racism in America?

The lurid images of the status and conditions of the lives of African Americans and some whites that dominated the media during and in the wake of Hurricane Katrina's onslaught on New Orleans challenged the public's perceptions of the progress concerning race and poverty that had been achieved within that city and, metaphorically, within the nation at large. These searing images of literally thousands of mostly African American people gathered on rooftops, herded into the Superdome, and essentially abandoned at the Convention Center shook the consciences of many Americans. Most victims were found not to possess bank accounts, automobiles, or other resources necessary to escape the ravages of Katrina. They seemed not to have been able to achieve meaningful progress in pursuit of the American dream, despite the social reforms of the post-1960s. Virtually all of the comparative empirical evidence on variables that include average life expectancy, distribution of wealth and income, educational achievement, poverty and unemployment, and most other social indicators that are available from the Census Bureau and other databases confirm that African Americans are disadvantaged as compared with their white counterparts within New Orleans.

At the same time, the argument for individual responsibility suggests that anyone who finishes high school will avoid extreme poverty. Juan Williams makes this point in a *New York Times* op-ed piece on September 1, 2006. His point is that "poverty didn't arrive with the tide and high winds" of Katrina. Williams' position supports Steele on this issue. Blacks must place more emphasis on the role of social responsibility.

So, is the racial inequality that one confronts within New Orleans a result of persistent racism, or does individual responsibility play a stronger role? Social scientists tend not to explain complex phenomena with a single causation. Rather, a more comprehensive set of factors tends to be employed for such analysis. How does one explain some of the responses within the external American society to the plight of those African Americans whose misery and poverty were revealed by Katrina? One report indicated that blacks who attempted to cross a bridge to seek refuge in a predominately white community on the mainland of Louisiana had shots fired over their heads to discourage their efforts. Were these African Americans perceived as potential criminals and a threat to the security of their neighbors? Were blacks who were fleeing the debacle of Katrina seen as refugees, or citizens? What was revealed in the comments of the president's mother, Barbara

Bush, who observed that blacks placed in the various shelters were doing better than ever and, therefore, had no reason to complain?

To place this issue in proper context, students would be well served to explore the history of race relations in Mississippi and Louisiana. Background information on New Orleans and the Gulf Coast can be found in *Black New Orleans: 1860–1880* (University of Chicago Press) by John W. Blassingame. More relevant to the issue of race relations in New Orleans is D. R. Goldfield's *Black, White, and Southern: Race Relations and Southern Culture 1940 to the Present* (Louisiana State University Press). General studies of the devastating effects of Hurricane Katrina include *The Great Deluge: Hurricane Katrina, New Orleans and the Mississippi Gulf Coast* (William Morrow/HarperCollins Publishers, 2006) by Douglas Brinkley, a professor of history at Rice University, and *Breach of Faith: Hurricane Katrina and the Near Death of a Great American City* (Random House, 2006) by Jed Horne. *Come Hell or High Water: Katrina and the Color of Disaster* by Michael Eric Dyson (Basic Civitas, 2006) examines race and Katrina from a conflict perspective.

For a more critical examination of the issue, see a series of articles appearing in the January 2, 2006, issue of *The Nation,* including "In the Shadow of Disaster: Can People and Nature Co-Exist in New Orleans?" by Ari Kelman, "Katrina Lives: The Country Has Moved On, But Black Americans Have Not Finished with Her," by Susan Straight, and "Left to Die: New Orleans Abandoned Its Citizens in Jail," by Billy Sothern. Another critical article, "Who Is Killing New Orleans?" by Mike Davis in *The Nation* appeared in the April 10, 2006, issue.

In contrast, Wilfred M. McClay's "The Storm Over Katrina" (*Commentary,* December 2005) argues that public officials played upon the race theme and that racial disparities in the rates of death did not materialize. The September 26, 2005, issue of *National Review* featured several articles on the hurricane, including "Hard Truths About the Big Easy: Your Government at Work." Relevant to the Steele article above is John McWhorter's "Racism! They Charge: When Don't They?". Also, in agreement with Steele's position is James Q. Wilson. In "American Dilemma: Problems of Race Still Cry to Be Solved," he argues that discrimination and racism are not problems in New Orleans; rather, it is the condition of the black family that is at the root of the criminal lower class. For in-depth analysis on race and class in post-Katrina New Orleans and the impact of the government response to Katrina on changing perceptions of the persistence of discrimination, see "The Black Scholar" (Winter 2006). The entire volume is devoted to a study of Hurricane Katrina.

# ISSUE 12

## Is the Reservation the Only Source of Community for Native Americans?

**YES: Frank Pommersheim,** from *Braid of Feathers. American Indian Law and Contemporary Tribal Life* (University of California Press, 1995)

**NO: Susan Lobo,** from "Is Urban a Person or a Place? Characteristics of Urban Indian Country," in Susan Lobo and Kurt Peters, eds., *American Indians and the Urban Experience* (Altamira Press, 2001)

### ISSUE SUMMARY

**YES:** Frank Pommersheim lived and worked on the Rosebud Sioux Reservation for 10 years and currently teaches at the University of South Dakota School of Law where he specializes in Indian law. Additionally, he is currently providing legal services within India. Emphasizing the critical role played by land within Indian country. He develops the argument for the significance of "measured separatism."

**NO:** Susan Lobo, a cultural anthropologist and an expert on Native American studies, presents the case of Native Americans in the Bay Area in California. She demonstrates the richness of Indian community life that extends beyond the reservation.

Among all the peoples that comprise the diverse population of United States, Native Americans have a unique legacy. In their encounter with Euro settlers, they were subjected to a genocidal ethnic cleansing that was essentially sanctioned by Congress in the passage of the Indian removal Act of 1830. In the process of being removed from their ancestral lands, in order to clear these lands for white settlement, Congress developed a system of land reserves as the new homeland for native peoples. These reservations tended to be barren, lacking the resources to facilitate prosperity. Yet, it is within these restricted enclaves that Native Americans were expected to pursue their destiny within America.

One may argue that the reservations have had a constraining influence upon Native peoples in their efforts to envision and pursue a positive future for themselves. However, it is indisputable that the reservations have provided Native Americans with real opportunities to promote Indian identity, cultural renewal, and a vision of Red empowerment, relatively free from the pressures of assimilation.

In 1924, citizenship was conferred upon Native Americans through the passage of the Indian Citizenship Act. This development, along with an urbanization policy that was implemented by the Bureau of Indian Affairs after World War II, led to the establishment of significant Native American communities in some American cities. There is evidence that within these urban enclaves Native Americans have been able to maintain their identity, cultures, and pride in their "Indianess" as they continue to struggle for justice and empowerment within American society.

Frank Pommersheim makes the case for "measured separatism." He emphasizes the significance of land and place for the promotion of Native American identity and culture. For him, reservations are valued spaces in pursuit of those goals.

Making the expanded argument for community, Susan Lobo illustrates the re-creation of a Native American community in the San Francisco area with institutions, a shared identity and associations and consistent features of social organization. She challenges the notion held by the larger public that American Indians have "vanished" within the urban landscape or live overwhelmingly on reservations in rural areas.

# YES

Frank Pommersheim

# The Reservation as Place

From the Indians we learned a toughness and a strength; and we gained
> A freedom: by taking theirs: but a real freedom: born
> From the wild and open land our grandfathers heroically stole.
> But we took a wound at Indian hands: a part of our soul scabbed over."

*Thomas McGrath,* Letter to an Imaginary Friend

**I**ndian reservations are often described as islands of poverty and despair torn from the continent of national progress. Less often, they are extolled as places luckily isolated from the predations of the twentieth century. Each of these descriptions invokes, in part, the complex field of Indian law as a touchstone of both the past and future, as either the wedge that will break up the Indians' natural resources, land, and culture or as a countervailing force of restraint that promises cultural renewal. Hidden in this web of description and claims lies the important notion of the reservation as place: a physical, human, legal, and spiritual reality that embodies the history, dreams, and aspirations of Indian people, their communities, and their tribes. It is a place that marks the endurance of Indian communities against the onslaught of a marauding European society; it is also a place that holds the promise of fulfillment. As Lakota people say, *"Hecel lena Oyate nipikte"* (That these people may live). The reservation constitutes an abiding place full of quotidian vitality and pressing dilemmas that continue to define modern Indian life.

There is little doubt that the states of the West, and South Dakota in particular, have often resisted the notion that the reservations possess any positive significance for the individual states or the region. The history of litigious animosity is long and bitter, with continuous and ongoing disputes about reservation boundaries, water rights, the Black Hills, and state authority on the reservation, to name only the most prominent. Yet at this juncture it may be worthwhile to suggest another angle of vision which might, in turn, suggest an angle of repose—a vision infused by mutual understanding and common interest.

From *Braid of Feathers: American Indian Law and Contemporary Tribal Life* by Frank Pommersheim (University of California Press, 1995), pp. 11–15, 19, 21, 22–23, 26–27, 33, 34–35 (excerpts). Copyright © 1995 by the Regents of the University of California. Reprinted by permission.

This chapter centers on the continuing process of cultural self-scrutiny and intercultural contact between Indians and non-Indians and between Indian tribes and the state and federal governments. This "contact," which began with the arrival of the first Europeans, is continuous. The process should not, of course, be understood in terms of the ethnocentric concepts of manifest destiny, progress, and cultural superiority; rather, we must examine the forces at play in the "contact" and the rubric of *choices* that emerges in the process. Choice, whether conscious or not, has very real implications for individuals, communities, and tribes. Choice is not always apparent, and the failure to be aware of it often results in loss and forfeited opportunity. It is therefore important to highlight and clarify these choices as they emerge from the consideration of the reservation as place and eternal center. These choices are not merely grounded in considerations of efficiency but are also located in the larger space of culture and meaning.

There are no "answers," and the imposition of "answers" in the past—answers such as cultural assimilation, religious conversion, and the concept of individual property—resulted in substantial cultural loss and the severe erosion of political and personal autonomy. These were answers to the wrong questions, for the questions were framed against the desires and beliefs of a European, expansionary society, not against the needs and values of tribal communities. Sovereignty and freedom have no meaning apart from the ability to make informed choices. My intention here is to elucidate the contours of some of the right questions about the reservation—their texture, their import, and the options they suggest. Doing so honors my obligation that flows from my friendship with people and communities who have done so much, with lasting good humor, to highlight the issues and enhance the choices in my own life and those of my family.

More broadly, I write from two overarching assumptions. One is that, despite grinding poverty and widespread despair, there is nevertheless a flame of hope and a broadening range of choices in almost all aspects of reservation life. If the most observable and detrimental aspect of the dominance of the majority society in Indian country has been the presence of substantial constraints and a reduced flexibility of choice, this situation has been successfully reversed. Despite the difficult and often inimical conditions, renaissance and struggle at the grassroots level have accomplished important changes in options for growth and fulfillment.

The second assumption is that, whatever the conditions, tribal members have been committed to remaining indelibly Indian, proudly defining themselves as a people apart and resisting full incorporation into the dominant society around them. Yet Indians and their tribes must encounter and transform modern social, economic, and political conditions in order to achieve a meaningful and flourishing future; the encounter and transformation must be governed by wise choice and mediated through deeply held cultural values.

A new understanding and willingness by the non-Indian community to listen to and to engage in dialogue and discussion with the Indian community may also help accomplish this formidable task of transformation.

Such mutual efforts may, in turn, redefine and redirect the political, legal, and social relationships between Indians and non-Indians and the tribes and the state. Yet the realization of any of these aspirations must rest on a firm understanding of the role of the reservation as the irreducible touchstone of tribal posterity and well-being.

## Figures on Mother Earth

Land is basic to Indian people: they are part of it and it is part of them; it is their Mother. Nor is this just a romantic commonplace. For most Indian groups, including the Lakota people, land is a cultural centerpiece with wide-ranging implications for any attempt to understand contemporary reservation life.

The importance of the land is severalfold. Beyond the obvious fact that land provides subsistence, it is the source of spiritual origins and sustaining myth, which in turn provide a landscape of cultural and emotional meaning. The land often determines the values of the human landscape. The harsh lands of the prairie helped to make Lakota tribal communities austere and generous, places where giving and sharing were first principles. The people needed the land and each other too much to permit wanton accumulation and ecological impairment to the living source of nourishment. Much of this is, of course, antithetical to European history and culture. As Frederick Turner suggests, the Western ethos reflects a commitment

> to *take* possession without being possessed: to take secure hold on the lands beyond and yet hold them at a rigidly maintained spiritual distance. It was never to merge, to mingle, to marry. To do so was to become an apostate from Christian history and so be kept in an eternal wilderness.

Such differing conceptions between Indians and non-Indians about the nature of land only added tinder to the flame of adversity and misunderstanding. And sure enough, one of the results of over three centuries of contact has been the nearly complete severing of this cultural taproot connecting Indian people to the land. Impaired but not eradicated, this root is being rediscovered and tended with renewed vigor and stewardship. In fact, this is so prevalent that it has been noted as a recurrent theme in contemporary Indian literature. The theme involves the loss of the old guardian spirits of place and the process by which they might be made to speak again—how the land may become numinous once more and speak to its dwellers.

This then is one pull of the land, the source of vital myth and cultural well-being. But there is also the complementary notion of a homeland where generations and generations of relatives have lived out their lives and destiny—that it is, after all, one's home, one's community, one's reservation in Indian country. Many reservations may seem rural and isolated, and indeed they are; but many, like the Rosebud Sioux Reservation in South

Dakota, are; quite beautiful, captivating in the way the subtle canvas of the prairie often is. The Rosebud Reservation and others like it do not possess (fortunately) the grandeur that attracts tourists, but a long stay makes lasting impressions on one's psyche. This notion of homeland is not, of course, unique to Indians, and despite the obvious irony, it is valued by many non-Indians, including non-Indian residents of the reservation.

These attractions and connections do not prevent people from leaving the reservation, but they do make leaving hard. People do depart, most often for greater economic opportunity, and sometimes to escape violence and perceptions about inferior schools. But most who leave return. Maybe Robert Logterman, a long-time non-Indian rancher on the Rosebud Reservation, said it best: "[T]hey ought to send someone from the reservation into outer space because then they would be sure that they would return safely." Even the federal government learned this lesson and abandoned its program of "relocation," which attempted to take people from the reservation and resettle them in major urban areas with greater economic opportunities. Few participated, and most of those who did refused to stay long on the fringes of urban ghettos.

The reservation is home. It is a place where the land lives and stalks people; a place where the land looks after people and makes them live right; a place where the earth provides solace and nurture. Yet, paradoxically, it is also a place where the land has been wounded; a place where the sacred hoop has been broken; a place stained with violence and suffering. And this painful truth also stalks the people and their Mother. . . .

The concept of an Indian reservation is best defined as the concrete manifestation of a guarantee of a "measured separatism" to Indian people as the result of negotiated treaties and settlements reached between Indian tribes and the federal government. Most of these treaties between mutual sovereigns were agreed upon in the nineteenth century through negotiations which represented political and legal adjustments between an expansionary, westward-marching American society and established, staunchly resistant tribal societies. . . .

Despite this history of bargained-for exchange, treaties and reservations are often misconstrued as unilateral, revocable acts of federal largesse. Tribes gave up much for what they received in return—homelands, often reduced in size, with the right to govern their own affairs. If this mutuality had been preserved and legally vouchsafed, perhaps the original purpose of reservations might have been achieved and maintained. Yet these treaty-based promises were often quickly eroded and the "strong fences" of federal protection torn down.

## "Measured Separatism" Under Assault

The pressure of western expansion did not abate with the signing of treaties, and the federal policy of measured separatism soon gave way to a policy of vigorous assimilation, which had dire consequences for reservations as islands of Indianness. The homelands were cut open. The bright line separating Indians and non-Indians was obliterated. Much land was lost as many non-Indian settlers came into Indian country. Cultural ways were strained, and traditional tribal institutions were undermined and weakened. For many, this was the most devastating historical blow to tribalism and Indian life. . . .

The missionaries in particular wreaked havoc with their religious and educational programs, particularly the boarding school program which took Indian children away from their families for substantial periods of time and specifically forbade the speaking of tribal languages in school. It is not difficult to perceive the strain and pressure placed on traditional culture under these circumstances. This is even more apparent when these policies were joined to BIA directives outlawing traditional religious practices such as the Sun Dance. As a result, the core of the culture was driven underground into a shadow existence.

Many people on the reservation vividly recall these times. Albert White Hat, an instructor of Lakota thought and Philosophy at Sinte Gleska University on the Rosebud Sioux Reservation, speaks of the many instances in which he and his classmates at St. Francis Indian School had their mouths washed out with soap for speaking Lakota in school. As Mr. White Hat eloquently summarized without rancor: "You gave us the Bible, but stole our land. You taught us English only so we could take, orders, not so that we might dream.". . .

Federal government endorsement of these policies was reversed with the Indian Reorganization Act of 1934 (IRA), which ended the allotment process and supported the development of tribal self-government. The reforms of the IRA, including explicit authorization and assistance in the adoption of tribal constitutions, sought to engender recovery from stultification. Yet the "new" opportunity held out in the IRA has long been perceived on the reservation as further evisceration of traditional tribal government, since the "modern" tribal governments rely on the "white man's way" of elections, the use of English, and the written word. For some, the apparatus of IRA tribal governments further disturbed and unsettled the cultural balance necessary to support traditional forms of self-rule often associated with tribal governance in force when the treaties were made. As a result, IRA-elected tribal governments often remain controversial and occasionally have a hint of illegitimacy about them.

The dismal effects of allotment and assimilation have been halted and the thrust of self-rule reworked and reinvigorated. But the scars of the sever loss of land and the reminders of social weakening verify the inextricable bond among the people, the culture, and the land. . . .

Vine Deloria, Jr., a leading Sioux intellectual, has noted that this flooding of ancestral lands ruthlessly took away old memories and led to material and spiritual impoverishment. He has characterized the Pick-Sloan Plan as "the single most destructive act ever perpetrated on any tribe by the United States." Yet this legacy of loss has not reduced, but rather has extended and deepened, the emotional and cultural commitment of Lakota people to the land as the enduring repository of their ultimate well-being. Without the land, there is no center to resist the historical pressures created by the dominant society. . . .

During the time I taught at Sinte Gleska University, I was repeatedly struck by the transformative nature of these exchanges, particularly as they affected non-Indians. Non-Indians reacted most favorably in three areas: (1) to the rigor and quality of education they were receiving; (2) to the fact that they were welcomed and not discriminated against; and (3) to the opportunity to meet Indians and their cultures in a nonthreatening, non-stereotyped situation.

The most striking attributes of these exchanges are legitimacy and humanity: legitimacy in the sense that most non-Indians begin to recognize and appreciate the legal and ethical thrust of Indian people to develop and to improve their institutions and government; and humanity in the sense that they begin to appreciate the human faces behind these exertions. . . .

The questions of the land have profound implications. They suggest the primary role of the land as the mediator of unity and wholeness, the central intercessor for a people. The bond to the land was almost completely severed by the grievous loss of so much of it through enforced assimilation and changed land tenure patterns and by almost total eradication of an economic relation to it as a material provider of sustenance. As Gerald Clifford, an Oglala and Chairman of the Black Hills Steering Committee, has said, "Our relationships to one another as Lakota are defined by our relationship to the earth. Until we get back on track in our relationship to the earth, we cannot straighten out any of our relationships to ourselves, to other people." The difficult question is *how* to get back on track in the relationship to the earth. There are no easy or simple answers. . . .

The land needs to be retained, restored, and redefined. Its economic role—long dormant—must be resuscitated. Its spiritual role—long atrophied—must be revivified. Its healing role—long obscured—must be revitalized. The land must hold the people, and give direction to their aspirations and yearnings. In this way of looking at the reservation as place, the land may be seen as part of the "sacred text" of Lakota religion and culture.

As part of the sacred text, the land—like sacred texts in other traditions—is *not* primarily a book of answers but rather a principal symbol of—perhaps *the* principal symbol of and thus a central occasion of recalling and heeding—the fundamental aspirations of the tradition. It summons the heart and the spirit to difficult labor. In this sense, the sacred text constantly *disturbs:* it serves a prophetic function in the life of the community. The land constantly evokes the fundamental Lakota aspirations to live in harmony with Mother Earth and to embody the traditional virtues of wisdom, courage, generosity, and fortitude. The "sacred text" itself guarantees nothing, but it does hold the necessary potential to mediate the past of the tradition with its present predicament.

The vindication of any tradition—including Lakota tradition—cannot be assumed. Yet the potential for the vindication and the flowering of the tradition is contingent, in part, on the commitment and exertions of the tradition's followers. This process is richly described by Jaroslav Pelikan, a leading commentator within the Christian community:

> Ultimately, however, tradition will be vindicated for us as an individual and for us as communities, by how it manages to accord with our own deepest intuitions and highest aspirations. . . . Those intuitions and aspirations tell us that there must be a way of holding together what the vicissitudes of our experience have driven apart—a realism about a fallen world and our hope for what the world may still become, our private integrity and our public duty, our hunger for community and our yearning for personal fulfillment, what Pascal called "the grandeur and the misery" of our common humanity.

# Is Urban a Person or a Place? Characteristics of Urban Indian Country

Is urban a person or a place? Urban is a place, a setting where many Indian people at some time in their lives visit, "establish an encampment," or settle into. Urban doesn't determine self-identity, yet the urban area and urban experiences are contexts that contribute to defining identity. The intent of this chapter is to delineate some of the general structural characteristics of urban Indian communities in the United States and to indicate the ways that urban communities interplay with individual and group identity. While most of the focused research lot this discussion has been carried out since 1978 in the San Francisco Bay Area and the principal examples are specific to this region, many of the comments are also applicable on a general level to other urban Indian communities such as those found in Seattle, Los Angeles, and Chicago. . . .

## The Community

For American Indians living in the Bay Area, and for our definitional purposes here, the Indian community is not a geographic location with clustered residency or neighborhoods, but rather it is fundamentally a widely scattered and frequently shifting network of relationships with locational nodes found in organizations and activity sites of special significance. It is a distinct community that answers needs for affirming and activating identity; it creates contexts for carrying out the necessary activities of community life; and it provides a wide range of circumstances and symbols that foster "Indian" relationships at the family and community levels.

The American Indian community in the San Francisco Bay Area is characterized here on a general level as a social group in which:

1. community members recognize a shared identity;
2. there are shared values, symbols, and history;
3. basic institutions have been created and sustained; and

4. there are consistent features of social organization such as those related to social control and the definition of distinctive and specialized gender- and age-related roles.

There are geographic markers around the Bay that set the stage for community activities: the enclosing hills, the Bay, the bridges that connect the East Bay with San Francisco and San Francisco with Marin County. However, these geographical features only set the stage for the "Indian map" of the area. This "map" charts the shared abstract connotations of people who speak of "going to the Healing Center," a residential treatment center for women and their children, or nodding with the head to the north of downtown Oakland and saying, "over by CRC," an American Indian family and child assistance agency. People in the Indian community know where these points of reference are; those not participating in the community would not know. Another example of such shared connotations is when an Indian person comments, quite possibly totally out of context. "You going to Stanford?" the question is not, "Do you attend Stanford University?" but rather, "Will I see you at the Stanford pow-wow this May?" Or when someone says, "I saw your niece up at Hilltop," the reference is to a high-profile Indian bar, not to be confused with a shopping mall of the same name. Each of these examples illustrates one of the ways in which Indian people in the Bay Area talk about or interpret their environment as both a setting for community as a place and also as deeply intertwined with the network of relatedness that ties members together as a community. Theodoratus and LaPena express this idea well in reference to Wintu sacred geography: "[This paper] is about topographical features that are the embodiment of Wintu expression of an ordinary and nonordinary world. It is about a concept of land and interpretations of that natural universe that translate into a coherent world." In the case of the Bay Area Indian vision of community, both the topographical features and the built environment are a part of creating this "coherent world."

The physical environment, while the backdrop and the grounding for much of the community activity, is not "the community," which instead finds its focus in relationship dynamics and the more abstract realm of shared knowledge that informs and shapes actions. An urban Indian community is not situated in an immutable, bounded territory as a reservation is, but rather exists within a fluidly defined region with niches of resources and boundaries that respond to needs and activities, perhaps reflecting a reality closer to that of Native homelands prior to the imposition of reservation borders. For example, with the development and flourishing of D-Q University, an Indian-controlled community college, the conceptualization of the Bay Area Indian community extended sixty miles to the north to include this institution as an outlying entity.

On tribal homelands a major source of identity is embodied in the land, and often in the old stories and songs that tie personal reality to time and place. As Basso notes, "Knowledge of place is therefore closely linked to knowledge of the self, to grasping one's position in the larger scheme of things, including one's own community, and to securing a confident sense of who one is as a person." Yet in an urban community there is essentially no land base, except for those few recently purchased buildings and properties. Or, on the other hand, as someone recently pointed out to one, "all of it is our urban territory." In this urban context, the Indian organizations come to powerfully represent Indian "space" or "a place that is Indian" and are intimately tied to identity. Consequently, the control, the programs, and the guiding values of these organizations are under constant scrutiny, negotiation, and adjustment by more community members who act as arbitrators.

To many outside the urban Indian community it is an invisible population, both because of the abstract and nongeographically clustered nature of the community, but also because of the continued existence of a series of stereotypes regarding Indian people. A widespread and mistaken assumption held by the general public is that American Indians have "vanished" or live overwhelmingly on reservations in rural areas. In reality, this is an expanding population, and the majority of Indian people now live in urban areas. In much of the social science literature and federal and state policy, as well as in criteria frequently utilized by funding sources, there is a mindset that imposes a dichotomy between urban and rural, based on the lingering stereotype that "Indian" is synonymous with rural and that urban is somehow not genuinely Indian. While there are certainly differences in these two types of settings, establishing rural/urban as the defining characteristic of identity is not realistic from an Indian point of view and serves to further officially alienate Indian people from homelands. One of the most notorious recent policies reflecting this attitude was Relocation, initiated in the 1950s and based on government assumptions that Indian people, once removed or relocated from tribal homelands, would become urban . . . definitively. Conversely, for many Indian people the urban areas are visualized more as an extension of home territory, or as one person put it, "our urban encampment out here" For those living in the city, even those a few generations removed from tribal homelands, these strong linkages to "back home" are, for the most part, not broken. One simply extends the sense of territory, often keenly aware, for example, that sacred places are found at home and that after death one will very likely be buried there. For third- and fourth-generation urban people, this connection to Home may change and take new forms, but nevertheless continues.

The underlying Native sense of community—if viewed fundamentally as a network of relatedness that has become subsequently structured in many tribal homelands into formalized, federally prescribed tribes— reemerges in the city as the rigid, bounded "tribe demanded by the government of federally recognized tribes falls away. In this volume Straus also discusses this aspect of urban communities. The federal government's image of a tribe as a bounded entity within a geographically rigid, demarcated territory or reservation, governed by a body of elected officials, and with stringently designated criteria for membership is not transferred to urban Indian communities. In contrast, here in cities, the social entity is reconstituted with a structuring based on a network of relatedness. The fluid territory has changing outer limits, there is no over-arching formalized governing body, and membership is defined by a series of strongly situational, and to some degree, negotiable criteria.

The most striking urban parallel to the tribal political structuring found on rural reservations is the legal non-profit status of many urban Indian organizations in which there is a governing board of directors, by-laws, and possibly membership lists. However, Indian people in the city, in contrast to the situation in a reservation tribal setting, are not governed by these organizations, nor do the organizations establish and enforce criteria for community membership. In the city, people may choose whether to become active in any particular organization at any specific time.

Although structured differently, the urban community comes to hold many connotations for Indian people that are similar to those of the tribe. The urban community gives a sense of belonging, meets a need to look inward to this social entity, and fosters a feeling of responsibility to contribute to the well-being of the members via support of the continuity and flourishing of urban institutions. In the Bay Area one occasionally hears joking reference to the Indian community as "The Urban Tribe."

One of the underlying objectives of the federal relocation program initiated in the 1950s was the assimilation of American Indians into an envisioned mainstream. Yet to many Indian people in the Bay Area, the existence and resiliency of the Indian community is an expression of resistance to pressure and domination by the non-Indian world. One factor in this persistence is the fluid, network-based social structure. As Indian people often explain it, the community itself has the potential for regeneration. The community is ephemeral in nature, as Coyote has taught people to appreciate, with the power to continually take new forms and thus endure. Or it is described as being like the old-time warrior's strategy to disperse, vanish, become invisible, and then to regroup to fight again another day. This dynamic is a familiar one to Indian people, who throughout the history of Indian–White relations and before have sought ways to persist as individuals and as peoples. The institutions in the Indian community are in continual flux, able to disassemble and reassemble. Yet through all of this motion, there is an underlying network structure that allows for persistence.

The urban community, in addition to having become the doorway to urban jobs and education, also functions as a doorway and a refuge for those who have unsolvable problems or who are deemed undesirable in their home reservation areas. Emo, the villain in Silko's classic novel *Ceremony,* is last mentioned leaving New Mexico. "'They told him to never come back around here. The old man said that. I heard he went to California.' . . . 'California', Tayo repeated softly, 'that's a good place for him.'" The urban community is also a gateway for those, such as Jackson discusses in this volume, who have been alienated from their tribal roots and who wish to reidentify as Indian. There are also those with hazily defined, distant Indian ancestry who create a niche for themselves in the urban Indian community and who are generally accepted if they make a substantial contribution to the community wellbeing. Increasingly the urban community is a doorway into Indian Country for Indian people who were "adopted out" in infancy—that is, raised in foster care or adopted by non-Indian families—and who seek to reestablish their Indianness in adulthood. Snipp has discussed some of these mechanisms of reidentification in regard to the increasing U.S. census count of American Indians.

The American Indian community is also characterized by a geographic mobility as people move in and out of the city, make return visits to their rural home territories or reservations, or sometimes return there for good. People speak of circulating through, or of establishing a temporary urban living situation as a way of indicating that living in the Bay Area is viewed by some as an extension of their original territory. At the same time, people often speak longingly of "back home," and there are shared in-group and tribally specific understandings of the connotations that "back home" holds. These are expressed in jokes ("You know that one about the Doggy Diner down on East Twelfth and the two Sioux guys who just come into town?"), in music (rap group WithOut Rezervation–WOR's CD cover speaks of the group's tie to "the mean streets of Oakland"), and in reference to aspects of the natural world. Movement through space, as movement through time, is a part of living.

In addition to increasing dramatically in population over the past fifty years, the Bay Area Indian community, as characteristic of many urban Indian communities, has become increasingly diverse and complex in the following ways.

1. *There has been proliferation of organizations,* the crucial nodes on the network of community. This array of organizations has become increasingly specialized as community needs become apparent and funding and human resources become available. For example, the generalized multiservice Indian Center has spawned a now-separate preschool and a number of other educational efforts, as well as many specialized cultural arts and social activities and social-service–focused organizations and projects.
2. *The community is now multigenerational.* Whereas the first generation to come to the Bay Area through relocation in the 1950s was primarily young single people and young families, the infant fourth generation is now often seen playing at their mothers' feet during meetings. This generational layering means that experiences, urban personal histories, and orientation toward both urban and rural contexts have become increasingly varied. The urban angst expressed in the now-classic Floyd Red Crow Westerman songs of the 1970s such as "Quier Desperation" and "Going Home" are contrasted with the more hard-hitting contemporary urban Indian music.
3. *The community is multitribal.* And, as intertribal marriages continue to occur, the children and grandchildren are themselves often multitribal. This has the potential to enrich each child's identity, but also to create complexities related to tribal enrollment and tribally based cultural knowledge. Recent research in the Bay Area, in which 290 women were interviewed indicated 90 tribes represented, 35 in-state tribes and 57 from out of state.

4. *The community is linked* in increasingly diverse ways to often geographically distant people and places in Indian homelands. The term *Indian Country* has come to include the urban communities. Family members visit from home and visits to home are made to attend funerals, see relatives, or to take children there for the summer. Many people return home for personal and spiritual renewal. Some return home to avoid problems with the law. Some older people decide to retire back home. Medicine people frequently come out to the city for ceremonies, or people return home for ceremonies. There is the recent and increasing presence in the city of the nearby "Casino Tribes" via their in-town offices and staff: There are also those living on the streets who follow an annual seasonal route between various cities and rural areas.

5. *There is increased economic and class diversity* in the Bay Area Indian community, with some resulting from educational opportunities that first became available in the late 1960s, and some the result of business and professional successes. There are those living hand-to-mouth on the streets, and there are those arriving in splendor at the gala annual American Indian Film Festival at the Palace of Fine Arts in San Francisco. Those living on the streets are not excluded from the community; nor are those living in the hills of Berkeley. In fact, they may all sit at the same long table at the Indian Center during a community feast. There are the many whose education does not include high school graduation and there are those completing their doctorates in ethnic studies, anthropology, or education at the University of California at Berkeley or Stanford, or those taking advanced computer courses at the community-based United Indian Nations in Oakland.

6. *There is now a recognized urban history,* and a community persona that is frequently referenced and that creates a framework for shared identity. A series of events and people, tied to dates, is shared in the minds of community members as being symbolically significant. For example, particularly memorable are the occupation of Alcatraz, the Bay Area Princess competitions, the old Intertribal Friendship House music festivals, and the annual Stanford powwow. Everyone knows who is being referred to when there is mention of Floyd or Bill within specific contexts. And the old-timers have full recollections of Walter and Mrs. Carnes. Remembrances are filled with shared connotations. "Remember when they drew the ticket for that raffled car, there was standing room only, and it was the director's girlfriend who got it!" Ah, yes, and what about the meeting twenty-three years ago, "And your grandmother stood up and, in front of everyone, said *that* about my aunt at that board meetings." Everyone gives "that look," remembering this event well; if they weren't there they certainly heard about it in detail. A well-known activist leader recalled recently to a group. "And we started right here. We started the Longest Walk to Washington D.C. right at this door." Many nodded in agreement and remembrance. These are parables of life in the city and a means of validating the shared historical content of urban living as a community.

# Identity

With their implications of inclusion and exclusion, the defining of who is Indian and the issue of who does the identifying are complicated and emotion-laden topics anywhere in Indian Country. For example, there is self-identity, there is identity externally imposed, there are the situationally appropriate shifts in identity, and there are the shifts in identity that may occur over a lifetime. In urban areas, although no roles exist comparable to tribal roles, there are a number of other ways by which one is identified by self and others as a community member and as Indian. Gonzales also discusses many of the nuances related to the question of identity in this volume. The urban Indian community is most frequently invisible to the non-Indian world, both informally in the general public mind that has not discarded the stereotype that everything Indian is rural and in the past, but also formally via institutions such as the U.S. Census Bureau that has yet to adequately count urban Indian people. Likewise, the federal emphasis on ancestry as the outstanding defining criteria, represented in a "blood quantum" model, is a much narrower and limiting criteria than that found in urban Indian communities.

Within the urban community there is a very different perspective regarding membership from that found on those tribal homelands structured by federally imposed criteria. As with the fluidity of defining the urban "territory," membership in the urban Indian community and the link to Indianness as defined by the community is likewise fluid. Membership in the Indian community is known and agreed upon through informal consensus. Indian people feel comfortable with this approach. This is the way it is, through consensus, rather than written on a piece of paper, a document. There is a shared understanding by participants of the social boundaries of the American Indian community, as well as the membership within the community. These boundaries and sense of membership are fluid, however, and always under review and negotiation. Those non-Indians who do not participate, who are external to the community, are not aware of these dynamics that tie the community together and mark who is "in the community" and who is not. Defining Indianness in the city is therefore essentially released from the burden of the formalized documentation imposed on federally recognized tribes. For example, as a strategy to channel the outcome of the board election at one of the urban organizations in the Bay Area, a board member recently sent out a letter indicating that in order to vote, community members should bring documentation proving they were Indian. Many people—those who could bring forward documentation and those who could not—were acutely offended. The strategy backfired and the board member was roundly criticized for taking an inappropriate stance. Her request was ignored at the polls.

Another example of the rejection and disdain in an urban setting for federally imposed tribal formulae, emanating from governmental demands for enrollment numbers, was demonstrated by a group of Bay Area Indian artists in protest of laws requiring proof of Indianness in order to exhibit their art as Indian artists. One artist, Hulleah Tsinhnahjinnie, took a series of defiant photographs of herself with numbers painted across her forehead. In essence, these people are assessing, "I am Indian because I say I am," "I am Indian because you know me and my family and see me participate in the community," and "I am Indian because I know what it is to be Indian: the protocols, the jokes, the knowledge of shared history, the racism and struggle that are a part of who we all are." "Trying to identify me as a number is fucked."

Thus, in urban areas Indian identity is defined through:

1. *Ancestry:* Does a person have Indian relatives and ancestors, and function as a member of an Indian extended family?
2. *Appearance:* Does a person look "Indian"?
3. *Cultural knowledge:* Is the person knowledgeable of the culture of their People and of those pan-Indian values and social expectations shared within the urban Indian community?
4. *Indian community participation:* Does the person "come out" for Indian events and activities in the Indian community and contribute to the community well-being?

The weight and combination given to these elements to determine Indian identity vary situationally and, to some extent, are always under community assessment, shifting with the changing times. For example, there are many people well accepted in the Bay Area Indian community who may not "look very Indian," who may not have verifiable documented Indian ancestry, yet—through a long history of actively participating in and contributing to the community well-being, as well as demonstrating a thorough understanding of Indian values and protocols—will be deemed without hesitation to be a member of the Indian community . . . until a conflict arises, then this combination may be critically scrutinized.

In an urban area there is an element of choice as each individual determines to what degree and in what circumstances tribal membership and urban Indian community participation is actualized. Thus, situationally, individuals may choose which criteria of Indianness may be activated and when. Some Indian people living in the Bay Area are affiliated with a home tribe but do not choose to participate in, or identify with, the urban Indian community during a particular time in their life. Others are actively engaged as members of their home tribes, and are also participants in, and identify with, the Bay Area American Indian community. Others may not be enrolled or active participants in their home tribes, yet they may be very involved and active in the urban community. Logically there are also some people who, though identifying as Indian, do not participate in or identify with either the urban community or a home tribe. There are some people who have chosen at some point in their life as a result of racism, assimilation pressures, or out-marrying, to pass as a non-Indian—for example as Mexican, Italian, or White. Increasingly, many of these individuals are choosing to reevaluate their racial self-identity, and often to reestablish their American Indian identity by reintegrating into, and becoming active in, an urban Indian community.

The position of children in the urban community is a telling one. In an urban community as tribally diverse as that of the Bay Area, there may come to be, after two or three generations, a number of children who, while undeniably Indian genetically, may have difficulty becoming enrolled in any one particular tribe due to mixed tribal ancestry and tribally specific criteria for enrollment. There is also the consideration that some children with a mother from a patrilineal tribe and a father from a matrilineal tribe may not be recognized by or enrolled in either tribe. These children of mixed tribal heritage and those of Indian/non-Indian heritage who may have difficulties related to formal tribal enrollment are, nevertheless, often active and accepted participants in the urban Indian community. Indian parents who are involved in the Bay Area community and whose children, for one of the reasons sketched here, do not have strong ties to a home tribe, often express concern that their children will lose their identity as American Indians and anguish over the problems that may be associated with tribal enrollment. A major theme of activities in the Bay Area Indian community is that participation validates and heightens Indian identity, and parents frequently facilitate their children's participation, knowing that this participation will foster a strong sense of Indian identity, as well as acceptance by the community. For example, children may join in special educational efforts such as attending Hintil Ku Caa's preschool and after-school programs, participate with the family in pow-wows and other activities, or come with their families to events such as the Wednesday night dinner at intertribal friendship House.

## Concluding Remarks

This chapter raises the caution that a much used concept such as "community" may not be as simple or as one-dimensional as it appears. It is important to pay close attention to the ways that people and communities of people perceive and define their environment, in terms of both its physical and social aspects.

Some of the fundamental ways in which the complex urban Indian community in the San Francisco Bay Area has constituted itself and, in turn, how this community structuring relates to identity, have been delineated here. Conceptually, the community here is primarily abstract, based as it is on a series of very dynamic relationships and shared meanings, history, and symbols, rather than on the more commonly assumed clustered residential and commercial neighborhood. It is particularly noteworthy that, although most Indian people living in the San Francisco Bay Area take advantage of the recreational opportunities the parks offer, live in a wide range of apartments and houses, and are, by and large, adept users of the roads and freeways, this physical environment, while the backdrop and the physical grounding for much of the community activity, is not "the community." The community instead finds its focus in relationship dynamics and the more abstract realm of shared knowledge that informs and shapes actions.

# POSTSCRIPT

## Is the Reservation the Only Source of Community for Native Americans?

**W**hether they reside on reservations or in urban areas, the 4.4 million Native Americans face the same challenges in dealing with the larger American society. Issues of identity, culture, and empowerment are fundamental to their American experience. It is interesting that the larger public views this issue very differently than is presented here. The larger public tends to view Native Americans through a distorted lens, which emphasizes that, "all Indians live on reservations," or through the "casino identity." This false dichotomy deprives students of the opportunity to develop a more comprehensive view of the status and conditions of Native peoples. Students are encouraged to think through the different perspectives from the point of view of Native Americans, which are presented throughout the selections.

The two selections chosen for this issue address a central theme in Native American life. The role of place, the reservation as a homeland, is a centerpiece of Native American culture that is unlike that of European immigrants or any other minorities. Thus, any discussion of multiculturalism and American identity is incomplete without this perspective.

Despite their respective positions on the reservation and the Indian community, both Pommersheim and Lobo emphasize the importance of place among Native peoples. Pommersheim stresses the importance of "measured separatism," while Lobo demonstrates the extension of Indian community life beyond the reservation.

For a comprehensive look at the history of Native Americans see *American Indians in U.S. History* by Roger Nichols (Oxford University Press, 2004). Additional sources dealing with Native American issues include "American Indians in the United States," by Russell Thornton, which is part of an edited volume, *America Becoming: Racial Trends and Their Consequences by National Research Council,* edited by Neil Smelser, William Julius Wilson, and Faith Mitchell. It deals with the issue of Indian sovereignty. *American Indian Ethnic Renewal: Red Power and the Resurgence of Identity and Culture* by Joane Nagel (Oxford University Press, 1996) deals with issues of empowerment (Red Power ideology) and emphasizes resuscitation of Native culture and identity. *American Indians, American Justice* by Vine, Jr. Deloria and Clifford M. Lytle (University of Texas Press, 1983) details the major policies developed by the U.S. federal government in Native American affairs and the ongoing struggles for justice resulting from the policies.

Sources related to the issue of the role of place in the history and life of Native Americans is "Keeping One Foot in the Community: Inter-generational Indigenous Women's Activism from the Local to the Global (and Back Again)," *American Indian Quarterly* (Summer 2003) by Elizabeth A. Castle. She discusses women's issues including activism and the college experience. More importantly, she argues that leaving the reservation is not an either-or choice. *The Urban Indian Experience in America* by Donald L. Fixico (University of New Mexico Press, Albuquerque, 2000) is a classic book on the topic. Among its strengths is a chapter on retention of traditionalism in urban environments. "Native Americans: Will the Columbus Quincentenary Highlight Their Problems?" by Richard Worsnop, *CQ Researcher* (May 8, 1992) will provide students with a good introduction of the role of land when studying issues of Native Americans. Despite its age, the article provides a sound background to understanding the current Native American community. A subsequent article in *CQ Researcher* (April 28, 2006), "American Indians: Are They Making Meaningful Progress at Last?" by Peter Katel, updates the socioeconomic conditions of Native Americans in light of the impact of gambling on American Indian communities.

Additional reading includes "The Racial Formation of American Indians: Negotiating Legitimate Identities Within Tribal and Federal Law," by Eva Marie Garroutte, *The American Indian Quarterly* (vol. 25, 2001), which shows the differences in the social construction of race between federal and tribal law. "'Playing Indian': Why Native American Mascots Must End," by Charles Fruehling Springwood and C. Richard King, challenges the use of Native American symbols within the popular culture. Does this contribute to the permanence of racism (see Issue 9)?

# Internet References . . .

## Teaching Tolerance

*Teaching Tolerance* is a web project of the Southern Poverty Law Center, which offers educators and students with a wide range of resources used for promoting multicultural understanding in schools and communities. Also available are an e-newsletter and an online version of the magazine, *Teaching Tolerance,* which is published twice a year.

### http://www.teachingtolerance.org

## U.S. Department of State

The U.S. Department of State Web site will enable students to read official texts and speeches dealing with race and immigration issues such as racial profiling, affirmative action, black colleges, racism, voting rights, and immigrant labor.

### http://usinfo.state.gov/usa/civilrights/homepage.htm

## The Sociological Imagination: Race and Ethnicity

This is the "race and ethnicity" part of the "Exercising the Sociological Imagination Tour" from the Trinity University Department of Sociology and Anthropology Web site. Helpful to students is the "Sociological Tour Through Cyberspace," which offers links to resources in race and ethnicity along with brief reports on American minority groups.

### http://www.trinity.edu/~mkearl/index.html#in

## Race in the 21st Century

This is the Web site of a political science professor at Michigan State University. Among the many offerings dealing with multiculturalism, education, civil rights, standardized tests, and citizenship is William B. Allen's "Race in the 21st Century" (3/22/99), dealing with race as a consideration in college admissions. Allen represents a conservative perspective.

### http://www.msu.edu/~allenwi/presentations /Race_in_21st_Century_America.htm

## Human Rights Watch

This is the Web site of Human Rights Watch, an organization dedicated to protecting the rights of people around the world with offices in Europe and the United States. It contains a general statement on reparations.

### http://www.hrw.org/campaigns/race/reparations.htm

## MIT: Asian American Resources

The Massachusetts Institute of Technology (MIT) offers this site for Asian American resouces. It lists links to Asian American organizations, activities, media, and art resources. Students researching Asian American life in the United States will be able to connect to sites that are mostly sponsored by colleges and universities.

### http://www.ai.mit.edu/people/irie/aar

# Persistent Challenges in a Changing America

*T*hestruggles *for civil rights and social justice and the increasing immigration of Asians and Latinos have led to an increased emphasis on diversity and multiculturalism within American society. Recent census data have confirmed that significant immigration of Asians and Latinos is altering the demographic composition of the American population. How are these various peoples of color to be included within the prevailing institutions of the society? What are the appropriate strategies for achieving policies of institutional inclusion? Are multiculturalism and increasing racial diversity contributing to the strength of American institutions and social life, or are these phenomena contributing to racial polarization and disunity within the nation? Persistent challenges in a constantly changing America include the resegregation of America's public schools, bilingualism, racial and ethnic diversity, and the model minority status of Asian Americans.*

- Are America's Public Schools Resegregating?

- Is There Room for Bilingualism in American Education?

- Is It Time to De-Emphasize Diversity?

- Are Asian Americans a Model Minority?

# ISSUE 13

# Are America's Public Schools Resegregating?

**YES: Gary Orfield and Susan E. Eaton,** from *Dismantling Desegregation* (The New Press, 1996)

**NO: Ingrid Gould Ellen,** from "Welcome Neighbors?" *The Brookings Review* (Winter 1997)

## ISSUE SUMMARY

**YES:** Gary Orfield, professor of education and social policy at the Harvard Graduate School of Education, and Susan E. Eaton, author, demonstrate that America's public schools are resegregating. Their argument is based on a series of legal decisions beginning in the 1970s that have successfully reversed the historic *Brown* decision.

**NO:** Ingrid Gould Ellen, writer for *The Brookings Review,* argues that neighborhood racial integration is increasing. She thinks researchers must balance their pessimistic findings of resegregation with increased integration.

**A**fter the Civil War and the Reconstruction Era, segregation replaced slavery as the primary basis for defining and developing race relations within the United States. In the wake of the *Plessy v. Ferguson* decision of the U.S. Supreme Court in 1896, segregation became the official policy of the U.S. government. Before and after 1896, segregation took shape and form almost as if designed by an architect. The *Plessy* case, a public transportation issue, led to the "separate but equal" doctrine that extended to most areas of life including transportation, public accommodations, housing, employment, marriage, and education. Blacks who challenged the architecture of segregation risked losing jobs, places to live, and worse of all—especially for young black men—lynching. Countless "forced acts of humiliation" kept blacks separate from whites.

It was with the *Brown v. Board of Education* decision of 1954 that legal segregation was reversed. In actuality, there were two *Brown* decisions rendered by the Court. In *Brown I*, the Court ruled that segregated schools are "inherently unequal," and *Plessy* was reversed. In *Brown II*, the Court challenged the school systems of the states to proceed to desegregate public schools "with all deliberate speed." The latter ruling was sufficiently vague and without a time line, so that it provided those who were opposed to integration the social and legal room to stay segregated.

The issues of American public education and residence are inextricably linked. Segregated schools are created through a variety of circumstances. Schools can be segregated because the community is segregated. Within "mixed" communities, schools may be segregated as the result of district mapping practices or neighborhood "redlining." This is known as *de jure* segregation and is illegal. However, *de facto* segregation, or school segregation resulting from housing patterns, is pervasive across the country today. And, the *Brown* decision has had little impact on those communities that practice *de facto* segregation.

Gary Orfield and Susan E. Eaton point out that in recent years, the Supreme Court has reversed itself and authorized school districts to return to segregation. Though little media attention has been given to the decisions, the cases have led to new school resegregation policies. Perhaps the best known of the cases, *Milligan v. Bradley*, in 1974, blocked desegregation plans that would have integrated Detroit with its suburbs. Orfield and Eaton trace the origins of the shift from *Brown* to President Richard Nixon's "southern strategy," which attacked school desegregation policies. Orfield and Eaton point a finger at former Justice William Rehnquist and his steadfast refusal to vote in favor of desegregation.

Ingrid Gould Ellen argues that integrated neighborhoods are growing in number and will most likely remain racially mixed in the future. Using census data that link households to neighborhoods, she found that certain demographic groups are more likely to move into racially mixed neighborhoods. Whites who are more likely to move into racially mixed neighborhoods are young and single. Thus, she argues that communities with a larger proportion of rental housing are more likely to be integrated. Further, Ellen sees no evidence of white flight. Lastly, she points out that stability is an important factor in maintaining integrated neighborhoods and schools. In other words, the longer a community has been integrated, the more likely that it will remain integrated.

To understand resegregation, students must connect patterns of residential neighborhood formation to public education. Ellen's optimistic argument about the possibility of racial integration could be seen as a new way of looking at housing patterns. At the same time, Orfield and Eaton point to a number of Court decisions that have contributed to an increasing trend of segregation. They call this trend resegregation. What kinds of neighborhoods remain integrated? Segregated? What factors cause neighborhoods to change from integrated to segregated? How has the Court reversed school integration?

# YES

Gary Orfield and
Susan E. Eaton

# Turning Back to Segregation

Four decades after the civil rights revolution began with the Supreme Court's unanimous 1954 school desegregation decision, *Brown v. Board of Education,* the Supreme Court reversed itself in the 1990s, authorizing school districts to return to segregated and unequal public schools. The cases were part of a general reversal of civil rights policy, which included decisions against affirmative action and voting rights. After decades of bitter political, legal, and community struggles over civil rights, there was surprisingly little attention to the new school resegregation policies spelled out in the Court's key 1990s decisions in *Board of Education of Oklahoma City v. Dowell,*[1] *Freeman v. Pitts,*[2] and *Missouri v. Jenkins.*[3] The decisions were often characterized as belated adjustments to an irrelevant, failed policy. But in fact, these historic High Court decisions were a triumph for the decades-long powerful, politicized attacks on school desegregation. The new policies reflected the victory of the conservative movement that altered the federal courts and turned the nation from the dream of *Brown* toward accepting a return to segregation.

*Dowell, Pitts,* and *Jenkins* spelled out procedures for court approval of the dismantling of school desegregation plans—plans that, despite the well-publicized problems in some cities, have been one of the few legally enforced routes of access and opportunity for millions of African American and Latino schoolchildren in an increasingly polarized society. Though now showing clear signs of erosion, the school desegregation *Brown v. Board of Education* made possible had weathered political attacks better than many had predicted it would.

But *Dowell, Pills,* and *Jenkins* established legal standards to determine when a local school district had repaid what the Court defined as a historic debt to its black students, a debt incurred during generations of intentional racial segregation and discrimination by state and local policies and practices. Under these decisions, districts that, in the eyes of a court, had obeyed their court orders for several years could send students back to neighborhood schools, even if those schools were segregated and inferior. With the 1995 *Jenkins* decision, the Court further narrowed educational remedies.

This is a troubling shift. *Brown* rested on the principle that intentional public action to support segregation was a violation of the U.S. Constitution. Under *Dowell and Pitts*, however, public decisions that re-create segregation, sometimes even more severe than before desegregation orders, are now deemed acceptable. These new resegregation decisions legitimate a deliberate return to segregation. As long as school districts temporarily maintain some aspects of desegregation for several years and do not express an intent to discriminate, the Court approves plans to send minority students back to segregation.

*Dowell* and *Pitts* embrace new conceptions of racial integration and school desegregation. These decisions view racial integration not as a goal that segregated districts should strive to attain, but as a merely temporary punishment for historic violations, an imposition to be lifted after a few years. After the sentence of desegregation has been served, the normal, "natural" pattern of segregated schools can be restored. In just two years in the early 1990s, *Dowell* and *Pitts* had reduced the long crusade for integrated education to a formalistic requirement that certain rough indicators of desegregation be present briefly.

These resegregation decisions received little national attention, in part because their most dramatic impact was on the South, the region that became the most integrated after *Brown*. The Supreme Court's 1974 *Milliken* decision had already rendered *Brown* almost meaningless for most of the metropolitan North by blocking desegregation plans that would integrate cities with their suburbs. Resegregation decisions made no difference to Washington and New York City since there were no desegregation plans in place.

In this chapter, we analyze the effects of the *Dowell, Pitts,* and *Jenkins* decisions and describe the social and political forces that shaped their underlying philosophy. These three cases largely displace the goal of rooting out the lingering damage of racial segregation and discrimination with the twin goals of minimizing judicial involvement in education and restoring power to local and state governments, whatever the consequences.

The Supreme Court handed down the first of the three resegregation decisions in 1991. *Board of Education of Oklahoma City v. Dowell* outlined circumstances under which courts have authority to release school districts from their obligation to maintain desegregated schools.[4] A previously illegally segregated district whose desegregation plan was being supervised by a court could be freed from oversight if the district had desegregated its students and faculty, and met for a few years the other requirements laid out in the Supreme Court's 1968 *Green v. School Board of New Kent County* decision.[5] *Green* ordered "root and branch" eradication of segregated schooling and specified several areas of a school system—such as students, teachers, transportation, and facilities—in which desegregation was mandatory. Under *Dowell*, a district briefly taking the steps outlined in *Green* can be termed "unitary" and is thus freed from its legal obligation to purge itself of segregation. Unitary might best be understood as the opposite of a "dual" system, in which a school district, in essence, operates two separate systems, one black and one white. A unitary district is assumed to be one that has repaired the damage caused by generations of segregation and overt discrimination.

Under *Brown*, proof of an intentionally segregated dual system triggers desegregation mandates. But once the formerly dual system becomes unitary, according to the decisions of the 1990s, minority students no longer have the special protection of the courts, and school districts no longer face any requirement to maintain desegregation or related education programs.

In 1992, a year after *Dowell*, the *Freeman v. Pitts*[6] decision went even further; holding that various requirements laid out in *Green* need not be present at the same time. This meant, for example, that a once-segregated system could dismantle its student desegregation plan without ever having desegregated its faculty or provided equal access to educational programs.

The Court's 5–4 decision in the 1995 case, *Missouri v. Jenkins,* found the Court's majority determined to narrow the reach of the "separate but equal" remedies provided in big cities after the Supreme Court blocked city-suburban desegregation in 1974. Its 1995 decision prohibited efforts to attract white suburban and private school students *voluntarily* into city schools through excellent programs. Kansas City spent more than a billion dollars upgrading a severely deteriorated school system. The goal here was to create desegregation by making inner city schools so attractive that private school and suburban students would choose to transfer to them. Because possible desegregation was limited within the city system by a lack of white students, the emphasis was put on upgrading the schools. When the district court said that it would examine test scores to help ensure that the remedy actually helped the black children who had been harmed by segregation, the Supreme Court said no, emphasizing the limited role of the courts and the need to restore state and local authority quickly, regardless of remaining inequalities. Ironically, the conservative movement that claimed it would be more productive to emphasize choice and "educational improvement" over desegregation, won a constitutional decision in *Jenkins* that pushed desegregation in big cities toward simple, short-term racial balancing within a city, even where the African American and Latino majority is so large that little contact with whites is possible.

Under *Dowell, Pitts,* and *Jenkins,* school districts need not prove actual racial equality, nor a narrowing of academic gaps between the races. Desegregation remedies can even be removed when achievement gaps between the races have widened, or even if a district has never fully implemented an effective desegregation plan. Formalistic compliance for a time with some limited requirements was enough, even if the roots of racial inequality were untouched.

This profound shift of judicial philosophy is eerily compatible with philosophies espoused by the Nixon, Reagan, and Bush administrations. This should not be much of a surprise, since the Supreme Court appointees of these presidents generally shared conservative assumptions about race, inequality, and schooling with the presidents who appointed them.

Furthermore, under the Reagan and Bush administrations, even the federal civil rights agencies actively undermined desegregation while embracing a "separate but equal" philosophy. Clarence Thomas, first named by President Reagan to begin dismantling enforcement activities in the civil rights office at the Education Department, was appointed by President Bush to the Supreme Court and became the deciding vote on the Supreme Court in the 1995 *Jenkins* decision.

Civil rights groups, represented by only a handful of lawyers, had little money to resist powerful dismantling efforts by local school districts and their legal teams. The fiscal and organizational crises that in the 1990s plagued the NAACP, the most visible and important civil rights organization, compounded the problem. Local school boards seeking to dismantle their desegregation plans were allied in court not only with powerful state officials but also, in the 1980s, with the U.S. Department of Justice.

After *Dowell* and *Pitts,* many educational leaders thought that, with courts out of the way, racial issues might be set aside and attention would shift from the divisiveness of imposed desegregation plans to educational improvement for all children. With this idea in mind, many school systems, including some of the nation's largest, have filed or are now considering filing motions for unitary status that will make it easier for them to return to neighborhood schools. Living under antidesegregation rhetoric and loosening desegregation standards, still other school districts have adopted policies based on "separate but equal" philosophies. Such policies pledge to do what *Brown* said could not be done—provide equality within segregated schools. Some have tried new and fashionable approaches that focused less and less on desegregation and incorrectly view segregation and its accompanying concentration of poverty as irrelevant to educational quality.

# Development of Law Before the Resegregation Cases

The school desegregation battle was for a lasting reconstruction of American education, not for desegregation as a temporary punishment for the quickly absolved sin of racial segregation. The significance of the *Dowell, Pitts,* and *Jenkins* decisions, in fact, is best understood within the historical context of this long, difficult and yet unfinished post-*Brown* struggle toward desegregated schooling. The quiet, gradual movement from the holdings of *Brown* to those of *Dowell, Pitts,* and *Jenkins,* expressed allegiance to *Brown* while chipping away at its spirit and its power. In many communities, *Brown* is left intact today in theory only.

The path toward *Brown* and the movement away from it reflect the larger social and political contexts in which the Supreme Court makes its decisions. It handed down the *Brown* decision less than a decade after the end of a world war against a racist Nazi dictatorship. Both the Truman and Eisenhower administrations had explicitly urged the High Court to act against racial segregation in the South.

Harry Truman, in fact, was the first president since Reconstruction to propose a serious civil rights program. In 1947, the Truman-appointed Committee on Civil Rights issued "To Secure These Rights," which called for ending segregation in American life. The report offered forty suggestions for eliminating segregation, among them a proposal for the Justice Department to enter the legal battle against segregation and discrimination in housing. Later that year, Truman called on Congress to prohibit lynching, the poll tax, and segregation in all interstate transportation.[7]

Dwight D. Eisenhower desegregated the military. His Justice Department urged the Supreme Court to end school segregation in the South, and he appointed a chief justice, Earl Warren, who wrote the Brown decision.[8] Although Eisenhower never publicly endorsed the *Brown* decision, the civil rights tradition of the party of Abraham Lincoln still had important echoes in his administration.

The Supreme Court justices who handed down the *Brown* decision were appointed by Presidents Franklin D. Roosevelt, Truman, and Eisenhower. The Court that later expanded and crystallized *Brown's* mandate through the 1968 *Green* decision and the *Keyes* and *Swann* decisions of the early 1970s, which expanded desegregation requirements to the North and approved student transportation as a means for integration, had been changed by the appointments made by Presidents John F. Kennedy and Lyndon B. Johnson.

After 1968, however, no Democratic president would make a Supreme Court appointment for nearly twenty-five years; all appointees in the 1970s and 1980s were chosen by presidents whose campaigns had promised a more conservative judiciary and weaker civil rights policies. Perhaps the starkest symbol of reversal was the appointment of Clarence Thomas, a staunch critic of civil rights policy, to the chair of Justice Thurgood Marshall, who had argued *Brown* as an NAACP Legal Defense Fund lawyer.

Amid all the changes, the central constitutional provision of the Fourteenth Amendment—the guarantee of "equal protection of the laws"—remained unaltered. The broad policy changes generally reflected the political views of the presidents who appointed the justices.

## *Brown* and Its Unanswered Questions

The *Brown* decision had tremendous impact upon the consciousness of the country and was an important catalyst and support for the civil rights movement. It challenged the legitimacy of all public institutions embracing segregation. The decision established a revolutionary principle in a society that had been overtly racist for most of its history. But the statement of principle was separated from the commitment to implementation, and the implementation procedures turned out not to work. For this reason, *Brown* and its implementation decision, *Brown II*, might most accurately be viewed as flawed compromises that combined a soaring repudiation of segregation with an unworkable remedy.

*Brown* announced, in no uncertain terms, that intentional segregation was unconstitutional; unanimity was obtained, however, by putting off the decision about how to enforce the new constitutional requirement.[9] In order to win a unanimous vote, the High Court diluted the subsequent 1955 *Brown II* decision on enforcement. The enforcement decision was so weak that it could not overcome resistance from the Southern political leaders who were prepared to close public education to resist desegregation. The 1955 decision on enforcement, *Brown II,* ordered desegregation with "all deliberate speed." The Court did not define what either "desegregation" or "all deliberate speed" meant. *Brown II's,* ambiguity left decisions about implementing *Brown* to the federal district courts in the South, which were without clear guidance from either the High Court or the federal government for more than a decade.[10]

Under fierce local political pressure, most Southern federal courts reacted to the vague mandates by delaying desegregation cases for long periods and then, in the end, ordering limited changes. Often these plans amounted to allowing a few black schoolchildren to attend a few grades in white schools, while maintaining a school district's essentially segregated character. Sometimes this meant that no whites were ever transferred to the previously all-black schools, faculties remained segregated, and black-and-white schools offered educational programs that differed in content and quality.[11]

The Southern segregated school system remained largely intact a full decade after *Brown*. By 1964, only one-fiftieth of Southern black children attended integrated schools. Northern segregation, meanwhile, was virtually untouched until the mid-1970s. Most Northern districts even refused to provide racial data that could be used to measure segregation. For nearly two decades following *Brown*, the Supreme Court denied hearings to school desegregation cases from the North.

After the rise of the civil rights movement, Congress passed the 1964 Civil Rights Act, the first major civil rights law in ninety years. It was only when serious executive enforcement was tied to the principles of *Brown* that the revolutionary potential of the constitutional change became apparent. The 1964 law, which barred discrimination in all schools and other institutions receiving federal dollars, forced rapid and dramatic changes on the South. Under President Johnson, the federal government vigorously enforced desegregation. Federal rules and sanctions took hold in 1965, backed by cutoffs of federal aid to school districts and extensive litigation by Justice Department civil rights lawyers.[12] This commitment lasted for only about three years, dying shortly after Richard Nixon was elected president in 1968.

Just a few years of intensive enforcement was enough to transform Southern schools and create much stricter and clearer desegregation standards. Following the enactment of the 1964 Civil Rights Act and the issuance of executive branch desegregation standards, the Supreme Court established a clear obligation for rapid and thorough desegregation of the South. The guiding principle here was that far-reaching desegregation must be accomplished by immediate change in an unequal opportunity structure. Finally, districts were told what they must do to eliminate segregation, how their progress toward a unitary, nonsegregated system would be measured, and what would be done to force change if they resisted.[13] By 1970, the schools in the South, which had been almost totally segregated in the early 1960s, were far more desegregated than those in any other region. The few years of active enforcement had had huge impacts.

Even when the mandates for action were clear, some key questions remained unanswered. No one really knew how long it would take to repair the corrosive damage caused by many generations of segregation or when the courts' responsibility for oversight would be fulfilled. By the late 1970s, lawyers, educators, and politicians were asking when a court order would cease and what obligations to desegregate would continue once judicial supervision ended. In what would become an increasingly important question well into the 1990s, they asked: Would courts view a return to neighborhood schools, a move with the foreseeable effect of recreating segregation, as a "neutral" act, or as another constitutional violation? Through the 1980s, the Supreme Court justices left these questions unanswered.

## A Turn to the Right: Nixon and His Court

Civil rights politics turned sharply to the right following the triumph of Nixon's "Southern strategy" in the 1968 presidential election, a strategy that wooed the Southern vote by attacking early busing policies and other targets of Southern conservatives.[14]

Following Nixon's election, H. R. Haldeman, Nixon's chief of staff, recorded in his diary the President's directives to staff to do as little as possible to enforce desegregation. An excerpt from early 1970 is typical of comments found throughout Haldeman's diary:

> Feb. 4 . . . he plans to take on the integration problem directly. Is really concerned about situation in Southern schools and feels we have to take some leadership to try to reverse Court decisions that have forced integration too far, too fast. Has told Mitchell [Attorney General] to file another case, and keep filing until we get a reversal.[15]

Early on in his first term, Nixon had fired Leon Panetta, then director of the Department of Health, Education, and Welfare's civil rights office, because Panetta had enforced school desegregation requirements. Nixon supported strong congressional action, even a constitutional amendment, to limit urban desegregation.[16]

Against the strong opposition of the Nixon administration, the Supreme Court's 1971 *Swann* decision ruled that busing was an appropriate means of achieving desegregation. That same year, President Nixon named the deeply conservative Justice Department lawyer, William Rehnquist, to the Supreme Court. During his tenure, Nixon appointed four Supreme Court justices. Rehnquist, elevated to chief justice by Ronald Reagan fifteen years later, became the member of the Supreme Court most hostile to desegregation issues. In Rehnquist's first twelve years on the Court, a law review analysis concluded, he had "never voted to uphold a school desegregation plan."[17] When the Rehnquist Court was firmly installed by the end of the 1980s, the stage would be set for dismantling desegregation.

Rehnquist had been a clerk at the Supreme Court during the *Brown* case, and he wrote a memo expressing approval for the "separate but equal" doctrine established by the 1896 *Plessy v. Ferguson* decision, which was the very doctrine that *Brown v. Board of Education* overturned. (Rehnquist later claimed that the memo did not express his views, but was actually an expression of Justice Jackson's early views on the *Brown* case.)[18]

The Rehnquist memo said:

> I realize that it is an unpopular and unhumanitarian position, for which I have been excoriated by "liberal" colleagues, but I think *Plessy v. Ferguson* was right and should be reaffirmed.[19]

Professor Sue Davis's analysis of Rehnquist's actual decisions on the Supreme Court in the 1970s and early 1980s showed that, although Rehnquist accepted *Brown* in theory, he gave it a narrow interpretation and disagreed with many of the later Supreme Court decisions that spelled out *Brown's* mandate.[20] Rehnquist was the first clear dissenter on school desegregation in the eighteen years after *Brown*. In the 1973 *Keyes* decision, Rehnquist argued against extending desegregation law to the North, calling the decision a "drastic extension of *Brown*." In a 1975 dissent, he attacked a decision from Wilmington, Delaware, which provided a metropolitan-wide desegregation remedy, calling it "more Draconian than any ever approved by this Court" and accused his colleagues of "total substitution of judicial for popular control of local education."[21]

In a 1979 case in which the Court decided to continue to desegregate entire urban districts rather than just individual schools, Rehnquist accused the majority of favoring a policy of "integration *über alles*," suggesting a parallel with the Nazi anthem, *"Deutschland über alles."*[22] By the time of the resegregation decisions of the 1990s, Rehnquist's views, long expressed in lonely dissents, would become the majority view of the Supreme Court. Rehnquist himself wrote the 1995 *Jenkins* decision.

# Accepting Segregation in the North: The Turning Point in Detroit

The impetus of *Brown* and the civil rights movement for desegregating American schools hit a stone wall with the 1974 *Milliken v. Bradley* decision. The metropolitan Detroit decision, known as *Milliken I*, represented the first major Supreme Court blow against school desegregation. With *Milliken*, the Supreme Court was forced to grapple with the basic barrier to achieving urban school desegregation. After the Second World War, the pattern of white suburbanization in Northern cities intensified; many districts were left with too few white students to achieve full and lasting desegregation. In response to this demographic pattern, lower courts hearing the *Milliken* case approved a desegregation plan that would include not only Detroit's central city, but the predominantly white suburbs around it. But, in the face of intense opposition from the Nixon administration and many state governments, the High Court rejected the metropolitan remedy by a 5–4 vote.

This decision was particularly devastating to civil rights advocates, because only the year before, the Court in *Rodriguez* had ruled that children had no constitutional right to equal school expenditures.[23] Taken together, *Rodriguez* and *Milliken* meant that illegally segregated minority students in school districts with high numbers of minority students had a right to neither equalization nor desegregation.

*Milliken* viewed desegregation as unfairly punishing the suburbs. The Court ruled that unless it could be shown either that suburban communities or discriminatory state action created the pattern of all-white suburbs and heavily black city schools, Detroit would have to desegregate by mixing its dwindling white enrollment with its huge and rapidly growing black majority. Chief Justice Warren Burger cited the "deeply rooted tradition" of local control of public schools as the legal rationale for denying a metropolitan remedy and allowing segregated schools to persist. Since the minority population in the industrial North is much more concentrated in a few big cities than it is in the South, this decision guaranteed that segregation would be limited and temporary in much of the North.

In his dissent, Justice Byron White challenged Burger, noting that school districts and municipal governments are not sovereign. State governments and state law created and empowered these districts; thus states have the power to change or dissolve them, White said. The basic tradition of U.S. law is not the independence of local government and school systems, but their existence as subdivisions of state government. He argued that the Supreme Court had ample authority to order the state to craft an interdistrict remedy. Justice William O. Douglas argued in his dissent that "metropolitan treatment" of various problems, such as sewage or water, is "commonplace" and that regional approaches could be used to accomplish the basic constitutional mandate of desegregation.[24]

Justice Thurgood Marshall challenged his colleagues about what he thought was the Court's real reason for denying the suburban-city remedy: suburban political and racial resistance.

The Court did not even consider the ways in which suburban governments around Detroit had perpetuated and contributed to the segregation of housing that led to the segregated schools across Detroit's metropolitan area.

Three years later, in the second Detroit case, *Milliken II*, the Court approved a plan ordering the state to pay for compensatory programs to redress the harms of segregation. But as the judge who later presided over the monetary remedies in Detroit said in 1993, *Milliken II* has been a "limited form of reparations." In Detroit and other cities . . . , the *Milliken II* remedy has not been implemented successfully.[25]

Rejection of city-suburban desegregation brought an end to the period of rapidly increasing school desegregation for black students, which began in 1965. No longer was the most severe segregation found among schools within the same community; the starkest racial separations occurred between urban and suburban school districts within a metropolitan area. But *Milliken* made this segregation almost untouchable. By 1991, African Americans in Michigan were more segregated than those in any other state. When the Supreme Court, through *Milliken I*, slammed the door on the only possible desegregation strategy for cities with few whites, it shifted the attention of urban educators and civil rights lawyers away from desegregation and toward other approaches for helping minority children confined to segregated and inferior city schools.

The outcome in *Milliken v. Bradley* reflected Nixon's goal of weakening desegregation requirements. His four appointees made up four of the five votes to protect the suburbs. *Milliken* was consistent with Nixon's fervent attacks on busing and on efforts to open up suburban housing to black families. He had derided suburban housing initiatives as "forced integration of the suburbs" just before firing the leading advocate for the initiatives, Housing and Urban Development Secretary George Romney. John Ehrlichman, Nixon's top domestic policy advisor, said the strategy was based on politics and on Nixon's conviction that blacks were *genetically inferior* to whites.[26]

Writing to his chief of staff early in 1972, the year of his reelection campaign, Nixon called for emphasis on three domestic issues in the campaign: inflation, the drug problem, and his opposition to busing.[27] Writing two months later to Ehrlichman, Nixon said it was time for the administration to abandon "the responsible position" on desegregation and "come to a Constitutional Amendment" in order to express a clear difference with the Democrats.[28] "We are not going to gain any brownie points whatsoever by being so responsible that we appear to be totally ineffective," he wrote.[29]

Nixon repeatedly declared that mandatory measures to achieve desegregation were unnecessary, and that Congress must stop courts from imposing "complicated plans drawn up by far-away officials in Washington, D.C." Fearing a constitutional crisis if Congress tried to override the authority of the Supreme Court to interpret the Constitution, the Senate narrowly blocked Nixon's attempt to limit judicial power by statute.[30] After he was reelected, the Watergate crisis diverted his attention from the desegregation issue.

By the mid-1970s, the United States had become an increasingly suburban country with a corresponding powerful suburban political perspective. Presidential elections were largely about the suburban vote, reapportionment was about expanding suburban representation, and older suburbs themselves were struggling with the problems of aging facilities and an antitax, antigovernment mood.

After the sudden changes of the civil rights era, the country denied the need to deal with race and income differences. White suburbanites were increasingly isolated from, and more fearful of, rapidly declining central cities. Between the mid-1960s and the early 1970s, Gallup Polls showed that racial inequality and race relations fell from the top concern of Americans to one of their lowest priorities.[31]

But although Nixon's triumph in the *Milliken* case did lock millions of minority schoolchildren into inferior, isolated schools, it did not resegregate the South. In a handful of cases outside the South—in Louisville, Wilmington, and Indianapolis—federal courts found grounds to mandate city-suburban desegregation in spite of *Milliken*. Civil rights advocates crushed by the *Milliken* defeat could at least celebrate the fact that millions of African American and Latino schoolchildren were enrolled in Southern school districts where desegregation was feasible and an increasingly accepted part of community life. This enduring desegregation was the special target of the 1990s resegregation decisions.

## The South's Comparative Success in Desegregation

The South was the target of the most aggressive and persistent desegregation enforcement. In the late 1960s, the Justice Department had launched a fullscale attack on Southern segregation under *Green's* "root and branch" mandate. In the early 1970s, after the Supreme Court's *Swann* decision rejected the Nixon administration's efforts to ban busing, the Justice Department reluctantly enforced urban desegregation. In a compromise between Congress and the Nixon administration, a substantial federal aid program for desegregated schools—the Emergency School Aid Act—was passed in 1972.[32] After the Nixon White House halted administrative enforcement of urban school desegregation, federal courts in Washington found the administration in violation of the 1964 Civil Rights Act, which mandated cutoff of federal funds to school districts not complying with desegregation law, and ordered that enforcement resume. As a result, scores of Southern school districts were required to end local desegregation.[33]

The *Green* and *Swann* decisions, which required full and immediate desegregation, had more impact on the South than they did in the North. First of all, there were already hundreds of school districts in the South that had been required, by *Brown* and the 1964 Civil Rights Act, to adopt some kind of desegregation plan. Even though many of these strategies were inadequate— they often consisted of "freedom of choice" transfer options that did not lead to desegregation—there was at least some plan in existence. This was not the case in much of the North. In the South, plans were already on the books and districts were under court jurisdiction or federal administrative supervision. Thus it was a simple matter to file motions or issue regulations to have a plan updated to the newer standards required by *Green* and *Swann*. After *Swann*, more than a hundred districts rapidly implemented new desegregation plans, imposing a move to districtwide orders for immediate and total desegregation of students, faculties, and transportation.

It had been easy to find school districts in the South guilty of segregation, but the question of guilt in the North was always more ambiguous. The South had overt segregation laws requiring separate schools; reading the state laws was enough to prove that government had imposed segregation, which itself was linked to many government actions. Northern segregation was compounded by many complex school policies such as the drawing of attendance zones or the construction of schools serving residentially segregated areas. This meant that civil rights lawyers in the North often had a more arduous task and a less certain outcome in their school desegregation cases. It would take years to prove guilt before anyone even began to talk about a remedy. By the time a plan could be drawn up, shifting demographics often made full, lasting desegregation within the city school system impossible.

Where a northeastern or midwestern metropolitan area had dozens of separate school districts, many metropolitan areas in some Southern states were contained within a single school district. Therefore, the South was much better equipped to institute long-term desegregation within single districts. Florida was an excellent example of this, with countrywide districts including cities and suburbs across the state. The Supreme Court's decision against crossing district lines was much more damaging to Northern desegregation.

Many areas of the booming Sunbelt were experiencing white immigration from the North. This trend was in stark contrast to the declining cities and some metropolitan areas of the North that were losing white residents rapidly.

After *Milliken I*, desegregation law remained relatively stable through the 1980s, and the South maintained the relatively high levels of school integration achieved under *Green, Swann,* and civil rights regulations through 1988. The struggle over the meaning of the law was ongoing. In two 1970s cases originating in the Ohio cities of Dayton and Columbus, Justice Rehnquist failed in his attempt to roll back the citywide desegregation requirements laid out in *Keyes,* which had ruled that once intentional segregation was found in one part of a school system, lower courts should presume that segregation found in other parts of that system was also unconstitutional. This presumption meant that desegregation plans would be drawn for entire districts rather than for just a few schools. Trying to reverse the *Keyes* requirement, Rehnquist, on his own initiative, blocked the desegregation of 43,000 Columbus students just before school opened in 1978. The next year, in the Ohio cases, however, the Supreme Court reaffirmed its citywide desegregation stand.[34]

President Jimmy Carter expressed reservations about busing policies both as governor of Georgia and during his presidential campaign. Griffin Bell, Carter's attorney general, also had a record of opposition.[35] Once Carter was in office, however, he appointed civil rights officials who favored school desegregation, and a few important cases were filed by the Justice Department. These included the Indianapolis case, resulting in a metropolitan-wide desegregation remedy despite the *Milliken* constraints. In fact, the first successful lawsuit to link school and housing desegregation in a single city (Yonkers, N.Y.) was filed under Carter's presidency.

During this time, though, Congress voted to limit mandatory desegregation by prohibiting the use of the federal fund cutoff sanction in the 1964 Civil Rights Act to enforce civil rights compliance if busing was needed. Without this enforcement power, there was no potential for a nationwide executive branch desegregation policy. By the end of its term, however, the Carter administration was trying to craft coordinated school and housing desegregation policies. But the belated effort was aborted by President Reagan's election. Carter did not have the opportunity to appoint a Supreme Court justice.

## The Reagan Era and the Movement to Dismantle

Opposition to mandatory desegregation reached a new intensity during the Reagan administration. Although desegregation orders were still sufficiently well-rooted to prevent a clear trend toward resegregation, the shift toward a "separate but equal" philosophy manifested itself at the end of the 1980s. Not even the South's favorable demographics and enforcement history could withstand the dismantling policies and court appointments of the Reagan administration.

In its first months, the administration won congressional action to rescind the Emergency School Aid Act of 1972, cutting off the only significant source of public money earmarked for the educational and human relations dimensions of desegregation plans. This was the largest federal education program deleted in the vast Omnibus Budget Reconciliation Act, which slashed hundreds of programs with a single vote.[36] Only the part that provided funds to specialized "magnet schools" was later restored. This restoration reflected the administration's desire to focus on choice. (Magnet schools relied upon parent's choosing to send their children to a particular school in an effort to achieve desegregation.) The Reagan administration also tried to eliminate Desegregation Assistance Centers, the only federally funded organizations that provide even limited assistance to desegregating school districts. Congress refused wholesale elimination, but funding cuts meant that the number of centers declined by three-fourths during this time.

During President Reagan's administration, the Justice Department, under the direction of Assistant Attorney General for Civil Rights William Bradford Reynolds, supported some of the school districts the Justice Department had once sued for intentional segregation, but failed to file any new desegregation lawsuits.[37] The administration proposed reliance on voluntary parental "choice" measures, like those the Supreme Court had rejected as inadequate in 1968 in *Green*. The administration also shut down research on ways to make desegregation more effective, took control of the formerly independent U.S. Civil Rights Commission, and used it to assail urban desegregation and other civil rights policies.

In 1981, Assistant Attorney General Reynolds told a congressional committee that "compulsory busing of students in order to achieve racial balance in the public schools is not an acceptable remedy." This position, Reynolds said, "has been endorsed by the President, the Vice President, the Secretary of Education, and me." At that time, however, Reynolds said that the administration would not try to apply the anti-desegregation principle to end desegregation plans already in force. He said: "Nothing we have learned in the 10 years since *Swann* leads to the conclusion that the public would be well-served by reopening wounds that have long since healed."[38] This resolve was quickly abandoned. Soon Reynolds and others intervened in older cases in an effort to dismantle settled desegregation plans.

As early as 1982, the administration called on the Supreme Court to restrict busing in metropolitan Nashville.[39] The Justice Department also supported an ultimately successful move in Norfolk, Virginia, to dismantle desegregation and become the first district to get court approval to return to segregated neighborhood schools. The department actively encouraged similar moves toward dismantling in other cities.

By the mid-1980s, educators and policymakers in a number of cities were actively discussing the option of dismantling their desegregation plans. This discussion picked up steam in 1986, soon after the Rehnquist Supreme Court refused to hear the Norfolk case, thus allowing a federal court to permit a return to racially segregated schools.

During this period, the Justice Department insisted that the plans were failures, unfair to whites and to local school systems. The plans should be seen as temporary punishments only, and districts should be allowed to return to segregated neighborhood schools. The department supported neighborhood schools, even in cities with no history of neighborhood schools, where the pre-desegregation policy had sent students to black or white schools, often well outside their neighborhoods.

For most of the 1980s, however, desegregation was surprisingly persistent. In contrast to the widespread belief that desegregation was a fragile, self-destructing policy, school desegregation endured year after year of attacks. Although the Reagan administration continually denounced desegregation as a failure, segregation levels for black students declined slightly during the Reagan years, showing the durability of many local plans, even in the face of opposition from Washington. Public opinion became more supportive of desegregation, even of busing. As the notion that widespread desertion of public schools was caused by integration won favor, the proportion of U.S. students attending public schools actually rose during the decade. Between 1984 and 1991, public school enrollment rose 7.1 percent, while enrollment in private schools dropped 8.9 percent.[40] The political leadership had succeeded in creating the false impression that desegregation policy had failed and families were deserting public education.

The Reagan administration's campaign against desegregation was successful after Reagan left because it was built upon appointments to the

Supreme Court and the lower federal courts. Presidents Reagan and Bush appointed a new majority in the Supreme Court, and President Reagan elevated Justice William Rehnquist, the Court's leading opponent of school desegregation, to chief justice. With this new elevation, Rehnquist gained power to assign opinions, thereby gaining tremendous influence within the Court, and became the nation's leading legal figure. A full 60 percent of sitting federal judges in 1995 had been appointed by Presidents Reagan and Bush.[41] They had been screened for ideology to an unprecedented degree with elaborate investigations by the Justice Department and the White House.[42] This is significant because lower federal court judges have extensive power to decide whether a school district is unitary, whether it has complied "in good faith" with the desegregation order, and, finally, whether the district can return to segregated schooling.

The impact of the conservative agenda was finally clear when the Supreme Court handed down the 1991 *Dowell* decision that spelled out the process by which districts could resegregate schools. *Dowell,* and then *Pitts* in 1992, created the means by which even the South might return to segregated education. *Milliken* had blocked desegregation in the North and Midwest; now the South, where rigorous enforcement had led to better levels of desegregation, was vulnerable.

## The 1990s' Definition of Unitary Status

The Court expressed its philosophical shift away from *Brown's* principles most clearly by redefining the legal term "unitary status." In doing so, the Court managed to invent a kind of judicial absolution for the sins of segregation. Under the new resegregation decisions, if a court declared a school district "unitary," that school district could knowingly re-create segregated schools with impunity.

This new use of unitary status represented an important change. Ironically, unitary status had been first used by the Court in its 1968 *Green* decision as a standard that segregated school districts should strive to attain. *Green* posited a unitary school system with equitable interracial schools as a long-term, permanent goal, viewing any school board action that worked against or ignored the goal of total desegregation to be impermissible.

By 1990, unitary status in that sense—discrimination-free, racially integrated education—was no longer the objective; it became merely a method of getting out of racial integration. The Court rejected not only the ideal of lasting integration, but also the idea that elements of a desegregation plan were part of an inseparable package necessary to break down the dual school system and create desegregated education.

Thus unitary status decisions now have profound consequences for racial integration in U.S. schools. A court-supervised district that has never been declared unitary is obligated under the law to avoid actions that create segregated and unequal schools. But after a declaration of unitary status, the courts presume any government action creating racially segregated schools to be innocent, unless a plaintiff proves that the school officials intentionally decided to discriminate. This burden of proof is nearly impossible to meet, as contemporary school officials can easily formulate plausible alternative justifications. They certainly know better than to give overtly racist reasons for the policy change. With local authorities expressing innocence and the courts inclined to accept any professed educational justification regardless of consequences, minority plaintiffs face overwhelming legal obstacles when they try to prevent resegregation and other racial inequalities. Many of the very same actions that were illegal prior to a unitary status declaration become perfectly legal afterward.

The unitary status ruling assumes two things: that segregation does not have far-reaching effects and that a few years of desegregation, no matter how ineffective, could miraculously erase residual "vestiges" or effects of segregation. In this way, the courts implied that generations of discrimination and segregation could be quickly overcome through formal compliance with *Green* requirements for just one-tenth or one-twentieth as much time as the segregation and discrimination had been practiced.

Many courts do not even investigate whether or not vestiges of segregation are ever remedied. For example, under *Pitts, Dowell,* and *Jenkins,* school districts do not need to show that education gains or opportunities are equal between minority and white children. Nor do courts require solid evidence that discriminatory attitudes and assumptions growing out of a history of segregation have been purged from the local educational system.

In practice, the shift in the burden of proof that results from the unitary status declaration may be the key difference that allows a system to resegregate its schools. For example, after an Austin, Texas Independent School District was declared unitary in 1983, the federal district court relinquished jurisdiction completely in 1986; one year later, the school board redrew attendance zones to create segregated neighborhood schools. By 1993, nearly one-third of the elementary schools had minority enrollments of more than 80 percent non-white in a district that still had a white majority.[43] The judge allowed this segregation, though the student reassignments created the segregation in fourteen of the nineteen imbalanced schools.[44] Since the school district had been officially proclaimed unitary, actions that created segregation were assumed to be nondiscriminatory as long as the school leaders claimed an educational justification for the new plans. In contrast, an attendance plan in Dallas, then a nonunitary system, was rejected because it would have created too many one-race schools.[45] (Dallas has since been declared unitary.)

After the *Dowell* and *Pitts* decisions of 1991 and 1993, the road to resegregation seemed to be wide open. Teams of lawyers and experts were available, usually at steep fees, to help school districts fight for a return to segregated schools.

By the mid-1990s, several large systems had already moved to reinstitute segregated neighborhood schools, at least for the elementary school grades, by going into court to win unitary status. In some cases, civil rights lawyers, desperate to hang on to whatever remedies they could, simply settled these cases for fear that a trial would result in courts ending all desegregation immediately.

By 1995, courts had granted unitary status in a number of cases. Oklahoma City had been allowed to operate segregated neighborhood schools with only perfunctory consideration of the issues in the Supreme Court guidelines. Austin, Texas, had been allowed to reinstate segregated elementary schools. In Savannah-Chatham County, the district was declared unitary after implementing a purely voluntary plan that failed to meet the guidelines of a 1988 order. In that case, District Judge B. Avant Edenfield's language expressed the views of many judges now supervising desegregation cases. He praised the district's "momentous efforts," claiming that requiring more would be "imposing an exercise in futility." His ruling terminated all supervision of the system.[46] Older central city desegregation plans were closed with settlement agreements. Such agreements were adopted in such cities as Cincinnati and Cleveland.[47] In September 1995, the plan that produced the first Supreme Court decision in the North (Denver) was dissolved and the plan that had made metropolitan Wilmington the most integrated urban center on the east coast was dropped the month before.[48]

Today, a great many school districts remain under desegregation orders and have not filed motions to dissolve their plans. Some, including many in Florida, have plans that are increasingly ineffective because of the tremendous growth of white suburbs and the expansion of city ghettos without any adjustment of attendance areas set up in the old court order.

Many communities are on the brink of initiatives to dissolve plans that had provided an important, if imperfect, route of access for minority schoolchildren. Even in the regions that integrated most successfully and stably in the decades following the *Brown* decision, school systems were debating a return to segregation.

Themes about the "failure" or irrelevance of desegregation echo in public debates in city after city. Proposals for resegregation and attacks on desegregation often sail smoothly through school boards without objection, not because they will produce gains or because they represent the goals of the public, but because the civil rights side has been weakened, poorly funded, and struggling for survival in an increasingly conservative society with deepening racial and economic divisions.

The NAACP, by far the largest civil rights organization and the one with the most influential local chapters, has been in decline during the mid-1990s. It has experienced bitter internal struggles, the removal of its executive director and board chairman, division, and bankruptcy, all of which threaten its viability. With all of the major civil rights programs and many substantive programs crucial to the black community under political and legal attack, weakened civil right groups have been overwhelmed.

## Does It Matter?

All this might be of only academic interest if it really were true that school desegregation had "failed," or had already been dismantled, or if the country had learned how to make separate institutions truly equal in a racially divided and extremely unequal society.

The truth, however, is that although urban desegregation has never been popular with whites, it is viewed as a success by both white and minority parents whose children experienced it. In the 1990s, there remains a widely shared preference in the society for integrated schools, though there is deep division about how to get them. Meanwhile, there is simply no workable districtwide model that shows that separate schools have actually been made equal in terms of outcomes or opportunities. A return to "separate but equal" is a bet that some unknown solution will be discovered and successfully implemented, and that local politics will now be sufficiently responsive to the interests of African American and Latino students that they can safely forgo the protection of the courts before ever actually experiencing equal education.

# Notes

1. *Bd. of Educ. of Oklahoma City v. Dowell*, 498 U.S. 237 (1991).
2. *Freeman v. Pitts*, 112 S. Ct. 1430 (1992).
3. *Missouri v. Jenkins*, 115 S. Ct. 2038 (1995).
4. *Bd. of Educ. of Oklahoma City v. Dowell*, 498 U.S. 237 (1991).
5. *Green v. Sch. Bd. of New Kent County*, 391 U.S. 430 (1968).
6. *Freeman v. Pitts*, 112 S. Ct. 1430 (1992).
7. Richard Kluger, *Simple Justice* (New York: Vintage Books, 1975), p. 253.
8. Herbert Brownell with John P. Burke, *Advising Ike: The Memoirs of Attorney General Herbert Brownell* (Lawrence: University of Kansas Press, 1993); Mark Stern, "Presidential Strategies and Civil Rights: Eisenhower, the Early Years, 1952–54," *Presidential Studies Quarterly* 19, no. 4 (Fall 1989), pp. 769–95.
9. G. Edward White, *Earl Warren: A Public Life* (New York: Oxford University Press, 1982), pp. 166–8.
10. J. W. Peltason, 58 *Lonely Men: Southern Federal Judges and School Desegregation* (New York: Harcourt, Brace and World, 1961).
11. Ibid.; Reed Sarratt, *The Ordeal of Desegregation* (New York: Harper and Row, 1966).
12. Gary Orfield, *The Reconstruction of Southern Education: The Schools and the 1964 Civil Rights Act* (New York: John Wiley, 1969).
13. *Green v. Sch. Bd. of New Kent County*, 391 U.S. 430 (1968).
14. Harry S. Dent, *The Prodigal South Returns to Power* (New York: John Wiley & Sons, 1978).
15. H. R. Haldeman, *The Haldeman Diaries: Inside the Nixon White House* (New York: G. P. Putnam's Sons, 1994), p. 126.
16. Ibid., pp. 126–30, 142, 183–4, 276; Leon Panetta and Peter Gall, *Bring Us Together: The Nixon Team and the Civil Rights Retreat* (Philadelphia: Lippincott, 1971).
17. Sue Davis, "Justice Rehnquist's Equal Protection Clause: An Interim Analysis," *University of Nebraska Law Review* 63 (1984), pp. 288, 308.

18. Senate Committee on the Judiciary, *Hearings on the Nomination of Justice William Hobbs Rehnquist,* 99th Cong. 2d. Sess., 1986, pp. 161–2.

19. Ibid., p. 325.

20. Davis, "Equal Protection," pp. 308–9.

21. *Delaware State Bd. of Educ. v. Evans,* 446 U.S. 923 (1975).

22. *Columbus Bd. of Educ. v. Penick,* 443 U.S. 449 (1979).

23. *San Antonio Indep. Sch. Dist. v. Rodriguez,* 541 U.S. 1 (1973).

24. *Milliken v. Bradley,* 94 S. Ct. 3112, 3134–41 (1974).

25. Judge Avram Cohn, letter to author, May 4, 1994.

26. Bruce Oudes, ed., *From: The President: President Nixon's Secret Files* (New York: Harper and Row, 1989), p. 399.

27. Oudes, *From: The President, Nixon to John Ehrlichman,* May 19, 1972, p. 451.

28. Ibid.

29. Ibid.

30. Gary Orfield, *Congressional Power: Congress and Social Changes* (New York: Harcourt Brace Jovanovich, 1975), pp. 182–4; G. Orfield, *Must We Bus? Segregated Schools and National Policy* (Washington, D.C.: Brookings Institution, 1978), pp. 247–54.

31. George H. Gallup, *The Gallup Poll: Public Opinion 1935–1971* (New York: Random House, 1972), pp. 1934, 2009.

32. Orfield, "Desegregation Aid and the Politics of Polarization," *Congressional Power,* ch. 9.

33. *Adams v. Richardson,* 356 F. Supp. 92 (D.D.C. 1973), was the first of many orders.

34. *Columbus Bd. of Educ. v. Penick,* 443 U.S. 449 (1979); *Dayton Bd. of Educ. v. Brinkman,* 443 U.S. 526 (1979).

35. "What Carter Believes: Interview on the Issues," *U.S. News & World Report,* May 24, 1976, pp. 22–3; Bell record is summarized in 95th Cong. 1st sess., *Congressional Record* daily ed., (January 25, 1977), pp. S1301–6.

36. See John Ellwood, ed., *Reductions in U.S. Domestic Spending* (New Brunswick, N.J.: Transaction Books, 1982), pp. 191–8.

37. Ibid., p. 35.

38. House Committee on the Judiciary, Subcommittee on Civil and Constitutional Rights, *Hearings on School Desegregation,* 97th Cong. 1st sess., 1981, pp. 614, 619.

39. *Education Week,* November 24, 1982.

40. U.S. National Center for Education Statistics, *The Condition of Education* (Washington, D.C.: U.S. Government Printing Office, 1993), p. 100. The trends had shown falling public and rising private enrollment in the 1970–84 period. (Ibid.)

41. Herman Schwartz, *Packing the Courts: The Conservative Campaign to Rewrite the Constitution* (New York: Charles Scribner's Sons, 1988); *New York Times,* November 30, 1995.

42. Edwin Meese III, *With Reagan: The Inside Story* (Washington, D.C.: Regnery Gateway, 1992), pp. 316–17.

43. P. Karatinos, *"Price v. Austin Indep. Sch. Dist.:* Desegregation's Unitary Tar Baby," 77 W. *Educ. L. Rep.* 15 (1992); see also *Price v. Austin Indep. Sch.* Dist., 729 F. Supp. The Austin Independent School District, Planning and Development Office, March 1994.

44. Karatinos, *"Price v. Austin."*

45. *Tabsy v. Wright,* 713 F. *2d* 90 (5th Cir. 1993).

46. *Stell v. Board of Public Education,* 860 F. Supp. 1563 (S.D. Ga. 1994).

47. *Cleveland Plain Dealer,* August 25, 1994, p. 6-B.

48. Patrice M. Jones, "School District Seeks Release From Edict on Cross-Town Busing," *Cleveland Plain Dealer,* January 5, 1995, p. 1-B; "Court Oversight of Denver Schools Is Ended," *New York Times,* September 13, 1995, p. B7; Peter Schmidt, "U.S. Judge Releases Wilmington Districts from Court Oversight," *Education Week,* September 6, 1995, p. 9.

Ingrid Gould Ellen

 **NO**

# Welcome Neighbors? New Evidence on the Possibility of Stable Racial Integration

The conventional wisdom on racial integration in the United States is that there are three kinds of neighborhoods: the all-white neighborhood, the all-black neighborhood, and the exceedingly rare, highly unstable, racially mixed neighborhood. The only real disagreement is about why so few neighborhoods are successfully integrated. Some attribute it to white discrimination pure and simple: whites, that is, have consciously and determinedly excluded blacks from their communities. Others contend that it is a matter of minority choice. Like Norwegians in Brooklyn's Bay Ridge and Italians in Manhattan's Little Italy, African Americans, they explain, prefer to live among their own kind. Finally, others maintain that segregation is driven mainly by income differences across racial groups. But almost all agree that when African Americans do manage to gain a foothold in a previously all-white community, the whites move away in droves—a phenomenon well known as "white flight." Integration is no more than, in the words of Saul Alinsky, the "time between when the first black moves in and last white moves out."

But while there is no denying that the United States remains a remarkably segregated country, such views are too pessimistic. Racially mixed neighborhoods are not as rare as people think. In 1990, according to nationwide census tract data, nearly 20 percent of all census tracts— which generally include a few thousand residents, roughly the size of the typical neighborhood— were racially integrated, defined as between 10 percent and 50 percent black. (Defining an "integrated" neighborhood is inevitably somewhat arbitrary. The 10–50 percent range takes into account both that African Americans make up just 12 percent of the total U.S. population and that most people consider integration to involve a fairly even racial split.) In 1990 more than 15 percent of the non-Hispanic white population and nearly one-third of the black population lived in these mixed neighborhoods. And the proportion is increasing. The number of households, both white and black, living in integrated communities grew markedly between 1970 and 1980 and even faster between 1980 and 1990.

From *Brookings Review,* Winter 1997, pp. 18–21. Copyright © 1997 by the Brookings Institution Press. All rights reserved. Reprinted by permission.

Most strikingly, the share of white residents living in overwhelmingly white census tracts—those in which blacks represent less than 1 percent of the total population—fell from 63 percent in 1970 to 36 percent in 1990.

Not only are racially mixed neighborhoods more numerous than people think, they are also more stable. An examination of a sample of 34 large U.S. metropolitan areas with significant black populations reveals that more than three quarters of the neighborhoods that were racially mixed in 1980 were still mixed in 1990. And in more than half, the share of non-Hispanic whites remained constant or grew. Most significantly, perhaps, a comparison with data from the 1970s suggests that neighborhoods are becoming more stable over time. The mean white population loss in integrated neighborhoods was lower in the 1980s than in the 1970s; a greater share of integrated tracts remained steady in the 1980s; and fewer tracts experienced dramatic white loss. In sum, neighborhood racial integration appears to be becoming both more widespread and more stable. Again, this is not to claim that America's neighborhoods are no longer dramatically segregated. But it may no longer be accurate to describe them, as have some, as a system of "American Apartheid."

How is it that certain neighborhoods seem to turn rapidly from white to black as soon as a few black households move in, while others hardly seem to change at all? The conventional account of racial mixing has, I think, discouraged people from seriously investigating this question— either by theorizing about what might be different about the more stable areas or by examining matters empirically. Because all mixed neighborhoods are presumed to be highly unstable, explaining the variance in the rate of racial change has hardly seemed pressing. But examining the conditions under which integration seems to thrive offers considerable insight not only into the causes of our nation's racial segregation, but also into the prospects for mitigating it.

## Why Are Some Mixed Neighborhoods Stable?

It is possible to devise a variety of theories to explain why some mixed neighborhoods remain integrated. One theory is simply that neighborhoods with fewer minority residents are more likely to be stable. The argument is that white households basically dislike living with minorities and that once the minority population of a given community reaches a concentration greater than they can tolerate, whites abandon the community, which quickly becomes all black. But while this argument has some intuitive appeal in light of our nation's long history of racism, the degree of integration in a mixed community appears to have no bearing on its future racial mix. Whether a community is 10 percent black or 50 percent black, the likelihood of white loss is the same.

A second theory is that communities are more stable when black and white residents have similar incomes and education levels. This theory has an intuitive appeal to those who think that our country has gotten beyond race. But it is not borne out by the data either. Indeed, neighborhoods where blacks and whites are more equal in status are, if anything, less stable.

A third theory—and the one that best fits the evidence—is that residential decisions, especially those of white households, are indeed heavily shaped by negative racial attitudes. But it is not a simple matter of racial animus, of white households being unwilling to live, at any particular moment in time, in neighborhoods with moderately sized black populations. Rather, it is a matter of white households tending to assume that all mixed neighborhoods quickly and inevitably become predominantly black and being uncomfortable with the prospect of living in such an environment in the future.

As for the sources of this discomfort, I would emphasize two. First, whites may simply fear being "left behind" as a racial minority as the community becomes largely black. Second, and more important, white households (and potentially black households as well) may have negative preconceptions about what an all-black neighborhood will be like. Specifically, black neighbors may be thought to bring with them, or at least to portend, a deterioration in what Richard Taub and others have called the "structural position," or strength, of a neighborhood: the aggregate of school quality, public safety, property values, and the like. In other words, white households may not necessarily dislike living next to blacks per se; but many white households, rightly or wrongly, associate blacks with decreasing structural strength. Whether such stereotyped associations should be distinguished from simple racial prejudice on moral grounds deserves lengthy discussion, but certainly they are analytically distinct and have distinct policy implications.

This proposed hypothesis—call it the "racial neighborhood stereotyping" hypothesis—generates some powerful predictions that can be tested empirically. First, it suggests that households who are less invested in the structural strength of the community—renters and households with no children, for instance—will be more open to racial mixing and thus more likely to live in mixed communities. Significantly, if whites simply dislike living near blacks, the opposite should hold true. For white renters—who can enter and exit neighborhoods more easily than homeowners—will be less likely to live in mixed communities.

Second, this hypothesis suggests that—contrary to the conventional view that racial transition is caused by "white flight"—racial concerns are more influential in decisions whether to move into a community than whether to move out. For residents of a community should be fully aware of its structural strength and therefore have less need to rely on race as a signal of this strength. Consequently, entry decisions should be far more important to racial change than exit decisions.

Third, racial mixing should be more stable in communities that seem sheltered in some way from further black growth (either because they are distant from the central area of black residence or because they have been racially stable in the past) or in which school quality, property values, and other neighborhood attributes seem particularly secure.

# Testing the Theory

Using a unique census data set that links households to the neighborhoods in which they live, I have tested each of these predictions. The data generally bear them out. First, as predicted, households who are likely to be less invested in the structural strength of a neighborhood appear to be far more open to racial mixing. White households moving into racially mixed areas tend, for instance, to be younger than those opting for predominantly white areas. They also tend to be single rather than married and not to have children. Significantly, childless black households are similarly more open to increasingly black communities than their counterparts with children. Finally, white renters are considerably more willing to move into and remain in racially mixed areas than homeowners are. Thus, communities with relatively larger proportions of rental housing are more likely to remain integrated. Again, this finding runs counter to the pure-prejudice view of neighborhood choice, since renters can leave much more quickly than homeowners.

The data support the second prediction as well. Indeed, there is virtually no evidence of white flight or accelerated departure rates in the face of racial mixing. White households are no more likely to leave a community that is 80 percent black than one that is 2 percent black. And the moving decisions of black households appear insensitive to racial composition as well. Thus, to the extent that integrated neighborhoods do tip, or become increasingly black, entry decisions, rather than exit decisions, appear to be the cause. The point is, residents living in a community are far less likely to consider race as a signal of neighborhood quality than outsiders considering moving in.

As for the third prediction, the evidence confirms that mixed neighborhoods that seem sheltered from further black growth are more stable. In fact, the most crucial determinant of a community's future course of racial change is its past racial stability. The longer a community has been integrated, the more likely it is to remain so. And analysis of individual decisionmaking confirms this. Controlling for present racial composition, white households are both less likely to leave a mixed community and more likely to enter one if its black population has been fairly steady in the past and thus seems likely to remain steady in the future. Moreover, integrated neighborhoods located farther from black inner-city communities are more likely to remain stable. Of course, the added distance may discourage blacks from entering these communities as quickly, but it seems likely that white expectations play a role too. For white households may view communities closer to the core black area as both more apt to gain black population and more vulnerable to the social dislocation that whites associate with such gain.

Furthermore, mixed neighborhoods in which the housing market is thriving and in which neighborhood amenities seem particularly secure are more likely to remain stable. For example, the data appear to show that communities with large stabilizing institutions, such as universities or military bases, that promise to provide a continual source of people, both white and black, who desire to live in the area provide just such strength and security.

## Policy Implications, Big and Small

To the extent the racial neighborhood stereotyping hypothesis is sound, the obvious question arises: what light does it shed on the moral and economic justification for government intervention to maintain mixed neighborhoods or to promote integration generally, and what kinds of policies would most effectively promote integration consistent with this justification? This is not the place to address such a grand question. Suffice it here simply to point out a few salient implications of the hypothesis for existing government policies designed to maintain mixed communities.

One policy that is occasionally used is the setting of an explicit quota on the number of blacks or minorities who may move into a particular mixed community or development where black or minority demand is high. For example, several years back, the owners of Starrett City, a large middle-income apartment complex in Brooklyn built with substantial government subsidies, set a quota on the number of blacks and Hispanics who could live there. In 1987 a federal court found that the quota violates the Fair Housing Act of 1968. But such quotas may also not make much sense as a matter of policy, since, as noted, no specified level of minority representation triggers white departure from a community.

Mixed communities have also tried to stem panic-selling by restricting realtors' unsolicited efforts to encourage homeowners to sell and by banning the display of "For Sale" signs. But if exit decisions are less sensitive than entry decisions to racial composition and less critical to long-run stability, such strategies are poorly targeted. Integration, my results show, would be more effectively promoted by encouraging outsiders to move in, not discouraging insiders from leaving.

Some communities have tried to do just this. For example, some have tried to attract outsiders by public relations campaigns that advertise their particular strengths: their housing stock, their parks, their community solidarity. Such efforts also directly counter white households' fears about the structural decline they associate with predominantly black neighborhoods.

Efforts in mixed communities to raise amenity levels also address white households' fears of community decline. For example, programs to improve the appearance of a community—restoring local playgrounds, cleaning up commercial strips, repairing broken windows—can build social capital and bolster people's faith in a neighborhood's strength.

Finally, the racial neighborhood stereotyping hypothesis has important implications for government policies that have nothing to do with promoting racial integration. For example, policies designed to increase homeownership, such as the homeowner mortgage interest deduction, may have the unintended consequence of exacerbating racial segregation.

# Unwarranted Pessimism

The real story about America's neighborhoods, though far from revealing anything close to a color-blind society, is less pessimistic and more dynamic than we have tended to believe. Integrated neighborhoods may be a minority, but their numbers are growing, and many appear likely to remain racially mixed for many years. Researchers must not overlook them. For the question of when and where households seem content to live in racially mixed environments is in many ways the flip side of the ultimate question of why our nation's residential neighborhoods are as segregated as they are. And any progress toward answering the first question is progress toward answering the second. More important, white households should not overlook the facts either, for their overly pessimistic assumption that rapid racial transition is inevitable has helped, by its self-fulfilling nature, to undermine racial mixing.

In hindsight, the optimism of many people during the civil rights era that integration was just around the corner seems hopelessly naive. But the pessimism that has replaced it in recent years does not seem appropriate either. It seems based more on weariness in the face of an endlessly daunting challenge than on the facts, and it has, in my view, slowed our progress toward understanding neighborhood racial segregation.

# POSTSCRIPT

## Are America's Public Schools Resegregating?

With the increase of suburbanization in the 1970s, America has gradually become more segregated. Segregation is generally imposed by a dominant group on a minority racial or ethnic group. Historically, housing practices in the United States have forced minorities into certain specific neighborhoods. At the same time, members of ethnic groups may seek the safety of a community of racial and ethnic peers. Typically, segregated minority neighborhoods are less desirable. Often poverty, poor government services and low achieving, segregated schools characterize them. On the other hand, all-white neighborhoods—indeed, they too are segregated—must be recognized as a significant factor in racial isolation today.

According to the Civil Rights Project at Harvard, as of 1999, "more than 70% of all Blacks attended schools that were predominantly Black," while white students were even more segregated with the vast majority attending schools "with few or no students of any other race." The Project points out that changes in segregation patterns are taking place in the general context of "an increasingly diverse public schools enrollment." Latinos, for example, have become increasingly segregated. Today more than 7 million Latinos attend public schools. Thus, two interesting trends are developing in the public schools—rising segregation and increasing diversity.

The example of Detroit illustrates the segregation issue. As one of the country's most segregated cities, almost 90% of its residents would have to move from segregated neighborhoods to achieve integration. Further, the vast majority of the residents of Buffalo, Chicago, Cincinnati, St. Louis, New York, Atlanta, Boston, Los Angeles, Houston, Dallas, and Washington, D.C. would also have to move for their cities to achieve racial integration. So, despite magnet schools, charter schools, and voucher programs, the school systems of these cities are becoming increasingly segregated.

Public schools have contributed to racial inequities. The embrace of education as a basis for social advancement is a core value of American culture. So long as blacks, Latinos, and other students of color are subjected to low-quality, poor-performing schools, their prospects for economic advancement and achieving equity with whites will continue to lag. Indeed, the Civil Rights Project points out that "patterns of segregation by race are strongly linked to segregation by poverty, and poverty concentrations are strongly linked to unequal opportunities and outcomes."

To address the issue of resegregation is to assess public education in America. School populations reflect the ethnic and racial composition of the community. Clearly, if the neighborhoods are all-white, then the schools will be too. No policies exist to remedy *de facto* segregation in the schools. Ellen's finding that stable mixed neighborhoods are increasing obscures the fact that many white neighborhoods are segregated.

It is possible that the student will find that both positions articulated here reflect contradictory twenty-first century trends. Large cities may reflect increasing diversity. At the same time, the communities and local neighborhoods in those cities continues to remain racially and ethnically isolated. This is a major paradox.

A general historical background of the imposition of legal segregation in the South following Reconstruction is in *The Strange Career of Jim Crow* (Oxford University Press, 1974) by C. Vann Woodward. For an extensive collection of maps and illustrations of slavery, Reconstruction, and segregation, see *The Atlas of African-American History and Politics: From the Slave Trade to Modern Times* (McGraw-Hill, 1998) by Arwin D. Smallwood. Andrew Hacker's *Two Nations: Black and White, Separate, Hostile, Unequal* (Charles Scribner's Sons, 1992) examines different forms of segregation. For a study of race and class, see Douglas S. Massey and Nancy A. Denton, *American Apartheid: Segregation and the Making of the Underclass* (Harvard University Press, 1993). William Julius Wilson's *The Truly Disadvantaged: The Inner City, the Underclass and Public Policy* (University of Chicago Press, 1987) looks at the economic effects of segregation. Students will find chapters 1 and 6 of *The American Civil Rights Movement: Readings and Interpretations* (McGraw/Dushkin, 2000) by Raymond D'Angelo helpful in this area.

A study of the historic *Brown* decision can begin with *Simple Justice: A History of Brown v. Board of Education and Black America's Struggle for Equality* (Vintage, 1975) by Richard Kluger. It is considered the definitive study of Brown. *Brown v. Board of Education: A Brief History with Documents* (Bedford, 1998) by Waldo Martin offers near complete versions of the important legal briefs and court decisions. *Teaching Tolerance* (Spring 2004) featured a special section entitled "50 Years Later: Brown v. Board of Education." The *Magazine of History* (January 2004, vol. 18, no. 2) is devoted to research on Jim Crow.

Hartford, Connecticut's effort to reverse the resegregation trend is examined by Monte Piliawsky in "Remedies to De Facto School Segregation: The Case of Hartford," in *Black Scholar* (Summer 1998).

Recent data on resegragation can be found in "Race in American Public Schools: Rapidly Resegregation School District" (August 2002) by Erica Frankenberg and Chungmei Lee. They are part of The Civil Rights Project at Harvard University. In contrast, Abigail and Stephan Thernstorm, in *America in Black and White: One Nation, Indivisible* (Simon & Schuster, 1997) defend the laissez-faire progress of U.S. race relations. They attack liberals and civil rights activists who seek to promote legislation to promote desegregation. For a critique of the Thernstroms' position, see Peter Schrag's "How the Other Half Learns," in *The Nation* (November 10, 2003).

# ISSUE 14

# Is There Room for Bilingualism in American Education?

**YES: Kendra Hamilton**, from "Bilingual or Immersion? A New Group of Studies Is Providing Evidence That It's Not the Language of Instruction That Counts, but the Quality of Education," *Diverse Issues in Higher Education* (April 20, 2006)

**NO: Rosalie Pedalino Porter**, from "The Case Against Bilingual Education," *The Atlantic Monthly* (May 1998)

## ISSUE SUMMARY

**YES:** Kendra Hamilton, editor of *Black Issues in Higher Education*, argues that the studies available for assessing the quality of such programs are inconclusive. She makes the argument that the outcomes of bilingual education programs are often jeopardized by the quality of the instruction provided. Thus, the significant question of the quality of the programs is being ignored.

**NO:** Rosalie Pedalino Porter, author of *Forked Tongue: The Politics of Bilingual Education* and affiliate of The Institute for Research in English Acquisition and Development (READ), makes the case against bilingual education. She presents a negative view of the contributions of such programs to the academic achievement of non–English speaking students. Also, she is greatly concerned that such programs retard the integration of such students within the larger, English-speaking society.

T he changing demographics of the American population, and most especially, the rapid increase in the Latino population have brought new challenges to the nation. One area of concern that has emerged in association with increasing immigration to the United States is reflective of the society's efforts to provide equal educational opportunities for all. So, the question of how best to educate non–English speaking students, especially Latinos, has arisen.

Public schools across the nation have responded to this challenge by developing and implementing comprehensive bilingual language programs that feature English as a second language. The federal government has passed legislation that facilitated this development, including The Bilingual Education Act (1968), also known as Title VII. However, it was eliminated as part of a larger "school reform" measure known as No Child Left Behind in 2002.

Bilingual education is not new to America. Such programs were introduced from the eighteenth through the twentieth centuries to facilitate the academic progress of European immigrants. Despite this historical experience, bilingual educational programs have come under increasing scrutiny in recent years, and opposition to such initiatives has grown. The value of such programs as reflected in the academic outcomes and progress, which they generate among non–English speaking students, is increasingly questioned.

Rosalie Pedalino Porter is a strong opponent of bilingual education programs. In support of her position, she states that accumulated research does not support any claim of educational efficacy for such programs. Additionally, she argues that such programs tend to reinforce the separate cultural identity of non–English speaking students and the speaking of the native language rather than a proper adaptation to the English-speaking society.

With a different approach, Kendra Hamilton argues that there is no conclusive evidence that bilingual education is superior to English immersion. However, Hamilton makes the case for bilingualism. In fact, she references a study by Dr. Tim Shanahan that is a synthesis of all the available research on second-language literacy. He concludes, "in fact, kids did somewhat better if they received some amount of instruction in their home language." Further, Hamilton is concerned that a significant question regarding this issue is being ignored. She argues that a consideration of the quality of instruction in bilingual education is critical to any assessment of the outcomes it produces.

Further questions for students to consider are as follows: How are issues of immigration and identity (Issues 1, 2, and 4) related to one's position on bilingualism? Does a bilingual education complicate the increasing demands on educational resources? In your educational experience, how has exposure to languages other than English enhanced or diminished your appreciation of American culture? How can educators best assess bilingual education programs? Does bilingualism threaten assimilation into American culture?

# YES

Kendra Hamilton

## Bilingual or Immersion? A New Group of Studies Is Providing Fresh Evidence That It's Not the Language of Instruction That Counts, But the Quality of Education

Eight years ago, Proposition 227 virtually eliminated bilingual education in California's K-12 schools. Since then, the English-only approach has made inroads in states like Arizona and Massachusetts, where ballot initiatives have created even more restrictive "English immersion" programs than California's. In Colorado, backers of a failed ballot initiative are trying again, this time with a campaign for a constitutional amendment.

But a group of new studies is providing fresh evidence of what many researchers have been saying all along: English immersion has more political appeal than educational merit.

"We're saying it's not possible given the data available to definitively answer the question 'which is better—bilingual or immersion?'" says Dr. Amy Merickel, co-author of "Effects of the Implementation of Proposition 227 on the Education of English Learners K-12." The five-year, $2.5 million study was conducted for the state of California by the American Institutes for Research and WestEd.

"We don't see conclusive evidence that bilingual education is superior to English immersion, and we don't see conclusive evidence for the reverse," Merickel says. "We think it's the wrong question. It's not the model of instruction that matters—it's the quality."

Dr. Tim Shanahan, professor of curriculum and instruction at the University of Illinois-Chicago and director of its Center for Literacy, agrees.

Shanahan and a team of more than a dozen researchers from institutions across the nation recently completed a synthesis of all the available research on literacy, including second language literacy for the U.S. Department of Education.

"When we looked at all the past attempts to get at this issue and analyzed their data, essentially what we concluded was that, in fact, kids did somewhat better if they received some amount of instruction in their home language," Shanahan says. "How much? It was not clear from the available data. What should it look like? That wasn't entirely clear either. But across the board, the impact of some instruction in home language seemed to be beneficial.

"But one of the things that surprised me and that stood out for me was the sheer volume of the research that was not devoted to these issues," he adds. "If you look at the data, most of the research is on [which] language of instruction [is better]. That issue has so sucked up all the oxygen that all those other issues of quality clearly are being neglected."

Such conclusions run sharply counter to the assertions of many defenders of English immersion. In 1997, millionaire Ron Unz began a campaign against bilingual education, forming an advocacy organization with a simple name and message—English for the Children. That organization helped push Proposition 227 to a landslide victory in California, claiming 61 percent of the vote. Two years later, citing dramatic gains on test scores for immigrant children, the English for the Children movement moved to Arizona, where Proposition 203 notched 63 percent of the vote. In 2002, Massachusetts followed suit with Question 2, which was passed with 70 percent support. But in Colorado, voters rejected the English-immersion philosophy, turning it down 55 percent to 44 percent at the polls.

But the movement began to fizzle after 2002. The offices of English for the Children have closed, and studies have consistently been punching holes in core tenets of the English-only argument.

First to fall were the "dramatic gains" in test scores. Proponents of English-immersion stated emphatically that test scores for immigrant students had shot up 40 percent between 1998 and 2000. But research teams from Stanford University, Arizona State University and others pointed out that scores had risen for all students during that period. They also noted that the rising test scores were due to the fact that California had introduced a new achievement test and not to the effects of Prop 227.

More damning was the failure of Prop 227 to hold up its central promise. English for the Children had repeatedly claimed that results could be achieved with only a one-year transition period for English learners.

"The one-year limit is a fantasy," says Dr. Stephen Krashen, professor emeritus at the University of Southern California's Rossier School of Education. "In California and Arizona, English learners are currently gaining less than one level per year out of five, where level five means 'ready for the mainstream.'

"That means that a child starting with no English will take at least five years before 'transitioning.' In Massachusetts, after three years of study, only half of the English learners are eligible to be considered for regular instruction," he says.

Merickel's AIR/WestEd research team noted several exemplary programs during the course of their study. Some of the programs were bilingual, others were English immersion and some were "dual immersion"—providing instruction in both Spanish and English.

Prop 227 has actually been a useful tool, she says, for forcing the state to focus much-needed attention on the non-English speaking population.

Some former foes of the proposition, she says, "have come to see it as a positive thing."

But Shelly Spiegel-Coleman, president of Californians Together, an advocacy coalition formed in 1998, isn't willing to go so far.

"The truth is Prop 227 was a horrible blow for us, but if that was all that happened to us since 1998, we could have galvanized attention, made our points" and worked to ease the law's most restrictive elements, she says.

But Prop 227 was the first of a wave of reform movements, each more restrictive than its predecessor. First came a flurry of one-size-fits-all, skill-based reading programs, crafted to meet the curricular needs specified in Prop. 227.

"They allow no accommodation for non-native speakers, and they're sweeping the country." Spiegel-Coleman says.

And then there are the harsh accountability systems mandated by No Child Left Behind.

"There are these people who have so much invested in these English-only reading programs and accountability systems who do not want to admit that what they're doing is wrong for kids," Spiegel-Coleman says.

Indeed, the stakes in these political battles over education could not be higher. According to U.S. Census figures, the number of children living in homes where English is not the primary language more than doubled from 1979 to 1999, from 6 million to 14 million. California was home to more than 1.4 million English learners—or nearly 40 percent of all such public school students in the nation (excluding Puerto Rico).

These "language minority" students lace formidable obstacles in school, according to the National Center for Education Statistics. The dropout rate is 31 percent for language minority children who speak English, compared with 51 percent for language minority kids who do not and only 10 percent for the general population.

"At some point," says Shanahan, "we better get serious about immigration, about integrating immigrants as productive, tax-paying and social security-supporting parts of our work force. To do these things, they have to be able to do the work that we do in the United States—that means we have to be making quality choices to provide them with a quality education."

But the discussion about quality has only begun, says Shanahan, noting that his review found only 17 studies concerned with educational quality, compared with more than 450 studies examining types of reading programs.

Meanwhile the discussion about the language of instruction—a discussion Shanahan says is deeply political—seems never-ending.

RELATED ARTICLE: Six myths about bilingual education.

*Myth 1:*  Bilingual programs are mostly concerned with maintaining the ethnic culture of the family.

*Response:*  While some bilingual programs encourage development of a student's native language after English has been mastered, the major goal of bilingual education is the rapid acquisition of English and mastery of academic subjects.

*Myth 2:* Bilingual education doesn't work; it prevents children from acquiring English.

*Response:* Scientific studies consistently show that children in bilingual programs typically score higher on tests of English than do children in all-English immersion programs. In fact, three major reviews coming to this conclusion were published last year in professional, scientific journals.

*Myth 3:* Children languish in bilingual programs for many years, never learning enough English to study in mainstream classes.

*Response:* According to a recent report from New York City for children entering school at kindergarten and grade 1, only 14 percent were still in bilingual education after six years. From data provided by the state of Texas, I have estimated that for those who started at kindergarten, only 7 percent were still in bilingual education after grade 5.

Most students in bilingual programs in upper grades are those who came to the United States at an older age. These late-comers face a daunting task: Many come with inadequate preparation in their country of origin, and need to acquire English as well as assimilate years of subject matter knowledge.

*Myth 4:* Bilingual programs teach only in the native language.

*Response:* Some critics have claimed that bilingual education requires that children spend five to seven years mastering their native language before they can learn English. This is not correct. In properly organized bilingual programs, English is introduced immediately. ESL [English as a Second Language instruction] begins from the first day, and subjects are taught in English as soon as they can be made comprehensible. Research confirms that English is not delayed by bilingual education. According to one study of bilingual programs, by the time children are in third grade, 75 percent of their subject matter is in English, and it is 90 percent by grade 5.

*Myth 5:* Immigrants, especially Spanish-speakers, are refusing to learn English.

*Response:* They aren't refusing to learn English. According to the most recent census, only 7 percent of those who said another language was spoken at home cannot speak English. These figures include newcomers. Census data also tells us that Spanish speakers are acquiring English at the same rate as other groups.

Spanish speakers born in the United States report that they speak, read and write English better than they do Spanish by the time they finish high school. One does, of course, occasionally run into immigrants who don't speak English. These are usually new arrivals, or those who have not been able to find the time or opportunity to acquire English.

*Myth 6:* Bilingual education is not done in other countries, only in the United States.

*Response:* Bilingual education is not the most widely used approach for children acquiring a second language, but it is widespread. Most European countries provide bilingual education for immigrant children, and studies done by European scholars show that children in these programs acquire the second language of the country as well as and usually better than those in "immersion" programs. There are also numerous programs for the languages spoken by indigenous minority communities. No member of the European Economic Community has passed the equivalent of California's Proposition 227.

 **NO**

# The Case Against
# Bilingual Education

**B**ilingual education is a classic example of an experiment that was begun with the best of humanitarian intentions but has turned out to be terribly wrongheaded. To understand this experiment, we need to look back to the mid-1960s, when the civil-rights movement for African-Americans was at its height and Latino activists began to protest the damaging circumstances that led to unacceptably high proportions of school dropouts among Spanish-speaking children—more than 50 percent nationwide. Latino leaders borrowed the strategies of the civil-rights movement, calling for legislation to address the needs of Spanish-speaking children—Cubans in Florida, Mexicans along the southern border, Puerto Ricans in the Northeast. In 1968 Congress approved a bill filed by Senator Ralph Yarborough, of Texas, aimed at removing the language barrier to an equal education. The Bilingual Education Act was a modestly funded ($7.5 million for the first year) amendment to the Elementary and Secondary Education Act of 1965, intended to help poor Mexican-American children learn English. At the time, the goal was "not to keep any specific language alive," Yarborough said. "It is not the purpose of the bill to create pockets of different languages through the country . . . but just to try to make those (children fully literate in English."

English was not always the language of instruction in American schools. During the eighteenth century classes were conducted in German, Dutch, French, and Swedish in some schools in Pennsylvania, Maryland, and Virginia From the mid nineteenth to the early twentieth century, classes were taught in German in several cities across the Midwest. For many years French was taught and spoken in Louisiana schools, Greek in Pittsburgh. Only after the First World War, when German was proscribed, did public sentiment swing against teaching in any language but English.

These earlier decisions on education policy were made in school, church, city, or state. Local conditions determined local school policy. But in 1968, for the first time, the federal government essentially dictated how non-English-speaking children should be educated. That action spawned state laws and legal decisions in venues all the way up to the Supreme Court. No end of money and effort was poured into a program that has since become the most controversial arena in public education.

In simplest terms, bilingual education is a special effort to help immigrant children learn English so that they can do regular schoolwork with their English-speaking classmates and receive an equal educational opportunity. But what it is in the letter and the spirit of the law is not what it has become in practice. Some experts decided early on that children should be taught for a time in their native languages, so that they would continue to learn other subjects while learning English. It was expected that the transition would take a child three years.

From this untried experimental idea grew an education industry that expanded far beyond its original mission to teach English and resulted in the extended segregation of non-English-speaking students. In practice, many bilingual programs became more concerned with teaching in the native language and maintaining the ethnic culture of the family than with teaching children English in three years.

Beginning in the 1970s several notions were put forward to provide a rationale, after the fact, for the bilingual-teaching experiment. José Cárdenas, the director emeritus of the Intercultural Development Research Association in San Antonio, and Blandina Cárdenas (no relation), an associate professor of educational administration at the University of Texas at San Antonio, published their "theory of incompatibilities." According to this theory, Mexican-American children in the United States are so different from "majority" children that they must be given bilingual and bicultural instruction in order to achieve academic success. Educators were convinced of the soundness of the idea—an urgent need for special teaching for non-English-speaking children—and judges handed down court decisions on the basis of it.

Jim Cummins, a bilingual-education theorist and a professor of education at the University of Toronto, contributed two hypotheses. His "developmental interdependence" hypothesis suggests that learning to read in one's native language facilitates reading in a second language. His "threshold" hypothesis suggests that children's achievement in the second language depends on the level of their mastery of their native language and that the most-positive cognitive effects occur when both languages are highly developed. Cummins's hypotheses were interpreted to mean that a solid foundation in native-language literacy and subject-matter learning would best prepare students for learning in English. In practice these notions work against the goals of bilingual education—English-language mastery and academic achievement in English in mainstream classrooms.

Bilingual education has heightened awareness of the needs of immigrant, migrant, and refugee children. The public accepts that these children are entitled to special help; we know that the economic well-being of our society depends on maintaining a literate population with the academic competence for higher education and skilled jobs. The typical complaint heard years ago, "My grandfather came from Greece [or Sicily or Poland]

and they didn't do anything special for him, and he did okay," no longer figures in the public discussion.

Bilingual education has brought in extra funding to hire and train para-professionals, often the parents of bilingual children, as classroom aides. Career programs in several school districts, among them an excellent one in Seattle that was in operation through early 1996, pay college tuition for paraprofessionals so that they may qualify as teachers, thus attracting more teachers from immigrant communities to the schools. Large school districts such as those in New York and Los Angeles have long had bilingual professionals on their staffs of psychologists, speech therapists, social workers, and other specialists.

Promoting parental understanding of American schools and encouraging parental involvement in school activities are also by-products of bilingual education. Workshops and training sessions for all educators on the historical and cultural backgrounds of the rapidly growing and varied ethnic communities in their districts result in greater understanding of and respect for non-English-speaking children and their families. These days teachers and school administrators make an effort to communicate with parents who have a limited command of English, by sending letters and school information to them at home in their native languages and by employing interpreters when necessary for parent-teacher conferences. In all these ways bilingual education has done some good.

⋅⋆⊙⋆⋅

But has it produced the desired results in the classroom? The accumulated research of the past thirty years reveals almost no justification for teaching children in their native languages to help them learn either English or other subjects—and these are the chief objectives of all legislation and judicial decisions in this field. Self-esteem is not higher among limited-English students who are taught in their native languages, and stress is not higher among children who are introduced to English from the first day of school—though self-esteem and stress are the factors most often cited by advocates of bilingual teaching.

The final report of the *Hispanic Dropout Project* (issued in February) states,

> While the dropout rate for other school-aged populations has declined, more or less steadily, over the last 25 years, the overall Hispanic dropout rate started higher and has remained between 30 and 35 percent during that same time period . . . 2.5 times the rate for blacks and 3.5 times the rate for white non-Hispanics.

About one out of every five Latino children never enters a U.S. school, which inflates the Latino dropout rate. According to a 1995 report on the dropout situation from the National Center on Education Statistics, speaking Spanish at home does not correlate strongly with dropping out of high school; what does correlate is having failed to acquire English-language ability. The NCES report states,

> For those youths that spoke Spanish at home, English speaking ability was related to their success in school. . . . The status dropout rate for young Hispanics reported to speak English 'well' or 'very well' was . . . 19.2 percent, a rate similar to the 17.5 percent status dropout rate observed for enrolled Hispanic youths that spoke only English at home.

In the past ten years several national surveys of the parents of limited-English schoolchildren have shown that a large majority consider learning English and having other subjects taught in English to be of much greater importance than receiving instruction in the native language or about the native culture. In 1988 the Educational Testing Service conducted a national Parent Preference Study among 2,900 Cuban, Mexican, Puerto Rican, and Asian parents with children in U.S. public schools. Although most of the parents said they wanted special help for their children in learning English and other subjects, they differed on whether their children should be taught in their native languages. Asian parents were the most heavily opposed to the use of native languages in the schools. Among Latino groups, the Puerto Rican parents were most in favor, the Mexicans somewhat less, and the Cubans least of all. A large majority of the parents felt that it is the family's duty, not the school's, to teach children about the history and traditions of their ancestors. When Mexican parents were asked if they wanted the school to teach reading and writing in Spanish and English, 70 percent answered yes. But when they were asked if they wanted Spanish taught in school if it meant less time for teaching English, only 12 percent were in favor.

In the most recent national survey of Latino parents, published by the Center for Equal Opportunity, in Washington, D.C., 600 Latino parents of school-age children were interviewed (in Spanish or English) in five U.S. cities—Houston, Los Angeles, Miami, New York, and San Antonio. A strong majority favored learning English as the first order of business for their children, considering it more important than learning other subjects, and much more important than reading and writing in Spanish.

Having begun quietly in the 1980s and gained momentum in the 1990s, Latino opposition to native-language teaching programs is now publicly apparent. Two actions by communities of Latino parents demonstrate this turn of events.

A hundred and fifty parents with children in Brooklyn public schools filed a lawsuit in September of 1995, charging that because their children routinely remained segregated in bilingual programs in excess of three years, and in some cases in excess of six years, contrary to section 3204 (2) of the State Education Law, these children were not receiving adequate instruction in English, "the crucial skill that leads to equal opportunity in schooling, jobs, and public life in the United States."

New York State law limits participation in a bilingual program to three years, but an extension can be granted for up to three years more if an individual review of the student's progress seems to warrant it. And here is the nub of the lawsuit: thousands of students are routinely kept in native-language classrooms for six years or longer without even the pretense of individual progress reviews.

Unfortunately, even with the help of a strong champion of their cause, Sister Kathy Maire, and the pro bono services of a prestigious New York law firm, Paul, Weiss, Rifkind, Wharton & Garrison, the parents lost their case. Under New York law these parents in fact have the right not to enroll their children in bilingual classes, or to remove them from bilingual classes, but in practice pressure from school personnel is almost impossible to overcome. Teachers and principals tell parents that their children will fail in English-language classrooms. They play on ethnic pride, asserting that children of a Latino background need to be taught in Spanish to improve their self-esteem.

In May of last year the Court of Appeals of the State of New York ruled that there could be no further appeals. But the publicity attracted by the case may encourage other Latino parents to take action on behalf of their children. And one concrete improvement has already occurred: the New York city Board of Education announced an end in 1996 to the automatic testing for English-language skills that children with Spanish surnames had undergone when they started school.

On the other coast an equally irate group of Latino parents moved against the Ninth Street School in Los Angeles. Seventy families of mostly Mexican garment workers planned the protest through Las Familias del Pueblo, a community organization that provides after-school child care. Typical of the protesters are Selena and Carlos (I have changed their names because they are undocumented immigrants), who left the poverty of a rural Mexican village in 1985 to come to work in Los Angeles. Their children were born in Los Angeles, but the school insisted that they not be taught in English until they had learned to read and write in Spanish, by the fourth or fifth grade. The parents complained to the school for years that children who lived in Spanish-speaking homes and neighborhood needed to study in English in the primary grades, when children find it easier to learn a language than they will later on.

Persistent stonewalling by administrators finally moved the parents to keep their children out of school for nearly two weeks in February of 1996, a boycott that made national news. The parents demanded that their children be placed in English-language classes, a demand that has since been met. The school administrators waited too long to make this change: the previous spring only six students (about one percent of enrollment) had been deemed sufficiently fluent in English to "graduate" to regular classrooms in the next school year.

In the early 1970s almost all the students in bilingual classes spoke Spanish. Today, of the three million limited-English students in U.S. public schools, more than 70 percent speak Spanish at home; the rest speak any of 327 other languages. California alone enrolls 1.4 million limited-English children in its schools—one of every four students in the state. According to the 1990 U.S. census, 70 percent of limited-English students are concentrated in California, Florida, Illinois, New Jersey, New York, and Texas.

⁓⚙⁓

Controversy over native-language education is at the boil in California. In our most multicultural state, where minorities now constitute 46 percent of the population, a revolution is brewing. In 1987 the California legislature failed to reauthorize the Bilingual-Bicultural Education Act, allowing it to expire. However, the California Department of Education immediately notified all school districts that even without the state law the same requirements would be enforced and bilingual programs continued. In July of 1995 the state Board of Education announced two major policy changes: the "preference" for native-language programs would henceforth be revoked and school districts would be given as much flexibility as possible in choosing their own programs; and school districts were ordered to be more diligent in recording evidence of student achievement than in describing the teaching methods used.

Yet in two years only four school districts have succeeded in obtaining waivers from the department, permitting them to initiate English-language programs for limited-English students. Why should schools have to seek waivers when no state or federal law, no court decision, no state policy, bars them from teaching in English? The most important case to date is that of the Orange Unified School District, with 7,000 limited-English students.

Orange Unified applied in early May of last year for permission to focus on English-language teaching in kindergarten through sixth grade while using a small amount of Spanish. The Department of Education strongly opposed the district, as did the California Association for Bilingual Education, California Rural Legal Assistance, and the organization Multicultural Education, Training, and Advocacy (META). Local Latino activists publicly criticized the district's change of plan, and some bilingual teachers resigned.

Nevertheless, the Board of Education last July granted Orange permission to try an English-language program for one year. A lawsuit was filed, and a temporary restraining order granted. But last September, U.S. District Court Judge William B. Shubb lifted the restraining order. In his seventeen-page decision the judge wrote, "The court will not second-guess the educational policy choices made by educational authorities." And he added a ruling with much broader application:

> It is clear that "appropriate action" does not require "bilingual education." . . . The alleged difference between two sound LEP [Limited-English Proficient] educational theories—ESL [English as a Second Language] and bilingual instruction—is inadequate to demonstrate irreparable harm.

The federal court ruling allowed Orange to proceed with its English-language program. But the case was returned to Sacramento County Superior Court, where Judge Ronald B. Robie ruled that nothing in California state law requires primary-language instruction, and therefore no waiver is needed for a district to provide an English-language program; and that federal law permits educational programs not to include native-language instruction. Soon after Robie's ruling the Board of Education rescinded the policy that schools must obtain waivers in order to eliminate bilingual programs. Although the court decision may be appealed, these two actions signal a victory for Orange Unified and have implications for other California districts as well. The legal battle has already cost the Orange district $300,000, which no doubt would have been better spent on students. It is estimated that the new program will cost an additional $60,000 the first year, but the superintendent of Orange Unified schools, Robert French, says, "We're not doing this to save money. We're doing this to save kids."

Ron Unz, a Silicon Valley entrepreneur, has long been concerned about the California education system's failures, especially as they affect its 1.4 million limited-English students. He has decided to put his time, energy, and money into an initiative—"English for the Children"—meant to give all California voters a say on the language of public education. If the initiative passes, in elections to be held on June 2, it will give "preference" to English-language programs for immigrant children, reduce the length of time children may remain in special programs, and make the state spend $50 million a year to teach English to adults. Bilingual programs will be allowed only in localities where parents actually request native-language teaching for their children.[*]

Last November, Unz and the co-chairman of the drive, Gloria Matta Tuchman, submitted more than 700,000 signatures to put the petition on the California ballot. The drive has the support of several Latino leaders in California, most notably Jaime Escalante, who is its honorary chairman. Escalante is the Los Angeles high school teacher whose success in teaching his Latino students advanced calculus gained him national fame in the film *Stand and Deliver*.

Though some opponents characterize the petition as "anti-immigrant," Unz and Matta Tuchman have strong pro-immigrant credentials. In 1994 Unz ran against the incumbent Pete Wilson in the Republican primary for governor and forcefully opposed the referendum to deny schooling and health benefits to illegal immigrants—a referendum that passed with Wilson's support. Matta Tuchman is a recognized Latina advocate for improved schooling for all immigrant children, but especially Spanish-speakers. The measure is likely to pass, some believe with strong ethnic support. A *Los Angeles Times* poll last October found Latino voters backing the initiative by 84 percent, and Anglos by 80 percent. A more recent survey showed a reduced amount of support—66 percent of respondents,

---

[*][It did pass.—Eds.]

and 46 percent of Latinos, in favor. But whether or not the initiative passes, bilingual education has had a sufficient trial period to be pronounced a failure. It is time finally to welcome immigrant children into our society by adding to the language they already know a full degree of competency in the common language of their new country—give these chidren the very best educational opportunity for *inclusion.*

# POSTSCRIPT

## Is There Room for Bilingualism in American Education?

**A**s noted above, bilingual education is not new to American public education. Prior to the reform era of the 1960s, American educators tended to accept that the best method for educating immigrants and incorporating them within the wider American society was through "Americanization." Today, this is called the English immersion approach. Some of this history is detailed in Porter's "The Case Against Bilingual Education."

The rise of bilingualism can be dated to the late I 960s when American educators became increasingly concerned with the challenge of providing equal opportunities for quality education to all students. Not without controversy early on, bilingualism spread rapidly within America's public schools. At the same time, a backlash developed that culminated in a California initiative to end bilingual education in public schools, Proposition 227. In 1998, the measure passed by a wide margin among voters. The quality of such programs and the outcomes that they produced in student learning and advancement came under serious questioning. Criticisms ranged from the claim that they perpetuated separate identities to the notion that they retarded assimilation.

Craig Donegan's "Debate Over Bilingualism: Should English Be the Nation's Official Language," *CQ Researcher* (January 19, 1996) provides a historical overview of bilingualism in light of recent large-scale immigration from Latin America and Asia. "The DEbilingualization of California's Prospective Bilingual Teachers," by Montano et al., *Social Justice* (vol. 32, no. 3, 2005), documents the many attacks on bilingual education in California and the subsequent impact on teacher education and the overall quality of the program.

Critical of bilingual education is P. K. Hart, in "Why Juan Can't Read," *Texas Monthly* (October 2006). Hart is concerned with the development and implementation of bilingual education programs over time. Adding to the sources in support of bilingual education as well as citing the detrimental effects on bilingual programs, S. N. Forrest in "Implications of No Child Left Behind on Family Literacy in a Multicultural Community," *The Clearing House* (September/October 2004, pp. 41–45), examines the destructive impact of this policy. Edward M. Olivos and Lilia E. Sarmiento, in "Is There Room for Biliteracy? Credentialing California's Future Bilingual Teachers," *Issues in Teacher Education*, (Vol. 15, No. l, Spring 2006), argue that such programs are necessary, given the diversity of the American population, and that they do contribute to academic achievement for non–English speaking students. They are also concerned about the quality of those who offer such instruction.

# ISSUE 15

## Is It Time to De-emphasize Diversity?

**YES: Walter Benn Michaels**, from "The Trouble with Diversity," *The American Prospect* (September 2006)

**NO: Henry A. Giroux**, from "Insurgent Multiculturalism and the Promise of Pedagogy," in David Theo Goldberg, ed., *Multiculturalism: A Critical Reader* (Blackwell, 1994)

### ISSUE SUMMARY

**YES:** Walter Benn Michaels, a literary theorist and English professor, is concerned that the emphasis on diversity and race obscures the scientific reality that there is only one race of which we all are members. As such, we tend to focus on racial identities instead of emphasizing that race does not or should not matter. Lastly, Michaels is concerned that the focus on diversity obscures the very real problems of class distinctions within American society.

**NO:** Henry A. Giroux is an author on multiculturalism and related topics and current chair of Communication Studies at McMaster University, Ontario, Canada. He emphasizes the need to focus on the cultural categories (black vs. white) that are promoted within multiculturalism and diversity in order to understand power relations and other issues that are reflective of racialized identities in society. For Giroux, one significant way to get to the problem of inequality is through identity politics.

**W**.E.B. DuBois' classic reference to America's race problem, "The problem of the twentieth century is the problem of the color line," can be seen as a precursor to the issue of diversity. Written in 1899, during the peak years of Jim Crow America, DuBois foresaw the next 100 years in terms of the struggle for equality and how race would limit that struggle. At the same time, as stated in Issues 1 and 2, immigration, especially surrounding the turn of the twentieth century, would challenge the dominant American identity. During the early twentieth century, there was no emphasis on diversity as something desirable.

Ethnic groups, consisting of immigrants from southern and eastern Europe, would seek to claim a part of the new-world culture. Indeed, the United States in the early twentieth century and throughout was becoming more and more multicultural. However, diversity, as we know it today, was not a part of the vocabulary of the time. In contrast, cultural emphasis was on assimilation and Americanization.

The emphasis on a need for diversity within American institutions was a positive response to the challenges presented to society by the Civil Rights Movement. The heightened sensitivity toward diversity and the need to be institutionally inclusive became a significant component of the struggles against racism and the racially exclusionary policies that prevailed at this time. The idea that institutions, ranging from universities to the military and including much of the corporate sector, have a legitimate interest in racial diversity gained wide acceptance within society. Hiring practices, in both the corporate and public sectors of the economy, as well as the admission policies of some colleges and universities reflected this embrace of diversity as appropriate institutional goals.

As the nation emerged within the post–civil rights era and conservative ideology has been embraced by a substantial portion of the body politic, a critical orientation toward diversity has arisen. One of the leading contributors to this critical discourse is Arthur Schlesinger, Jr., a leading liberal historian (see Issue 1) in the writing of his book *The Disuniting of America*. The critics associate racial diversity with the promotion of separate identities rather than the unifying theme of an American identity. Such critics raise the question of whether it is good for society to emphasize separate racial identities or should the notion that race does not/should not matter gain ascendancy. Lastly, critics argue that the emphasis upon racial diversity has contributed to the problems that it was designed to resolve.

Michaels sees the current emphasis on diversity as contributing to increasing inequality in America. The concept of diversity originated from the *Bakke v. University of California Board of Regents* in 1978, when the U.S. Supreme Court ruled "that taking into consideration the race of an applicant to the University was acceptable if it served **'the interest of diversity.'**" He argues strongly that diversity advocates' preoccupation of supporting programs based on cultural identity such as affirmative action has not stemmed the tide of a growing inequality in recent decades.

Has diversity become a sacred concept in American life today, as Walter Benn Michaels asks? In an ideal universe would we celebrate diversity? Cultural conservatives want everyone to be assimilated to one American culture (see Issue 1). Liberals want a truly inclusive multiculturalism. What about inequality? What about redistributing wealth? Michaels sees our commitment to diversity as a distraction that prevents us from looking at inequality.

The editors urge students to understand the issue of diversity in the context of the long history of race and ethnic relations in America. How do you want to characterize the issue? It can be viewed in terms of identity politics (see Issue 1), and it can also be viewed as obscuring a proper concern with class and inequality. This is an important issue for students because it does not fall into the "either-or" analysis. Further, since racial and ethnic identity concerns intersect with class distinctions, the latter must be addressed.

# YES

**Walter Benn Michaels**

# The Trouble With Diversity

"The rich are different from you and me" is a famous remark supposedly made by F. Scott Fitzgerald to Ernest Hemingway, although what made it famous—or at least made Hemingway famously repeat it—was not the remark itself but Hemingway's reply: "Yes, they have more money." In other words, to Hemingway, the rich really aren't very different from you and me. Fitzgerald's mistake, he thought, was that he mythologized or sentimentalized the rich, treating them as if they were a different kind of person instead of the same kind of person with more money. It was as if, according to Fitzgerald, what made rich people different was not what they *had*—their money—but what they were, "a special glamorous race."

To Hemingway, this difference–between what people owned and what they were—seemed obvious. No one cares much about Robert Cohn's money in *The Sun Also Rises,* but everybody feels the force of the fact that he's a "race conscious . . . little kike." And whether or not it's true that Fitzgerald sentimentalized the rich, it's certainly true that he, like Hemingway, believed that the fundamental differences—the ones that really mattered—ran deeper than the question of how much money you had. That's why in *The Great Gatsby,* the fact that Gatsby has made a great deal of money isn't quite enough to win Daisy Buchanan back. Rich as he has become, he's still "Mr. Nobody from Nowhere," not Jay Gatsby but Jimmy Gatz. The change of name is what matters. One way to look at *The Great Gatsby* is as a story about a poor boy who makes good, which is to say, a poor boy who becomes rich—the so-called American Dream. But *Gatsby* is not really about someone who makes a lot of money; it is instead about someone who tries and fails to change who he is. Or, more precisely, it's about someone who pretends to be something he's not; it's about Jimmy Gatz pretending to be Jay Gatsby. If, in the end, Daisy Buchanan is very different from Jimmy Gatz, it's not because she's rich and he isn't but be- cause Fitzgerald treats them as if they really do belong to different races, as if poor boys who made a lot of money were only "passing" as rich. "We're all white here," someone says, interrupting one of Tom Buchanan's racist outbursts. Jimmy Gatz isn't quite white enough.

What's important about *The Great Gatsby,* then, is that it takes one kind of difference (the difference between the rich and the poor) and rede- scribes it as another kind of difference (the difference between the white

As seen in *The American Prospect,* September 2006. Adapted from the Introduction of *The Trouble with Diversity: How We Learned to Love Identity and Hate Inequality* (Metropolitan Books, 2006). Copyright © 2006 by Walter Benn Michaels. Reprinted by permission of Henry Holt & Co.

and the not-so-white). To put the point more generally, books like *The Great Gatsby* (and there have been a great many of them) give us a vision of our society divided into races rather than into economic classes. And this vision has proven to be extraordinarily attractive. Indeed, it has survived even though what we used to think were the races have not. In the 1920s, racial science was in its heyday; now very few scientists believe that there are any such things as races. But many of those who are quick to remind us that there are no biological entities called races are even quicker to remind us that races have not disappeared; they should just be understood as social entities instead. And these social entities have turned out to be remarkably tenacious, both in ways we know are bad and in ways we have come to think of as good. The bad ways involve racism, the inability or refusal to accept people who are different from us. The good ways involve just the opposite: embracing difference, celebrating what we have come to call diversity.

⋯⊙⋯

Indeed, in the United States, the commitment to appreciating diversity emerged out of the struggle against racism, and the word diversity itself began to have the importance it does for us today in 1978 when, in *Bakke v. Board of Regents,* the Supreme Court ruled that taking into consideration the race of an applicant to the University of California (the medical school at UC Davis, in this case) was acceptable if it served "the interest of diversity." The Court's point here was significant. It was not asserting that preference in admissions could be given, say, to black people because they had previously been discriminated against. It was saying instead that universities had a legitimate interest in taking race into account in exactly the same way they had a legitimate interest in taking into account what part of the country an applicant came from or what his or her nonacademic interests were. They had, in other words, a legitimate interest in having a "diverse student body," and racial diversity, like geographic diversity, could thus be an acceptable goal for an admissions policy.

Two things happened here. First, even though the concept of diversity was not originally connected with race (universities had long sought diverse student bodies without worrying about race at all), the two now came to be firmly associated. When universities publish their diversity statistics today, they're not talking about how many kids come from Oregon. My university—the University of Illinois at Chicago—is ranked as one of the most diverse in the country, but well over half the students in it come from Chicago. What the rankings measure is the number of African Americans and Asian Americans and Latinos we have, not the number of Chicagoans.

And, second, even though the concept of diversity was introduced as a kind of end run around the historical problem of racism (the whole point was that you could argue for the desirability of a diverse student body without appealing to the history of discrimination against blacks and so without getting accused by people like Alan Bakke of reverse discrimination against whites), the commitment to diversity became deeply associated with the struggle against racism. Indeed, the goal of overcoming racism—of creating a "color-blind" society—was now reconceived as the goal of creating a diverse, that is, a color-conscious, society. Instead of trying to treat people as if their race didn't matter, we would not only recognize but celebrate racial identity. Indeed, race has turned out to be a gateway drug for all kinds of identities, cultural, religious, sexual, even medical. To take what may seem like an extreme case, advocates for the disabled now urge us to stop thinking of disability as a condition to be "cured" or "eliminated" and to start thinking of it instead on the model of race: We don't think black people should want to stop being black; why do we assume the deaf want to hear?

Our commitment to diversity has thus redefined the opposition to discrimination as the appreciation (rather than the elimination) of difference. So with respect to race, the idea is not just that racism is a bad thing (which of course it is) but that race itself is a good thing.

And what makes it a good thing is that it's not class. We love race—we love identity—because we don't love class. We love thinking that the differences that divide us are not the differences between those of us who have money and those who don't but are instead the differences between those of us who are black and those who are white or Asian or Latino or whatever. A world where some of us don't have enough money is a world where the differences between us present a problem: the need to get rid of inequality or to justify it. A world where some of us are black and some of us are white—or bi-racial or Native American or transgendered—is a world where the differences between us present a solution: appreciating our diversity. So we like to talk about the differences we can appreciate, and we don't like to talk about the ones we can't. Indeed, we don't even like to acknowledge that they exist. As survey after survey has shown, Americans are very reluctant to identify themselves as belonging to the lower class and even more reluctant to identify themselves as belonging to the upper class. The class we like is the middle class.

But the fact that we all like to think of ourselves as belonging to the same class doesn't, of course, mean that we actually do belong to the same class. In reality, we obviously and increasingly don't. "The last few decades," as *The Economist* puts it, "have seen a huge increase in inequality in America." The rich *are* different from you and me, and one of the ways they're different is that they're getting richer and we're not. And while it's not surprising that most of the rich and their apologists on the intellectual right are unperturbed by this development, it is at least a little surprising that the intellectual left has managed to remain almost equally unperturbed. Giving priority to issues like affirmative action and committing itself to the celebration of difference, the intellectual left has responded to the increase in economic inequality by insisting on the importance of cultural identity. So for 30 years, while the gap between the rich and the poor has grown larger, we've been urged to respect people's identities—as if the problem of poverty would be solved if we just appreciated the poor. From the economic standpoint, however, what poor people want is not to contribute to diversity but to minimize their contribution to it—they want to stop being poor. Celebrating the diversity of American life has become the American left's way of accepting their poverty, of accepting inequality.

⌑

Our current notion of cultural diversity—trumpeted as the repudiation of racism and biological essentialism—in fact grew out of and perpetuates the very concepts it congratulates itself on having escaped. The American love affair with race—especially when you can dress race up as culture—has continued and even intensified. Almost everything we say about culture (that the significant differences between us are cultural, that such differences should be respected, that our cultural heritages should be perpetuated, that there's a value in making sure that different cultures survive) seems to me mistaken. We must shift our focus from cultural diversity to economic equality to help alter the political terrain of contemporary American intellectual life.

In the last year, it has sometimes seemed as if this terrain might in fact be starting to change, and there has been what at least looks like the beginning of a new interest in the problem of economic inequality. Various newspapers have run series noticing the growth of inequality and the decline of class mobility; it turns out, for example, that the Gatsby-style American Dream—poor boy makes good, buys beautiful, beautiful shirts—now has a better chance of coming true in Sweden than it does in America, and as good a chance of coming true in western Europe (which is to say, not very good) as it does here. People have begun to notice also that the intensity of interest in the race of students in our universities has coincided with more or less complete indifference to their wealth. We're getting to the point where there are more black people than poor people in elite universities (even though there are still precious few black people). And Hurricane Katrina—with its televised images of the people left to fend for themselves in a drowning New Orleans—provided both a reminder that there still are poor people in America and a vision of what the consequences of that poverty can be. At the same time, however, the understanding of these issues has proven to be more a symptom of the problem than a diagnosis. In the *Class Matters* series in *The New York Times,* for example, the differences that mattered most turned out to be the ones between the rich and the really rich and between the old rich and the new rich. Indeed, at one point, the *Times* started treating class not as an issue to be addressed in addition to race but as itself a version of race, as if the rich and poor really were different races and so as if the occasional marriage between them were a kind of interracial marriage.

But classes are not like races and cultures, and treating them as if they were—different but equal—is one of our strategies for managing inequality rather than minimizing or eliminating it. White is not better than black, but rich is definitely better than poor. Poor people are an endangered species in elite universities not because the universities put quotas on them (as they did with Jews in the old days) and not even because they can't afford to go to them (Harvard will lend you or even give you the money you need to go there) but because they can't get into them. Hence the irrelevance of most of the proposed solutions to the systematic exclusion of poor people from elite universities, which involve ideas like increased financial aid for students who can't afford the high tuition, support systems for the few poor students who manage to end up there anyway, and, in general, an effort to increase the "cultural capital" of the poor. Today, says David Brooks, "the rich don't exploit the poor, they just out-compete them." And if out-competing people means tying their ankles together and loading them down with extra weight while hiring yourself the most expensive coaches and the best practice facilities, he's right. The entire U.S. school system, from pre-K up, is structured from the very start to enable the rich to out-compete the poor, which is to say, the race is fixed. And the kinds of solutions that might actually make a difference—financing every school district equally, abolishing private schools, making high-quality child care available to every family—are treated as if they were positively un-American.

•◦۞◦•

But it's the response to Katrina that is most illuminating for our purposes, especially the response from the left, not from the right. "Let's be honest," Cornel West told an audience at the Paul Robeson Student Center at Rutgers University, "we live in one of the bleakest moments in the history of black people in this nation." "Look at the Super Dome," he went on to say. "It's not a big move from the hull of the slave ship to the living hell of the Super Dome." This is what we might call the "George Bush doesn't care about black people" interpretation of the government's failed response to the catastrophe. But nobody doubts that George Bush cares about Condoleezza Rice, who is very much a black person and who is fond of pointing out that she's been black since birth. And there are, of course, lots of other black people—like Clarence Thomas and Thomas Sowell and Janice Rogers Brown and, at least once upon a time, Colin Powell—for whom George Bush almost certainly has warm feelings. But what American liberals want is for our conservatives to be racists. We want the black people George Bush cares about to be "some of my best friends are black" tokens. We want a fictional George Bush who doesn't care about black people rather than the George Bush we've actually got, one who doesn't care about poor people.

Although that's not quite the right way to put it. First because, for all I know, George Bush does care about poor people; at least he cares as much about poor people as anyone else does. What he doesn't care about—and what Bill Clinton, judging by his eight years in office, didn't much care about, and what John Kerry, judging from his presidential campaign, doesn't much care about, and what we on the so called left, judging by our willingness to accept Kerry as the alternative to Bush, don't care about either—is taking any steps to get them to stop being poor. We would much rather get rid of racism than get rid of poverty. And we would much rather celebrate cultural diversity than seek to establish economic equality.

Indeed, diversity has become virtually a sacred concept in American life today. No one's really against it; people tend instead to differ only in their degrees of enthusiasm for it and their ingenuity in pursuing it. Microsoft, for example, is very ingenious indeed. Almost every company has the standard racial and sexual "employee relations groups," just as every college has the standard student groups: African American, Black and Latino Brotherhood, Alliance of South Asians, Chinese Adopted Sibs (this one's pretty cutting-edge) and the standard GLBTQ (the Q is for *Questioning*) support center. But (as reported in a 2003 article in *Workforce Management*) Microsoft also includes groups for "single parents, dads, Singaporean, Malaysian, Hellenic, and Brazilian employees, and one for those with attention deficit disorder." And the same article goes on to quote Patricia Pope, CEO of a diversity management firm in Cincinnati, describing companies that "tackle other differences" like "diversity of birth order" and, most impressive of all, "diversity of thought." If it's a little hard to imagine the diversity of birth order workshops (all the oldest siblings trying to take care of each other, all the youngest competing to be the baby), it's harder still to imagine how the diversity of thought workshops go. What if the diversity of thought is about your sales plan? Are you supposed to reach agreement (but that would eliminate diversity) or celebrate disagreement (but that would eliminate the sales plan)?

❧

Among the most enthusiastic proponents of diversity, needless to say, are the thousands of companies providing "diversity products," from diversity training (a $10-billion-a-year industry) to diversity newsletters (I subscribe to *Diversity Inc.*, but there are dozens of them) to diversity rankings to diversity gifts and clothing—you can "show your support for multiculturalism" *and* "put an end to panty lines" with a "Diversity Rocks ß Thong" ($9.99). The "Show Me the Money Diversity Venture Capital Conference" says what needs to be said here. But it's not all about the benjamins. There's no money for the government in proclaiming Asian Pacific American Heritage Month (it used to be just a week, but the first President Bush upgraded it) or in Women's History Month or National Disability Employment Awareness Month or Black History Month or American Indian Heritage Month. And there's no money for the Asians, Indians, blacks, and women whose history gets honored.

In fact, the closest thing we have to a holiday that addresses economic inequality instead of identity is Labor Day, which is a product not of the multicultural cheerleading at the end of the 20th century, but of the labor unrest at the end of the 19th. The union workers who took a day off to protest President Grover Cleveland's deployment of 12,000 troops to break the

Pullman strike weren't campaigning to have their otherness respected. And when, in 1894, their day off was made official, the president of the American Federation of Labor, Samuel Gompers, looked forward not just to a "holiday" but to "the day for which the toilers in past centuries looked forward, when their rights and wrongs would be discussed." The idea was not that they'd celebrate their history but that they'd figure out how to build a stronger labor movement and make the dream of economic justice a reality.

Obviously, it didn't work out that way, either for labor (which is weaker than it's ever been) or for Labor Day (which mainly marks the end of summer). You get bigger crowds, a lot livelier party and a much stronger sense of solidarity for Gay Pride Day. But Gay Pride Day isn't about economic equality, and celebrating diversity shouldn't be an acceptable alternative to seeking economic equality.

In an ideal universe we wouldn't be celebrating diversity at all—we wouldn't even be encouraging it—because in an ideal universe the question of who you wanted to sleep with would be a matter of concern only to you and to your loved (or unloved) ones. As would your skin color; some people might like it, some people might not, but it would have no political significance whatsoever. Diversity of skin color is something we should happily take for granted, the way we do diversity of hair color. No issue of social justice hangs on appreciating hair color diversity; no issue of social justice hangs on appreciating racial or cultural diversity.

If you're worried about the growing economic inequality in American life, if you suspect that there may be something unjust as well as unpleasant in the spectacle of the rich getting richer and the poor getting poorer, no cause is less worth supporting, no battles are less worth fighting, than the ones we fight for diversity. While some cultural conservatives may wish that everyone should be assimilated to their fantasy of one truly American culture, and while the supposed radicals of the "tenured left" continue to struggle for what they hope will finally become a truly inclusive multiculturalism, the really radical idea of redistributing wealth becomes almost literally unthinkable. In the early 1930s, Senator Huey Long of Louisiana proposed a law making it illegal for anyone to earn more than $1 million a year and for anyone to inherit more than $5 million. Imagine the response if—even suitably adjusted for inflation—any senator were to propose such a law today, cutting off incomes at, say, $15 million a year and inheritances at $75 million. It's not just the numbers that wouldn't fly; it's the whole concept. Long's proposal never became law, but it was popular and debated with some seriousness. Today, such a restriction would seem as outrageous and unnatural as interracial—not to mention gay—marriage would have seemed then. But we don't need to purchase our progress in civil rights at the expense of a commitment to economic justice. More fundamentally still, we should not allow—or we should not continue to allow—the phantasm of respect for difference to take the place of that commitment to economic justice. Commitment to diversity is at best a distraction and at worst an essentially reactionary position that prevents us from putting equality at the center of the national agenda.

Our identity is the least important thing about us. And yet, it is the thing we have become most committed to talking about. From the standpoint of a left politics, this is a profound mistake since what it means is that the political left—increasingly invested in the celebration of diversity and the redress of historical grievance—has converted itself into the accomplice rather than the opponent of the right. Diversity has become the left's way of doing neoliberalism, and antiracism has become the left's contribution to enhancing market efficiency. The old Socialist leader Eugene Debs used to be criticized for being unwilling to interest himself in any social reform that didn't involve attacking economic inequality. The situation now is almost exactly the opposite; the left today obsessively interests itself in issues that have nothing to do with economic inequality.

And, not content with pretending that our real problem is cultural difference rather than economic difference, we have also started to treat economic difference as if it were cultural difference. So now we're urged to be more respectful of poor people and to stop thinking of them as victims, since to treat them as victims is condescending—it denies them their "agency." And if we can stop thinking of the poor as people who have too little money and start thinking of them instead as people who have too little respect, then it's our attitude toward the poor, not their poverty, that becomes the problem to be solved, and we can focus our efforts of reform not on getting rid of classes but on getting rid of what we like to call classism. The trick, in other words, is to stop thinking of poverty as a disadvantage, and once you stop thinking of it as a disadvantage then, of course, you no longer need to worry about getting rid of it. More generally, the trick is to think of inequality as a consequence of our prejudices rather than as a consequence of our social system and thus to turn the project of creating a more egalitarian society into the project of getting people (ourselves and, especially, others) to stop being racist, sexist, classist homophobes. The starting point for a progressive politics should be to attack that trick.

 **NO**

# Insurgent Multiculturalism and the Promise of Pedagogy

## Introduction

Multiculturalism has become a central discourse in the struggle over issues regarding national identity, the construction of historical memory, the purpose of schooling, and the meaning of democracy. While most of these battles have been waged in the university around curriculum changes and in polemic exchanges in the public media, today's crucial culture wars increasingly are being fought on two fronts. First, multiculturalism has become a "tug of war over who gets to create public culture."[1] Second, the contested terrain of multiculturalism is heating up between educational institutions that do not meet the needs of a massively shifting student population and students and their families for whom schools increasingly are perceived as merely one more instrument of repression.

In the first instance, the struggle over public culture is deeply tied to a historical legacy that affirms American character and national identity in terms that are deeply exclusionary, nativist, and racist. Echoes of this racism can be heard in the voices of public intellectuals such as George Will, Arthur Schlesinger Jr, and George Gilder. Institutional support for such racism can be found in neoconservative establishments such as the Olin Foundation and the National Association of Scholars.

In the second instance, academic culture has become a contested space primarily because groups that have been traditionally excluded from the public school curriculum, and from the ranks of higher education, are now becoming more politicized and are attending higher education institutions in increasing numbers. One consequence of this developing politics of difference has been a series of struggles by subordinate groups over access to educational resources, gender and racial equity, curriculum content, and the disciplinary-based organization of academic departments.

While it has become commonplace to acknowledge the conflicting meanings of multiculturalism, it is important to acknowledge that in its conservative and liberal forms multiculturalism has placed the related

From *Multiculturalism: A Critical Reader* by David Theo Goldberg, ed. (Blackwell, 1994), pp. 325–343. Copyright © 1994 by David Theo Goldberg. Reprinted by permission of Wiley-Blackwell.

problems of white racism, social justice, and power off limits, especially as these might be addressed as part of a broader set of political and pedagogical concerns. In what follows, I want to reassert the importance of making the pedagogical more political. That is, I want to analyze how a broader definition of pedagogy can be used to address how the production of knowledge, social identities, and social relations might challenge the racist assumptions and practices that inform a variety of cultural sites, including, but not limited to, the public and private spheres of schooling. Central to this approach is an attempt to define the pedagogical meaning of what I will call an insurgent multiculturalism. This is not a multiculturalism that is limited to a fascination with the construction of identities, communicative competence, and the celebration of tolerance. Instead, I want to shift the discussion of multiculturalism to a pedagogical terrain in which relations of power and racialized identities become paramount as part of a language of critique and possibility.

In part, this suggests constructing "an educational politics that would reveal the structures of power relations at work in the racialization of our social order" while simultaneously encouraging students to "think about the invention of the category of whiteness as well as that of blackness and, consequently, to make visible what is rendered invisible when viewed as the normative state of existence: the (white) point in space from which we tend to identify difference."[2] As part of a language of critique, a central concern of an insurgent multiculturalism is to strip white supremacy of its legitimacy and authority. As part of a project of possibility, an insurgent multiculturalism is about developing a notion of radical democracy around differences that are not exclusionary and fixed, but that designate sites of struggle that are open, fluid, and that will provide the conditions for expanding the heterogeneity of public spaces and the possibility for "critical dialogues across different political communities and constituencies."[3] . . .

## Toward an Insurgent Multiculturalism

To make a claim for multiculturalism is not . . . to suggest a juxtaposition of several cultures whose frontiers remain intact, nor is it to subscribe to a bland "melting-pot" type of attitude that would level all differences. It lies instead, in the intercultural acceptance of risks, unexpected detours, and complexities of relation between break and closure.[4]

Multiculturalism like another broadly signifying term is multiaccentual and must be adamantly challenged when defined as part of the discourse of domination or essentialism. The challenge the term presents is daunting given the way in which it has been appropriated by various mainstream and orthodox positions. For example, when defined in corporate terms it generally is reduced to a message without critical content. Liberals have used multiculturalism to denote a pluralism devoid of historical contextualization and the specificities of relations of power or they have depicted a view of cultural struggle in which the most fundamental contradictions "implicating race, class, and gender can be harmonized within the prevailing structure of power relation."[5] For many conservatives, multiculturalism has come to signify a disruptive, unsettling, and dangerous force in American society. For some critics, it has been taken up as a slogan for promoting an essentializing identity politics and various forms of nationalism. In short, multiculturalism can be defined through a variety of ideological constructs, and signifies a terrain of struggle around the reformation of historical memory, national identity, self- and social representation, and the politics of difference.

Multiculturalism is too important as a political discourse to be exclusively appropriated by liberals and conservatives. This suggests that if the concept of multiculturalism is to become useful as a pedagogical concept, educators need to appropriate it as more than a tool for critical understanding and the pluralizing of differences; it must also be used as an ethical and political referent which allows teachers and students to understand how power works in the interest of dominant social relations, and how such relations can be challenged and transformed. In other words, an insurgent multiculturalism should promote pedagogical practices that offer the possibility for schools to become places where students and teachers can become border crossers engaged in critical ethical reflection about what it means to bring a wider variety of cultures into dialogue with each other, to theorize about cultures in the plural, within rather than outside "antagonistic relations of domination and subordination."[6]

In opposition to the liberal emphasis on individual diversity, an insurgent multiculfuralism also must address issues regarding group differences and how power relations function to structure racial and ethnic identities. Furthermore, cultural differences cannot be merely affirmed to be assimilated into a common culture or policed through economic, political, and social spheres that restrict full citizenship to dominant groups. If multiculturalism is to be linked to renewed interests in expanding the principles of democracy to wider spheres of application, it must be defined in pedagogical and political terms that embrace it as a referent and practice for civic courage, critical citizenship, and democratic struggle. Bhikhu Parekh provides a definition that appears to avoid a superficial pluralism and a notion of multiculturalism that is structured in dominance. He writes:

> Multicultualism doesn't simply mean numerical plurality of different cultures, but rather a community which is creating, guaranteeing, encouraging spaces within which different communities are able to grow at their own pace. At the same time it means creating a public space in which these communities are able to interact, enrich the existing culture and create a new consensual culture in which they recognize reflections of their own identity.[7]

In this view, multiculturalism becomes more than a critical referent for interrogating the racist representations and practices of the dominant culture, it also provides a space in which the criticism of cultural practices is inextricably linked to the production of cultural spaces marked by the

formation of new identities and pedagogical practices that offers a powerful challenge to the racist, patriarchal, and sexist principles embedded
in American society and schooling. Within this discourse, curriculum is
viewed as a hierarchical and representational system that selectively produces knowledge, identities, desires, and values. The notion that curriculum represents knowledge that is objective, value free, and beneficial to
all students is challenged forcefully as it becomes clear that those who
benefit from public schooling and higher education are generally white,
middleclass students whose histories, experiences, language, and knowledge largely conform to dominant cultural codes and practices. Moreover,
an insurgent multiculturalism performs a theoretical service by addressing
curriculum as a form of cultural politics which demands linking the production and legitimation of classroom knowledge, social identities, and
values to the institutional environments in which they are produced.

As part of a project of possibility, I want to suggest some general
elements that might inform an insurgent multicultural curriculum. First,
a multicultural curriculum must be informed by a new language in which
cultural differences are taken up not as something to be tolerated by as
essential to expanding the discourse and practice of democratic life. It
is important to note that multiculturalism is not merely an ideological
construct, it also refers to the fact that by the year 2010, people of color
will be the numerical majority in the United States. This suggests that
educators need to develop a language, vision, and curriculum in which
multiculturalism and democracy become mutually reinforcing categories.
At issue here is the task of reworking democracy as a pedagogical and
cultural practice that contributes to what John Dewey once called the creation of an articulate public. [Historian and intellectual] Manning Marable
define some of the essential parameters of this task.

> Multicultural political democracy means that this country was not
> built by and for only one group—Western Europeans; that our coun-
> try does not have only one language—English; or only one religion-
> Christianity; or only one economic philosophy—corporate capitalism.
> Multicultural democracy means that the leadership within our society
> should reflect the richness, colors and diversity expressed in the lives
> of all of our people. Multicultural democracy demands new types of
> power sharing and the reallocation of resources necessary to great eco-
> nomic and social development for those who have been systematically
> excluded and denied.[8]

Imperative to such a task is a reworking of the relationship between culture and power to avoid what Homi Bhabha has called "the subsumption
or sublation of social antagonism . . . the repression of social divisions . . .
and a representation of the social that naturalizes culfural difference and
turns it into a 'second'-nature argument."[9]

Second, as part of an attempt to develop a multicultural and
multiracial society consistent with the principles of a democratic society,
educators must account for the fact that men and women of color are

disproportionately underrepresented in the cultural and public institutions of this country. Pedagogically this suggests that a multicultural curriculum must provide students with the skills to analyze how various audio, visual, and print texts fashion social identities over time, and how these representations serve to reinforce, challenge, or rewrite dominant moral and political vocabularies that promote stereotypes that degrade people by depriving them of their history, culture, and identity.

This should not suggest that such a pedagogy should solely concentrate on how meanings produce particular stereotypes and the uses to which they are put. Nor should a multicultural politics of representation focus exclusively on producing positive images of subordinated groups by recovering and reconstituting elements of their suppressed histories. While such approaches can be pedagogically useful, it is crucial for critical educators to reject any approach to multiculturalism that affirms cultural differences in the name of an essentialized and separatist identity politics. Rather than recovering differences that sustain their self-representation through exclusions, educators need to demonstrate how differences collide, cross over, mutate, and transgress in their negotiations and struggles. Differences in this sense must be understood not through the fixity of place or the romanticization of an essentialized notion of history and experience but through the tropes of indeterminacy, flows, and translations. In this instance, multiculturalism can begin to formulate a politics of representation in which questions of access and cultural production are linked to what people do with the signifying regimes they use within historically-specific public spaces.

While such approaches are essential to giving up the quest for a pure historical tradition, it is imperative that a multicultural curriculum also focus on dominant, white institutions and histories to interrogate them in terms of their injustices and their contributions for "humanity." This means, as [author and Harvard professor] Cornel West points out that

> to engage in a serious discussion of race in America, we must begin not with the problems of black people but with the flaws of American society—flaws rooted in historical inequalities and longstanding cultural stereotypes. . . . How we set up the terms for discussing racial issues shapes our perception and response to these issues. As long as black people are viewed as "them," the burden falls on blacks to do all the "cultural" and "moral" work necessary for healthy race relations. The implication is that only certain Americans can define what it means to be American—and the rest must simply " fit in."[10]

In this sense, multiculturalism is about making whiteness visible as a racial category that is, it points to the necessity of providing white students with the cultural memories that enable them to recognize the historically- and socially-constructed nature of their own identities. Multiculturalism as a radical, cultural politics should attempt to provide white students (and others) with the self-definitions upon which they can recognize their own complicity with, or resistance to, how power works within and across differences to legitimate some voices and dismantle others. Of course, more is at stake here than having whites reflect critically on the construction of their own racial formation and their complicity in promoting racism. Equally important is the issue of making all students responsible for their practices, particularly as these serve either to undermine or expand the possibility for democratic public life.

Third, a multicultural curriculum must address how to articulate a relationship between unity and difference that moves beyond simplistic binarisms. This is, rather than defining multiculturalism against unity or simply for difference, it is crucial for educators to develop a unity-in-difference position in which new, hybrid forms of democratic representation, participation, and citizenship provide a forum for creating unity without denying the particular, multiple, and the specific. In this instance, the interrelationship of different cultures and identities become borderlands, sites of crossing, negotiation, translation, and dialogue. At issue is the production of a border pedagogy in which the intersection of culture and identity produces self-definitions that enable teachers and students to authorize a sense of critical agency. Border pedagogy points to a self/other relationship in which identity is fixed as neither other nor the same; instead, it is both and, hence, defined within multiple literacies that become a referent, critique, and practice of cultural translation, a recognition of no possibility of fixed, final, or monologically authoritative meaning that exists outside of history, power, and ideology.

Within such a pedagogical cartography, teachers must be given the opportunity to cross ideological and political borders as a way of clarifying their own moral vision, as a way of enabling counterdiscourses, and, as Roger Simon points out, as a way of getting students "beyond the world they already know in order to challenge and provoke their inquiry and challenge of their existing views of the way things are and should be."[11]

Underlying this notion of border pedagogy is neither the logic of assimilation (the melting pot) nor the imperative to create cultural hierarchies, but the attempt to expand the possibilities for different groups to enter into dialogue to understand further the richness of their differences and the value of what they share in common.

Fourth, an insurgent multiculturalism must challenge the task of merely representing cultural differences in the curriculum; it must also educate students of the necessity for linking a justice of multiplicity to struggles over real material conditions that structure everyday life. In part, this means understanding how structural imbalances in power produce real limits on the capacity of subordinate groups to exercise a sense of agency and struggle. It also means analyzing specific class, race, gender, and other issues as social problems rooted in real material and institutional factors that produce specific forms of inequality and oppression. This would necessitate a multicultural curriculum that produces a language that deals with social problems in historical and relational terms, and uncovers how the dynamics of power work to promote domination within the school and the wider society. In part, this means multiculturalism as a curricula discourse and pedagogical practice must function in its dual capacity as collective memory and alternative reconstruction. History, in this sense, is not merely resurrected but interrogated and tempered by "a sense of its liability, its contingency, its constructedness."[12] Memory does not become the repository of registering suppressed histories, albeit critically, but of reconstructing the moral frameworks of historical discourse to interrogate the present as living history.

Finally, a multicultural curriculum must develop, in public schools and institutions of higher education, contexts that serve to refigure relations between the school, teachers, students, and the wide community. For instance, public schools must be willing to develop a critical dialogue between the school and those public cultures within the community dedicated to producing students who address the discourse and obligations of power as part of a larger attempt at civic renewal and the reconstruction of democratic life. At best, parents, social activists, and other socially-concerned community members should be allowed to play a formative role in crucial decisions about what is taught, who is hired, and how the school can become a laboratory for learning that nurtures critical citizenship and civic courage. Of course, the relationship between the school and the larger community should be made in the interest of expanding "the social and political task of transformation, resistance, and radical democratization.[13] In both spheres of education, the curriculum needs to be decentralized to allow students to have some input into what is taught and under what conditions. Moreover, teachers need to be educated to be border crossers, to explore zones of cultural difference by moving in and out of the resources, histories, and narratives that provide different students with a sense of identity, place, and possibility. This does not suggest that educators become tourists traveling to exotic lands; on the contrary, it points to the need for them to enter into negotiation and dialogue around issues of nationality, difference, and identity so as to be able to fashion a more ethical and democratic set of pedagogical relations between themselves and their students while simultaneously allowing students to speak, listen and learn differently within pedagogical spaces that are safe, affirming, questioning, and enabling.

In this instance, a curriculum for a multicultural and multiracial society provides the conditions for students to imagine beyond the given and to embrace their identities critically as a source of agency and possibility. In addition, an insurgent multiculturalism should serve to redefine existing debates about national identity while simultaneously expanding its theoretical concerns to more global and international matters. Developing a respect for cultures in the plural demands a reformulation of what it means to be educated in the United States and what such an education implies for the creation of new cultural spaces that deepen and extend the possibility of democratic public life. Multiculturalism insists upon challenging old orthodoxies and reformulating new projects of possibility. It is a challenge that all critical educators need to address.

# Notes

1. Alice Kessler-Harris, "Cultural Locations: Positioning American Studies in the Great Debate," *American Quarterly,* 44, 3 (1992), p. 310.

2. Hazel Carby, "The Multicultural Wars," in *Black Popular Culture,* ed. Gina Dent (Seattle: Bay Press, 1992), pp. 193–4.

3. Kobena Mercer, "Back to my Routes: A Postscript on the 80s," *Ten.* 8, 2, 3 (1992), p. 33.

4. Trinh T. Minh-Ha, *Woman, Native, Other: Writing Postcoloniality and Feminism* (Bloomington: Indiana University Press, 1989), p. 232.

5. E. San Juan, Jr, *Racial Formations/Critical Transformations: Articulations of Power in Ethnic and Racial Studies in the United States* (Atlantic Highlands, NJ: Humanities Press, 1992), p. 101.

6. Hazel Carby, "Multi-Culture," *Screen Education,* 34 (Spring 1980), p. 65.

7. Bhabha and Parekh, "Identities on Parade: A Conversation," p. 4.

8. Manning Marable, *Black America: Multicultural Democracy* (Westfield, NJ: Open Media, 1992), p. 13.

9. Homi K. Bhabha, "A Good Judge of Character: Men, Metaphors, and the Common Culture: in *Racing Justice, Engendering Power: Essays on Anita Hill, Clarence Thomas, and the Construction of Social Reality,* ed. Toni Morrison (New York: Pantheon, 1992), p. 242.

10. Cornel West, "Learning to Talk of Race," p. 24.

11. Roger I. Simon, *Teaching Against the Grain* (New York: Bergin and Garvey Press, 1992), p. 17.

12. Henry Louis Gates, Jr, "The Black Man's Burden," *Black Popular Culture,* ed. Gina Dent (Seattle: Bay Press, 1992), p. 76.

13. Judith Butler, "Contingent Foundations: Feminism and the Question of 'Post modernism'," in *Feminists Theorize the Political,* eds. Judith Butler and Joan Scott (New York: Routledge, 1991), p. 13.

# POSTSCRIPT

## Is It Time to De-emphasize Diversity?

Just as in the early- and mid-twentieth centuries, public schools play a critical role in teaching American history. However, in contemporary American schools, ethnic and racial differences are celebrated rather than de-emphasized.

*The Journal of Blacks in Higher Education* (November 23, 2000) reported that more than half of American colleges have a diversity study requirement. Considering the role that colleges and universities play in forming a foundation for intellectual understanding, learning about diversity through required courses suggests that now is not the time to deemphasize diversity. Moreover, this academic requirement to include diversity as a core curriculum requirement appears to be increasing. Programs in diversity studies and multicultural education have grown in recent years. *The Journal of Higher Education,* Special Issue: The Social Role of Higher Education (March–April 2001, pp. 172–204) speaks of the commitment of higher education to diversity. There is evidence that such programs have gained significant favor within the military and private business.

"Racial Diversity in Public Schools: Has the Supreme Court Dealt a Blow to Integration?" by Kenneth Jost in *CQ Researcher* (September 14, 2007) addresses a recent U.S. Supreme Court decision that bars school districts from using race as a factor in individual pupil assignments. "Dealing with Diversity: Mapping Multiculturalism in Sociological Terms," by Joseph Gerteis, *Sociological Theory* (vol. 23, no. 2, 2005) offers sociological information on the topic.

Walter Benn Michaels' *The Trouble with Diversity: How We Learned to Love Identity and Ignore Inequality* (Henry Holt & Co., 2006) argues that diversity fails to offer a premise for social justice. He challenges the benefits of affirmative action, multiculturalism, heritage, and identity politics. "The Diversity Myth," *The Atlantic Monthly* (May 1995), by Benjamin Schwartz, takes the position that the emphasis on diversity is a distorted view of American history. It is ethnic domination, not ethnic pluralism, which characterizes America's history of cultural homogeneity. Thus, American foreign policy, which encourages other nations to be some multi-ethnic states, is seen as hypocritical in that we have not yet found a workable solution to ethnic differences here at home.

Two classic conservative pieces critical of diversity include Arthur M. Schlesinger, Jr.'s *The Disuniting of America: Reflections on a Multicultural Society* (W.W. Norton & Company, 1992), from which a selection appears in Issue 1 of this edition of *Taking Sides,* and E.D. Hirsch's "American Diversity and Public Discourse," in *Cultural Literacy: What Every American Needs to Know* (Houghton Mifflin, 1987). Also of interest is Peter Schrag's "The Diversity Defense," *The American Prospect* (September 1, 1999).

# ISSUE 16

# Are Asian Americans
# a Model Minority?

**YES: David A. Bell,** from "America's Greatest Success Story: The Triumph of Asian-Americans," *The New Republic* (July 15 & 22, 1985)

**NO: Frank H. Wu,** from *Yellow: Race in America Beyond Black and White* (Basic Books, 2002)

## ISSUE SUMMARY

**YES:** David A. Bell, journalist and historian, agrees that Asian Americans are a "model minority" and expresses a great appreciation for the progress and prominence they have achieved within the nation.

**NO:** Frank H. Wu, Howard University law professor, rejects the characterization of Asian Americans as a "model minority" based on the belief that this characterization tends to obscure problems facing Asians in America.

$\mathbf{T}$he labeling of Asian Americans as a model minority group emerged in a nation with long experience with conflict-ridden intergroup relations. As a model minority, the Asian Americans are viewed as industrious, frugal, and possessing a strong achievement orientation. These are among the values that are promoted within the dominant white culture. Asian Americans also tend to be associated with the promotion of a success ethic and achievement at much higher levels in significant areas of American life than other minority groups, especially African Americans and Latinos.

The Asian-American population of the United States is rapidly expanding as the nation becomes more diverse. There is great ethnic diversity among these Asian ethnic peoples whose demographic composition extends from the Hmong immigrants of the highlands of Vietnam to Bengali people of the Indian subcontinent. Thus, Asian peoples are contributing to the ongoing expansion of the ethnic composition of the United States.

Although written in 1985, David Bell's selection presents the standard argument in support of Asian Americans for the model minority thesis. Bell is impressed with the fact that Asians have become prominent out of all proportion to their share of the U.S. population. He presents an examination of data gleaned from the Census Bureau and the State Department to demonstrate that the rapid expansion of the Asian-American population will likely intensify in the future.

Bell draws our attention to the new prominence of Asian Americans in business and the professions. He presents evidence of progress that these model citizens have achieved in areas of business, such as the ownership of grocery stores, motels, fishing boats, and the computer industry, and in the professions of medicine and architecture.

It is important to note that Asian Americans have not always been embraced by American society. Throughout most of their history, Asians have experienced prejudice, discrimination, exclusion, and violence at the hands of whites and other groups. Bell provides us with a significant examination of these aspects of Asian-American social history in order to provide a proper social context for understanding these developments. Thus, the "spectacular" success that they have achieved that has earned them the status of America's "model minority" has come at a substantial cost.

Education tends to be viewed as a key factor in achieving socioeconomic progress in America. Asian Americans have embraced this "education ethic," and Bell views this development as a major contributor to the "spectacular" success that he claims they have achieved. Wu, however, is concerned with the disparity between Asians' educational achievements and their institutional success. The claim that Asian Americans have succeeded in certain fields is beyond dispute. However, Wu is wary of the facile tendency of the post–civil rights era to label Asian Americans as a "model minority." For Wu, this label has been employed to promote an exaggerated image of Asian-American "success," and it fails to account for significant inequalities within their lives. He notes "that the only good Asian American is a genius workaholic, not an average or normal man or woman."

The economic achievements of Asians are less than those promoted within the "model minority" imagery according to Wu. There are a number of additional reasons why Wu challenges the "model minority" imagery. The utilization of this label by America's leaders to criticize or inspire other racial and ethnic groups can foster resentment from members of these outgroups, thus undermining the security of Asian Americans.

Lastly, Asian Americans have been subjected to stereotyping throughout the nation's history, and Wu views this "model minority" image as the latest of that line. So Wu has concluded that the "model minority" claim as applied to Asian Americans is a myth that tends to obscure much more than it illuminates in the lives of Asians in America.

# YES

David A. Bell

## America's Greatest Success Story: The Triumph of Asian-Americans

It is the year 2019. In the heart of downtown Los Angeles, massive electronic billboards feature a model in a kimono hawking products labeled in Japanese. In the streets below, figures clad in traditional East Asian peasant garb hurry by, speaking to each other in an English made unrecognizable by the addition of hundreds of Spanish and Asian words. A rough-mannered policeman leaves an incongruously graceful calling card on a doorstep: a delicate origami paper sculpture.

This is, of course, a scene from a science-fiction movie, Ridley Scott's 1982 *Blade Runner.* It is also a vision that Asian-Americans dislike intensely. Hysterical warnings of an imminent Asian "takeover" of the United States stained a whole century of their 140-year history in this country, providing the back-drop for racial violence, legal segregation, and the internment of 110,000 Japanese-Americans in concentration camps during World War II. Today integration into American society, not transformation of American society, is the goal of an overwhelming majority. So why did the critics praise *Blade Runner* for its "realism"? The answer is easy to see.

The Asian-American population is exploding. According to the Census Bureau, it grew an astounding 125 percent between 1970 and 1980, and now stands at 4.1 million, or 1.8 percent of all Americans. Most of the increase is the result of immigration, which accounted for 1.8 million people between 1973 and 1983, the last year for which the Immigration and Naturalization Service has accurate figures (710,000 of these arrived as refugees from Southeast Asia). And the wave shows little sign of subsiding. Ever since the Immigration Act of 1965 permitted large-scale immigration by Asians, they have made up over 40 percent of all newcomers to the United States. Indeed, the arbitrary quota of 20,000 immigrants per country per year established by the act has produced huge backlogs of future Asian-Americans in several countries, including 120,000 in South Korea and 336,000 in the Philippines, some of whom, according to the State Department, have been waiting for their visas since 1970.

The numbers are astonishing. But even more astonishing is the extent to which Asian-Americans have become prominent out of all proportion

From *The New Republic*, July 15 & 22, 1985. Copyright © 1985 by The New Republic, LLC. Reprinted by permission of The New Republic.

to their share of the population. It now seems likely that their influx will have as important an effect on American society as the migration from Europe of 100 years ago. Most remarkable of all, it is taking place with relatively tittle trouble.

The new immigration from Asia is a radical development in several ways. First, it has not simply enlarged an existing Asian-American community, but created an entirely new one. Before 1965, and the passage of the Immigration Act, the term "Oriental-American" (which was then the vogue) generally denoted people living on the West Coast, in Hawaii, or in the Chinatowns of a few large cities. Generally they traced their ancestry either to one small part of China, the Toishan district of Kwantung province, or to a small number of communities in Japan (one of the largest of which, ironically, was Hiroshima). Today more than a third of all Asian-Americans live outside Chinatowns in the East, South, and Midwest, and their origins are as diverse as those of "European-Americans." The term "Asian-American" now refers to over 900,000 Chinese from all parts of China and also Vietnam, 800,000 Filipinos, 700,000 Japanese, 500,000 Koreans, 400,000 East Indians, and a huge assortment of everything else from Moslem Cambodians to Catholic Hawaiians. It can mean an illiterate Hmong tribesman or a fully assimilated graduate of the Harvard Business School.

Asian-Americans have also attracted attention by their new prominence in several professions and trades. In New York City, for example, where the Asian-American population jumped from 94,500 in 1970 to 231,500 in 1980, Korean-Americans run an estimated 900 of the city's 1,600 corner grocery stores. Filipino doctors—who outnumber black doctors—have become general practitioners in thousands of rural communities that previously lacked physicians. East Indian-Americans own 800 of California's 6,000 motels. And in parts of Texas, Vietnamese-Americans now control 85 percent of the shrimp-fishing industry, though they only reached this position after considerable strife (now the subject of a film, *Alamo Bay*).

Individual Asian-Americans have become quite prominent as well. I. M. Pei and Minoru Yamasaki have helped transform American architecture. Seiji Ozawa and Yo Yo Ma are giant figures in American music. An Wang created one of the nation's largest computer firms, and Rocky Aoki founded one of its largest restaurant chains (Benihana). Samuel C. C. Ting won a Nobel prize in physics.

*◦◉◦*

Most spectacular of all, and most significant for the future, is the entry of Asian-Americans into the universities. At Harvard, for example, Asian-Americans ten years ago made up barely three percent of the freshman class. The figure is now ten percent—five times their share of the population. At Brown, Asian-American applications more than tripled over the same period, and at Berkeley they increased from 3,408 in 1982 to 4,235 only three years later. The Berkeley student body is now 22 percent Asian-American, UCLA's is 21 percent, and MIT's 19 percent. The Julliard School of Music in New York is currently 30 percent Asian and Asian-American. American medical schools had only 571 Asian-American students in 1970, but in 1980 they had 1,924, and last year 3,763, or 5.6 percent of total enrollment. What is more, nearly all of these figures are certain to increase. In the current, largely foreign-born Asian-American community, 32.9 percent of people over 25 graduated from college (as opposed to 16.2 percent in the general population). For third-generation Japanese-Americans, the figure is 88 percent.

By any measure these Asian-American students are outstanding. In California only the top 12.5 percent of high school students qualify for admission to the uppermost tier of the state university system, but 39 percent of Asian-American high school students do. On the SATs, Asian-Americans score an average of 519 in math, surpassing whites, the next highest group, by 32 points. Among Japanese-Americans, the most heavily native-born Asian-American group, 68 percent of those taking the math SAT scored above 600—high enough to qualify for admission to almost any university in the country. The Westinghouse Science Talent search, which each year identified 40 top high school science students, picked 12 Asian-Americans in 1983, nine last year, and seven this year. And at Harvard the Phi Beta Kappa chapter last April named as its elite "Junior Twelve" students five Asian-Americans and seven Jews.

Faced with these statistics, the understandable reflex of many non-Asian-Americans is adulation. President Reagan has called Asian-Americans "our exemplars of hope and inspiration." *Parade* magazine recently featured an article on Asian-Americans titled "The Promise of America," and *Time* and *Newsweek* stories have boasted headlines like "A Formula for Success," "The Drive to Excel," and "A 'Model Minority.'" However, not all of these stories come to grips with the fact that Asian-Americans, like all immigrants, have to deal with a great many problems of adjustment, ranging from the absurd to the deadly serious.

Who would think, for example, that there is a connection between Asian-American immigration and the decimation of California's black bear population? But Los Angeles, whose Korean population grew by 100,000 in the past decade, now has more than 300 licensed herbal-acupuncture shops. And a key ingredient in traditional Korean herbal medicine is *ungdam,* bear gallbladder. The result is widespread illegal hunting and what *Audubon* magazine soberly called "a booming trade in bear parts."

As Mark R. Thompson recently pointed out in *The Wall Street Journal,* the clash of cultures produced by Asian immigration can also have vexing legal results. Take the case of Fumiko Kimura, a Japanese-American woman who tried to drown herself and her two children in the Pacific. She survived but the children did not, and she is now on trial for their murder. As a defense, her lawyers are arguing that parent-child suicide is a common occurrence in Japan. In Fresno, California, meanwhile, 30,000 newly arrived Hmong cause a different problem. "Anthropologists call the custom 'marriage by capture,'" Mr. Thompson writes, "Fresno police and prosecutors call it 'rape.'"

A much more serious problem for Asian-Americans is racial violence. In 1982 two unemployed whites in Detroit beat to death a Chinese-American named Vincent Chin, claiming that they wanted revenge on the Japanese for hurting the automobile industry. After pleading guilty to manslaughter, they paid a $3,000 fine and were released, More recently, groups of Cambodians and Vietnamese in Boston were beaten by white youths, and there have been incidents in New York and Los Angles as well.

# ASIANS AND JEWS

Comparing the social success of Asian-Americans with that of the Jews is irresistible. Jews and Asians rank number one and number two, respectively, in median family income. In the Ivy League they are the two groups most heavily "over-represented" in comparison to their shares of the population. And observers are quick to point out all sorts of cultural parallels. As Arthur Rosen, the chairman of (appropriately) the National Committee on United States–China Relations, recently told *The New York Times,* "There are the same kind of strong family ties and the same sacrificial drive on the part of immigrant parents who couldn't get a college education to see that their children do."

In historical terms, the parallels can often be striking. For example, when Russian and Polish Jews came to this country in the late 19th and early 20th centuries, 60 percent of those who went into industry worked in the garment trade. Today thousands of Chinese-American women fill sweatshops in New York City doing the same work of stitching and sewing. In Los Angeles, when the Jews began to arrive in large numbers in the 1880s, 43 percent of them became retail or wholesale proprietors, according to Ivan Light's essay in *Clamor at the Gates.* One hundred years later, 40 percent of Koreans in Los Angeles are also wholesale and retail proprietors. The current controversy over Asian-American admission in Ivy League colleges eerily recalls the Jews' struggle to end quotas in the 1940s and 1950s.

In cultural terms, however, it is easy to take the comparison too far. American Jews remain a relatively homogeneous group, with a common religion and history. Asian-Americans, especially after the post-1965 flood of immigrants, are exactly the opposite. They seem homogeneous largely because they share some racial characteristics. And even those vary widely. The label "Chinese-American" itself covers a range of cultural and linguistic differences that makes those between German and East European Jews, or between Reform and Orthodox Jews, seem trivial in comparison.

The most important parallels between Jews and the various Asian groups are not cultural. They lie rather in the sociological profile of Jewish and Asian immigration. The Jewish newcomers of a hundred years ago never completely fit into the category of "huddled masses." They had an astonishing high literacy rate (nearly 100 percent for German Jews, and over 50 percent for East European Jews), a long tradition of scholarship even in the smallest shtetls, and useful skills. More than two-thirds of male Jewish immigrants were considered skilled workers in America. Less than three percent of Jewish immigrants had worked on the land. Similarly, the Japanese, Korean, Filipino, and Vietnamese immigrants of the 20th century have come almost exclusively from the middle class. Seventy percent of Korean male immigrants, for example, are college graduates. Like middle-class native-born Americans, Asian and Jewish immigrants alike have fully understood the importance of the universities, and have pushed their children to enter them from the very start.

Thomas Sowell offers another parallel between the successes of Asians and Jews. Both communities have benefited paradoxically, he argues, from their small size and from past discrimination against them. These disadvantages long kept both groups out of politics. And, as Sowell writes in *Race and Economics:* "those American ethnic groups that have succeeded best politically have not usually been the same as those who succeeded best economically . . . those minorities that have pinned their greatest hopes on political action—the Irish and the Negroes, for example—have made some of the slower economic advances." Rather than searching for a solution to their problems through the political process, Jewish, Chinese, and Japanese immigrants developed self-sufficiency by relying on community organizations. The combination of their skills, their desire for education, and the gradual disappearance of discrimination led inexorably to economic success.

—D.A.B.

---

Is this violence an aberration, or does it reflect the persistence of anti-Asian prejudice in America? By at least one indicator, it seems hard to believe that Asian-Americans suffer greatly from discrimination. Their median family income, according to the 1980 census, was $22,713, compared to only $19,917 for whites. True, Asians live almost exclusively in urban areas (where incomes are higher), and generally have more people working in each family. They are also better educated than whites. Irene Natividad, a Filipino-American active in the Democratic Party's Asian Caucus, states bluntly that "we are under-paid for the high level of education we have achieved." However, because of language difficulties and differing professional standards in the United States, many new Asian immigrants initially work in jobs for which they are greatly overqualified.

Ironically, charges of discrimination today arise most frequently in the universities, the setting generally cited as the best evidence of Asian-American achievement. For several years Asian student associations at Ivy League universities have cited figures showing that a smaller percentage of Asian-American students than others are accepted. At Harvard this year, 12.5 percent of Asian-American applicants were admitted, as opposed to 16 percent of all applicants; at Princeton, the figures were 14 to 17 percent. Recently a Princeton professor, Uwe Reinhardt, told a *New York Times* reporter that Princeton has an unofficial quota for Asian-American applicants.

The question of university discrimination is a subtle one. For one thing, it only arises at the most prestigious schools, where admissions are the most subjective. At universities like UCLA, where applicants are judged largely by their grades and SAT scores, Asian-Americans have a higher admission rate than other students (80 percent versus 70 percent for all applicants). And at schools that emphasize science, like MIT, the general excellence of Asian-Americans in the field also produces a higher admission rate.

Why are things different at the Ivy League schools? One reason, according to a recent study done at Princeton, is that very few Asian-Americans are alumni children. The children of alumni are accepted at a rate of about 50 percent, and so raise the overall admissions figure. Athletes have a better chance of admission as well, and few Asian-Americans play varsity sports. These arguments, however, leave out another admissions factor: affirmative action. The fact is that if alumni children have a special advantage, at least some Asians do too, because of their race. At Harvard, for instance, partly in response to complaints from the Asian student organization, the admissions office in the late 1970s began to recruit vigorously among two categories of Asian-Americans: the poor, often living in Chinatowns; and recent immigrants. Today, according to the dean of admissions, L. Fred Jewett, roughly a third of Harvard's Asian-American applicants come from these groups, and are included in the university's "affirmative action" efforts. Like black students, who have a 27 percent admission rate, they find it easier to get in. And this means that the *other* Asian-Americans, the ones with no language problem or economic disadvantage, find things correspondingly tougher. Harvard has no statistics on the two groups. But if we assume the first group has an admissions rate of only 20 percent (very low for affirmative action candidates), the second one still slips down to slightly less than nine percent, or roughly half the overall admissions rate.

Dean Jewett offers two explanations for this phenomenon. First, he says, "family pressure makes more marginal students apply." In other words, many Asian students apply regardless of their qualifications, because of the university's prestige. And second, "a terribly high proportion of the Asian students are heading toward the sciences." In the interests of diversity, then, more of them must be left out.

✦

It is true that more Asian-Americans go into the sciences. In Harvard's class of 1985, 57 percent of them did (as opposed to 29 percent of all students) and 71 percent went into either the sciences or economics. It is also true that a great many of Harvard's Asian-American applicants have little on their records except scientific excellence. But there are good reasons for this. In the sciences, complete mastery of English is less important than in other fields, an important fact for immigrants and children of immigrants. And scientific careers allow Asian-Americans to avoid the sort of large, hierarchical organization where their unfamiliarity with America, and management's resistance to putting them into highly visible positions, could hinder their advancement. And so the admissions problem comes down to a problem of clashing cultural standards. Since the values of Asian-American applicants differ from the universities' own, many of those applicants appear narrowly focused and dull. As Linda Matthews, an alumni recruiter for Harvard in Los Angeles, says with regret, "We hold them to the standards of white suburban kids. We want them to be cheerleaders and class presidents and all the rest."

The universities, however, consider their idea of the academic community to be liberal and sound. They are understandably hesitant to change it because of a demographic shift in the admissions pool. So how can they resolve this difficult problem? It is hard to say, except to suggest humility, and to recall that this sort of thing has come up before. At Harvard, the admissions office might do well to remember a memorandum Walter Lippmann prepared for the university in 1922. "I am fully prepared to accept the judgment of the Harvard authorities that a concentration of Jews in excess of fifteen per cent will produce a segregation of cultures rather than a fusion," wrote Lippmann, himself a Jew and a Harvard graduate. "They hand on unconsciously and uncritically from one generation to another many distressing personal and social habits. . . .

The debate over admissions is abstruse. But for Asian-Americans, it has become an extremely sensitive issue. The universities, after all, represent their route to complete integration in American society, and to an equal chance at the advantages that enticed them and their parents to immigrate in the first place. At the same time, discrimination, even very slight discrimination, recalls the bitter prejudice and discrimination that Asian-Americans suffered for their first hundred years in this country.

Few white Americans today realize just how pervasive legal anti-Asian discrimination was before 1945. The tens of thousand of Chinese laborers who arrived in California in the 1850s and 1860s to work in the goldfields and build the Central Pacific Railroad often lived in virtual slavery (the words kuli, now part of the English language, mean "bitter labor"). Far from having the chance to organize, they were seized on as scapegoats by labor unions, particularly Samuel Gompers's AFL, and often ended up working as strikebreakers instead, thus inviting violent attacks. In 1870 Congress barred Asian immigrants from citizenship, and in 1882 it passed the Chinese Exclusion Act, which summarily prohibited more Chinese from entering the country. Since it did this at a time when 100,600 male Chinese-Americans had the company of only 4,800 females, it effectively sentenced the Chinese community to rapid decline. From 1854 to 1874, California had in effect a law preventing Asian-Americans from testifying in court, leaving them without the protection of the law.

Little changed in the late 19th and early 20th centuries, as large numbers of Japanese and smaller contingents from Korea and the Philippines began to arrive on the West Coast. In 1906 San Francisco made a brief attempt to segregate its school system. In 1910 a California law went so far as to prohibit marriage between Caucasians and "Mongolians," in flagrant defiance of the Fourteenth Amendment. Two Alien Land Acts in 1913 and 1920 prevented noncitizens in California (in other words, all alien immigrants) from owning or leasing land. These laws, and the Chinese Exclusion Act, remained in effect until the 1940s. And of course during the Second World War, President Franklin Roosevelt signed an Executive Order sending 110,000 ethnic Japanese on the West Coast, 64 percent of whom were American citizens, to internment camps. Estimates of the monetary damage to the Japanese-American community from this action range as high as $400,000,000, and Japanese-American political activists have made reparations one of their most important goals. Only in Hawaii, where Japanese-Americans already outnumbered whites 61,000 to 29,000 at the turn of the century, was discrimination relatively less important. (Indeed, 157,000 Japanese-Americans in Hawaii at the start of the war were *not* interned, although they posed a greater possible threat to the war effort than their cousins in California.)

In light of this history, the current problems of the Asian-American community seem relatively minor, and its success appears even more remarkable. Social scientists wonder just how this success was possible, and how Asian-Americans have managed to avoid the "second-class citizenship" that has trapped so many blacks and Hispanics. There is no single answer, but all the various explanations of the Asian-Americans' success do tend to fall into one category: self-sufficiency.

The first element of this self-sufficiency is family. Conservative sociologist Thomas Sowell writes that "strong, stable families have been characteristic of . . . successful minorities," and calls Chinese-Americans and Japanese-Americans the most stable he has encountered. This quality contributes to success in at least three ways. First and most obviously, it provides a secure environment for children. Second, it pushes those children to do better than their parents. As former Ohio state demographer William Petersen, author of *Japanese-Americans* (1971), says "They're like the Jews in that they have the whole family and the whole community pushing them to make the best of themselves." And finally, it is a significant financial advantage. Traditionally, Asian-Americans have headed into family businesses, with all the family members pitching in long hours to make them a success. For the Chinese, it was restaurants and laundries (as late as 1940, half of the Chinese-American labor force worked in one or the other), for the Japanese, groceries and truck farming, and for the Koreans, groceries. Today the proportion of Koreans working without pay in family businesses is nearly three times as high as any other group. A recent *New*

*York* magazine profile of one typical Korean grocery in New York showed that several of the family members running it consistently worked 15 to 18 hours a day. Thomas Sowell points out that in 1970, although Chinese median family income already exceeded white median family income by a third, their median personal income was only ten percent higher, indicating much greater participation per family.

Also contributing to Asian-American self-sufficiency are powerful community organizations. From the beginning of Chinese-American settlement in California, clan organizations, mutual aid societies, and rotating credit associations gave many Japanese-Americans a start in business, at a time when most banks would only lend to whites. Throughout the first half of this century, the strength of community organizations was an important reason why Asian-Americans tended to live in small, closed communities rather than spreading out among the general population. And during the Depression years, they proved vital. In the early 1930s, when nine percent of the population of New York City subsisted on public relief, only one percent of Chinese-Americans did so. The community structure has also helped keep Asian-American crime rates the lowest in the nation, despite recently increasing gang violence among new Chinese and Vietnamese immigrants. According to the 1980 census, the proportion of Asian-Americans in prison is one-fourth that of the general population.

The more recent immigrants have also developed close communities. In the Washington, D.C., suburb of Arlington, Virginia, there is now a "Little Saigon." Koreans also take advantage of the "ethnic resources" provided by a small community. As Ivan Light writes in an essay in Nathan Glazer's new book, *Clamor at the Gates,* "They help one another with business skills, information, and purchase of ethnic commodities; cluster in particular industries; combine easily in restraint of trade; or utilize rotation credit associations." Light cites a study showing that 34 percent of Korean grocery store owners in Chicago had received financial help from within the Korean community. The immigrants in these communities are self-sufficient in another way as well. Unlike the immigrants of the 19th century, most new Asian-Americans come to the United States with professional skills. Or they come to obtain those skills, and then stay on. Of 16,000 Taiwanese who came to the U.S. as students in the 1960s, only three percent returned to Taiwan.

⋅⟨◉⟩⋅

So what does the future hold for Asian-Americans? With the removal of most discrimination, and with the massive Asian-American influx in the universities, the importance of tightly knit communities is sure to wane. Indeed, among the older Asian-American groups it already has: since the war, fewer and fewer native-born Chinese-Americans have come to live in Chinatowns. But will complete assimilation follow? One study, at least, seems to indicate that it will, if one can look to the well-established Japanese-Americans for hints as to the future of other Asian groups.

According to Professor Harry Kitano of UCLA, 63 percent of Japanese now intermarry.

But can all Asian-Americans follow the prosperous, assimilationist Japanese example? For some, it may not be easy. Hmong tribesmen, for instance, arrived in the United States with little money, few valuable skills, and extreme cultural disorientation. After five years here, they are still heavily dependent on welfare. (When the state of Oregon cut its assistance to refugees, 90 percent of the Hmong there moved to California.) Filipinos, although now the second-largest Asian-American group, make up less than ten percent of the Asian-American population at Harvard, and are the only Asian-Americans to benefit from affirmative action programs at the University of California. Do figures like these point to the emergence of a disadvantaged Asian-American underclass? It is still too early to tell, but the question is not receiving much attention either. As Nathan Glazer says of Asian-Americans, "When they're already above average, it's very hard to pay much attention to those who fall below." Ross Harano, a Chicago businessman active in the Democratic Party's Asian Caucus, argues that the label of "model minority" earned by the most conspicuous Asian-Americans hurt less successful groups. "We need money to help people who can't assimilate as fast as the superstars," he says.

Harano also points out that the stragglers find little help in traditional minority politics. "When blacks talk about a minority agenda, they don't include us," he says. "Most Asians are viewed by blacks as whites." Indeed, in cities with large numbers of Asians and blacks, relations between the communities are tense. In September 1984, for example, *The Los Angeles Sentinel,* a prominent black newspaper, ran a four-part series condemning Koreans for their "takeover" of black businesses, provoking a strong reaction from Asian-American groups. In Harlem some blacks have organized a boycott to Asian-American stores.

Another barrier to complete integration lies in the tendency of many Asian-American students to crowd into a small number of careers, mainly in the sciences. Professor Ronn Takaki of Berkeley is a strong critic of this "maldistribution," and says that universities should make efforts to correct it. The extent of these efforts, he told *The Boston Globe* last December, "will determine whether we have our poets, sociologists, historians, and journalists. If we are all tracked into becoming computer technicians and scientists, this need will not be fulfilled."

Yet it is not clear that the "maldistribution" problem will extend to the next generation. The children of the current immigrants will not share their parents' language difficulties. Nor will they worry as much about joining large institutions where subtle racism might once have barred them from advancement. William Petersen argues, "As the discrimination disappears, as it mostly has already, the self-selection will disappear as well. . . . There's nothing in Chinese or Japanese culture pushing them toward these fields." Professor Kitano of UCLA is not so sure. "The submerging of the individual to the group is another basic Japanese tradition," he wrote in an article for *The Harvard Encyclopedia of American Ethnic Groups.* It is a tradition that causes problems for Japanese-Americans who wish to avoid current career patterns: "It may only be a matter of time before some break out of these middleman jobs, but the structural and cultural restraints may prove difficult to overcome."

In short, Asian-Americans face undeniable problems of integration. Still, it takes a very narrow mind not to realize that these problems are the envy of every other American racial minority, and of a good number of white ethnic groups as well. Like the Jews, who experienced a similar pattern of discrimination and quotas, and who first crowded into a small range of professions, Asian-Americans have shown an ability to overcome large obstacles in spectacular fashion. In particular, they have done so by taking full advantage of America's greatest civic resource, its schools and universities, just as the Jews did 50 years ago. Now they seem poised to burst out upon American society.

The clearest indication of this course is in politics, a sphere that Asian-Americans traditionally avoided. Now this is changing. And importantly, it is *not* changing just because Asian-Americans want government to solve their particular problems. Yes, there are "Asian" issues: the loosening of immigration restrictions, reparations for the wartime internment, equal opportunity for the Asian disadvantaged. Asian-American Democrats are at present incensed over the way the Democratic National Committee has stripped their caucus of "official" status. But even the most vehement activists on these points still insist that the most important thing for Asian-Americans is not any particular combination of issues, but simply "being part of the process." Unlike blacks or Hispanics, Asian-American politicians have the luxury of not having to devote the bulk of their time to an "Asian-American agenda," and thus escape becoming prisoners of such an agenda. Who thinks of Senator Daniel Inouye or former senator S. I. Hayakawa primarily in terms of his race? In June a young Chinese-American named Michael Woo won a seat on the Los Angeles City Council, running in a district that is only five percent Asian. According to *The Washington Post,* he attributed his victory to his "links to his fellow young American professionals." This is not typical minority-group politics.

Since Asian-Americans have the luxury of not having to behave like other minority groups, it seems only a matter of time before they, like the Jews, lose their "minority" status altogether, both legally and in the public's perception. And when this occurs, Asian-Americans will have to face the danger not of discrimination but of losing their cultural identity. It is a problem that every immigrant group must eventually come to terms with.

For Americans in general, however, the success of Asian-Americans poses no problems at all. On the contrary, their triumph has done nothing but enrich the United States. Asian-Americans improve every field they enter, for the simple reason that in a free society, a group succeeds by doing something better than it had been done before: Korean grocery stores provide fresher vegetables; Filipino doctors provide better rural health care; Asian science students raise the quality of science in the universities, and go on to provide better medicine, engineering, computer technology, and so on. And by a peculiarly American miracle, the Asian-Americans' success has not been balanced by anyone else's failure. Indeed, as successive waves of immigrants have shown, each new ethnic and racial group adds far more to American society than it takes away. This Fourth of July, that is cause for hope and celebration.

Frank H. Wu  **NO**

# The Model Minority:
# Asian American "Success"
# as a Race Relations Failure

*Student* "Asians are threatening our economic future. . . . We can see it right here in our own school. Who are getting into the best colleges, in disproportionate numbers? Asian Kids! It's not fair."

*Teacher* "Uh . . . That certainly was an unusual essay. . . . Unfortunately, it's racist."

*Student* "Um . . . are you sure? My parents helped me."

—Garry Trudeau
*Recycled Doonesbury: Second Thoughts on a Gilded Age*

## Revenge of the Nerds

I am not the model minority. Before I can talk about Asian American experiences at all, I have to kill off the model minority myth because the stereotype obscures many realities. I am an Asian American, but I am not good with computers. I cannot balance my checkbook, much less perform calculus in my head. I would like to fail in school, for no reason other than to cast off my freakish alter ego of geek and nerd. I am tempted to be very rude, just to demonstrate once and for all that I will not be excessively polite, bowing, smiling, and deferring. I am lazy and a loner, who would rather reform the law than obey it and who has no business skills. I yearn to be an artist, an athlete, a rebel, and above all, an ordinary person.

I am fascinated by the imperviousness of the model minority myth against all efforts at debunking it. I am often told by nice people who are bewildered by the fuss, "You Asians are all doing well. What could you have to complain about anyway? Why would you object to a positive image?" To my frustration, many people who say with the utmost conviction that they would like to be color blind revert to being color conscious as soon as they look at Asian Americans, but then shrug off the contradiction. They are nonchalant about the racial generalization, "You Asians are all doing well," dismissive in asking "What could you have to complain about anyway?," and indifferent to the negative consequences of "a positive image."

From *Yellow: Race in America Beyond Black and White*, (Basic Books, 2002) excerpts from pp. 39–77. Copyright © 2002 by Frank H. Wu. Reprinted by permission of Basic Books, a member of Perseus Books Group, L.L.C.

Even people who are sympathetic to civil rights in general, including other people of color, sometimes resist mentioning civil rights and Asian Americans together in the same sentence. It is as if Asian American civil rights concerns can be ruled out categorically without the need for serious consideration of the facts, because everyone knows that Asian Americans are prospering. . . .

And so it is with Asian Americans. "You Asians are all doing well anyway" summarizes the model minority myth. This is the dominant image of Asians in the United States. Ever since immigration reforms in 1965 led to a great influx of Asian peoples, we have enjoyed an excellent reputation. As a group, we are said to be intelligent, gifted in math and science, polite, hard working, family oriented, law abiding, and successfully entrepreneurial. We revere our elders and show fidelity to tradition. The nation has become familiar with the turn-of-the-century Horatio Alger tales of "pulling yourself up by your own bootstraps" updated for the new millennium with an "Oriental" face and imbued with Asian values.

This miracle is the standard depiction of Asian Americans in fact and fiction, from the news media to scholarly books to Hollywood movies. From the 1960s to the 1990s, profiles of whiz kid Asian Americans became so common as to be cliches. . . .

Conservative politicians especially like to celebrate Asian Americans. President Ronald Reagan called Asian Americans "our exemplars of hope." President George Bush, California Governor Pete Wilson, House Speaker Newt Gingrich—all have been unduly awed by the model minority myth. In a brief for the *Heritage Foundation Policy Review,* California politician Ron Unz said that Asian Americans come from an "anti-liberal Confucian tradition" that "leaves them a natural constituency for conservatives." In the *National Review,* author Willian McGurn made the model minority myth a partisan parable: "Precisely because Asian Americans are making it in their adoptive land, they hold the potential not only to add to Republican rolls but to define a bona-fide American language of civil rights."

According to the model minority myth, Asian immigrants have followed the beacon of economic opportunity from their homes in China, Japan, Korea, the Philippines, India, Vietnam, and all the other countries on the Asian continent and within the Pacific Rim. They might be fleeing despotism or Communism, backwardness or the deprivations or war and famine, but whatever the conditions of their past they know that the legend of Golden Mountain, to use the Cantonese phrase, guides their future.

They arrive in America virtually penniless. They bring barely more than the clothes on their backs. Their meager physical possessions are less important than their mental capacity and work ethic. Thanks to their selfless dedication to a small business or an advanced degree in electrical engineering—or both—they are soon achieving the American Dream. . . .

They were doctors, nurses, engineers, scientists, professors, and librarians, but they have problems pursuing their professions because the requisite license is denied to them owing to their foreign education, or they are discriminated against because they have a heavy accent. Even if they are reduced to the drudgery of jobs for which they are overqualified, they are earning what they could never have in conditions of a developing country. Although they may be sweating as a janitor despite holding a doctorate, the toil is only temporary, until they can secure the patent for their discovery. In the interim, they can save enough to send remittances home to kinfolk who want very much to come here, too.

Whatever endeavor they pursue, Asian Americans are astonishing for their gung-ho enthusiasm. They remain busy with the chores called for by their enterprise twenty-four hours a day, seven days a week, through the holidays. After they sweep out their storefront entryway, they wash down the public sidewalk.

They come to dominate their trades after less than a decade, reducing their competition to the verge of bankruptcy and then buying up their warehouse stocks. Their associations become monopolies, lending money cooperatively among their own members to preserve their collective advantage. In some cities, they hold more than half the commercial licenses and operate a majority of the downtown "mom and pop" retail outlets. Hospitals and universities have departments wholly staffed by Asian immigrants. Private industries ranging from automobile manufacturers to software developers to government agencies, such as the Defense Department, depend on them for research and development.

In turn, their American-born progeny continue the tradition with their staggering academic prowess. They start off speaking pidgin, some of them even being held back a grade to adjust. They are willing to do as they are told, changing their given names to Anglicized Christian names chosen with the help of their teachers and their friends and told matter of factly to their parents. Above all, they study, study, study. . . .

The no-nonsense regimen works wonders. A parade of prodigies named Chang, Nguyen, and Patel takes the prizes at piano recitals and proceeds to graduate from high school with honors as valedictorian, salutatorian, and the rest of the top ten of the class, receiving full scholarships to the Ivy League colleges en route to graduate school and advanced professional training.

In any course on campus, Asian Americans are the best (or worst) classmates. In a physics class, they wreck the grade curve, idly twirling their pens back and forth with thumb and forefinger during lectures, solving problem sets late into the night with their peers, breaking for fried rice seasoned with pungent fish sauce and accompanied by smelly kim chee. In the laboratory, they are polishing up projects begun when they were adolescents, making breakthroughs in biology and chemistry, and publishing papers that make the faculty envious as they strive toward a Nobel prize. If they engage in frivolous activities after hours, as they rarely do, they are betrayed by their telltale red faces, which they develop after drinking just half a glass of beer.

Eventually, they land a job at a high-tech company or they start their own. Making millions, they buy big houses in the suburbs or build monstrosities right up to the property line on vacant lots. They bring their relatives over, starting the cycle over again.

In the view of other Americans, Asian Americans vindicate the American Dream. A publicity campaign designed to secure the acceptance of Asian Americans could hardly improve perceptions. They have done better here than they ever could have dreamed of doing in their homelands. They are living proof of the power of the free market and the absence of racial discrimination. Their good fortune flows from individual self-reliance and community self-sufficiency, not civil rights activism or government welfare benefits. They believe that merit and effort pay off handsomely and justly, and so they do. Asian Americans do not whine about racial discrimination; they only try harder. If they are told that they have a weakness that prevents their social acceptance, they quickly agree and earnestly attempt to cure it. If they are subjected to mistreatment by their employer, they quit and found their own company rather than protesting or suing.

This caricature is the portrait of the model minority. It is a parody of itself. . . .

Cartoonist Garry Trudeau satirized the model minority myth while recognizing its continuity with the earlier treatment of Jewish immigrants. In an installment of his "Doonesbury" comic strips devoted to the subject, another excerpt from which serves as the epigraph to this chapter, he portrays the following exchange between a white boy and an Asian American girl:

> "Hey, good goin' on the National Merit Scholarship, Kim! Fairly awesome."
> "Thanks, Sean."
> "Must be easier to be a grind if you grow up in an Asian family, huh?"
> "I wouldn't know."
> "Huh?"
> "I'm adopted. My parents are Jewish."
> "Jewish? Yo! Say no more!"
> "I wasn't planning to."

Non-Asian American college students have been similarly sarcastic about the model minority myth. On campuses at the end of the twentieth century, non-Asian American students joke that "MIT" stands for "Made In Taiwan" rather than "Massachusetts Institute of Technology"; "UCLA" (pronounced "UCRA" to mock the reputed Asian inability to enunciate a proper "R") means "United Caucasians Lost Among Asians"; and the initials of University of California at Irvine, "UCI," mean "University of Chinese Immigrants." The University of California-Berkeley Engineering school has been spray-painted with graffiti calling on school authorities to "Stop the Asian Hordes."

The model minority myth is daunting. The white president of Stanford University related an apocryphal story about a professor who asked a white student about a poor exam answer in an engineering course, only to receive the comeback, "What do you think I am, Chinese?" The student body president of Berkeley has said, "Some students say that if they see too many Asians in a class, they are not going to take it because the curve will be too high." A Yale student has said, "If you are weak in math or science and find yourself assigned to a class with a majority of Asian kids, the only thing to do is transfer to a different section."

The model minority myth appears to have the twin virtues of being true and being benevolent. It seems to be more benefit than burden for its subjects. It is unlike theories that array human beings in racial hierarchies. On its face, it is neither outlandish nor objectionable. It does not depend on allegations that Asian blood is better or even different than European blood. It relies more on acquired behavior than on inborn biology. It is not presented as some sort of tortured justification for outright oppression, such as incredible stories about African Americans told to legitimize the "peculiar institution" of chattel slavery.

The model minority myth also looks modern. It seems to be the product of scientific research rather than reflexive superstition. It cancels out prejudices of only a generation ago. It is ostensibly founded on empirical findings of social science, primarily Census tabulations. Since the 1980s, the figures have suggested that some Asian ethnic groups, notably Japanese Americans, have attained household incomes equal to or greater than those of white Americans. The numbers are averages, but they seem about as adequate a foundation as could be found for a racial proposition.

For all these reasons, it is a considerable challenge to explain how an apparent tribute can be a dangerous stereotype and why it presents a problem to be overcome. A person who demurs to praise seems to be "politically correct." Yet declining the laudatory title of model minority is fundamental to gaining Asian American autonomy. The model minority myth deserves a thoughtful critique. It would be foolish to condemn it as wrong or racist, without discussion. It is too complex, as well as too common.

Regrettably, the model minority myth embraced by the pundits and the public alike is neither true nor truly flattering. Instead, it is a stock character that plays multiple roles in our racial drama. Like any other myth forming our collective narrative of race, it is ultimately more revealing than reassuring. Complimentary on its face, the model minority myth is disingenuous at its heart.

As well-meaning as it may be, the model minority myth ought to be rejected for three reasons. First, the myth is a gross simplification that is not accurate enough to be seriously used for understanding 10 million people. Second, it conceals within it an invidious statement about African Americans along the lines of the inflammatory taunt: "They made it; why can't you?" Third, the myth is abused both to deny that Asian Americans experience racial discrimination and to turn Asian Americans into a racial threat.

## Germs of Truth Within the Myth

Like many racial stereotypes, the model minority myth has a germ of truth. The problem, however, is that the germ becomes exaggerated and distorted. On its own terms, the myth is not even persuasive as a description of the status of Asian Americans. In earning power, for example, the evidence points toward a disparity between what individual white Americans and what individual Asian Americans are paid—and not for lack of trying on the part of Asian Americans.

To figure out the facts, University of Hawaii sociology professor Herbert Barringer led a team that conducted the most comprehensive review of the research literature ever done. Barringer concludes that with respect to income, "in almost every category . . . whites showed advantages over most Asian Americans." . . .

That interpretation, however, is most favorable to white Americans and not Asian Americans. Translated into practical terms, it means that white Americans are paid more than Asian Americans who are equally qualified. Either Asian Americans are not hired for the higher-paying jobs, or they are hired but are still paid less. . . .

The fact that Asian Americans are better educated than white Americans on average undermines, rather than supports, the model minority myth. The gap between Asian Americans and white Americans that appears with income reverses itself with education. It was consistent throughout the 1980s and 1990s. In 1980, approximately 36 percent of foreign-born Asian Americans had finished college compared with 16 percent of native-born citizens. In 1990, about 42 percent of Asian Americans had finished college compared with 25 percent of the general population. . . . As of 1993, Asian Americans made up 5.3 percent of the college student body but approximately 2.9 percent of the general population. Their desire for education is increasing even as that of other groups is decreasing. Between 1979 and 1989, Asian Americans increased their numbers of Ph.D. recipients by 46 percent while whites and blacks decreased their numbers by 6 and 23 percent, respectively. By 1997, Asian Americans were receiving 12 percent of the doctorates conferred by U.S. universities, and they received more than one-quarter of the doctorates in engineering disciplines.

Although the average educational levels of Asian Americans might be taken as substantiating the model minority myth, the more plausible reading is that Asian Americans have had to overcompensate. Asian Americans receive a lower return on their investment in education. They gain less money than white Americans on average for each additional degree. They are underrepresented in management, and those who are managers earn less than white Americans in comparable positions. . . .

Moreover, Asian immigrants start off relatively privileged. This admission must be made gingerly, so that it will not be taken as corroboration of the model minority myth. In actuality, it undercuts the myth. Most Asian Americans are not rich. But some Asian immigrants are relatively fortunate compared to the many Asians who reside in Asia, and some of them are relatively fortunate compared to native-born Americans (including, incidentally, native-born Asian Americans), even though they have not had an easy time of it in coming to the United States and even though they experience prejudice. A major study of diversity in the power elite found that almost none of the Chinese Americans who served on the boards of directors for Fortune 1000 companies were "authentic bootstrap-pers." Almost all of them had come from well-to-do families in China, Taiwan, and Hong Kong.

University of California at Santa Cruz sociologist Deborah Woo exam-ined more closely the media coverage of "a Korean-born immigrant who once worked the night shift at 7-Eleven to put himself through school" and who sold his company for $1 billion, as well as another Korean-born immigrant, a Silicon Valley entrepreneur who lived on ramen noodles and had to pawn his belongings to pay his phone bill, but gave $15 million to the San Francisco Asian Art Museum, "mak[ing] Horatio Alger look like a slacker." Woo delved into the backgrounds of these examples of the model minority myth. In the former instance, the individual was able to start his company because he had received a government contract through a minority set-aside program. In the latter, the man was descended from the royal family that ruled Korea until the Japanese takeover of 1905, and he had been a university professor and an executive in the family business in Korea before emigrating. They are still impressive people, but they have not come from the ghetto. The sheen comes off the model minority myth once the real stories are revealed. . . .

Asian Americans are more likely than white Americans to be self-employed. Self-employed individuals with the same income as corporate employees tend to put in longer hours, with fewer benefits and increased risks of bankruptcy and other setbacks. The average employee of an Asian-owned enterprise is paid less than $10,000 per year. . . .

The model minority myth also masks great disparities among Asian ethnic groups. Japanese Americans and Chinese Americans are closest to equality with whites, but Vietnamese Americans and other Southeast Asian refugees languish at the bottom of the economic pyramid, along with blacks. In the 1980 Census, for example, Vietnamese Americans were below African Americans on average. According to the 1990 Census, 25 percent of Vietnamese Americans and 45 percent of other Southeast Asians lived in poverty. Those poverty rates were higher than the rates for Africans (21 percent) and Hispanics (23 percent).

Finally, the figures for Asian Americans are rendered unreliable by the careless inclusion of Asians who reside in the United States but who are not Asian Americans at all. Hundreds of business executives with Japanese-based multinational companies spend stints of up to a few years here. Their upper-management salaries add to the average Asian American income, but they are no more representative of either Asians overseas or Asian immigrants than a white American vice-president of a Fortune 500 company who was an expatriate manager in Europe would be either average of Americans or of Europeans themselves. They are part of a transnational overclass. . . .

The model minority myth persists, despite violating our societal norms against racial stereotyping and even though it is not accurate. Dozens of amply documented and heavily annotated government studies and schol-arly papers, along with a handful of better magazine and newspaper articles supplemented by television segments and public speeches, all intended to destroy the myth, have had negligible effect on popular culture. In the latest college textbook on Asian Americans, professors Lucie Cheng and Philip Q. Yang comment, "despite an unending barrage of attacks, the model minority image has persisted into the 1990s, quite alive if not entirely unscathed."

The myth has not succumbed to individualism or facts because it serves a purpose in reinforcing racial hierarchies. Asian Americans are as much a "middleman minority" as we are a model minority. We are placed in the awkward position of buffer or intermediary, elevated as the preferred racial minority at the expense of denigrating African Americans. Asian American writers and scholars have not hesitated to call the phenomenon what it is. Novelist Frank Chin has described it as "racist love," contrasting it with "racist hate" of other people of color. DePaul University law professor Sumi Cho has explained that Asian Americans are turned into "racial mascots," giving right-wing causes a novel messenger, camouflaging arguments that would look unconscionably self-interested if made by whites about themselves. University of California at Irvine political scientist Claire Kim has argued that Asian Americans are positioned through "racial triangulation," much as a Machiavellian would engage in political triangulation for maximum advantage. Law professor Mari Matsuda famously declared, "we will not be used" in repudiating the model minority myth.

Whatever the effects are called, Asian Americans become pawns. We are not recognized in our own right but advanced for ulterior motives. Michael S. Greve, a leading advocate against racial remedies, said that the controversy over anti-Asian discrimination could be used to attack affirmative action: It presented "an opportunity to call, on behalf of a racial minority (i.e., the Asian applicants), for an end to discrimination. It was an appeal that, when made on behalf of whites, is politically hopeless and, perhaps, no longer entirely respectable."

The model minority myth is resilient because it is a "meme." Scientist Richard Dawkins's concept of a "meme"—a piece of cultural material that can be passed on from person to person, society to society, and generation to generation—advises us that any information and any image can survive and evolve. Dawkins posits that memes are to culture what genes are to biology, replicating themselves in an evolutionary process that selects the bits most likely to survive. Whether they are information or rumor, stereotypes take on their own social life. The longevity and propagation of information depends on its usefulness, not necessarily its truth. The myth is useful, even if it is not true. Its content assuages the conscience and assigns blame, a function that is psychologically needed and socially desired. It tells a comforting narrative of America as having progressed to become a place where race does not matter anymore, and it offers a cautionary parable about the good minority and the bad minority. Author Michael Lind has written that "in addition to fulfilling their immediate functions—selling egg rolls, measuring blood sugar—Vietnamese vendors and Filipino lab technicians serve an additional function for the white overclass: they relieve it of guilt about the squalor of millions of native-born Americans, not only ghetto blacks and poor Hispanics but poor whites." To condemn the myth is not the same as to condemn the individual who has lived it or repeated it. We all like fables with happy endings, especially when we are the actors in the story. . . .

## Backlash from the Myth

The model minority myth hurts Asian Americans themselves. It is two-faced. Every attractive trait matches up neatly to its repulsive complement, and the aspects are conducive to reversal. If we acquiesced to the myth in its favorable guise, we would be precluded from rejecting its unfavorable interpretations. We would already have accepted the characteristics at issue as inherent. . . .

Upside down or right side up, the model minority myth whitewashes racial discrimination. "People don't believe it," as one Asian American leader told the *L.A. Times* in 1991, in discussing the prevalence of anti-Asian bias. An Asian American student leader said that, like whites, other people of color doubt claims about attacks: "Some simply didn't see us as minorities. . . . They think if you're Asian you're automatically interning at Merrill Lynch and that you're never touched by racism." The myth implies that bigotry has been brought on by the victims, who must defeat it, rather than that it is the responsibility of the perpetrators, who could be compelled to eliminate it. Senator Alan Simpson, an opponent of immigration, coined the term "compassion fatigue" to describe his sense that Americans were tired of hearing about other peoples' problems (as if those other people weren't tired of their problems). Under Simpson's concept, even if Asian Americans press complaints about bias for which they have evidence, the incidents should be treated as inconsequential or written off as the cost of being a newcomer. The reasoning seems to be that because Asian Americans have theoretically surmounted the deleterious effects of racial discrimination, we cannot be actually aggrieved even if real wrongs are done to us. . . .

The model minority myth does more than cover up racial discrimination; it instigates racial discrimination as retribution. The hyperbole about Asian American affluence can lead to jealousy on the part of non-Asian Americans, who may suspect that Asian Americans are too comfortable or who are convinced by . . . others telling them Asian American gains are their losses. Through the justification of the myth, the humiliation of Asian Americans or even physical attacks directed against Asian Americans become compensation or retaliation. . . .

It would be bad enough if the model minority myth were true. Everyone else would resent Asian Americans for what Asian Americans possess. It is worse that the model minority myth is false. Everyone else resents Asian Americans for what they believe Asian Americans possess. Other Americans say that their resentment is about riches and not race, but they assume that Asian Americans are rich on the basis of race; there is no escaping that the resentment is racial. Above all, the model minority myth is a case study in the risks of racial stereotypes of any kind. It is the stereotyping itself, not the positive or negative valence it assumes temporarily, that is dangerous. A stereotype confines its subjects. The myth was neither created by, nor is it controlled by, Asian Americans. It is applied to but not by Asian Americans.

The model minority myth tells us that the only good Asian American is a genius workaholic, not an average or normal man or woman. The expectations of being a supergeek can be debilitating. Asian American children are not allowed to be like other children. They must be superstudents, because their parents, their teachers, and society overall expect nothing less. They become misfits to their classmates. Their rarified upbringing is like that of John Stuart Mill, the great utilitarian philosopher whose father was determined to produce a polymath of the first order. Mill's homeschooling routine, sitting at a desk opposite his father for the entirety of the day except during walks when he would recite his lessons, worked brilliantly, producing a formidable scholar who was publishing learned papers as an adolescent but who also underwent a grave emotional breakdown at an early age. Other than through the model minority myth, few Americans today wish to force their children to endure the box of psychologist B. F. Skinner, with its positive and negative reinforcements to condition behavior as if we were rats to be rewarded for running a maze. Asian American adults are directed into specific occupations. Yet Asian Americans cannot sustain communities in which we all are engineers, no matter how good a profession it is. If we are not to be stunted as communities, we must have artists, journalists, lawyers, crafts-people, police officers, firefighters, social workers, and the myriad others with contributions to make to our civic culture. We should have communities that contain the spectrum of human pursuits, or we will live down to our stereotype. . . .

# POSTSCRIPT

## Are Asian Americans a Model Minority?

**W**hen one examines Asian American's "success" within the United States, it is important to be more specific concerning the group or groups that are the focus of analysis. Such specificity is required because all Asian ethnic groups have not achieved the same levels of success based on traditional measures that are employed in such assessments.

Asian Americans have been involved in the development of the nation for approximately one and a half centuries. This diverse aggregation of immigrant peoples brought cultures to the New World from some of the oldest civilizations to evolve in human history. The tendency to lump such culturally disparate minority groups into a singular macro-level category does not provide an adequate basis for understanding the distinctions that exist among the Asian-American ethnic groups that are impacting their life chances and prospects for advancement within society.

The two selections chosen for this issue present positions on opposite sides of the question: Is the glass half empty, or is it half full? Bell views Asian Americans as Americans' "greatest success story." Though he recognizes that all of the problems facing Asians in the quest for acceptance and advancement in society have not been resolved, he chooses to downplay such concerns. Bell is certain that Asian Americans are poised to achieve even greater success in a future America where they will become fully assimilated to the extent that they will lose their minority status within society.

Wu is cognizant of the real successes that some Asians have achieved, but he does not endorse the "model minority" notion. He is concerned that this imagery is being attached to Asian Americans at a time when they have not achieved equality with whites in important areas of economic life, and that they are lagging behind on significant indices of success, especially administration and other areas of leadership. And he is seriously concerned about the backlash against Asians that is expressed through stereotyping, hostile sentiments, and violence. Wu feels that the "model minority" rhetoric of U.S. leaders and their supporters tends to obscure these issues and concerns, thus mitigating the prospects of developing meaning and effective strategies for their resolution.

Among the Asian-American ethnic groups, Koreans have achieved more then the Hmong people or other boat people who arrived on America's shores in the wake of the Vietnam War. So, it is important to engage in an analysis of the stratification that exists, both among the various Asian ethnicities and within each of these groups, in order to gain a clearer and more meaningful assessment of their socioeconomic status and the success that they are experiencing in the society.

One question that arises is whether it is possible to establish a scientifically acceptable method to establish a meaningful comparison of the "successes" achieved by different minority groups? For example, how does the fact that African Americans have established over 100 black colleges and universities figure into the determination of success? The creation of these institutions is a major demonstration of the embrace of an ethic of self-reliance an educational achievement by African Americans.

Wu notes that the pitting of one ethnic group against another by American leaders, such as former President Ronald Reagan, is dangerous and irresponsible. Such conservative leaders have employed the "model minority" rhetoric to delegitimize the demands of other ethnic groups for the government to be active and effective in resolving social problems. The message to groups such as blacks and Latinos emanating from these leaders is: Why can't you be like them (i.e., quiet and self-reliant)? The countervailing question that such leaders must address is: What would be the quality of race and ethnic relations today if African Americans had not been in the vanguard of the civil rights movement, and what would be the nature of Asian Americans' successes if the movement had not achieved the more open society that exists in the United States today? What value should be accorded African Americans for their Herculean contributions that they have exerted on behalf of freedom and justice for all minorities in America?

For an overview of Asian-American groups, see *Asian Americans: Emerging Minorities* (Prentice-Hall, 1988) by Harry Kitano and Roger Daniels. The June 1998 issue of the *Population Bulletin* was devoted to "Asian-Americans: Diverse and Growing." The volume, written by Sharon M. Lee, is a good introduction to the study of Asian Americans. An article that deals with Asians and assimilation is "In Asian America," by Tamar Jacoby in *Commentary* (July–August 2000). *Everybody Was Kung Fu Fighting: Afro-Asian Connections and the Myth of Cultural Purity* (Beacon Press, 2001) by Vijay Prashad discusses links between black and South Asian experiences. Eric Liu, in *The Accidental Asian: Notes of a Native Speaker* (Random House, 1998), articulates a vision of Asian-American identity.

Stanford Lyman's *The Asian in the West* (Western Studies Center, Desert Research Institute, 1970) is a little known but important discussion on Asians and the beginnings of American institutional racism. Critical of the model minority notion is Won Moo Hurh and Kwang Chung Kim's "The 'Success' Image of Asian Americans: Its Validity, and Its Practical and Theoretical Implications" in *Ethnic and Racial Studies* (1989). *Asian American Dreams: The Emergence of an American People* (Farrar, Straus, 2000) by Helen Zia is a book about the transformation of Asian Americans from "aliens" into Americans with dreams of equality.

# Internet References . . .

## Brookings

America's oldest think tank, the Brookings Institute, sponsors this Web site. It offers students high quality research on many relevant topics dealing with race, ethnicity, and immigration. Over the past 90 years, its research has contributed to countless public policy decisions in large part, because of its centrist approach.

**http://brookings.edu**

## The Heritage Foundation

This is the Web site for the well known conservative think tank, The Heritage Foundation, which states that it is committed to building an America where freedom, opportunity, prosperity, and civil society flourish. The site offers information including research on many issues including race, ethnicity, and immigration.

**http://www.heritage.org**

## The American Enterprise Institute

The Web site for the American Enterprise Institute for Public Policy Research (AEI) indicates that it is a conservative think tank, founded in 1943. It is associated with neoconservative thought and policy recommendations. Approximately 35 conservative public intellectuals and activists contribute to the site.

**http://www.aei.org**

## Latin American Network Information Center: University of Texas

The Latin American Network Information Center sponsors this Web site. It seeks to facilitate access to Internet-based information to, from, or on Latin America. It provides information about Latin America for students, teachers, and researchers, and potential research to hundreds of sites on Hispanics in the United States. There are excellent academic resources available on the site.

**http://www1.lanic.utexas.edu**

## Policy and People

This Web site offers current information on national issues including immigration, education, and other social issues. It aims to take the spotlight off politics and politicians and put it back on policy and the people. The site is nonpartisan and nonprofit, featuring moderates, liberals, and conservatives. It highlights national policy debates.

**http://www.citizenjoe.org**

## Immigration Policy Center

This is the Web site for the Immigration Policy Center, a Division of the American Immigration Law Foundation. It offers data and research on several aspects of immigration including asylum, refugees, undocumented immigrants, the labor market, and enforcement of immigrant policy.

**http://www.immigrationpolicy.org**

# UNIT 5

# Policy Issues for the Twenty-First Century

*T*wenty-first century America is truly a nation of diverse ethnicities. As indicated earlier, the Asians and Latinos are the fastest growing groups within the American population. Latinos have passed African Americans as the country's largest minority group. Yet despite the darkening of the skin color of the American population, issues of race, sometimes intertwined with immigration, continue to confront this nation. Among the issues to be resolved in twenty-first century America are race and immigration, race and other factors involved in college admissions, affirmative action, and reparations for African Americans, among other policy concerns. These issues continue to generate conflict within the American population and its political and economic elites.

- Does Latino Immigration Threaten African American Workers?

- Should Race Be Included Among the Many Factors Considered for Admission to Selective Colleges?

- Is Affirmative Action Necessary to Achieve Racial Equality in the United States Today?

- Is Now the Time for Reparations for African Americans?

# ISSUE 17

# Does Latino Immigration Threaten African American Workers?

**YES: Douglas P. Woodward and Paulo Guimarães**, from "Latino Immigration," *Business and Economic Review* (April 1, 2008)

**NO: David C. Ruffin**, from "Immigration: 5 Black Leaders Lend Their Voices to the Debate," *The Crisis* (July/August 2006)

## ISSUE SUMMARY

**YES:** Douglas P. Woodward, director of the Division of Research and Professor of Economics, and Paulo Guimarães, a Clinical Research Professor of Economics, both of the Moore School of Business at the University of South Carolina, in a strongly researched case study of the impact of Latino immigration on the workers of South Carolina, present significant statistical evidence that African American workers have lost both jobs and wages.

**NO:** David C. Ruffin, a writer and political analyst in Washington, D.C., interviews five black leaders who respond negatively to this question. It is their considered judgment that other factors including technological advancement and high rates of incarceration are major contributors to the lagging prospects of African American workers.

The various ethnic groups that comprise the nation have tended to celebrate their immigrant origins and contributions to the building of America. Americans also have tended to take pride in the fact that we are a nation of immigrants. Given these facts, one may find it difficult to comprehend that immigration, especially Latino immigration, has become such a divisive issue within the American body politic in recent years. This issue has not just generated controversy and division among the mass public, it has also generated schisms within our political parties. It has provided hate groups with fodder for recruitment and expansion, and has fostered increasing sentiments of white nationalism within a portion of the American population.

Lastly, advocates for these immigrants argue that they are doing work that other Americans refuse to do and provide a convenient scapegoat for those who desire to divert attention from the prevailing contradictions and challenges confronting the society.

White Americans tend to view this controversy in terms of identity politics and potential losses that they incur within labor markets. Other areas of concern that are expressed include crime and welfare dependency. African Americans tend to focus on competition with Latino immigrants in lower status labor markets and the concomitant loss of jobs and wages that they might suffer.

Douglas P. Woodward has written a research-based article in which he presents significant empirical evidence that African American workers have indeed suffered from a recent influx of Latino immigrants within South Carolina. In this case study, he presents clear evidence that black workers have suffered economic losses, that is, job losses, declining wages, or both, in three important labor markets, including construction, animal slaughtering, and landscaping.

Five prominent African American leaders offers their views on this controversial issue, and they tend to take a negative view of the matter. They cite such factors as technology, automation, and mass incarceration as the greatest threats to the economic prospects of low-skilled black workers. They also see the need to coalesce with Latinos to elevate their status so that they and low-skilled black workers do not retain the status of an exploitable pool of cheap labor.

Questions for students to consider, which will enhance their understanding of this issue, include: Does immigration complicate the already dire job crisis for African Americans? Is the claim that immigrants perform jobs that the rest of the American population including African Americans refuses to do correct? How do issues of class and race intersect in the relationship between African Americans and Latino workers?

# YES

**Douglas P. Woodward
and Paulo Guimarães**

# Latino Immigration

The number of Latino immigrants in South Carolina, like the rest of the Southeast, is growing rapidly. What does this mean for wages and jobs in the state?

In 1924, South Carolina Senator Ellison DuRant Smith ("Cotton Ed") argued before the U.S. Congress, "I think that we have sufficient stock in America now for us to shut the door, Americanize what we have, and save the resources of America for the natural increase of our population. . . . We ought to Americanize our factories and our vast material resources, so that we can make each contribute to the other and have an abundance for us under the form of the government laid down by our fathers. . . ."

The United States is again engaged in an often emotional debate about immigration, but this time about Latinos, not Europeans, flooding across our borders. Over the past decade, the influx of Latino immigrants has been driven by economic forces both in the United States and in Latin America.

For many immigrants, jobs seem to be plentiful in the United States, with wages far above the norm for Latin America, and the immigrants are willing to accept wages and benefits below that expected by U.S. workers. In addition, Latin American immigrant workers are known to be highly motivated and extremely productive, which is often the case for immigrants. At the same time, as a competitive business strategy some firms seek immigrant workers because they are vastly less expensive relative to native U.S. workers.

The southeastern United States has seen an especially large increase in immigration. Along with neighboring states, the Latino population in South Carolina is growing rapidly as we reported earlier in the Business & Economic Review (Volume 52, Number 4, July-August-September 2006). According to the U.S. Bureau of the Census, South Carolina led the nation in the growth of its foreign-born population between 2000 and 2005 (with a 47 percent increase), and Hispanics/Latinos comprise a sizeable portion of the foreign-born in the state. In South Carolina, Latino numbers increased by 350 percent during that same period, or from roughly 30,000 to 135,000, while growing by only 87 percent in the nation as a whole (from 22,354,059 to 41,870,703). Given the rapid rise of undocumented workers, the actual number of Latinos in South Carolina is much higher than reported by the Census Bureau.

Until the late 1990s, there was only a minimal presence of Latinos in the workforce in the state. Since then, Latino immigrant labor has spread across a variety of industries and occupations in South Carolina. A few industries dominate, however. Like many states, Latino immigrant labor first appeared in agriculture. Since 2000, much of the increase in immigration can be traced to the demand for labor in construction, landscaping, and food processing. It is not surprising that some firms in these industries seek cheap Latino labor. After all, while industries like apparel can relocate offshore and export from developing countries, a construction or landscaping firm cannot move its activities to foreign locations to lower its costs.

## The Latino Labor Market in South Carolina

According to the simple economics of supply and demand, an influx of low-skilled immigrants into the labor market could cause a decrease in the wages for the existing low-skilled workers. Some low-skilled native workers may even choose to leave the labor force if the wage would leave them impoverished or working conditions become less desirable, at least by U.S. standards.

Prominent economists have examined this issue. Notably, Harvard economist George Borjas has studied the labor market effects of immigration extensively. Generally, he has found negative effects on wages from increased immigration, especially for low-skilled workers in the United States. Not all economists concur with his conclusions, however. Sharp differences have emerged about the size of the wage impact from immigration.

Beyond the effects on the labor market, many economic studies conclude that immigration does not adversely affect the U.S. economy as a whole; rather it provides many benefits. The output of products and services may be greater than would be possible without immigrant labor. Direct benefits include higher profits for firms and an increased standard of living for skilled, educated labor.

No doubt Latino immigration has a varied effect on the South Carolina economy–both positive and negative. However, the impact on wages and employment in low-skill occupations is particularly crucial to understand, for there is a relatively large segment of the population with low skills and low wages.

## Construction

A clearer picture of South Carolina workforce trends can be seen in specific industries where the Latino labor force growth has been most pronounced. Particularly noteworthy is construction's dominance, which accounts for 37.6 percent of Latino employment reported in the USC survey. Even restaurants and landscaping, often thought to be leading employers of Latinos, are eclipsed by construction, as Table 4 reveals. These results confirm that more than anything else, the 2000–2005 construction boom was a major pulling force, drawing new Latinos to South Carolina.

Given the strong representation of Latinos in South Carolina's construction sector, it is worth examining the earnings trends in comparison
with Black and White workers. According to ACS-U.S. Census data, real
median earnings dropped 5.1 percent for full-time South Carolina workers.
At the same time, Hispanic workers saw real wages drop 12.1 percent (as the
number of construction workers expanded 181 percent). Black construction
labor saw inflation-adjusted earnings fall 2.4 percent. It is also surprising to
find that total Black employment sank 23.7 percent during the construction boom. Meanwhile, White construction employment grew 4.3 percent,
but the corresponding median earnings fell by more than that of Black
construction workers.

The USC survey found that the median annual wage for the Latinos
identified as working in construction is $21,840, higher than that reported
in the ACS-U.S Census for 2005 ($18,549). In the survey, construction labor
included painters, carpenters, roofers, electrical workers, and others who
reported that they worked in construction trades.

## Animal Slaughtering

After construction, the U.S. Census records the greatest numbers of
Hispanics working in South Carolina's animal slaughtering industry. For
this industry, which includes poultry processing, employment grew overall
as real wages fell: Hispanic employment increased by 12.6 percent between
2000–2005, while real annual median earnings for full-time workers
declined 18.9 percent. By 2005, meanwhile, Black workers in this industry
saw jobs dramatically drop 43.4 percent when compared with 2000. In
this case, however, the median earnings for the remaining Black workers
retained in the animal slaughtering industry rose 14.6 percent. Thus, it
could be said the lack of employment opportunities, not falling wages,
has been the trend in the sector. One could speculate the Black workers
remaining in animal slaughtering were more highly skilled, while low-skill
work went to Latino labor.

In the USC survey, food processing workers (including poultry
slaughtering, vegetable packing, and meat packing) had a median wage of
$15,600. This is higher than the U.S. Census median wage ($14,269) for
animal slaughtering.

## Landscaping

The U.S. Census records that the third-largest sector of South Carolina's
economy employing Hispanics is landscaping services. From 2000–2005,
employment in this industry surged. In this case, a different picture emerges
once the data are broken into different groups. Many Hispanics found
full-time jobs over the period in landscaping services (rising 66.7 percent),
although again, real median earnings fell (14.2 percent). For Blacks, landscaping service employment grew substantially over the period (unlike the

other two sectors). But real earnings fell 9.6 percent. For Whites working in landscaping services, employment and earnings declined by 1.5 percent and 5.5 percent, respectively.

## Employment and Wage Trends: A Summary

For each of the three sectors with the largest Hispanic workforce in South Carolina, Blacks either lost jobs, saw earnings decline, or both (as in construction). In contrast to the deterioration of employment and earnings in sectors with a large Hispanic presence, Blacks did make significant employment and wage gains from 2000–2005 in some industries. Especially pronounced were the improvements found in the job market for the motor vehicle and motor vehicle equipment industry (see Table 6). This important manufacturing backbone of the South Carolina economy supported a 63.1 percent increase in Black full-time employment, and the total number of workers is almost 10,500 (still smaller than construction, but far larger than animal slaughtering and landscape services). Blacks also witnessed a dramatic rise in real earnings: 36.8 percent. Whites also fared well, both in earnings and employment. But Hispanics have only a minor presence in motor vehicle and motor vehicle equipment. In fact, employment and median earnings both fell from 2000–2005.

Overall, our labor market analysis suggests that Blacks are losing ground in industries with a large, growing Hispanic workforce. Real earnings have declined, but they have been falling even in sectors with high labor demand during the survey period, like construction. Blacks have lost employment in construction, despite a record expansion in activity. The good news is that Blacks have made notable progress in the motor vehicle and motor vehicle equipment sector, which was also expanding during 2000–2005.

## Poverty Trends

Consider the poverty differences among Hispanics, Blacks, and Whites. Since Hispanics have seen real earnings fall from 2000 to 2006, we would expect poverty status may have been adversely affected. In fact, for the Hispanic population as a whole, the poverty rate went down from 24.8 percent to 22.3 percent. At the same time, Black poverty in South Carolina rose from 26.2 percent in 2000 to 28.9 percent in 2006. Whites exhibit a much smaller poverty rate: 10.0 percent in 2006. Even so, the poverty rate has risen since 2000, despite a strong economy in 2006.

## Conclusion

With a surging Latino population, South Carolina's workforce in the first decade of the 21st century is changing. As elsewhere, the forces pulling Latino immigrants to South Carolina are straightforward: employment opportunities and much higher wages than remotely possible in the home country. Immigrants are pressed to travel thousands of miles because of limited employment prospects in many Latin American communities (especially in rural areas). For the immigrant-sending communities south of the border, employment in the United States is perceived as a solution to endemic poverty and economic instability.

This trend is likely to continue. For some U.S. businesses, the Latino labor force offers a strong work ethic combined with lower wages. The USC survey reveals that annual earnings for Latinos totaled $20,400. This falls in line with U.S. Census figures that show a median of $21,199 in earnings for full-time Latino workers. In either case, Latino earnings are about $10,000 below the norm for South Carolinians.

Construction has been the sector most responsible for enticing immigrants to work in South Carolina. The downturn in housing construction, however, may lead to less labor demand and a much slower growth of Latino immigration, at least in the short term. As for the recent past, this industry witnessed the largest increase in Latino workers, by far. At the same time, we have seen that Black construction employment fell even as residential and nonresidential building was booming across the state through 2005. Real wages also fell for Latino construction labor during this expansion.

Beyond construction, the entry of Latinos into the South Carolina economy has had varied effects. We have seen that median real wages have fallen for Black workers from 2000–2005, even as the economy expanded. In general, it appears that median wages for Latinos have, in fact, been the most negatively impacted as the Latino workforce has grown.

In sum, for a variety of reasons, including growth of low-skilled immigrant workers and low levels of educational attainment for many native workers, wages are stagnating across the state. Is the solution, then, to cut off the supply of new labor?

It would be foolish, then, to "shut the door" at a time when the economy will demand more labor. With a sensible, comprehensive national immigration policy, this increased demand could be met. For native U.S. workers, enhanced skills and better educational attainment, along with a steadily growing economy, offer the best prospects for increasing living standards.

David C. Ruffin

 **NO**

# Immigration: 5 Black Leaders Lend Their Voices to the Debate

**I**mmigration has been a problem in America since the first European settlers arrived and disrupted the civilizations of the natives they encountered. Enslaved Africans followed shortly and, together with White indentured servants, formed the first pool of a long line of exploited workers who generated for others much of the wealth that built this country. Through the 19th and 20th centuries, new waves of immigrants came—Irish driven from their homeland by the potato famine, Jews fleeing oppression in Eastern Europe and peoples from dozens of Southern and Eastern European ethnic groups seeking better lives within these shores. As in the past, strong and vocal groups have risen to oppose the relatively recent influx that comprises mainly people of color from Latin America, the Caribbean and Asia. Immigrants and their supporters have pushed back with nationwide protests against draconian legislation that would mark illegal immigrants as felons.

Caught in the middle are African Americans, many of whom make up a large portion of low-skilled workers who have competed with each successive surge of newcomers for jobs at the bottom of the pay scale. Rising out of the current furor over immigration are concerns emanating from within Black communities that seem to echo those from the past: Are immigrants taking jobs from Black workers and depressing wages? How significant is immigration compared with other causes of Black unemployment? What do African Americans lose if undocumented immigrants are provided a pathway to citizenship? Are there issues on which Black and immigrant communities can find common ground?

*The Crisis* sought answers to these and other questions through a series of interviews with five prominent Black leaders and activists. We talked to: **Constance Rice**, a human rights and civil rights lawyer and co-director of the Advancement Project in Los Angeles; **Gerald Hudson**, executive vice president of the Service Employees International Union; **Ronald Walters**, professor of government and politics at the University of Maryland at College Park; **Bruce S. Gordon**, president and CEO of the NAACP; and U.S. Rep. **Sheila Jackson Lee** (D-Texas).

The McGraw-Hill Companies wishes to thank the Crisis Publishing Co., Inc., the publisher of the magazine of the National Association for the Advancement of Colored People, for the use of this material first published in the July/August 2006 issue of *The Crisis*, pp. 20–25. Reprinted by permission.

# Constance Rice, Advancement Project

*CRISIS    How would you characterize the U.S. immigration issue?*

*Rice*   It must be really rich for Native Americans to hear European descendents talk about proper immigration. I mean, the Europeans came over here and basically did grand theft nation and genocide. If you think about it, the only folks who have a right to be here are Native Americans. So I start there.

Immigration has always been problematic for the groups that come here and for African Americans as a whole. There has always been this demonization of immigrants, even though we have needed them to do cheap labor.

*How does immigration affect African Americans?*

*Rice*   When you talk about the intersection between African Americans and immigrants, you have to ask which African Americans. If you are talking about my friends, the Buppies—Black urban professionals who are Ivy League-educated—we benefit from immigration because these folks are mowing our lawns and taking care of our children.

*But does the pressure of undocumented workers have an impact on Black workers at the low end of the workforce?*

*Rice*   The three biggest threats to low-skilled [and] no-skilled African American laborers are as follows: number one, America's mass incarceration strategy; number two is technology and automation—tollbooths and cashier jobs are now automated.

The third thing is the downsizing of the public sector, because African Americans are disproportionately employed in government jobs as postal workers, public school teachers and nurses in public hospitals. All my relatives drove trucks for the government. They were clerks and teachers. These are at least three major dynamics that have had a bigger impact on low-skilled, no-skilled African American job prospects before you even get to immigration.

*How would you respond to those who depict immigration as an "invasion"?*

*Rice*   You have to ask why these people leave their children behind and come here. Who in the world would risk gang rape, being robbed by the police and by bandits, and a long walk into a desert where more than 500 people a year perish? The reason that we have this massive tide of immigrants is because Mexico is a failed state. There is not enough of an economic engine there to employ their own people.

So I don't blame the immigrants who are desperate to provide for their families. When we allow an employer to get away with exploiting immigrant labor, is that the immigrant's fault or is that our fault? Have you ever seen

CEOs marched off in leg irons for presiding over a conspiracy to hire undocumented illegal alien labor so that they can lower wages and make bigger profits? They get away with it and there are no real employer sanctions. We've got reverse Robin Hood going on in this country right now.

*Is this a civil rights issue?*

**Rice**   Do you think Martin Luther King Jr. would for a moment stand for the fact that you have a group of totally exploitable people in this country who are treated just like the slaves were? Not for a nanosecond. So we need to go back and reclaim the leadership on this issue until our *European* cousins and fellow Americans get a grip. Let's figure out how we set a path so that these folks will become full-fledged Americans.

*Are there opportunities for African Americans and Latinos to work together on important issues?*

**Rice**   I see it here in Los Angeles all of the time. Is it Kumbaya? No. It's like a hostile standoff in some communities. But we at the Advancement Project represented Latinos and African Americans who joined together to go to court to bring back a quarter of a billion dollars for school construction. We've banded together to fight police abuse. Multiracial coalitions are a way of life out here in Los Angeles.

# Gerald Hudson, Seiu

**CRISIS**   *What is SEIU's position on the immigration issue?*

**Hudson**   We at SEIU think of ourselves as trying to build a movement that lifts people of color and the poor out of poverty. A significant chunk of the poor people in the country are immigrants of color from various parts of the world. We can't figure out how to deal with poverty and race unless we figure out a way to deal with the issues around immigration.

*How would you compare immigration today with the waves of immigrants of the past?*

**Hudson**   This wave is significantly of color, and it is coming from the Third World—not from Europe. It's coming from Central and South America. It's coming from the Caribbean. It's coming from Asia. It's coming from parts of the world that traditionally have been excluded from other immigration policies designed to let folks in.

*Are immigrants a threat to vulnerable African American workers? Do immigrants depress wages?*

**Hudson**   To the extent to which there's unemployment inside of the Black community, almost anybody who comes in is going to be some sort of a threat. But the question is, who is the threat coming from? It's not coming from the immigrants. It's coming from the people who hire them. At the moment, employers can hire an immigrant to undercut other people's labor standards. The way to handle that is not to block the immigrants from coming in. The way to deal with it is for African Americans and immigrants to team up to try to make sure that they have the right to advocate for the best possible wages for the labor that they provide.

We're stronger in some relationship with each other rather than battling for crumbs. I think that it's going to take something on the part of both Black leadership and Latino leadership to reimagine how to get poor people of color together to organize for power and against their own poverty as well as to promote racial equality.

*Forty or 50 years ago, the labor movement was essentially anti-immigrant. Why has the labor movement embraced immigrant workers in recent decades?*

**Hudson** Some of us who have always been against the way people of color—immigrants and otherwise—have been dealt with in the labor movement have tried to force a different conversation about immigrants. A large number of the folks who make up the workforce in the service industry, for example, are immigrants. So if we were going to agitate on behalf of our own membership, we had to change.

*How should Congress frame legislation to deal with immigration?*

**Hudson** I think that immigrants should be legalized and afforded a path to citizenship. And for those who are here, we should try to figure out a way to allow them to reunite with their families. I would set realistic limits on future flow. I'm not sure what that is. I'm certainly not interested in saying the policy should be disproportionately aimed at Latinos and nobody from the Caribbean or Africa. Immigration is a bigger problem than just Latinos.

*What do you think the consequences are if we don't solve this in an equitable way?*

**Hudson** I think that you will continue to have huge numbers of illegal immigrants come to this country with employers committed to continuing some of the ugliest forms of exploitation of those workers.

## Ronald Walters, U. of Maryland

*CRISIS Why is there such a national furor over immigration now?*

**Walters** The voices of undocumented workers have been relatively silent. When President George W. Bush proposed his guest worker plan, conservative congressional Republicans countered with a draconian measure that would make felons of immigrants for being undocumented. In response, a critical mass of the immigrant community, mostly Latinos, became political and began to mobilize around this issue. They're now forcing demands for legalization of their status, the right to work and human rights.

*Are immigrants a threat to the economic security of African Americans?*

**Walters** That's a legitimate concern. There are studies that show half of Black males were unemployed in cities like New York and Milwaukee. According to a study that appeared in *USA Today*, the fastest growing segment of the economic recovery has been among low-wage jobs for which Black and Latino workers compete. This is especially true in the restaurant and construction industries. An increase in the number of low-wage jobs has a depressive effect on wages overall. Another *USA Today* study shows that the hourly wage of jobs in [the majority of] low-wage industries declined.

*Are there other factors that have had an impact on African Americans?*

**Walters** I wouldn't argue that immigration was the whole ball of wax. We have to talk about globalization and the outsourcing of American jobs. There isn't any question that we are suffering competition from two directions—indirectly from the global market and directly from immigrants. We also have to consider the decline of the industrial sector of the economy. Since 2001, the U.S. economy has lost nearly 3 million industrial jobs.

*Does the African American community benefit from immigration?*

**Walters** Immigrants contribute to economic growth and they keep the prices of goods down. That's an ironic effect of their expansion of the low-wage labor sector. They purchase cheap goods which helps keep prices down for everybody. This is especially beneficial to low-income African Americans.

*Do you see areas of cooperation between the Black and immigrant communities?*

**Walters** The Voting Rights Act is a big one. Studies show that Hispanics have been able to take advantage of the language provisions [which state that ballots and instructions must be available in a variety of languages]. They have been a part of the civil rights coalition for a long time. African Americans have worked with Cesar Chavez as far as back as 1972, when he began the lettuce boycotts designed to raise wages and provide some protections for Hispanic agricultural workers. That was when Chavez was putting together the United Farm Workers organization. I was with Jesse Jackson in 1984 when he marched in South Texas with 2,000 Hispanic agricultural workers to secure healthcare and human rights.

African Americans and Hispanics have identical interests politically in making and maintaining what I call a respectful political coalition. What I mean by that is that we legitimize each other's issues. Hispanic workers ought to fight with us to raise wages in this country, and that should be a common agenda.

Also in the area of coalitions, immigrants have a responsibility to join labor unions. They can't just work for anything and not seek to get unionized. It's the same argument that the NAACP applied to Black workers who were coming up to the North as strike breakers in the 1920s. The NAACP said the future of Blacks is in the labor movement, and so you ought to become unionized with White workers, then both of you can have a raise in wages. That's what happened then. That's what ought to happen today.

# Bruce S. Gordon, NAACP

*CRISIS   As the leader of the nation's oldest civil rights organization, how do you view the immigration issue?*

*Gordon*   It is suggested by some that the employment conditions affecting Blacks are substantially damaged by the presence of more Hispanics in this country. And I would suggest that we not fall into that trap. We have dealt with and faced employment disparities in this country for years. Those disparities, whether they are unemployment rates or household income disparities, have preceded the current discussion around immigration.

*Do you see immigration as a civil rights issue?*

*Gordon*   It is certainly a human rights issue. I think that people in this country should have an equal opportunity to compete for a decent job and decent wages. And that I do view as a civil rights issue.

*Do you see parallels between the massive protests against the House immigration reform bill, HR 4437, and the civil rights marches of the 1960s?*

*Gordon*   I think the people in this country who are disadvantaged; who don't have economic resources; don't have control over the media; don't have control over state or federal legislative bodies, have to use whatever means available to them to express themselves. In the 1950s and 1960s, we found that mobilization, agitation and protest were ways to make ourselves heard and exert pressure on the system. I think that the rallies that we've seen around immigration certainly are taking a page out of that book.

*Should undocumented immigrants be perceived as felons?*

*Gordon*   For years, this country has opened its arms and said, "Give me your tired, your poor, your huddled masses yearning to breathe free." There are people around the globe who have taken us at our word and have come to take advantage of what the American dream offers.

At the end of the day, people want to have the ability to care for their families—to feed, clothe and educate them and to do whatever is in their power to provide the highest quality of life available. That's what Black folks have wanted to do in this country since the moment we came here.

That's what Hispanics in this country want to do today. They want a piece of the dream.

*What do you think that Black and Latino leaders can do to build coalitions around their mutual concerns?*

**Gordon**   We need to focus on where our agendas intersect. And that only comes from open and candid two-way communication. I have worked closely with the National Council of La Raza and the Mexican American Legal Defense and Educational Fund in protesting two [of Bush's] recent Supreme Court Justice nominees. LULAC [the League of United Latin American Citizens) is another important ally of ours.

*You mentioned the fight over judges. Are there other areas where you can see opportunities for cooperation?*

**Gordon**   I think we could pool our resources to deal with the criminal justice system, racial profiling, disparate convictions and incarceration rates—every major social concern, whether it's healthcare or education—poor people have many issues in common. And the probability of being poor is higher if you are African American or Hispanic.

*How does immigration fit into the overall issue of race in America?*

**Gordon**   We should be thinking about it in terms of a multiracial, multicultural country. Some in this country are still trying to keep people of color out. This is a country whose model has worked. And I think America is strong because of the diversity of its population.

# Sheila Jackson Lee, U.S. Congress

**CRISIS**   *How would you describe America's immigration policy?*

**Jackson Lee**   It's broken. It is an unequal and unfair system.

*You represent a diverse congressional district. What does this issue look like on the ground in Houston?*

**Jackson Lee**   We live with the immigration issue. My district includes not only Hispanics from Mexico, but also from Central and South America. It includes a wide range of other immigrants, Jamaicans for example, and other people from the Caribbean. The largest Nigerian population in the nation is in Houston. We have large Indo-American and Pakistani communities. But we view all of them as our neighbors.

*Is that the way all Americans should view immigrants, as neighbors?*

*Jackson Lee*  There still are problems, of course. The fact that African Americans are made to compete for some lower-paying jobs certainly gives the appearance that the single biggest problem has to be the undocumented immigrants. The key questions that rage across all communities when it comes to immigration are: What will I lose out on, and what do I get in return if this road to citizenship through earned access to legalization becomes a reality?

*How should the United States address those questions?*

*Jackson Lee*  You acknowledge the equality of work. You ensure that there is a fair minimum wage that all workers are paid so that no employer can undermine the value of a worker by suggesting that they will hire someone who is undocumented they can pay less. And you must confront the issue of unemployment, which is raging in America, especially in certain African American communities. You invest in education and job training programs that work. And you wage major job preservation and job creation efforts. Fix the employment and wage opportunity issues and I believe you can fix the immigration problem.

*What should national policy be toward undocumented immigrants inside U.S. borders?*

*Jackson Lee*  My Save America Comprehensive Immigration bill would provide for earned access to legalization—and I emphasize the word "earned"—not amnesty. It means get in line, learn the language, do community service, pay fines and wait for five or six years. Ultimately, you may not make it. If you meet the criteria, we will consider giving you legal permanent resident status, which then allows you to get on the pathway to citizenship.

    The bill would include opportunities for people to go to college if they are in high school. We tried to address the situation of individuals who've got children and [spouses] here who are on the verge of being deported. That is a big problem among Africans who are usually high on the list for deportation.

*Massive street protests were aimed at the House-passed immigration reform bill HR 4437 sponsored by Rep. James Sensenbrenner (R-Wisc.). What's your take on the bill?*

*Jackson Lee*  When the U.S. House of Representatives passes a bill that makes felons out of people who simply want to come to America for an opportunity for a better life, it's an outrage. Some of this has to do with persecution. Why don't Haitians get the same treatment as Cubans? We have previously asked for relief for the Liberians. The Sudanese are fleeing absolute persecution. If you went to most African Americans and asked them about these immigrants, they wouldn't deny them the right to come into this country.

It would take 200,000 buses to deport these 12 million undocumented immigrants and billions of dollars, which could be utilized for historically Black colleges and invested in Pell grants and job creation. I spent time in my city's high schools trying to calm down youngsters who believe that their mothers and fathers will be deported. Securing the border makes a lot of sense, but making felons out of economic immigrants is ridiculous.

*There are loud calls from certain quarters to secure U.S. borders.*

*Jackson Lee*   I'm not here to suggest that immigration should be without restraints. Six years ago, I started discussing the idea of reinforcing the border with more Border Patrol agents, more power boats, more night vision goggles and more computers. If we had done that then we wouldn't be in the predicament we are today. We would have at least been able to stem the flow of immigration, because we would have more trained personnel on the border, including the [Canadian] border, which everyone is ignoring.

# POSTSCRIPT

## Does Latino Immigration Threaten African American Workers?

**D**espite the current controversy over immigration policy, it appears that Latino emigration to the United States will continue. Latinos are expected soon to comprise 25 percent of the U.S. population. It is likely therefore that there will be some competition between Latino immigrant workers and African Americans in certain labor markets, especially among low and unskilled jobs. However, African American leaders are not willing to blame Latino workers for the economic woes of blacks. These black elites contend that black workers are facing fundamental economic inequities that pre-date this recent Latino immigration trend, and on which these migrants have little or no influence. With the above as preface, one can expect that the debate over this issue will continue unabated.

For a historical perspective, *Mexican Workers and American Dreams Immigration, Repatriation, and California Farm Labor, 1900–1939* (Rutgers University Press, 2004) by Camille Guerin-Gonzales, suggests that immigrant Mexican workers were tolerated as long as there was enough work to go around. However, during the Great Depression, white American sentiment turned against the Mexicans and demanded they return to Mexico. *Crossing the Border: Research from the Mexican Migration Project* (Russell Sage Foundation, 2004), edited by Jorge Durand and Douglas S. Massey, discusses Mexican migration to the United States.

For an overview of Latino labor in the United States, see *Latino Labor Report, 2004: More Jobs for New Immigrants but at Lower Wages* (Pew Hispanic Center) by Rakesh Kochhar. Recently arrived Latinos are an increasing source of labor for low-wage jobs. Interesting selections dealing with this topic include: Stephen Steinberg, "Immigration, African Americans, and Race Discourse" (*New Politics*, vol X, no. 3), and Jack Miles, "Blacks vs. Browns," *Atlantic Monthly* (October 1992). Also, *Help or Hindrance? The Economic Implications of Immigration for African Americans*, edited by Daniel S. Hamermesh and Frank D. Bean (Russell Sage Foundation, 1998), and Steven Shulman and Robert C. Smith, "Immigration and African Americans," in Cecilia A. Conrad, et al., eds., *African Americans in the U.S. Economy* (Lanham, MD: Rowman & Littlefield, 2005).

Additional reading to assess immigrant Latino labor can be found in *Latino Workers in the Contemporary South* (University of Georgia Press, 2001) by Arthur D. Murphy, Colleen Blanchard, and Jennifer A. Hill.

# ISSUE 18

## Should Race Be Included Among the Many Factors Considered for Admission to Selective Colleges?

**YES: William G. Bowen and Neil L. Rudenstine,** from "Race-Sensitive Admissions: Back to Basics," *The Chronicle of Higher Education* (February 7, 2003)

**NO: Roger Clegg,** from "Time Has Not Favored Racial Preferences," *The Chronicle of Higher Education* (January 14, 2005)

### ISSUE SUMMARY

**YES:** William G. Bowen, former president of Princeton University, and Neil L. Rudenstine, former president of Harvard University, make the case for race-sensitive admissions in higher education. With a focus on selective colleges, they cite empirical data that demonstrate the success of beneficiaries of race-sensitive admission policies. In their opinion, both public and private selective colleges should continue such policies.

**NO:** Roger Clegg, general counsel of the Center for Equal Opportunity in Sterling, Virginia and contributor to *The Chronicle of Higher Education,* argues that universities should put racial groupings aside and give "individualized consideration" to all applicants. His center serves as a place where students can file complaints about illegal racially approved programs.

$\mathbf{A}$mong the many issues considered in this edition of *Taking Sides,* that of college admissions may be the most interesting for students. The highly competitive quest to gain admission to the college of one's choice is perhaps the most important decision high school seniors have to face. Hence, the intense focus on the process of selection to elite colleges and universities. Annual college ratings and long-standing reputations weigh heavily on college-bound seniors. In this context alone, admissions policies face scrutiny from potential applicants. This scrutiny has illuminated the issue of race in college admissions.

Recalling Supreme Court decisions including *Bakke, Milligan,* and most recently, *Bollinger,* race remains a factor—among many others—to be considered in admissions, and debated in the early part of the twenty-first century.

The position of William G. Bowen and Neil L. Rudenstine, both of whom have spent many years in higher education at two of America's most selective colleges, is that race-sensitive admissions policies are both necessary and good. Behind their position is the argument that race matters profoundly in America. To consider race as "just another" dimension of diversity is to trivialize the African American experience and to diminish American history. The aftermath of this history is "to place racial minorities in situations in which embedded perceptions and stereotypes limit opportunities and create divides that demean us all." In effect, they recognize the persistence of race prejudice and racism. Thus, institutional racism along with subtle and complex stereotyping exists in ways that belie the notion of equality.

Bowen and Rudenstine incorporate data from *The Shape of the River: Long Term Consequences of Considering Race in College and University Admissions,* written by Bowen and Derek Bok, which demonstrates the success of race-preference programs. They address the "reverse discrimination" claim often advanced by some whites. Merely to proclaim that a school is an affirmative action institution does not insure admission to an elite college to a reasonably qualified minority. The research of Bowen and Bok tells us that among the elite colleges they studied, "a very considerable number of high-scoring minority students were turned down." For example, they cite, "At the very top of the SAT distribution (in the 1400-plus range), nearly two out of five [minority applicants] were not admitted." One should note the recent (July 2006) report on National Public Radio of African American students with SAT scores of 1400 and over who were denied admission to the University of California at Los Angeles, a selective public university.

Roger Clegg is a lawyer and head of an organization that is opposed to hiring preferences for minorities and women. He claims that such programs are in fundamental violation of Title 7 of the 1964 Civil Rights Act, which was designed to promote equal employment opportunities. Clegg embraces the criticism of affirmative action programs for allegedly hiring less than the best qualified for the positions available in higher education. To Clegg, affirmative action programs to date have represented "affirmative discrimination."

# YES

**William G. Bowen and
Neil L. Rudenstine**

# Race-Sensitive Admissions: Back to Basics

The controversy (and confusion) surrounding the White House's recent statements on the use of race in college and university admissions indicate the need for careful examination of the underlying issues. The Justice Department has filed a brief with the U.S. Supreme Court urging it to declare two race-sensitive policies at the University of Michigan unconstitutional; however, the brief does not rule out ever taking race into account, but argues that institutions should first exhaust all "race-neutral" alternatives. Secretary of State Colin Powell has publicly said that he supports not just affirmative action, but also the Michigan policies. National Security Advisor Condoleezza Rice says she opposes the specific methods used by Michigan, but recognizes the need to take race into account in admissions.

As the Supreme Court prepares to hear oral arguments in a case that will shape college admissions processes in the coming decades, those of us who believe that such processes should be permitted to include a nuanced consideration of race must speak out clearly as well as forcefully. Too often, we fear, the key issues have been oversimplified or overlooked. Having been personally involved with this highly contentious subject for more than 30 years, we would like to try to frame the discussion by offering a set of nine connected propositions about race and admissions that derive from core human values and substantial empirical research.

1. The twin goals served by race-sensitive admissions remain critically important.

The debate over race-sensitive admissions has relevance only at public and private institutions of higher education that have to choose among considerably more qualified candidates than they can admit. Essentially all of these "academically selective" colleges and universities have elected to take race into account in making admissions decisions, a fact that, in itself, has considerable import. Race-sensitive admissions programs are intended to serve two important purposes:

- To enrich the learning environment by giving *all* students the opportunity to share perspectives and exchange points of view with classmates from varied backgrounds. The recognition of the educational power of diversity led many colleges and universities—well before the mid-1960s, when the term affirmative action began to be used—to craft incoming classes that included students representing a wide variety of interests, talents, backgrounds, and perspectives. *The Shape of the River,* written by William G. Bowen and Derek Bok, provides abundant evidence that graduates of these institutions value educational diversity and, in general, are strong supporters of race-sensitive admissions. Survey responses from more than 90,000 alumni of selective colleges and universities show that nearly 80 percent of those who enrolled in 1976 and 1989 felt that their alma mater placed the right amount of emphasis—or not enough—on diversity in the admissions process. That same survey also found that there is much more interaction across racial lines than many people suppose. In the 1989 entering cohort, 56 percent of white matriculants and 88 percent of black matriculants indicated that they "knew well" two or more classmates of the other race.

- To serve the needs of the professions, of business, of government, and of society more generally by educating larger numbers of well-prepared minority students who can assume positions of leadership—thereby reducing somewhat the continuing disparity in access to power and responsibility that is related to race in America. Since colonial days, colleges and universities have accepted an obligation to educate individuals who will play leadership roles in society. Today, that requires taking account of the clearly articulated needs of business and the professions for a healthier mix of well-educated leaders and practitioners from varied racial and ethnic backgrounds. Professional groups like the American Bar Association and the American Medical Association, and businesses like General Motors, Microsoft, and American Airlines (among many others), have explicitly endorsed affirmative-action policies in higher education. Leading law firms, hospitals, and businesses depend heavily on their ability to recruit broadly trained individuals from many racial backgrounds who are able to perform at the highest level in settings that are themselves increasingly diverse. A prohibition on the consideration of race in admissions would drastically reduce minority participation in the most selective professional programs. Does it make any sense to resegregate, de facto, many of the country's most respected professional schools and to slow the progress that has been made in achieving diversity within the professions? We don't think so.

2. Private colleges and universities are as likely as their public counterparts to be affected by the outcome of this debate.

The fact that litigation over affirmative action has, thus far, centered on public universities should not lead us to believe that private institutions will be unaffected. The 1996 federal-court ruling in *Hopwood v. Texas,* banning race-sensitive admissions policies in Texas, Louisiana, and Mississippi, has been understood to cover Rice University as well as public universities such as the University of Texas, Title VI of the Civil Rights Act of 1964 subjects all institutions that receive federal funds to any court determinations as to what constitutes "discrimination." Because many private colleges and universities have invested substantial resources in creating diverse entering classes, they might well be *more* dramatically affected by any limitation on their freedom to consider race than would most public institutions. That is especially true because they are, in general, smaller and more selective in admissions than their public counterparts.

It matters that minority applicants have access to the most selective programs, at both undergraduate and graduate levels, in both private and public institutions. The argument that they will surely be able to "get in somewhere" rings hollow to many people. As one black woman quoted in *The Shape of the River* observed wryly to a white parent: "Are you telling me that all those white folks fighting so hard to get their kids into Duke and Stanford are just ignorant? Or are we supposed to believe that attending a top-ranked school is important for their children but not for mine?" That interchange was not just about perceptions. Various studies show that the short-term and long-term gains associated with attending the most selective institutions are, if anything, greater for minority students than for white students, and that academic and other resources are concentrated increasingly in the top tier colleges and universities.

> 3. Race-sensitive admissions policies involve much "picking and choosing" among individual applicants; they need not be mechanical, are not quota systems, and involve making bets about likely student contributions to campus life and, subsequently, to the larger society.

Contrary to what some people believe, admissions decisions at academically selective public and private colleges and universities are much more than a "numbers game." They involve considerations that extend far beyond test scores and GPAs. Analysis of new data from leading private research universities for the undergraduate class entering in 1999 (reported in the forthcoming *Reclaiming the Game,* by William G. Bowen and Sarah A. Levin) indicates that a very considerable number of high-scoring minority students were turned down. For instance, among male minority applicants with combined SAT scores in the 1200 to 1299 range (which put them well within the top 10 percent of minority test-takers and the top 20 percent of all test-takers, regardless of race), the odds of admission were about 35 percent: That is, roughly two out of three of these minority applicants were denied admission. At the very top of the SAT distribution (in the 1400-plus range), nearly two out of five were *not* admitted. Public universities are larger and somewhat less selective, but they also turn down very high-scoring minority candidates. At two public universities for which detailed data are available, one out of four minority candidates in the 1200 to 1399 SAT range was rejected.

In short, admissions officers at both private and public universities have been doing exactly what Justice Powell, in the landmark 1978 decision.

*Regents of the University of California v. Bakke,* said that they should be allowed to do: pursuing "race-sensitive" admissions policies that entail considering race among other factors. They have been weighing considerations that are both objective (advanced-placement courses taken in high school, for example) and subjective (indications of drive, intellectual curiosity, leadership ability, and so on). And they have been selecting very well. According to all the available evidence, minority students admitted to academically selective colleges and universities as long ago as the mid-1970s have been shown to be successful in completing rigorous graduate programs, doing well in the marketplace, and, most notably, contributing in the civic arena out of all proportion to their numbers.

Minority candidates are, of course, by no means the only group of applicants to receive special consideration. Colleges and universities have long paid special attention to children of alumni, to "development cases," to applicants who come from poor families or who have otherwise overcome special obstacles, to applicants who will add to the geographic (including international) diversity of the student body, to students with special talents in fields such as music, and, especially in recent years, to athletes. Some readers may be surprised to learn from *Reclaiming the Game* that recruited athletes at many selective colleges are far more advantaged in the admissions process (that is, are much more likely to be admitted at a given SAT level) than are minority candidates.

A related topic deserves some emphasis, and that is the issue of "quotas." There is not space here to discuss the subject in detail, but one point is important to clarify. The fact that the percentage of minority students in many colleges and universities does not fluctuate substantially from year to year is in no sense prima facie evidence that quotas are being used. Anyone familiar with admissions processes—and with their basic statistics— knows that percentages for virtually all subgroups of any reasonable size are remarkably consistent from year to year. That is because the size of the college going population does not change significantly on an annual basis, nor do the number and quality of secondary schools from which institutions draw applications, nor does the number of qualified candidates. All of these numbers are very stable, and it is therefore not at all surprising that incoming college classes should change very little in their composition from year to year. (For example, we suspect that the fraction of an entering class wearing eyeglasses is remarkably consistent from year to year, but that would hardly persuade us that an eyeglass quota is being imposed.)

4. Selectivity and "merit" involve predictions about on-campus learning environments and future contributions to society.

One of the most common misconceptions is that candidates who have scored above some level or earned a certain grade-point average "deserve" a place in an academically selective institution. That "entitlement" notion is squarely at odds with the fundamental principle that, in choosing among a large number of well-qualified applicants, all of whom are over a high threshold, colleges and universities are making bets on the future, not giving rewards for prior accomplishments. Institutions are meant to take well-considered risks. That can involve turning down candidate "A" (who is entirely admissible but does not stand out in any particular way) in favor of candidate "B" (who is expected to contribute more to the educational milieu of the institution and appears to have better long-term prospects of making a major contribution to society). All applicants, of course, deserve to be evaluated fairly, which means treating them the same way as other similarly situated candidates; but, in the words of Lee Bollinger, president of Columbia University and former president of the University of Michigan, "there is no right to be admitted to a university without regard to how the overall makeup of the student body will affect the educational process or without regard to the needs of the society. . . ." "Merit" is not a simple concept. It has certainly never meant admitting all the valedictorians who apply, or choosing students strictly on the basis of test scores and GPAs.

An elaborate admissions process, which focuses on the particular characteristics of individuals within many subgroups—and on those of the entire pool of applicants—is designed to craft a class that will, in its diversity, be a potent source of educational vitality. Colleges use a variety of procedures to take account of race, and it is essential that differences of opinion concerning the wisdom (or even the legality) of any single approach not lead to an outcome that precludes other approaches.

5. Paying special attention to any group in making admissions decisions entails costs; but the costs of race-sensitive admissions have been modest and well-justified by the benefits.

The "opportunity cost" of admitting any particular student is that another applicant will not be chosen. But such choices are rarely "head-to-head" decisions. For example, there is no reason to believe—as reverse-discrimination lawsuits generally assume—that if a particular minority student had not been accepted, his or her place would have been given to a complainant with comparable or better test scores or grades. The choice might, instead, have been an even higher-scoring minority student who had not been admitted, a student from a foreign country, or a lower-scoring white student from one of several subgroups that are given extra consideration in the admissions process. Making hard choices on the margin is never easy and always—fortunately—involves human judgments made by experienced admissions officers. It is, in any case, wrong to assume that race-sensitive admissions policies have significantly reduced the chances of well-qualified white students to gain admission to the most selective colleges. Findings reported in *The Shape of the River,* based on data for a subset of selective colleges and universities, demonstrate that elimination of race-sensitive policies would have increased the admission rate for white students by less than two percentage points: from roughly 25 percent to 26.5 percent.

It should be emphasized that taking race into account in making admissions decisions does *not* appear to have two kinds of costs often mentioned by critics of these policies.

- First, there is no systemic evidence that race-sensitive admissions policies tend to "harm the beneficiaries" by putting them in settings in which they are overmatched intellectually or "stigmatized" to the point that they would have been better off attending a less selective institution. On the contrary, extensive analysis of data reported in *The Shape of the River* shows that minority students at selective institutions have, over all, performed well. The more selective the institution that they attended, the more likely they were to graduate and earn advanced degrees, the happier they were with their college experience, and the more successful they were in later life.

- Second, the available evidence disposes of the argument that the substitution of "race-sensitive" for "race-neutral" admissions policies has led to admission of many minority students who are not well-suited to take advantage of the educational opportunities they are being offered. Examination of the later accomplishments of those students who would have been "retrospectively rejected" under race-neutral policies shows that they did just as well as a hypothetical reference group that might have been admitted if GPAs and test scores had been the primary criteria (which is, itself, a questionable assumption). There are no significant differences in graduation rates, advanced-degree attainment, earnings, civic contributions, or satisfactions with college. In short, the abandonment of race-sensitive admissions would not have removed from campuses a marginal group of mediocre students. Rather, it would have deprived campuses of much of their diversity and diminished the capacity of the academically selective institutions to benefit larger numbers of talented minority students.

6. Progress has been made in narrowing test-score gaps between minority students and other students, but gaps remain.

A frequently asked question is: Are we getting anywhere? Data on average test scores in *Reclaiming the Game* are encouraging. At a group of liberal-arts colleges and universities examined in 1976 and 1995, average combined SAT test scores for minority students rose roughly 130 points at the liberal-arts colleges and roughly 150 points at the research universities. Test scores for other students rose, too, but by much smaller amounts (roughly 30 points at the liberal-arts colleges and roughly 70 points at the research universities). Test-score gaps narrowed over this period, and the average rank-in-class of minority students on college graduation improved even more than one would have predicted on the basis of test scores alone. As anyone who has studied campus life can attest, there are also many impressionistic signs of progress. Minority students are more involved in a wide range of activities, and increasing numbers of children of minority students of an earlier day are now reaching the age where they are beginning to enroll as "second generation" college students. Graduates are also increasingly making their presence known in the professions and business world.

Still, test-score gaps remain (of roughly 100 to 140 points in the private colleges and universities for which we have data), and so there is still more progress to be made. That is hardly surprising, given the deep-seated nature of the factors that impede academic opportunity and achievement among minority groups—including the fact that a very large proportion of such students continue to attend primary and secondary schools that are underfinanced, insufficiently challenging, and often segregated. It would be naive to expect that a problem as long in the making as the racial divide in educational preparation could be eradicated in a generation or two.

7. There are alternative ways of pursuing diversity, but all substitutes for race-sensitive admissions have serious limitations.

Many of us have a strong appetite for apparently painless alternatives, and it is natural to look for ways to achieve "diversity" without directly confronting the emotion-laden issue of race. Several alternatives to race-sensitive admissions have been suggested. For example, colleges and universities have been urged to:

- Focus on the economically disadvantaged. The argument is that, since racial minorities are especially likely to be poor, racial diversity could be promoted in this way (an approach sometimes referred to as "classbased affirmative action"). The results, however, would not be what some people might expect. Several studies have shown that there are simply very few minority candidates for admission to academically selective institutions who are *both* poor and academically qualified.
- Adopt a "percentage plan" whereby all high-school students in a state who graduate in the top X percent of their classes are automatically guaranteed a place in one of the state's universities. In states like Texas, where the secondary-school system is highly segregated, that approach can yield a significant number of minority admissions at the undergraduate level (although the actual effects, even at the undergraduate level, have been shown by the social scientists Marta Tienda and John F. Kain to be more limited than many have suggested). Moreover, the process is highly mechanical. Students in the top X percent are not simply awarded "points," as the undergraduate program at the University of Michigan does. Rather, they are given automatic admission without any prior scrutiny, and without any consideration of the fact that some high schools are much stronger academically than others.

Even if one considered the top-X-percent plan to be viable at state institutions, it could not work at all at private institutions, which admit from national and international pools of applicants and are so selective that they must turn down the vast majority who apply—including very large numbers of students who graduate at or near the top of their secondary-school classes. Private institutions could not conceivably adopt a policy that would automatically give admission to students in the top X percent of their class at the hundreds and hundreds of schools—worldwide—from which they attract applicants.

The top-X-percent plan is also entirely ineffective at the professional and graduate-school level, because (like selective undergraduate colleges) these schools have national and international applicant pools, with no conceivable "reference group" of colleges to which they could possibly give such an admission guarantee. Even if there were a set of undegraduate colleges whose top graduates would be guaranteed admission to certain professional schools, the result would not represent any marked degree of racial diversity. For example, if the top 10 percent of students in the academi-cally selective colleges and universities studied in *Reclaiming the Game* were offered admission to a professional school (an unrealistically high percent-age given the intensely competitive nature of the admissions process), only 3 percent of the students included in that group would be underrep-resented minorities—and, of course, only some modest fractions of those students would be interested even in applying to such programs. If we are examining a top-5-percent plan, the minority component of the pool would be about *one-half of 1 percent*. Without some explicit consideration of race, professional schools (and Ph.D. programs) that ordinarily admit a significant number of their students from selective colleges would simply not be able to enroll a diverse student body.

Other troubling questions include: Do we really want to endorse an admissions approach that depends on de facto segregation at the secondary-school level? Do we want to impose an arbitrary and mechanical admis-sions standard—based on fixed rank-in-class—on a process that should involve careful consideration of all of an applicant's qualifications as well as thoughtful attention to the overall characteristics of the applicant pool?

- Place heavy weight on "geographic distribution" and so-called "expe-riential" factors, such as a student's ability to overcome obstacles and handicaps of various kinds, or the experience of living in a home where a language other than English is spoken. The argu-ment here is that, if special attention were given to those and anal-ogous criteria, then a sizable pool of qualified minority students would automatically be created.

But, as we have mentioned, colleges have been using precisely such criteria for many decades, and they have discovered—not surprisingly—that there are large numbers of very competitive "majority" candidates in all of the suggested categories. For example, if a student's home language is Russian, Polish, Arabic, Korean, or Hebrew, will that be weighted by a college as strongly as Spanish? If not, then the institutions will clearly be giving conscious preference to a group of underrepresented minority students—Hispanic students—in a deliberate way that explicitly takes ethnicity (or, in other cases, race) into account.

Similar issues arise with respect to other experiential categories, as well as geographic distribution. There is no need to speculate about (or experiment with) such approaches, because colleges have already had nearly a half-century of experience applying them, and there is ample evidence that the hoped-for results, in terms of minority representation, are not what many people now suggest or claim. Moreover, insofar as such categories were to become surreptitious gateways for minority students, they would soon run the risk of breeding cynicism, and probably inviting legal challenges.

All of the indirect approaches just described pose serious problems. Nor can they be accurately described as "race-neutral." "They have all been conceived with the clear goal (whether practicable or not) of producing an appreciable representation of minority students in higher education. In some cases, they involve the conscious use of a kind of social engineering decried by critics of race-sensitive admissions.

Surely the best way to achieve racial diversity is to acknowledge candidly that minority status is one among many factors that can be considered in an admissions process designed to judge individuals on a case-by-case basis. We can see no reason why a college or university should be compelled to experiment with—and "exhaust"—all suggested alternative approaches before it can turn to a carefully tailored race-sensitive policy that focuses on individual cases. The alternative approaches are susceptible to systematic analysis, based on experience and empirical investigation. A preponderance of them have been tested for decades. All can be shown to be seriously deficient. Indeed, if genuinely race-neutral (and educationally appropriate) methods were available, colleges and universities would long ago have gladly embraced them.

8. Reasonable degrees of institutional autonomy should be permitted—accompanied by a clear expectation of accountability.

As the courts have recognized in other contexts (for example, in giving reasonable deference to administrative agencies), a balance has to be struck between Judicial protection of rights guaranteed to all of us by the Constitution and the desirability of giving a presumption of validity to the judgements of those with special knowledge, experience, and closeness to the actual decisions being made. The widely acclaimed heterogeneity of the American system of higher education has permitted much experimentation in admissions, as in other areas, and has discouraged the kinds of government-mandated uniformity that we find in many other parts of the world. Serious consideration should be given to the disadvantages of imposing too many "dos" and "don'ts" on admissions policies.

The case for allowing a considerable degree of institutional autonomy in such sensitive and complex territory is inextricably tied, in our view, to a clear acceptance by colleges and universities of accountability for the policies they elect and the ways such policies are given effect. There is, to be sure, much more accountability today than many people outside the university world recognize. Admissions practices are highly visible and are subject to challenge by faculty members, trustees and regents, avid investigative reporters, disappointed applicants, and the public at large. Colleges and universities operate in more of a "fishbowl" environment than the great majority of other private and public entities. Nonetheless, we favor even stronger commitments by colleges and universities to monitor closely how specific admissions policies work out in practice. Studies of outcomes should be a regular part of college and university operations, and if it is found, for example, that minority students (or other students) accepted with certain test scores or other qualifications are consistently doing poorly, then some change in policy—or some change in the personnel responsible for administering the stated policy—may well be in order.

That point was made with special force by a very conservative friend of ours, Charles Exley, former chairman and CEO of NCR Corporation and a onetime trustee of Wesleyan University. In a pointed conversation that one of us (Bowen) will long remember, Exley explained that he held essentially the same view that we hold concerning who should select the criteria and make admissions decisions. "I would probably not admit the same class that you would admit, even though I don't know how different the classes would be," he said. "You will certainly make mistakes," he went on, "but I would much rather live with your errors than with those that will inevitably result from the imposition of more outside constraints, including legislative and judicial interventions." And then, with the nicest smile, he concluded: "And, if you make *too* many mistakes, the trustees can always fire you!"

> 9. Race matters profoundly in America; it differs fundamentally from other "markers" of diversity, and it has to be understood on its own terms.

We believe that it is morally wrong and historically indefensible to think of race as "just another" dimension of diversity. It is a critically important dimension, but it is also far more difficult than others to address. The fundamental reason is that racial classifications were used in this country for more than 300 years in the most odious ways to deprive people of their basic rights. The fact that overt discrimination has now been outlawed should not lead us to believe that race no longer matters. As the legal scholar Ronald Dworkin has put it, "the worst of the stereotypes, suspicions, fears, and hatreds that still poison America are color-coded. . . .

The aftereffects of this long history continue to place racial minorities (and especially African-Americans) in situations in which embedded perceptions and stereotypes limit opportunities and create divides that demean us all. This social reality, described with searing precision by the economist Glenn C. Loury in *The Anatomy of Racial Inequality,* explains why persistence is required in efforts to overcome, day by day, the vestiges of our country's "unlovely racial history." We believe that it would be perverse in the extreme if, after many generations when race was used in the service of blatant discrimination, colleges and universities were now to be prevented from considering race at all, when, at last, we are learning how to use nuanced forms of race-sensitive admissions to improve education for everyone and to diminish racial disparities.

The former Attorney General Nicholas Katzenbach draws a sharp distinction between the use of race to exclude a group of people from educational opportunity ("racial discrimination") and the use of race to enhance learning for all students, thereby serving the mission of colleges and universities chartered to serve the public good. No one contends that white students are being excluded by any college or university today simply because they are white.

Roger Clegg

**NO**

# Time Has Not Favored Racial Preferences

T he end of 2004 brought plenty of news to make college officials uneasy at institutions that treat their students and applicants differently on account of their skin color or what country their ancestors came from.

At the end of November, the Office for Civil Rights at the Education Department pressured the state of Wisconsin into changing a minorities-only scholarship program to one that allows participation by students of all races. In early December, *The Chronicle* reported that the civil-rights office had also begun investigating the use of racial and ethnic admission preferences at the University of Virginia, and had pending complaints against a number of other colleges and universities. The former head of that office, Gerald A. Reynolds, was appointed the same week as the new chairman of the U.S. Commission on Civil Rights, where his skepticism about affirmative action will continue to be relevant. At about the same time, the Center for Individual Rights filed its claim for $1.2-million on behalf of nonminority applicants who were denied admission to the University of Michigan because of admissions policies that were declared illegally discriminatory in 2003 by the Supreme Court.

Then there are the November elections. They leave the Republican Party—which has clearly stated in its platform that it rejects racial preferences—firmly in charge of all three branches of the federal government.

All of which is to say: Oh, what a difference a year and half makes.

In June 2003, after the U.S. Supreme Court struck down the University of Michigan's use of racial and ethnic preferences in its undergraduate admissions in *Gratz v. Bollinger* and narrowly upheld their use in law-school admissions in *Grutter v. Bollinger,* the mood of the pro-preference forces was unreservedly euphoric. They had, indeed, dodged a bullet. The anti-preference groups had thought a court decision banning affirmative action in college admissions was likely, but it didn't happen, and the preference supporters felt like winners.

Yet the law, in fact, has not improved for them. To the contrary: Except in the three states making up the federal Fifth Circuit—Louisiana, Mississippi, and Texas—where the court of appeals has banned preferences outright, the law is actually now a little tougher on preferences than it was

From *The Chronicle of Higher Education*, January 14, 2005, pp. B10-B11. Copyright © 2005 by Roger Clegg. Reprinted by permission of the author.

when colleges and universities could claim Justice Lewis F. Powell Jr.'s 1978 opinion in *Regents of the University of California v. Bakke* as their guide. Not only have preferences been struck down in *Gratz*, but in *Grutter* the court established new rules for determining when the use of preferences is "narrowly tailored."

To be sure, neither *Gratz* nor *Grutter* is a marvel of clarity, and if the federal agencies enforcing them were willing to ignore their limitations on preferences, perhaps the legal landscape would be more hospitable to them. But that hasn't happened—nor is it likely to.

Republican control of not only the executive branch, but both houses of Congress, makes it impossible for preferences to receive any shoring up from the political branches—even if the Democrats were inclined to make that a priority, which they aren't. Democratic politicians have concluded that racial preferences are not a winning issue for them. Indeed, their erstwhile standard-bearer, Sen. John Kerry, stated his own misgivings about them earlier in his career, before his base jerked him back into line.

The judiciary, meanwhile, is going to become more and more conservative as President Bush makes more and more appointments. What's more, one of the key ways that a conservative judge can be distinguished from a liberal one is his or her stance on racial preferences. *Gratz* and *Grutter* contain plenty of language that judges who are so inclined can cite in limiting the use of preferences. Nor will they feel guilty or "activist" in doing so, given the clear language banning preferences in Title VI of the Civil Rights Act of 1964, and the lack of any footnote to the Constitution's Equal Protection Clause saying that some races are more equal than others.

So there is every indication that the powers-that-be in charge of all three branches of the federal government are unlikely to come to the rescue of racial preferences if the pressure is kept on them. And there is every indication that the pressure will be kept on, even increased.

The civil-rights office of the Education Department has demonstrated that it takes seriously the requirement in *Grutter* that admissions preferences be prohibited in circumstances where diversity is attainable by race-neutral means. It has published and is continuing to publish materials elaborating on those means. Likewise, it has stated that it views racially exclusive scholarships, internships, summer programs, and the like as "extremely difficult to defend." It has pressured individual colleges and, most recently, the state of Wisconsin to open up such programs to students of all colors. The Justice Department's Civil-Rights Division—headed by R. Alexander Acosta, who is no friend of affirmative action—has recently begun to investigate such programs itself, and it had pushed (unsuccessfully) a brief categorically rejecting admissions preferences in the *Grutter* and *Gratz* cases.

Organizations outside the federal government are being even more aggressive. My own Center for Equal Opportunity has contacted well over a hundred colleges about illegal faculty discrimination and racially exclusive programs for students. We have filed complaints in some of those cases with the Office for Civil Rights, and have now also begun bringing such cases—where they involve state institutions—to the attention of the

Justice Department. Significantly, the overwhelming majority of colleges that we have contacted—Carnegie Mellon University, Harvard University, Indiana University, the Massachusetts Institute of Technology, Northwestern University, Princeton University, the University of Illinois at Urbana-Champaign, Williams College, Yale University, and dozens of others—have opened up racially exclusive programs to all students, regardless of race. That, in turn, makes it much more difficult for other institutions to claim any necessity for their programs' racial exclusivity.

Meanwhile, the National Association of Scholars has systematically sent out freedom-of-information requests to dozens of state universities to determine whether they are using racial and ethnic preferences—particularly in admissions—and, if so, whether the manner in which they do so is within the constraints set out by the Supreme Court in the University of Michigan cases.

The association's efforts have had two important results. First, they have put colleges and universities on notice that they will not be able to keep their use of preferences secret and that they run the risk of legal challenge if their preferences are not carefully limited. Recently, for instance, the Virginia Association of Scholars—a state affiliate of the NAS—released a study based on data it obtained from North Carolina State University, the University of Virginia, and the College of William and Mary's law school, concluding that all three institutions weighed race and ethnicity heavily in their admission decisions.

That information was passed along to the Center for Individual Rights—the same organization that had sued not only the University of Michigan but also the University of Texas and University of Washington law schools—and my organization, which already had pending Title VI complaints with the Education Department's civil-rights office against North Carolina State University and William and Mary's law school. And, as it happens, a complaint against UVa, filed by the parent of a rejected student, is already being investigated by the civil-rights office.

The more that the use of preferences is made public, the less prevalent they will be. Even those who support preferences are hard-pressed to explain what right colleges—especially taxpayer-supported ones—have to keep their use secret. Peter N. Kirsanow, of the U.S. Commission on Civil Rights, has already sent information requests to colleges about the role that race plays in their admissions policies and procedures. The chairman of the commission at the time, Mary Frances Berry, who opposed the requests, is being replaced by the conservative Reynolds. So higher-education institutions may soon face commission subpoenas for admissions information.

The other important result of the National Association of Scholar's freedom-of-information requests is their revelation that many perfectly fine undergraduate institutions do not use racial and ethnic preferences (19 of the 66 schools that the association has so far contacted, or 29 percent). Here again, the more colleges and universities that show they can thrive without preferences, the harder it is for other institutions to claim a necessity for such discrimination.

The responses to the association's document requests indicate that public universities in states like Arizona, Connecticut, Iowa, Kentucky, and North Carolina are eschewing preferences. Added to that list are the public colleges and universities in California, Washington, and Florida, where by law preferences have been ended statewide. And we must also add the public and private institutions in the federal Fifth Circuit—Texas, Louisiana, and Mississippi—and the University of Georgia, because they had for years used, and in some cases are still using, no preferences in light of judicial decisions there. Clearly, colleges can prosper without preferences.

In 2006 the University of Michigan—and the other public universities in the state—may be added to the list as well. After a shaky start, the Michigan Civil Rights Initiative, led by Ward Connerly, has gathered more than half of the necessary signatures and will probably be on the ballot in less than two years.

The continuing decline of preferences and their lack of political support demonstrate that treating students differently on the basis of their race or ethnicity is unpopular among the vast majority of Americans—and for good reason. The use of preferences has undeniable costs: It is personally unfair, passes over better qualified students, and sets a disturbing legal, political, and moral precedent in allowing racial discrimination. It involves states and colleges in unsavory activities like deciding which racial and ethnic minority groups will be favored and which ones not, and how much blood is needed to establish group membership. It stigmatizes the so-called beneficiaries, reinforcing old stereotypes of black intellectual inferiority. It fosters a victim mind-set, removes the incentive for academic excellence, and encourages separatism. It compromises the academic mission of the university, creates pressure to discriminate in grading and graduation, and lowers the overall academic quality of the student body. It mismatches students and institutions, guaranteeing failure for many of the former. And it sweeps under the rug the real social problems of the poor academic performance of so many African-American and Latino students.

And what of the benefits? Many people have doubted all along the crucial assumption underlying preferences: that, by providing acceptance to more selective institutions, they ensure a better future for the beneficiaries. And now growing empirical evidence suggests that, indeed, preferences are actually *hurting* the people they were supposed to be helping.

The most dramatic example is the research by Richard H. Sander, professor of law at the University of California at Los Angeles, recently published in the *Stanford Law Review* that finds that, by mismatching students with law schools, the use of preferences results in fewer black lawyers than there would be otherwise. His findings are in line with other work; for example, in *Increasing Faculty Diversity* (Harvard University Press, 2003), Stephen Cole and Elinor Barber found that preferences have resulted in lower grades and thus fewer academic careers by those minority groups supposedly being helped.

Preferences are at bay, then, not only because of their legal and political vulnerability, but because a consensus is growing among even one-time supporters that they just don't make sense anymore and need to be recast.

The rationales behind affirmative action have generally been, after all, either that some people deserve special help because of past injustice, or that some people have special outlooks and experiences that will add something important to the campus mix. But colleges are now giving preferences not to slaves, not to former slaves, not to people who were even alive during the Jim Crow era, but to young men and women born in the latter part of the 1980s. That is not to say that those young people may not have faced discrimination. Undoubtedly they did—albeit much less than their parents or grandparents did—but it no longer makes sense to assume that, say, *all* African-American people and *only* African-American people can have suffered disadvantages in life or that they and only they can add diversity.

Rather, we should put racial groupings aside and give individualized consideration. Nice phrase, "individualized consideration"—the linchpin, by the way, of the Supreme Court's command in *Gratz* and *Grutter* to college admission offices.

# POSTSCRIPT

## Should Race Be Included Among the Many Factors Considered for Admission to Selective Colleges?

**W**hen we reduce the admissions issue to "well, if it comes down to the admissions committee having to choose between a white student and a black student with identical records, then the black student will be admitted," we lose sight of the larger picture of race-sensitive admissions. That picture is best understood in light of all preferences. Colleges and universities "select" students based on many criteria to insure a diverse student body. Both white parents and minority parents want the best opportunities for their children. Clearly, race has become a contentious college admissions issue for whites. Historically, it has been an issue of exclusion for blacks. Whites have now been forced to examine an advantage previously taken for granted. That privilege was not examined before affirmative action programs.

Preferential treatment in college admissions is not limited to racial minorities. Indeed, there is a long history of preference for children of alumni ("legacies") and athletes. The selection process of qualified applicants leads many colleges to admit lesser-qualified men (at former woman's schools), and lesser-qualified women at traditionally men's colleges. A recent *Princeton Review Guide to the 331 Best Colleges (2006 edition)* makes reference to a selective college known for engineering, "Underrepresented minorities and women are high on the list of desirables in the applicant pool here, and go through the admissions process without any hitches if reasonably well qualified." Clearly middle-class white women, along with underrepresented minorities, benefit directly from this admissions policy. Why is there a lack of outcry dealing with white women? Does the argument for merit in these cases exist? Are the public reactions concerning "reverse discrimination" used only to contest race-sensitive policies?

A random search of college Web sites shows the many "qualitative" factors in college admissions. Also, it is interesting to observe that the University of Michigan case in 2003 revealed that white students from the Upper Peninsula are overwhelmingly given preference for admission to the university.

Further reading about race and selective college admissions can be found in *The Wall Street Journal* (April 25, 2003) "College Ties: For Groton Grads, Academics Aren't Only Keys to Ivies," by Daniel Golden. "The Birth of a New Institution," by Geoffrey Kabaservice in the Yale alumni magazine,

*Yale* (December 1999), looks at how two Yale presidents utilized minority admissions to strengthen the school. There are numerous guides to colleges and universities that are available to students. They can be used for data on race and higher education. Routinely, journals including *The Chronicle of Higher Education* and *Journal of Blacks in Higher Education* offer data and contemporary accounts of race and college admissions.

A complete social history of the many factors used for admission and exclusion to three prominent universities is brilliantly analyzed and explored by Jerome Karabel in *The Chosen: The Hidden History of Admission and Exclusion at Harvard, Yale and Princeton* (Houghton Mifflin, 2005). Analyzing the many factors considered for admission to selective colleges, Daniel Golden's *The Price of Admission: How America's Ruling Class Buys Its Way into Elite Colleges—and Who Gets Left Outside the Gates* (Crown Publishing Group, 2006) exposes the myth of meritocracy and higher education at elite colleges. Both the Karabel and Golden books are must reading for students researching race, class, and college admissions.

# ISSUE 19

# Is Affirmative Action Necessary to Achieve Racial Equality in the United States Today?

**YES: Robert Staples**, from "Black Deprivation-White Privilege: The Assault on Affirmative Action," *The Black Scholar* (Summer 1995)

**NO: Roger Clegg**, from "Faculty Hiring Preferences and the Law," *The Chronicle of Higher Education* (May 19, 2006)

### ISSUE SUMMARY

**YES:** Robert Staples, an African-American sociologist, views affirmative action as a positive policy designed to provide equal economic opportunities for women and other minorities.

**NO:** Roger Clegg, general counsel of the Center for Equal Opportunity in Sterling, Virginia and contributor to *The Chronicle of Higher Education,* argues against affirmative action, citing the 2003 Supreme Court decision. He makes the case for universities to hire the best-qualified faculty.

**A**ffirmative action emerged as a primary policy of government to remedy prevailing racial discrimination and to promote equal opportunity consistent with the requirements of the Civil Rights Act of 1964. Yet, despite its noble intentions, the application of this policy in attempts to end bias and promote racial diversity has provoked much controversy.

Those who favor affirmative action programs such as Professor Robert Staples, reject the premise that the United States has achieved the status of a color-blind society, thus obviating the need for the preferences that they provide for members of the "protected classes." Rather, he views American society as one afflicted with an embedded racism that persists today. So, Staples is concerned that the attack on affirmative action is part of a plan designed to maintain white privilege at the expense of the continued suffering and subordination of African Americans and other minorities to include women within society.

Staples points out that affirmative action is not a "black" program. Rather, he concludes that affirmative action programs were initiated to provide equal economic opportunities for minorities and women. Thus, Staples is very critical of politicians and others who play the "race card" by promoting the myth that most of the benefits of affirmative action programs accrue to blacks, when in fact the primary beneficiaries are white females. To Staples, the targeting of blacks in such a fashion reflects a historical tradition of scapegoating blacks within a strategy of "divide and conquer" politics.

Racial politics are a significant aspect of American political life. Staples locates the attack on affirmative action policies as a significant manifestation of the white backlash against civil rights advancement of 1990's politics. He decries the tendency of the opponents of these policies to use them to target African Americans, a group that represents a relatively small minority (12.5%) among the potential beneficiaries of affirmative action, while ignoring the fact that white women are the majority of those targeted for the assistance, which they provide. So, Staples has concluded that the opponents of affirmative action will have accomplished the elimination of an "innocuous" remedial program that has achieved some progress in the pursuit of society's diversity goals if their efforts to abolish such programs are successful.

Opponents of affirmative action view such reforms as bad public policy. As one who tends to view the policy negatively, Clegg believes that affirmative action programs violate the principle of equal opportunity and promote the untenable notion that a group is entitled to a guarantee of success. He believes that this evolutionary orientation of affirmative action is divisive and contributes significantly to the perpetuation of racial intolerance within the nation.

Another concern expressed by opponents of this issue is the claim that affirmative action reinforces feelings of self-doubt and stifles individual initiatives among blacks and other minorities, thus causing them to miss opportunities that are available to them. They also deny blacks and others the full opportunity to promote the perception within the dominant culture that their hiring was based on merit rather than quotas or preferential hiring.

# YES

**Robert Staples**

# Black Deprivation-White Privilege: The Assault on Affirmative Action

$T$he current furor over affirmative action has many of us perplexed. Somehow, black Americans have shifted, in image, from being violent criminals, drug dealers, wife beaters, sexual harassers, welfare cheaters and underclass members to privileged members of the middle-class, who acquired their jobs through some racial quota system at the expense of white males who had superior qualifications for those same jobs. It is a testament to the ingenuity of white male politicians, using the race card, that they can exploit the historically ingrained prejudice against black Americans in the direction of the small black middle-class. For the last twenty-five years, the use of racial code issues, such as law and order, revising the welfare system and the tax revolt has served to transform the southern states from a Democratic stronghold to a Republican majority among its white population.

However, Republicans are increasingly becoming victims of their own success. White Democratic candidates have become as vigilantly anti-crime and welfare as their Republican opponents. In the Louisiana gubernatorial race of 1995, even the black candidates reached out to those whites seeking harsher sentences for criminals, the overwhelming majority of offenders being black in that particular state. While this situation illustrates that there is no honor among thieves, i.e. politicians, it also demonstrates that the diminishing returns of the racial code issues have created a dilemma among the Republican right. Into this void steps the issue of affirmative action, an innocuous program devised more than thirty years ago by President John F. Kennedy to increase the employment of blacks in the public sector. It was expanded by President Richard M. Nixon, who personally believed blacks were intellectually inferior, to include other people of color and white women.

All this occurred at a time when white males held an almost total monopoly of all top and mid-level professional and managerial jobs in the US. Blacks and women who were qualified could not penetrate the barriers to white collar employment except in very special niches for white women (e.g. nursing, home economics or teaching) and a small number of professional blacks who serviced the black community. Subsequently, there was some reduction in the exclusive white male monopoly in the white collar

From *The Black Scholar,* vol. 25, no. 3, Summer 1995, pp. 2–6. Copyright © 1995 by The Black Scholar. Reprinted by permission.

occupations and affirmative action was only one of the reasons for the change. The shift from a manufacturing to a service-based economy was a big factor in increasing female employment. And the racial violence of the late 1960s convinced the ruling elites that some blacks had to be brought into white dominated institutions to bring about racial tranquility.

As for affirmative action, there is no consensus on what it is, who are its beneficiaries or what it has achieved. I will not try to define it, since the practice runs the gamut from including people of color and women in the pool of applicants for vacant positions to establishing explicit racial and gender quotas in some institutional spheres. The beneficiaries are generally blacks, Latinos, American Indians, sometimes Asians and women, the disabled, and military veterans. It is estimated that as many as five million people of color have gotten their jobs directly through affirmative action. However, such figures cannot be validated because affirmative action operates in such a complex and convoluted way.

What we do know is that there has been a small shift in the number of blacks who can be regarded as middle-class. Most estimates are generally in the range of one-third of the Afro-American population. The progress for black women has been greater, as recent census figures show that among young black college graduates, women earn more than men. The progress for white women is more complicated to measure, because the majority of them are married to white men and share the same standard of living. Nonetheless, there has been some economic and educational progress for all affected groups and affirmative action is, at least, partly responsible for this progress because it requires employers to be racial and gender inclusive. What has been overshadowed in this debate is that these groups make up about 70 percent of the American population. White males, the alleged victims of affirmative action compose about 30 percent of the population and still hold about 75 percent of the highest earning occupations in this country, and 95 percent at the very top.

Somehow, some way, this whole issue has been distorted into a prevailing belief that white men are the victims of affirmative action and that their rights have been trampled on. Underlying this belief is the assumption that white males are entitled to 100 percent of the high paying occupations, as they had prior to 1965, because they are intellectually superior to people of color and women. That such a notion could have any credence should be absurd on the face of it. Still, it will be upheld in an initiative on the California ballot in 1996, as it was in July of 1995, when the University of California Regents abolished affirmative action in admissions and employment. And this occurred in a state where half the population are people of color and white, non-Hispanic, males compose twenty percent of the state's population.

I will now address the issue of affirmative action in the state of California and at the University of California, where I have lived and taught for the last three decades. About the state: it is a mosaic of geographic, cultural, social and political elements. Its borders house both the radicals of Berkeley and the John Birch Society of Orange County. Not only is California the most populous of the 50 states, it is one of the most racially diverse. Latinos, Asians, blacks and American Indians make up one half of the state's population. Politically it can be a progressive state, since blacks and women have held a higher number of elective offices there than in any other state. Yet, in the last thirty years the state has experienced (1) the passage of a state proposition to legalize racial discrimination in housing, which was declared unconstitutional by the courts, (2) the uprooting of every black person, by white groups, from their homes in the town of Taft, (3) the election of a member of the Ku Klux Klan as the Democratic candidate for a US Congressional seat and (4) the passage of proposition 187, which denies medical treatment and education to undocumented aliens and their children, most of whom are considered people of color.

With this historical backdrop, the Board of Regents of the University of California met in San Francisco on July 20, 1995 to vote on the issue of abolishing affirmative action in admissions and employment. Until this date, there had been no ground swell of public desire to end a program that had existed for 25 years, in a state where blacks and Latinos compose 40 percent of the pool of potential students. But, the Governor, Pete Wilson, who is running for the Republican nomination for president, was way behind in the polls and needed to show he could actually do something about this "wedge issue" that the Republican party discovered in 1995. Typical of 1990s politics, Wilson has a black man, Ward Connerly, himself a beneficiary of affirmative action, to lead the fight to abolish affirmative action. All those involved in the university—the faculty, administration, student groups and alumni were opposed to its abolishment. The vote was a mere formality, as almost all the white male regents were Republican appointees, and by a vote of 15–10, became the first public university to abolish affirmative action.

One would think it a risky political move in a state where people of color make up 50 percent of the population. However, because many Latinos and Asians are recent immigrants, some undocumented, the voting population is 80 percent white. As Mark Di Camillo, of the California Poll commented, "when you do public opinion polling, you see that whites are much more sensitive to issues that relate to the future of California and the position of whites. They probably have greater concern about their own self-interest." Of course, a substantial number of Asians and some Latinos were also opposed to affirmative action at the University of California. The issue is often framed as a black/white one, though blacks make up only 8 percent of the state's population, less than 6 percent of the UC student body and 2 percent of the faculty. By far, the greatest beneficiaries of affirmative action, due to their larger numbers, are white women. Yet they are hardly mentioned in this debate, partly because they are also 52 percent of white voters and their husbands depend on them for their standard of living. The polls show that about two-thirds of white women would vote to abolish affirmative action.

It is not clear what effect the UC Regents' votes will have on the racial and gender balance of the UC campuses. The president of the University of

California, Jack Petalson, issued a statement saying, "Few significant changes are likely because UC's employment and contracting programs are governed by state and federal laws, regulations, executive orders and the US Constitution." Because affirmative action is such an innocuous program, it has created strange political bedfellows. Richard Butler, a leading white supremacist and head of the Church of Jesus Christ Christian Aryan Nation hailed Governor Wilson for his support of the UC Regents' decision. He said that "Wilson is beginning to wake up to Aryan views." At the same time, arch conservatives such as Jack Kemp and William Bennett, who are not running for public office, have reaffirmed their support for affirmative action.

This whole debate tends to obscure some of the real issues for the black community. As Jesse Jackson has noted, "There is substantial evidence that affirmative action is inadequately enforced and too narrowly applied." Blacks hold only 4 percent of professional and managerial positions in the US and are a fraction of 1 percent of senior managers in America's major corporations. At the same time, almost a majority of black males are not in the civilian labor force. About 25 percent of young black males are in prison, on probation or parole. Even if white males can reclaim that 4 percent of the executive positions, it will do little to restore them to the 100 percent monopoly they once held.

An essential piece of the attack on affirmative action is that it unfairly discriminates against white males. To accept this premise is to assume that every white male is superior to every woman and person of color. Why else should they control 100 percent of the top positions in the society: for example, in the government contract set asides about 25 percent of the work is often delegated to people of color and women. Presumably, the other 75 percent is held by "deserving" white males. If that aspect of affirmative action is eliminated, white males will get all the hundreds of billions of dollars in taxpayer funds that go to private companies. As for how white males have achieved such an advantage in this one sphere, far in excess of their percentage of the population, it may have more to do with the fact that other white males are making the decisions on whom to award those contracts—not on the merits of a true competition for them.

The center of the white male argument is that they possess skills other groups do not have, particularly as measured by their performance on standardized tests. Thus, they pretend that those tests are valid measures of merit and use them to exclude all but white males from the top paying occupations. It is, indeed, true that they are better test takers than women and people of color—in part because they created and administer the tests. Other research, also by white males, suggests that many of those exams have no relevance to job performance, contain a cultural bias that favors middle-class Anglo males and are not required for most jobs in the US. In many cases, affirmative action was a tool to consider other—often more relevant—measures to evaluate job applicants. And the opponents of affirmative action is hard pressed to name many cases where individuals, hired under affirmative action, lack the necessary skills to do a job for which they are hired.

In reality, most people in this country are capable of performing well at a variety of occupations, because most of what they learn, in performing occupational tasks, is on the job itself. Since there are not enough "desirable and high paying jobs for all the qualified applicants, the system devises arbitrary screening devices such as educational requirements and standardized tests to weed out people. Because white males in the US are socialized into a sense of entitlement to the most prestigious and highest paying positions, they are generally better positioned to take advantage of the those arbitrary screening devices. Moreover, studies over the years have found that between 35–65 percent Americans find their jobs through contacts made via the friends and kinship network, a practice that partly accounts for the white male dominance of senior positions in both the private and public sector.

Affirmative action has experienced some abuses. Why people of color and women are held responsible for the abuses is a mystery, since white males are chiefly responsible for administering affirmative action programs. The greatest abuses seem to occur in the contract set asides, where a few black and Latinos have served as fronts to get government contracts that actually go to Anglo contractors. Another problem has been the classification of racial minorities. Because people with a small percentage of Indian ancestry can live as white Americans, they face no disadvantage different from other whites in this society. Yet, they have often qualified for affirmative action treatment. The problem of white usurpation of Indian identity was so prevalent that American Indians wanted to retain their original name, albeit a misnomer, because so many whites were claiming the title of Native Americans and receiving benefits designed for oppressed American Indians.

Some opponents of affirmative action have suggested replacing its racial/gender components with that of socioeconomic status, which would also include poor whites. Of course poor whites are already included in university recruitment and admission of students, as well as being part of the disabled and military veteran category. However it is unfair to equate a low socioeconomic status with the disadvantages of race and gender. A poor white male who gets a college education and a middle-class job simply increases the number of white males in the ruling elite. His problems are over, while women and people of color will continue to encounter glass ceilings in education and employment. And blacks who are middle-class do not escape anything but the economic problems associated with being black. Because the oppression is aimed at the entire group, the political remedies should go to all visible members of the black population.

Finally, this attack on affirmative action is nothing more than a replay of history for Afro-Americans. Slavery was defended with a variety of rationalizations, including the inferiority of blacks, the need to make blacks Christians and the slaveowners' property rights. Racial segregation in schools was defended by the separate but equal doctrine. Southern apartheid was maintained politically under the states' rights defense. Now, we have the anomaly of having white males, a third of the population who make up 95 percent of those who run America, control and distribute 90 percent of the nation's wealth, trying to portray themselves as victims because women and people of color finally broke their grip on all the society's resources. Their attack on affirmative action can only be characterized as political and economic overkill.

However, despite its absurdity, the assault has the potential to succeed. Politicians have had the wisdom to target blacks as the main recipients of affirmative action, while ignoring the fact that white women make up as much as 80 percent of the beneficiaries. This allows them to get the votes of white women, who may act on their interests as whites and ignore their interests as women. To the degree that they empathize and share households with white males, they have less to lose. Single white women, female heads-of-households and lesbians, will be sacrificed on the altar of larger white interests. Blacks, historically, make a convenient scapegoat for the decline of capitalism and the whites who are casualties of that decline. While they comprise a small percentage of those subject to affirmative action, they remain a national target of prejudice and stereotyping in every corner of the nation.

The notion of a color blind society, with no need for affirmative action, is a fantasy at this point. Race is the most divisive variable extant in the US. Whites commonly betray their class interests on its behalf and individual life chances for both blacks and whites are a direct function of it. Affirmative action is but one tool—not a very effective one—to mitigate its effect. The attack on it is part of a white plan to make people of color their servants again, while they continue to obligate them to pay taxes to subsidize white privilege. What whites may find is they may not want to live in the world they are creating.

Roger Clegg  **NO**

# Faculty Hiring Preferences and the Law

**S**ince the U.S. Supreme Court's rulings on affirmative action in 2003, colleges have begun to reconsider how they give preference to students according to race, ethnicity, and sex—not only in admissions, but in financial aid, internships, and various other programs. They need to do the same thing now for employment preferences. It is an open and ugly secret that many colleges still weigh such factors in faculty hiring decisions. That practice is flatly at odds with, among other laws, Title VII of the 1964 Civil Rights Act, which bans employers from such discrimination. In fact, legal challenges concerning faculty hiring are mounting, and it is emerging as the next big front in the battle against racial preferences.

Consider the collision between law and common practice in higher education at every stage of the employment process:

*Posting job notices.* Advertisements for job applicants commonly single out minority and female candidates as especially welcome. But Title VII specifically makes it generally illegal "to print or publish or cause to be printed or published any notice or advertisement relating to employment . . . indicating any preference . . . based on race, color, religion, sex, or national origin." My organization, the Center for Equal Opportunity, has recently suggested that the U.S. Equal Employment Opportunity Commission spell out what that means for academic institutions, whose refusal to follow the law makes them virtually unique among employers. We are also challenging ads that seem to suggest not just preference but racial exclusivity.

*Offering graduate fellowships.* Another track to a faculty position is through a graduate fellowship. In early February, the U.S. Department of Justice forced the Southern Illinois University system to end its policy of giving preferential treatment to minority groups and women in its awarding of such fellowships. The department had argued that, because such positions are typically paid, discrimination in selection for them would violate Title VII. The university denied that it had done anything illegal, but said it would open its paid fellowships to all applicants.

My organization had brought that matter to the Justice Department's attention after students and faculty members unhappy with the university's

From *The Chronicle of Higher Education*, May 19, 2006, pp. B13. Copyright © 2006 by Roger Clegg. Reprinted by permission of the author.

approach contacted us. That illuminates an important point: Surveys, like a 1996 study by the Roper Center for Public Opinion Research and a 2000 study in Connecticut by the Center for Survey Research and Analysis, show that most professors are opposed to preferences. Many are happy to bring such discrimination to the attention of federal agencies or private antidiscrimination organizations.

*Defining the applicant pool.*   Once applications have been received, some colleges deliberately halt the process if they don't think the pool is "diverse" enough. They will then insist on adding candidates—so long, of course, as those candidates are members of a minority group or female.

But a panel for the U.S. Court of Appeals for the Seventh Circuit ruled last August in *Rudin v. Lincoln Land Community College* that such a practice constitutes evidence of illegal discrimination. And rightly so. It is fair to assume that the practice is going to result in some instances where a non-"diversity" candidate, who would have been hired absent the practice, won't get hired. Further, there will be situations in which the pool does not contain a diversity candidate, and so the college will add such a candidate, but in doing so will not add a nondiversity candidate with the same or better qualifications. In those instances, too, a nondiversity candidate is denied an employment opportunity.

*Setting aside special funds for "targets of opportunity."*   Colleges sometimes establish special pools of money from which a department can draw to hire underrepresented minority scholars whenever there is an opportunity to do so; those minority scholars are called "targets of opportunity." But such pools are indistinguishable from the racially exclusive scholarships for students that colleges have, quite rightly, been abandoning—and that the federal government has, quite rightly, been successfully challenging. Indeed, the Justice Department challenged an "opportunity hire" program as illegally discriminatory against white males in a June 17, 2005, letter to a university.

Jonathan Bean, a professor of history at Southern Illinois University at Carbondale, and an expert on and critic of racial preferences, has observed that those pools of money have been "like the weather—many people complained about them, but nobody did anything about them." "But," he predicts, "that is about to change, as more professors and universities conclude that the racially exclusive approach is legally untenable."

*Making hiring decisions.*   Colleges, when they hire, often grant preferences to women or "underrepresented minorities" ("underrepresented" being a clever way to avoid having to give a preference to some minority groups, like Asians or Arab Americans). The bias is supposedly justified by one of three rationales, but none has any legal merit.

The first and oldest justification is that discrimination in favor of a minority person is somehow fair because members of that racial group have historically been discriminated against. That is illogical, inasmuch as the individual beneficiary is not claimed to have been an actual victim. The courts have in all events rejected that "societal discrimination" rationale—for instance, Justice Sandra Day O'Connor's 1989 opinion in *City of Richmond v. J.A. Croson Company,* citing Justice Lewis F. Powell Jr.'s opinions in *Wygant v. Jackson Board of Education and University of California Regents v. Bakke.* Hiring preferences, then, can be justified only when evidence exists that the particular employer was at some point discriminating.

The Supreme Court's Title VII decisions—like *Steelworkers v. Weber* and *Johnson v. Transportation Agency*—likewise require showing a "manifest imbalance" in a "traditionally segregated" position. In 2006 it seems unlikely that many faculties will be able to point to any recent discrimination against "underrepresented minorities," when colleges have been cheerfully discriminating in their favor for years, if not decades.

The second excuse is a desire for greater faculty diversity. But that justification has fared no better in the courts. While discrimination in the name of student-body diversity has been narrowly upheld in the Supreme Court's latest decisions on affirmative action, Title VII—the law that applies specifically to hiring—explicitly declines to carve out a "bona fide occupational qualification" for race. So it is unlikely that a court, particularly the current Supreme Court, would make one up.

Nor has any federal court. In the leading case on the matter, *Taxman v. Board of Education of the Township of Piscataway* (1996), the U.S. Court of Appeals for the Third Circuit refused to carve out a diversity exception for faculty-employment discrimination under Title VII. The Fifth Circuit has ruled the same way, and there is no federal decision to the contrary.

In addition, it is important to note that the Justice Department rejected the "diversity" rationale when it moved against Southern Illinois University a few months ago. The rationale proves too much: It could be used to discriminate against women and members of minority groups if they become "overrepresented."

The third excuse is a desire to provide more "role models" for underrepresented minority students. But the Supreme Court rejected the role-model justification for employment discrimination with respect to teachers 20 years ago in *Wygant v. Jackson Board of Education.* Justice Powell wrote, "Carried to its logical extreme, the idea that black students are better off with black teachers could lead to the very system the Court rejected in *Brown v. Board of Education.*" Besides, are we to believe that white students cannot be inspired by black teachers, or black students by white teachers, or either by Asian or Latino teachers?

*Setting pay differences.*    Colleges sometimes offer pay bonuses to faculty hires of the right color. That is flatly prohibited by Title VII for all colleges, and by the Constitution for all state colleges (and by the Equal Pay Act with respect to sex discrimination). Here again, the Justice Department has recently fired a warning shot, successfully confronting Langston University this year on behalf of a white female professor who was paid less than her African and African-American counterparts.

*Retaliating against complainants.* Title VII is explicit that colleges may not retaliate against faculty members or applicants who challenge illegal discrimination. The EEOC recently brought a successful lawsuit—which was settled this year for $125,000—against Macalester College for retaliating against a white male professor who complained to the provost that he had been discriminated against.

Sometimes the pressure to engage in hiring discrimination is brought to bear on colleges from the outside—specifically, from accreditation authorities. The Center for Equal Opportunity, the Center for Individual Rights, the National Association of Scholars, and five of the seven members of the U.S. Commission on Civil Rights have asked that the Education Department not renew the accreditation authority of the American Bar Association's Council of the Section of Legal Education and Admissions to the Bar because the ABA is attempting to use that authority to coerce law schools into using illegal preferences in student admissions and faculty hiring. My organization has also asked the Education Department and Justice Department to jointly investigate past abuses of this sort by the ABA.

Colleges that refuse to conform their hiring practices to the law risk hefty legal judgments—and they will have to pay not only their own lawyers but also the opposing side's. Unlike most cases, in which you pay only your own lawyers, win or lose, the civil-rights laws provide for such lawyer "fee shifting." Bean points out that his (state) university ultimately concluded that it should not "spend taxpayer dollars defending the indefensible"; presumably, private colleges would be even more reluctant to waste their own money. Bean also notes that, "after years of brazen racial discrimination on all fronts, colleges have left a trail of evidence that could be used against them in court." He's right.

The law aside, neither the interests of students nor the research mission of a college are furthered by hiring less than the best-qualified faculty members. Nor does a double standard in hiring and promotion encourage faculty collegiality.

Universities are free—indeed, they are obliged—to make sure that women and minority groups—underrepresented and otherwise—are not discriminated against. They are free to make sure that their hiring committees "cast a wide net," not relying on old-boy networks but instead trying to ensure the best possible applicant pool from which to draw. That sort of affirmative action is fine. Affirmative discrimination is not.

# POSTSCRIPT

## Is Affirmative Action Necessary to Achieve Racial Equality in the United States Today?

In 2003, the U.S. Supreme Court rendered its highly anticipated ruling on *Grutter v. Bollinger* concerning the University of Michigan Law School's affirmative action policy. The justices ruled that race may be employed as one factor among others in the decision-making processes of college admissions. Thus the Court upheld the "Bakke standard" that was enunciated by Justice Powell within the ruling on that case in 1978. Since that earlier decision, a standard that permits the use of race as one factor among others has prevailed within the admission policies of the nation's colleges and universities.

Sociologist Orlando Patterson argues "no issue better reveals the American tension between principle and pragmatism than the debate over affirmative action." The principles of fairness, equality, and meritocracy all inform this debate. The discourse on affirmative action policies contains significant misconceptions. There is a tendency to view such programs as remedies for past racism and sexism. It is difficult to comprehend or accept a claim that a limited policy of affirmative action is an adequate response to the legacy of slavery and racial segregation that continues to challenge the nation. In this context, Issue 20 deals with reparations. On the other hand, any racial preferences call into question the prevailing commitment to equal opportunity.

Roger Clegg and other opponents of affirmative action think that such programs are no longer necessary because African Americans and other members of the "protected classes" have made sufficient progress. He and others raise questions about merit in employment and education. Further, Clegg expresses concern that the recognition of black achievement will be undermined by such policies. Legitimate concerns about divisiveness and a backlash against such policies are also raised.

Robert Staples and proponents of affirmative action policies must confront the fact that these programs are not applied properly in certain situations. In its 1978 ruling in the *Bakke* case and the recent *Bollinger* case, the court found that racial or gender-based quotas are impermissible applications of affirmative action policies. So, gender or racial preferences that are based on some numerical scheme that utilizes a point system to give protected class members a boost are unconstitutional and must be changed. Quotas, therefore, are unacceptable in affirmative action policy.

Supporters of affirmative action programs embrace the proposition that the goal of achieving racial diversity within the institutions of society is a compelling national interest. They believe that social institutions should reflect the diverse composition of America's population within the profile of their employees. Those who affirm support for such programs are concerned that they will not be able to meet their diversity goals if affirmative action is curtailed or abolished. It is not just the traditional membership of the civil rights community who express such concerns. Leaders of the military establishment and the private corporate world have expressed such concerns, and they were the basis for the *amicus curae* briefs that were filed in support of the University of Michigan's affirmative action policies before the U.S. Supreme Court. Their concern is based on a clear understanding that education and life experiences garnered within diverse environments are vital preparation for one to meet the challenges and function effectively in an increasingly global and multicultural social reality. The achievement of racial and class diversity within educational settings, from preschool to graduate school, is a critical component of any meaningful response to these concerns.

Further reading that supports affirmative action can be found in "Racism Has Its Privileges," by Roger Wilkins in *The Nation* (March 22, 1995). Stephen Carter's *Reflections of an Affirmative Action Baby* (HarperCollins, 1991) furthers the case for affirmative action. An argument in support of affirmative action as a redistributive measure in American society is made by Cornel West in "Equality and Identity," in *The American Prospect* (Spring 1992). Orlando Patterson's op-ed piece "Affirmative Action: The Sequel" (*The New York Times,* June 6, 2003) written just before the *Bollinger* decision, argues "using diversity as a rationale for affirmative action also distorts the aims of affirmative action." Ronald Dworkin in "Is Affirmative Action Doomed?" (*New York Review of Books* November 5, 1998) makes the case for the constitutionality of affirmative action. The entire Fall/Winter edition of *The Black Scholar* (2003) is devoted to an analysis of the rulings on admissions policy at the University of Michigan, June 16, 2003.

A critique of affirmative action by Shelby Steele, an African American educator is developed in *The Content of Our Character* (St. Martin's Press, 1990). Charles Murray attacks affirmative action programs in his article "Affirmative Racism," which appeared in *The New Republic* (December 31, 1984). Carl Cohen, in "Race Preference and the Universities—A Final Reckoning," in a *Commentary* (September 2001) article, argues that the most recent Supreme Court case will end quotas in college admissions. In another *Commentary* (February 1999) article, Stephan and Abigail Thernstrom argue against racial preferences in admissions in "Racial Preferences: What We Now Know." Clarence Thomas argues against numerical measures of affirmative action in "Affirmative Action Goals and Timetables: Too Tough? Not Tough Enough!" in the *Yale Law and Policy Review* (Summer 1987).

*The Affirmative Action Debate* (Perseus Books Group, 1996) edited by George E. Curry and Cornel West includes several different perspectives of the subject. Another anthology on affirmative action is *Debating Affirmative Action: Race, Gender, Ethnicity, and the Politics of Inclusion* (Delta, 1994) edited by Nicholaus Mills.

# ISSUE 20

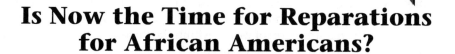

# Is Now the Time for Reparations for African Americans?

**YES: Robert L. Allen**, from "Past Due: The African American Quest for Reparations," *The Black Scholar* (Summer 1998)

**NO: *The Economist*,** from "Slavery and the Law: Time and Punishment," *The Economist* (April 14, 2002)

## ISSUE SUMMARY

**YES:** Robert L. Allen, professor and senior editor of *The Black Scholar,* argues that reparations for African Americans are necessary to achieve an economically just society within the United States.

**NO:** Staff writers from *The Economist* oppose reparations and question whether such a policy is appropriate in a nation where the victims of slavery are difficult to identify and the perpetrators of past racial oppressions are no longer among us.

T he debate over the proposal for reparations for African Americans has generated even more controversy than affirmative action policies. Many Americans believe that since the African Americans currently residing in the nation did not experience slavery and racial segregation—the two major components of the society's racist legacy—they are not entitled to such a benefit. Other commentators, including some African Americans, oppose reparations because they believe that the acceptance of such a payout would result in a foreclosure of opportunities to have future racial grievances dealt with by meaningful and effective means. Others are concerned with the financial and budgetary pressures that reparations would place upon the U.S. treasury. Still others strongly believe that reparations are a meaningful and appropriate response to the dilemma of race within the American experience and the legacy of racial inequalities that it has bequeathed to the nation. It is abundantly clear, therefore, that the proposal to grant reparations to African Americans is a significant wedge issue of American society and politics where race relations are concerned.

Robert L. Allen favors reparations for African Americans and employs an historical perspective to support his position. He presents an historical examination of the quest for reparations as African-American leaders and organizations throughout history have advanced it in order to document the strong support that this policy has received within society. Allen proceeds to examine the problems that African Americans have experienced in acquiring property and income, and accumulating wealth in this country throughout history. These inequities/disparities are the direct result of the racist legacy of slavery and segregation. Thus, Robert Allen argues: "Reparations provides a framework for the redistribution of wealth within the existing political economy, and thereby moving towards economic equality between whites and blacks." Finally, Allen presents a significant body of evidence concerning the precedents that are available for supporting reparations for African Americans and the legal principles upon which the claim for such restitution rests.

The authors of the article from *The Economist* are opposed to reparations and begin their disagreement with such a policy by focusing upon the complexity of this issue of American race relations. These authors state the view that identifying the victims and the perpetrators of past oppressions, such as slavery, is so complex that it is virtually impossible to do so. They also claim that the corporations that were involved in the economic exploitation of slave labor have long since mended their ways and should no longer be held responsible for the historical plight of African Americans.

For the reader who has just now been introduced to this topic, a consideration of general related questions may help gain insight into the issue. Historically, what is the justification of reparations for any group? Under what circumstances should a group be granted reparations? Is it possible to "settle" claims of past exploitation and injustice with a lump sum of money? For those in favor of reparations for African Americans, is there a danger that a monetary award will foreclose opportunities for resolving future racial grievances? Will reparations minimize racial prejudice and discrimination? Will reparations contribute to American unity or further racial polarization?

# YES

Robert L. Allen

# Past Due: The African American Quest for Reparations

In recent years the quest for reparations for Africa and Africa's children in the Diaspora has emerged as an important issue. A growing number of activists, scholars and political leaders, such as British M.P. Bernie Grant and U.S. Congressman John Conyers, have taken up the call for reparations. Organizations have been formed to press the issue, and a foundation for engagement with governments, particularly in Britain and (perhaps) the United States, is being laid. The issue of reparations is truly global and it has many dimensions—moral, cultural, social, psychological, political and economic. In this article, I will focus chiefly on reparations as a matter of social justice for African Americans, but I am cognizant of the fact that the struggle for reparations is a global issue requiring a unified, international mobilization.

## History of the Quest for Reparations

The quest for reparations has a long and deeply rooted history in the life and struggles of the African American community. Reparations have been proposed and fought for by individuals and organizations representing a wide range of social and political viewpoints. As early as 1854 a black emigrationist convention called for a "national indemnity" as a "redress of our grievances for the unparalleled wrongs, undisguised impositions, and unmitigated oppression which we have suffered at the hands of this American people."[1] After the Civil War the anti-slavery activist Sojourner Truth organized a petition campaign seeking free public land for the former slaves.[2] In support of her campaign Sojourner Truth said: "America owes to my people some of the dividends. She can afford to pay and she must pay. I shall make them understand that there is a debt to the Negro people which they can never repay. At least, then, they must make amends."[3] Her valiant campaign was unsuccessful.

In the 1890s another black woman, Callie House, filed lawsuits and petitioned Congress for reparations payments to African Americans. Her efforts were endorsed by Frederick Douglass, but again there was no success.[4]

From *The Black Scholar,* vol. 28, no. 2, Summer 1998, pp. 2–13 & 16. Copyright © 1998 by The Black Scholar. Reprinted by permission.

Religious leaders have also called for reparations. Bishop Henry McNeal Turner once declared: "We have worked, enriched the country and helped give it a standing among the powers of the earth. . . ." Turner estimated that the United States owed black people $40 billion for unpaid labor.[5] Most recently Rev. Amos Brown, pastor of Third Baptist Church in San Francisco, called for reparations in the form of tax credits and automatic tuition for African American youths who qualify for higher education.[6]

Marcus Garvey's call of "Africa for Africans at home and abroad" echoed the quest for restitution. In the "Declaration of the Rights the Negro People of the World" adopted in 1920 by the Universal Negro Improvement Association, Point 15 declared: "We strongly condemn the cupidity of those nations of the world who, by open aggression or secret schemes, have seized the territories and inexhaustible natural wealth of Africa, and we place on record our most solemn determination to reclaim the treasures and possession of the vast continent of our forefathers."[7]

One of the foremost proponents of reparations was the venerable Queen Mother Moore. An activist in the Garvey movement and many other organizations during a long life spanning nearly a century, she insisted that restitution was required to make amends for the great injustice of slavery.[8]

The Nation of Islam also made a reparations demand. In its program for establishing a separate state the Nation asserted that "our former slave masters are obligated to provide such land and that the areas must be fertile and minerally rich. We believe that our former slave masters are obligated to maintain and supply our needs in this separate territory for the next 20 to 25 years—until we are able to produce and supply our own needs."[9]

The quest for reparations was voiced in the Ten-Point Program of the Black Panther Party. Point Number Three states: "We believe that this racist government has robbed us and now we are demanding the overdue debt of forty acres and two mules. Forty acres and two mules was promised 100 years ago as restitution for slave labor and mass murder of Black people. We will accept payment in currency which will be distributed to our many communities. The Germans are now aiding the Jews in Israel for the genocide of the Jewish people. The Germans murdered six million Jews. The American racist has taken part in the slaughter of over fifty million Black people; therefore, we feel that this is a modest demand that we make."[10]

In the late 1960s, two of the most dramatic demands for reparations were put forward by former SNCC leader James Forman and by the nationalist Republic of New Africa.

In 1969 Forman strode into Riverside Church in New York City and presented a Black Manifesto calling for $500 million in reparations from white Christian Churches and Jewish synagogues. The Manifesto stemmed from a Black Economic Development Conference held in Detroit under the auspices of Christian churches. Commenting on the thinking behind the reparations demand, Forman wrote in *The Making of Black Revolutionaries:* "Reparations did not represent any kind of long-range goal to our minds, but an intermediate step on the path to liberation. We saw it as a politically correct step, for the concept of reparation reflected the need to adjust past wrongs—to compensate for the enslavement of black people by Christians and their subsequent exploitation by Christians and Jews in the United States. Our demands—to be called the Black Manifesto—would not merely involve money but would be a call for revolutionary action, a Manifesto that spoke of the human misery of black people under capitalism and imperialism, and pointed the way to ending these conditions."[11] The Manifesto proposed that reparations be used for helping black farmers, establishing black print and electronic media, funding training, research and community organizing centers, assistance in organizing welfare recipients and black workers, funding research on black economic development and links with Africa, and funding a black university.[12]

The Republic of New Africa (RNA) was founded in 1968 with the purpose of establishing an independent Black Republic in five southern states with large black populations. (South Carolina, Georgia, Alabama, Mississippi and Louisiana) In 1972 the RNA developed what it called an Anti-Depression Program that called for $300 billion in reparations from the U.S. government, part of which would be used to finance establishment of new communities in the proposed black republic.[13] The program featured three "legislative requests" to be presented to the U.S. Congress. One proposal called for the ceding of land to the RNA in areas where black people voted for independence. A second proposal called for reparations of $300 billion. The third proposal called for negotiations between the U.S. Government and the RNA with regard to the details of reparations.

The RNA reparations proposal noted that reparations are commonly paid by one nation to another to compensate for damage caused by unjust acts of war. For example, the document pointed to payments made to various nations by the Federal Republic of Germany for damage caused by the Nazi regime during World War II. The document argued that slavery constituted a form of unjust warfare against the African nation in America, and the damage caused by this warfare provided the basis for a demand for reparations.[14]

In comparing the Black Manifesto and the RNA Anti-Depression Program several things stand out. The Black Manifesto was directed not at the government but at church institutions, and its monetary demands were much more modest. Reparations payments were to be used fund a Southern land bank, independent media, training and organizing efforts, and educational initiatives. The RNA demand was directed to the government and sought reparations to fund new self-sustaining communities as part of an independent black nation. These communities were to develop their own industries, health and educational systems, media, and public infrastructure. Both the Black Manifesto and the RNA program stressed the need for independence from white control. Both the RNA and Forman deployed the concept of domestic colonialism. For the RNA reparations were a means of establishing a separate black nation. For Forman reparations were a step in the process of liberation of an oppressed black community and socialist transformation of America.

Neither program made much headway. The Black Manifesto was ridiculed by most whites, although it did gain a respectful response in journals such as *Commonweal, Christian Century,* and *World Outlook. Christian Century* wrote: "We do not believe the idea of reparations is ridiculous. This generation of blacks continues to pay the price of earlier generations' slavery and subjugation; this generation of whites continues to enjoy the profits of racial exploitation." Nevertheless, the monetary response was minimal; the churches increased their contributions to black organizations by $1 million.[15]

The RNA program was also ridiculed, although the RNA garnered a more dangerous form of attention. In 1971 RNA headquarters in Jackson, Mississippi was the target of a COINTELPRO-type attack by local policemen and FBI agents. In the ensuing shootout a local policeman was fatally wounded. Eleven RNA members, including President Imari Obadele I, were arrested and charged with murder, assault, and treason against the state of Mississippi.[16]

Despite government repression, the RNA pressed its program, lobbying for it at both the Democratic National Convention and the National Black Political Convention held in Gary in 1972.[17]

## NBPC Endorses Reparations

The National Black Political Convention (NBPC) endorsed the demand for reparations, which had been raised by a number of delegates. A resolution passed by the NBPC stated: "The economic impoverishment of the Black community in America is clearly traceable to the historic enslavement of our people and to the racist discrimination to which we have been subjected since 'emancipation.' Indeed, much of the unprecedented economic wealth and power of American capitalism has obviously been built upon this exploitation of Black people." The resolution asserted that "we must not rest until American society has recognized our valid, historic right to reparations, to a massive claim on the financial assets of the American economy. At the same time, it is necessary Black people realize that full economic development for us cannot take place without radical transformation of the economic system which has so clearly exploited us these many years."[18] The Convention recommended that a presidential convention be established, with a majority of black members, to determine appropriate reparations and methods of payment.

The Black Manifesto, RNA program, and the Black Political Convention resolution brought the issue of reparations into a wider public discourse.

As early as 1970 maverick black businessman Dempsey Travis came up with a proposal for a new homestead act as a form of reparations. Travis calculated that if the government had granted 40 acres to the each of the former slaves, the value of this land would have been $21.6 billion (valued at $150 an acre). Travis called for establishing a fund in this amount to assist black people in buying land and homes.[19]

In 1973 white law professor Boris Bitker wrote a book entitled *The Case for Black Reparations*. Noting the "paucity of analysis" that followed Forman's presentation of the Black Manifesto, Bitker offered a narrowly legalistic argument for black reparations. Unlike most black advocates of reparations, Bitker dismissed any reparations demand based on the "ancient injustice" of slavery as largely moot.[20] Instead he argued for reparations that "seek to redress injuries caused by a system of legally imposed segregation that was eventually held in *Brown v. Board of Education* to violate the equal-protection clause of the Fourteenth Amendment."[21]

Bitker's argument made use of the authority of Section 1983, Title 42 of the United States Code. Section 1983, enacted more than a century ago as part of an act to control the Ku Klux Klan, provided that "Every person who, under color of any statute . . . of any State or Territory, subjects . . . any citizen of the United States . . . to the deprivation of any rights . . . secured by the Constitution and laws, shall be liable to the party injured in an action at law, suit in equity, or other proper proceeding for redress."[22] Bitker suggested that a valid claim for reparations could be brought on the grounds that segregation and Jim Crow statutes were found in 1954 to be unconstitutional and therefore subject to a "proceeding for redress" under Section 1983.

In 1974 black economist Robert S. Browne, at the time the director of the Black Economic Research Center, wrote of reparations as requiring "a massive capital transfer of a sizable chunk of America's wealth to the black community."[23] Racial disparities in both economic status and political power could be traced to disparities in ownership of capital assets, according to Browne. Echoing the position that was most widely adopted by black advocates of reparations, Browne said a moral justification for reparations derived from "the debt owed to Blacks for the centuries of unpaid slave labor which built so much of the early American economy, and from the discriminatory wage and employment patterns to which Blacks were subjected after emancipation." Browne also invoked white America's "national self-interest" and desire for racial peace when he further suggested that such "gross inequities" in wealth distribution would exacerbate racial tensions if not redressed.

Following Browne's lead other economists took up serious discussion and advocacy of reparations. They produced a body of work on the economics of slavery, the present value of past labor performed by slaves, the value of black labor since emancipation and racial disparities in distribution of wealth.[24] A good summary statement of this research and its implications for reparations was provided by economist David Swinton: "Discrimination and racism reduced the historic accumulation of capital by blacks and increased the accumulation by whites. The resulting disparities in ownership of capital are transmitted intergenerationally. These capital disparities would prevent attainment of racial equality even if current discrimination ended and blacks and whites had identical tastes and preferences. It would, therefore, be necessary to repair historic damage to the black capital stock in order to ensure attainment of equality."[25]

# New Activism Emerges

In the last decade reparations have again become an activist issue with the establishment of the National Coalition of Blacks for Reparations in America (N'COBRA)[26] in the U.S., and the Africa Reparations Movement (ARM)[27] internationally. Founded in 1989 N'COBRA is an umbrella group that sponsors a Reparations Awareness Day each February 25th and holds an annual convention. The organization has done much to create public awareness in the U.S. about the issue of reparations.[28] Similarly, the Africa Reparations Movement, founded in 1993 as an outgrowth of a conference on reparations held in Nigeria, has worked in the international arena to promote the idea of reparations, including cancellation of the external debt of African nations and return of stolen art objects to their home countries. British M.P. Bernie Grant is Chairperson of ARM, and he has taken an active role in pushing the British government to begin to take the issue of reparations seriously.[29]

In the arena of public policy in the U.S. there have been growing efforts to get reparations on the agenda. In 1987 the Republic of New Africa again drafted a reparations bill and circulated it to members of Congress.[30] In 1989, seventeen years after the Gary Black Political Convention, Congressman John Conyers introduced a bill in Congress calling for creation of a presidential commission to study the question of reparations for African Americans. The Conyers bill (originally HR 40, now HR 891) followed the passage of the Civil Liberties Act of 1988 which granted reparations to Japanese Americans who were unjustly interned during World War II. With the success of the reparations effort by Japanese Americans, black activists succeeded in getting several cities, including Detroit, Cleveland, and the District of Columbia to pass resolutions endorsing the tenets of reparations.[31] The Conyers bill, which has been put forward every year since 1989, presents "findings" that "the institution of slavery was constitutionally and statutorily sanctioned by the Government of the United States from 1798 through 1865" and that slavery "constituted an immoral and inhumane deprivation of Africans' life, liberty, African citizenship rights, and cultural heritage, and denied them the fruits of their own labor." So far, every year the Conyers bill has been bottled up in committee and prevented from coming before Congress. Nevertheless, the bill has become a significant rallying point for those individuals and organizations seeking to get a serious hearing for reparations.

The Conyers bill calls for appropriating $8 million to establish a commission to study reparations proposals for African Americans. Specifically the commission would:

1. examine the institution of slavery which existed from 1619 through 1865 within the United States and the colonies that became the United States, including the extent to which the Federal and State governments constitutionally and statutorilysupported the institution of slavery;

2.  examine de jure and de facto discrimination against freed slaves and their descendants from the end of the Civil War to the present, including economic, political, and social discrimination;
3.  examine the lingering negative effects of the institution of slavery and the discrimination described in paragraph (2) on living African Americans and on society in the United States;
4.  recommend appropriate ways to educate the American public of the Commission's findings;
5.  recommend appropriate remedies in consideration of the Commission's findings on the matters described in paragraphs (1) and (2); and
6.  submit to the Congress the results of such examination, together with such recommendations.[32]

If deemed appropriate, the remedies to be considered include the possibility of a formal apology from the government and payment of compensation to the descendants of African slaves. The commission would recommend what form any compensation should take and who would be eligible.

The commission would have seven members; three to be appointed by the President, three to be appointed by the Speaker of the House of Representatives; and one to be appointed by the President pro tempore of the Senate.

This past year we have seen a maneuver by President Clinton to coopt the Conyers bill by creating a Race Commission with a mandate to conduct a dialogue on race. The Race Commission has not gotten beyond the usual debates over access to jobs and discussion of ways to reduce discrimination. Meanwhile, the *New York Times* reported that over the past two years federal government agencies slashed affirmative action funding and "conducted the most sweeping reductions of [affirmative action] measures since they were instituted."[33] Seen in this light, Clinton's Race Commission is a cynical cosmetic gesture designed to deflect attention from the administration's dismantling of affirmative action programs.

In June 1998 a Black Radical Congress held in Chicago brought together activists from around the country. A draft of a "Black Freedom Agenda for the 21st Century" proposed for the Congress included a demand for reparations. Point number ten of the Freedom Agenda stated: "We demand just compensation and reparations for the systematic brutality and exploitation our people have suffered historically and continue to experience today. We claim the legal and moral right to demand and receive just compensation for oppression which was responsible for the destruction of millions of Black people's lives."

## Political Economy and Reparations

With the destruction of affirmative action programs the quest for reparations gains added urgency. However, let me stress that my discussion of reparations is not meant to dismiss issues of access to employment and the necessity of challenging racial discrimination in education and other areas of social life. Social movements and public policies that address racial discrimination in employment, education and elsewhere are clearly important in bringing about any progressive change. However, such remedies do not address the systematic long-term de-capitalization of the African American community. Struggles for civil rights are important, but not sufficient. Transfers of capital resources into the African American community must also occur. Such transfers, to be most effective, must be class-based, aimed at benefitting first and foremost the black working class—those who have been most ravaged by the depredations of capitalism and who have benefitted least from the social reforms of the civil rights era.

From the standpoint of political economy I think the *process of underdevelopment* of the African American community and the *role of the state* in this process of underdevelopment are critical in understanding the unfolding of the quest for reparations.

Manning Marable has argued convincingly that capitalism is the fundamental cause of the underdevelopment of black America. At the same time, the wealth produced by slave labor enormously enhanced the economic and political development of North America. In his seminal book, *How Capitalism Underdeveloped Black America,* Marable wrote: "Capitalist development has occurred not in spite of the exclusion of Blacks, but because of the brutal exploitation of Blacks as workers and consumers. Blacks have never been equal partners in the American Social Contract, because the system exists not to develop, but to *underdevelop Black people.*"[34]

He goes on to write:

> The ordeal of slavery was responsible for accelerating the economic and political power of Europe and North America over the rest of the mostly nonwhite world. Since the demise of slavery, and the emergence of modern capitalism, the process of Black underdevelopment has expanded and deepened. To understand this dynamic of degradation, first, is to recognize that development itself is comparative in essence, a relationship of inequality between the capitalist ruling class and those who are exploited. Underdevelopment is not the absence of development; it is the inevitable product of an oppressed population's integration into the world market economy and political system. Once "freed," Black Americans were not compensated for their 246 years of free labor to this country's slave oligarchy. The only means of survival and economic development they possessed was their ability to work, their labor power, which they sold in various forms to the agricultural capitalist. Sharecropping and convict leasing were followed by industrial labor at low wages. . . . Throughout the totality of economic relations, Black workers were exploited—in land tenure, in the ownership of factories shops and other enterprises, in the means of transportation, in energy, and so forth. *The constant expropriation of surplus value created by Black labor is the heart and soul of underdevelopment.*"[35]

Underdevelopment manifests in the restriction of black labor to certain functions: chattel slavery, sharecropping, low-paid industrial work, a reserve army of labor (aka the "underclass"). Underdevelopment manifests in the restricted and distorted development of black landownership, home ownership and black business enterprises. It manifests in chronic impoverishment, the fostering of retrograde political leadership, the destruction of black education, the spread of racist violence, and the wholesale incarceration of black youth.

The role of the state, as Marable and others have noted, was critical to the process of underdevelopment. Specifically, the underdevelopment of Black America occurred not because of the "normal" operation of capitalist economic and property relations, rather the state apparatus was directly and intimately involved in the expropriation of surplus value *from* black workers and the blocking of capital accumulation *by* African Americans.

From the earliest colonial period the passage of laws establishing racial slavery ensured that black labor could be exploited without compensation and in perpetuity. Virginia colony, with a plantation economy based on tobacco, led the way. By the 1640s *de facto* African slavery existed in Virginia colony; in the 1660s slavery became institutionalized in law. This was done in two ways. Laws were passed effectively excluding Africans as non-Christians from limitation of the number of years they could be held in bondage.[36] A Virginia law in 1661 regarding punishment of runaway servants recognized that some black workers were already enslaved for life; it referred to "any Negroes who are incapable of making satisfaction by addition of time."[37] Secondly, the status of slavery was made hereditary. In 1662 the Virginia Assembly decreed that the children of a slave mother shall themselves be slaves, regardless of the status of the father.[38] This law flew in the face of English patriarchal tradition, but it guaranteed that African bondage could be passed down through the generations without interruption.

At the same time European indentured servants were granted privileges based on whiteness. They were protected from enslavement by statutes limiting the period of servitude (typically 4–6 years). Moreover, capital accumulation by whites was privileged. In 1705 in Virginia the colonial assembly passed a law granting white servants 50 acres of land, 30 shillings, a musket and food upon completion of their term of service.[39] No such landstake would be granted to black workers.

Free black people also found their freedom circumscribed by the state. Licensing was used to exclude them from certain occupations. They could not own land in many areas, and they were largely excluded from the franchise. In California and elsewhere they could not testify in court against whites, further undermining their ability to protect themselves.[40] In 1668, Virginia, seemingly always in the forefront of new ways to oppress black people, made free African American women liable to taxes on the ground that black women should not admitted to the "exemptions and impunities of the English."[41]

Theodore Allen, in the second volume of his important work, *The Invention of the White Race,* notes one consequence of such state intervention. He reports that in Virginia landholding by blacks declined from about

11 percent in 1666 to one-quarter of one percent in 1860. Allen concludes that this precipitous decline was the result not of normal capitalist economic development but due to a system of racial oppression enforced by the state.[42]

# Role of U.S. Government

The formation of the U.S. government after the American War for Independence continued the process of state-sanctioned black oppression. The U.S. Constitution itself recognized and approved the existence of slavery. The Constitution declared that the abolition of the slave trade was prohibited for twenty years; that runaway slaves must be returned to the slaveholders; and that, for purposes of determining the number of representatives each state shall have in Congress, slaves were to be counted as three-fifths of a person. After the American Revolution slavery was abolished in many northern states, but the federal government aided the long arm of slavery in reaching into those states. In 1850 Congress passed a Fugitive Slave Law that required all federal marshals to assist slaveholders in capturing fugitive slaves, even in those states where slavery had been abolished. Then in 1857 the U.S. Supreme Court overturned the last limitations on slavery and made it a *national* institution. In the Dred Scott case the Court ruled that even if a slave lives for years in a free territory in the North the slave does not become free. Chief Justice Roger Taney argued that under the U.S. Constitution slaves were property just like any other property, and that therefore a slaveholder had the right to take his slaves to any part of the country and to maintain ownership of them, just as he would any other form of property. Under this ruling it became possible for slaveholding to legally exist even in states that had abolished slavery.

But Taney went even further and argued that no black person, whether slave or free, could ever be a citizen because black people were "a subordinate and inferior class of beings." The Dred Scott decision fixed in law the subordinate *racial* status of black people as an "inferior class" denied citizenship rights and other legal protections. In the words of the Court black people "had no rights which a white man was bound to respect."

The prospects for black economic emancipation were dealt a severe blow after the Civil War. Black people had hoped for land redistribution by the federal government. Land redistribution was justified, as an Alabama black convention put it, on the grounds that "the property which [the planters] hold was nearly all earned by the sweat of *our* brows."[43] The failure of Congress to enact land redistribution guaranteed black economic subservience. Black people would be exploited as sharecroppers and agricultural workers and denied access to land. The original Freedman's Bureau Act, passed by Colmongress in 1865, assigned 40 acres of land to "every male citizen, whether refugee or freedman," for their use for a term of three years at a nominal rent. This was vetoed by President Andrew Johnson, Lincoln's successor. In 1867 Thaddeus Stevens introduced a plan to confiscate the lands of the big planters—almost 400 million acres. The families of the former slaves would each receive 40 acres and $50 dollars, and the remaining land was to be sold off for $10 per acre. Stevens' plan would have created one million black landowners in the South, an independent class of small farmers. But Congress rejected the idea of wholesale confiscation of the big plantations.[44] Indeed, the Freedmen's Bureau Act that became law in 1866 provided for the restoration of abandoned and confiscated plantations to former white owners in the South. The property rights of the planter class, now protected by northern capital, took precedence over the claims of black workers without whose labor the plantations would be worthless. Even efforts by blacks to buy land were obstructed so that white planters could continue to exploit their labor.[45] As one white landowner put it bluntly, "Who'd work the land if the niggers had farms of their own?"[46]

Commenting on the significance these developments W.E.B. Du Bois observed that Lincoln even considered compensating the slaveholders for their losses, but not the slaves. "Lincoln was impressed by the loss of capital invested in slaves, but curiously never seemed seriously to consider the correlative loss of wage and opportunity of slave workers, the tangible results of whose exploitation had gone into the planters' pockets for two centuries."[47] In 1864, Lincoln momentarily considered paying the South $400 million as compensation for the loss of slaves. He later abandoned this idea. Regardless of Lincoln's views, black people hoped for land redistribution. "So far as the Negroes were concerned," Du Bois writes, "their demand for a reasonable part of the land on which they had worked for a quarter of a millennium was absolutely justified, and to give them anything less than this was an economic farce. On the other hand, to have given each of the million Negro free families a forty-acre freehold would have made a basis of real democracy in the United States that might easily have transformed the modern world." Du Bois concludes that "The restoration of the lands [to the planters] not only deprived Negroes in various ways of a clear path toward livelihood, but greatly discouraged them and broke their faith in the United States Government."[48]

Black people did seize some abandoned plantations, and some land was parcelled out by General Sherman in the Sea islands off the coast of South Carolina. But the government later sought to regain this land.[49] Meanwhile the Southern Homestead Act of 1866 opened up 46 million acres of land to settlers. The vast majority of this land went to whites, with blacks being excluded by various means including discriminatory court rulings.[50] At the same time the government handed out another 23 million acres of land to the railroads.

The Civil War and its aftermath emancipated black workers from slavery but fixed on them a new subordinate status as propertyless sharecroppers and wage workers. The overthrow of Reconstruction rolled back the political gains blacks had made. In 1883 the U.S. Supreme Court overturned the Civil Rights Law of 1875 which had guaranteed equal access to public accommodations without regard to race, color or previous condition of servitude. This was capped by the Court's decision in 1896 in *Plessy vs. Ferguson* affirming the segregationist doctrine of "separate but equal."

Disfranchisement and peonage followed in the wake of these rulings by the nation's highest court.

Landowning by black farmers did increase after the Civil War, despite the absence of widespread land redistribution to the freed people, nevertheless the systematic transfer of black-owned land to white hands, facilitated by state policies with regard to subsidies and loans, would insure that land-ownership by black farmers would dwindle until today it is negligible.[51] The state assiduously protected the interests of the landed classes and their demand for a propertyless work force that could be bound by debt to the plantations. When this required racially discriminatory laws and practices these were readily put in place. In the modern era, as in the slave era, the state has been the chief instrument shaping the exploitation of black labor and blocking the accumulation of capital assets by black people.

## Impact on Wealth Accumulation

While black workers and farmers have been hardest hit by the policies of the state, the black middle class is not exempt. Melvin Oliver and Thomas Shapiro in *Black Wealth/White Wealth* note that the much celebrated progress of the new black middle class that has emerged since World War II is highly deceptive. While it is true, the authors observe, that middle class blacks are approaching middle class whites in terms of annual income, when it comes to wealth and capital assets, the black middle class lags far behind. White families typically have a net worth 8 to 10 times as large as the net worth accumulated by black families.[52] This discrepancy remains even when occupation and income are comparable. Oliver and Shapiro contend that this disparity does not result from the normal operation of a capitalist economy but is the result of what they call the "racialization of the state," by which they mean systematic, state-sanctioned mining of the wealth created by black labor and the blocking of asset accumulation by African Americans. For example, in the period from 1933 to 1978 over 35 million American families benefitted from homeowner equity accumulation as a result of suburban home ownership polices of the federal government. Blacks were largely excluded from this process due to such practices as restrictive covenants and "redlining" (refusing to make loans in certain areas). The Federal Housing Authority endorsed restrictive covenants on the grounds that "if a neighborhood is to retain stability, it is necessary that properties shall continue to be occupied by the same social and racial classes."[53]

"The FHA's actions have had a lasting impact on the wealth portfolios of black Americans," Oliver and Shapiro write. "Locked out of the greatest mass-based opportunity for wealth accumulation in American history, African Americans who desired and were able to afford home ownership found themselves consigned to central-city communities where their investments were affected by the 'self-fulfilling prophecies' of the FHA appraisers: cut off from sources of new investment their homes and communities deteriorated and lost value in comparison to those homes and communities that FHA appraisers deemed desirable."[54]

The difficulty of gaining access to credit has enabled banks and finance companies to strip mine black communities of housing equity through unscrupulous backdoor loans and by charging higher interest rates and points for conventional mortgages. As many as half of borrowers who must opt for high-interest loans end up losing their homes through foreclosure.[55]

Home ownership is the primary means for accumulating capital among middle class Americans. Housing equity can underwrite the cost of college education for children and provide for a comfortable retirement for parents. It is a major form of inheritance passed on to the next generation. Oliver and Shapiro calculated what they called the cost of being black in the housing market in terms of higher interest rates, lost home equity, and mortgages denied to qualified borrowers. That cost came to $82 billion in 1992.

"The main consequence for future generations of current discrimination or past discrimination is that it reduces capital accumulation," commented David Swinton, an economist and president of Benedict College in South Carolina. "If it is desirable to equalize the status of the races in the future, then there must be some make up, some compensation, some reparations . . . for the capital that these groups were prevented from accumulating. Otherwise, the past will continue to perpetuate itself throughout the future."[56]

Most recently Clarence Munford's bold and important new book, *Race and Reparations,* offers a thoughtful and provocative discussion of reparations. Taking civilization as his unit of analysis, Munford argues that racism is deeply embedded in white, Western civilization. The oppression and exploitation of Africa, Africans in the Diaspora and people of color generally, he argues, stems from the racist impulse of white colonialism and imperialism growing out of the Atlantic slave trade.[57] In turn, the racist reality of slavery underlies the demand for reparations. Emancipation and ending of legal segregation were not enough, he writes, because they leave intact a disparity in wealth and resources that will remain for centuries.[58] "Reparations—and its Siamese twin, Black empowerment," Munford writes, "are imperative if the end of formal segregation is ever to amount to anything but a sham leading absolutely nowhere."[59]

Munford calls for a reparations program that "should be broadly construed as encompassing affirmative action, employment equity, race-conscious quotas, parity, minority set-asides, equality of results, free, state-of-the-art health care and, above all, legislated and government-administered remittances of assets and monies."[60] Munford also proposes a family income plan, to be extended to all citizens, to prevent families from falling below a specified income level. He also suggests channeling reparations funds into housing, education and job skills; funding of investments with dividends allocated on a per capita or per household basis; government-funded urban land reform; and financing of the purchase of productive industries.[61]

Interestingly, Munford offers a reason for for whites to support reparations on an international basis. He argues that a massive reparations program in Africa and the western hemisphere could greatly stimulate the global economy much as the Marshall Plan did following World War II. "Reparations could function as the post-Cold War spark plug, helping to keep the world economy from spinning its wheels."[62]

However, Munford is not so sanguine as to think that whites will welcome his reparations program. On the contrary he thinks that what will be required is "a mass political campaign in favor of reparations encompassing all the main components of the Black community."[63] Munford argues that reparations is also an issue for Africa and the Diaspora requiring coordinated action. He cites the 1993 Pan-African Congress on Reparations held in Nigeria, and growing interest in reparations on the part of black people in Brazil, the Caribbean and other areas of the Diaspora, as evidence of an emerging global campaign.

"The cry for reparations on both sides of the Atlantic," Munford concludes, "represents two sides of a single coin, as it were. One side of the coin is white aggression, 550 years of Caucasian assault on the people and continent of Africa. The other side of the coin is history's greatest Diaspora, the scattering of Blacks to live lives of exile outside Mother Africa, in communities of suffering. . . . Both the Diaspora and the continent have irrefutable claims to reparations."[64]

## Conclusion: The Cost of Being Black

Much discussion of the plight of African Americans has centered on disparities in access to jobs and income between blacks and whites. Underlying these differences are fundamental disparities in the distribution of wealth and capital. The political economy of white hegemony and black subordination is based on these disparities—disparities that are structured into the functioning of the capitalist economic system and maintained by the political power of the state.

The cost of being black amounts to a tax unfairly imposed solely because of race. It is analogous to the tax that Virginia imposed on free black women in 1668. The state must bear responsibility for abolishing such an unjust tax and making restitution for the period that it was imposed. Not only does the race tax harm the present generation, its effects are cumulative—it deprives the present generation and denies an inheritance to the next. Imposed by the state, the burdensome and unfair race tax can only be remedied by the federal government. More than a matter of individuals or regions, the state must be held accountable to remove the burden and make appropriate restitution for value lost.

The concept of reparations provides a framework for thinking about such restitution. The basic argument I would make is that the African American community has a just claim to compensation for that part of the wealth of the United States that was derived from violating the human rights, citizenship and property rights of black people. In particular, the vast wealth created by slave labor stands as the most egregious example of the expropriation without compensation of black labor's product. But the race tax, the cost of being black, continued after slavery and it continues today. Reparations must address both the human and economic costs of slavery, and the human and economic injustices that have been imposed on African Americans from the end of the Civil War until the present.

The quest for reparations is deeply embedded in the African American experience and black consciousness. It cuts across all ideological lines in the black community, finding advocates among emigrationists, nationalists, integrationists, religious figures, black elected officials, capitalists, socialists, liberals and radicals.

The widespread and frequent recurrence of this quest in African American history suggests that it reflects a deeply felt sense of catastrophic racial injustice—an unconscionable and still unremedied past injustice that continues to be produced and reproduced in new forms in the present.

The issue of reparations also involves critical issues of political economy insofar as it calls our attention to (1) the importance of structured racial inequities of wealth and capital; (2) the role that this structure of inequality has played in the development of U.S. capitalism and the underdevelopment of black America; and (3) the role of the state in structuring racial inequalities of wealth; (4) the fact that elimination of present discrimination is not sufficient to reverse the cumulative and continuing effects of state-sanctioned racial inequities in distribution of wealth and capital.

As many advocates of reparations have argued, if we are seeking a more economically just society, a society in which equality (or parity) is more than rhetoric, then the issue of reparations must be addressed. Reparations provides a framework for the redistribution of wealth within the existing political economy, and thereby moving towards economic equality between whites and blacks. Transfers of wealth in the form of capital assets and resources—black community ownership of national and local economic enterprises, housing and home ownership, educational scholarships—are critical to the success of any effort aimed at reversing the present underdevelopment of the black community. In my view, such transfers must first and foremost benefit the black workingclass and the poor.

I would argue that the quest for reparations also raises questions about the nature and legitimacy of the capitalist political economy, most fundamentally capitalist alienation of labor from ownership of the wealth that labor produces, and the role of the state in this process. At its most radical, the demand for reparations stands as a critique of capitalist property relations. It also underscores the need for *general* redistribution of wealth and resources. Seen in this light, the struggle for racial reparations can be convergent with the struggle for a socialist society in which black people would have full and equal access to the total wealth and resources of society. Only in the presence of such full and equal access to the total wealth and resources of society could we conclude that racial discrimination has been eliminated.

Finally, it must be said again that the issue of reparations is a global issue, for the enslavement of Africans and the colonization of Africa is a global issue. The situation of African Americans cannot be divided from the situation of Africans in Africa and the Diaspora. If civil rights alone are insufficient to assure full equality for black Americans, then national independence alone is insufficient to assure national liberation for the former colonies. As Frantz Fanon commented in *The Wretched of the Earth:*

> We are not blinded by the moral reparation of national independence; nor are we fed by it. The wealth of the imperial countries is our wealth too. . . . Europe is literally the creation of the Third World. The wealth which smothers her is that which was stolen from the under-developed peoples. The ports of Holland, the docks of Bordeaux and Liverpool were specialised in the Negro slave-trade, and owe their renown to millions of deported slaves. So when we hear the head of a European state declare with his hand on his heart that he must come to the help of the poor under-developed peoples, we do not tremble with gratitude. Quite the contrary; we say to ourselves: 'It is a just reparation which will be paid to us.' . . . This help should be the ratification of a double realisation: the realisation by the colonised peoples that *it is their due,* and the realisation by the capitalist powers that in fact *they must pay.* For if, through lack of intelligence . . . the capitalist countries refuse to pay, then the relentless dialectic of their own system will smother them.[65]

The African American quest for reparations is part of a much larger, global reparations movement by black people in Africa, the Caribbean, South America and Britain. This global movement has been gaining strength in recent years. Africa and black people in the Diaspora represent a powerful force, a sleeping giant, that has been drugged by the poisons of colonialism, slavery and racism. But the giant is awakening, fitfully but certainly, from the nightmare, and justice must be served. In the words of Fanon, a just reparation must be paid for the lives that were lost and for the wealth and labor that were stolen.

# Notes

1.  Mary Frances Berry and John W. Blassingame, *Long Memory: The Black Experience in America* (New York: Oxford University Press, 1982), p. 405.
2.  *Ibid,* p. 406; Nell Irvin Painter, *Sojourner Truth: A Life, A Symbol* (New York: W.W. Norton & Co., 1996), p. 244.
3.  Quoted in Jeanette Davis-Adeshote, *Black Survival in White America* (Orange, NJ: Bryant and Dillon Publishers, 1995), p. 87.
4.  Berry and Blassingame, *Long Memory,* p. 406.
5.  *Ibid,* p. 405.
6.  *San Francisco Chronicle,* February 10, 1998.
7.  William L. Van Deburg (ed.), *Modern Black Nationalism* (New York: New York University Press, 1997), p. 27.
8.  Herb Boyd, "Longtime Activist Queen Mother Moore, 98, Dies," in *The Black Scholar,* Vol. 27, No. 2 (Summer 1997), inside front cover.
9.  John H. Bracey, Jr., August Meir and Elliot Rudwick (eds.), *Black Nationalism in America* (New York: Bobbs-Merrill Co., 1970), p. 404.
10. Huey P. Newton, *To Die for the People: Selected Writings and Speeches* (New York: Writers and Readers Publishing, 1995), p. 3.

11. James Forman, *The Making of Black Revolutionaries* (Seattle: University of Washington Press, 1997), p. 545.
12. E. Franklin Frazier and C. Eric Lincoln, *The Negro Church in America/The Black Church Since Frazier* (New York: Schocken Books, 1974), pp. 184–86.
13. Imari Abubakari Obadele I, *Foundations of the Black Nation* (Detroit: House of Songhay, 1975), p. 68.
14. *Ibid,* 80–89.
15. Berry and Blassingame, *Long Memory,* p. 406.
16. "The Repression of the RNA," in *The Black Scholar,* Vol. 3., No. 2 (October, 1971), p. 57.
17. Obadele, *Foundations,* pp. 112–13.
18. Quoted in Boris I. Bitker, *The Case for Black Reparations* (New York: Random House, 1973), p. 79–80.
19. Dempsey J. Travis, "The Homestead Act," in *The Black Scholar,* Vol. 1, No. 6 (April, 1970), p. 15.
20. Bitker, p. 9.
21. *Ibid,* p. 18.
22. Quoted in Bitker, p. 31.
23. Quoted in William Darity, Jr., "Forty Acres and a Mule: Placing a Price Tag on Oppression," in Richard F. America (ed.), *The Wealth of Races: The Present Value of Benefits from Past Injustices* (New York: Greenwood Press, 1990), p. 5.
24. See Richard F. America (ed.), *The Wealth of Races: The Present Value of Benefits from Past Injustices* (New York: Greenwood Press, 1990), Melvin L. Oliver and Thomas M. Shapiro, *Black Wealth/White Wealth: A New Perspective on Racial Inequality* (New York: Routledge, 1995).
25. David H. Swinton, "Racial Inequality and Reparations," in America, *The Wealth of Races,* p. 157.
26. Address: N'COBRA, P.O. Box 62622, Washington, D.C. 20020–2622. . . .
27. Address: ARM, 3 Devonshire Chambers, 557 High Road, Tottenham, London, N17 6SB, United Kingdom. . . .
28. Lori Robinson, "Righting a Wrong," in *Emerge* magazine, Vol. 8, No. 4 (February, 1997), pp. 44, 46.
29. Interview in *West Africa* magazine, 27 October–9 November, 1997.
30. Van Deburg, *Modern Black Nationalism,* p. 333.
31. *Ibid.*
32. U.S. House of Representatives, H.R. 891.
33. *The New York Times,* March 16, 1998, p. A5.
34. Manning Marable, *How Capitalism Underdeveloped Black America* (Boston: South End Press, 1983), p. 2 (emphasis in original).
35. *Ibid,* p. 7 (emphasis in original).
36. Theodore W. Allen, *The Invention of the White Race (Vol. Two): The Origins of Racial Oppression in Anglo-America* (New York: Verso, 1997), p. 179. The loophole allowing possible freedom for Christian Africans was closed in 1662. Allen, p. 197.
37. *Ibid,* p. 187.
38. *Ibid,* p. 197.
39. Ronald Takaki, *A Different Mirror: A History of Multicultural America* (Boston: Little, Brown & Co., 1993), p. 66.
40. Berry and Blassingame, *Long Memory,* p. 35.
41. Allen, *Invention of the White Race,* p. 187.

42. *Ibid*, pp. 184–85.
43. Quoted in Eric Foner, *Reconstruction: America's Unfinished Revolution, 1863–1877* (New York: Harper & Row, 1988), p. 105.
44. William Z. Foster, *The Negro People in American History* (New York: International Publishers, 1954), p. 300.
45. *The Negro in Virginia* (Winston-Salem, NC: John F. Blair, Publisher, 1994), p. 249.
46. Quoted in Oliver and Shapiro, *Black Wealth/White Wealth*, p. 15.
47. W.E.B. Du Bois, *Black Reconstruction in America* (New York: Atheneum, 1979), p. 150.
48. *Ibid*, pp. 602–3.
49. Foster, *The Negro People in American History*, pp. 302–3.
50. Oliver and Shapiro, *Black Wealth/White Wealth*, p. 14.
51. Marable, *How Capitalism Underdeveloped Black America*, p. 49.
52. Oliver and Shapiro, *Black Wealth/White Wealth*, pp. 116–17.
53. *Ibid*, pp. 16–18.
54. *Ibid*.
55. *Ibid*, pp. 20–21.
56. Quoted in Lori Robinson, "Righting a Wrong," in *Emerge* magazine, p. 45.
57. Clarence J. Munford, *Race and Reparations: A Black Perspective for the 21st Century* (Trenton, NJ: Africa World Press, 1996), pp. 57–58.
58. *Ibid*, pp. 421, 427–28.
59. *Ibid*, p. 414.
60. *Ibid*, pp. 430–31.
61. *Ibid*, pp. 432–34.
62. *Ibid*, p. 416.
63. *Ibid*, p. 431.
64. *Ibid*, p. 439.
65. Frantz Fanon, *The Wretched of the Earth* (New York: Grove Press, 1963), pp. 80–81 (emphasis in original).

# Slavery and the Law:
# Time and Punishment

**W**hat would Abraham Lincoln have made of Edward Fagan? In the past few weeks, the New York lawyer has launched a war against firms that he claims profited from slavery, filing legal complaints against FleetBoston, a bank, Aetna, and CSX, a transport company. New York Life, Lehman Brothers, Norfolk Southern, Liggett and Lloyd's of London will follow next week. In all, some 60 companies are in his sights.

The suits are being filed on behalf of all descendants of slaves in America, a 30m-strong group. The defendants are the legal successors of entities that existed when slavery was still legal: FleetBoston, for example, is the present-day incarnation of the Providence Bank of Rhode Island. Economists put the current value of the companies' ill-gotten gains in the trillions. . . . Mr. Fagan reckons a settlement would fall somewhere "in the tens of billions." The lawyers will collect a percentage of that.

Calls for reparations date back to the 1960s. In 2000 Mr. Fagan was approached by Deadria Farmer-Paellmann, a black activist who has provided much of the research (and is one of the plaintiffs). The current plan seems to rely on two things: a few companies tiring of the lawsuits and agreeing to pay up, and others lobbying the government to shoulder its share.

In 1988 Congress authorised payments to 80,000 Japanese-Americans who had been interned during the second world war. Some $1.6 billion was paid out. But the precedent for the present lawsuits is Nazi slave labour. After the war the German government made big reparations, particularly to Israel, for its role in the Holocaust. In the 1990s Mr. Fagan and other lawyers sued German firms on behalf of former slave-labourers. Legally, the case was fiddly: much revolved around whether slave labour was legal under the Nazi regime and whether too much time had passed to prosecute the firms. Two suits, against Degussa and Siemens, were dismissed by a judge who decided that reparations were a matter of foreign policy and politics, not of the law.

But public opinion proved decisive. With New York regulators deeming Deutsche Bank's recalcitrance over the issue to be a barrier to its purchase of Bankers Trust, and with hundreds of local authorities threatening regulatory sanctions, the Germans worried about their ability to do business in

America. Bill Clinton assured them that a settlement would protect them against future suits. A fund of $5.2 billion, created by the firms and the German government, is now being disbursed.

The legal merits of slavery lawsuits are even more contentious. Last year a United Nations conference on racism in Durban (from which America walked out) branded slavery "a crime against humanity" which "should have always been so." Mr. Fagan argues that there should be no statute of limitations for such a crime. But the legal idea of a crime against humanity was invented decades after slavery was banned in America, so a court will have to define that crime retroactively. The UN conference steered clear of doing that.

The plaintiffs' case may be undermined by the money involved. They say that every dollar a firm should have paid to a slave 150 years ago should be subject to compound interest at a rate tied to the firms' growth. Each dollar could be worth anything from $6,250 to over $400,000. "This is exactly the kind of ridiculous lawsuit that a statute of limitations is designed to prevent," says Richard Epstein, a law professor at the University of Chicago.

Assessing the profits banks and insurers made from slavery is also hard. Fleet-Boston's ancestor, for instance, profited from financing the slave trade when it was already illegal under American law. Its contracts were thus all technically unenforceable, frauds for which the statute of limitations has long since expired. And although slavery itself was certainly profitable, it is less clear whether Aetna made money from insuring it.

When quizzed about such obstacles, Mr Fagan and his clients reply that public opinion will sway the courts again. Mr Fagan predicts boycotts, shareholder lawsuits, even race riots. Local politicians are being urged to hold hearings and create commissions to study the impact of slavery in their jurisdictions. A "Millions for Reparations" march is planned for August in Washington, DC.

Will it work? Cleverly, Mr. Fagan will multiply his chances of success not just by suing more companies, but by launching complaints in more jurisdictions across the country. In recent years, American juries have often found against big companies in such celebrity cases. John McWhorter, a black conservative at the Manhattan Institute, bets that all three companies sued so far would rather settle out of court.

If they do, they will surely lobby Congress to contribute its share. Until the civil war, the American government was as complicit in slavery as its German equivalent. Mr Fagan reckons a fund like the September 11th victims' compensation fund, where the airlines and the federal government paid in to a government-administered pot, would be a good resolution.

## A Nation Decides

But it is not clear that public opinion will rally to Mr. Fagan's cause as readily as he hopes. The Germans—foreigners who had committed crimes against Americans, many of whom were still alive—were easier targets.

Polls have shown 70% of whites objecting even to a public apology for slavery. Despite a longstanding campaign for reparations by Charles Ogletree, a Harvard professor, black leaders also seem divided on the issue. Jesse Jackson supports the suits. Others think that the government alone should pay up. Some want the money to support a fund devoted to black education; others would prefer a cash payment and a national apology. A few worry that the lawsuits could distract Americans from re-examining the role of slavery. "If a lawsuit does not lead to a general discussion in society about slavery," argues Elazar Barkan, the author of "The Guilt of Nations" (Norton, 2000), "then the lawsuits are not very helpful."

One lawyer who advised the German firms to settle says that their American counterparts should "go to court and fight like hell." Such tough talk may not last long: companies that come under pressure from Mr Jackson's boycotts tend to settle quickly. But it is hard to see how all this will help America understand its past.

# POSTSCRIPT

## Is Now the Time for Reparations for African Americans?

$\mathbf{A}$ significant basis for the movement for reparations resides in the claim that African Americans should receive compensation for the unpaid labor that they provided during the Slave Era and for the ongoing discriminatory and exclusionary policies. The opponents of reparations, in contrast, tend not to accept the alleged connection between the racist past of American social history and the lagging position of blacks today. The anti-reparations advocates are not convinced that the current generation of African Americans hold their white counterparts or other groups account-able for what they consider the sins of America's past. Rather, opponents of reparations tended to view contemporary white Americans as having broken with the racist past of the United States experience and committed themselves to supporting reasonable policies designed to produce a genu-ine multiracial society in the United States.

Slavery produced wealth, income, and status for whites, while blacks lagged behind. Exploitation of black labor during the era of segregation coupled with the loss of voting rights meant that blacks could not employ their potential political and economic power to alter their condition. In contrast, despite the difficult challenges that immigrant groups such as the Irish had in establishing a footing in the New World, they were able to vote and to use the power of the franchise and government to advance their interests. Due to the loss of political rights, African Americans were virtually foreclosed from opportunities to employ these vehicles to ad-vance in society until the Voting Rights Act was passed in 1965.

Robert L. Allen has identified seven important precedents in support of reparations. In this regard, it should be noted that in addition to the survivors of the Holocaust, Native Americans, Japanese Americans, and aboriginal peoples of Alaska and Canada have all received reparations. It is also noteworthy that compensation is accepted within American jurisprudence as a just award to those who have suffered wrongs. The writers from *The Economist* do not think you can connect today's white population with the injustices of the past. Are today's blacks victims of slavery? Is there a meaningful connection between slavery, segregation, and the contemporary status of African Americans? How do we identify victims of injustice racially?

Reparations is a very difficult issue confronting race relations within the United States. It is an issue that is surrounded by a good deal of controversy and resistance. Clearly, it is a wedge issue within American politics, and despite the arguments in support of reparations, this policy faces significant challenges to its adoption and implementation.

Two contemporary African Americans extend the reparations debate. Charles Ogletree, a Harvard law professor and reparations activist, thinks that the reparations movement has more "vigor and vitality in the 21st century" than it has ever had. Opponents such as John H. McWhorter, who agrees with the writers from *The Economist,* continue to argue that the idea of reparations is based on a fallacy that the problem for blacks in America is lack of cash. This fallacy, he argues, stands in the way of better ideas regarding reparations.

An explanation of the intellectual origins of the global reparations movement in *The Guilt of Nations: Restitution and Negotiating Historical Injustices* (W.W. Norton, 2000) by Elazar Barkan includes the case of Holocaust victims. *CQ Researcher* devoted its June 22, 2001 issue to the reparations movement. It provides a historical overview. The economic benefits of slavery to America are demonstrated in Robert F. Starobin's *Industrial Slavery in the Old South* (Oxford University Press, 1970), and in *Capitalism and Slavery* (Capricorn Books, 1966) by Eric Williams.

For further reading, advocates of reparations will find in *The Debt: What America Owes to Blacks* (Dutton, 2000) by Randall Robinson a strong supportive argument. Wole Soyinka, in *The Burden of Memory, The Muse of Forgiveness* (Oxford University Press, 2003) argues that reparations are a key to real social justice. Another selection in support of reparations is "The Growing Movement for Reparations," in *When Sorry Isn't Enough: The Controversy over Apologies and Reparations for Human Injustice,* edited by Roy L. Brooks (New York University Press, 1999). *Slavery by Another Name: The Re-Enslavement of Black Americans from the Civil War to World War II,* by Douglas A. Blackmon (Doubleday, 2008), is a groundbreaking account of how thousands of free black men labored without compensation for white southerners in a form of "neoslavery." His argument would strengthen the case for reparations. *Driven Out: The Forgotten War Against Chinese Americans* (Random House, 2007) by Jean Pfaelzer describes the purging of thousands of Chinese immigrants in the Pacific Northwest and Rocky Mountain region between 1850 and 1906. Pfaelzer points out that the country's first reparations lawsuit was filed by Chinese Americans in response to racist actions.

Opponents of reparations for African Americans will find support in "The Case Against Reparations" (*Progressive,* December 2000) by Adolph L. Reed. A strong case against reparations appeared in a *St. Petersburg Times* (June 25, 2000) article, "Our Country Has Paid the Bill for Slavery," by Martin Dyckman. Similarly, an article opposing Holocaust reparations can be found in "Holocaust Reparations—A Growing Scandal," by Gabriel Schoenfeld in *Commentary* (September 2000).

The reparations debate is covered in seminal essays collected and edited by Raymond A. Winbush in *Should America Pay? Slavery and the Raging Debate on Reparations* (HarperCollins Publishers, 2003). It is the best treatment of the reparations issue to date.

# Contributors to This Volume

## EDITORS

**RAYMOND D'ANGELO** is a professor of sociology at St. Joseph's College in New York where he serves as Chair of the Department of Social Sciences. He has been involved with teaching and research in race and ethnic studies throughout his academic career. He is a recipient of two fellowships from the National Science Foundation and a research award from the National Institute of Justice, and is a recent recipient of a National Endowment for the Humanities award. D'Angelo is author and editor of *The American Civil Rights Movement: Readings and Interpretations* (McGraw Hill/Dushkin, 2000) and has contributed to the *Arena Review: Journal for the Study of Sport and Sociology* and *Civil Rights in the United States*. He is active in historic preservation.

**HERBERT DOUGLAS** is a professor of Law and Justice Studies at Rowan University in Glassboro, New Jersey, where he also serves as an African American Studies and International Studies faculty member. He graduated from Duquesne University and received his Ph.D. from the University of Toledo. He was a recipient of a Fulbright-Hays Fellowship to study in the Soviet Union in summer 1990, and he recently received the Gary Hunter Award for Excellence in Mentoring at Rowan University. He is involved in social causes including membership on the governing board of the Fair Share Housing Center in Camden, New Jersey, an organization designed to promote the housing needs of low and moderate income families. Douglas contributed "Migration and Adaptations of African American Families within Urban America," to *Minority Voices: Linking Personal Ethnic History and the Sociological Imagination* (Allyn & Bacon, 2005) edited by John Myers. He has been involved with teaching and research in race and ethnic studies throughout his academic career.

# AUTHORS

**ROBERT L. ALLEN** is senior editor of *The Black Scholar*. A long-time activist and professor, he is author of *The Port Chicago Mutiny* (Amistad Press, 1993) and coeditor with Herb Boyd of *Brotherman: The Odyssey of Black Men in America* (Sagebrush Education Resources, 1996).

**GORDON W. ALLPORT** (1897–1967) was a social psychologist and author of *The Nature of Prejudice* (1954).

**PETER BEINART** is a senior editor to *The New Republic*. He has also written for *The New York Times, The Wall Street Journal, The Financial Times, The Boston Globe, The Atlantic Monthly, Newsweek,* and *Time*.

**DAVID A. BELL**, journalist and historian, is a former reporter and researcher for *The National Review*.

**DERRICK BELL** is a visiting professor of law at New York University School of Law. He is author of many books including *Faces at the Bottom of the Well: The Permanence of Racism* (Basic Books, 1992) and the classic *Race, Racism and American Law* (Aspen Publishers Inc., 2000).

**HERBERT BLUMER** (1900–1987) was a former professional football player who became a sociology professor at the University of Chicago and the University of California, Berkeley. He helped to establish symbolic interactionism as a major paradigm in sociology.

**EDUARDO BONILLA-SILVA** is a professor of sociology at Texas A&M University and the author of several books on race and ethnicity including *Racism Without Racists* (Rowan & Littlefield, 2003).

**WILLIAM G. BOWEN** is president of the Andrew W. Mellon Foundation. He is coauthor, along with Derek Bok, of *The Shape of the River: Long-Term Consequences of Considering Race in College and University Admissions* (Princeton University Press, 1998).

**PETER BRIMELOW** is senior editor of *Forbes* and *National Review*. He is the author of *Alien Nation: Common Sense About America's Immigration Disaster* (Perennial, 1996).

**ROGER CLEGG** is general council of the Center for Equal Opportunity and frequent contributor to *The Chronicle of Higher Education*.

**WARD CONNERLY** is a political activist and conservative commentator. He is best identified with Proposition 209, a California ballot initiative in opposition to affirmative action programs.

**ELLIS COSE** is the author of *The Press, A Nation of Strangers* and *The Rage of a Privileged Class*. He is now a writer and essayist for *Newsweek*.

**DINESH D'SOUZA** is the John Olin Research Fellow at the American Enterprise Institute. He is author of *The End of Racism: Principles for a Multicultural Society* (Free Press, 1995) and *Illiberal Education: The Politics of Race and Sex on Campus* (Free Press, 1991).

**SUSAN E. EATON,** formerly assistant director of the Harvard Project On School Desegregation, has written for newspapers in Massachusetts and Connecticut.

**INGRID GOULD ELLEN** is a writer for *The Brookings Review.* She is author of *Sharing America's Neighborhoods: The Prospects for Stable Racial Integration* (Harvard University Press, 2000).

**CARLOS FUENTES** is a social commentator and distinguished Mexican writer.

**CHARLES A. GALLAGHER** is a professor of sociology at Georgia State University and author of *Rethinking the Color Line: Readings in Race and Ethnicity* (McGraw-Hill, 2006).

**HENRY A. GIROUX,** an expert on cultural studies, education, multiculturalism, and related topics, is current chair of communication studies at McMaster University, Ontario, Canada. He is the author of several books including *Education Still Under Siege,* co-authored with Stanley Aronowitz (Bergin & Garvey, 1993).

**PAULO GUIMARAES** is a Research Associate Professor in the Division of Research and Economics Department at the Moore School of Business, the University of South Carolina.

**KENDRA HAMILTON** is the editor of *Black Issues in Higher Education.* Her background is in English and creative writing. She has published poems in *Callaloo* and written and researched on Gullah, the language and culture of the South Carolina and Georgia's Low Country.

**DAVID A. HARRIS** is a professor of law and values at the University of Toledo College of Law and Soros Senior Justice Fellow at the Center of Crime, Communities and Justice in New York City. He is author of *Profiles in Injustice: Why Racial Profiling Cannot Work* (New Press, 2003).

**SAMUEL P. HUNTINGTON** is a political scientist and Albert J. Weatherhead III University Professor at Harvard University. He is author of *The Clash of Civilizations and the Remaking of World Order* (Touchstone, 1996).

**SCOTT JOHNSON** is a fellow of the Claremont Institute, an attorney, and senior vice president of TCF National Bank in Minnesota. Also, he is co-author of The Power Line blog.

**PAUL KIVEL** is a teacher, writer, and antiracist social activist. He is author of *Uprooting Racism: How White People Can Work for Racial Justice* (New Society Publishers, 1995).

**PHILIPPE LEGRAIN** is a British journalist, economist, and author of *Immigrants: Your Country Needs Them* (Princeton University Press, 2007) and *Open World: The Truth about Globalisation* (Ivan R. Dee Publishers, 2003).

**SUSAN LOBO** is a cultural anthropologist and an expert on Native American studies. She is the author of numerous books on Native Americans. Along with Kurt Peters, she is the editor of *American Indians and the*

*Urban Experience* (Altamira Press, 2001). Currently, she is distinguished visiting scholar in the American Indian Studies Program at Arizona University.

**WALTER BENN MICHAELS** is a literary theorist and English professor at the University of Illinois at Chicago. He is the author of *The Trouble with Diversisty: How We Learned to Love Identity and Ignore Inequality* (Metropolitan Books, 2006).

**GARY ORFIELD** is a professor of education at Harvard University where he is involved with the Civil Rights Project. He is author of *Dismantling Desegregation: The Quiet Reversal of Brown v. Board of Education* (The New Press, 1996).

**FRANK POMMERSHEIM** lived and worked on the Rosebud Sioux Reservation for 10 years and currently teaches at the University of South Dakota School of Law where he specializes in Indian law. He is the author of *Braid of Feathers: American Indian Law and Contemporary Tribal Life* (University of California Press, 1995).

**ROSALIE PEDALINO PORTER** is the author of *Forked Tongue: The Politics of Bilingual Education* (Basic Books, 1990) and *Educating Language Minority Children: An Agenda for the Future* (Transaction Publishers, 2000). She is the chairman and director of the READ Institute (Research in English Acquisition and Development).

**ADOLPH REED** is a professor of political science at the University of Pennsylvania and author of *Without Justice for All: The New Liberalism and Our Retreat from Racial Equality* (Westview Press, 1999).

**NEIL L. RUDENSTINE** is a scholar and educator. A former president of Harvard University, he is author of *"Pointing Our Thoughts: Reflections on Harvard and Higher Education, 1991–2001,"* and with William Bowen, *"In Pursuit of the PhD."*

**DAVID C. RUFFIN** is a writer and political analyst in Washington, D.C.

**ARTHUR M. SCHLESINGER, JR.,** is a historian and former speech writer to President John F. Kennedy. He is the author of many books including *The Disuniting of America: Reflections on a Multicultural Society* (W.W. Norton, 1992).

**ROBERT STAPLES** is a professor of sociology at the University of California, San Francisco, and author of *Black Masculinity: The Black Male's Role in American Society* (Black Scholar Press, 1982) and *Families at the Crossroads: Challenges and Prospects* (Jossey-Bass Inc., 1993), coauthored with Leanor Boulin Johnson.

**SHELBY STEELE** is a research fellow at the Hoover Institution and author of *White Guilt: How Blacks and Whites Together Destroyed the Promise of the Civil Rights Era* (Harper Collins, 2006).

**STEPHEN STEINBERG** is a professor of sociology at Queens College of the City University of New York. He is the author of *The Ethnic Myth: Race, Ethnicity, and Class in America* (Beacon Press, 1982).

**BEVERLY DANIEL TATUM** is a clinical psychologist and current president of Spelman College. She is author of *Why Are All the Black Kids Sitting Together in the Cafeteria? And Other Conversations About Race* (Basic Books, 1997).

**MICHAEL WALZER** is a political philosopher and professor at the Institute for Advanced Study. He is author of *On Toleration* (Yale University Press, 1997) and *Exodus and Revolution* (Basic Books, 2000).

**TIM WISE** is author of *White Like Me: Reflections from a Privileged Son* (Soft Skull Press, 2005) and director of the newly formed Association for White Anti-Racist Education (AWARE) in Nashville, Tennessee.

**DOUGLAS P. WOODWARD** is the director of the Division of Research and professor of economics at Moore School of Business at the University of South Carolina. He has published extensively in *The Journal of Urban Economics, The Journal of Regional Science,* and the *Review of Economics and Statistics.* He is the co-author with Norman J. Glickman of *The New Competitors: How Foreign Investors Are Changing the U.S. Economy* (Harper Collins, 1990).

**FRANK H. WU** is a law professor at the Howard University School of Law. He writes for many publications and is the author of *Yellow: Race in America Beyond Black and White* (Basic Books, 2002).

## DATE DUE

| | | | |
|---|---|---|---|
| DEC 0 7 2009 | | | |
| | | | |
| | | | |
| | | | |
| | | | |
| | | | |
| | | | |
| | | | |
| | | | |
| | | | |
| | | | |